BASIC FEDERAL INCOME TAX

BASIC FEDERAL INCOME TAX

Gwendolyn Griffith Lieuallen
Speer, Hoyt, Jones, Feinman, Poppe, Wolf & Griffith, P.C.

The *Emanuel Law Outlines* Series

ASPEN
PUBLISHERS

111 Eighth Avenue, New York, New York 10011
www.aspenpublishers.com

About Aspen Publishers

Aspen Publishers, headquartered in New York City, is a leading information provider for attorneys, business professionals, and law students. Written by preeminent authorities, our products consist of analytical and practical information covering both U.S. and international topics. We publish in the full range of formats, including updated manuals, books, periodicals, CDs, and online products.

Our proprietary content is complemented by 2,500 legal databases, containing over 11 million documents, available through our Loislaw division. Aspen Publishers also offers a wide range of topical legal and business databases linked to Loislaw's primary material. Our mission is to provide accurate, timely, and authoritative content in easily accessible formats, supported by unmatched customer care.

To order any Aspen Publishers title, go to *www.aspenpublishers.com* or call 1-800-638-8437.

To reinstate your manual update service, call 1-800-638-8437.

For more information on Loislaw products, go to *www.loislaw.com* or call 1-800-364-2512.

For Customer Care issues, e-mail *CustomerCare @aspenpublishers.com;* call 1-800-234-1660; or fax 1-800-901-9075.

Aspen Publishers
A Wolters Kluwer Company

**Dedicated
to
Peyton, with love**

Summary of Contents

Table of Contents

CHAPTER 1

GETTING STARTED IN FEDERAL INCOME TAX

CHAPTER 2
IDENTIFYING GROSS INCOME

Chapter 3
SPECIFIC INCLUSIONS IN GROSS INCOME

CHAPTER 4

SPECIFIC EXCLUSIONS FROM GROSS INCOME

CHAPTER 5

DEDUCTIONS—IN GENERAL

CHAPTER 6

PERSONAL DEDUCTIONS

CHAPTER 7

BUSINESS AND INVESTMENT DEDUCTIONS

Chapter 8
MIXED BUSINESS AND PERSONAL EXPENSES

CHAPTER 9
TRANSACTIONS IN PROPERTY

CHAPTER 10

NONRECOGNITION TRANSACTIONS

CHAPTER 11

TIMING OF INCOME AND EXPENSES

CHAPTER 12

CHARACTER OF INCOME AND LOSS

CHAPTER 13

TAX RATES AND CREDITS

CHAPTER 14

IDENTIFYING THE TAXPAYER

CHAPTER 15

TIME VALUE OF MONEY: PRINCIPLES AND APPLICATIONS

CHAPTER 16

RECOGNIZING RELATED TAX STATUTES: A TRANSACTIONAL APPROACH TO TAX

Preface

Thank you for buying this book!

In my many years in the classroom, and now as a practicing tax lawyer, I have spent countless hours listening to students and tax professionals alike describe the study of tax law as both fascinating and frustrating.

It's a fascinating subject, not only because it touches almost everyone's life in a very real and direct way, but also because it serves as a pretty good mirror for our society's beliefs and values. But learning tax law can be frustrating as well. It requires learning a whole new language—the language of the Internal Revenue Code and its seemingly endless pages of regulations. It requires faith that what may seem to be a jumble of obscure statutes is really a coherent system whose parts work together in a sensible fashion. Finally (and this is what keeps tax practitioners up at night) Congress changes these laws *every year*—creating new challenges for both taxpayers and their advisors.

This book offers some of the techniques I've developed over the years to help students and practitioners overcome these frustrations. Chapter 1 begins with the basics, including a method for reading the Internal Revenue Code *and* understanding it. (I recently received an email from a former student, who now is a tax lawyer. He found himself using this "parsing" technique years after taking my course and wanted to let me know that he still "parses" statutes when he finds himself in unfamiliar tax territory.) I hope this approach works for you as well.

The succeeding chapters of this book describe in detail the five basic issues of individual taxation: what is "income''; what expenses are deductible; the character of income or loss; what tax rates apply; and what tax credits are available. Chapter 16 summarizes the well-established themes and issues of basic income tax, collecting the "families" of tax statutes that govern these issues. We'll never prevent Congress from tinkering with the Code (nor should we), but these essential themes will remain as long as there is an individual income tax.

This book can't substitute for the hard work of tax study: understanding the Code and regulations, working through example after example, and participating in the discussion in your tax class. What it can do is supplement those sources and help explain the concepts you encounter in class. To make the best use of this book, I suggest that you:

- Skim the appropriate sections of this outline before the material is covered in class (you will find a casebook correlation chart at the front of the book).

- Review the material in this book in detail after it is discussed in class. Note in the margins of this outline the emphasis that your particular professor places on the various aspects of the material.

- Work through the examples and "Quiz Yourself" questions. Make sure you can explain the result in each example, using the Code and case law. Consider creating new examples to work through alone or in your study group.

- Use the outline material to supplement the notes or your own outline that you prepare to study for the exam.

- Use the "Capsule Summary" as a review just prior to your exam.

My warmest thanks to Aspen's Carol McGeehan and Barbara Lasoff for their optimism and sensible suggestions—and to my family for their infinite patience—during the writing of this book.

I wish you the best in your first tax course and hope most of all that you will discover that tax can be interesting and even fun. Good luck!

Gwendolyn Griffith Lieuallen
Speer, Hoyt, Jones, Feinman, Poppe, Wolf & Griffith, P.C.
Eugene, Oregon

Casebook Correlation Chart

(Note: general sections of the outline are omitted for this chart. NC = not directly covered by this casebook.)

Basic Federal Income Tax Emanuel Law Outline *(by chapter and section heading)*	Burke & Friel: *Taxation of Individual Income* (7th ed., 2004)	Klein, Bankman, & Shaviro: *Federal Income Taxation* (13th ed., 2003)	Dodge, Fleming, & Geier: *Federal Income Tax: Doctrine, Structure, and Policy* (3rd ed., 2004)	Freeland, Lathrope, Lind, & Stephens: *Fundamentals of Federal Income Taxation* (13th ed., 2004)	Guerrin & Postlewaite: *Problems and Materials in Federal Income Taxation* (6th ed., 2002)
CHAPTER 1 **GETTING STARTED IN FEDERAL INCOME TAX**					
I. Introduction—The Big Picture	8-19	NC	767-771	2-6	NC
II. The Sources of Federal Income Tax Law	5-8	16-22, 32-36	9-16	6-32	1-3, 14-25, 28-37
III. Tax Ethics—Tax Return Positions and Sanctions	5-6	NC	178-183	956-976	25-28
IV. Reading the Code	NC	22-30	NC	NC	NC
V. A Few Words on Tax Policy	NC	NC	NC	32-46, 987-990	4-8
VI. Relationship of Income Tax to Other Tax Systems	NC	NC	18-23	NC	17-19
CHAPTER 2 **IDENTIFYING GROSS INCOME**					
II. IRC Section 61	9-10, 24-26	22, 72	43-45	48-68	39-63
III. Definitions of Income	24-41	7-8, 37-62, 69-73, 191-201, 257-266	37-41, 205-208, 423, 431-435	34-35, 48-60	42-49
IV. Items That Are Not Income	30-32, 161-164	62-69, 104-106	228-233	NC	48-56
CHAPTER 3 **SPECIFIC INCLUSIONS IN GROSS INCOME**					
II. Compensation for Services	26-27, 207, 218	149	203-208	92-102, 244-255	41-42
III. Gross Income from Business	238-239	NC	208-211	NC	149-163
IV. Gains Derived from Dealings in Property	76-79	NC	53-57	255-275	94-96
V. Investment Income	148-151, 248-249, 257-61	406-414, 671-675, 114-18	567-77, 673-675	159-164, 444-448	229-230, 400-407, 632-633, 651-663, 671
VI. Alimony and Separate Maintenance Payments	833-840	306-311	188-192, 504-510	195-208	255-262
VII. Income from Discharge of Indebtedness	157-171	144-179	303-320	165-181	50-56

Basic Federal Income Tax Emanuel Law Outline *(by chapter and section heading)*	Burke & Friel: *Taxation of Individual Income* (7th ed., 2004)	Klein, Bankman, & Shaviro: *Federal Income Taxation* (13th ed., 2003)	Dodge, Fleming, & Geier: *Federal Income Tax: Doctrine, Structure, and Policy* (3rd ed., 2004)	Freeland, Lathrope, Lind, & Stephens: *Fundamentals of Federal Income Taxation* (13th ed., 2004)	Guerrin & Postlewaite: *Problems and Materials in Federal Income Taxation* (6th ed., 2002)
CHAPTER 3 continued					
VIII. **Several Items Not Usually Crucial in the Basic Tax Course**	NC	266-271, 603-614	817-831	282-303, 665-671	423
IX. **Some Odds and Ends— Prizes, Helpful Payments, and Embezzlements**	127-128	91-93, 183-184, 453-454	197-199	63-65, 107-113, 537-543, 547-552	61-62, 69-77, 189-207
CHAPTER 4 SPECIFIC EXCLUSIONS FROM GROSS INCOME					
I. **Where are We?**	NC	NC	NC	NC	121-122
II. **Death Benefits—§101**	141-145	108-114	166-168, 177-178	155-164	140-141
III. **Gifts—§102**	26, 90-108	72-94	169-177	70-83	122-128
IV. **Interest on State and Local Bonds—§103**	229-230	22-23, 186-187	79	236-240	188-189
V. **Compensation for Personal Injury or Sickness—§104**	178-202	140-144	268-281	186-194	176-180
VI. **Discharge of Indebtedness Income—§108**	160-173	144-179	308-311	165-181	181-188
VII. **Qualified Scholarships— §117**	128-130	91-92	199-202	113-116	141-149
VIII. **One-Time Exclusion for Gain on Sale of Principal Residence—§121**	109-122	189-190	79-80	221-227	386-389
IX. **Employment-Related Exclusions**	203-228	42-62	208-222	92-106	149-174
X. **Educational Incentives**	415-439	465-468	NC	228-236	425-436, 468-475, 892
XI. **Child Support**	836-837	148, 311-314	469-471	212-214	259
XII. **Gain from Sale of Stock**	NC	285-286	NC	NC	297-303
CHAPTER 5 DEDUCTIONS—IN GENERAL					
II. **Role of Deductions**	11-12, 15-18	233, 383-384	533-537	314-316, 565-569, 770	391-393
III. **Common Themes of Deduction Controversies**	16-18	NC	NC	314-316, 319-328	394-424
CHAPTER 6 PERSONAL DEDUCTIONS					
II. **Above-the-Line and Below-the-Line Deductions**	NC	335-337, 468	NC	NC	391-392
III. **Alimony**	833-836	306-311	501-510	195-208	255-261
IV. **Moving Expenses**	449-451	453-454	611	547-552	170
V. **Contributions to Regular IRAs**	154-156	13	NC	668-670	NC
VI. **Losses**	344-349	NC	267-268, 522-531	400-403	642-663

Basic Federal Income Tax Emanuel Law Outline (by chapter and section heading)	Burke & Friel: *Taxation of Individual Income* (7th ed., 2004)	Klein, Bankman, & Shaviro: *Federal Income Taxation* (13th ed., 2003)	Dodge, Fleming, & Geier: *Federal Income Tax: Doctrine, Structure, and Policy* (3rd ed., 2004)	Freeland, Lathrope, Lind, & Stephens: *Fundamentals of Federal Income Taxation* (13th ed., 2004)	Guerrin & Postlewaite: *Problems and Materials in Federal Income Taxation* (6th ed., 2002)
CHAPTER 6 continued					
VII. Interest on Education Loans	502, 504	382-383	NC	496-498	468-475
VIII. Qualified Education Expenses	418-446	465-468	NC	384-392, 563-565	468-475, 678-680
IX. Certain Contributions to Medical Accounts	NC	NC	518-522	552-563	NC
X. Costs Incurred in Civil Rights Actions	NC	NC	NC	NC	NC
XI. The Choice: Standard or Itemized Deduction	16-18	NC	516-517	567-580	391, 718-729
XII. Interest—§163	500-514	400, 378-380, 551-553	559-564	494-504	670-680
XIII. Taxes—§164	517-524	383-384	550-556	504-508	680-684
XIV. Casualty Losses—§165(c)(3)	528-543	338-351	257-260	806-817	684-695
XV. Medical Expenses—§213	547-554	351-360	512-522	552-563	708-712
XVI. Charitable Contributions—§170	558-584	360-378	537-550	784-806	695-707
XVII. Miscellaneous Expenses—2% Floor	1055 n.4	NC	NC	571-572	717-718
XVIII. Personal Exemption—§151	17-18	384-385	NC	565-569	836-845
CHAPTER 7 **BUSINESS DEDUCTIONS**					
II. Trade or Business Expenses—§162	238-266	503-521	577-579	314-345, 360-384	394-408, 425-426
III. Capital Recovery for Business Assets	270-296, 312-314	28, 476, 481-482, 523, 527	94-115, 693-696, 701-05	328-337, 403-443	408-424, 485-496, 503-506
IV. Other Deductions	350-260, 517-519, 531	NC	550-556, 561-563, 576	NC	663-672, 680-682
V. Rental and Royalty Activities	NC	NC	389-392	NC	NC
VI. Special Rules for Losses	NC	NC	NC	NC	NC
CHAPTER 8 **MIXED BUSINESS AND PERSONAL EXPENSES**					
II. Origin Test	456-457	459-465	623-628	NC	394-395, 399-400, 477-481
III. Hobby Losses—§183	461-475	391-399	588-596	516-518	642-650
IV. Section 274 Restrictions	391-413	427-437	648-653	392-400	448-459, 467-468
V. Home Offices and Vacation Homes—§280A	480-495	399-406	614-622	518-523	506-510
VI. "Luxury" Automobiles and Listed Property—§280F	487-492	418	700-701	434-438	496-502
VII. Gambling Losses	NC	119-120	585-588	NC	NC

Basic Federal Income Tax Emanuel Law Outline *(by chapter and section heading)*	Burke & Friel: *Taxation of Individual Income* (7th ed., 2004)	Klein, Bankman, & Shaviro: *Federal Income Taxation* (13th ed., 2003)	Dodge, Fleming, & Geier: *Federal Income Tax: Doctrine, Structure, and Policy* (3rd ed., 2004)	Freeland, Lathrope, Lind, & Stephens: *Fundamentals of Federal Income Taxation* (13th ed., 2004)	Guerrin & Postlewaite: *Problems and Materials in Federal Income Taxation* (6th ed., 2002)
CHAPTER 12 continued					
IV. Section 1231—Real and Depreciable Property Used in a Trade or Business	767-776	673-674	732-735	741-753	568-575
V. Calculating Net Capital Gain and Net Capital Loss	721-726	NC	NC	695-702, 711-718	518-521
CHAPTER 13 TAX RATES AND CREDITS					
II. Tax Rates	NC	28-30, 573-574	459-468	914-929	854-865, 869-875
III. The Alternative Minimum Tax	1051-1060	24, 559-568	772-774	942-953	878
IV. Tax Credits—In General	NC	NC	243-245	929-941	879-880
V. Dependent Care Credit	NC	437-440	469-474	931-932	880-881
VI. Earned Income Tax Credit	NC	385-386	475-476	939-940	881-883
VII. Education Credits	424-428	465-468	600-607	933	NC
VIII. Other Credits	NC	386-388	470-471	931-941	883
CHAPTER 14 IDENTIFYING THE TAXPAYER					
II. "Persons" Subject to Tax	NC	14-16	480-493	916-917, 921-922	854-856
III. Assignment of Income	785-708	575-591, 599-603	481-501	242-275	209-229
IV. Statutory Responses to Assignment of Income and Related Problems	809-813	574, 620-629	488-498	243	238-239
CHAPTER 15 TIME VALUE OF MONEY: PRINCIPLES AND APPLICATIONS					
II. Time Value of Money Principles—the Basics	NC	30-32	23-29	NC	605-622
III. Original Issue Discount (OID)	1007-1029	239-243	665-673	847-855	607-610
IV. Imputed Interest—§483	27, 1027	NC	387-388	847-848	610-622
V. Below-Market Loans—§7872	815-828	274	288-291	485-494	240-254
VI. The Basic Tax Strategies—Deferral of Income and Acceleration of Deductions	427, 1031-1049	NC	856-881	432-434, 509-512	733-758, 776-780

Basic Federal Income Tax Emanuel Law Outline *(by chapter and section heading)*	Burke & Friel: *Taxation of Individual Income* (7th ed., 2004)	Klein, Bankman, & Shaviro: *Federal Income Taxation* (13th ed., 2003)	Dodge, Fleming, & Geier: *Federal Income Tax: Doctrine, Structure, and Policy* (3rd ed., 2004)	Freeland, Lathrope, Lind, & Stephens: *Fundamentals of Federal Income Taxation* (13th ed., 2004)	Guerrin & Postlewaite: *Problems and Materials in Federal Income Taxation* (6th ed., 2002)
CHAPTER 16 **RECOGNIZING RELATED TAX STATUTES: A TRANSACTIONAL APPROACH TO TAX**					
II. **A Problem-Solving Approach to Tax**	NC	NC	NC	NC	NC
III. **Applying the Study Tax FIRST! Approach to Common Types of Transactions**	NC	NC	NC	NC	NC

Capsule Summary

This Capsule Summary is intended for review at the end of the semester. Reading it is not a substitute for mastering the material in the main outline. Numbers in brackets refer to the pages in the main outline where the topic is discussed.

CHAPTER 1
GETTING STARTED IN FEDERAL INCOME TAX

I. UNDERSTANDING THE BIG PICTURE

The process of computing tax liability is summarized below and can be traced in the Form 1040, included in the Outline. [4-5]

> Gross Income
> − <u>Certain Deductions</u>
>   Adjusted Gross Income
> − Standard Deduction *or*
>   Itemized Deduction
> − <u>Personal Exemption</u>
>   Taxable Income
> × <u>Tax Rate(s)</u>
>   Tentative Tax
> − <u>Tax Credits</u>
>   Tax Due or Refund

A. Gross income—§61

Gross income includes all income from whatever sources derived. IRC §61(a). Income from compensation, dividends, gains from dealings in property, and discharge of debt are common types of income. However, particular Code sections exclude certain types of income from gross income. [2]

B. Deductions

Deductions are subtractions from income in computing taxable income. [2] There are two types of deductions available in computing taxable income:

1. **Deductions from gross income in computing adjusted gross income:** Certain expenditures are deducted (subtracted) from gross income in computing adjusted gross income (AGI).

2. **Deductions from adjusted gross income in computing taxable income:** The taxpayer subtracts his or her personal exemptions and then takes the larger of either the standard deduction or the itemized deduction. The standard deduction is a statutorily set amount, and the itemized deduction is the sum of all allowable itemized deductions.

C. Multiply taxable income by the tax rate(s)

The taxpayer's tax rate, which depends on his or her filing status, is multiplied by taxable income to produce the "tentative tax." The tax rates applicable to individuals range from 10% to 35% for ordinary income and 5% to 28% for capital gain. IRC §1. The alternative minimum tax is a separate tax imposed on some taxpayers, with tax rates of 26% and 28%. [2]

D. Subtract available tax credits

A tax credit is a dollar-for-dollar reduction in the amount of tax due. Available tax credits are subtracted from the tentative tax to produce the actual tax due. [2]

E. Six Fundamental Tax Questions

Tax problems—and the material in this book—can be summarized into six fundamental issues. [2-3]

1. **Who is the taxpayer?** Identifying the right taxpayer is critical. Families often try to rearrange income and deductions so as to minimize the tax on the family as a whole, while the IRS seeks to match income and deductions to the right taxpayer. [2] and Chapter 14.

2. **Does the taxpayer have income?** To begin the analysis of a taxpayer's tax liability, it is necessary to identify his or her income in a theoretical sense and in the sense of §61. We construe income broadly. [2-3] and Chapters 2 through 4, 9, and 10.

3. **What deductions may the taxpayer claim?** The income tax is a tax on net income, not gross income. Therefore, taxpayers are entitled to reduce gross income by certain deductions, principally personal and business deductions. We construe deductions narrowly. [3] and Chapters 5 through 8 and 9 through 12.

4. **Timing issues:** Once income and deductions are identified, the next question is when—*in which taxable year*—a taxpayer must include an item of income in gross income and when a taxpayer may claim a deduction. Taxpayers seek to defer income as far into the future as possible, and accelerate deductions to the earliest possible year. [3] and Chapters 11 and 15.

5. **Character of income and loss:** When income or loss arises from the sale or exchange of property, it is necessary to characterize it as ordinary or capital. Taxpayers prefer capital gain to ordinary income, because capital gain is subject to preferential, lower tax rates. Taxpayers prefer ordinary loss to capital loss because the deductibility of capital losses is restricted. [3] and Chapter 12.

6. **Rates and credits:** The final step in calculating a taxpayer's tax liability is determining the appropriate rate of tax and subtracting available tax credits. The tax rate depends on the character of the taxpayer's income and also on the imposition of the alternative minimum tax. [3] and Chapter 13.

II. SOURCES OF TAX LAW

Title 26 of the United States Code is the statutory base for all federal tax law, including the federal income tax. The Department of the Treasury, through the Internal Revenue Service (IRS), and the courts offer guidance on ambiguous provisions of the Code. [6-7]

A. Administrative interpretation

The Department of the Treasury issues regulations (temporary, final, or proposed) interpreting various Code provisions as well as revenue rulings, revenue procedures, notices, announcements, private letter rulings, and technical advice memoranda on various issues. [7-9]

B. Judicial interpretation

The U.S. Tax Court, the U.S. District Court, the U.S. Court of Federal Claims, and the U.S. Bankruptcy Courts are trial courts for tax matters. Cases are appealed to the appellate court for the circuit in which the taxpayer lives and then to the U.S. Supreme Court. [9-12]

1. U.S. Tax Court—Litigate without first paying tax: A taxpayer may adjudicate tax matters in the U.S. Tax Court without first paying the tax, if the taxpayer files a petition within 90 days of the date of the Statutory Notice of Deficiency (90-day letter).

2. U.S. Bankruptcy Court: A bankruptcy court has jurisdiction over tax matters of the debtor, and may stay proceedings in the U.S. Tax Court regarding tax matters.

3. Other courts—Pay first, then litigate: In order to litigate in the U.S. District Court or the U.S. Court of Federal Claims, the taxpayer must first pay the tax and file a claim for refund. If that claim is either denied or ignored, the taxpayer can sue for refund.

C. Deference to IRS interpretation

The courts interpret ambiguous statutory material in cases properly brought before them. The courts will properly give deference to an IRS-published, prelitigation interpretation of a Code provision. This means that the court will adopt the IRS's interpretation of a Code provision if it is a "reasonable" interpretation of the statute. The IRS's interpretation need not be the only reasonable interpretation or even the "best" interpretation. It need only be a reasonable interpretation. If, however, there is no published, prelitigation interpretation by the IRS, the courts need not give deference to the IRS's interpretation, and may select the interpretation that seems most reasonable. [12]

III. TAX ETHICS

A taxpayer has a responsibility to file an accurate tax return, and a lawyer can advise a client to take a return position only if he or she abides by the applicable ethical rules imposed by the state bar association. The IRS itself regulates practice before it by imposing certain standards and the ABA has promulgated its recommended standard: A position must have a "realistic possibility of success on the merits if litigated." Certain civil and criminal penalties attach to an inaccurate tax return. [14-15]

IV. READING TAX STATUTES

Any statute is made up of two parts: its domain (the set of facts to which it applies) and its effect (the consequences of the statute applying). Consider using a five–step process—called parsing—to understand the domain and effect of an unfamiliar statute. [15-20]

A. The general rule

Find the statute's general rule, and underline it in red.

B. Definitions

Find the statute's terms of art and definitions, and highlight these in yellow.

C. Exceptions and special rules

Find the statute's exceptions and special rules, and mark them with a green "X."

D. Related statutory material

Find the statute's explicit and implicit references to related material, and circle these in blue.

E. Summarize domain and effect

Summarize the statute's domain and effect in the margin in your own words.

V. TAX POLICY

The wisdom of a particular tax statute can be evaluated using three criteria: fairness of the system; its administrative practicality; and its economic impact. [20-21]

A. Fairness

The U.S. income tax burden is allocated among taxpayers based on their "ability to pay." A "fair" system imposes similar taxes on those with similar abilities to pay (horizontal equity). It is impossible to measure each taxpayer's ability to pay directly, and thus taxable income is the surrogate for a taxpayer's ability to pay. If a tax statute causes the system to be more accurate in distinguishing among various taxpayers' abilities to pay, it is more "fair" than a provision that does not do so. [20-21]

B. Administrative practicality

A good tax statute will assess and collect tax in a cost-effective manner and will not require undue governmental interference with a taxpayer's life. [21]

C. Economic effects

Taxpayers change their behavior in response to tax statutes, and proponents of a taxing measure must consider the effects (both intended and unintended) that the measure likely will have on taxpayer behavior. [21]

CHAPTER 2

IDENTIFYING GROSS INCOME

I. IRC SECTION 61—INCOME

The linchpin of the Code, §61, defines gross income as "all *income* from whatever source derived" (emphasis added). Thus it is important to define "income" in order to determine what is included in gross income (even if later it is excluded by another statute). [26]

II. DEFINITIONS OF INCOME

A. Haig-Simons definition: Theoretical approach

Under this approach, income is the sum of (1) the market value of rights exercised in consumption, plus (2) the change in the value of the store of property rights between the beginning and end of the period in question (usually a taxable year). The Haig-Simons definition defines a comprehensive tax base, but difficulties may arise in measuring all consumption and in valuing assets each year. [26-27]

B. "Economic benefit": A more practical approach

Under this approach, income is the value of any economic benefit received by the taxpayer regardless of the form of the benefit. [27-28]

1. **Tangible items:** The receipt of cash or other property generates income under this approach, even if it comes from an unusual source, such as a windfall.

2. **Barter:** The exchange of services for services constitutes income to both service providers. See Rev. Rul. 79-24, 1979-2 C.B. 60.

3. **Intangible benefits:** The receipt of an intangible benefit would be included in gross income under this approach. For example, if one taxpayer satisfies another taxpayer's legal obligation, the latter has income in the amount of the satisfaction. *Old Colony Trust Co. v. Commissioner,* 279 U.S. 716 (1929). But noneconomic benefits (such as a sunny day in Oregon) are not income under this principle.

III. CERTAIN ITEMS THAT ARE NOT INCOME

Certain items are not considered income by general understanding of that term in federal tax law, even though they might qualify as "income" under a theoretical definition of income.

A. Imputed income

The value of any services one performs for oneself or one's family and the value of any property used that one owns are imputed income, which is not considered income for purposes of federal income tax. [29-30]

B. Capital recovery

A taxpayer's income from the sale or exchange of property is his or her profit on the transaction, not the total amount received. A taxpayer is entitled to receive his or her capital investment in the property tax free, although the timing of this recovery is a matter for legislative determination. [30-31]

C. Loans

Neither the creation nor the repayment of a loan is a taxable event. However, forgiveness or discharge of a loan may generate income to the debtor. [31]

CHAPTER 3

SPECIFIC INCLUSIONS IN GROSS INCOME

I. SECTION 61

Section 61 provides that gross income includes "all income" from all sources. Courts construe §61 broadly to include most types of income in gross income, unless they are specifically excepted by statute.

II. SPECIFIC ITEMS

Section 61(a) provides a nonexclusive list of types of income specifically included in gross income.

A. Compensation income—§61(a)(1)

Compensation income is the consideration transferred for the performance of services, whether in the form of salary, fees, commissions, or fringe benefits, and whether in the form of cash, property, or other services. [35-37]

1. **Amount included:** The amount of compensation income is the amount of cash received or the fair market value of the property or services received.

2. **Timing issues:** The taxable year in which a taxpayer will include an amount of compensation income will depend on the taxpayer's method of accounting, and if restricted property is involved, the rules of §83.

3. **Character:** Compensation income is ordinary income, potentially taxable at the highest tax rate.

B. Gross income from business—§61(a)(2)

A taxpayer engaged in business as a sole proprietor will include his or her gross income from business and will subtract available deductions from that amount, reporting the net result (income or loss) on the tax return. Entities such as corporations report their income and deductions from business, and pass–through entities such as partnerships report these results to their owners for inclusion in the owners' tax return. [37-38]

C. Gains derived from dealings in property—§61(a)(3)

These are discussed fully in Chapters 9 and 10.

D. Investment income—§61(a)(4)-(7)

Various types of investment income are included in gross income, including dividends, interest (both explicit and imputed), rents, royalties, and income from annuities. [38-43]

1. **Imputed interest—OID rules, §§483, 7872:** Most loans explicitly provide for interest to be paid. Some, however, provide for no interest or a below-market rate of interest, and the Code often will recharacterize these loans or investments to impute interest to the transactions. [39] and generally See Chapter 15.

2. **Annuities—§§61(a)(9), 72:** A taxpayer receiving a regular annuity payment is receiving a partial return of his or her invested capital, and the balance of the payment is income. To determine the amount of a payment that is excluded from gross income, multiply the payment by the exclusion ratio. The exclusion ratio is the following fraction:

$$\frac{\text{Investment in the contract}}{\text{Total expected return under the contract}}$$

The amount of the payment in excess of the excluded amount is included in gross income of the taxpayer, subject to certain limitations. [40-43]

E. **Alimony—§§61(a)(8), 71**

A taxpayer receiving alimony must include it in his or her gross income. The federal definition of alimony governs the tax consequences of alimony payments, regardless of the label used under state law for the payment. [43-47]

     1. **Definition of alimony:** In order for a payment to qualify as alimony, it must meet six requirements: (1) it must be paid in cash, not in property or services; (2) the payment must be received by or on behalf of the spouse or former spouse pursuant to a divorce decree or separation instrument; (3) the decree must not designate the payment as nondeductible and nonincludable; (4) the payor and recipient must not be members of the same household at the time of the payment; (5) there must be no obligation to make a payment after the death of the recipient spouse; and (6) the payment must not be, in substance, support for the child of the payor (there is an incentive to characterize child support as alimony because alimony is deductible to the payor, and child support is not deductible).

     2. **Front-end loaded alimony:** If alimony payments vary by more than $15,000 in the first three years, and the payments are greater in the beginning than at the end of the three–year period, they will be "front-end loaded." In that case, the "excess alimony amount" is included in the gross income of the payor spouse and is deducted from the income of the recipient spouse in the third post-separation year.

     3. **Property settlements:** If an amount payable in divorce is not alimony or child support, it may be a property settlement. See Chapter 10.

F. **Discharge of indebtedness income—§61(a)(12)**

Creation of a loan is not a taxable event to either the creditor or the debtor, for neither has a net economic benefit. If, however, the creditor forgoes collection under the debt, the debtor will have a benefit equal in amount of the debt forgone. This is discharge of indebtedness income and must be included in the debtor's gross income. [47-51]

     1. **Enforceable debt:** In order to have discharge of indebtedness income, there must be an enforceable debt in the first place. See *Zarin v. Commissioner,* 916 F.2d 110 (3d Cir. 1990).

     2. **Identifying discharge:** A discharge occurs when the creditor agrees to take something less than he or she originally agreed to take, in satisfaction of the loan. Payment is not discharge, nor is payment by another, or payment deferral. If the creditor receives what he or she bargained for, even if that amount is different from the amount loaned, there is no discharge.

     3. **Contested liability doctrine:** If a taxpayer in good faith disputes the amount of the debt, a subsequent settlement of the debt is treated as the amount of the debt for tax purposes.

     4. **Possible exclusion—§108:** Certain types of discharge of indebtedness income are excluded from the gross income of the taxpayer, if the taxpayer also reduces his or her "tax attributes."

III. PRIZES, AWARDS, HELPFUL PAYMENTS, AND EMBEZZLEMENTS

Code sections other than §61 provide for specific inclusions in gross income, and judicial doctrines also include some amounts in gross income. [53-55]

A. Prizes and awards—§74

Prizes and awards are included in gross income unless the recipient did nothing to be selected, the recipient is not required to render substantial future services as a condition of receiving the prize, and immediately transfers the prize to charity. [54]

B. Helpful payments—§§82, 85, 86

Various types of helpful payments are included in gross income, such as unemployment compensation, and a portion of social security benefits received, depending on the income of the recipient. [54-55]

C. Embezzled funds

Embezzlers must include the proceeds of their embezzlements in their gross income unless they can show that the transaction is akin to a loan. See *Gilbert v. Commissioner,* 552 F.2d 478 (2d Cir. 1977). [55]

IV. SOME ITEMS NOT USUALLY CRUCIAL TO THE BASIC TAX COURSE

Section 61 specifically includes in gross income several items that are not usually the focus of the basic tax course. These include income from pensions, a partner's distributive share of partnership income (see business income, above), income from an interest in an estate or trust, and income in respect of a decedent. [51-53]

CHAPTER 4

SPECIFIC EXCLUSIONS FROM GROSS INCOME

I. EXCLUSIONS—IN GENERAL

When an item is excluded from gross income, even though it may be income in the sense of §61, a specific statute provides that it will not be included in gross income. Exclusions are construed narrowly; an item must fit within the precise domain of an exclusion statute in order to be excluded from gross income. [61-62]

II. DEATH BENEFITS—§101

Amounts received under a life insurance policy by reason of the death of the insured are excluded from gross income. [62-65]

A. Transfer for valuable consideration

The exclusion does not apply to payments made under policies that were transferred for valuable consideration; in that case, the exclusion is limited to the purchaser's purchase price under the contract. [64]

B. Chronic or terminal illness

The exclusion extends to amounts paid to or for the care of chronically or terminally ill insureds. [64]

III. GIFTS—§102

The recipient of a gift or an inheritance may exclude the cash or value of the property received from gross income regardless of amount. [65-67]

A. Definition

A gift is a transfer made with detached and disinterested generosity. See *Duberstein v. Commissioner,* 363 U.S. 278 (1960). [66]

B. Exceptions

1. **Income from property:** The exclusion does not apply to the income derived from property received by gift.

2. **Employee gifts:** The exclusion does not apply to any transfer made by an employer to an employee; these amounts are considered compensation income, not gifts.

C. Basis—§1015

A recipient of property by gift or inheritance must determine the basis he or she has in the property. [66] and Chapter 9.

1. **Property received by gift:** The recipient of property by gift takes the donor's basis in the gift, plus a portion of any gift tax paid on the transfer. However, if at the time of the gift the fair market value of the property was less than its basis, for purposes of determining loss on subsequent sale or disposition, the donee takes the fair market value of the gift on the date of the gift. IRC §1015(a).

2. **Property received by inheritance—§1014:** The recipient of property through inheritance takes as his or her basis in the property the fair market value of the property on the date of the decedent's death or the alternate valuation date if that date is elected.

IV. COMPENSATION FOR PERSONAL INJURY OR SICKNESS—§104

Section 104 excludes from gross income amounts received as a result of personal physical injury or sickness. This excludes compensatory damages from suit or settlement of personal physical injury actions (in lump sums or in structured settlements), but does not exclude punitive damages (except in very limited situations), previously deducted medical expenses, and pre- or postjudgment interest. [67-69]

V. DISCHARGE OF INDEBTEDNESS INCOME—§108

Certain types of discharge of indebtedness income may be excluded from gross income. The exclusion is generally conditioned on the taxpayer giving up certain tax benefits. [69-72]

A. Types of discharge of indebtedness income excluded

Only certain types of discharge of indebtedness income are excluded under §108. Of these, the principal types are the following:

1. **Bankruptcy—§108(a)(1)(A):** If the discharge occurs in a title 11 (bankruptcy) case, the discharge of indebtedness income is excluded from gross income.

2. **Insolvency—§108(a)(1)(B):** If the discharge occurs at a time the taxpayer is insolvent, the discharge of indebtedness income is excluded from gross income to the extent of the insolvency. Insolvency is the amount of the taxpayer's debts over the fair market value of his or her property.

3. **Certain farm debt—§108(a)(1)(C):** If the discharge is of "qualified farm indebtedness" the discharge of indebtedness income will be excluded from gross income.

4. **Certain real property debt—§108(a)(1)(D):** If the discharge is qualified real property business indebtedness, and the taxpayer is not a C corporation, the discharge of indebtedness will be excluded from gross income. Qualified real property business indebtedness is generally debt incurred in connection with real property used in a trade or business, and which is secured by that property.

B. **"Paying the piper"—§108(b)**

Each dollar of exclusion generally requires a reduction in the taxpayer's tax benefits, i.e., net operating losses, tax credits, capital loss carryovers, and other carryovers. The taxpayer may elect in some circumstances to apply the exclusion amount to reduce the basis of depreciable property. The result of this reduction is that the taxpayer will have a greater amount of income in the future. [70]

VI. QUALIFIED SCHOLARSHIPS—§117

Amounts received as a "qualified scholarship," which generally means amounts received by degree candidates at regularly operated educational institutions for tuition, books, fees, and supplies, are excluded from gross income. A qualified scholarship does not include room and board or amounts paid for services. [72-73]

VII. EXCLUSION FOR GAIN ON PRINCIPAL RESIDENCE—§121

Section 121 allows a taxpayer to exclude from gross income $250,000 ($500,000 for joint returns) of gain on the sale of a principal residence, if the taxpayer has owned and used the dwelling as a principal residence for at least two of the past five years. [73-76]

VIII. EMPLOYMENT-RELATED EXCLUSIONS

The Code provides a variety of employment-related exclusions. [76-83]

A. **Meals and lodging—§119**

An employee may exclude from gross income the value of meals and lodging provided by an employer if the meals or lodging are provided for the convenience of the employer, are provided on the business premises of the employer, and in the case of lodging, the employee is required to accept the lodging as a condition of employment. [76-78]

1. **Convenience of the employer:** "Convenience of the employer" means that the employer has a "substantial noncompensatory business reason" for supplying the meals and lodging, considering all the facts and circumstances of the situation.

2. **Business premises:** The business premises of an employer are the grounds of the employer's place of business. The circuits have split on whether the business premises for state police include all public roads and contiguous restaurants.

3. **Condition of employment:** The condition of employment requirement is generally satisfied by showing that the employee is on call for the business of the employer.

B. Statutory fringe benefits—§132

The value of any fringe benefit that qualifies as any of eight fringe benefits is excluded from the gross income of the employee. In some cases, the provision of the benefit must meet antidiscrimination rules. [78-80]

1. **No additional cost service—§132(b):** If the employer regularly provides the service to the public and provides it to the employee without incurring any significant additional cost, it will be excluded from the gross income of the employee who receives the service.

2. **Qualified employee discounts—§132(c):** If employees enjoy a discount on property or services provided to the public by the employer, and the discount does not exceed a stated percentage, the value of the discount will be excluded from the gross income of the employees taking advantage of the discount.

3. **Working condition fringe—§132(d):** An employee receiving a benefit that would have generated a deduction as a trade or business expense or as depreciation to the employee had he or she purchased the benefit individually may exclude the benefit from gross income.

4. **De minimis fringe—§132(e):** If the benefit provided to the employees is so small that accounting for it would be unreasonable or administratively impractical, it will be excluded from the gross income of the employees receiving it.

5. **Qualified transportation fringe—§132(f):** An employee who receives transit passes, van transportation, or parking may exclude the benefit from gross income, within specified dollar limitations.

6. **Qualified moving expense reimbursement—§132(g):** If an employee receives reimbursement for amounts that would be deductible as moving expenses under §217, he or she may exclude these amounts from gross income.

7. **Athletic facility—§132(j):** The value of an on-premises athletic facility may be excluded from the gross income of an employee if it is operated by the employer and is used mostly by employees.

8. **Qualified retirement planning services—§132(m):** An employer may provide financial planning services, if certain conditions are met.

C. Insurance premiums and payments—§§79, 105, 106

The cost of employer-provided health insurance premiums is excluded from the gross income of the employee. When an employee receives benefits, these are excluded from gross income up to the amount of the employee's medical expenses. The employee may also exclude the cost of employer-provided term life insurance attributable to coverage up to $50,000; premiums attributable to excess coverage are includable in the employee's gross income. [80-82]

D. Dependent care assistance—§129

The employee may exclude up to $5,000 of employer-provided dependent care assistance in the form of actual care provided or as reimbursement. [82]

E. Educational assistance—§127

The employee may exclude up to $5,250 of qualifying educational assistance provided by the employer. [82]

F. Adoption expenses—§137

An employer may provide up to $10,630 of adoption assistance to employees, which may be excluded from their gross incomes, subject to certain income limitations. [83]

IX. EDUCATIONAL INCENTIVES—EXCLUSIONS

A. Interest on U.S. savings bonds—§135

To the extent the redemption proceeds of U.S. savings bonds are used for qualified education expenses, the income element of such redemption is excluded from gross income. Income level restrictions apply. IRC §135. [83-85]

B. Section 529 plans—§529

Distributions from §529 plans, which are state-sponsored plans for education savings, are excluded from gross income to the extent they are used for qualified education expenses. Unlike many education incentives, these funds can be used for K–12 as well as post-secondary education. [85]

C. Education savings accounts—§530

Distributions from education savings accounts (formerly known as Education IRAs) are excluded from gross income to the extent they are used for qualified education expense. Unlike many education incentives, these funds can be used for K–12 as well as post-secondary education. [85]

X. CHILD SUPPORT—§71

A custodial parent may exclude child support received from his or her gross income. [86]

XI. INTEREST ON STATE AND LOCAL BONDS—§103

A taxpayer may exclude the interest on qualifying state and local bonds. [67]

CHAPTER 5

DEDUCTIONS—IN GENERAL

I. DEFINITION OF DEDUCTION

A deduction is a subtraction from income in computing adjusted gross income or taxable income. [91-92]

A. Compare exclusion

By contrast, an exclusion causes an item of income not to be included in gross income. An exclusion and a deduction will have the same tax effect for taxpayers, but will reach this result by very different paths. [92] and Chapter 4.

B. Compare tax credit

A tax credit is a dollar-for-dollar reduction in the amount of tax due. [92] and Chapter 13.

II. ROLE OF DEDUCTIONS

Deductions figure prominently in two phases of computation of taxable income. One group of deductions is subtracted from gross income in computing adjusted gross income (AGI). Another group is subtracted from AGI in computing taxable income. See Figure 5A, in text. [92-93]

III. COMMON THEMES OF DEDUCTION CONTROVERSIES

Three common themes arise in deduction controversies. [94-95]

A. An event

A taxpayer must experience an outlay, an outflow, or a loss in which there is no realistic possibility of recovery of the item. Deductions are narrowly construed, and each and every requirement of a deduction statute must be met. [94]

B. Personal versus business expenses

A common theme in the analysis of deductions is the question whether an expense is "personal" or "business." This distinction is important because, as a general rule, personal expenses are not deductible unless a specific statute provides otherwise. Business expenses are generally deductible. Taxpayers seek to characterize deductions as business-related, rather than personal, in order to deduct them. [94-95]

C. Expense or capital expenditure

An expense may be deducted currently, but if an expenditure is for a capital item (a capital expenditure), its cost must be added to basis and be recovered in accordance with the statutory scheme governing capital recovery. Taxpayers prefer to characterize expenditures as expenses rather than capital expenditures in order to accelerate capital recovery. [95]

CHAPTER 6

PERSONAL DEDUCTIONS

I. IN GENERAL—§262

While personal expenditures are not generally deductible, specific Code provisions allow a taxpayer to deduct certain personal expenses if the statutory requirements are met.

II. TWO KINDS OF PERSONAL DEDUCTIONS

A. "Above-the-line" deductions

This group of deductions is subtracted from gross income in computing AGI. Taxpayers seek to increase "above-the-line" deductions because AGI serves as a measure for certain itemized deductions, and lowering AGI will potentially increase the deductible portion of these itemized deductions. [99]

B. "Below-the-line" deductions

This group of deductions is subtracted from AGI in computing taxable income and includes the personal exemption and either the standard or the itemized deduction. The itemized deduction is the sum of a number of deductions including home mortgage interest, taxes, casualty losses, medical expenses, charitable contributions, bad debts, and miscellaneous expenses. [99]

III. "ABOVE-THE-LINE" PERSONAL DEDUCTIONS

A. Alimony—§215

A taxpayer may deduct the amount of alimony or separate maintenance paid during the year. Alimony has a special definition under federal tax law. [100]

B. Moving expenses—§217

A taxpayer may deduct qualifying moving expenses associated with a move to a new place of employment 50 or more miles from the taxpayer's former employment. [100-101]

C. Contributions to regular IRAs—§219

A taxpayer may claim a deduction for certain retirement savings. In general, an individual may deduct the lesser of $4,000 or his or her earned income to an individual retirement account (IRA). If the taxpayer participates in a qualified plan and has income in excess of a certain amount, the contribution may be made, but no deduction is allowable. [101-102]

D. Losses—§165

A taxpayer may deduct losses incurred during a taxable year that are not compensated for by insurance or otherwise. However, an individual taxpayer may deduct only three types of loss. [102]

1. Trade or business losses—§165(c)(1): A taxpayer may deduct losses incurred in a trade or business. A trade or business is defined below? [132] and Chapter 7.

2. Investment losses—§165(c)(2): A taxpayer may deduct losses incurred in an activity engaged in for profit, which does not constitute a trade or business. For example, losses on the sale of stock would be investment losses, but losses on the sale of a principal residence would not be, as a principal residence is held for personal, rather than investment, purposes.

3. Casualty losses—§165(c)(3): A taxpayer may deduct certain casualty losses, such as losses from theft, fire, storm, and flood. Casualty losses up to the amount of casualty gains are deducted from gross income in computing AGI. The remaining deductible losses constitute an itemized deduction. [112-114]

E. Interest on student loans—§221

Up to $2,500 of the interest paid on certain student loans is potentially deductible, as an above-the-line deduction, depending on income limitations. [103-104]

F. Qualified education expenses—§222

Before 2006, up to $4,000 of qualified education expenses for post-secondary education is potentially deductible, as an itemized deduction, depending on income limitations. [104-105]

G. Medical savings accounts—§223

A taxpayer subject to a high-deductible health plan can deduct certain contributions to a Health Savings Account (HSA). [105-106]

H. Costs incurred in civil rights actions

A taxpayer who incurs attorneys' fees or other costs in certain civil rights actions may deduct such expenses. There are only a limited number of actions that qualify, and otherwise the taxpayer would probably be required to deduct these amounts as miscellaneous itemized deductions. [106]

IV. THE CHOICE: STANDARD OR ITEMIZED DEDUCTION

A taxpayer may deduct either the standard or the itemized deduction, but not both. The rational taxpayer will choose the larger of the two. The standard deduction is a specified amount based on filing status, and the itemized deduction is the sum of the taxpayer's itemized deductions. [107-108]

V. ITEMIZED DEDUCTIONS

A number of deductions are available to the taxpayer only if he or she claims the itemized deductions. The principal itemized deductions are discussed below.

A. Interest—§163

Personal interest is not deductible. Personal interest is interest other than (1) trade or business interest; (2) investment interest; (3) qualified residence interest; or (4) passive activity interest. [108-109]

1. **Investment interest—§163(d):** A taxpayer may deduct interest to finance the purchase of investments, but only to the extent of net income from those investments.

2. **Qualified residence interest—§163(h):** Qualified residence interest is deductible by individuals. There are two types of qualified residence interest attributable to loans on the taxpayer's principal residence and one other qualifying residence (which the taxpayer uses at least 14 days per year for personal purposes).

   a. **Acquisition indebtedness:** Interest is deductible on loans up to $1 million, the proceeds of which are used to acquire or construct a qualifying residence, and which are secured by that residence.

   b. **Home equity indebtedness:** Interest is deductible on loans up to $100,000, which are secured by a principal residence and do not exceed the taxpayer's "equity" in the residence, i.e., the difference between the fair market value and any indebtedness secured by that residence.

B. Taxes—§164

A taxpayer may deduct state, local, and foreign real property, personal property, and income taxes, and, in 2004-2005, sales taxes. [112]

C. Casualty losses—§165(c)(3), (h)

A casualty loss is a loss through complete or partial destruction of property from a sudden, unexpected, and unusual cause such as fire or storm. A taxpayer may deduct casualty losses to the extent that they exceed (1) $100 per event, and (2) 10% of the taxpayer's adjusted gross income. [112-115]

D. Medical expenses—§213

A taxpayer may deduct medical expenses, but only to the extent that they exceed 7.5% of his or her AGI. Medical expenses are expenses for the cure, treatment, or management of a disease or accident and include health insurance premiums paid by the taxpayer but do not include certain other items such as nonprescription drugs and certain elective cosmetic surgery. [115-118]

E. Charitable contributions—§170

A taxpayer may deduct contributions to qualifying charitable organizations. The amount of the deduction is the amount of cash or the fair market value of any property contributed. Limitations based on a taxpayer's AGI are imposed; usually, this is 50% of AGI. The taxpayer must not receive a personal benefit as a result of the contribution. [118-120]

F. Miscellaneous expenses—§67

A number of expenses are deductible only to the extent that they, in the aggregate, exceed 2% of the taxpayer's AGI. These include employee's unreimbursed business expenses and certain investment expenses. [120-121]

VI. PERSONAL EXEMPTION—§151

A taxpayer is entitled to deduct a personal exemption for him- or herself and for any dependent of the taxpayer. [121-122]

CHAPTER 7

BUSINESS AND INVESTMENT DEDUCTIONS

I. IN GENERAL

Net business income is included in a taxpayer's gross income, and net loss from a business constitutes a deduction subject to certain limitations. To compute net income or loss from business, a taxpayer begins with gross income from the business and subtracts available deductions. [123] A taxpayer doing business as a sole proprietor reports this income and the available deductions on Schedule C and the net result (income or loss) is then reported on his or her own tax return, subject to certain limits on losses. A taxpayer who owns rental or royalty property will compute the income and deductions associated with this activity on Schedule E and report the net result (profit or loss) on his or her own tax return, subject to certain limitations. In both situations, it is critical to identify available deductions. [129-130]

II. ORDINARY AND NECESSARY BUSINESS EXPENSES—§162

A taxpayer may claim a deduction for all the ordinary and necessary expenses paid or incurred in carrying on a trade or business, or while away from home, and rental payments for business property. [130-133]

A. Five Requirements

There are five distinct requirements for deduction of an expenditure under §162.

1. Ordinary: Ordinary means "usual in the course of general and accepted business practice," arising from a transaction commonly encountered in the type of business in question, even if the expenditure is unique for the particular taxpayers. See *Deputy v. DuPont,* 308 U.S. 488 (1940).

In addition, the expenditure must be reasonable in amount, and this particular issue often arises in the area of compensation.

2. **Necessary:** There must be a reasonable connection between the expense and the furtherance of the business. Necessary means "appropriate and helpful" to the business, but the courts are reluctant to second-guess the judgment of business people except in extreme cases.

3. **Expense:** The expense requirement distinguishes between expenses (which may be deductible) and capital expenditures, which must be capitalized.

4. **Trade or business:** In order to be deductible, the expense must be incurred in connection with a taxpayer's trade or business. The principal function of the trade or business requirement is to distinguish between personal activities and business activities.

   a. **Definition:** To be engaged in a trade or business, a taxpayer must be involved in an activity with continuity and regularity and must have the primary purpose of creating income or profit rather than merely engaging in a hobby. See *Commissioner v. Groetzinger,* 480 U.S. 23 (1987).

   b. **Hobbies:** A trade or business requires a profit motive, which is not characteristic of hobbies. Hobbies may generate income, and certain deductions may be available under §183.

5. **Carrying on:** The expense must be incurred during the time the taxpayer is actually engaged in carrying on a trade or business.

   a. **Going concern:** A taxpayer is carrying on a trade or business from the date that it is a going concern, i.e., has regular activity in the areas in which the business is organized.

   b. **Pre-opening expenses—§195:** Expenses incurred prior to opening must be capitalized. Up to $5,000 of expenses that would have been deductible if the taxpayer had been engaged in a trade or business when they were incurred can be deducted in the year of opening, but this amount is reduced by the amount by which pre-opening expenses exceed $50,000. Any remaining amount is amortized over 15 years.

B. **Limits on deduction**

Section 162 is riddled with exceptions and special rules; only the principal exceptions are discussed here. [132-133]

1. **Public policy:** No deduction is allowed for illegal bribes and kickbacks, for fines or similar penalties paid to the government, or for the two-thirds portion of the treble damages of antitrust damages.

2. **Excessive CEO compensation:** There is no deduction for compensation of a chief executive officer of a publicly traded company in excess of $1 million unless it is performance-based.

III. CAPITAL RECOVERY FOR BUSINESS ASSETS

A. **In general—§263**

A taxpayer may not claim a current deduction for capital expenditures, generally defined as "permanent improvements or betterments made to increase the value of any property or estate." [133-143]

1. **Capital recovery:** When a capital expenditure is made, the cost is said to be "capitalized." The taxpayer will be entitled to recover that capitalized amount at some point during his or her ownership of the asset (capital recovery). "Recovery" means that the taxpayer's economic investment in the asset will constitute a tax benefit, either as a deduction during the ownership of the asset, or at sale when the taxpayer reports as gain the amount received in excess of his or her investment in the property.

2. **Timing:** The timing of capital recovery is completely within the discretion of Congress. Taxpayers prefer to recover capital as soon as possible, preferring accelerated depreciation systems to systems that defer capital recovery until sale or other disposition of the asset.

B. Definition of capital expenditure

Neither the Code nor the regulations offer a precise definition of a capital expenditure. [134-136]

1. **Separate asset test:** If an expenditure creates a separate, identifiable asset with a useful life that will extend substantially beyond the taxable year, the expenditure is probably a capital expenditure. See *Commissioner v. Lincoln Savings & Loan Assn.*, 403 U.S. 345 (1971) and Reg. §1.263-2(a).

2. **Future benefits test:** Even if a separate asset is not created, if an expenditure creates more than an insignificant future benefit, it is a capital expenditure. See *Indopco, Inc. v. Commissioner*, 112 S. Ct. 1039 (1992).

C. Section 179 deduction

Section 179 allows a taxpayer to deduct up to a specified amount attributable to capital expenditures for equipment and tools purchased for the business. This deduction also reduces the basis of the asset(s) by the amount of the deduction claimed. In 2005, this amount is $105,000 or the taxable income of the taxpayer, whichever is less. [142-143]

D. Modified accelerated cost recovery system (MACRS) deduction for tangible business assets—§§167, 168

MACRS is the method by which taxpayers claim capital recovery for tangible business assets. [137-141]

1. **Dual function of deduction:** The MACRS deduction is a deduction from gross income in computing net business income or loss. Each time the taxpayer claims an MACRS deduction, the basis of the asset is reduced by the same amount (producing the "adjusted basis" of the asset).

2. **Calculation of MACRS deduction:** The MACRS deduction is computed by applying the "applicable recovery method" to the "basis" of the asset over the "applicable recovery period," taking into account "applicable conventions."

    a. **Applicable recovery method:** Three different recovery methods are available under MACRS: straight-line and two accelerated methods.

    b. **Basis:** The basis of an asset is generally its cost, unless it is acquired by some other means.

    c. **Applicable recovery period:** The recovery period for an asset is the period of years over which the taxpayer claims capital recovery for the item. The recovery period for assets is defined by statute or by the IRS.

    i. Real property: Residential real property has a recovery period of 27.5 years. Non-residential real property has a recovery period of 39 years.

    ii. Personal property: Personal property can be 3, 5, 7, 10, 15, or 20-year property. For example, office furniture is 10-year property.

  d. Applicable conventions: The applicable convention expresses the beginning date of capital recovery. Recovery generally begins when property is placed in service, and the conventions provide that regardless of when the property is actually placed in service, it will be deemed placed in service on a particular date. Real property uses a midmonth convention, and personal property a midyear convention.

E. Section 197 intangibles

Section 197 allows a taxpayer to amortize the cost of "section 197 intangibles" ratably over 15 years. A §197 intangible includes purchased goodwill, going-concern value, covenants not to compete, patents, copyrights, secret formulas or processes, and various other intangibles. [141-142]

IV. OTHER BUSINESS DEDUCTIONS

A taxpayer engaged in business may deduct taxes, interest, losses, bad debts, and charitable contributions incurred in his or her business endeavors. [143-145]

V. RENTAL AND ROYALTY ACTIVITIES

A taxpayer who owns rental property, or property that generates royalties, probably is not engaged in a "trade or business." Nevertheless, the taxpayer may deduct the ordinary and necessary expenses incurred to generate this income and may depreciate or amortize assets that are subject to periodic capital recovery. [145]

VI. SPECIAL RULES FOR LOSSES

Net loss from a trade or business, or from rental or royalty activities may be limited if the taxpayer does not materially participate or does not have sufficient amounts "at risk." [145]

CHAPTER 8

MIXED BUSINESS AND PERSONAL EXPENSES

I. IN GENERAL

Business expenses are usually deductible, while personal expenses are not. Some expenses, however, have a mixed character. They are connected to the taxpayer's business, but also have a connection to his or her personal life. This mixed character raises questions about their deductibility. The Code takes a variety of approaches to these types of expenses. [151-152]

II. ORIGIN TEST

In order for an expense to be deductible as a business expense, it must have its origin in the taxpayer's business, not his or her personal life. In making this determination, the courts will inquire into the

C
A
P
S
U
L
E

S
U
M
M
A
R
Y

so-called "origin" of the expense—the reason the expense was incurred—considering all the facts and circumstances of the situation. See *United States v. Gilmore,* 372 U.S. 39 (1963). [152]

III. HOBBY LOSSES—§183

A taxpayer who has no profit motive for an activity may only deduct the expenses associated with the activity to the extent that such expenses are deductible under Code sections that do not require a profit motive (nonbusiness expenses) plus expenses in the amount equal to the gross income from the activity minus the nonbusiness expenses. [152-155]

A. Existence of profit motive—Reg. §1.183-2

Whether a taxpayer has engaged in an activity for profit is to be determined from all of the facts and circumstances of the situation. The regulations offer nine factors indicative of a profit motive. [153-154]

B. Exception—§183(d)

If an activity produces income in three out of the five consecutive years ending in the year in question, it is rebuttably presumed to be engaged in for profit. [155]

IV. SECTION 274 LIMITATIONS

Section 274 imposes significant limitations on the deduction of certain business expenses. [155-159]

A. Meals

A taxpayer must be physically present at meals, and the expense for the meal must not be lavish or extravagant. Only 50% of the cost of meals is deductible. [155-156]

B. Entertainment

The taxpayer must be present at the entertainment, and the expense for the entertainment must not be lavish or extravagant.

1. Directly related standard: For entertainment that does not occur in connection with a business meeting, the taxpayer must establish that the expense was directly related to the active conduct of the trade or business. [156-158]

2. Associated with standard: If the entertainment occurs immediately before or after a substantial and bona fide business meeting, the taxpayer must establish that the expense was associated with the active conduct of the trade or business.

C. Foreign travel

A taxpayer who engages in substantial personal activity while traveling outside the United States for more than one week is subject to significant restrictions on the deduction of travel expenses. In addition, significant restrictions are placed on expenses of travel on cruise ships outside the United States. [158-159]

D. Gifts

Regardless of the cost of a gift, a business-related gift can only generate a deduction of $25. [158]

E. Substantiation

A taxpayer must be able to prove his or her expenses (which is true for all expenses) by adequate substantiation. [159]

V. HOME OFFICES AND VACATION HOMES—§280A

When a taxpayer uses a portion of his or her residence as an office or rents out a vacation home while still using it for part of the year for personal purposes, an allocation must be made between deductible (business) and nondeductible (personal) expenses associated with use of the residence. [159-165]

A. Home offices

In order to deduct any expenses attributable to a home office, the taxpayer must use the office as the principal place of business, or as a place where the taxpayer regularly meets with patients, clients, or customers. [159-160]

1. **Restriction on deductions:** If the taxpayer meets this test, a portion of the expenses allocable to the business activity may be deducted, but not in excess of the gross income from the business minus the sum of the nonbusiness deductions plus business deductions not related to the use of the property

2. **Remember §121:** Section 121 allows a taxpayer to exclude from gross income some or all of the gain on the sale of a principal residence. This exclusion does not apply to deductions previously claimed for depreciation on a home. Thus, taxpayers must carefully consider whether it is worthwhile it to claim such a deduction.

B. Vacation homes

Deductions attributable to rental use of a home cannot exceed the percentage of those expenses equal to the total expenses multiplied by a fraction. The numerator of the fraction is the total number of days the unit is rented at fair rental value, and the denominator is the total number of days during the year in which the unit is used. This limitation does not apply to deductions that are allowable regardless of rental use, such as qualified residence interest. [160-163]

VI. "LUXURY" AUTOMOBILES AND LISTED PROPERTY—§280F

A. Automobiles

Section 280F limits the amount of MACRS deductions that may be claimed each year for passenger automobiles, thus essentially disallowing depreciation for "luxury" automobiles. [165-169]

B. Listed property

For certain types of property, the taxpayer will be required to use the straight-line method of depreciation unless the predominant use of the property is for business. [168]

VII. GAMBLING LOSSES

Gambling losses are deductible only to the extent of gains from gambling. [170]

CHAPTER 9

TRANSACTIONS IN PROPERTY

I. IN GENERAL

A six-step approach to sales or exchanges of property will ensure that all issues are addressed: (1) identifying transactions in "property"; (2) identifying a realization event; (3) computing realized gain or loss; (4) determining the amount of recognized gain or loss; (5) determining the basis of property (not cash) received in the transaction; and (6) determining the character of any recognized gain or loss. [177-179]

II. TRANSACTIONS IN PROPERTY

While most transactions in property are easy to identify—sales or trades of real estate, personal property, or stocks—in some situations it can be difficult to distinguish between sales of property and acceleration of streams of ordinary income. Only the former potentially generates capital gain. [179]

III. REALIZATION EVENT—§1001

A realization event occurs when a taxpayer exchanges property, receiving some materially different item. A "materially different" item of property is one that bestows on a taxpayer a different legal interest than what he or she had before. See *Cottage Savings Association v. Commissioner*, 499 U.S. 554 (1991). Thus, all sales and most exchanges will be realization events. [180-181]

IV. REALIZED GAIN OR LOSS—§1001(a)

Realized gain or loss is equal to the difference between the amount realized on a sale or other disposition of property and the adjusted basis of the property transferred. [181-186]

A. Amount realized—§1001(b)

A taxpayer's amount realized on the sale or other disposition of property is equal to the sum of the cash and fair market value of property or services received, plus the amount of liabilities assumed by the other party to the transaction. [181-182]

B. Adjusted basis

The adjusted basis of property is equal to its initial basis adjusted upward for improvements and downward for capital recovery (depreciation) deductions. [182-186]

1. **Basis—purchases—§1012:** The basis of property is usually equal to its cost. If a taxpayer performs services and receives property in payment, the amount the taxpayer includes in gross income as payment will constitute the basis of the property.

2. **Basis—other transactions:** The basis of property received other than by purchase is determined under specific Code sections.

    a. **Property received from a decedent—§1014:** Property received from a decedent takes a basis equal to its fair market value on the date of death.

    b. **Property received by gift—§1015:** If property is received by gift, the donee generally takes the property with the same basis as the donor had in the property, increased by a portion of any gift tax paid. If, at the time of the gift, the adjusted basis of the property in the donor's hands is greater than its fair market value, for purposes of determining loss on sale or other disposition by the donee, the donee's basis is the fair market value of the property on the date of the gift.

c. **Property received in divorce—§1041(d):** Property received incident to a divorce has the same basis that it had immediately prior to the transfer.

V. RECOGNIZED GAIN OR LOSS—§1001(c)

Realized gain or loss is generally recognized unless a specific Code section prohibits or limits recognition. [186-188] and Chapter 10.

VI. BASIS OF PROPERTY RECEIVED IN THE SALE OR DISPOSITION

If the taxpayer sells property for cash, there is no need to determine the basis of the property received (since cash neither appreciates nor depreciates in value, there is no need to assign cash a basis for tax purposes). If, however, the taxpayer receives property in an exchange, the basis of that property must be determined, for later the taxpayer may sell or otherwise dispose of the property.

A. Full-recognition transactions

In a transaction in which the selling taxpayer recognizes all realized gain or loss, the property received will have a basis equal to its fair market value. [182]

B. Nonrecognition transactions

In transactions in which the selling taxpayer does not recognize all or part of the realized gain or loss, the property received will have a basis different than its fair market value, determined under specific Code sections. See Chapter 10.

VII. CHARACTER

The character of the gain or loss recognized will depend on the nature of the asset in the hands of the transferor. See Chapter 12.

VIII. TRANSFERS OF ENCUMBERED PROPERTIES

In most sales or other dispositions of property, the selling taxpayer satisfies all mortgages or other encumbrances prior to sale. The repayment of a mortgage or other debt is not, in itself, a taxable event. In some situations, however, the taxpayer transfers the property subject to the debt; in other words, the buyer assumes the mortgage as part of the purchase price. In this situation, the consequences to the seller and purchaser must be considered. [187-198]

A. Mortgage amount less than fair market value

If the mortgage on the seller's property is less than the fair market value of that property, the seller's amount realized includes the assumption of debt regardless of the nature of the debt as recourse or nonrecourse. The seller will compute realized gain in the usual fashion: amount realized (including the debt assumption) minus the adjusted basis of the property transferred. The buyer will include the debt assumption in basis as part of the cost of the property. [191-193]

B. Mortgage amount greater than fair market value

If the mortgage on the seller's property exceeds the fair market value of that property, the nature of the mortgage as recourse or nonrecourse becomes important in determining the tax consequences of sale. [194-198]

1. **Nonrecourse debt:** If the mortgage is nonrecourse, the seller's amount realized will include the full amount of the assumption, and the seller will compute realized gain in the usual fashion: amount realized (including the mortgage assumption) minus the adjusted basis of the property. Whether the buyer can include the total debt assumed as part of the purchase price is unclear; the buyer may be limited to the fair market value of the property as basis.

2. **Recourse debt:** If the mortgage is recourse, the buyer will not assume it because to do so would place the buyer's other assets at risk. Instead, a number of different transactions may occur with different consequences to the seller/debtor.

CHAPTER 10

NONRECOGNITION TRANSACTIONS

I. IN GENERAL

In some property transactions, realized gain or loss is not recognized in whole or in part at the time of the transaction. These transactions are called nonrecognition transactions and include like-kind exchanges, involuntary conversions, divorce transactions, and other transactions. When realized gain or loss is deferred rather than recognized, the property received in the transaction takes a basis that preserves that realized gain or loss for later recognition. [201-203]

II. LIKE-KIND EXCHANGES—§1031

A. Requirements

There are five requirements for a qualifying like-kind exchange. [203-204]

1. **Exchange of property:** The taxpayer must exchange property for property, rather than selling property or engaging in some other transaction. See *Jordan Marsh Co. v. Commissioner,* 269 F.2d 453 (2d Cir. 1959).

2. **Nature of property transferred—§1031(a)(2):** The property transferred must not be inventory, stocks, bonds, notes, other evidences of indebtedness, interests in a partnership, certificates of trust or beneficial interest, or choses in action.

3. **Property transferred—use:** The taxpayer must have held the property transferred for use in a trade or business, or for investment.

4. **Property received—use:** The taxpayer must intend to hold the property received for use in a trade or business, or for investment.

5. **Like kind:** The property received must be like-kind to the property transferred in the exchange. Like kind refers to the nature and character of the property rather than to its grade or quality.

   a. **Real property:** An exchange of real property for real property is a like-kind exchange regardless of the development status of the two properties. *Koch v. Commissioner*, 71 T.C. 54 (1978).

    b. Depreciable personal property—Reg. §1.1031(a)-1(b): The regulations offer a safe harbor for determining whether depreciable personal properties are like-kind, in which properties of the same "class" are considered like-kind. Properties outside the same class must be examined under the general like-kind test.

    c. Other personal property: Intangible and nondepreciable personal property and personal property held for investment must be examined under the general like-kind test.

B. Effect of qualifying like-kind exchange

If a taxpayer engages in a qualifying like-kind exchange of property for property, he or she will not recognize any of the realized gain or loss on the transaction. [204-207]

    1. Effect of boot—§1031(b): If the taxpayer receives boot (non-like-kind property), the taxpayer will recognize gain, but not loss, in the amount of the lesser of the fair market value of the boot or the realized gain.

    2. Basis of property received—§1031(d): The basis of like-kind property received in a like-kind exchange is equal to the basis of the property transferred, plus the gain recognized, minus the fair market value of the boot received, minus any loss recognized, plus any boot paid (additional investment in the property). The basis of any boot (nonlike-kind property) received is its fair market value.

C. Deferred and three-party exchanges—§1031(a)(3)

A potential problem arises when the taxpayer wishes to transfer property in a like-kind exchange, but the potential buyer who wants the taxpayer's property does not have suitable property to exchange. This problem can be overcome by creating a deferred exchange, but the property to be received by the taxpayer must be identified within 45 days after the taxpayer relinquishes his or her property and must be received before the earlier of the 180th day after the date the taxpayer relinquishes his or her property or the due date of the taxpayer's return for the year of transfer of the relinquished property. Any intermediary used must meet specific identity requirements to avoid agent status. [210-212]

D. Effect of mortgages in like-kind exchanges [212-218]

    1. One mortgage: If the property transferred in a like-kind exchange is subject to a mortgage, the transferee's assumption of that mortgage as a part of the transaction is treated as boot to the transferor. The mortgage assumption is also treated as boot for purposes of computing the taxpayer's basis in the property received.

    2. Two mortgages: If both the property transferred and the property received are subject to mortgages assumed in the like-kind exchange, the regulations allow the "netting" of the mortgages. The party with the net relief from liabilities (i.e., whose property was subject to the higher mortgage at the outset) is treated as having received boot in the amount of the net relief from liability. The mortgage netting rule applies only to the computation of gain recognition; the full amounts of the mortgages are considered in the computation of basis of the properties received by each party.

    3. Two mortgages plus boot: The mortgage netting rule allows the party with net assumption of debt to avoid recognition of gain. But this applies only to the mortgage portion of the transaction. If the person with net assumption of debt receives boot, the usual recognition rules will apply so that realized gain will be recognized to the extent of the fair market value of the boot received.

III. INVOLUNTARY CONVERSIONS—§1033

A taxpayer may be able to defer, in whole or in part, recognition of gain on the "involuntary conversion" of property. [219-224]

A. Conversion into similar property

If a taxpayer's property is involuntarily converted into property that is similar or related in service or use, the taxpayer will not recognize any of the realized gain on the conversion. [220-221]

B. Conversion into money

If the taxpayer's property is involuntarily converted into money, the taxpayer may elect to recognize gain in the amount of proceeds that are not reinvested in property similar or related in service or use to the converted property. [220-221]

C. Similar property

Real property used in a trade or business or held for investment must be like kind to the property converted, invoking the same standard as in §1031. All other property must meet the "similar" standard, which is a stricter standard than "like-kind." The similar standard requires that the properties have the same physical characteristics and that the taxpayer use the properties in the same way. [221-222]

D. Statutory replacement period

The taxpayer must reinvest within two years after the close of the taxable year in which the taxpayer realizes any portion of the gain on conversion. [222]

E. Basis of replacement property

The basis of the replacement property will be the basis of the property converted, plus the gain recognized, minus the unreinvested proceeds of conversion, minus any loss recognized on the conversion. [220-221]

F. Inapplicable to loss

Section 1033 does not apply to loss realized on the involuntary conversion of property; those losses would be casualty losses, potentially deductible under §165(c)(3) and (h).

IV. SPOUSAL AND DIVORCE TRANSFERS—§1041

A. Nonrecognition

Section 1041 provides that no gain or loss will be recognized on transfers of property between spouses or on transfers incident to a divorce. [224-227]

1. **Incident to a divorce:** A transfer of property is incident to a divorce if it occurs within one year of the date the marriage is terminated, or if it is contemplated by the divorce decree and occurs within six years of the date of termination of the marriage (or later if there is a good reason for the delay).

2. Indirect transfers: A transfer usually occurs directly from one spouse to the other. However, a qualifying transfer also can be made to a third person if made by direction or ratification of the other spouse or provided for in the divorce decree.

B. Effect of qualifying transfer to spouse or former spouse

The transferor in a §1041 transfer will not recognize gain or loss on the transfer. In addition, the recipient of property will not include any amount in gross income, and will take the property with the same basis as the property had immediately prior to the transfer. [225-226]

C. Related material

Consider in connection with §1041 the rules relating to alimony and child support.

V. OTHER NONRECOGNITION PROVISIONS

The Code contains a number of other nonrecognition provisions, including provisions relating to tax-free transfers to corporations and partnerships, allowing the tax-free exchange of stock in the same corporation, and allowing the tax-free exchange of life insurance policies. [227-228]

Chapter 11

TIMING ISSUES

I. THE ANNUAL ACCOUNTING CONCEPT

Federal income tax returns are filed on an annual basis in which taxpayers tote up their income, deductions, and allowable credits for their taxable year, and apply the tax rates for that year to their taxable income. [236-242]

A. Calendar and fiscal years

A taxpayer may use a calendar year or a fiscal year (which is a year other than a calendar year). Most individuals use a calendar year. [236]

B. Problems with annual accounting

While annual accounting is administratively easy, it can inaccurately measure a taxpayer's ability to pay, particularly for transactions that span more than one taxable year. Several Code sections have evolved to address these difficulties. [236-237]

1. The net operating loss deduction—§172: A taxpayer's excess of deductions over expenses constitutes a net operating loss that the taxpayer may carry back two years and forward 20 years. This allows the taxpayer to more accurately reflect income over a period of years.

2. Claim of right doctrine and §1341: A taxpayer must include amounts in gross income over which he or she has a claim of right and unfettered use, even if the taxpayer may be required to return all or a portion of the amount to another person. Section 1341 calculates the tax due if the taxpayer is required to return items previously included in gross income, in a taxpayer-friendly way.

3. Tax benefit rule—§111: The recovery of an item that constituted a deduction or credit in a prior year will be income to the taxpayer to the extent of the prior tax benefit. A "recovery" is an event that is fundamentally inconsistent with the previous deduction or credit.

II. METHODS OF ACCOUNTING

A. Cash method of accounting

A taxpayer using the cash method of accounting will report income when it is received, actually or constructively, and will claim deductions when amounts are actually paid (regardless of when they are due). [243-245]

1. Constructive receipt: A taxpayer will be considered to have received items to which he or she had a right and had the ability to claim but did not do so.

2. Restrictions on use of the cash method: Some taxpayers may not use the cash method of accounting, as Congress has determined that it would unreasonably accelerate deductions for these taxpayers.

B. Accrual method of accounting

A taxpayer using the accrual method of accounting will report income when all events that fix the taxpayer's right to the income have occurred, and the amount thereof can be determined with reasonable accuracy. Accrual-method taxpayers will deduct expenses when all events that fix the liability have occurred and its amount can be determined with reasonable accuracy, subject to special rules that defer deductions until "economic performance." [245-249]

III. ACCOUNTING FOR INVENTORIES

Taxpayers engaged in manufacturing and retail activities are required to account for inventories. Under an inventory approach, the taxpayer deducts from gross sales the cost of goods sold to determine the profit from sales for the year. Included in inventory are amounts attributable to the cost of manufacturing or purchasing the product, and certain taxpayers also must include in inventory an amount attributable to indirect costs (administrative costs, for example) under the UNICAP rules. Taxpayers identify inventory that is deemed sold in the cost of goods sold by adopting the LIFO (last-in, first-out) or FIFO (first-in, first-out) inventory methods. [249-253]

IV. INSTALLMENT METHOD OF REPORTING INCOME—§453

When a taxpayer sells property other than inventory in a sale in which at least one payment will be received after the close of the taxable year, the taxpayer may report the gain realized on the sale over the period of time payments are received by using the installment method. [252-259]

A. Applicable to gain

The installment method is applicable to gain, not loss. It is also not applicable to the interest portion of the transaction; interest is determined and accounted for separately. [252]

B. Amount includable in gross income

The amount of gain to be reported each year is the payment for the year multiplied by the gross profit ratio, which is a fraction the numerator of which is the gross profit (sales price minus adjusted basis) and the denominator of which is the total contract price (amount to be received under the contract). The remaining amount of any payment is excluded from gross income as capital recovery. [253-255]

V. RESTRICTED PROPERTY—§83

In many deferred compensation situations, the taxpayer receives property in exchange for the performance of services that is restricted in some fashion as to transfer or enjoyment. Section 83 defines (1) whether the taxpayer has income; (2) when the taxpayer has income; and (3) how much income the taxpayer has in these situations. [260-263]

A. Income?

A taxpayer potentially has income if there is a "transfer" of property to the taxpayer. An employer's setting aside of funds or property for the taxpayer's benefit is not income if the property can be reached by the employer's general creditors. But if the taxpayer has rights in the property that are not subject to the employer's creditors' claims, the taxpayer may have income. [260]

B. When?

A taxpayer must include the value of the property in gross income in the earlier of the first year in which the taxpayer owns the property without a requirement that he or she perform significant future services (i.e., the property is not subject to a "substantial risk of forfeiture") or the first year in which the property is transferable. [260-262]

C. How much?

The taxpayer includes in gross income the value of the property minus the amount the taxpayer paid for it. A taxpayer who receives restricted property may make what is known as a §83(b) election, in which the taxpayer includes in gross income the value of the property (minus amounts paid for it) within 30 days of receiving it, even though it is restricted. This would be appropriate for restricted property that is expected to greatly increase in value. [260-263]

VI. SPECIAL LIMITATIONS ON LOSS DEDUCTIONS

In addition to the restrictions on deductible losses of §165(c), discussed above, the Code imposes additional loss restrictions on certain types of losses. These are properly viewed as timing rules because they potentially cause losses incurred in a particular taxable year to be deferred to future taxable years. [263-265]

A. Capital losses—§1211

Capital losses are deductible only to the extent of capital gains plus, for individuals, $3,000 of ordinary income. Disallowed capital losses carry forward to future taxable years subject to the same limitation. See Chapter 12.

B. Passive losses—§469

Passive losses are losses from passive activities, i.e., activities that qualify as trades or businesses but in which the taxpayer does not materially participate. Passive losses incurred during a taxable year may only be deducted to the extent of the taxpayer's passive income for that year, and losses that are disallowed under this rule carry forward to future years when the taxpayer has passive income or disposes of the investment generating the passive loss. [263-264]

C. Amounts at risk—§465

A taxpayer's losses from certain activities are limited to a taxpayer's amount "at risk," i.e., the amount by which the taxpayer can be held liable to third parties upon failure of the venture. Losses disallowed by the at risk rules carry forward to future years in which the taxpayer has amounts at risk. [264-265]

CHAPTER 12

CHARACTER OF INCOME AND LOSS

I. IN GENERAL

When a taxpayer sells or exchanges property and recognizes gain or loss, the character of that gain or loss—as capital or ordinary—must be determined. [270]

II. CAPITAL/ORDINARY DISTINCTION

The capital/ordinary distinction has implications for both income and loss. [270-272]

A. Income—§1(h)

Tax is imposed on an individual's ordinary income at rates up to 35%. However, the maximum rate on "net capital gain" is potentially much lower, ranging from 5% to 28%. Thus, taxpayers prefer to characterize income as capital gain subject to the preferential rate. [270]

B. Loss—§1211

Section 1211 imposes a significant restriction on the deductibility of capital losses. Corporations may only deduct capital losses to the extent of their capital gains. IRC §1211(a). Individuals may deduct capital losses to the extent of their capital gain income, plus $3,000 of ordinary income. IRC §1211(b). Unused capital losses carry forward (and for corporations, carry back) to other taxable years. [270-271]

III. AN APPROACH TO CHARACTERIZING GAIN OR LOSS

A. An approach to characterization problems [272-273]

Figure 12A (in text) offers an approach to characterizing gain or loss as capital or ordinary, which requires analysis of the following issues, discussed in the sections that follow. [273-283]

1. **Has there been a recognized gain or loss?**

2. **Has there been a sale or exchange of property?**

3. **Is the property a capital asset?**

4. **Does §1231 apply to treat gains as capital?**

5. **Do any special recharacterization rules apply?**

B. Has there been a recognized gain or loss?

In order for a taxpayer to have a capital gain or loss, there must be a realization event, and any gains or losses from that event must be recognized. The item in question must constitute a sale or exchange of property, not the prepayment of income. See *Hort v. Commissioner*, 313 U.S. 28 (1941) (lease cancellation payment). [273-274] and Chapter 9.

C. Has there been a sale or exchange?

In order for the taxpayer to have a capital gain or loss, the recognized gain or loss must arise from the "sale or exchange" of property. This generally requires a "giving, a receipt, and a causal connection between the two." See *Yarbro v. Commissioner,* 737 F.2d 479 (5th Cir. 1984). Some events that might not otherwise meet this standard are deemed to be sales or exchanges by statute, such as losses from the worthlessness of stock or securities. [274-276]

D. Is the property a capital asset?

In order for the taxpayer to have a capital gain or loss, the recognized gain or loss must be from sale or exchange of a property that qualifies as a "capital asset." [276-281]

1. Excluded categories: Section 1221 defines a capital asset as "property held by the taxpayer (whether or not in connection with his trade or business)" except for eight enumerated categories of property, of which only five are usually important in the basic tax class. Thus, an item is a capital asset *unless* it falls within any of these five categories.

    a. Inventory/stock in trade—§1221(1): A taxpayer's stock in trade or inventory held primarily for sale to customers in the ordinary course of business is not a capital asset.

        i. Definition: "Primarily" means "of first importance" or "principal." See *Malat v. Riddell,* 383 U.S. 569 (1966).

        ii. Dealers: In order to have inventory, the taxpayer must hold the property primarily for sale to customers in the ordinary course of business. It is the relationship of the taxpayer to the assets, not the taxpayer's status generally, that determines whether assets constitute inventory. See *Van Suetendael v. Commissioner,* 3 T.C.M. 987 (1944), *aff'd,* 152 F.2d 654 (2d Cir. 1945).

        iii. Real estate: Whether a taxpayer holds real estate as an investor or as a dealer depends on the analysis of seven factors discussed in *United States v. Winthrop,* 417 F.2d 905 (5th Cir. 1969).

    b. Real and depreciable property—§1221(2): Real property used in a trade or business or property used in a trade or business that is subject to depreciation under §167 is not a capital asset. This type of property is §1231 property, discussed below.

    c. Creative works—§1221(3): Creative works generated by the taxpayer, such as material subject to copyright, letters, and memoranda are not capital assets.

    d. Accounts/notes receivable—§1221(4): A taxpayer's accounts or notes receivable from the sale of inventory are not capital assets.

    e. Supplies—§1221(a)(8): Supplies and similar items used in a taxpayer's business.

2. "Related to" the trade or business: Relying on the case of *Corn Products Refining Co. v. Commissioner,* 350 U.S. 46 (1955), taxpayers asserted that items that were integrally connected with their trade or business should be treated as noncapital assets. In *Arkansas Best Corp. v. Commissioner,* 485 U.S. 212 (1988), the U.S. Supreme Court reexamined *Corn Products,* concluding that the relation of an asset to a taxpayer's business was irrelevant in determining its status as a capital or noncapital asset. In determining whether an item was included in the noncapital category of inventory, certain "inventory substitutes" could be included in that category. The Court limited the holding of *Corn Products* to an application of the inventory substitute idea.

E. Does §1231 apply to characterize gains as capital?

Section 1221(2) excludes from the definition of a capital asset real and depreciable property used in a trade or business or held for investment. [268-271] But all is not lost. Section 1231 may apply to treat net gains from this kind of property as capital. [283-286]

1. **An approach to §1231:** Figure 12D (in text) offers an approach to characterizing gain or loss arising from §1231 property. The first question is whether the property sold is §1231 property. If the property is not §1231 property, its character is determined under the usual rules set forth in Figure 12A. If the property is §1231 property, the next question is whether the recapture rules of §§1245 or 1250 apply, because recapture income cannot be classified as §1231 gain. Then, the taxpayer determines all of the recognized gains and losses from §1231 assets involving casualties, and if such losses exceed such gains, all are removed from the calculation. If such losses do not exceed gains, all are included, along with all other §1231 gains and losses, and the losses and gains are netted against one another. If the final result is a net loss, all §1231 gains and losses are ordinary. If the final result is a net gain, all gains and losses are capital, except to the extent of unrecaptured §1231 losses during the previous five years.

2. **Section 1231 property:** Section 1231 gains and losses arise from the sale of property used in the trade or business of the taxpayer, or from the involuntary or compulsory conversion of property used in the trade or business, or any capital asset held for more than a year and held in connection with the taxpayer's trade or business.

3. **Recapture rule:** The recapture rule may limit the recharacterization of gains as capital under §1231. If the taxpayer has had, within the previous five years, §1231 losses that were characterized as ordinary, the current year's gain must be characterized as ordinary to the extent of the previous loss.

F. Do any special recharacterization rules apply?

Recognized gain or loss on the sale or exchange of a capital asset will usually be capital. However, the Code may, in certain circumstances, require all or a part of the gain or loss to be characterized as ordinary. [281-283]

1. **Recapture for personal and real property:** The recapture provisions require that upon sale or exchange of property that would otherwise generate capital gain, a portion of the recognized gain be characterized as ordinary. Recapture thus seeks to account for the previous benefit of depreciation deductions taken with respect to the property.

   a. **Personal tangible property—§1245:** On the sale or exchange of depreciable personal property that otherwise qualifies as a capital asset or a §1231 asset generating capital gain, the portion of the gain equal to the lower of the realized gain or depreciation previously claimed with respect to the property will be characterized as ordinary. Any remaining balance will be capital.

   b. **Real property—§1250:** Section 1250 requires recapture of the accelerated portion of depreciation taken with respect to real property to be recaptured upon sale. However, since real property acquired since 1987 has been depreciated using the straight-line method, the practical impact of this provision is minimal today.

2. **Small business stock—§1244:** Individual taxpayers and partnerships may claim a portion of the loss on the sale or worthlessness of small business stock as ordinary rather than capital. The maximum amount considered ordinary is $50,000 for a single taxpayer or $100,000 for a married couple filing a joint return. A small business corporation is a corporation that issues the stock to the taxpayer in exchange for property and must have derived more than 50% of its income from active business sources during the five-year period ending on the date of the loss.

IV. CALCULATING CAPITAL GAIN AND LOSS

The final step in addressing character issues is determining the taxpayer's net capital gain (which is included in the taxpayer's gross income and is taxed at preferential rates) or deductible capital loss, and the net capital loss carryforward. [286-294]

A. Definitions

Section 1222 sets forth a number of definitions relating to capital gains and losses that are relevant in calculating capital gain and loss. There are three baskets of capital gain/loss: the 28% group (collectibles); the 25% group (unrecaptured §1250 gain); and the 15/5% group (everything else). [288-292]

B. Holding period

Capital gains and losses must be characterized as long-term or short-term. Long-term gain or loss is gain or loss from the sale of an asset held for more than one year. Short-term gain or loss is gain or loss from the sale of an asset held for one year or less. The period of time during which a taxpayer owns (or is deemed to own) an asset is his or her holding period for the asset. The calculation of a taxpayer's capital gain and loss depends on the taxpayer's holding period of the assets generating capital gain and loss. The holding period usually begins with the taxpayer's acquisition of the asset, but in some cases, the taxpayer's holding period will include another person's holding period for the asset or the taxpayer's holding period for another asset. [288-289]

1. **Exchanged basis property—§1223(1):** For exchange transactions involving the transfer of capital or §1231 assets in which a taxpayer's gain is deferred in whole or in part, the taxpayer's holding period for the property received in the transaction will include the period the taxpayer held the property he or she transferred in the transaction. An example of this is the holding period for property received in a qualifying like-kind exchange.

2. **Transferred basis property—§1223(2):** If a taxpayer receives property in a transaction in which the taxpayer's basis is determined by reference to another person's basis in the same property, the taxpayer's holding period includes the period of time that other person held the property. An example of this is the holding period for a gift.

C. An approach to calculating net capital gain and net capital loss

Figure 12E provides a systematic approach for calculating net capital gain and net capital loss. First, the taxpayer's long- and short-term capital gains and losses are categorized into each group (28%; 25%; and 15/5%). Then, the gains and losses in each group are netted against one another to produce gain or loss in each category. Then, any losses in the short term, 28%, or 15/5% groups are applied to reduce gains in the other categories. This produces a net gain or a net loss in each category. The maximum rate of tax is the tax rate applicable to the group (such as 28%), but if the taxpayer's regular rate is lower, that rate will apply. [286-288]

CHAPTER 13

TAX RATES AND CREDITS

I. IN GENERAL

The applicable tax rate is applied to taxable income to produce the tentative tax. Available tax credits are subtracted from the tentative tax to produce the actual tax due. [299-300]

II. CURRENT TAX RATES

The current tax rate on ordinary income is progressive within a limited range, with tax rates for individuals ranging from 10% to 35% (in 2005). The specific rate applicable to an individual depends on his or her taxable income and filing status. [300-301]

A. Phase-outs

As income rises, certain tax benefits are phased out, including the full benefit of the itemized deduction and the personal exemption. [300]

B. Children

Children with sufficient income to owe tax file their own tax returns reporting their gross income and available deductions and credits. In some circumstances a child's parents may claim the child's investment income on the parents' return pursuant to the "kiddie tax." [301] and see Chapter 14.

C. Preferential rates on capital gains

Net capital gain is taxed at a maximum rate of 28% (collectibles), 25% (net unrecaptured §1250 gain); or 15% (everything else). If the taxpayer's rate on ordinary income is lower, the taxpayer gets the benefit of that rate. A taxpayer with gain in the 15% category, whose tax rate is 10%, will pay a 5% capital gains tax. [302]

D. Qualified dividend income

Qualified dividend income is subject to the 15/5% tax rate regime applicable to capital gains in the 15/5% category, removing the distinction between capital gain and ordinary income for many corporate distributions. [302]

III. THE ALTERNATIVE MINIMUM TAX

A. In general

The alternative minimum tax (AMT) is a surtax imposed on taxpayers with certain kinds of income or deductions. The purpose of the AMT is to ensure that every taxpayer, even those with the kinds of activities that reduce tax through tax-exempt income or significant deductions, pay some amount of tax. [303-306]

B. AMTI

The AMT is imposed on "alternative minimum taxable income"(AMTI). AMTI is computed by taking regular taxable income and adding back in certain items that were excluded and certain items that were deducted in the computation of regular taxable income. Important adjustments include the deduction for state taxes, the deduction for personal exemptions, the inclusion of certain tax-exempt interest, and a longer, slower depreciation period for certain assets. [303-304]

C. Exemption/tax rates

The AMT is imposed on AMTI in excess of an exemption amount. The first $175,000 is taxed at 26% and the rest is taxed at 28%. [304-305]

IV. TAX CREDITS

A tax credit is a dollar-for-dollar reduction in the amount of tax due. A refundable credit can reduce tax below zero, generating a refund. A nonrefundable credit can only reduce tax to zero and will not generate a refund. [306-314]

A. Contrast deductions and exclusions

While a tax credit is a dollar-for-dollar reduction in the amount of tax due, a deduction is a subtraction from either gross income or adjusted gross income in computing taxable income. Moreover, if an amount is excluded from gross income, it is never included in the computation of gross income. [306]

B. Credit for tax withheld—§31

Perhaps the most familiar tax credit is the credit for the amount of tax withheld from wages, salaries, bonuses, and similar payments. [306]

C. Dependent care credit—§21

Expenses for care of a dependent are not deductible, because they are personal expenses. Section 21 allows a taxpayer who maintains a household with at least one qualifying individual to claim a nonrefundable tax credit for certain expenses, equal to the taxpayer's "applicable percentage" multiplied by the "employment-related expenses." [307-309]

1. **Qualifying individual:** A qualifying individual is a dependent under the age of 13 for whom the taxpayer is entitled to a deduction as a dependent, or any other dependent or a spouse of a taxpayer who is physically or mentally unable to care for him- or herself.

2. **Applicable percentage:** The taxpayer's applicable percentage ranges from 35% for taxpayers with AGI of $15,000 or less, to 20% for taxpayers with AGI above $43,000.

3. **Employment-related expenses:** Employment-related expenses are those incurred for care of a qualifying individual while the taxpayer works, subject to two limitations.

    a. **Dollar limitation:** Employment-related expenses are limited to $3,000 for one qualifying individual and $6,000 for two or more qualifying individuals.

4. **Earned income limitation:** Employment-related expenses are limited to the earned income of a single taxpayer, or if a married couple files a joint return, to the earned income of the lesser-earning spouse. Special rules impute an amount of income to students and disabled taxpayers for purposes of this limitation.

4. Coordination with §129: Section 129 allows a taxpayer to exclude from gross income up to $5,000 of dependent care assistance provided by an employer. A taxpayer may not claim both the exclusion and the tax credit for the same dollar of dependent care assistance.

D. Earned income tax credit

A low income "eligible individual" may claim a refundable tax credit. To compute the amount of the credit, the "credit percentage" is multiplied by the taxpayer's earned income, up to a certain amount known as the "earned income amount." Then, from that figure is subtracted the taxpayer's "phase-out percentage" multiplied by the taxpayer's AGI, reduced (but not below zero) by the phase-out amount. These percentages and amounts vary depending on the income and family status of the taxpayer. [309-311]

1. Eligible individual: An eligible individual is an individual with a dependent child under the age of 19 or a taxpayer who is a U.S. resident between the ages of 25 and 65 and who cannot be claimed as a dependent on another person's tax return.

2. Earned income amount: Earned income includes wages, salary, and self-employment income. See Figure 13A (in text) for earned income amounts.

E. Education credits

Section 25A allows taxpayers to claim tax credits for certain education expenses. The HOPE scholarship credit is a credit of up to $1,500 of qualified education expenses and the lifetime learning credit is a credit equal to 20% of certain expenses. Income level restrictions apply. [311]

F. Other tax credits

The Code contains a variety of other tax credits usually given less attention in the basic federal income tax course. [313-314]

1. Child tax credit—§24: A taxpayer may claim a credit for $1,000 per child, with income limitations starting at $75,000 for single taxpayers, and $110,000 for married taxpayers.

2. Blind/elderly/disabled tax credit—§22: A taxpayer who qualifies as blind, elderly, or disabled is entitled to an additional tax credit.

3. Adoption expense credit—§23: A taxpayer who incurs certain qualifying adoption expenses may claim a credit for these expenses, but this credit is phased out as AGI rises.

4. Foreign tax credit—§901: A taxpayer may claim a deduction for certain foreign income and other taxes paid or may choose to claim a credit for these taxes. A credit is usually more valuable than a deduction for foreign taxes paid or accrued.

CHAPTER 14

IDENTIFYING THE TAXPAYER

I. IN GENERAL

The identification of the proper taxpayer to report income and claim deductions is crucial in maintaining a tax system that fairly allocates income among various taxpayers. [321]

II. PERSONS SUBJECT TO TAX

Both natural persons and legal entities may be subject to tax.

A. Individuals—§1

Individuals are subject to tax at rates ranging from 10% to 35% (in 2005). Single individuals, including children, file a tax return reporting only their income. Married couples can, and usually do, file a joint return reporting their combined income and deductions. Married couples have the option of filing separately, but usually do not, as this can produce a higher joint tax liability. [321-322]

1. Child's services income—§73: Income from a child's services is reported on the child's tax return, even if the parent is entitled to the income under state law.

2. The kiddie tax—§1(g): A child's investment income may be subject to tax at the parental rate, and parents may elect to report a child's investment income on the parents' tax return.

B. Legal entities

A legal entity—such as a corporation, partnership, estate, or trust—may be required to file a tax return reporting its items of income, deduction, and credit. Corporate tax rates are set forth in IRC §11. [322]

III. ASSIGNMENT OF INCOME

In a progressive tax system, an incentive exists for those in high tax brackets to direct income to related persons in lower tax brackets in order to reduce the overall tax imposed on the group. This strategy is known as "assignment of income." Because assignment of income threatens to undermine the integrity of the progressive tax structure, a variety of judicial and legislative responses have arisen over the years to combat it. [322-328]

A. Judicial views on services income

A common scenario involves the taxpayer who performs services for compensation but attempts to direct the compensation to another person (usually a relative in a lower tax bracket) prior to receiving it. [323-324]

1. Diversion by private agreement: If a taxpayer who performs services attempts to direct the compensation to another person by private agreement, the taxpayer (not the transferee) will be required to include the amount in gross income. See *Lucas v. Earl,* 281 U.S. 111 (1930).

2. Diversion by operation of law: By contrast, if the law governing the legal relationships provides that both the taxpayer and another person have legal rights to the income, the tax consequences will follow from these legal relationships. As a result, the taxpayer and the other party will include their proportionate shares of the income in gross income. See *Poe v. Seaborn,* 282 U.S. 101 (1930).

B. Judicial views on income from property

If an owner of income-producing property gives some interest in the property to another person, the issue arises of which person (the donor or donee) should be taxable on the income from the property. [324-328]

1. **Transfers of property:** If the donor transfers the property itself, the donee will properly report the income from the property.

2. **Transfers of income only:** The general rule is that attempts to transfer only the income from the property to another, without a transfer of the property itself, will be respected only if the income interest is transferred for its entire duration. Otherwise, the donor will be taxed on the income and will be deemed to have made a gift of the income to the donee. See *Blair v. Commissioner,* 300 U.S. 5 (1937); *Helvering v. Horst,* 311 U.S. 112 (1940).

C. **Statutory responses to assignment of income and related problems [328-329]**

1. **The kiddie tax—§1(g):** Certain investment income of a child under the age of 14 must be taxed at his or her parents' tax rate. The special tax rate applies only to "unearned income" in excess of $1,600. The parents have the option of including the child's investment income on their own returns.

2. **Reallocation of income and deductions—§482:** Under the broad statutory authority granted in §482, the IRS may reallocate among related entities items of gross income, deduction, and credit if necessary to prevent the evasion of tax or clearly to reflect income. This statute goes far beyond assignment of income principles, giving the IRS a powerful tool with which to combat the misallocation of tax items among related entities.

CHAPTER 15
TIME VALUE OF MONEY: PRINCIPLES AND APPLICATIONS

I. IN GENERAL

While the concept of the time value of money is not specifically invoked in any tax statute, its principles permeate much tax-planning activity. Taxpayers invoke basic time value of money concepts when they attempt to defer income and accelerate deductions. The IRS and ultimately Congress may seek to block these strategies by accelerating income and precluding the early deduction of expenses. [333-334]

II. INTEREST

Interest is the cost of using money. A lender charges the borrower interest for the privilege of using the lender's funds during the period of the loan, and thus the lender is said to "earn interest" on the loan. Interest is what creates the concept of the "time value of money." A specified sum of money will earn interest at the market rate over a period of time; thus, the value of that sum a year in the future will be the sum plus the interest earned during the year. [334]

A. **Simple interest**

Simple interest is calculated as a percentage of the principal sum only. [334]

B. **Compound interest**

Compound interest is computed by applying the interest rate to both the principal sum and the accrued but unpaid interest. Compounding generally occurs daily, monthly, half-yearly, or annually. [334]

III. VALUING AMOUNTS

A. Future value

Future value is the value of a sum of money invested for a specified period at a specified interest rate. The future value of a sum will be the amount that an investor will have at the maturity of the investment, given the number of years to maturity and the rate of return (i.e., the interest rate) of the investment. Future value can be calculated using present and future value tables [see Figure 15A, in text] or by using the following formula: [334-335]

$$FV = PV(1 + i)^n$$

B. Present value

Present value is the current value, given an assumed interest rate, of the right to a stated amount in the future. Another way to express this is that present value is the sum that must be invested today at a given interest rate to produce a stated sum in the future. Present value can be calculated using present and future value tables [see Figure 15A, in text] or by using the following formula: [335-337]

$$PV = \frac{FV}{(1 + i)^n}$$

IV. SPECIFIC TIME VALUE OF MONEY APPLICATIONS

The Code recognizes time value of money principles in specific applications, even though it does not import the concept on a global basis.

A. Applicable federal rates

The IRS publishes interest rates monthly for calculations under various Code provisions such as imputed interest and interest on tax over- and underpayments. [336]

B. Tax under- and overpayments—§6621

The U.S. government pays interest on tax overpayments at the federal short-term rate plus 2%, and a taxpayer must pay interest on tax underpayments at the federal short-term rate plus 3%. [336]

C. Original issue discount (OID)

While most debt instruments provide for a market rate of interest payable currently or otherwise, some debt instruments may not specifically provide for market interest. Yet, these instruments do pay interest in an economic sense, for no creditor would lend money without compensation. Without the OID rules, such instruments might create two misstatements of tax reality. First, repayment of the principal plus an additional sum might be considered a return of capital and capital gain rather than interest, which is ordinary income. Second, the creditor might defer the inclusion of any income until maturity even though presumably the interest is accruing during the entire outstanding period of the loan. The OID rules, while complicated in the extreme, seek to address these character and timing issues. [338-341]

1. **General approach:** The holder of a debt instrument must include in gross income an amount equal to the daily portions of the original issue discount for each day during the year on which the instrument is held. IRC §1272(a)(1). Thus, the original issue discount is considered ordinary

income and is included during the outstanding period of the loan, rather than deferred until maturity.

    a. Debt instrument: A debt instrument includes a bond, debenture, note, certificate, or other evidence of indebtedness. IRC §1275(a)(1).

    b. Original issue discount: Original issue discount is the excess (if any) of the stated redemption price at maturity over the issue price. IRC §1273(a)(1).

    c. Stated redemption price at maturity: The stated redemption price at maturity is the fixed amount the debtor will pay the creditor to retire the debt. IRC §1273(a).

    d. Issue price: For bonds and similar instruments, the issue price generally is the offering price to the public for issuance of the debt instrument. IRC §1273(b). For property sales, the issue price is the stated principal amount if there is adequate stated interest. IRC §1274(a)(1). Otherwise, the issue price is the imputed principal amount. IRC §1274(a). The imputed principal amount is the present value of all payments to be made under the contract, using the applicable federal rate as the discount rate. IRC §1274(b)(1).

  2. Exceptions to OID treatment: The OID rules do not apply to certain types of transactions that are not considered abusive, including sales of farms by certain taxpayers for $1 million or less, sales of principal residences, and sales involving total payments of $250,000 or less. IRC §1274(c).

D. Imputed interest—§483

Section 483 imputes to the creditor interest on certain loans made in connection with sales or exchanges of property to which the OID rules do not apply. [341-343]

  1. General approach: The creditor must include in gross income the total unstated interest ratably over the term of the contract. IRC §483(a).

    a. Which loans? Section 483 applies to contracts for the sale or exchange of property for which at least one payment is due more than one year after the date of the contract. IRC §483(c).

    b. Total unstated interest: Total unstated interest is the excess of the total payments due under the contract, over the sum of the present values of those payments and the present value of any payment provided for in the contract, using a discount rate equal to the applicable federal rate. IRC §483(b).

  2. Correlative effects of imputed interest: The imputation of interest under §483 reduces the amount characterized as the amount realized (principal) by the parties to the transaction. This reduces the gain (usually capital) reported by the seller of the property and, in turn, reduces the basis of the purchaser in the property. Moreover, the purchaser of the property, who is deemed to pay interest, may be able to deduct that interest, if the deduction requirements of §163 are met.

  3. Exceptions to §483: Section 483 does not apply to sales not exceeding $3,000 and to any debt instrument to which the OID rules apply.

E. Below-market loans—§7872

If a taxpayer makes a loan to another that does not provide for market interest, the transaction may be recharacterized to ensure that the creditor includes market interest in his or her gross income and

C
A
P
S
U
L
E

S
U
M
M
A
R
Y

that any other aspects of the transaction (such as compensation or gifts, for example) are properly taken into account. IRC §7872(a). [343-346]

1. **General approach:** Below-market "demand," "term," and "gift" loans are recharacterized so that the creditor includes the appropriate amount of interest in gross income. IRC §7872(a)(1).

   a. **Demand and gift loans:** For demand and gift loans, the forgone interest is treated as transferred from the lender to the borrower and retransferred from the borrower to the lender on the last day of the taxable year. IRC §7872(a)(1). Each leg of the transaction is characterized in accordance with its substance. For a gift loan, for example, the first leg (lender to borrower) is treated as a gift, and the second leg (borrower to lender) is treated as interest.

   b. **Other types of loans:** For other types of loans, first compute the excess of the amount loaned over the present value of all payments to be received under the loan. The lender is deemed to have transferred this amount to the borrower on the date the loan is made, and the below-market loan is treated as having OID in that same amount. The transfer from the lender to the borrower is characterized in accordance with its substance (e.g., compensation), and the characterization of the loan as having OID means that the lender must include the OID in gross income over the period of the loan.

      i. **Demand loan:** A demand loan is a loan payable on demand of the creditor.

      ii. **Term loan:** A term loan is a loan payable on a certain date that is fixed or determinable. IRC §7872(f)(6).

      iii. **Gift loan:** A gift loan is a loan in the context of which the creditor's forbearance of interest is most appropriately viewed as a gift. IRC §7872(f)(3).

      iv. **Below-market loan:** A demand loan is below market if its stated interest rate is less than the applicable federal rate at the time the loan is made. IRC §7872(e)(1)(A). A term loan is below market if the amount loaned is greater than the present value of the payments due under the loan, using the applicable federal rate as the discount rate. IRC §7872(e)(1)(B).

2. **Exceptions to §7872:** Section 7872 doesn't apply to gift loans between individuals, to compensation-related loans, and to shareholder loans if the total outstanding principal amount of such loans does not exceed $10,000. IRC §7872(c)(2),(3). Section 7872 also does not apply to any loan to which either the OID rules or §483 applies. IRC §7872(f)(8).

V. BASIC TAX STRATEGIES: INCOME DEFERRAL, ACCELERATION OF DEDUCTIONS, AND CLAIMING TAX CREDITS

Time value of money principles inspire the most basic tax strategies. The best of all tax strategies from the taxpayer's point of view is the exclusion of amounts from gross income entirely (so that tax will never be due on these amounts) or a deduction for the full amount of an expenditure (that shelters the same amount of income from tax). However, exclusions are relatively rare in the Code, and deductions are limited. Most strategies rely on a delay in tax; the taxpayer invests the amount that would otherwise be paid in tax and earns interest on that amount. The tax ultimately will be due, but the taxpayer who has invested the saved tax will usually come out ahead. [347]

A. Income deferral

A taxpayer may seek to defer the inclusion of an amount of gross income to a future year. This requires that the taxpayer have a sufficient ownership interest in the funds so that they are invested for his or her benefit but have an interest that will not require the taxpayer to include the amounts in gross income currently. Many income deferral strategies also assume that the taxpayer will be in a lower tax bracket when amounts will be included in his or her gross income (e.g., at retirement). Examples of income deferral strategies include the following [347-350]:

1. **Method of accounting:** A taxpayer may attempt to take advantage of the rules of his or her particular method of accounting to defer income to future years. Consider in this context the limitations on the use of the cash method of accounting and the doctrine of constructive receipt as limitations on the cash method taxpayer's ability to defer items of gross income.

2. **Realization principle:** Because income from the sale or exchange of property must be realized before it can be recognized, taxpayers may invest in property to defer the recognition of income until sale. Consider also in this context the effect of §1014, which by giving an heir a fair market value basis in property received from a decedent, encourages taxpayers to hold property until death and thus to exclude from the income tax the appreciation in the property prior to death.

3. **Nonrecognition provisions:** Certain nonrecognition provisions may allow the taxpayer to defer the recognition of gain on the disposition of property. These include like-kind exchanges, spousal and divorce transactions, and involuntary conversions.

4. **Retirement planning:** Most of retirement planning is based on the income deferral strategy. Employers' contributions to retirement plans are not included in the gross income of the employee until retirement, and the fund earns interest for the benefit of the employee during the employee's working years.

5. **Education savings incentives:** Section 529 plans and education savings accounts allow taxpayers to invest money but not be taxed on the earnings until distribution, and then only if the distributions are not used for qualified education expenses.

B. Deduction acceleration strategies

Taxpayers prefer to accelerate and maximize deductions because a deduction "shelters" an amount of income from tax. The tax benefit from a deduction is equal to the amount of the deduction multiplied by the taxpayer's tax rate. Examples of deduction strategies include the following [350-352]:

1. **Method of accounting:** A taxpayer may attempt to take advantage of the particular rules of his or her method of accounting to accelerate deductions. Consider in this context the limitations placed on deductions of prepayments for cash method taxpayers and the economic performance rules for accrual method taxpayers.

2. **Capital recovery:** A taxpayer prefers accelerated capital recovery for investment in assets. For example, a taxpayer usually will claim double-declining balance depreciation rather than straight-line depreciation for an asset for which the double-declining balance method is available. Consider in this context §179 deductions, the MACRS method of capital recovery, §195

(amortization of pre-opening expenses), and §197 (amortization of intangibles). But consider the effect of recapture on the claiming of capital recovery deductions.

3. **Loss limitations:** Various loss limitations restrict taxpayers' ability to claim a deduction for certain losses. Consider in this context the capital loss restrictions (§1211), the passive loss restrictions (§469), the at-risk limitations (§465), and the rules against the recognition of losses in certain transactions (§165 and various nonrecognition rules).

CHAPTER 16
RECOGNIZING RELATED TAX STATUTES: A TRANSACTIONAL APPROACH TO TAX

I. AN APPROACH: STUDY TAX FIRST!

One approach to ensuring a complete analysis of a tax question is to take the approach of STUDY TAX FIRST! [357-359]

A. STUDY the transaction

The very first step in any tax problem is to study the facts of a transaction carefully. Be sure you understand who did what with whom, when, why, and how. It may be helpful to draw the transaction to ensure that you understand its various components. [359]

B. What is the TAX problem?

A specific tax question may accompany a set of facts. More commonly, however, the facts end with a general question such as "What are the tax consequences of these transactions?" or "Advise the taxpayer." These raise two different kinds of tax problems. [359]

1. **Reactive problem:** In a reactive problem, events have occurred already, and the problem is to determine their tax consequences. Consider the alternative characterizations of the transaction, and conclude as to which one is most appropriate.

2. **Proactive (planning) problem:** In a proactive problem, the taxpayer is typically considering a transaction and seeks advice on how best to structure it. Consider alternative means to achieve the taxpayer's goals, and choose the one that produces the best overall tax and nontax consequences.

C. FIRST! analysis: Facts, Issues, Rules, So what? and Taxpayer advice

This involves in-depth analysis of the tax issues. [359-363]

1. **Facts:** Characterize the transaction as one of the common transactions. Consider whether it is, for example, a sale or exchange of property or a compensation transaction.

2. **Issues:** There are six fundamental issues in tax, all or some of which may be relevant to a particular transaction.

   a. **Who is the relevant taxpayer?**

   b. **Does the taxpayer have income?**

   c. **What deductions may the taxpayer claim?**

d. **What is the character of income or loss?**

e. **Timing issues—When must a taxpayer include an item in gross income, and when may a taxpayer claim a deduction?**

f. **What is the taxpayer's rate of tax and is the taxpayer entitled to any credits?**

3. **Rules—What tax concepts and Code provisions apply?** This step of the FIRST! analysis identifies the concepts and Code provisions potentially applicable to the transaction at hand. The characterization of the transaction as a type (in the Facts step) is very helpful in identifying potentially applicable statutes and concepts. Once potentially applicable rules are identified, the domain of each is examined with the facts in mind to determine if the concept or statute actually applies.

4. **So what? Applying the rules:** The applicable rules identified in the previous step must be applied, i.e., their consequences in the particular transaction must be determined.

5. **Taxpayer advice:** In the final step, recall that the point of the exercise is tax advice. Whether advising the taxpayer or the government, the tax problem posed must be addressed. Consider in this context what would be an appropriate return position or structure for a transaction, advice with respect to a tax controversy, or an appropriate government position. Basic tax strategies such as income deferral, deduction acceleration, and the claiming of credits should be considered, along with Congressional and judicial responses to these techniques.

II. COMMONLY ENCOUNTERED TRANSACTIONS

Commonly encountered transactions can be analyzed using the STUDY TAX FIRST! approach.

A. Compensation transactions [363-367]

1. **Recognizing this transaction:** To recognize the basic transaction, look for a person performing services in exchange for value or a promise to transfer value.

2. **FIRST! analysis:** For the payor, the essential question is whether a deduction is available for amounts paid for services. For the service provider, the essential question is whether he or she has income, and if so, how much and when it will be included in gross income. The expenses of performing services may be deductible, and compensation income will be ordinary income, potentially taxable at the highest tax rate. Advice to taxpayers in compensation transactions generally focuses on strategies to accelerate the deduction to the payor and defer the inclusion of income to the service provider.

B. Transactions in property [367-370]

A second major category of commonly encountered transactions is the sale or other disposition of property, including sales and various types of exchanges. (Gifts are treated as intrafamilial transfers, discussed below.)

1. **Recognizing this transaction:** Transactions in property involve a taxpayer transferring an item of property that he or she owns, usually in exchange for value. In a gift transaction, the donor will not receive value for the property, but in nongift contexts, we assume that the seller will dispose of the property at fair market value.

2. **FIRST! analysis:** The tax problem may be posed for the buyer, the seller, or both. For the seller, the essential questions are the amount of gain or loss to be recognized on the transaction and the character of that gain or loss. Sales or exchanges of property may generate capital gain or loss, subject to the preferential rate for net capital gain and the capital loss restrictions of §1211. If the seller has received something other than cash in the transactions, the basis of that property must be computed. For the buyer, the essential question is the basis of the property acquired. Advice to taxpayers in this situation centers on the computation of realized and recognized gain or loss and strategies to exclude or defer income and accelerate loss.

C. Personal expenditure transactions [370-376]

1. **Recognizing this transaction:** In a personal expenditure transaction, the taxpayer is making expenditures for essentially personal items that would not be deductible but for specific Code sections that allow deduction.

2. **FIRST! analysis:** The crucial questions for the taxpayer are whether he or she is entitled to claim a deduction for these amounts, and when. Income issues may arise if the taxpayer has been compensated for personal losses or physical injuries. Advice to taxpayers in personal expenditure transactions involves identification of allowable deductions and acceleration of these deductions to the earliest possible year.

D. Education incentives [372-376]

1. **Testing:** The number and relative newness of many education incentives suggests that this area of personal expenditure is fertile ground for testing.

2. **Exclusions:** The following provisions potentially allow exclusions for educationally related savings and expenses:

   a. **Scholarships—§117**

   b. **Employer assistance—§127**

   c. **Interest on U.S. savings bonds—§135**

   d. **Section 529 plans**

   e. **Education savings accounts—§530**

3. **Deductions:** The following provisions potentially allow deductions associated with educational expenses:

   a. **Student loan interest deduction—§221**

   b. **Deduction for qualified education expenses—§222**

4. **Credits:** Two provisions potentially allow a credit for educational expenses:

   a. **HOPE credit—§25A**

   b. **Lifetime learning credit—§25A**

E. Business transactions [376-378]

1. **Recognizing this transaction:** Business transactions generally involve a taxpayer's sale of inventory or services for profit. Look for a taxpayer potentially engaged in business—the regular undertaking of an activity for profit.

2. **FIRST! analysis:** For the business taxpayer, the essential question is the net income from the business, which requires a determination of the taxpayer's gross business income and available deductions. Timing issues (including inventory issues) generally figure prominently in the computation of income and deductions. The character of the business income generally will be ordinary, potentially subject to the highest rate of tax. Advice in business transactions involves calculation of gross income from business and identification of available deductions and credits.

F. Intrafamilial transfers [378-380]

1. **Recognizing this transaction:** In this type of transaction, members of a family are transferring money or property among themselves, and the typical transactions include gifts, divorce transfers, and inheritances.

2. **FIRST! analysis:** The tax consequences to the transferor and transferee of any intrafamilial transfer must be considered.

   a. **Gifts—§§102, 1015:** The making of a gift is not a taxable event to the transferor, and thus the transferor realizes and recognizes no gain or loss on the transfer (unless it is a partial sale, which is properly treated as a sale transaction). The transferee generally receives property tax-free, i.e., without being required to include its value in gross income. The recipient of a gift takes the property with the same basis the property had in the hands of the donor, unless the property's fair market value was less than its basis at the time of the gift. In that situation, for purposes of determining loss only, the donee takes the fair market value of the property on the date of the gift as his or her basis.

   b. **Inheritances—§§102, 1014:** The recipient of property by bequest or inheritance need not include its value in gross income, and takes the property with a basis equal to fair market value on the date of death or at the alternate valuation date six months later, if elected.

   c. **Divorce transfers—§§71, 215, 1041:** The payment of alimony (federally defined) constitutes a deduction to the payor and is includable in the gross income of the recipient. The payment of child support, by contrast, generates no deduction to the payor and no income to the recipient. The transferor of property "incident to a divorce" recognizes no gain or loss on the transfer, and the recipient of the property need not include its value in gross income. The recipient takes the property with the same basis it had immediately before the transfer.

   d. **Assignment of income and the "kiddie tax"—§1(g):** Taxpayers in high tax brackets may attempt to allocate income from services or property to related taxpayers in lower tax brackets. Attempted assignments of services income or income from property that constitutes a "carved-out interest" will not be respected by the IRS or courts, and the transferor will be taxed on the income purportedly assigned. Taxpayers may, however, transfer property to another so that the income from that property is properly taxed to the transferee. The "kiddie tax," however, serves as a check on this strategy by requiring certain unearned income of children to be taxed at their parents' tax rate rather than their lower individual rates.

   e. **Advice:** Advice in intrafamilial transfers centers around ensuring that the transfer is tax-free to both the transferor and transferee, computing the basis of the property transferred, and identifying proper (and improper) assignments of income.

CHAPTER 1

GETTING STARTED IN FEDERAL INCOME TAX

ChapterScope _____

To help a student get started in the process of learning federal income tax, this chapter provides some background information on the U.S. tax system, the Code and its administrative and judicial interpretations, and calculation of tax.

Key concepts in this chapter include:

- **Calculation of tax:** The process of calculating the tax and the six fundamental tax questions.

- **Sources of federal tax law:** The sources of tax law, including the U.S. Constitution, the ***Internal Revenue Code,*** and various judicial and administrative interpretations of the Code.

- **Tax procedure:** How tax controversies become tax cases, the administrative pathway they follow, and the various courts with jurisdiction over tax matters.

- **Process of statutory interpretation:** How courts typically derive meaning for ambiguous statutory tax terms.

- **Tax ethics:** The standards governing clients and lawyers in taking a position on a tax return.

- **Parsing—a five-step approach to tax statutes:** Parsing offers a five-step approach to understanding an unfamiliar tax statute.

- **Tax policy:** The concepts of ***fairness, administrative practicality,*** and ***rational economic effects*** often serve as measures of a "good" tax system.

I. INTRODUCTION—THE BIG PICTURE

Learning tax law requires an understanding of general tax concepts, an array of tax statutes, and a grasp of the "big picture"—the role of specific concepts and statutes in the tax law as a whole. Along the way, the student of federal income tax will learn a new language (the language of the Code and regulations) as well as the process of statutory interpretation.

A. Computation of tax

The federal income tax imposes a tax on the ***taxable income*** of an individual (or other taxable entity). The computation of that tax is the point of the Code, regulations, and judicial and administrative interpretations of the law. Computation of the tax due for an individual can be expressed most simply as the following process:

> Gross Income
>   — <u>Certain Deductions</u>
>   = Adjusted Gross Income (AGI)
>   — Standard or Itemized Deductions
>   — <u>Personal Exemptions</u>
>   = Taxable Income
>   × <u>Tax Rate</u>
>   = Tentative Tax
>   — <u>Tax Credits</u>
>   = Tax Due (if positive number) or Refund (if negative number)

1. **Explanation of process:** The computation of the tax due begins with *gross income,* which means all of a taxpayer's income. IRC §61. From gross income, certain *deductions* are subtracted to produce *adjusted gross income* (AGI). IRC §62. From AGI, a taxpayer subtracts either the *standard* or the *itemized deduction* (but not both) and his or her *personal exemptions.* IRC §63. This produces taxable income, against which the applicable tax rate is multiplied to produce the tentative tax. It is "tentative" because one step remains: to subtract, on a dollar-for-dollar basis, any available *tax credits.* The ending point is the actual tax due (if a positive number) or a possible refund for the taxpayer (if a negative number).

2. **Multiple processes, multiple rates:** As later chapters will discuss, there isn't just one tax rate. Different kinds of income are subject to different rates of tax. Also, the process described above is used to calculate a taxpayer's *regular tax liability.* A second, shadow process is also involved: the computation of the *alternative minimum tax.* But for now, we can focus solely on a taxpayer's regular tax liability.

3. **A note on arithmetic:** Tax requires no advanced math skills, just the ability to add, subtract, multiply, and divide. Later in the text, some formulas will be presented; while these may at first seem intimidating, they are based on these simple arithmetic functions. Outside of some graduate tax schools, professors are usually less interested in computations than in analysis of the legal issues that arise in the computation of taxable income. If you are math-wary, don't despair. You will probably find tax less arithmetically oriented than you think.

B. Six fundamental tax questions

Tax concepts and Code sections cluster around six fundamental questions. These issues provide an organizational structure for this outline and for many tax casebooks. And, as discussed in detail in Chapter 16, these issues can be used to successfully analyze unfamiliar tax problems on exams and in practice.

1. **Who is the taxpayer?** Tax is a transactional subject, typically involving two or more taxpayers. Identifying the relevant taxpayer is crucial, as is identifying strategies a taxpayer may use to direct income or *deductions* to others to improve his or her own tax situation. Because analysis of these types of issues assumes an understanding of income and deduction, the discussion of "Who is the taxpayer?" is deferred until Chapter 14.

2. **Does the taxpayer have income?** The federal income tax is concerned with a tax on income, and therefore the starting place is whether the taxpayer has items of income that will be included in his or her gross income. This requires an understanding of income theoretically and

practically and a grasp of the myriad tax statutes that include particular items of income in a taxpayer's gross income. Chapters 2, 3, and 4 address these issues.

3. **What deductions may the taxpayer claim?** Because the income tax is a tax not on gross income but on something less, *deductions* constitute an essential step in the computation of the tax base. Deductions may be business-related or personal, but whatever their nature, they are a matter of legislative grace: A taxpayer must be able to point to a specific statute as justification in order to claim a deduction. Chapters 5-8 address deduction issues.

4. **Timing issues:** When must a taxpayer include an amount in gross income, and when may the taxpayer claim a deduction? The federal income tax is computed on an annual basis. The entry of an item of income or deduction on a return constitutes the taxpayer's claim that the year of the return is the proper year for reporting the item. For many items, the proper reporting year is clear. But for transactions that occur over several years, selection of the proper year can have important tax implications for the taxpayer. Moreover, taxpayers invoke timing rules in the *income deferral* and *deduction acceleration* strategies they use to save taxes. Chapter 11 addresses timing issues, and Chapter 15 discusses the time value of money principles that underlie many tax planning strategies.

5. **Character of income and loss:** The federal income tax differentiates among some types of *income and loss,* giving tax preference to some types and imposing limits on others. Principal among these is the distinction between *ordinary income or loss* and *capital gain or loss. Net capital gain* is subject to a preferential rate as compared to the rates for *ordinary income,* and the *deduction* for *capital losses* is limited to an individual's *capital gains* plus $3,000 of *ordinary income.* Thus, characterizing income and loss as capital or ordinary can have a significant impact on tax liability. Character issues are discussed in Chapter 12.

6. **Rates and credits:** The particular tax rate(s) to be applied to a taxpayer depends on the taxable income and status of that taxpayer. The tax rate multiplied by the taxpayer's taxable income produces the tentative tax from which available *tax credits* are subtracted on a dollar-for-dollar basis. Issues surrounding tax rates and credits are the subject of Chapter 13.

C. Tax form 1040—A detailed roadmap

The basic federal income tax course is *not* a tax preparation course. But the individual income tax return, the Form 1040, provides an excellent roadmap for the course and a way to organize the massive amounts of information in the course. Figure 1A reproduces the 2004 basic form. Take a moment now to see how Form 1040 presents the six basic issues of tax. The schedules to the 1040 and additional forms can be found on the IRS Website in .pdf format at *www.irs.gov.*

1. **Who is the taxpayer?** Notice that Form 1040 begins with issues relating to the status of the taxpayer. Filing status (Lines 1–3) and *dependents* (Lines 6a–d) are important in defining the *personal exemption* (line 41) and tax rate (line 43).

2. **Income issues:** Notice that the Form 1040 continues by addressing items of income. Lines 7-21 list common types of income that must be included in gross income.

3. **Deduction issues:** In lines 23 through 34a Form 1040 addresses *deductions* for various expenses. Lines 23-34a list the items deductible in computing adjusted gross income, and the *itemized deductions* are listed in Schedule A, which in turn are summarized on Line 39 of Form 1040.

Figure 1A
Form 1040

Form **1040**	Department of the Treasury—Internal Revenue Service **U.S. Individual Income Tax Return** 2004	(99)	IRS Use Only—Do not write or staple in this space.

For the year Jan. 1–Dec. 31, 2004, or other tax year beginning _____ , 2004, ending _____ , 20 ___   OMB No. 1545-0074

Label

(See instructions on page 16.)

Use the IRS label. Otherwise, please print or type.

L A B E L   H E R E

Your first name and initial	Last name	Your social security number
If a joint return, spouse's first name and initial	Last name	Spouse's social security number
Home address (number and street). If you have a P.O. box, see page 16.	Apt. no.	▲ **Important!** ▲
City, town or post office, state, and ZIP code. If you have a foreign address, see page 16.		You **must** enter your SSN(s) above.

Presidential Election Campaign
(See page 16.) ▶

Note. Checking "Yes" will not change your tax or reduce your refund.
Do you, or your spouse if filing a joint return, want $3 to go to this fund? . . . ▶

	You		Spouse	
	☐ Yes	☐ No	☐ Yes	☐ No

Filing Status

Check only one box.

1 ☐ Single
2 ☐ Married filing jointly (even if only one had income)
3 ☐ Married filing separately. Enter spouse's SSN above and full name here. ▶
4 ☐ Head of household (with qualifying person). (See page 17.) If the qualifying person is a child but not your dependent, enter this child's name here. ▶ _____
5 ☐ Qualifying widow(er) with dependent child (see page 17)

Exemptions

6a ☐ **Yourself.** If someone can claim you as a dependent, **do not** check box 6a . . . .
b ☐ **Spouse** . . . .

c **Dependents:**

(1) First name Last name	(2) Dependent's social security number	(3) Dependent's relationship to you	(4)✔ if qualifying child for child tax credit (see page 18)
			☐
			☐
			☐
			☐

If more than four dependents, see page 18.

Boxes checked on 6a and 6b ___
No. of children on 6c who:
● lived with you ___
● did not live with you due to divorce or separation (see page 18) ___
Dependents on 6c not entered above ___

d Total number of exemptions claimed . . . .

Add numbers on lines above ▶ ☐

Income

Attach Form(s) W-2 here. Also attach Forms W-2G and 1099-R if tax was withheld.

If you did not get a W-2, see page 19.

Enclose, but do not attach, any payment. Also, please use **Form 1040-V.**

7	Wages, salaries, tips, etc. Attach Form(s) W-2	7	
8a	**Taxable** interest. Attach Schedule B if required	8a	
b	Tax-exempt interest. **Do not** include on line 8a . . .	8b	
9a	Ordinary dividends. Attach Schedule B if required . . .	9a	
b	Qualified dividends (see page 20)	9b	
10	Taxable refunds, credits, or offsets of state and local income taxes (see page 20) . .	10	
11	Alimony received	11	
12	Business income or (loss). Attach Schedule C or C-EZ . .	12	
13	Capital gain or (loss). Attach Schedule D if required. If not required, check here ▶ ☐	13	
14	Other gains or (losses). Attach Form 4797	14	
15a	IRA distributions . . [15a] b Taxable amount (see page 22)	15b	
16a	Pensions and annuities [16a] b Taxable amount (see page 22)	16b	
17	Rental real estate, royalties, partnerships, S corporations, trusts, etc. Attach Schedule E	17	
18	Farm income or (loss). Attach Schedule F	18	
19	Unemployment compensation	19	
20a	Social security benefits . [20a] b Taxable amount (see page 24)	20b	
21	Other income. List type and amount (see page 24) _____	21	
22	Add the amounts in the far right column for lines 7 through 21. This is your **total income** ▶	22	

Adjusted Gross Income

23	Educator expenses (see page 26)	23	
24	Certain business expenses of reservists, performing artists, and fee-basis government officials. Attach Form 2106 or 2106-EZ	24	
25	IRA deduction (see page 26)	25	
26	Student loan interest deduction (see page 28)	26	
27	Tuition and fees deduction (see page 29)	27	
28	Health savings account deduction. Attach Form 8889 . .	28	
29	Moving expenses. Attach Form 3903	29	
30	One-half of self-employment tax. Attach Schedule SE . .	30	
31	Self-employed health insurance deduction (see page 30) .	31	
32	Self-employed SEP, SIMPLE, and qualified plans . . .	32	
33	Penalty on early withdrawal of savings	33	
34a	Alimony paid b Recipient's SSN ▶ _____	34a	
35	Add lines 23 through 34a	35	
36	Subtract line 35 from line 22. This is your **adjusted gross income** . . . ▶	36	

For Disclosure, Privacy Act, and Paperwork Reduction Act Notice, see page 75.   Cat. No. 11320B   Form **1040** (2004)

Figure 1A [continued]

Form 1040 (2004)   Page **2**

Tax and Credits	**37**	Amount from line 36 (adjusted gross income)	**37**
	38a	Check if: { ☐ **You** were born before January 2, 1940, ☐ Blind. ☐ **Spouse** was born before January 2, 1940, ☐ Blind. } Total boxes checked ▶ **38a**	
Standard Deduction for—	**b**	If your spouse itemizes on a separate return or you were a dual-status alien, see page 31 and check here ▶ **38b** ☐	
• People who checked any box on line 38a or 38b **or** who can be claimed as a dependent, see page 31.	**39**	**Itemized deductions** (from Schedule A) **or** your **standard deduction** (see left margin) . .	**39**
	40	Subtract line 39 from line 37	**40**
	41	If line 37 is $107,025 or less, multiply $3,100 by the total number of exemptions claimed on line 6d. If line 37 is over $107,025, see the worksheet on page 33	**41**
	42	**Taxable income.** Subtract line 41 from line 40. If line 41 is more than line 40, enter -0-	**42**
	43	**Tax** (see page 33). Check if any tax is from: **a** ☐ Form(s) 8814 **b** ☐ Form 4972 . .	**43**
• All others:	**44**	**Alternative minimum tax** (see page 35). Attach Form 6251 . .	**44**
Single or Married filing separately, $4,850	**45**	Add lines 43 and 44 . . . . ▶	**45**
	46	Foreign tax credit. Attach Form 1116 if required	**46**
	47	Credit for child and dependent care expenses. Attach Form 2441 . .	**47**
Married filing jointly or Qualifying widow(er), $9,700	**48**	Credit for the elderly or the disabled. Attach Schedule R . .	**48**
	49	Education credits. Attach Form 8863	**49**
	50	Retirement savings contributions credit. Attach Form 8880 . .	**50**
	51	Child tax credit (see page 37)	**51**
Head of household, $7,150	**52**	Adoption credit. Attach Form 8839	**52**
	53	Credits from: **a** ☐ Form 8396 **b** ☐ Form 8859 . . .	**53**
	54	Other credits. Check applicable box(es): **a** ☐ Form 3800 **b** ☐ Form 8801 **c** ☐ Specify _____ . .	**54**
	55	Add lines 46 through 54. These are your **total credits**	**55**
	56	Subtract line 55 from line 45. If line 55 is more than line 45, enter -0- . . . . . ▶	**56**
Other Taxes	**57**	Self-employment tax. Attach Schedule SE	**57**
	58	Social security and Medicare tax on tip income not reported to employer. Attach Form 4137 . .	**58**
	59	Additional tax on IRAs, other qualified retirement plans, etc. Attach Form 5329 if required .	**59**
	60	Advance earned income credit payments from Form(s) W-2 . .	**60**
	61	Household employment taxes. Attach Schedule H	**61**
	62	Add lines 56 through 61. This is your **total tax** . . . . ▶	**62**
Payments	**63**	Federal income tax withheld from Forms W-2 and 1099 . .	**63**
	64	2004 estimated tax payments and amount applied from 2003 return	**64**
If you have a qualifying child, attach Schedule EIC.	**65a**	**Earned income credit (EIC)**	**65a**
	b	Nontaxable combat pay election ▶ **65b**	
	66	Excess social security and tier 1 RRTA tax withheld (see page 54)	**66**
	67	Additional child tax credit. Attach Form 8812	**67**
	68	Amount paid with request for extension to file (see page 54)	**68**
	69	Other payments from: **a** ☐ Form 2439 **b** ☐ Form 4136 **c** ☐ Form 8885	**69**
	70	Add lines 63, 64, 65a, and 66 through 69. These are your **total payments** . . . . ▶	**70**
Refund	**71**	If line 70 is more than line 62, subtract line 62 from line 70. This is the amount you **overpaid**	**71**
Direct deposit? See page 54 and fill in 72b, 72c, and 72d.	**72a**	Amount of line 71 you want **refunded to you** . . . . ▶	**72a**
	▶ **b**	Routing number [ ][ ][ ][ ][ ][ ][ ][ ][ ] ▶ **c** Type: ☐ Checking ☐ Savings	
	▶ **d**	Account number [ ][ ][ ][ ][ ][ ][ ][ ][ ][ ][ ][ ][ ][ ][ ][ ][ ]	
	73	Amount of line 71 you want **applied to your 2005 estimated tax** ▶ **73**	
Amount You Owe	**74**	**Amount you owe.** Subtract line 70 from line 62. For details on how to pay, see page 55 ▶	**74**
	75	Estimated tax penalty (see page 55) **75**	

Third Party Designee

Do you want to allow another person to discuss this return with the IRS (see page 56)? ☐ **Yes.** Complete the following. ☐ **No**

Designee's name ▶   Phone no. ▶ ( )   Personal identification number (PIN) ▶ [ ][ ][ ][ ][ ]

Sign Here

Joint return? See page 17.

Keep a copy for your records.

Under penalties of perjury, I declare that I have examined this return and accompanying schedules and statements, and to the best of my knowledge and belief, they are true, correct, and complete. Declaration of preparer (other than taxpayer) is based on all information of which preparer has any knowledge.

Your signature	Date	Your occupation	Daytime phone number ( )
Spouse's signature. If a joint return, **both** must sign.	Date	Spouse's occupation	

Paid Preparer's Use Only

Preparer's signature ▶	Date	Check if self-employed ☐	Preparer's SSN or PTIN
Firm's name (or yours if self-employed), address, and ZIP code ▶		EIN	Phone no. ( )

Form **1040** (2004)

4. **Timing issues:** Timing issues are not immediately apparent on the Form 1040. Yet each item of income and deduction raises the issue of whether the current tax year is the proper year for claiming a deduction or reporting income.

5. **Character:** Schedule D to Form 1040 requires information for the sale or exchange of *capital assets,* and the result of the computations on Schedule D are reported on Line 13 of the Form 1040.

6. **Tax rate and credit issues:** Once the appropriate tax rate is applied to a taxpayer's taxable income, tax *credits* produce a dollar-for-dollar reduction in the amount of tax due. The basic question really is simple: is the taxpayer entitled to a tax *credit,* and if so, how much? Lines 46 through 54 of Form 1040 address *credit* issues.

II. THE SOURCES OF FEDERAL INCOME TAX LAW

A. The U.S. Constitution—And how the Code is created

The U.S. Constitution is a source of tax law just as it is a source of law for other kinds of law. Article I, §8 of the Constitution allows Congress "to lay and collect Taxes, Duties, Imposts and Excises. . . ." However, §8 limits the taxing power in three ways: direct taxes must be apportioned among the states; bills for raising revenue must originate in the U.S. House of Representatives; and taxes must be "uniform throughout the United States." Although the U.S. Constitution is a source of tax law, modern courts rarely rely on the Constitution to limit Congress' taxing authority.

1. **Direct taxes:** The "direct tax" issue is no longer controversial because the Sixteenth Amendment (adopted in 1913, the year of the first individual income tax) allows Congress to tax "incomes" without apportionment.

2. **Origination:** Although tax bills must originate in the House of Representatives, the Senate may delete what it finds undesirable and add any amendment it chooses when it receives the bill.

3. **Uniformity:** Taxes must be geographically uniform throughout the United States. However, the uniformity clause does not prohibit a tax statute from distinguishing among various types or sources of income or from imposing different rate structures on taxpayers of different status (as long as that status is not based on geographic locale).

B. The Internal Revenue Code

1. **The Code:** Title 26 of the U.S. Code, known in this outline as "the Code," contains income, gift, estate, excise, and employment taxes. The basic federal income tax course is devoted to the income taxation of *individuals,* with a nod to basic income taxation of entities such as trusts or corporations. The starting place for analysis of any tax problem is the Code, with an inquiry into the tax statutes potentially applicable to the problem.

2. **Don't forget—Tax law is how the federal government raises *money*:** The process of tax legislation is intimately tied to the creation and implementation of the federal budget. The House and Senate receive the budget from the President, and then begin their own process of creating, ultimately, a joint resolution approving the budget. Then, the tax-writing committees get busy writing their tax bills. The budget resolution isn't law, but it acts as a guide for both taxing and spending bills, which must conform to the budget resolution.

3. **Some things, like sausage and legislation, you *don't* want to see made:** The House generates a tax bill, which goes to the Senate. The Senate objects to some provisions, wants to change others, and wants new provisions included. So, the Joint Committee on Taxation—made up of representatives from the House and the Senate—convenes to generate agreement, and produce a tax bill. This bill also coordinates the taxing provisions with the budget revenue provisions, and the result is a "reconciliation bill." The chairs of the House and Senate tax committees manage this bill through Congress on an increasingly short schedule which allows for limited debate.

   a. **More than you want to know—The Byrd rule:** The Byrd rule was enacted originally in 1974, and made permanent in 1990. It is a Senate rule, which functions as a way of enforcing the budget resolution during the debate on reconciliation acts. This rule permits Senate members to object to any "extraneous" provisions in a reconciliation bill; if the objection is carried, it requires three-fifths of the Senate to waive the rule with respect to the provision to keep it in the bill. There aren't very many kinds of objections a Senator can make, but one kind that is available is an objection to a provision that would increase net outlays or decrease revenues for a fiscal year beyond those covered by the reconciliation bill.

   b. **So what?** The Economic Growth and Tax Relief Reconciliation Act of 2001 (P.L. 107-16), the provisions of which feature prominently in this book, changed tax rates and other tax provisions in the years 2001 through 2010. In order to avoid objections from Senate members that would have required a three-fifths majority override, the Act included a "sunset provision" that provided that all provisions and amendments made by the Act would not apply to any taxable year beginning after December 31, 2010. This means that at midnight, December 31, 2010, the tax code reverts back to its pre-2001 Act incarnation, unless Congress acts to extend or change these provisions. Will Congress act to prevent this result? For some provisions, it already has. Important sections subject to this sunset provision are indicated by the asterisk symbol (*) followed by "Sunset" in this text.

   c. **Tax law changes every year:** One of the challenges of understanding tax law is that the statutes change every year—and often more than once a year. Fortunately, income tax principles remain largely the same year after year, and most tax professors focus on these principles and not on the arcane details of obscure Code provisions.

      i. **Inflation adjustments:** Many Code provisions have dollar amounts that are adjusted for inflation each year. The IRS publishes the new numbers annually in the Internal Revenue Bulletin.

      ii. **Scheduled increases/decreases:** Some Code provisions have dollar amounts, percentages, etc., that are scheduled to increase or decrease over time.

      iii. **Check the Website:** The latest numbers for these changing provisions are listed on the Speer Hoyt Website at *www.speerhoyt.com.*

C. **Administrative interpretations of the Code**

Section 7805 authorizes the Secretary of the Treasury or the Secretary's delegate to prescribe "all needful rules and regulations" for the administration of the tax system.

1. **The Internal Revenue Service:** The Internal Revenue Service (referred to in this outline as the **IRS**), a bureau of the Department of the Treasury, issues various types of administrative interpretations of the Code.

2. **Regulations:** In issuing regulations, the Department of the Treasury must comply with the Administrative Procedures Act (APA), which requires public notice of new rules and opportunity for public comment. Transcripts of hearings and other opportunities for comments often provide insight into the purpose and proper interpretation of a tax statute.

   a. **Legislative versus interpretive regulations:** A regulation that simply provides guidance on a statutory provision under the general authority granted by §7805 is known as "interpretive regulation." Sometimes, however, Congress will specifically instruct Treasury to issue regulations interpreting a provision; regulations issued under this type of authority are known as "legislative regulations." While the courts give *deference* to both types of regulations, they tend to grant legislative regulations a greater degree of deference than interpretive regulations. See discussion of deference, this chapter, at Section II(D)(2).

   b. **Types of regulations:** Legislative or interpretive regulations can be final, temporary, or proposed.

      i. **Final regulations:** These regulations have the force and effect of law. They are typically cited as "Treas. Reg." or simply "Reg."

      ii. **Temporary regulations:** These regulations are in force, but their "temporary" label suggests that the IRS will probably revise them in the future. Temporary regulations are identified by their "T" designation. See, for example, Reg. §1.1041-1T.

      iii. **Proposed regulations:** These regulations are still in the public comment stage of development and are not yet in force, but do serve to indicate the IRS's position on a particular subject. They are cited as "Prop. Reg."

3. **Other published administrative guidance:** The IRS issues other types of guidance that are not subject to the APA. These are published weekly in the *Internal Revenue Bulletin* (cited as I.R.B.) and compiled annually in the *Cumulative Bulletin* (cited as C.B.).

   a. **Revenue Rulings:** Revenue Rulings apply the law to a specific set of facts and draw conclusions on the application of the law. Taxpayers may rely on revenue rulings in preparing their tax returns if their own facts and circumstances are substantially the same as in the ruling.

   b. **Revenue Procedures:** A Revenue Procedure sets forth the rights and duties of taxpayers in dealing with the IRS on an administrative matter, such as seeking a private letter ruling. Revenue Procedures do not deal with substantive tax issues. If the IRS deviates from its stated policy published in a Revenue Procedure, a taxpayer has no right to the benefit of a particular procedure.

   c. **Notices and Announcements:** These authorities set forth the IRS's views or a procedure on a matter of transitory importance, such as the procedure for seeking relief from filing due to natural disasters. Taxpayers may rely on notices and announcements in preparing their tax returns.

4. **Forms, instructions, and publications:** An important source of guidance for taxpayers are the forms and instructions, as well as information publications, issued by the Internal Revenue Service. However, IRS forms, instructions, and publications do not bind the IRS with respect to a particular interpretation of the law.

5. **Internal Revenue Manual:** The Internal Revenue Manual (I.R.M.) sets forth the IRS's internal procedures in the administration of the Code. It provides useful information on how the IRS will conduct *audits* and related matters, but taxpayers are not entitled to rely on it to require any particular IRS action.

6. **Unpublished administrative authority:** The IRS issues several kinds of unpublished authority. These are subject to public disclosure (in redacted form) and are generally available from commercial services but are not published in the Internal Revenue Bulletin.

   a. **Private Letter Rulings:** Taxpayers in some circumstances may seek a ruling by the IRS on the application of the law to a specific set of facts. Only the taxpayer who seeks the ruling can rely on them, and PLRs cannot be used or cited as precedent by other taxpayers. IRC §6110(k)(3). However, tax lawyers use PLRs to get a sense of the IRS' views on a particular transaction.

   b. **Technical Advice Memoranda:** During an *audit,* the IRS revenue agent or the taxpayer may request technical advice from the National Office of the IRS. The response is a Technical Advice Memorandum that interprets the law and applies it to the specific set of facts submitted by the agent and taxpayer. It is binding on the IRS, even if the local IRS authorities do not agree with its conclusions.

   c. **Chief Counsel Advice:** The Chief Counsel's office of the IRS often will issue a memorandum interpreting the law on a specific issue. Known as *Chief Counsel Advice* or a *General Counsel Memorandum* (cited as G.C.M.), these sometimes evolve into Revenue Rulings.

   d. **Actions on decisions:** The IRS will often publish its decision to follow, appeal, or not follow without appeal, a decision of a trial court in what is known as an *Action on Decision* (cited as A.O.D.). In addition, the IRS will indicate its agreement to abide by an unfavorable decision or intention to continue to contest the issue in an *acquiescence* or *nonacquiescence* published in the Internal Revenue Bulletin.

D. Judicial interpretation of the Code

A number of courts have jurisdiction over tax controversies between the IRS and taxpayers.

1. **How a tax case gets to court:** Figure 1B—How a Tax Case Gets to Court—summarizes the steps by which a tax case arrives at court. In Figure 1B, the boxes in dashed lines represent the administrative process that a tax controversy goes through before ripening into an actual case.

   a. **Filing a tax return:** The U.S. tax system is a "self-assessment system," which means that each taxpayer calculates his or her tax on a tax return he or she files with the IRS.

   b. **Audit:** The IRS may review all or part of a return, raising questions about items reported (or not reported) by the taxpayer. At the conclusion of an audit, the IRS issues a Revenue Agent's Report (also known as a "30-day letter") setting forth proposed changes and giving the taxpayer 30 days in which to agree (and have additional taxes assessed) or to request an administrative conference. The taxpayer may agree to these changes.

   c. **Administrative controversies:** If the taxpayer does not agree with the changes proposed by the Revenue Agent's Report, he or she may request a conference with the Appeals Division of the IRS.

Figure 1B
How a Tax Case Gets to Court

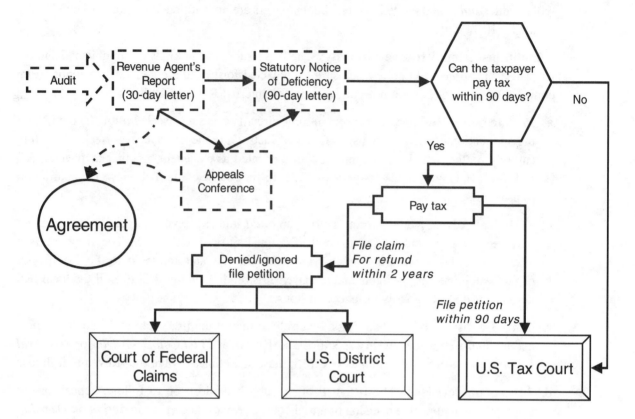

i. **Protest, conference, and settlement:** The taxpayer submits a Protest (similar to a brief) setting forth the basis for his or her disagreement with the Revenue Agent's Report. At the conference and thereafter, the appeals agent has the authority to settle the case with the taxpayer.

ii. **No settlement—Statutory Notice of Deficiency:** If the case is not resolved at the Appeals Division, the IRS will issue a Statutory Notice of Deficiency (also known as a "90-day letter") seeking to assess additional taxes and setting forth the basis for the IRS's position.

d. **Judicial determinations:** After receiving a Statutory Notice of Deficiency, the taxpayer must make a decision as to which trial forum he or she prefers. See Figure 1C—Comparison of Trial Forums for Tax Disputes.

i. **U.S. Tax Court:** A taxpayer may file a petition with the *U.S. Tax Court* (formerly the Board of Tax Appeals) within 90 days of receiving a Statutory Notice of Deficiency from the IRS. This is the only forum in which the taxpayer does not have to pay the tax prior to filing. The taxpayer may choose to pay the tax, however, in order to stop the accumulation of interest. All collection efforts are suspended during pendency of the suit. The trial is to a Tax Court judge, not a jury. The Tax Court will apply the law of the circuit to which the taxpayer would appeal. See *Golsen v. Commissioner,* 54 T.C. 742 (1970), *aff'd on another issue*, 445 F.2d 985 (10th Cir.), *cert. denied*, 404 U.S. 940 (1971). The U.S.

Tax Court issues three kinds of opinions: regular opinions (cited as "T.C."); memorandum decisions (cited as "T.C. Memo" and usually fact-intensive); and summary decisions (less than $50,000 at issue).

ii. U.S. District Court: If the taxpayer does not file a petition in the Tax Court within 90 days, his or her only other option for contesting the assessment is to pay the tax and file a claim for refund, and have that claim denied (or ignored for six months). Then the taxpayer may file a complaint in U.S. District Court for a refund of taxes paid, following a denial of the taxpayer's application for refund prior to filing suit. This is the only forum in which a jury trial is available.

iii. U.S. Court of Federal Claims: As an alternative to filing in U.S. District Court, a taxpayer may file for refund of taxes paid in the U.S. Court of Federal Claims. The taxpayer must have paid the tax, and filed a claim for refund, which was denied (or ignored for six months) prior to filing suit. The trial is to a judge of the U.S. Court of Federal Claims, not a jury.

iv. Jurisdiction of the U.S. Bankruptcy Courts: The Bankruptcy Court has jurisdiction over any tax issue of a debtor or a bankruptcy estate for which a bankruptcy petition has been filed. 11 U.S.C. §505(a). If a taxpayer commences a proceeding in Bankruptcy Court, actions pending in the Tax Court for that taxpayer are automatically stayed. 11 U.S.C. §362(a)(8). The Bankruptcy Court may decide all tax matters, preempting the jurisdiction of the Tax Court. 11 U.S.C. §362(a), (f). If a Statutory Notice of Deficiency has been issued, the stay stops the running of the 90-day period, although the Bankruptcy Court may (but is not required to) lift the stay and allow the filing of a Petition with the Tax Court. 11 U.S.C. §362(c), (d).

e. Appellate jurisdiction

i. Circuit Courts of Appeal: From each trial court, appeal is to the circuit court for the jurisdiction in which the taxpayer lives or has its domicile.

ii. U.S. Supreme Court: Review of appellate courts' tax decisions is by application for a writ of certiorari from the U.S. Supreme Court.

f. Tax procedure: Numerous rules govern the actions of the IRS and taxpayers (and their representatives) in assessing, contesting, and collecting taxes. These rules are generally beyond the scope of the basic income tax course. A passing familiarity with the following rules will usually suffice.

Figure 1C
Comparison of Trial Forums for Tax Disputes

Question	U.S. Tax Court	U.S. District Court	U.S. Court of Federal Claims
Pay tax first?	No	Yes	Yes
Jury trial?	No	Available	No

i. **Burden of proof:** Under the Tax Court rules, the taxpayer generally bears the burden of proof. Tax Court Rule 142. There are a few exceptions in which the burden of proof is on the IRS. These generally involve situations in which the IRS is asserting a particular kind of taxpayer behavior, such as fraud, for which it should already have proof before asserting its argument.

ii. **Collection processes:** Two major pieces of legislation, in 1988 and 1996, both known as the Taxpayer Bill of Rights (I and II, respectively) addressed concerns with IRS collection and other internal processes. Taxpayers have the right to notice and special appeals in the collection process.

iii. **Taxpayer Advocate:** The Office of the Taxpayer Advocate is a special office in the IRS designed to address taxpayer's concerns and help move cases along if they become "stuck." This office is intended to be independent of other IRS functions and can require that the IRA respond to inquiries and recommend solutions.

2. **The process of statutory interpretation:** Because the federal income tax is a creature of statute, most judicial activity in the area focuses on the process of statutory interpretation. An interpretive question arises whenever the taxpayer and the IRS cannot agree on the proper meaning of an ambiguous statutory term.

a. **Deference:** Courts will give deference to the IRS's pre-litigation, published interpretation of a statutory term. This means that a court will adopt the IRS's interpretation of an unclear term (instead of the taxpayer's interpretation or an interpretation the court might devise) if the IRS's interpretation is a ***reasonable*** interpretation of congressional intent. The Commissioner's interpretation need not be the only possible interpretation, or even the best interpretation; it need only be a ***reasonable*** interpretation. *Chevron U.S.A., Inc. v. Natural Resources Defense Council, Inc.,* 467 U.S. 837 (1984).

i. **Types of authority given deference:** Courts give the greatest deference to legislative regulations. See discussion this chapter, at Section II(C)(2), above. But the courts also give deference to other regulations, and, to a lesser extent, to Revenue Rulings and other administrative interpretations. Generally, however, less deference is given to authorities whose promulgation was not subject to the Administrative Procedures Act.

ii. **No deference required:** Deference is not accorded an IRS interpretation that was not the subject of a prelitigation, published administrative position. In that situation, the court will determine which interpretation—the taxpayer's, the IRS's, or some other interpretation—is correct, without giving deference to the IRS's interpretation. In addition, courts will adopt a particular interpretation if they believe the term is clear; that is, the interpretation is obvious.

b. **Tools of interpretation:** In interpreting the Code, the courts rely on a variety of tools (useful sources of information) to guide them in choosing an interpretation of a statutory term. These include language tools, extrinsic tools, and functional tools.

i. **Language tools:** Courts often refer to the literal language of a statute as the "best guide" to its meaning. But if the language were so clear, there would be no controversy. Therefore, courts often turn to the "canons of statutory interpretation" as a language tool. Although commentators criticize the canons as unhelpful and contradictory, judges nevertheless continue to rely on them. See Figure 1D—Canons of Statutory Interpretation. In addition, courts consistently invoke two specific rules of interpretation for tax statutes: Construe income statutes broadly, and construe deduction and credit statutes narrowly.

ii. **Extrinsic tools:** Courts seek guidance in the meaning of a statutory term from a wide variety of extrinsic sources. These include legislative history (hearings, floor debates, statements of the sponsors, and committee reports), the Joint Committee on Taxation's "General Explanation" of a tax bill, legislative inaction, other statutory schemes, and commentary on a statute.

iii. **Functional tools:** Courts also seek to interpret tax statutes consistently with their purpose within a legislative scheme. This requires a court to discern the purpose of a statute and to interpret its particular terms consistently with that purpose. Functional analysis often will produce the same result reached by reference to language or extrinsic tools. Yet it can also provide answers where a statute defies interpretation using other tools. Courts develop the purposes of statutes from legislative history, the structure of the larger legislative scheme, and tax policy. See discussion of tax policy this chapter, Section V.

Figure 1D
Canons of Statutory Interpretation

Canon	Description
Plain Meaning Rule	Words are to be given their obvious or plain meaning.
Ordinary Meaning Rule	Words are to be given their ordinary or everyday meaning.
Technical Meaning Rule	When words are used in a technical or complex arena, their technical meaning is preferred over their ordinary meaning.
Expressio unius est exclusio alterius	The inclusion of an item in statute implies exclusion of other similar items.
Esjusdem generis	"Of the same kind or nature." When a statute takes the form of specific items followed by a general class, it may be inferred that the class includes only those of the same nature as those specifically listed. When a statute takes the opposite form with a general class followed by specific words, the interpretation of the general term must be consistent with the nature of the specific items.
Noscitur a sociis	"It is known from its associates." The meaning of an unclear term may be derived from the meaning of words connected with it in the statute or statutory scheme.
Grammatical Rules	The grammer of a statute, including its use of specific articles, prepositions or punctuation, will be considered in deriving meaning, particularly in technical areas.
The Whole Act Rule	The terms of a statute must be construed in accordance with the entire statute, including its other terms and overall function.

c. **A guide to statutory interpretation cases:** Most statutory interpretation deals with the meaning of one or two ambiguous terms within a tax statute. To understand the interpretative question, identify the following:

   i. **The ambiguous term(s):** Identify the statutory term(s) at issue.

   ii. **The consequences:** Focus on the different tax consequences of the competing interpretations. What results will flow from each interpretation?

   iii. **The process:** What process did the court use in reaching its result? Did the court give deference to the IRS's interpretation? Why or why not?

   iv. **The result:** Which interpretation did the court choose, and why?

III. TAX ETHICS—TAX RETURN POSITIONS AND SANCTIONS

A. Taxpayer's responsibility for accuracy

Section 6001 requires taxpayers to file tax returns and comply with the Secretary of the Treasury's regulations. Form 1040 requires a taxpayer to sign the return, declaring under penalties of perjury that the return is "true, correct, and complete." The standard for a taxpayer's return position is the same as the standard for positions to be litigated before the U.S. Tax Court: the position must not be "frivolous"—i.e., it must be well grounded in fact and warranted by existing law or a good faith argument for the extension, modification, or reversal of existing law. See Tax Court Rule 33.

B. Lawyer's duty in advising on tax return positions

A lawyer advising a client of a tax return position is subject to all of the rules and regulations governing law practice of his or her state. The IRS also governs practice before it, and has promulgated rules governing that practice in what is known as Circular 230. 11 C.F.R. pt. 10. Violation of those rules can lead to sanctions, including being prohibited from practicing before the IRS. The American Bar Association Formal Opinion 85-352 provides the ABA's view on what return positions a lawyer may advise a client to take, which is similar to the standard of Circular 230. Under that opinion, a lawyer may advise a tax return position only if it has a realistic possibility of success if litigated. This requires a good faith belief that the positions are warranted in existing law or can be supported by a good faith argument for an extension, modification, or reversal of existing law. A good faith belief can exist even if the lawyer believes that the position probably will not prevail; however, a good faith belief requires that there be a realistic possibility of success if the matter is litigated. This appears to impose a higher standard than the "not frivolous" standard for litigation in the Tax Court. Finally, the likelihood of audit is not an appropriate consideration in the development of a return position. Some state bar associations have issued their own ethics opinions regarding the standards of practice for tax lawyers.

C. The accuracy-related penalty

A penalty is imposed for any portion of a tax underpayment equal to 20% of any underpayment that is attributable to negligence, substantial understatement of tax, or certain other misstatements. IRC §6662(a).

1. **Negligence:** Negligence includes any failure to make a reasonable attempt to comply with the tax laws. Reg. §1.6662-3(b)(1).

2. **Substantial understatement of tax:** An understatement of tax is substantial if it exceeds the greater of 10% of the tax required to be shown on the return for the year, or $5,000. IRC §6662(d)(1); Reg. §1.6662-4(b)(1).

   a. **Understatement:** A tax understatement is the excess of the amount of tax required to be shown on the return over the amount actually shown. IRC §6662(d)(2).

   b. **Exception for supported, disclosed items:** The penalty will not be imposed for any understatement for which the taxpayer had substantial authority, or (1) which the taxpayer disclosed on the return, and (2) for which the taxpayer had a reasonable basis. IRC §6662(d)(2)(B).

      i. **Substantial authority:** A taxpayer has substantial authority for a position if the weight of authorities supports the position compared with the weight of authorities against it. Reg. §1.6662-4(d)(3). The regulations specify which authorities may be considered in making this comparison. Id.

      ii. **Disclosure:** The taxpayer makes the required disclosure on Form 8275.

      iii. **Reasonable basis:** The regulations refer to the reasonable basis standard as being "arguable, but fairly unlikely to prevail in court." Reg. §1.6662-4(d). The legislative history of the accuracy-related penalty suggests that it is somewhat higher than the "not frivolous" standard, but the precise outlines of this standard are not clear.

D. **The civil fraud penalty**

   If any part of a tax underpayment is due to fraud, a penalty is imposed equal to 75% of that portion of the underpayment. IRC §6663(a). Fraud is defined as an intentional wrongdoing by the taxpayer with the specific intent to evade a tax known to be owed. See *Stoltzfus v. United States,* 398 F.2d 1002 (3d Cir. 1968), *cert. denied,* 393 U.S. 1020 (1969).

E. **Criminal tax sanctions**

   Tax fraud is a crime for which criminal sanctions, including prison terms and fines, apply. See IRC §§7201-7207. Criminal tax penalties are generally beyond the scope of most basic tax courses.

IV. READING THE CODE

At first, the Code may seem like a foreign language. And indeed, learning to read the Code is like learning a new language—part vocabulary, part syntax. To help you with vocabulary, this outline provides you with definitions within the text. Learning the syntax requires a systematic approach to reading a tax statute, discussed below.

A. **Nomenclature of the Code**

   A Code section is divided into a number of subparts, separately identified by letters or numbers. The nomenclature is identical for every Code section. It is helpful to have in mind the name of each separate part, particularly when *parsing* complex Code sections.

   1. **From section to subclause:** A Code "section" is the entire statute. Subdivisions are made by parenthetical indicators. The first subdivision is indicated by a parenthetical lower-case letter, such as (a)—this is known as a subsection. A subsection may be divided into parts, indicated by a parenthetical Arabic numeral, such as (1)—these are known as paragraphs. A paragraph may

be divided into parts, indicated by parenthetical upper-case letters, such as (A)—these are known as subparagraphs. A subparagraph may be divided into parts, indicated by parenthetical lower-case Roman numerals, such as (iv)—these are known as clauses. Clauses may be sub-divided into parts, indicated by parenthetical upper-case Roman numerals, such as (I)—these are known as subclauses and are not further divided. Finally, language that begins at the left margin without a parenthetical indicator is known as "flush language."

2. **Summary:** To summarize, the Code's nomenclature is as follows:

- Section—§ symbol or Section

- Subsection—Parenthetical lower-case letter, e.g., (a).

- Paragraph—Parenthetical Arabic numeral, e.g., (1).

- Subparagraph—Parenthetical upper-case letter, e.g., (A).

- Clause—Parenthetical lower-case Roman numeral, e.g., (i).

- Subclause—Parenthetical upper-case Roman numeral, e.g., (II)

- Flush language—Begins at left margin without indicator

See Figure 1E—Code Nomenclature. Figure 1E provides an illustration of the Code's nomenclature for a Code section (§163(h)(1)) that students are likely to encounter later in the course.

B. Regulations

The Treasury has its own nomenclature for regulations as well. Income tax regulations generally begin with "1." and include the Code section number, followed by a dash and another number in a series, as in -1, -2, -3, etc. For example, "Treas. Reg. §1.102-1" is a regulation explaining the basics of the gift exclusion. You can locate regulations by Code section number. Procedural regulations usually begin with "301" (e.g., Reg. §301.7701-1") and estate/gift tax regulations usually begin with a "20" or "25"(e.g., Reg. §25.2502-1).

C. A systematic approach

Comprehension of a tax statute requires a firm grasp of its ***domain*** and ***effect.*** These two concepts are often expressed through "if . . . then" statements of varying degrees of complexity at the beginning of a statute.

1. **Domain:** A tax statute (like any statutes) does not apply universally. Instead, it applies only if certain preconditions exist. The domain of a statute is the set of facts that must exist for the statute to apply.

   a. **Domain and definitions:** A statute's domain will usually depend on the definition of various terms of art defined elsewhere in the statute.

   b. **Domain and exceptions:** A tax statute may contain exceptions—situations that otherwise would fit within the domain but are specifically excepted.

   c. **Domain and interpretation:** Much of tax work is deciding whether a particular set of facts falls within the domain of the statute. The interpretation of various ambiguous terms will either bring situations within or exclude them from the statutory domain.

Figure 1E
Code Nomenclature

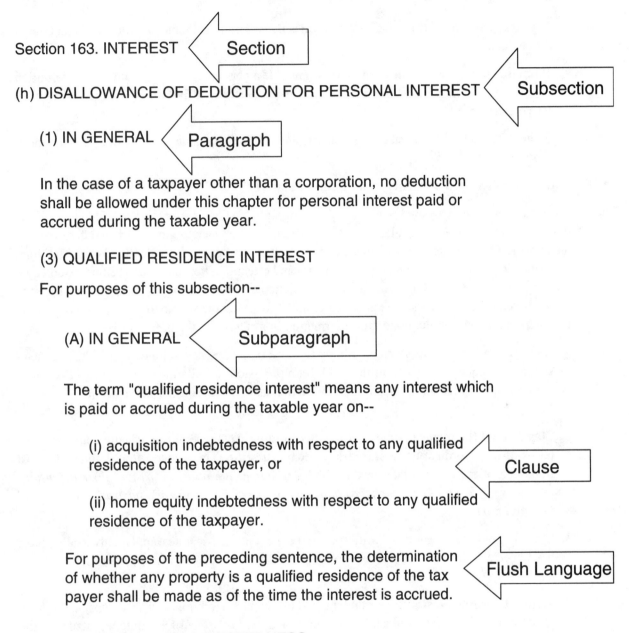

Section 163. INTEREST — Section

(h) DISALLOWANCE OF DEDUCTION FOR PERSONAL INTEREST — Subsection

(1) IN GENERAL — Paragraph

In the case of a taxpayer other than a corporation, no deduction shall be allowed under this chapter for personal interest paid or accrued during the taxable year.

(3) QUALIFIED RESIDENCE INTEREST

For purposes of this subsection--

(A) IN GENERAL — Subparagraph

The term "qualified residence interest" means any interest which is paid or accrued during the taxable year on--

(i) acquisition indebtedness with respect to any qualified residence of the taxpayer, or — Clause

(ii) home equity indebtedness with respect to any qualified residence of the taxpayer.

For purposes of the preceding sentence, the determination of whether any property is a qualified residence of the taxpayer shall be made as of the time the interest is accrued. — Flush Language

(B) ACQUISITION INDEBTEDNESS

(i) IN GENERAL

The term "acquisition indebtedness" means any indebtedness which--

(I) is incurred in acquiring, constructing, or substantially improving any qualified residence of the taxpayer, and — Subclause

(II) is secured by such residence.

2. **Effect:** Once the domain of a statute is defined, the effect of coming within the domain must be determined. In simple terms: If the statute applies, so what? What will be the tax consequences to the taxpayer?

Example: Section 71(a) of the Code provides that *alimony* is included in the Gross Income of the recipient.

Domain: The domain of this statute is simple: "If a person receives alimony." The definition of alimony is found elsewhere in §71, and is further refined in administrative and judicial interpretation.

Effect: The effect of the statute is equally simple: The recipient must include the amount in gross income.

D. Parsing—A five-step approach to unfamiliar statutes

Tax statutes are classic examples of what educators euphemistically refer to as "difficult texts." The *domain* and *effect* of a particular statute are difficult for novices to glean with standard reading techniques. The antidote to any difficult text is a systematic approach to identifying the important material within the text. Fortunately, the domain and effect of a tax statute can be understood by a five-step method of *parsing* a statute. Parsing a statute is like briefing a case—it identifies the important components of a statute and creates a tool for using the statute to solve problems. These five steps help you find the important information in a statute, in the proper order.

1. **Step 1. Find the general rule:** Almost every tax statute has a fundamental "if . . . then" statement, which is its general rule. Look for a provision (usually in subsection (a)) that states the basic conditions for application of the section and its consequences. *Underline the general rule in red.*

2. **Step 2. Find the terms of art and their definitions:** The general rule usually contains a few terms of art or ordinary terms used in a technical sense. The statute often defines the most important of these terms later in the statute. *Highlight the terms of art and their definitions in yellow. If a term is not defined, note this as a candidate for administrative or judicial interpretation.*

3. **Step 3. Find the exceptions and special rules:** Few tax statutes apply universally; most have special rules, limitations, and exceptions. *Mark these with a big green "X" for later analysis.*

4. **Step 4. Find related statutory material:** Many statutes work together in groups, and related statutory material must be identified to understand the full *effect* of a statute. Related material may appear as a reference to a Code section or as a reference to a concept discussed elsewhere in the Code. *Circle related material in blue.*

5. **Step 5. Summarize the domain and effect of the statute in the margin:** Summarizing information in your own words is the best way to remember it. For tax statutes, it is also useful to note a clear and uncomplicated example of the application of the statute. *Summarize the statute and an example in the margin in black.*

Example: See Figure 1F. (The black and white format of this book prevents this example from being parsed in color. However, use of color on your own will help you distinguish the various parts of a statute.)

Figure 1F
Example of a Parsed Statute

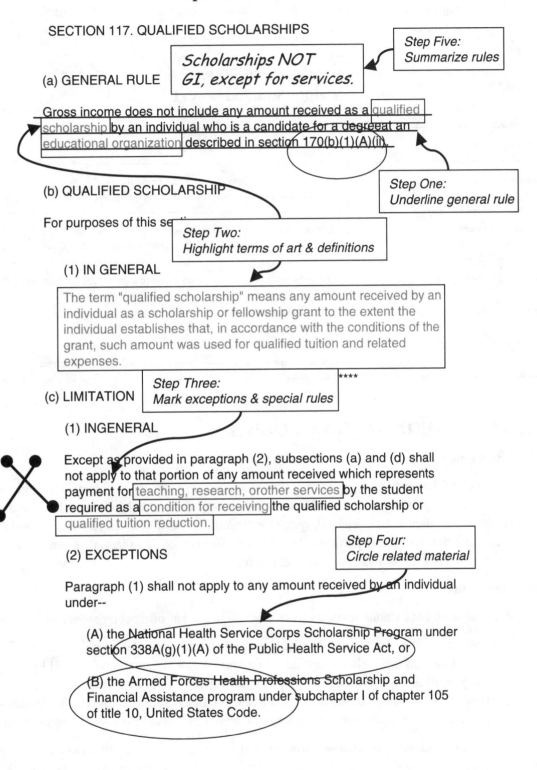

SECTION 117. QUALIFIED SCHOLARSHIPS

Step Five:
Summarize rules

(a) GENERAL RULE

Scholarships NOT GI, except for services.

Gross income does not include any amount received as a qualified scholarship by an individual who is a candidate for a degree at an educational organization described in section 170(b)(1)(A)(ii).

Step One:
Underline general rule

(b) QUALIFIED SCHOLARSHIP

For purposes of this section

Step Two:
Highlight terms of art & definitions

(1) IN GENERAL

The term "qualified scholarship" means any amount received by an individual as a scholarship or fellowship grant to the extent the individual establishes that, in accordance with the conditions of the grant, such amount was used for qualified tuition and related expenses.

****

(c) LIMITATION

Step Three:
Mark exceptions & special rules

(1) INGENERAL

Except as provided in paragraph (2), subsections (a) and (d) shall not apply to that portion of any amount received which represents payment for teaching, research, or other services by the student required as a condition for receiving the qualified scholarship or qualified tuition reduction.

(2) EXCEPTIONS

Step Four:
Circle related material

Paragraph (1) shall not apply to any amount received by an individual under--

(A) the National Health Service Corps Scholarship Program under section 338A(g)(1)(A) of the Public Health Service Act, or

(B) the Armed Forces Health Professions Scholarship and Financial Assistance program under subchapter I of chapter 105 of title 10, United States Code.

6. **Parsing boxes:** This outline presents statutory material using these five steps: the general rule, definitional issues, special rules and exceptions, related material, and summary. A chart summarizing the material is offered for particularly important statutes. See Figure 1G—Sample Statute Summary Box.

Figure 1G—Sample Statute Summary Box
Statute Summary—§71

Parsing Step	§71
General rule	Gross income includes alimony payments received Gross income does not include child support payments received
Definitional issues	Alimony: cash; divorce decree; not designated nondeductible; not same household; no liability to pay beyond recipient's death; not child support
Special rules and exceptions	Front-end loaded alimony: varies by more than $15,000 during first three years
Related material	§215: deductible to payor §1041: property transfers in divorce
Summary	Gross income includes alimony but not child support received

V. A FEW WORDS ON TAX POLICY

A. Importance

One tool of statutory interpretation is functional analysis, in which courts interpret the Code consistently with the policy considerations motivating Congress. Moreover, the federal income tax course is often policy-oriented, requiring students to be able to articulate a methodology for evaluating the wisdom of particular tax statutes. The debate is value-laden, but there are some accepted standards for evaluation of a tax statute.

B. Standards

Evaluation of a tax statute involves three general goals that often compete with one another.

1. **Fairness:** Is the statute fair? The income tax burden is intended to be allocated among taxpayers based on their relative abilities to pay tax. A fair tax statute would add to the system's ability to distinguish between taxpayers with different abilities to pay. It would ensure that taxpayers with similar ability to pay are treated similarly for tax purposes *(horizontal equity)*, and taxpayers with different abilities to pay would be treated differently *(vertical equity)*.

    a. **Ability to pay and taxable income:** It is difficult, if not impossible, to directly measure a taxpayer's ability to pay tax. This would require direct inquiry into a taxpayer's relative ability to contribute to the tax burden. "Taxable income" is viewed as a viable substitute or surrogate for direct measurement of a taxpayer's ability to pay.

   b. **A "fair" measure of taxable income:** Taxable income will never be a perfect surrogate for ability to pay. But if it is a good substitute, use of taxable income as the income tax base will tend to impose similar taxes on those with similar abilities to pay and will differentiate among taxpayers with different abilities to pay. Thus, the choice to include an item in gross income or to allow a deduction must make taxable income a closer measure of ability to pay if it is to be a "fair" statute.

2. **Administrative practicality:** Is a statute administratively practical? A statute must not be so complex as to be unworkable or require undue government intrusion into the lives of taxpayers. It must also collect revenue at a reasonable cost. The goal of administrative practicality often competes directly with the goal of *fairness.* As statutes make increasingly fine distinctions among taxpayers with different abilities to pay (presumably making the system fairer), these distinctions tend to increase the complexity of the system as a whole.

3. **Economic effects:** Does the statute have the intended economic effect? Taxpayers respond rationally to any statute, and if a statute creates an incentive to take a particular action, they may indeed do so. In addition, a statute may have some unintended effects on taxpayer behavior. In enacting a tax statute, Congress must attempt to predict its consequences and determine if they are desirable. While Congress has in the past used the tax code to induce behavioral changes, the modern trend is to make statutes as neutral as possible. Increasingly important in this debate is the budgetary impact of any particular tax measure.

VI. RELATIONSHIP OF INCOME TAX TO OTHER TAX SYSTEMS

A. Income Tax

The primary subject of the income tax is the tax levied by §1 of the Code on the "taxable income" of the individual.

B. Other tax regimes

Other tax systems exist independently of the federal income tax.

1. **Estate and gift tax:** The Code imposes a tax on lifetime gifts and estates of decedents in amounts in excess of stated amounts ($1,500,000 in 2005). This is not an income tax; it is a tax on transfers.

2. **Employment tax:** The Code imposes social security, unemployment, and Medicare taxes on the wages of employees and on employers. The employer must deduct and withhold the employee's portion of these taxes, and the employer must pay its share. Employers are also responsible for withholding federal *income* taxes, but this is merely a method of collection of the income tax, and employment taxes are a separate system of taxation.

3. **State and local tax:** The various states and their political subdivisions impose taxes on their residents. Many states adopt the federal income tax definitions and computations for their own income tax, but state income taxes are separately levied and collected. States and local governments also favor property and sales taxes in generating revenue.

4. **Foreign tax systems:** Foreign countries have their own taxing systems, which may extend to tax U.S. persons engaged in foreign transactions.

VII. WHERE ARE WE GOING?

With these preliminary matters out of the way, the next chapters turn to the technical matters of calculating a taxpayer's tax—the determination of gross income, deductions, tax rates, and credits. As a first step in this process, Chapter 2 addresses the theoretical concept of income to identify what items are potentially includable in gross income.

Quiz Yourself on
GETTING STARTED IN FEDERAL INCOME TAX

1. Why would a taxpayer disclose the details of a particular return position even though not required to do so by the usual reporting rules? _____

2. The IRS is assessing additional taxes, interest, and penalties against Leona. She is outraged, because in her opinion, "Only the little people pay taxes!" She is further outraged because she relied on an article in *Time* magazine and followed that advice in taking one of her return positions and disclosed that on the return. After calming her down, you must explain what authorities do and do not have "precedential value." How do you do that? _____

3. Willie received a Statutory Notice of Deficiency assessing $13,000,000 in back taxes, interest, and penalties. He hasn't a cent to his name, only a guitar, a collection of records, and an old pickup truck. If Willie wants to contest this assessment, how should he do so? _____

4. Carla is intent on taking a return position that saves her a lot of money in taxes, but which you (her advisor) suspect is not based in law or fact. What potential penalties apply to Carla if this position is ultimately not successful? _____

5. Assume the same facts as in Problem 4. May *you* advise Carla to take this position?
    _____

6. Your Congressman proposes a new Code provision that allows a person getting a divorce a deduction of $5,000 in the year the divorce is final. His rationale is that taxpayers have additional expenses in that year, and their taxable income should reflect that reality. You're his aide, and official tax guru. What do you tell him as to the advisability of this? (Disregard budget and budget process implications.) _____

7. Become facile in finding Code and regulations sections in your statute book *before* you need to do this in class. Can you find IRC §102(b)(2)? Or §117(b)(2)(A)? Or §108(f)(2)(C)(iii)? How about Treas. Reg. §1.61-2? Or Treas. Reg. §1.132-5? _____

Answers

1. In order to avoid the substantial understatement penalty of IRC §6662, the taxpayer might choose to fully disclose the details of a transaction.

2. Precedential value means, in the tax world, that authorities can be cited as precedent in the Tax Court and that, if they are administrative guidance, the IRS will be bound by such rulings. Court opinions,

temporary and final regulations, revenue rulings, and revenue procedures all have precedential value and all bind the IRS except for some court opinions (it is bound by the Supreme Court's opinions, and appellate courts' opinions for tax controversies appealable to that circuit). Authorities that do not have precedential value and do not bind the IRS: Private Letter Rulings and Technical Advice Memoranda addressed to other taxpayers; Chief Counsel Advice; Proposed Regulations; the Internal Revenue Manual; and forms and instructions issued by the IRS. Also (need it be said?) *Time* magazine—while possibly a source of tax information—does not generate opinions with precedential value.

3. Willie has two alternatives. He can file a petition in the U.S. Tax Court, if he files within 90 days of the date of the Statutory Notice of Deficiency. If he does so, he won't have to pay the tax unless and until the Tax Court decides against him. But he might want to consider coming under the wing of the Bankruptcy Court—this will stay enforcement proceedings. There is no guarantee that the taxes will be dischargeable in bankruptcy, but maybe he could get to keep his guitar and truck.

4. Because Carla is truly intent on taking the position, she should be warned about the following potential penalties, in order from least intrusive to most intrusive [it is impossible to advise her on which one(s) apply, without more facts]:

   ■ The substantial understatement penalty: 20% of any amount attributable to negligence (unless disclosed, see Question 1, above). IRC §6662.

   ■ The Civil Fraud Penalty: 75% of the understatement attributable to fraud, which is defined as the specific intent to evade a tax known to be owing. IRC §6663.

   ■ Criminal Tax Sanctions: Carla could find herself facing a big fine, and enjoying the hospitality of the federal government, courtesy of IRS special agents and prosecutors.

5. You would advise Carla *not* to take a return position that is not supportable in law and fact. To determine if it is supportable, you would first need to identify the applicable standard, which can vary from state to state. For a state that has adopted the ABA approach, you would need to determine if there is a realistic possibility of success on the merits if litigated. This requires an analysis of the authorities supporting the position and those against it along with careful analysis of the facts. Advising Carla to take an approach that doesn't meet this (or other applicable) standard(s) could result in preparer penalties (if you prepared the return), discipline (state and IRS), and malpractice claims.

6. In advising the Congressman, you would focus on the fairness, administrative practicality, and economic effects of this provision.

   Fairness: Does it treat persons similarly situated, as to their ability to pay, in a similar fashion? Doubtful. Certainly the good Congressman is correct, that many people getting a divorce have extra expenses associated with that divorce, and this reduces their ability to pay. But the proposal has two faults (at least) in the fairness arena. The first problem is the reach of the statute. It is not limited to people who really have extra expenses, nor does it distinguish the year in which those expenses actually occur. Second, divorce expenses are clearly personal expenses. While some personal expenses are deductible (such as certain medical expenses and casualty losses), in all of these cases you can be pretty sure that the taxpayer is really "out" a significant amount of money. Not so with divorces—in fact, some people (those married to compulsive shoppers, for example) may be saving money by getting a divorce.

   Administrative practicality: It seems to be easy to administer, at least in its current form. The year of divorce is easy to identify, and the people getting a divorce are also easy to identify. However, one might wonder how to distinguish between real divorces, and those designed to take advantage of this deduction (see below).

Economic effects: Here is where you tell your Congressman that "this dog won't hunt." Not only does it appear he is supporting divorce, he may in fact appear to be creating an economic incentive for people to get a divorce. It's a political dead end because of these effects.

Exam Tips on GETTING STARTED IN FEDERAL INCOME TAX

Make sure you understand the "big picture" of how the federal tax is imposed:

> Gross Income
> − <u>Certain Deductions</u>
> = Adjusted Gross Income (AGI)
> − Either Standard or Itemized Deduction
> − <u>Personal Exemptions</u>
> = Taxable Income
> × <u>Tax Rate</u>
> = Tentative Tax
> − <u>Tax Credits</u>
> = **Tax Due or Refund Owing**

☛ The most valuable thing you can do at the beginning of the course is to become comfortable reading the Code and applying it. When you read a tax case, read the statute that the case is based on. Analyze how the taxpayer interpreted the statute and how the IRS interpreted it—and ultimately how the court interpreted it.

☛ Tax professors almost universally allow students to take the Code book into the exam. By that time, you will have "parsed" the important statutes, for later reference. When discussing a tax problem on an exam, it never hurts to cite the statutes involved, but if pressed for time, don't cite to particular subsections, paragraphs, etc.

☛ An ingenious tax professor will offer up a "new" tax statute that you've never seen before, and pose problems from it. This tests your ability to read statutes. Use the parsing approach, and you'll be fine. (The good news: It's usually a relatively simple statute.)

☛ Tax procedure, including how cases get to court, is usually tested *indirectly* on tax exams.

   ☞ *Watch for:* A taxpayer who has filed a return with a problematic return position.

   ☞ *Analyze:* The likelihood of success if challenged on the merits, and the taxpayer's options for resolving this controversy.

☛ Policy questions place you in the position of a legislator, an aide, or even an advocate faced with a statute that arguably produces unfair, impractical, or absurd results. Be sure to present both sides of the issues. There is no "right" answer to these questions; you're being tested on your understanding of tax fairness, how tax statutes are administered, and your ability to see expected and unexpected consequences of tax statutes. These questions can be paired with the "new" statute described above.

CHAPTER 2

IDENTIFYING GROSS INCOME

ChapterScope

This chapter begins the analysis of the substantive rules governing the computation of taxable income. The starting place is the concept of gross income, which is defined in IRC §61 as including all "income" from all sources.

- **IRC Section 61:** Section 61 provides that gross income includes all income from whatever source derived. Section 61's use of the term "income" requires that a definition of income be developed so that transactions potentially generating gross income can be identified.

- **Haig-Simons definition of income:** Under this approach, a taxpayer's "income" is the sum of (1) the market value of rights exercised in consumption, plus (2) the change in the value of the store of property rights between the beginning and end of the period in question. This approach generates a comprehensive tax base and raises interesting issues of tax administration.

- **Economic benefit:** A second approach to the definition of income views a taxpayer as having income when he or she receives an economic benefit, whether in cash or property (tangible or intangible).

- **Imputed income:** Imputed income is the value one experiences from performing services for oneself or using one's own property. Imputed income, although perhaps income in a theoretical sense under the two approaches above, is not considered income under our tax system. The principal forms of imputed income are the value of household services by a nonworking spouse and the value of owner-occupied housing.

- **Capital recovery:** The income tax is a tax on "income," and thus taxpayers have the right to be taxed only on their profit on the sale or disposition of property. The capital they invested in the property will not be subject to the income tax.

- **Loans:** An inflow of funds from a loan is not considered income to the debtor because of the offsetting obligation to repay the loan.

I. WHERE ARE WE?

On the long road toward determination of a taxpayer's tax, gross income is the starting place. Section 61 requires the inclusion of all items of "income" in a taxpayer's gross income. Therefore, we begin our analysis with a discussion of the definition of "income." If a transaction produces no "income" for a taxpayer, no amount will be included in gross income, and the transaction will not generate tax for the taxpayer. By contrast, if an amount is considered "income" it will be included in gross income (and potentially subject to tax) unless specifically excluded by another Code section. Here, we examine two theoretical approaches to income and three items that are excluded from the concept of "income."

II. IRC SECTION 61

IRC Section 61(a) defines gross income as follows: "Gross income means all income from whatever source derived. . . ." Section 61 also provides a nonexclusive list of specific items that are included in gross income.

A. Interpretation

The courts interpret this language broadly, in order "to exert the full measure of [Congress'] taxing power under the Sixteenth Amendment to the United States Constitution." *Cesarini v. United States,* 296 F. Supp. 3 (N.D. Ohio 1969), *aff'd per curiam,* 428 F.2d 812 (6th Cir. 1970).

B. What is "income"?

Section 61 seems circular: It includes in gross income all items of "income." This requires a definition of "income" so that transactions potentially generating gross income can be identified.

III. DEFINITIONS OF INCOME

A. Haig-Simons definition—Theoretical approach

Under this approach, income is the sum of (1) the market value of rights exercised in consumption plus (2) the change in the value of the store of property rights between the beginning and the end of the period in question (usually the taxable year). H. Simons, *Personal Income Taxation* 50 (1938). This is known as the "Haig-Simons definition of income."

1. **Consumption rights:** This part of the equation measures the expenditures of a taxpayer for all items of consumption. Included are expenditures for basic necessities such as food, clothing, and shelter, and for luxuries such as vacations, automobiles, and cable TV. The definition potentially includes non-marketplace consumption, i.e., the value of services performed for oneself and the value of property owned and used by the taxpayer. This is known as *imputed income* and is discussed more generally at Section IV(A).

2. **Property rights:** This part of the equation measures the net change in savings over the taxable period. Savings includes bank accounts, stocks and bonds, real property, and other types of property. A net increase in savings would constitute an addition. A net decrease in savings (a fall in value of an asset, for example) would constitute a subtraction.

   Example: During the taxable year Heidi spent $32,000 on food, clothing, and shelter, another $5,000 on travel and other luxuries, and saved $4,000. Under the Haig-Simons definition of income, her income is $41,000; the sum of her market rights exercised in consumption ($37,000) and the net increase in her property rights ($4,000).

   Example—Changes in property rights: Assume the same facts as in the previous example, except that in the next year Heidi invests her $4,000 savings from the prior year in a mutual fund, which declines in value to $3,000. All of her expenditures remain the same. Her income for the year would be $36,000; the market rights exercised in consumption ($37,000) minus the net change in the value of her property interests (− $1,000).

3. **Broad definition:** The Haig-Simons approach constitutes a broad definition of income. It offers a "comprehensive tax base," i.e., a tax base that reflects all potential sources of income from which taxpayers may derive an ability to pay tax.

4. Practical limitations: It would be difficult (but not impossible) to measure the value of *imputed income* and to administer the yearly addition or subtraction of paper "profits or losses" for assets.

B. Another approach—Economic benefit

Under this approach, income is the value of *economic benefits* received by the taxpayer. A benefit is broadly defined to include inflows of both cash and noncash items that result in the taxpayer being "better off" as a result of the receipt. Only economic benefits are considered in this analysis, although "economic" is construed broadly to include not only cash and property but certain other benefits that cause the taxpayer's wealth to increase. Intangible, nonmaterial benefits are excluded, such as one's enjoyment of a job, the beauty of a spring day, or the personal satisfaction of being close to family. While important benefits to individuals, these are not quantified and considered benefits in the economic sense to be included in gross income.

Example: Ed works as an analyst for Bingo Corporation for a salary of $25,000. One morning a big truck drives up and unloads a number of paintings to beautify the workplace. Ed is an art lover, and his enjoyment of his job increases dramatically as a result of his employer's action. The value of the intangible benefit of a pleasant work place is not included in Ed's income under the economic benefit theory even though it is a benefit to him, because it is not an "economic" benefit.

1. Receipt of cash and property: The receipt of cash or property (whether tangible or intangible) is the receipt of an economic benefit by the taxpayer. The source of the cash or property is not important to this determination, so even receipts from unusual sources constitute "income."

    a. The usual economic benefits: The usual economic benefits include payments for goods or services, gifts, and transfers of property.

    b. *Commissioner v. Glenshaw Glass Co.,* **348 U.S. 426,** *rehearing denied,* **349 U.S. 925 (1955):** The taxpayers received exemplary damages for fraud and treble damages for anti-trust violations by other companies.

        i. Issue: Were exemplary and treble damages includable in the taxpayers' gross incomes?

        ii. Result and rationale: Treble damages under antitrust law and exemplary damages for fraud are included in recipient's gross income. According to the court, "[U]ndeniable accessions to wealth, clearly realized, and over which the taxpayers have complete dominion" are includable in gross income.

    c. *Cesarini v. United States,* **296 F. Supp. 3 (N.D. Ohio 1969),** *aff'd per curiam,* **428 F.2d 812 (6th Cir. 1970):** Husband and wife found $5,000 inside an old piano they had purchased.

        i. Issues: Must the taxpayers include the $5,000 in their gross income? If so, when the piano was purchased, or when the cash was discovered? And, if so, what is the character of the income?

        ii. Result and rationale: The taxpayers must include the $5,000 in their gross income. Reg. §1.61-14(a) requires taxpayers finding treasure to include it in gross income when reduced to undisputed possession. This regulation is consistent with §61's statutory scheme to include all income in gross income. The court rejected the taxpayers' arguments that §74 (prizes) or §102 (gifts) would exclude this amount from gross income.

(The regulation required the taxpayers to include the $5,000 in the year they found it, and its character was ordinary, but those issues are for a later chapter.)

2. **Receipt of intangible benefit:** What the taxpayer receives may be something other than cash or a property right. If it constitutes an **economic benefit** to the taxpayer, it is income within this definition.

    a. **Noncash compensation—*United States v. Drescher*, 179 F.2d 863 (2d Cir.), *cert. denied*, 340 U.S. 821 (1950):** Employer paid $5,000 for an annuity contract naming an employee as the annuitant. Under the terms of the contract, the employer retained possession of the contract until the employee reached age 65, and thereafter the insurance company would pay the annuitant $54.70 monthly until his death. If he died before receiving 120 payments, the remaining payments would be paid to a beneficiary named by the annuitant. The employee had no assignable rights in the contract, and it had no cash, surrender, or loan value.

        i. **Issue:** Must the employee include in his gross income the $5,000 paid by the employer for the annuity contract?

        ii. **Result and rationale:** The employee must include an amount in gross income equal to the value of the contract. The employee received an **economic benefit** for services rendered to his employer, thus receiving compensation. The absence of assignability or surrender value did not render the benefit valueless. The question of value was to be considered on remand.

    b. **Satisfaction of obligation—*Old Colony Trust Co. v. Commissioner*, 279 U.S. 716 (1929):** An employer entered into contract with employee in which the employer agreed to pay the income taxes of the employee.

        i. **Issue:** Did the employer's payment of the taxes constitute additional gross income to the employee?

        ii. **Result and rationale:** The Court concluded that the satisfaction of a taxpayer's obligation (taxes) by another person constitutes an **economic benefit** to him, resulting in income to the taxpayer.

        Example: Brad agrees to work for The Firm, a law firm offering a competitive salary and benefits. On the first day of work, much to Brad's surprise, the senior partner informs him that The Firm has paid all of his law school debt, a total of $50,000. This transaction will be viewed for tax purposes as the payment of $50,000 of compensation income to Brad followed by Brad's payment of the loans. Thus, Brad will be required to include the $50,000 in gross income. (Notice that because the creditors have been paid in full, Brad has no "discharge of indebtedness income," discussed in Chapter 3 at Section VII.)

    c. **Services—Revenue Ruling 79-24, 1979-1 C.B. 60:** A lawyer performs legal services for a housepainter, who in turn paints the lawyer's house.

        i. **Issue:** Do the lawyer and housepainter have income as a result of the transaction?

        ii. **Result and rationale:** The lawyer and the housepainter both have income as a result of the transaction, in an amount equal to the fair market value of the services each received. (This is presumed to be an equal amount of each, because no additional payments are made.)

IV. ITEMS THAT ARE NOT INCOME

A. Imputed income

Imputed income is the fair market value of the taxpayer's performance of services for his or her personal benefit and the value of the taxpayer's personal use of property that he or she owns. The amount of imputed income can be established by reference to what the taxpayer would have to pay to hire the service or rent the property in the marketplace. Imputed income is not considered income for purposes of inclusion in gross income.

1. **Importance:** The value of any service one performs for oneself, and the rental value of any property that one owns constitutes imputed income. However, there are two very significant types of imputed income in terms of dollar value.

   a. **Household services:** The value of housework and child care performed by stay-at-home spouses is an important type of imputed income in the U.S. economy. For example, some observers have estimated the annual value of U.S. unpaid housework at $1.5 billion.

   b. **Owner-occupied housing:** The rental value of the home owned by the occupier is also an important type of imputed income.

2. **Compare—Barter:** A barter transaction does not generate imputed income. If a housepainter paints a house for a lawyer in exchange for legal services, neither has *imputed income* because neither has performed services for him- or herself. Instead, each has performed services for the other and has gross income in the amount of the value of the services obtained from the other. See Rev. Rul. 79-24, 1979-1 C.B. 60, discussed in this chapter, at Section III(B).

3. **Is it income?** Imputed income appears in theory to be income under either the Haig-Simons or economic benefit definitions of income.

   a. **Haig-Simons:** The Haig-Simons definition includes the market value of rights exercised in consumption. Thus, the value of shelter (housing), child care, and housework constitute consumption, which in turn constitutes income, in theory.

   b. **Economic benefit:** The right to live in a home and the value of child care and housework are economic benefits to the taxpayer. Thus, they are income to the taxpayer, in theory.

   c. **Transactions only?** One possible explanation for the exclusion of imputed income from the definition of income is that a "transaction" is necessary to trigger income. A transaction requires more than one taxpaying unit and some sort of transfer of value between them.

4. **Policy**

   a. **Fairness:** Some commentators argue that it is unfair to exclude from gross income *imputed income* because the exclusion results in taxpayers with similar abilities to pay tax being treated differently (a violation of horizontal equity).

   Example: Compare Jack and Jill, a married couple with two children, with Kurt and Kathy, also married with two children. Jack works outside the home, earning taxable income of $50,000, and Jill cares for their two children and home. Kurt and Kathy both work outside the home, with Kurt earning $50,000 in taxable income and Kathy earning $25,000 in taxable income. Kurt and Kathy hire Lola to care for their two children at home while they work, and they pay her $20,000. Both couples are in a 30% tax bracket.

Current taxation. Kurt and Kathy will pay tax on $75,000 of income while Jack and Jill will pay tax on $50,000 of income. At a 30% rate, this would result in Kurt and Kathy paying $7,500 more in tax.

Compare consumption rights. Both couples have someone to care for their home and children, at an apparent value of $20,000 (Lola's wages). In fact, Kurt and Kathy have only $5,000 more in available consumption rights than do Jack and Jill and thus should have an additional tax of only $1,500.

Compare economic benefits. Same analysis as consumption rights; both couples have the economic benefit of a cared-for home and cared-for children.

A possible solution. Include in Jack and Jill's gross income the $20,000 of imputed income Jill earns taking care of the children and home. This would result in the two couples being taxed similarly.

b. Administrative practicality: It is difficult to measure the value of owner-occupied housing or the value of housework and child care, but it is hardly an impossible task. The annual value of owner-occupied housing could be set as a percentage of property tax value. The value of a stay-at-home spouse could be conservatively estimated based on the annual cost of hiring household help.

c. Economic effects: The exclusion of imputed income from gross income may cause desirable or undesirable economic effects, depending on one's value choices.

i. Marketplace or home? Lesser earning spouses may choose to stay home rather than work outside the home.

ii. Own or rent? Taxpayers may choose to own rather than rent items such as homes or equipment.

iii. Work or play? Taxpayers may choose to perform certain services (e.g., home repair) for themselves rather than hiring a professional. The time they devote to such activities may be more productively spent in other pursuits, such as their own job.

d. The political question: Imputed income is so far from the average taxpayer's view of the proper subject for taxation that it seems unlikely to become part of the federal income tax.

B. Capital recovery

''Capital'' is the taxpayer's unrecovered economic investment in property. Upon sale or disposition of that property, the taxpayer has a right to be taxed only on the income (profit) from the transaction, not his or her invested capital. Thus, the taxpayer is entitled to "recover" his or her invested capital. See discussion at Chapter 7, Section III(A).

Example: Ingrid purchases Blackacre, a parcel of raw land, for $10,000. Five years later she sells Blackacre for $30,000. Ingrid will be taxed only on her income from this sale, which is the difference between her sales price ($30,000) and what she paid for Blackacre ($10,000), or $20,000. She will not be taxed on her invested capital.

1. Capital recovery—Timing: While the right to obtain a tax-free recovery of invested capital in property is a constitutional issue, the timing of that recovery is within the discretion of Congress. See discussion at Chapter 7, Section III(E).

Example: In the above example, Ingrid received her tax-free recovery of capital upon sale at the end of her investment. If Blackacre had been a commercial office building, Ingrid would have been entitled to obtain her tax-free capital recovery during her ownership of the property (through depreciation or MACRS deductions).

2. **Basis:** A taxpayer's economic investment in property is reflected in his or her "basis" in that property. Basis is adjusted downward for capital recovery deductions, producing a taxpayer's "adjusted basis." See discussion at Chapter 9, Section III(B).

C. Loans

The creation of a loan does not generate income for either the debtor or the creditor. The inflow of funds (the loan proceeds) to the debtor, which might otherwise be viewed as an economic benefit, is offset by the debtor's promise to repay the debt. Similarly, the creditor's receipt of the debtor's note or other evidence of indebtedness, which could be viewed as the receipt of an economic benefit, is offset by the outflow of the loan proceeds. Repayment of the loan does not generate income for either party. The creditor's inflow (repayment) is offset by the creditor's return of the note. The debtor's receipt of his or her note, even if it qualifies as an economic benefit (which it may not), is offset by repayment. Thus neither the making of the loan nor repayment generates income to the parties to the loan.

1. **Discharge of indebtedness income:** If ultimately the debtor's obligation to repay is canceled in whole or in part, the debtor will have "discharge of indebtedness income" in the amount of the cancellation. See discussion at Chapter 3, Section VII.

2. **Possible exclusion—§108:** Section 108 provides an exclusion from gross income for discharge of indebtedness income in certain circumstances. See discussion at Chapter 4, Section VI.

V. WHERE ARE WE GOING?

With an idea of what theoretically constitutes income in mind, we now move to an analysis of items specifically included in gross income. Section 61 provides a nonexclusive list of items of income that are included in gross income, and other statutes supplement this list with additional inclusions in gross income. These are addressed in Chapter 3.

Quiz Yourself on
IDENTIFYING GROSS INCOME

8. Valley Girl Buffy asks, ""*Gross* income"? What's up with *that*?" Can you explain to her what "gross income" really is? _____

9. This year, Cally earned $300,000 in salary as a TV star. She spent $50,000 on housing, $100,000 on clothing, and $2,000 on food. She spent $100,000 on having fun: sporting events, galas, travel, and parties. The rest she invested in a Certificate of Deposit earning 5%. Using the Haig-Simons definition of income, what is Cally's income? _____

10. Assume that Cally (from the previous question) invested her surplus funds not in a CD but instead in EndRun Co., a high-flying stock recommended by her accountant. At the next year its value plummeted to $2,000. What effect does this have on her income in the later year, using the Haig-Simons definition of income? _____

11. Nick's grandparents pay off his student loans for him as a graduation present. Does this result in income to Nick? _____

12. Ken borrowed $15,000 from the bank. Does he have income when he receives the loan proceeds, under the economic benefit theory of income? Why or why not? _____

13. Martha is the ultimate stay-at-home mother. She raises the children, and in her spare time, she decorates the home she and her husband own, repairs their appliances if they break, creates fabulous meals on a shoestring, and gives advice on cooking, cleaning, crafts, and surviving prison life in style to her many friends, neighbors, and acquaintances. What is her "income" from these activities? _____

14. Don purchased Chump Chowder, a parcel unimproved real estate, for $500,000. His plans for building a seafood restaurant on the property never matured, and several years later, he sold it for $750,000. Assume no depreciation was claimed and no improvements to the property were made. What is Don's "income" from the sale of Chump Chowder and why? _____

15. A massage therapist and a graphic artist agree that the graphic artist will design a brochure for the massage therapist in exchange for five massages. Who has income from this transaction? _____

16. Lana has saved $10,000. She purchases 100 shares of ABC stock with this money. Does she have income as a result of this transaction? _____

Answers

8. Gross income is the term used in IRC §61 to mean all income, from whatever source derived. It is the beginning place for the calculation of taxable income, the tax base on which the income tax is levied. You can tell Buffy that the "gross" in "gross income" refers to the fact that no deductions are taken in determining it.

9. The Haig-Simons definition of income says that income is the sum of (1) all rights exercised in consumption, plus (2) the change in value of property rights from the beginning to the end of the taxable period. Cally exercised $252,000 in consumption rights. She also had a net increase in property rights of $48,000 (the CD) plus whatever interest accrued on that amount during that year. Thus, her total income (under this theory) is $300,000 for the year, exactly the same as what she earned.

10. Cally started with a property right worth $48,000 and ended with a property right worth $2,000. In the Haig-Simons definition of income, the net decrease in property rights ($46,000) is a reduction in her income for that year.

11. Yes, but . . . anyone's payment of Nick's obligations results in an economic benefit to him, and so he has income. Later chapters will discuss specific exclusions for gifts. See Chapter 4(III).

12. Ken does not have an economic benefit from taking out the loan, because he has an offsetting obligation to repay the loan. He is also out of pocket the fees, which is a decrease in economic rights.

13. Imputed income is the value of the use of property one owns, or the services one performs for oneself. The value of all of Martha's activities that she performs for herself and family (child care, decorating, cooking, etc.) constitute imputed income. Also, one-half of the rental value of her home is imputed income to her (the other one-half is imputed to her co-owner, her husband). The advice she gives to others is not imputed income, as it is not services she provides for herself (nor does she appear to be receiving income for this activity). However, under our system of taxation, imputed income is not included in gross income. This avoids the difficult question of how to value these services.

14. Don's income from the sale of Chump Chowder is $250,000, the difference between the sales price ($750,000) and his cost of the property ($500,000). Don is entitled to recover his capital investment in the property and be taxed only on the gain he experiences on the sale.

15. Both have income. This is a barter transaction, in which the value of the services exchanged will be income to both parties. It will probably be easier to value the services based on the standard fee for a massage, and thus the massage therapist will have income of five massages, and the graphic artist also will have the same amount of income.

16. No. Lana has simply transformed money into property; she has had no increase or decrease in income under any theory. However, if she receives dividends on the stock, that would be income to her.

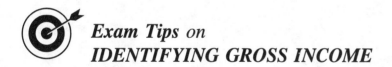

Exam Tips on
IDENTIFYING GROSS INCOME

☞ If the question is whether the taxpayer has "income," determine what theory is being used to define gross income. Is this a theoretical question of comparing a broad tax base (Haig-Simons) with the more practical statutory scheme? Or is this a question based solely on a single theory, or on the statutory system of the Code?

☞ Questions requiring identification of gross income focus on a taxpayer receiving "stuff" of value, including:

 ☞ Cash

 ☞ Property

 ☞ Services

 ☞ The use of the taxpayer's own property, or the value of the taxpayer's own services (imputed income)

 ☞ Discharge of debt

☛ Questions requiring identification of gross income also focus on the few things that are *not* income in our system:

  ☞ Loan proceeds are not income, because of the offsetting obligation to repay.

  ☞ Capital recovery is not income; a taxpayer is entitled to recover his or her invested capital without tax.

  ☞ Imputed income is not income in our system, but is income under other theories.

  ☞ Noneconomic benefits such as living in a beautiful place, or the enjoyment of one's job, are not income.

☛ Some questions combine a nontaxable receipt and a later development that might change the result.

  ☞ **Example:** In Year One, Kelly borrows $45,000 from Alex. That isn't income, because Kelly is required to pay Alex back. But later, Alex forgives the debt. This is income to Kelly in the year of forgiveness, because she has been discharged of the obligation. (It might, however, be excludable under a specific statutory rule, but that's for a later chapter.)

☛ Questions involving barter are common—on exams and in practice. A barter transaction involves the exchange of goods or services, and is distinguishable from imputed income, which involves the use of property or services for oneself.

CHAPTER 3

SPECIFIC INCLUSIONS IN GROSS INCOME

ChapterScope

The previous chapter discussed the definition of "income" as used in Section 61. This chapter addresses the specific items listed in §61 as included in gross income and discusses some items brought into the concept of income by other Code sections and judicial decisions. Some important kinds of income include:

- **Services income:** Compensation for services is included in gross income of the service provider, whether in the form of cash, property, or other services.

- **Investment income:** Income from investments, including interest, dividends, annuities, rents, and royalties, is included in the gross income of the recipient.

- **Alimony:** Alimony, which has a specific federal definition independent of state law labels, is includable in the gross income of the recipient.

- **Discharge of indebtedness income:** Income from the discharge or cancellation of indebtedness is included in the gross income of the debtor.

- **Other income:** Gross income includes a number of other items of income, including certain prizes and awards, a portion of social security payments, and a variety of payments that are normally beyond the scope of the federal income tax course.

I. WHERE ARE WE?

We are still at the starting gate of computing a taxpayer's ultimate tax liability. Remember: If an item is excluded from gross income, it will never be taxed. So it is very important to determine what is—and is not—included in gross income.

II. COMPENSATION FOR SERVICES

Section 61(a)(1) includes in gross income compensation for services, including fees, commissions, fringe benefits, and "similar items."

A. Identifying the transaction

To identify a transaction involving compensation for services, look for two related events.

1. **Provision of services:** One taxpayer provides services for another, or promises to do so (e.g., signing bonuses for athletes).

2. **Compensation:** The person receiving the benefit of the services (or a person related to the recipient of the benefit) transfers money or other property (or the promise of money or other property) to the service provider.

Example: *Compensation.* Mildred drafts a will for Nelson, who pays her $300. Mildred has $300 income from compensation for her services.

Example: *Compensation.* Ollie agrees to live in Paula's mountain cabin for the winter to tend Paula's livestock. Ollie is performing services for Paula in exchange for the benefit of living in the cabin. His income is the fair market value of the rental. This income may be excluded from his gross income by §119; see discussion at Chapter 4(IX)(2).

Example: *No compensation.* George agrees to fix two meals per week for Fred, who is disabled and cannot prepare his own food. George receives nothing in return for his meal preparation. This transaction is not compensation, for although George has provided services to Fred, George has received nothing tangible in return.

Example: *Compensation.* Rudy repairs Steve's car, and Steve gives Rudy a CD player worth $300 in exchange. Rudy has income from compensation equal to the fair market value of the CD player—$300. His basis in the CD player is $300, the amount he must include in gross income.

B. Forms of compensation

The form of the compensation does not matter for federal income tax purposes. The service provider includes in gross income the amount of money, or fair market value of the property or services, received as compensation.

1. **Cash/check:** The gross amount of wages or salary (not reduced by withholdings) is included in the gross income of the service provider. Wages include the gross amount of tips earned by a service provider.

2. **Property:** The fair market value of property received as compensation is included in gross income of the service provider. The service provider will then have a "basis" in the property equal to the amount he or she included in gross income. Property can include items such as the employer's inventory (a car or washing machine) or can include stock or stock options or other rights with respect to the employer. The timing of including the property in gross income often depends on whether it is "restricted," i.e., whether the recipient can sell it. See discussion at Chapter 11, Section IV.

3. **Barter of services:** If taxpayers exchange services, each has income equal to the fair market value of the services received. See discussion of Rev. Rul. 79-24, at Chapter 2, Section III(B).

C. Related issues

1. **Exclusions:** Various Code sections provide exclusions from gross income for certain types of compensation income, such as fringe benefits. See discussion at Chapter 4, Section IX(C).

2. **Timing:** The question of *whether* a taxpayer has income is related to—but independent of—the question of *when* a taxpayer has income. The taxpayer may provide services in one year but be paid in a later taxable year. This transaction will generate compensation income for the service provider, but *when* that person must include the income in gross income depends on a number of factors.

   a. **Method of accounting:** The taxpayer's method of accounting will often determine the year of taxation. See discussion at Chapter 11, Section III.

b. Restricted property: If the taxpayer's use of property received is restricted in some way, taxation may not occur until the restriction is removed. See discussion at Chapter 11 Section IV.

3. **Character:** Compensation income is ordinary income. See generally Chapter 12.

III. GROSS INCOME FROM BUSINESS

Although §61(a)(2) includes in gross income the taxpayer's gross income from business, the taxpayer actually reports the net result (net income or loss) from business activities on his or her own tax return, having calculated that result by tallying up gross income from business and subtracting available deductions. Net income is included in the taxpayer's gross income, and net loss may be deductible.

A. Identifying business income

To identify potential business income, look for a taxpayer selling goods or services or engaging in other regular activity with an intent to make a profit.

1. **Sole proprietorships:** The taxpayer conducting business through a sole proprietorship computes the net income or loss from the business on Schedule C of the tax return and the result is ultimately reported on Form 1040, Line 12 (see Figure 1A). Net income is included in gross income.

2. **Pass-through entities:** Entities such as trusts and partnerships (including limited-liability companies treated as partnerships) report their activities to their beneficiaries or partners, who report the net income from the entity as gross income on their own tax returns. Partners need not receive distributions from the partnership in order to be taxed.

3. **Corporations:** A corporation is an incorporated entity under state law or an unincorporated organization treated as a corporation under standards set forth in the regulations. See IRC §7701(a)(3) and Reg. §301.7701-2. A corporation is a separate taxable entity for federal income tax purposes.

   a. C corporations: A C corporation is a corporation that does not have in effect a valid election to be taxed as an S corporation. C corporations pay dividends to their shareholders, who must include the amount of dividends in gross income. Dividends are viewed as investment income rather than business income, because a shareholder's holding of stock is not a business activity.

   b. S corporations: An S corporation is a corporation that has made a valid election to be taxed as a small business corporation. IRC §1361(a). The S corporation is not subject to the corporate income tax, and the shareholders report their shares of the corporation's income on their own tax returns, much like partners in a partnership. IRC §1366(a)(1)(A),(B). Distributions from the S corporation are taxable to a shareholder only to the extent they exceed the basis of the shareholder's stock in the S corporation. IRC §1368(b)(2).

B. Related issues

1. **Trade or business expenses:** In computing net income or loss, the taxpayer deducts certain business expenses. See generally Chapter 7.

2. **Losses:** There are special restrictions on the deductibility of losses. See discussion at Chapter 11(VII).

3. **Character:** Income from business activity is ordinary, not capital. See discussion at Chapter 12.

IV. GAINS DERIVED FROM DEALINGS IN PROPERTY

Section 61(a)(3) includes gains derived from dealings in property in gross income. When a taxpayer sells or exchanges property, the taxpayer must compute the gain or loss from the transaction and determine if any statutes limit the amount of gain to be included in gross income or the amount of loss to be deducted. Losses generally offset gains, and the taxpayer will report the net figure as gain or loss from dealings in property. This very important topic in federal income tax is discussed fully in Chapters 9 and 10.

V. INVESTMENT INCOME

Section 61 includes in a taxpayer's gross income various types of investment income.

A. Identifying investment income

Investment income generally means income from profit-motivated activities that do not rise to the level of a *trade or business.*

1. **Trade or business:** In order to be engaged in a trade or business, the taxpayer must be involved in the activity with regularity and continuity and must have as his or her primary motivation for engaging in the activity an expectation of profit. *Commissioner v. Groetzinger,* 480 U.S. 23 (1987).

2. **Investment activity:** The activities of owning stock and buying and selling for one's own account are not a trade or business, regardless of frequency of trades or the amount of time devoted to the activity. *Higgins v. Commissioner,* 312 U.S. 212 (1941).

B. Dividends

Section 61(a)(7) includes dividends in a taxpayer's gross income. Dividends are amounts paid by a corporation to a shareholder in his or her capacity as a shareholder from the earnings and profits of the corporation. IRC §301(c)(1). Payments made to a shareholder other than in his or her capacity as a shareholder are *not* dividends and must be classified as some other type of payment, such as salary or rent.

Example: Victor is the sole shareholder of a profitable corporation. He also rents an office building to the corporation. The corporation pays Victor an annual lump sum of $100,000. This payment must be divided between Victor's rental payments for the building and dividends paid by the corporation. If a reasonable rental for the office building is $40,000, the remaining $60,000 must be a dividend, which must be included in Victor's gross income.

C. Interest

Section 61(a)(4) includes interest in a taxpayer's gross income.

1. **Definition:** Interest is the amount paid by a debtor to a creditor for the use of borrowed money. *Deputy v. DuPont*, 308 U.S. 488 (1940). Interest depends on the existence of an underlying debt, which is defined as the "unconditional and legally enforceable obligation for the repayment of money." *Autenreith v. Commissioner,* 115 F.2d 856 (3d Cir. 1940).

   Example: Wendy lends Yolanda $5,000 at 10% interest for five years. Each year that the debt is outstanding, Yolanda pays Wendy $500 as interest. Wendy must include the $500 yearly interest payment in her gross income.

2. **"Hidden" interest payments:** Federal income tax law assumes that creditors will extract market interest from debtors, even if the loan appears to provide for a below-market rate of interest or no interest at all. Such a transaction will be "recharacterized" for tax purposes, i.e., it will be recast in another form to reveal the hidden interest payment. In the recharacterization, the creditor will be deemed to receive, and the debtor will be deemed to pay, an appropriate amount of interest. See generally Chapter 15.

3. **Related issues**

   a. **Timing:** The year in which the creditor includes the interest in income depends on the creditor's method of accounting. See discussion at Chapter 11(III).

   b. **Character:** Interest is ordinary income. See generally Chapter 12.

   c. **Exclusion for interest on certain state and local bonds:** See discussion of §103, at Chapter 4(IV).

   d. **Deduction:** The payor of interest may be able to deduct the interest paid or accrued. See discussion at Chapters 6(XII) and 7(IV).

D. Rental income

Section 61(a)(5) includes rental income in a taxpayer's gross income.

1. **Definition:** Rental income is the amount paid by the lessee of property to the lessor for the use of tangible property. Reg. §1.61-8(a).

   Example: Felicia owns Whiteacre, an office building. She leases Whiteacre to Greg for ten years at an annual rent of $640,000. Felicia must include the rental income of $640,000 per year in her gross income.

2. **Related issues**

   a. **Timing of inclusion:** The year in which taxable year the taxpayer includes rental income depends on his or her method of accounting. See discussion at Chapter 11(III).

   b. **Deduction of rent by lessee:** The lessee may be able to deduct the rental payment. See discussion at Chapter 7(II).

E. Royalty income

Section 61(a)(6) includes royalty income in the gross income of the recipient.

1. **Identifying royalty income:** Royalty income is the amount paid for the use of intangible property, such as a copyright, trademark, or patent. Reg. §1.61-8(a). Royalty income also includes the payment (in money or in kind) made by an operator of oil and gas properties

to the owner as a portion of the oil and gas mined from the property. *Shamrock Oil and Gas Corp. v. Commissioner,* 346 F.2d 377 (5th Cir. 1965).

Example: Bonnie wrote a book about estate planning. Under her contract with the publisher, she is entitled to a royalty of 15% of the gross sales from the book. She receives her first royalty payment of $1,500 from the publisher, which she must include in her gross income.

2. Related issues

a. Timing: In which taxable year the taxpayer includes royalty income depends on his or her method of accounting. See discussion at Chapter 11(III).

b. Deduction: The payor may be able to deduct the royalty payment. See discussion at Chapter 7(II).

F. Income derived from annuities

Section 61(a)(9) includes income from annuities in a taxpayer's gross income.

1. What is an annuity?
When a taxpayer purchases an "annuity," the taxpayer pays premiums (in a lump sum or over time) for a promise from another person (usually an insurance company) to pay the taxpayer a sum of money in the future. The issuer of the annuity invests the premiums in order to satisfy its future promise to pay the taxpayer. The annuity contract can have any number of choices for the taxpayer to withdraw his or her money: withdrawing amounts from time to time; by electing to receive periodic (usually monthly or annual) amounts; or withdrawing the entire amount in a lump sum.

2. The tax problem:
Recall that a taxpayer can only be taxed on the "income" realized from property; he or she is entitled to a tax-free return of his or her investment. See discussion at Chapter 2(IV)(B). If a taxpayer receives a lump-sum payment pursuant to an annuity contract, there will be no problem in identifying the amount of income from the contract: it will be the excess of the sum received over the cost of the annuity to the taxpayer. But what if the taxpayer withdraws amounts from time to time, or receives periodic payments? How much of each payment is income and how much is a tax-free return of the taxpayer's invested capital? The annuity taxation rules allocate a portion of each payment between capital and income.

3. Statutory analysis—§72

a. General rule: Gross income includes amounts received as an annuity under an annuity, life insurance, or endowment contract. IRC §72(a). Section 72(b), however, excludes from gross income the portion of a periodic annuity payment equal to the payment multiplied by the *exclusion ratio.* IRC §72(b)(1).

b. Definitional issues: An annuity, life insurance, or endowment contract is a contract under the "customary practices" of life insurance companies under which an amount is paid to an annuitant at a time other than at his or her death. Reg. §1.72-2(a)(1). To determine the portion of an annuity payment that is excluded from gross income, multiply the payment by a fraction, called the "exclusion ratio." The numerator of this fraction is the taxpayer's "investment in the contract." The denominator is the "expected return under the contract." IRC §72(b)(1). Both figures are calculated at the annuity starting date. IRC §72(b)(1). See Figure 3A—Exclusion Ratio—§72.

Figure 3A
Exclusion Ratio—Section 72

Amount of an annuity payment = annuity payment $\times$ $\dfrac{\text{Investment in the Contract*}}{\text{Total Expected Return**}}$
excluded from Gross Income

* Investment in the Contract = total premiums paid, less amounts withdrawn tax-free.
**Total Expected Return = the total amount to be received under the contract.

i. **Investment in contract:** The taxpayer's investment in the contract is equal to the total premiums paid less any amounts previously withdrawn that were excluded from gross income. IRC §72(c)(1).

ii. **Total expected return:** The calculation of total expected return depends on the nature of the contract. If the contract pays a fixed amount, the total expected return is the total amount to be received under the contract. IRC §72(c)(3)(B). If the contract depends on the life of the annuitant (or the annuitant and spouse), the total expected return is the life expectancy of the taxpayer at the starting date multiplied by the annual amount to be received. IRC §72(c)(3)(A).

Example—Lump sum annuity: Gwyneth, age 25, purchases an annuity policy from Local Life Assurance Company. Under the terms of the policy, Gwyneth is to pay an annual premium of $1,200 for the twenty years from age 25 to 45. On her 65th birthday, she will be entitled to a lump-sum distribution of $125,000. To determine how much of that lump-sum payment Gwyneth must include in her gross income, we calculate the exclusion ratio:

Payment $\times$ $\dfrac{\text{Investment in the Contract}}{\text{Total Expected Return}}$

$125,000 $\times$ $\dfrac{\$24,000^*}{\$125,000}$

*($1,200 $\times$ 20 years)

$125,000 $\times$ 19.2% = $24,000 (amount excluded)

Thus, Gwyneth must include 80.8% ($101,000) in her income in the year of the distribution. This is obviously correct because she invested $24,000 and the remaining $101,000 is income on her original investment.

Example—Periodic payments: George, age 45, purchases a premium annuity contract from Friendly Insurance Company for a single premium of $50,000. Under the terms of the policy, he is entitled to a monthly payment of $500 beginning on January 1 of the year he turns 65 and continuing until his death. Assume he has a life expectancy of 20 years when he turns 65.

The purchase of the policy is not a taxable event to George. During the 20 years that Friendly invests George's $50,000, George is not taxed on the investment income.

In the year George turns 65, he receives monthly payments of $500 for a total annual payment of $6,000. To determine how much of this payment is income, George applies the exclusion ratio to the annual payment:

$$\text{Payment} \quad \times \quad \frac{\text{Investment in the Contract}}{\text{Total Expected Return}} \quad = \quad \text{Excluded percentage}$$

$$\$6,000 \quad \times \quad \frac{\$50,000^*}{\$120,000}$$

$$^*(6,000 \quad \times \quad 20 \text{ years})$$

$$\$6,000 \quad \times \quad 41.67\% \quad = \quad \$2,500 \text{ (amount excluded)}$$

Thus, of the $6,000 payment George receives each year, 58.33% ($3,500) must be included in gross income, and the remaining 41.67% ($2,500) is a tax-free return of capital.

c. Special rules and exceptions: For contracts based on the taxpayer's life, if the taxpayer's actual life span matches his or her actuarially determined life expectancy, at death he or she will have fully recovered invested capital and will have reported the proper amount of income. If the taxpayer dies earlier or lives longer than expected, the exclusion ratio will overstate or understate, respectively, the income from the contract. Two special rules address this problem.

i. Exclusion limitation: The total exclusion allowed under section 72(b) is limited to the taxpayer's investment in the contract (i.e., his or her basis). IRC §72(b)(2).

Example: Consider George from the previous example. Notice that if George lives exactly 20 years from the annuity payment starting date, he will have recovered his full $50,000 investment in the contract (20 years of excluding $2,500, from each annual payment, with some rounding error). Assume, however, that George lives past age 85. If the exclusion ratio were applied to payments in those years, George would be excluding more than his initial investment of $50,000, and thus his income would be understated. Therefore, once George fully recovers his invested capital, all additional payments are income to him.

ii. Deduction for unrecovered investment: If the taxpayer dies before recovering his or her investment in the contract, and the payments end by reason of the taxpayer's death, the taxpayer's executor will be able to claim a deduction on the taxpayer's last income tax return for the unrecovered portion of the investment. IRC §72(b)(3).

Example: Consider George from the previous two examples, but assume that George dies on January 1 exactly five years after the annuity starting date, rather than surviving to his life expectancy of 85. Having properly applied the exclusion ratio during the first five years of the annuity payments, George will have recovered, tax-free, only $12,500 of his $50,000 investment in the contract. On his income tax return for the year of his death, George's executor will claim a deduction equal to the unrecovered amount of $37,500 ($50,000 − $12,500).

iii. Withdrawals before annuitization: As a practical matter, annuities are often marketed and used by taxpayers as a tax-deferred investment. Amounts invested in an annuity compound tax-free until they are withdrawn. The approach described above in connection with the exclusion ratio applies after the annuity has been "annuitized," i.e., a payout time has been selected. In many cases, annuities are not annuitized. Instead, the owner withdraws a lump sum from the annuity from time to time. In that case, the entire amount is considered income, unless it exceeds the amount by which the cash value of the annuity exceeds the taxpayer's investment in the contract. Any amount by which the withdrawal exceeds that figure is excluded. IRC §72(e)(2)(B), (e)(3).

Example: Lisa purchased an annuity for $14,000. It has a cash value of $30,000. Lisa withdraws $8,000 from her annuity, which is not part of the periodic payments to which she would be entitled. All of the $8,000 is included in her gross income because it is less than the amount by which the cash value of the annuity ($30,000) exceeds her investment in the contract ($14,000). If, however, Lisa had withdrawn $22,000, $6,000 would be considered a tax-free return of her investment.

d. **Related material**

    i. **Life insurance contracts:** For a discussion of the exclusion of life insurance proceeds payable upon death, see Chapter 4(II)(A).

    ii. **Installment sales:** For similar timing rules in installment sales, see discussion at Chapter 11(V).

e. **Summary:** See Statute Summary—§72.

Statute Summary—§72

Parsing Step	**§72**
General rule	For annuity payments: Amount excluded from gross income = Payment $\times \dfrac{\text{Investment in Contract}}{\text{Total Expected Return}}$
Definitional issues	Annuity contract Investment in contract Total expected return
Special rules and exceptions	If insured dies early—deduction If insured lives beyond return of investment—all payments included
Related material	§101 (insurance) §453 (similar method for installment sales)
Summary	Only a portion of each annuity payment is included in gross income; apply exclusion ratio.

VI. ALIMONY AND SEPARATE MAINTENANCE PAYMENTS

Section 61(a)(8) includes alimony and separate maintenance payments in the recipient's gross income. Section 71(a) confirms this inclusion.

A. Identifying alimony income

Look for a divorce situation in which one former spouse pays support (other than ***child support***) to the other. Make sure that the payment meets the strict federal definition of alimony; its state law label is irrelevant.

B. Statutory analysis—§71

1. **General rule:** The recipient of alimony or separate maintenance must include it in his or her gross income. IRC §71(a).

2. **Definitional issues:** The Code defines alimony, and state law labels are irrelevant. In order to be "alimony," the payment must satisfy the following six requirements.

   a. **Cash:** The payment must be in cash, rather than any other type of property (*not* stocks, bonds, or diamond rings). IRC §71(b)(1).

   b. **Receipt under decree:** The payment must be received by (or on behalf of) the spouse pursuant to a divorce decree or separation instrument. IRC §71(b)(1)(A), (2)(A). The payor spouse may pay the recipient spouse directly, or the payor spouse may pay a third party on behalf of the former spouse. IRC §71(b)(1)(A); Temp. Reg. §1.71-1T(b), A-6. Common examples of payments on behalf of a former spouse include a mortgage payment, the payment of health insurance premiums, or the payment of the recipient spouse's tuition. Rev. Rul. 62-106, 1962-2 C.B. 21.

      Example: Toya and Frank are getting a divorce. Under the divorce decree, Toya is awarded the marital home and Frank is ordered to make the mortgage payment each month to Friendly Bank. Assuming the other requirements for alimony are met, this payment would qualify as a payment received "on behalf of" a spouse pursuant to a divorce decree and would constitute alimony.

   c. **Private ordering:** The divorce decree or separation instrument must not designate the payment as nondeductible/nonincludable. IRC §71(b)(1)(B). The parties have the power to determine which spouse will pay tax on the alimony income. Generally, the payor will wish to claim the deduction, because he or she will be in a higher tax bracket than the recipient. If, however, the payor's tax bracket is lower, the parties should specify in the decree that the payment is nondeductible to the payor and nonincludable to the recipient.

      Example: Karl and Linda are getting a divorce. Karl's tax bracket is 33%, and Linda's is 15%. Under the terms of the divorce decree, Karl is to pay Linda $1,000 per month for four years. Compare the effects of treating this $12,000 annual payment as deductible and nondeductible alimony:

      Treatment as deductible to payor and includable to recipient. Treating the payments as deductible to Karl and includable in Linda's gross income means that Linda will be taxed on the $12,000 annual payment. Linda includes the $12,000 in gross income and pays a tax of $1,800 on it ($12,000 × 15%). Thus, the total tax on the $12,000 is $1,800. Because Karl deducts the alimony payment, he is not taxed on the income that generated the payment.

      Treatment as nondeductible to payor and nonincludable to recipient. Treating the payments as nondeductible to Karl and excluded from Linda's gross income means that Karl will earn the funds to make the payment, and will be taxed on them without an offsetting deduction.

Linda will not be taxed on this amount. Karl will pay a tax of $3,960 ($12,000 × 33%) on this amount.

Comparison. Rational taxpayers would clearly opt to treat this payment as deductible to Karl (assuming it otherwise meets the requirements for alimony) because this treatment saves the parties $2,160 in tax, equal to the difference between the tax Karl would pay and the tax Linda would pay on the annual alimony payment.

d. No "live-in" divorces! The payor and recipient must not be members of the same household at the time of the payment. IRC §71(b)(1)(C).

e. No payment if recipient dies: There must be no liability to make payments beyond the death of the recipient spouse. IRC §71(b)(1)(D). Think of alimony as "support" for the recipient spouse. If that spouse dies, he or she no longer needs support. Thus, alimony must end at the death of the recipient spouse. If the parties intended an amount to be a deferred payment of property (rather than a support payment) they would make arrangements for payment to be made to the estate of the recipient spouse in the event of his or her death. This would not qualify as alimony. In addition, there must be no "substitute payments" to replace payments to the recipient spouse after the latter's death. Treas. Reg. §1.71-1T(b); see *Okerson v. Commissioner*, 123 T.C. 4 (2004). If the decree or order is silent on this issue, look to state law to determine whether the payment would be required if the recipient spouse dies.

Example: Karl and Linda are getting a divorce. Karl owns a business in which Linda has an interest. The parties agree that Karl will receive the business and will pay Linda $50,000 each year for seven years. In the event of Linda's death prior to the last payment, Karl will pay the amounts into a trust established by Linda's will for the benefit of her children from a prior marriage. The $50,000 annual payment does not qualify as alimony, because it survives the death of the recipient spouse. Instead, it is clearly a property settlement.

f. Not child support: Child support is excluded from gross income of the custodial spouse. IRC §71(c)(1); see discussion at Chapter 4(XII). Thus, in order to qualify as alimony, the payment must not be, in substance, a payment for the support of a child of the payor. IRC §71(c)(2); Reg. §1.71-1T(c), A-16. The decree will generally fix an amount for support of child; this amount is not alimony. If the payment is tied to a contingency of a child (such as attaining majority), it will be considered child support, even if it is called and otherwise qualifies as alimony. IRC §71(c)(2)(A).

Example: In Toya and Frank's divorce, Frank's obligation to pay the mortgage ends on the earlier of April 13, 2003 (which just happens to be the date on which his youngest daughter turns 18) or the date of the last-to-die of his children. This would be a payment tied to a contingency of a minor child and would be considered child support rather than alimony.

3. Special rules and exceptions—"Front-end loaded" alimony: This special rule ferrets out "disguised" property settlements, mitigating the benefit of the deduction to the payor and the detriment of the inclusion to the recipient.

a. General approach: If alimony payments are front-end loaded, the statute requires an adjustment in the third taxable year. In that year, the payor includes the "excess alimony payments" in gross income, and the recipient is entitled to a deduction in computing AGI in the same amount. IRC §71(f)(1)(A), (B).

b. **Third year:** The adjustment is made in the taxable year beginning in the third post-separation year. The first post-separation year is the first calendar year in which alimony is paid, and the next two years are the second and third post-separation years. IRC §71(f)(6).

   Example: Rita and Jeff are getting a divorce. Jeff is to pay Rita $100,000 on January 1, Year One; $50,000 on January 1, Year Two; and $25,000 on January 1, Year Three. Assume that the payments qualify as alimony. Because they are front-end loaded, in the third post-separation year Jeff will include in gross income, and Rita will deduct, the excess alimony amount.

c. **Identifying excess alimony payments:** A front-end loaded payment is exactly what it sounds like—a payment that is relatively large in the early year or years compared with later payments. The statute only requires analysis of the three years following the divorce; payments in the fourth year and thereafter are irrelevant. The statute provides a very complicated definition of excess alimony payments, the calculation of which is outlined in the steps of Figure 3B—Front-End Loaded Alimony Payments. In general, however, there must be a variance among the payments due during the three-year period of more than $15,000 in order for the front-end loading rules to apply.

Figure 3B
Front-End Loaded Alimony Payments

(Y = year)

Step 1   Calculate the excess alimony payment for the *second* post-separation year.
Alimony Y2 − (Alimony Y3 + $15,000) = excess payment for second post-separation year.

Step 2   Calculate the excess alimony payment for the *first* post-separation year.

$$\text{Alimony Y1} - \left[\left\{ \frac{(\text{Alimony Y2} - \text{Excess Payment Y2}) + \text{Alimony Y3}}{2} \right\} + \$15,000 \right] = \text{excess payment for the } \textit{first} \text{ post-separation year}$$

Step 3   Calculate the excess alimony payment: sum of steps 1 and 2.

Step 4   Determine the consequences to payor and recipient in third post-separation year:
Deduction to recipient in the amount of excess alimony payment.
Inclusion to payor in the amount of excess alimony payment.

Example: Molly and Neil are getting a divorce, and they agree that Molly will pay Neil $60,000 in the first year after their divorce, $30,000 in the second year, and $10,000 in the third year. Assume that the payments otherwise qualify as alimony, and Molly deducts these payments and Neil includes them in his gross income in the years the payments are made. These payments likely are front-end loaded because they vary by more than $15,000 during the three years. The calculation of the ***excess alimony payment*** confirms that indeed the amounts are front-end loaded. Neil will receive a deduction for the third year equal to the excess alimony payment, and Molly will include that amount in gross income in the third year. The excess alimony payment is calculated as follows:

- *Step 1:* Calculate the excess alimony payment for the *second* post-separation year.

   $$\$30,000 - (\$10,000 + \$15,000) = \$5,000$$

- *Step 2:* Calculate the excess alimony payment for the *first* post-separation year.

$$\$60,000 - \left[\left\{\frac{(\$30,000 - 5,000) + 10,000)}{2}\right\} + \$15,000\right]$$

$$\$60,000 - \$32,500 = \$27,500$$

- *Step 3:* Calculate the excess alimony payment: The sum of steps 1 and 2.

$$\$27,500 + 5,000 = \$32,500$$

- *Step 4:* Determine the consequences to payor and recipient in third post-separation year:

$32,500 deduction from AGI to Neil
$32,500 inclusion in gross income for Molly

4. Related material

a. Deduction: For a discussion of the deduction for alimony available to the payor, see Chapter 6(II).

b. Child support: For a discussion of the exclusion of child support from the gross income of the recipient, see Chapter 4(XI).

c. Property transfers: For a discussion of the treatment of property transfers in divorce, see Chapter 10(V).

5. Summary: See Statute Summary—§71.

Statute Summary—§71

Parsing Step	§71
General rule	Gross income includes alimony payments received. Gross income does not include child support payments received.
Definitional issues	Alimony: cash, divorce decree, not designated nondeductible, not same household, no liability to pay beyond recipient's death, not child support
Special rules and exceptions	Front-end loaded alimony: varies by more than $15,000 during first three years.
Related material	§215: deductible to payor §1041: property transfers in divorce
Summary	Gross income includes alimony but not child support received.

VII. INCOME FROM DISCHARGE OF INDEBTEDNESS

Section 61(a)(12) includes income from discharge of indebtedness in a debtor's gross income.

A. Recognizing the basic transaction

The making of a loan is not taxable event for either the debtor or the creditor. See discussion at Chapter 1(V)(C). But when the creditor forgives or discharges all or part of the loan, the debtor has income in the amount of the forgiveness or discharge. To identify a potential discharge of debt situation, look for a creditor accepting (or being required to accept), in satisfaction of a debt, less than the creditor originally contracted to receive.

B. Loan creation—A tax non-event

A loan is defined as the "unconditional and legally enforceable obligation for the repayment of money." *Autenreith v. Commissioner,* 115 F.2d 856 (3d Cir. 1940). As a general rule, the loan is treated as an independent transaction from the debtor's use of the loan proceeds. Each transaction generates its own tax consequences; the consequences of the use of proceeds do not affect the loan transaction. *Vukosovich, Inc. v. Commissioner,* 790 F.2d 1409 (9th Cir. 1986).

Example: Rita borrows $100,000 from Friendly Bank and uses it to purchase Blackacre, a parcel of raw land. She intends to hold Blackacre until the loan is due, then sell it, repay the loan, and keep the profit. Unfortunately, toxic wastes are found on Blackacre, and its value falls to $20,000. When the loan is due, Rita sells Blackacre and repays the bank in full, using $80,000 of her own savings. The tax consequences of the loan are independent of the real estate transaction. The loan and its repayment generate no tax consequences. On the real estate transaction, Rita has an $80,000 loss.

1. **Debtor's tax consequences—No income:** The debtor has no income as a result of taking out a loan. Even though the debtor is apparently "richer" by the amount of the loan proceeds, the debtor has an offsetting obligation to repay the proceeds to the creditor.

2. **Creditor's tax consequences—No income:** The creditor has no income as a result of making the loan. The creditor's receipt of the debtor's note or other evidence of indebtedness is offset by the outflow of the loan proceeds.

C. Loan repayment—A tax non-event

When the debtor repays the principal amount of the loan in full, this is not a tax event for either the debtor or the creditor. Neither party is better or worse off because of the repayment. Interest payments are treated separately. They constitute income to the creditor and may generate a deduction to the debtor. See discussion at Chapters 6(VII) and 7(IV)(A).

Example: Megan borrows $25,000 from Friendly Bank. Megan has no income as a result of the loan, and Friendly Bank has no deduction. When, five years later, Megan repays the debt in full, neither she nor Friendly Bank have any tax consequences as a result of the repayment. If Megan has paid interest during the five-year period, that transaction is accounted for separately, with Friendly Bank including the interest in its gross income and Megan potentially taking a deduction for the interest paid.

D. The "forgiveness" transaction—A tax event

In a forgiveness or discharge situation, the creditor accepts, in satisfaction of all or part of the debt, something less than the creditor originally agreed to receive in payment of the debt.

1. **Debtor's tax consequences—Income:** The debtor has income from a *discharge of indebtedness* event, in the amount of the discharge. There are two different rationales for this income.

a. **"Freeing of assets" theory—*United States v. Kirby Lumber Co.*, 284 U.S. 1 (1931):** *Kirby Lumber* suggests that the discharge event "frees up" assets of the debtor, generating income to the debtor. This rationale is problematic, because not every discharge frees assets of the debtor.

b. **Economic benefit rationale:** The more comprehensive explanation is that the debtor has income because discharge removes all or part of the offsetting obligation to repay, which prevented the debtor from having income at the creation of the loan. Thus the debtor has enjoyment of the loan proceeds (in whole or in part) without the offsetting obligation to repay, resulting in a net economic benefit to the debtor.

2. **Creditor's tax consequences—Possible deduction:** In a discharge situation, the creditor receives less than it had originally loaned and may be entitled to a deduction. See discussion at Chapter 7(IV).

E. Definition of discharge

Discharge is "forgiveness of, or release from, an obligation to repay." *United States v. Centennial Savings Bank FSB*, 499 U.S. 573, 580 (1991). Discharge occurs when the taxpayer is relieved of a liability through the creditor (voluntarily or not) canceling or forgiving the obligation to repay, thus taking less than the creditor originally bargained for in satisfaction of the debt.

1. **Common examples of discharge:** The following three examples of discharge illustrate the creditor accepting less than it originally bargained for in satisfaction of the loan.

a. **"Taking what you can get":** When the creditor perceives that the debtor is unlikely to pay the full amount, the creditor may opt to take what it can get rather than waiting (perhaps in competition with other creditors) for the full amount. The difference between the face amount and the amount paid is the discharge or forgiveness.

Example: Sam borrows $150,000 from Friendly Bank, promising to repay it in two years. Two years later, Sam is teetering on the brink of financial ruin, and offers Friendly Bank $35,000 in satisfaction of the debt. Friendly Bank accepts this offer. Sam has $115,000 of *discharge of indebtedness income* because the creditor has accepted $35,000 in satisfaction of a $150,000 debt.

b. **Retirement of bonds:** When a corporation issues bonds at a stated interest rate, it may seek to retire those bonds when interest rates fall in order to save interest costs. If the creditors (bondholders) take less than the face amount of the bonds in repayment of the bonds, the corporation will have discharge of indebtedness income in the amount of the difference.

c. **Antideficiency statutes:** Many states have antideficiency statutes, which protect mortgagors from personal liability when foreclosure proceeds are insufficient to satisfy the mortgage on a personal residence. If an antideficiency statute operates to cancel the underlying obligation, this cancellation should constitute a discharge. If it only protects a debtor from further action by the creditor, the result is uncertain but probably does not constitute discharge because the debt remains outstanding.

d. **Repayment obligation:** A cancellation of a debt that is conditional upon the obligation to repay sometime in the future upon the occurrence of certain events will be a discharge at the time of cancellation of the original debt. By contrast, a cancellation that takes effect sometime in the future is not a discharge until that future time. See, e.g., *Jelle v. Commissioner*, 116 T.C. 63 (2001).

2. **Common examples of nondischarge:** It is tempting to apply the discharge of debt concept to situations in which the basic requirements for discharge of indebtedness income are not present.

  a. **No real debt, No discharge—*Zarin v. Commissioner*, 916 F.2d 110 (3d Cir. 1990):** Zarin was a compulsive gambler. Resorts, a casino, extended credit to him in the form of allowing him to purchase gambling chips in the amount of $3,000,000 in violation of state law. Zarin and Resorts agreed that Zarin would pay $500,000 in satisfaction of the debt, and he did so.

    i. **Issue:** Did Zarin have $2,500,000 of discharge of debt income (the difference between the loan and the payment)?

    ii. **Result and rationale:** Zarin had no discharge of debt income because there was no debt. Section 108 requires either that (1) the taxpayer be liable for the debt, or (2) the taxpayer hold property subject to the debt. The debt was unenforceable under state law, so Zarin was not liable for the debt. Moreover, because the chips were not property under state law, they were not property securing a debt.

  b. **Contested liability doctrine:** If a taxpayer in good faith disputes the amount of the debt, a subsequent settlement of the debt is treated as the amount of the debt for tax purposes. *N. Sobel, Inc. v. Commissioner*, 40 B.T.A. 1263 (1939).

    Example: Paula borrowed $10,000 from Quark, and agreed to repay him in two years. In connection with this loan, both parties agreed to undertake certain tasks. When payment became due, Paula argued in good faith that Quark did not fulfill his obligations under the loan. They settled their dispute by agreeing that Paula would pay $8,500 to Quark in full payment of the debt. For tax purposes, the original loan is treated as $8,500, not $10,000.

  c. **Repayment by another:** Repayment of a taxpayer's debt by the taxpayer or another person does not create discharge of indebtedness income because the creditor has not taken less than the originally agreed-upon amount. Instead, the repayment by another may be another type of income to the taxpayer, includable in his or her gross income.

    Example: Stephanie owes $40,000 in student loans. The Firm offers her a job at a nice salary, and one of the fringe benefits is that if she works for a year, The Firm will pay off her student loans in full. If The Firm pays her loans, Stephanie will not have discharge of indebtedness income because her creditors have received payment in full. Instead, she will have compensation income in the amount the Firm paid the creditors. The distinction can make a big difference in the application of §108. See Chapter 4(VI).

  d. **No discharge event—No income:** If the creditor receives what it bargained for, there is no discharge. In the usual situation, it will be easy to see whether the creditor received the principal amount in repayment. But in some unusual situations, the creditor may receive exactly what it bargained for, even if that is not what it originally loaned the debtor.

    Example: Theresa borrowed $50,000 from Uly. Under the terms of the loan, Theresa was to repay Uly in two years in the amount of the lesser of $50,000 or her gross income for the year. Two years later, Theresa's gross income was $45,000 and she repaid Uly that amount.

Theresa has no discharge of indebtedness because Uly received in repayment exactly what he bargained for—no more and no less.

Example: Kay borrowed $1,000,000 from Friendly Bank to purchase Pinkacre, an office building. The loan was nonrecourse, which means that Friendly Bank's only recourse in the event of nonpayment was to foreclose against Pinkacre itself, and Friendly Bank could not proceed against Kay's personal assets. The real estate market crashed, Pinkacre's value dropped to $500,000, and Kay stopped making payments on the debt. The bank took Pinkacre in full satisfaction of the debt. Kay has no discharge of indebtedness because the Bank got exactly what it bargained for—Pinkacre. See discussion of *Commissioner v. Tufts* at Chapter 9(IV)(C).

F. Income excluded

A taxpayer with discharge of indebtedness income may be able to exclude the income from gross income because of a specific exclusion available under the Code.

1. **Gift:** If the discharge is intended as a gift, there is no income to the taxpayer. See discussion at Chapter 4(III).

   Example: Gerry borrows $1,500 from his father in order to study for the bar exam. When Gerry passes the exam, his father is so pleased that he forgives the debt. It is likely that the forgiveness is intended as a gift, and Gerry may therefore exclude from his gross income the $1,500 that would otherwise be included as discharge of indebtedness income.

2. **Section 108:** Section 108 provides an exclusion from gross income for certain types of discharge of indebtedness income. See discussion at Chapter 4(VI).

VIII. SEVERAL ITEMS NOT USUALLY CRUCIAL IN THE BASIC TAX COURSE

Section 61 includes in gross income several items for which only a passing understanding is usually required from the basic federal income tax student.

A. Income from pensions

Section 61(a)(11) includes income from a pension in the recipient's gross income.

1. **Vocabulary:** The pension area is stuffed with specialized terms and phrases. Here are the most important:

   a. **Deferred compensation plan:** A deferred compensation plan is a compensation arrangement in which an employer agrees to pay an employee in the future for services provided currently.

   b. **Qualified plan:** A qualified plan is a deferred compensation plan that meets the requirements of §401(a) of the Code, which sets forth stringent requirements for qualification based on contribution, participation, and eligibility.

   c. **Nonqualified plan:** A nonqualified plan is a deferred compensation plan that does not meet the requirements of §401(a) of the Code.

2. Qualified retirement plans

a. Contribution benefits:
The qualified plan offers three benefits for the participants in the transaction.

   i. Deduction to employer: The employer takes a deduction equal to the amount of contributions to the plan at the time the contribution is made.

   ii. Deferral for employee: The employee does not include the employer's contributions in gross income until the plan makes a distribution to the employee.

   iii. Tax-free buildup: The trust that holds the plan assets is not taxed on the investment income from those assets.

b. Taxation to employee upon withdrawal:
When the qualified plan makes a distribution to the employee, the employee includes the payment in gross income under the principles of §72. If the employee has made no after-tax contributions, the entire distribution will be included in his or her gross income. If the employee has made after-tax contributions, the portion excluded from gross income will be determined under §72, with the after-tax contributions being the employee's "investment in the contract." See discussion at Chapter 3(V)(F).

3. Nonqualified deferred compensation plans:
Nonqualified deferred compensation plans are not subject to the stringent regulations of qualified plans. Nor do they offer the same tax benefits. Under a nonqualified plan, the employer may not claim a deduction for contributions until the employee includes the amount in income. The employee includes the compensation in gross income when either he has the right to it or has received a substantial economic benefit as a result of it. For an example of a nonqualified plan, see *Minor v. United States*, discussed at Chapter 11(III). Employers often use nonqualified deferred compensation to offer additional compensation above the limits established by qualified plans.

4. Time value of money:
Deferred compensation plans are inspired by the principles of the time value of money. Taxpayers seek to defer income to future years to reduce current tax and invest the tax savings. See generally Chapter 15.

B. Partner's distributive share of partnership income

If an individual or an entity is a partner in a partnership (or a member of a limited liability company treated as a partnership), the partner or member reports his or her share of partnership gross income (and deductions) on his or her own tax return—as if the partner or member earned it directly. Similarly, losses pass through to the partners or members and may be deductible within, certain constraints. The entity itself is not subject to tax. IRC §701.

Example: XYZ Partnership has three partners, X, Y, and Z, all of whom are one-third partners. In the current year, XYZ Partnership earns $90,000 in gross rents, and has $30,000 of deductions associated with that rental income. Each partner will report his or her one-third share of the net income ($60,000) from the partnership on his or her own income tax return. Thus, X, Y, and Z will each report $20,000 of income from the partnership.

C. Income in respect of a decedent

If a decedent earns income prior to death, but that income is not properly included in any of his or her tax returns (including the final return), to whom should it be taxed? Section 691 offers explicit rules for allocating income among the various parties who may claim the income.

1. **Estate:** Income in respect of a decedent is taxed to the estate of the decedent, if the estate received the right to the income from the decedent (e.g., by will). IRC §691(a)(1)(A).

2. **Other—If right to income:** If the estate does not have the right to the income, the income is taxed to the person who ultimately has the right to receive it, such as the heir. IRC §691(a)(1)(B), (C).

3. **Character:** The character of the income is the same in the hands of the entity or person who is taxed as it would have been in the hands of the decedent, had he or she lived. IRC §691(a)(3).

4. **Deductions and credits:** The entity or person taxed on the income is also entitled to all deductions and credits associated with the income. IRC §691(c)(1)(A); Reg. §1.691(c)-1(a).

   Example: Victoria owned rental property, for which she typically received $10,000 each year as rent. In the year of her death, Victoria was in a disagreement with her tenant regarding payment of the rent, and the tenant had not paid the rent. The tenant paid the rent plus interest two years after Victoria's death to her executor, who included it as an asset of her estate pursuant to her will. Under the rules described above, Victoria's estate will include the income in its gross income.

D. Income from an interest in an estate or trust

A trust or estate may be a taxable entity, depending on its attributes. A beneficiary of an estate or trust may be taxed on his or her distributive shares of income from an estate or trust.

1. **Grantor trusts:** A grantor trust is a trust described in §§673-677 of the Code. In these trusts, the grantor typically retains significant control over the corpus of the trust. The income of a grantor trust is taxed to the grantor of the trust, and the trust is essentially ignored for tax purposes. IRC §671.

2. *Mallinckrodt* **or "demand" trusts:** A demand trust is one in which a person other than the grantor or trustee has the power to direct the disposition of the trust income or corpus. See *Mallinckrodt v. Nunan,* 146 F.2d 1 (8th Cir.), *cert. denied,* 324 U.S. 871 (1945). The income of such a trust is taxed to the person with the power or control over the trust. IRC §678.

3. **Other trusts:** Trusts in which the income is not taxed to another person will calculate their gross income, deductions, and credits and will pay tax on their taxable income. Distributions from such trusts typically generate a deduction to the trust, and must be included in the gross income of the distributee. IRC §§651, 652.

   Example: Walter is the beneficiary of a trust established by his grandfather for his support. Under the terms of the trust, the trustee must distribute at least $5,000 per year to Walter, and more if he needs it, in the sole discretion of the trustee. In this scenario, the trust will be a taxable entity but will take a deduction for the amount required to be paid, or actually paid, to Walter. Walter will include the amount distributed to him in his gross income.

IX. SOME ODDS AND ENDS—PRIZES, HELPFUL PAYMENTS, AND EMBEZZLEMENTS

Code sections other than §61 and certain judicial doctrines also specifically include items in gross income.

A. Prizes and awards—§74

1. **General rule:** Gross income includes amounts received as prizes and awards. IRC §74(a).

2. **Definitional issue—Prizes and awards:** Prizes and awards include amounts received in contests, door prizes, radio and television promotions and games, and employee prizes. Reg. §1.74-1(a)(1).

3. **Special rules and exceptions**

   a. **Exclusion:** The amount of the prize or award will be excluded from the gross income of the recipient if three conditions are met.

      i. **Passive recipient:** The recipient must have been selected without any action on his or her part to enter the contest, IRC §74(b)(1);

      ii. **No services:** The recipient must not be required to render substantial future services as a condition of receiving the prize, IRC §74(b)(2); and

      iii. **Charity:** The recipient must immediately transfer the prize to charity. IRC §74(b)(3).

      Example: Amy's mother secretly entered her name in a drawing for a trip to Hawaii. Much to Amy's surprise, she won the trip, and there were no conditions that she endorse any product or perform any services for any person. Amy enjoyed her trip to Hawaii immensely. However, she must include in her gross income the fair market value of the trip, as §74 includes this amount in gross income, and she fails the third of the three requirements for exclusion—she didn't immediately transfer the trip to charity.

   b. **Employee achievement awards:** Employee achievement awards are excludable up to the amount of the cost of the award to the employer that is deductible. IRC §74(c)(1).

4. **Related material**

   a. **Scholarships:** For a discussion of potential exclusions for scholarships, see Chapter 4(VII).

   b. **Fringe benefits:** For a discussion of potential exclusions for fringe benefits, see Chapter 4(IX).

B. Helpful payments

1. **Moving expenses:** Section 82 includes in gross income any payment or reimbursement for moving expenses relating to employment or self-employment. For a discussion of the deduction for moving expenses, see Chapter 6(IV).

2. **Unemployment compensation:** Section 85 includes unemployment compensation in gross income.

3. **Social Security benefits:** A portion of Social Security benefits (including disability benefits) is included in gross income if a taxpayer's modified adjusted gross income (MAGI) exceeds a certain "base amount." The amount included is either 50% or 85% of the Social Security benefits received. The computation of this inclusion is extremely complex and the entire concept of including Social Security benefits in gross income has been criticized as creating a double income tax—once on the income earned (from which Social Security taxes were withheld) and then again upon benefits being received.

4. **Disability payments:** If a taxpayer receives disability payments attributable to premiums paid by his or her employer, and excluded from gross income, the payments will be included in the taxpayer's gross income. See discussion at Chapter 4(IX)(D).

C. Embezzled funds

An embezzler must include the proceeds of embezzlement in his or her gross income, unless he or she repays the money in the same taxable year as the embezzlement. *James v. United States*, 366 U.S. 213 (1961). However, the person who makes unauthorized withdrawals from a corporation need not include the amounts in gross income when he or she can show four items.

1. **Intent to repay:** The taxpayer intends to repay the amount.

2. **Ability:** The taxpayer reasonably expects to be able to repay the amounts.

3. **Authority:** The taxpayer in good faith believes withdrawals will be approved by corporation.

4. **Security:** The taxpayer makes immediate assignment of assets to secure repayment. *Gilbert v. Commissioner*, 552 F.2d 478 (2d Cir. 1977).

X. WHERE ARE WE GOING?

This chapter has discussed the list of items of income specifically included in a taxpayer's gross income under §61 and related statutes. However, not all items that would otherwise qualify as "income" are actually included in gross income. Various Code sections exclude some items from gross income, and Chapter 4 explores these items in detail.

Quiz Yourself on
SPECIFIC INCLUSIONS IN GROSS INCOME

17. Diane forms a sole proprietorship engaged in the business of cleaning up crime scenes. She had $45,000 of income and $20,000 of deductible expenses this year. How will she be taxed on this result? _____

18. Shaq, a noted basketball player, realizes that he needs a plan for his retirement. He pays a $500,000 one-time premium for an annuity, which will pay him $100,000 per year beginning on January 1 of the year he turns 65 and continuing for the rest of his life. At age 65, he is deemed to have a life expectancy of 20 years. When Shaq receives his first year's payment of $100,000, must he include it in his gross income? _____

19. Assume Shaq, from the previous question, died on January 30 of the year he turned 67. The terms of the annuity provide that if the annuitant dies before the end of his life expectancy, the remaining amounts that would have been received, based on his life expectancy at the time the annuity began paying, will be paid to his estate or beneficiary. What are the tax consequences if $1,700,000 is paid to the estate or beneficiary in that year? _____

20. Hilary and Bill are getting a divorce. The divorce decree says that Hilary must pay Bill $100,000 within 30 days of the entering of the decree, $50,000 on the first anniversary of the divorce, and

$25,000 on the second anniversary of the divorce, unless Bill dies during this period. They have no children. Are these payments includable in Bill's income? _____

21. Bruce and Demi are getting a divorce. The divorce decree requires Bruce to transfer to Demi 1,000 shares of XYZ Corp. stock before the first anniversary of the divorce. Is the value of the XYZ stock includable in Demi's income as alimony? _____

22. Aging film star Greta's mansion in BelAire is virtually falling apart. She leaves for a trip around the world, and rents it to starving actor Harrison for $200 per month and Harrison's agreement to spend 20 hours a week fixing it up. What are the tax consequences to Greta of this arrangement? _____

23. Marc borrowed $1,000,000 from the bank. He absconded to Europe, and never paid it back. The bank determined that the amount was uncollectible, and wrote it off. The time period for collection expired. What are the tax consequences of this transaction to Marc? _____

24. Assume the same facts as in the previous question, except that Marc's mother is mortified at her son's behavior, and repays the loan. What are the tax consequences of the loan and its repayment to Marc? _____

25. Frieda owed $40,000 on her credit card. She contacted a credit counseling agency, which convinced the credit card company to accept a reduced amount of $25,000. What are the tax consequences of this transaction to Frieda? What if Frieda had been disputing some of the charges with the credit card company at the time of the discharge? _____

26. Rookie pitcher Greg listened to his parents' advice and purchased disability income insurance. It's a good thing he did, too, because in his very first major league game, he injured his shoulder and was released from the team. He receives payments from the insurance company. What is the tax treatment of these payments to Greg? _____

27. Carlotta was a bookkeeper for ABC Corp who felt she was underpaid. She took matters into her own hands, and embezzled $50,000 from the company before being discovered. She promises to repay the money as soon as possible. What are the tax consequences to Carlotta? _____

28. Of the following, which is *not* includable in an individual taxpayer's gross income?

    (a)   Dividends received from corporations

    (b)   Royalties received from the licensing of patents

    (c)   Rent received from tenants in a commercial building

    (d)   Interest on a loan made to a relative

    (e)   A periodic payment received under an annuity contract

---

Answers

17. IRC §61(a) provides that gross income includes all income from whatever source derived, including income from business. Diane has net income of $25,000 from her business ($45,000 − $20,000) which she must include in her gross income.

18. Shaq must include some of each payment in his gross income. IRC §72 determines the amount to be included. Shaq must multiply each payment by the "exclusion ratio," the numerator of which is his investment in the contract and the denominator of which is the expected total return of the contract. The resulting number will be the nontaxable amount (his capital recovery) and the rest he must include in gross income. The expected total return is calculated by taking Shaq's life expectancy and multiplying it by the annual payment on the contract ($100,000 × 20 years = $2,000,000). In Shaq's case, the exclusion ratio produces the following result for each payment:

$$\$100,000 \times \frac{\$500,000}{\$2,000,000} = \$25,000 \text{ (nontaxable)}$$

The remaining $75,000 of each payment is included in Shaq's gross income.

19. If Shaq died on January 30 of the year he turned 67, let us assume that he received a payment of $100,000 in each of the years in which he turned 65, 66, and 67. Thus, he had recovered $75,000 of his total $500,000 investment in the contract ($25,000 per year × 3 years). Let us assume also that the remaining amount of $1,700,000 (17 years × $100,000) is paid in the year of death to his estate or beneficiary. In that case, the estate or beneficiary is able to claim an exclusion of $425,000 of the total amount received, which is Shaq's unrecovered investment in the contract at the time of his death. Thus, of the $1,700,000 received, only $1,425,000 is includable in the estate or beneficiary's gross income.

20. These payments appear to meet the requirements of alimony: They are made in cash and received under a divorce decree; the parties aren't living together; the payments stop if the recipient dies; and they are not disguised child support. Thus, they should be included in the gross income of the recipient, Bill. However, because the payments vary by more than $15,000 per year, they will be considered "front-end loaded" and be subject to the special rules of §71(f). This section requires that the amount of so-called "excess alimony payments" be included in the income of the payor in the third post-separation year. To determine the excess alimony payment, a rather complex calculation must be completed, as follows:

Step 1: Compute the excess payment for the second post-separation year. (IRC §71(f)(4))

Alimony paid Y2 − (Alimony Y3 + $15,000)

$50,000 − ($25,000 + $15,000)

$50,000 − $40,000 = $10,000 + excess payment for second post-separation year.

Step 2: Compute the excess payment for the first post-separation year. (IRC §71(f)(3))

$$\$100,000 - \left\{ \left[\frac{(\$50,000 - 10,000) + \$25,000)}{2} \right] + \$15,000 \right\}$$

$100,000 − ($32,500 + $15,000)

$100,000 − $47,500

$52,500 = excess payment for first post-separation year.

Step 3: Add the two excess payments together:

$10,000   second year

+   52,500   first year

$62,500   total

The total amount is the amount that will be included in Hilary's gross income and deducted from Bill's gross income in computing AGI in the third post-separation year.

21. In this case, the payment does not fall within the definition of alimony, as the amounts are not paid in cash, but instead in stock. The value of the stock will not be included in the gross income of Demi, but instead will be treated as a transfer of property incident to a divorce. See Chapter 10.

22. Greta has income. But how much? Focus on the exchange: Greta is providing a home for Harrison, and thus what she receives in exchange is properly considered rental income. This would be $200 per month plus the fair market value of the services Harrison would perform. The best way to measure this is to determine the fair rental value of the house, or, if that is not possible because there simply isn't a rental market for dilapidated mansions, by determining the hourly rate for carpenters.

23. Marc did not have income in the year of the loan because of the offsetting obligation to repay it. However, in the year it is forgiven (written off by the bank) he has discharge of indebtedness income in the amount of $1,000,000 (plus any accrued interest left unpaid).

24. Marc does not have discharge of indebtedness income if his mother repays the loan. This is a benefit to him, which would be income, but would probably be considered a gift which would be excluded from his gross income.

25. Frieda has $15,000 of discharge of indebtedness income which is included in her gross income unless she can fall within any of the exceptions of IRC §108(b), such as the insolvency exception. If Frieda had a legitimate basis for disputing any of these charges, however, the discharge attributable to those amounts would not constitute discharge of indebtedness income under the disputed liability doctrine. Allocation of the discharge among disputed and accepted items is a question of fact.

26. If Greg paid for the disability insurance premiums with after-tax dollars, the amounts received would be excluded from his gross income. If the employer paid for the premiums, with before-tax dollars, the amounts received under the policy are includable in Greg's gross income.

27. Carlotta must include the $50,000 in her gross income. Her promise to repay the funds does not affect this result. In fact, it is very unlikely that any embezzler will be able to meet the four requirements of *James v. United States, supra.*

28. (e). Not all of the annuity payment will be included in gross income. When the taxpayer receives a periodic payment from an annuity, a portion of it is a tax-free return of capital (the amount paid for the annuity) and the rest is included in gross income. All of the other items (dividends, rents, royalties, and interest) are included in gross income.

Exam Tips *on*
SPECIFIC INCLUSIONS IN GROSS INCOME

☛ Make sure you read the call of the question. Tax questions typically involve transactions between two or more people. Which person's tax consequences are you asked to address in the question?

☛ Recall the principles of Chapter 2—some receipts aren't income, by definition. If these rules apply, you do not reach the specific statutory inclusions in gross income. These excluded amounts are:

   ☞ Loan proceeds

   ☞ Capital recovery

   ☞ Imputed income

☛ Questions about income inclusion involve the taxpayer's receipt of something of value. Identify the transfer of things of value, such as:

   ☞ Cash or check

   ☞ Services

   ☞ Property

☛ Compensation for services is a common transaction.

   ☞ *Watch for:* Someone providing services to another in exchange for something of value.

   ☞ *Analyze:* Focus on the service provider—what he or she did, and what is received. The fair market value of services or property received is gross income to the service provider.

☛ Most, if not all, kinds of investment income is includable in gross income. Dividends, rents, royalties, and interest are all includable.

☛ In a divorce setting, one party may pay alimony to the other. Be sure to analyze the transaction from both sides, and include any alimony in the gross income of the recipient.

   ☞ *Watch for:* The payment of cash from one party to the other in a divorce setting

   ☞ *Analyze:* Are the requirements for alimony met? Are the payments front-end loaded?

☛ Understand loan transactions. A loan isn't a taxable event, nor is the repayment of the loan principal. When a taxpayer takes out a loan, what he or she does with the proceeds (buys a house, for example) is an independent transaction, even if the seller of the property is the one making the loan (seller financing).

☛ Be able to identify discharge of debt situations.

   ☞ *Watch for:* A loan from one party to the other, and then the lender doing something that reduces or eliminates the debt, or a discharge by operation of law.

☞ *Analyze:* How much discharge income does the taxpayer have? In later chapters we will consider possible exclusions.

☛ Some payments are partially includable in gross income, such as:

☞ Some annuity payments

☞ Some Social Security payments

☛ Most receipts are includable in gross income. If in doubt, include an item in gross income, because gross income is a broad category that involves much more than what is specifically enumerated.

CHAPTER 4

SPECIFIC EXCLUSIONS FROM GROSS INCOME

ChapterScope

This chapter addresses specific statutory exclusions from gross income: items that constitute "income" within the meaning of IRC §61 but are not included in a taxpayer's gross income because of a specific Code exception.

- **Interpret narrowly:** Exclusions are matters of legislative grace, and in order for an item to be excluded from gross income, it must meet the specific requirements of a statute allowing an exclusion.

- **Life insurance payments:** Section 101 excludes from the gross income of the beneficiary the proceeds of life insurance policies payable upon the death of the insured.

- **Gifts and bequests:** Section 102 excludes gifts and bequests (regardless of amount) from the gross income of the recipient of the gift.

- **Damages for personal injury:** Section 104 excludes from gross income amounts received as compensation for personal physical injuries or sickness. Related Code sections address medical insurance premiums, and insurance payments.

- **Discharge of indebtedness income:** Section 108 excludes discharge of indebtedness income from gross income, if certain conditions are met. A taxpayer excluding amounts under §108 may be required to reduce certain tax benefits that he or she would otherwise enjoy.

- **Employment-related exclusions:** A variety of Code sections provide exclusions for certain types of compensation income, including certain meals and lodging (§119) life (§79) and health (§106) insurance premiums, and fringe benefits (§132).

- **Gain on sale of principal residence:** All or a portion of the gain on the sale of a taxpayer's principal residence is excludable from gross income if certain conditions are met.

- **Other exclusions:** Various other Code provisions allow a taxpayer to exclude certain items that would otherwise qualify as income from his or her gross income. These include interest on certain savings bonds, qualified scholarships, and child support.

I. WHERE ARE WE?

We are still trying to define gross income, the starting place for the computation of a taxpayer's tax. Although gross income is a very broad concept, Congress has determined that certain kinds of income are not appropriate for inclusion in gross income—if (and only if) certain conditions are met.

A. Exclusions—Definition

An exclusion from gross income means that the item is simply not included in gross income, so that it never enters the computation of taxable income.

1. **Compare deduction:** An exclusion means that the item is not included in gross income at all. A deduction is a subtraction from income in computing taxable income. Both a deduction and exclusion will reduce tax liability by the amount of the item multiplied by the taxpayer's tax rate. However, the process by which each works is very different. Excluding an item from gross income means that the item will forever escape the income tax. A deduction, by contrast, will offset (or shelter) an equal amount of income so that the amount of income will not be taxed.

    Example: Angela's taxable income is $40,000. Assume that she is in a flat 28% tax bracket, so that she pays $11,200. If she discovers that she is entitled to exclude $5,000 of income so that her taxable income is $35,000, she will pay only $9,800 of tax, saving $1,400. The tax savings of $1,400 is equal to the exclusion ($5,000) multiplied by Angela's tax rate (28%).

    Example: Dave's taxable income is $50,000, and assume that he is in a flat 31% tax bracket. He pays $15,500 in tax. If he discovers an additional $5,000 deduction to which he is entitled, he will reduce his taxable income to $45,000 and will pay a tax of $13,950. Dave's tax savings of $1,550 is equal to the deduction ($5,000) multiplied by his tax rate (31%).

2. **Compare credit:** A tax credit (discussed generally in Chapter 13) is a dollar-for-dollar reduction in the amount of tax due. An exclusion is very different from a credit in operation. An exclusion prevents an item from being included in the computation of taxable income, allowing it to escape taxation entirely. By contrast, a credit simply reduces the amount of tax imposed on taxable income. The value of an exclusion is the amount of the exclusion multiplied by the taxpayer's tax rate, and its value is higher for taxpayers in high brackets than for taxpayers at lower brackets. A tax credit, by contrast, results in a tax savings equal to the amount of credit and thus has the same value for high- and low-bracket taxpayers.

3. **Compare deferral:** An exclusion exempts an amount from gross income altogether, so that it is never subject to tax. Other statutes defer the inclusion of amounts in gross income, so they are included in a taxpayer's gross income in a later year. For example, amounts contributed by an employer to a ***qualified retirement plan*** are not included in gross income of an employee when the contribution is made, but *are* included in the employee's gross income when he or she receives distributions from the plan. See discussion at Chapter 3(VIII)(A) and discussion of *deferral* generally at Chapter 15.

B. Construction

While the courts construe §61 broadly, they construe exclusions narrowly. See *United States v. Centennial Savings Bank FSB*, 499 U.S. 573, 583-584 (1991).

II. DEATH BENEFITS—§101

Section 101(a) excludes from gross income amounts received under a ***life insurance*** policy by reason of the death of the insured.

A. Life Insurance—A primer

1. **Why buy insurance?** Taxpayers purchase *life insurance* for two reasons. First, taxpayers purchase life insurance to replace their earnings in the event of their untimely death. This is the "insurance element" of life insurance. But taxpayers also purchase life insurance as a savings device. Like an annuity, the increase in value of the life insurance contract over time is not included in the gross income of the insured.

   a. **Compare other investments:** The savings element in a life insurance policy is treated very differently from other types of savings vehicles such as bank accounts or mutual funds in which income is taxed currently to the owner.

   b. **Policy:** This represents a political preference for life insurance products, as opposed to other types of investment, perhaps in recognition of the importance of life insurance in the estates of many taxpayers and the strength of the insurance industry lobby.

2. **Vocabulary:** Life insurance has its own vocabulary.

   a. **Life insurance contract:** A life insurance contract is the promise by an insurance company to pay a fixed amount to the beneficiary named by the insured upon the death of the insured.

   b. **Insured:** The person whose life is insured under the contract, whose death triggers payment under the policy.

   c. **Premium:** The amount(s) paid for the life insurance contract. The premium may be paid in a single sum or, more often, over time. The insured may be the owner, or the owner may be some other person, e.g., a corporation, or a spouse, or a trust.

   d. **Term insurance:** A term insurance policy provides insurance for a stated period, usually a year. The premium pays for insurance for that period, and when that period is over, the insured has no further benefit under the contract. Term insurance becomes more expensive as the insured ages.

   e. **Permanent insurance (also known as "whole life" insurance):** A permanent insurance policy provides insurance for the entire period of the taxpayer's life, as opposed to the stated period of a term policy. Premiums may change over the period or be level throughout. If the premium is level throughout the life of the policy, the insured will be paying more in the early years of the policy than the cost of term insurance, and in later years, the annual premium will be less than required to fund term insurance. Investment of the sum in excess of the amount needed for insurance will earn interest and will pay for the more expensive insurance later in the policy.

   f. **Cash value (or "surrender value"):** In the early years of a permanent policy, the premium is greater than the amount needed to fund term insurance. The difference (reserve) earns interest that is not taxed to the taxpayer. The reserve is used in the later years of the policy to fund a portion of the premium in the years when the premium for term insurance would be high. During the years in which the reserve exists, the taxpayer may borrow this value from the insurance company.

B. Statutory analysis—§101

1. **General rule:** Section 101(a) excludes from gross income amounts received under a life insurance contract, whether in a lump sum or in a series of payments, by reason of the death of the insured.

Example: Bill purchases a single premium life insurance policy under which the insurance company promises to pay Bill's designated beneficiary $100,000 upon his death. Bill dies, and his son Corey receives the $100,000 proceeds. Corey need not include this amount in gross income, as it is excluded by §101(a).

2. **Definitional issues—Life insurance contract:** In general, a life insurance contract is the promise of an insurer to pay, upon the death of the insured, an amount to a designated beneficiary in exchange for the payment of premiums. To qualify for the advantageous tax treatment of IRC §101(a), a life insurance contract also must meet specific statutory tests. These are designed to exclude contracts that function primarily as investments rather than insurance.

3. **Special rules and exceptions**

   a. **Accelerated death benefits:** Although §101(a) requires amounts to be paid by reason of the death of the insured, a special rule allows certain accelerated death benefits to fall within the general rule's exclusion. Amounts received under a life insurance contract on the life of an individual who is terminally or chronically ill will be treated as paid by reason of the death of the insured. IRC §101(g)(1).

   b. **Transfer for valuable consideration:** The exclusion does not apply to those who receive proceeds by purchasing a life insurance contract for valuable consideration. In that situation, the exclusion is limited to the buyer's purchase price in the contract; amounts in excess of the purchase price must be included in gross income. IRC §101(a)(2). However, the transfer of a policy to allow payment for long-term care for a terminally or chronically ill insured is not considered assignment of the death benefit. IRC §101(g)(2)(A).

   Example: Diane purchased a single premium life insurance policy that will pay her designated beneficiary $100,000 upon her death. While in financial difficulty, Diane assigns her rights in the insurance contract to a creditor to whom she owes an $80,000 debt, in satisfaction of that debt. The creditor names himself beneficiary. When Diane dies, the creditor receives $100,000 in insurance proceeds. Only $80,000 of this amount is excluded from gross income under §101(a). The $20,000 balance is included in the creditor's gross income.

   c. **Employee death benefits:** Any amount paid by an employer for death benefits is generally included in the gross income of the recipient, unless the death benefit is part of a life insurance arrangement. However, §101(i) provides an exclusion from gross income for any amount paid by an employer with respect to the death of an employee who is a specified terrorist victim as defined by IRC §692(d)(4) or an astronaut killed in the line of duty.

4. **Related material**

   a. **Annuities:** For the treatment of amounts payable by reasons other than the death of the insured, see discussion of annuities at Chapter 3(V)(F).

   b. **Premiums:** For a discussion of exclusions for an employer's payment of life insurance premiums, see this Chapter, Section (IX)(D).

5. **Summary:** See Statute Summary—§101.

Statute Summary—§101

Parsing Step	§101
General rule	Amounts received under life insurance contract by reason of death or terminal or chronic illness of insured are excluded
Definitional issues	Life insurance contract Terminal or chronic illness
Special rules and exceptions	Acceleration of death benefits for chronic/terminal illness Does not apply to transfer for valuable consideration
Related material	Annuities
Summary	Exclude life insurance proceeds from gross income.

III. GIFTS—§102

Section 102 excludes from the gross income of the recipient the value of cash or property received by gift or inheritance, regardless of amount.

A. Policy

Possible justifications for exclusion of gifts include the following:

1. **Support/gifts:** Since most transfers by gift occur within families, it may be difficult to distinguish between gifts and support, and including gifts in gross income would require such a distinction.

2. **Estate and gift tax:** A frequently invoked rationale is that the income tax should not apply to gifts because a separate federal taxing scheme applies to estates and gifts. However, this justification is unfounded because the two tax systems operate independently, and have different rationales for their imposition.

B. Statutory analysis

1. **General rule:** Gross income does not include the value of property acquired by gift, bequest, devise, or inheritance. The value of the gift is excluded from the recipient's gross income, regardless of the amount of the gift.

   a. **Compare gift tax:** The donor may be required to pay gift tax on the transfer, and for federal gift tax purposes only, the amount of the gift is relevant.

   b. **Annual exclusion:** For gift tax purposes, the donor may make a nontaxable gift of up to a specified dollar amount per person per year. This amount is $11,000 in the year 2005 and is scheduled to increase over the coming years with cost-of-living adjustments. IRC §2503(b). Amounts in excess of the specified dollar amounts are applied to the donor's lifetime exclusion for estate and gift tax.

   Example: Frieda gives stock in ABC Corporation worth $50,000 to her son Greg as a holiday gift. Greg does not include the $50,000 in his gross income. (Frieda does not take a deduction for the gift, either.) Frieda may have to pay gift tax on the gift because it exceeds the amount she can give free of gift tax each year, but the amount of the gift does not affect its excludability for federal income tax purposes.

2. Definitional issue—Gift

a. **Intent of transferor:** A gift is a transfer made by a transferor motivated by "detached and disinterested generosity." *Commissioner v. Duberstein,* 363 U.S. 278 (1960).

b. **Compare compensation:** Transfers made to compensate another for services rendered or in expectation of services to be rendered are not gifts and thus are included in the recipient's gross income. *Olk v. United States,* 536 F.2d 876 (9th Cir.), *cert. denied,* 429 U.S. 920 (1976).

c. **Intrafamilial transfers:** In the gift tax context, intrafamilial transfers are rebuttably presumed to be gifts. In the income tax field, by contrast, courts do not apply a presumption but instead examine the facts and circumstances surrounding a transfer. Intrafamily transfers usually qualify as gifts because they are motivated by affection and generosity. If, however, the transferor has an expectation of receiving economic value, the transfer will not be considered a gift even if it is made from one family member to another.

Example: Frieda sends her son Greg a check for $1,000. This would probably be a gift, but if there was evidence that the $1,000 was payment for services provided by Greg, the exclusion for gifts would not apply.

3. Special rules and exceptions

a. **Income:** The exclusion does not apply to income from the property received by gift. IRC §102(b)(1).

Example: Connie's mother gives her Blueacre, a rental property. While Connie may exclude the value of Blueacre from her gross income, she nevertheless must include in her gross income the rental income from Blueacre during her ownership of the property.

b. **Employee gifts:** The exclusion of §102 does not extend to any transfer made by an employer to an employee. IRC §102(c)(1). These amounts are considered compensation, not gifts.

Example: Hilda works for XYZ Corp. as a bookkeeper. Each year at the holiday season, XYZ Corp. gives each employee a 25-pound turkey and a $50 gift certificate to a local department store. These items are not excluded from Hilda's gross income under §102 (although the turkey might be excluded under §132, relating to *fringe benefits*).

4. Related material

a. **Basis:** The recipient of a gift generally takes the same basis as the donor had in the property increased by a portion of any gift tax paid. See discussion at Chapter 9(III)(B).

b. **Fringe benefits:** For transfers by employers to employees that may be excluded, see discussion of fringe benefits this chapter, Section (IX)(C).

c. **Assignment of income:** The transfer of income from property, as compared to the transfer of the property itself, may constitute a prohibited assignment of income. See discussion at Chapter 14(III).

5. Summary: See Statute Summary—§102.

Statute Summary—§101

Parsing Step	§102
General rule	Gross income does not include amounts received by gift.
Definitional issues	Gift = transfer made with detached and disinterested generosity.
Special rules and exceptions	Does not apply to income from gift Does not apply to transfers by employers to employees
Related material	Basis of property received—§1015
Summary	Exclude gifts from recipient's gross income.

IV. INTEREST ON STATE AND LOCAL BONDS—§103

Section 61(a)(4) includes interest in gross income, but §103 allows a taxpayer to exclude from gross income interest on any state or local bond. Certain exceptions to this rule, relating to bonds issued for "private activities" and "arbitrage bonds," are generally beyond the scope of a basic tax class. See IRC §§141, 148.

V. COMPENSATION FOR PERSONAL INJURY OR SICKNESS—§104

Section 104(a) excludes from gross income amounts received as compensation for personal physical injury or sickness.

A. Policy

The following rationales have been offered for this exclusion.

1. **No income:** Because the taxpayer is merely placed back in his or her original (undamaged) state, the taxpayer has no benefit and therefore no income from the transaction.

2. **Measurement:** Even if the taxpayer has some amount of income, it is too difficult to measure.

3. **Adding insult to injury:** It would be cruel to an injured taxpayer to include these amounts in income.

B. Statutory Analysis—§104

1. **General rule:** A taxpayer may exclude from his or her gross income amounts received for personal physical injury or physical sickness in the form of workers' compensation payments, damages received, certain amounts received from health insurance, and certain other personal injury payments not commonly encountered. IRC §104(a).

   a. **Damages—Method of payment:** The exclusion applies whether the damages are received in a lump sum or as periodic payments. IRC §104(a).

   b. **Damages—Suit or settlement:** Damages may be received either as a judgment or in settlement of a claim. IRC §104(a)(2). If in settlement, the proper allocation of damages among claims and types of damages is a question of fact.

Example: Ian slips and falls on his neighbor's icy steps, and injures his back. His neighbor's insurance company pays Ian $5,000 in settlement of his claim for injury to his back. Ian may exclude the $5,000 from his gross income.

c. Disability insurance payments: Amounts received through disability insurance payments are excluded from gross income if the premiums were either paid by the insured person or were paid by the employer but included in the gross income of the insured employee.

Example: Dolores was an employee of Company X. Company X provided disability insurance to each of its employees on a group disability plan and was responsible for paying the premium on the group policy every month. However, each employee was deemed to have received as salary the amount paid for his or her premium each month, and this was included in the employee's taxable salary. If Dolores becomes disabled, the amounts received from the disability policy should be excluded from her gross income.

2. Definitional issue—"Personal" injury or sickness: Only amounts received on account of "personal physical injuries" or "physical sickness" are excludable. IRC §104(a)(2). Business injuries, and personal nonphysical injuries, such as discrimination, are not excluded.

3. Special rules and exceptions

a. Previously deducted medical expenses: The exclusion does not apply to amounts the taxpayer has deducted as medical expenses under §213. IRC §104(a). See Chapter 6(XV).

Example: Ian slipped on his neighbor's steps and hurt his back. In the year of his injury he incurs medical expenses, and he properly claims $2,000 as a deduction on that year's tax return. In the next year he receives $5,000 in payments from his neighbor's insurance company. Assuming the entire amount is compensation for personal physical injuries, only $3,000 is excludable from gross income, as the other $2,000 is attributable to previously deducted medical expenses and must be included in gross income. See also Chapter 11(II)(F).

b. Punitive damages: Punitive damages are included in gross income even if received on account of personal physical injury or physical sickness. IRC §104(a)(2). The one exception to this rule is that punitive damages received for wrongful death under a state statute that does not allow for compensatory damages will be excludable. IRC §104(c).

c. Interest on judgments: The exclusion from gross income does not extend to prejudgment interest. *Brabson v. United States,* 73 F.3d 1040 (10th Cir. 1996); *Kovacs v. Commissioner,* 100 T.C. 124 (1993), *aff'd without published opinion,* 25 F.3d 1048 (6th Cir. 1994). Delay damages are treated like prejudgment interest as nonexcludable. *Francisco v. United States,* —F.3d—, 2001–2 USTC ¶50,662 (3d Cir. 2001).

4. Related material

a. Fringe benefits: For the treatment of employer-provided health insurance plans, see discussion in this chapter, Section IX(D).

b. Deduction: For the deduction of medical expenses, see discussion at Chapter 6(XV).

c. Attorneys' fees: For the treatment of attorneys fees and the alternative minimum tax, see discussion at Chapter 13(III).

5. Summary: See Statute Summary—§104.

Statute Summary—§101

Parsing Step	§104
General rule	Gross income does not include amounts received as compensation for personal physical injury or sickness
Definitional issues	Personal physical injury or sickness
Special rules and exceptions	Does not usually exclude punitive damages Does not exclude interest
Related material	Health insurance—§§105, 106 Deduction for medical expenses—§213
Summary	Exclude compensation for personal physical injury or sickness from gross income.

VI. DISCHARGE OF INDEBTEDNESS INCOME—§108

Section 108 allows an exclusion for discharge of indebtedness income in certain specified circumstances. The exclusion is generally conditioned upon the taxpayer giving up certain tax benefits.

Example: Jolene owes Friendly Bank $100,000. Jolene's assets are $50,000, and her debts total $150,000. In recognition of her dire financial straits, the bank agrees to take $20,000 in satisfaction of the debt. Jolene has discharge of indebtedness income of $80,000, but if she meets one of the conditions of exclusion of §108, she will be able to exclude all or part of the $80,000 of discharge of indebtedness income from her gross income.

A. Policy

Various rationales justify this exclusion.

1. Blood from a turnip? It is difficult to collect tax from insolvent taxpayers, so deferral of the tax is the best option.

2. Subsidy: For certain types of taxpayers, such as farmers, exclusion or deferral represents a political decision to offer a tax benefit.

B. Statutory analysis—§108

1. General rule: A taxpayer may exclude from his or her gross income discharge of indebtedness income if any of the following four conditions apply.

a. Bankruptcy: The discharge occurs in a title 11 (bankruptcy) case. IRC §108(a)(1)(A).

b. Insolvency: The discharge occurs while the taxpayer is insolvent (in this case, the exclusion is limited to the amount of the insolvency). IRC §108(a)(1)(B).

c. Farm debt: The indebtedness discharged is "qualified farm indebtedness." IRC §108(a)(1)(C).

d. Real property debt: The taxpayer is not a C corporation, and the indebtedness discharged is qualified real property business indebtedness. IRC §108(a)(1)(D).

2. Definitional issues

a. Indebtedness: In order for §108 to apply, there must be an "indebtedness," which is defined as a debt for which the taxpayer is liable or a debt secured by the taxpayer's property. IRC §108(d)(1). See discussion of *Zarin v. Commissioner,* at Chapter 3(VII)(E), above.

b. Discharge of indebtedness income: In order for §108 to potentially apply, there must be discharge of indebtedness income. See discussion at Chapter 3(VII).

c. Insolvency: A taxpayer is insolvent if, and to the extent that, his or her liabilities exceed the fair market value of his or her assets. IRC §108(d)(3). Insolvency is determined immediately prior to discharge. IRC §108(d)(3).

d. Qualified farm indebtedness: This definition is quite technical, but generally means commercial or governmental debt incurred by a person whose primary business is farming. IRC §108(g)(2).

e. Qualified real property business indebtedness: This definition is also technical, but generally means debt incurred in connection with real property used in a trade or business and secured by that property. IRC §108(g)(3)(C).

3. Special rules and exceptions

a. Paying the piper: The exclusion from gross income is not "free." For each dollar of exclusion claimed by the taxpayer because of any exclusion other than real property business indebtedness, the taxpayer must also give up a dollar of tax attributes or reduce the basis of his or her depreciable property. IRC §108(b)(1).

    i. Effect: Although §108 will protect the taxpayer from the inclusion of discharge of debt income in gross income, the taxpayer will experience a burden in the future—by having fewer tax benefits to enjoy or having property with a lower basis for depreciation and a larger gain on sale.

    ii. Tax attributes: Tax attributes are reduced in this order:

- net operating losses and carryovers,

- certain tax credits,

- capital loss carryovers,

- passive activity loss carryovers, and

- foreign tax credit carryovers.

    IRC §108(b)(1), (2)

    iii. Basis reduction: The taxpayer may elect in certain cases to apply the exclusion amount to reduce the basis of his or her depreciable property, up to the basis of that property. IRC §108(b)(5)(A).

    Example: Kathy has discharge of indebtedness income of $80,000, which is discharged in a Title 11 case. She also has a net operating loss carryforward of $50,000 and depreciable property with a basis of $40,000. Kathy elects to apply the exclusion amount of $80,000 first to the basis of her depreciable property ($40,000), and thereafter she reduces her net operating loss carryover from $50,000 to $10,000.

b. **Purchase price adjustment:** A discharge of debt will be treated as a purchase price adjustment (which has no tax consequences) if the seller of property reduces the debt incurred to acquire the property, and the reduction does not occur in a Title 11 case or when the purchaser is insolvent. IRC §108(e)(5).

Example: Larry purchases a backhoe for $35,000, giving the seller $5,000 in cash and a promissory note for $30,000. Later, the purchaser agrees to reduce the amount of the note to $20,000, in light of difficulties Larry is having with the equipment. Assuming Larry is not insolvent and is not participating in a bankruptcy proceeding, the $10,000 reduction (which would otherwise be discharge of indebtedness income) will be treated as a reduction of the original purchase price from $35,000 to $25,000. Therefore, Larry will not have any discharge of indebtedness income.

c. **Student loans:** Gross income does not include any discharge of a student loan if the discharge occurs because the student works for a certain period of time for a nonprofit or governmental organization. IRC §108(f)(1).

Example: Mary incurs $40,000 in student loans to attend medical school. The lender offers a program under which, if she works for five years in a publicly funded poverty medical program, $25,000 of her loans will be discharged. Mary works for five years in a qualifying program and receives the benefit of the $25,000 discharge. This discharge of indebtedness income is not included in Mary's gross income.

d. **Stock for debt:** If a corporation issues stock to a creditor in satisfaction of the debt it owes to that creditor, the corporation is considered to have satisfied the debt with an amount of money equal to the fair market value of the stock. This may lead to discharge of indebtedness income, which in turn may (or may not) be excluded under §108. IRC §108(e)(8).

Example: Nota Bene Corporation owes $50,000 to a creditor. Being in dire financial straits, Nota Bene issues common stock worth $25,000 to the creditor, who accepts it in full satisfaction of the debt. This transaction results in $25,000 of discharge of indebtedness income to Nota Bene Corporation (the difference between the face amount of the debt and the fair market value of the stock accepted in satisfaction of the debt). If Nota Bene is insolvent or qualifies under any of the other exclusions, it may exclude all or a portion of the income from gross income. Otherwise, Nota Bene must include the income in its gross income.

e. **Qualified farm indebtedness:** The total qualified farm indebtedness that can be excluded is limited to an amount roughly equal to three times the taxpayer's tax attributes plus the bases of assets. IRC §108(g)(3)(A), (B).

4. Related material

a. **Discharge:** In order for §108 to apply, there must be discharge of indebtedness income. See discussion at Chapter 3(VII)(E).

b. **Sales of encumbered properties:** A sale of encumbered property may generate discharge of indebtedness income potentially subject to §108. See discussion at Chapter 9(IV).

c. **Net operating losses (*NOLs*):** For a discussion of *NOLs,* a tax attribute, see Chapter 11(II)(D).

5. Summary: See Statute Summary—§108.

Statute Summary—§108

Parsing Step	§108
General rule	Gross income does not include discharge of indebtedness income incurred in certain situations
Definitional issues	Discharge of indebtedness income Insolvency Title 11 case Qualified farm indebtedness Qualified real property indebtedness
Special rules and exceptions	Reduction of tax attributes—paying the piper Student loans Stock for debt
Related material	Sales of encumbered properties—§1001 Net operating losses—§172
Summary	Exclude discharge of indebtedness income from gross income only if requirements met.

VII. QUALIFIED SCHOLARSHIPS—§117

Section 117 excludes from gross income the amount received as a "qualified scholarship" by students at qualifying educational institutions.

Example: Tina, a high school senior, receives an offer of a scholarship from a local university that will cover her tuition, books, and room and board for the first three years of her college education. She wishes to know the tax consequences of the offer as part of her decisionmaking process. As discussed below, §117 will exclude from Tina's gross income the portion of the scholarship attributable to tuition and books, but will not exclude the portion attributable to room and board.

A. Policy

The legislative history for §117 reveals no rationale for its exclusion of scholarships from gross income. It may reflect a desire to treat similarly those who receive gifts from family to attend school and those who receive "institutional gifts" such as scholarships. While such a rationale is consistent with §117's restrictions as to services, it does not explain the denial of an exclusion for amounts attributable to room and board.

B. Statutory analysis—§117

1. General rule: A candidate for a degree at a qualifying educational organization may exclude from his or her gross income the amount he or she receives as a qualified scholarship or as a qualified tuition reduction. IRC §117(a).

2. Definitional issues

    a. Qualifying educational organization: The educational organization must qualify as one under §170(b)(1)(A)(ii), i.e., one that normally maintains a regular faculty and curriculum and normally has a regularly enrolled body of students in attendance where its educational activities are regularly carried on. IRC §117(a).

   b. **Qualified scholarship:** The scholarship or fellowship must be for tuition, books, fees, and supplies (not room and board). IRC §117(b).

   c. **Qualified tuition reduction:** This is a reduction in tuition provided to an employee (or family member of the employee) of the qualifying educational organization, if the benefit does not discriminate in favor of highly compensated employees and is used for under-graduate study. IRC §117(d).

   Example: Victor is the son of Wanda, a professor at a small college in the Pacific North-west. Under the terms of Wanda's employment agreement, her children may attend the college for four years of undergraduate study by paying only 20% of the tuition charged students whose parents are not employees. Victor opts to do so and thus enjoys a tuition reduction of 80%. Assuming this benefit does not discriminate in favor of highly compensated employees of the college, it is excluded from the gross income of both Victor and Wanda because it is a qualified tuition reduction.

3. **Special rules and exceptions—Not for services:** The exclusion does not apply to any portion of the amount received that represents payment for services—teaching, research, or other services—required as a condition of the grant. IRC §117(c). Athletic scholarships, in which (1) students are expected but not required to participate in athletic events, (2) no particular activity is required in lieu of participation, and (3) no cancellation will occur if the student cannot participate, do not carry with them a service requirement that would result in the amounts received being taxable. Rev. Rul. 77-263, 1977-2 C.B. 47.

   Example: Zach is offered a fellowship at a nationally acclaimed graduate program. As a condition of the fellowship he must teach a section of Economics 101. The portion of the fellowship attributable to teaching activities will not be excluded from Zach's gross income.

4. **Related material**

   a. **Prizes and awards:** For a discussion of prizes and awards, see Chapter 3(IX)(A).

   b. **Educational incentives:** For descriptions of other educational incentives, see discussion in this chapter, Section X.

5. **Summary:** Section 117 excludes from gross income amounts received as scholarships for tuition, books and fees, and supplies. It does not apply to room and board or for any amount attributable to services.

VIII. EXCLUSION FOR GAIN ON SALE OF PRINCIPAL RESIDENCE—§121

A taxpayer may exclude from gross income up to $250,000 ($500,000 for joint filers) of the gain on the sale of his or her principal residence.

Example: Amanda, who files as a single person, owns Whiteacre, her principal residence, in which she has a basis of $40,000. Amanda sold Whiteacre for $190,000. Amanda's gain on the sale is $150,000 ($190,000 – $40,000). She may exclude all of this gain from gross income pursuant to §121.

A. Policy

Section 121 is one of several Code provisions favoring investment in real estate, particularly homes. As a practical matter, §121 will result in most sales of taxpayers' principal residences being tax free.

B. Statutory analysis—§121

1. General rule: A taxpayer may exclude up to $250,000 ($500,000 for joint filers) of gain on the sale of a principal residence if the following two conditions are met.

   a. Principal residence: The taxpayer must have owned and used the property as a principal residence for a period aggregating two or more years during the five-year period ending on the date of the sale or exchange. IRC §121(a).

   b. Once every two years only: A taxpayer can only take advantage of this provision once every two years.

2. Definitional issues

   a. Principal residence: The principal residence is the residence where the taxpayer actually lives, based on all the facts and circumstances of the situation. A principal residence can be a nontraditional dwelling, such as a houseboat, a recreational vehicle, or stock in a tenant cooperative. Reg. §1.121-1(b).

   b. Ownership and use: Ownership and use may be satisfied with nonconcurrent periods of time. For the use requirement, occupancy of the dwelling is required, but short absences, such as for vacation or illness, do not interrupt a period of use. Reg. §1.121-1(c). If a dwelling is used partly for business and partly for residence, only the part attributable to the residence use is eligible for the §121 exclusion. Reg. §1.121-1(e). Gain attributable to depreciation taken on the property after May 6, 1997 is not eligible for the exclusion. Reg. §1.121-1(d).

   Example: Calvin lived in a townhouse that he rented from 1997 through 2001. On January 1, 2002, he purchased this townhouse. On February 1, 2002, Calvin moved into his daughter's home. On March 1, 2004, while still living in his daughter's home, Calvin sold his townhouse. The §121 exclusion will apply to gain from the sale because Calvin owned the townhouse for at least two years out of the five years preceding the sale (from January 1, 2002 until March 1, 2004) and he used the townhouse as his principal residence for at least two years during the five-year period preceding the sale (from February 1, 2000 until February 1, 2002).

3. Special rules and exceptions

   a. Reduced exclusion: When a taxpayer cannot satisfy the use/ownership test, or needs to use the exclusion more than once in a two-year period, special rules may apply to allow a reduced exclusion. The taxpayer's need to sell must arise from a change in place of employment, health, or other unforeseen circumstances acceptable to the IRS. If so, the reduced exclusion is applied by multiplying the maximum gain ($250,000, or $500,000 for joint filers) by a fraction, the numerator of which is the amount of time the taxpayer did own or use the property, or the period of time since the last §121 sale, and the denominator is two years, expressed as days or months. This produces the reduced exclusion to which the taxpayer is entitled.

Example: Lois, who files as a single taxpayer, purchases a house that she uses as her principal residence. Twelve months after the purchase, Lois sells the house due to a change in place of her employment. Lois has not excluded gain under §121 on a prior sale or exchange of property within the last two years. Lois is eligible to exclude up to $125,000 of the gain from the sale of her house (12/24 × $250,000).

Example: Peter, who files as a single taxpayer, sold a home on January 1, 2004, excluding $150,000 of gain under §121. He purchased another home, and because of serious health problems, was forced to sell it on July 1, 2005. He has $60,000 of gain on that sale. May he exclude this $60,000 gain from his gross income? To determine the maximum exclusion, multiply $250,000 by a fraction, the numerator of which is the total number of days he owned the home (365 + 181) and the denominator of which is 730 (2 × 365). $250,000 × 546/730 = $186,986. Peter will be able to exclude his $60,000 gain.

b. Husbands and wives: A husband and wife will meet the requirements of §121 if *both* or *either* of them meet the ownership and use tests, and *neither* of them has used the §121 exclusion in the past two years. If they don't meet this test, their maximum exclusion will be the sum of their individual exclusions. Reg. §1.121-2(b)(1), (2).

Example: During 2004, newly married taxpayers Harlan and Wynona each sell a residence that each had separately owned and used as a principal residence before their marriage. Each spouse meets the ownership and use tests for his or her respective residence. Neither spouse meets the use requirement for the other spouse's residence. Harlan and Wynona file a joint return for the year of the sales. The gain realized from the sale of Harlan's residence is $200,000. The gain realized from the sale of Wynona's residence is $300,000. Because the ownership and use requirements are met for each residence by each respective spouse, Harlan and Wynona are eligible to exclude up to $250,000 of gain from the sale of each of their residences. However, Wynona may not use Harlan's unused exclusion to exclude gain in excess of her exclusion amount. Therefore, Harlan and Wynona must recognize $50,000 of the gain realized on the sale of Wynona's residence.

c. Disabled taxpayer: An elderly or disabled taxpayer who moves to an assisted care facility may have difficulty meeting the use requirement. A special rule allows such taxpayers to claim the exclusion if the taxpayer uses the property as a residence for at least one year out of the five ending on the date of sale. IRC §121(d)(7).

d. Estates and trusts: An estate or heir of a decedent, or at trust that was a revocable living trust just before the decedent's death, may take advantage of the exclusion of §121. These taxpayers may add the period of time the property was owned/used by the decedent to their ownership/use period to meet the statutory requirements. IRC §121(d)(9).

4. Related material

a. Involuntary conversions: For a discussion of the deferral of gain on the involuntary conversion of property, see Chapter 10(IV).

b. Office in home: When a taxpayer claims depreciation for use of part of his or her home as an office, IRC §121 will not protect the gain attributable to that deduction from recognition.

5. **Summary:** A taxpayer may exclude up to $250,000 ($500,000 for joint filers) of gain on the sale of a principal residence. IRC §121.

IX. EMPLOYMENT-RELATED EXCLUSIONS

In the employment relationship, the employer typically pays the employee wages or salary, but also may provide certain other benefits such as health insurance, child care, or the ubiquitous holiday turkey. Some of these benefits may be excludable from gross income; others are not. In order to exclude an amount from gross income, the employee must be able to point to a specific statutory exclusion that applies to the particular benefit.

A. Policy

While it is clear that amounts paid—whether in cash or property—by an employer to an employee are compensation income to the employee, several rationales exist to exclude some common noncash benefits from the employee's gross income. Some benefits may be difficult to value. Others may be so small that the expense of accounting for them would exceed their value to the employee. Still others are the result of a congressional purpose to encourage the provision of a certain benefit.

For many years the Code simply ignored many widely available fringe benefits, and the tax treatment of these items varied widely among employees. In 1984, Congress enacted §132 to deal definitively with commonly encountered fringe benefits. While §132 was intended to resolve the treatment of all miscellaneous fringe benefits, it has not resolved all controversies. Various specific benefits continue to raise questions about whether such amounts constitute compensation and, if so, whether any exclusion applies.

B. Meals and lodging—§119

1. **Judicial limitation on gross income—*Benaglia v. Commissioner*, 36 B.T.A. 838 (1937),** *acq.* **1940-1 C.B. 1:** Mr. Benaglia was the manager of the Royal Hawaiian Hotel, where he was on call 24 hours a day. He and his wife lived in a suite of rooms at the hotel and ate their meals in the hotel dining room.

   a. **Issue:** Should Mr. Benaglia's gross income be increased by the fair market value of the room and board ($7,845 per year) provided to him by his employer?

   b. **Result and rationale:** Mr. Benaglia may exclude the value of the room and board from his gross income. Because he was required to live in the hotel for the convenience of his employer, the advantage to him was merely incidental, even though it relieved him of an expense he would otherwise bear.

   c. **Comment—Fairness:** It is almost impossible to justify this result on statutory or fairness grounds. Mr. Benaglia did have an economic benefit (food and shelter), and as there was no exclusion in the Code at that time, it seems clear that some amount should be included in his income. To hold otherwise seems patently unfair to similarly situated employees whose employers do not provide food and shelter.

   Example: Consider two employees, Alvin and Betty, both subject to a flat 30% tax rate. Alvin's taxable income is $50,000, and he pays $15,000 in tax. From his remaining $35,000 he pays $10,000 for rent and $5,000 for food. Betty is a fire chief who lives at the fire station.

Her taxable income is $35,000, but she lives at the station rent-free, and her food is provided by the fire district. Assuming the room and board are not included in her income, Betty pays $10,500 in tax—$4,500 less than Alvin. Is this fair? Not if Alvin and Betty's living quarters and food consumption are equivalent—Alvin is paying more tax for the same consumption.

    d. Comment—Administrative practicality: If any amount were included in Mr. Benaglia's gross income, determining what that amount should be may be difficult. Fair market value—what a tourist would have paid? Or the "corporate rate"? Or the employer's cost?

    e. Comment—Economic effects: The result reached in *Benaglia* might well encourage other employers to require their employees to eat and live on the business premises, which may alter the working relationship in undesirable (or perhaps desirable) ways.

2. Statutory analysis—§119: *Benaglia* was decided before the enactment of §119, which now governs the inclusion of room and board provided to employees.

    a. General rule: An employee may exclude from his or her gross income the value of the meals and lodgings provided by an employer if the following three conditions are met.

        i. Convenience of employer: The meals or lodging must be provided for the convenience of the employer. IRC §119(a).

        ii. Business premises: The meals or lodging must be provided on the business premises of the employer. Id.

        iii. Lodging—Condition of employment: For lodging, the employee must be required to accept such lodging as a condition of employment. Id.

    b. Definitional issues

        i. Convenience of the employer: This requires that there be a "substantial noncompensatory business reason" for supplying the meals or lodging. Reg. §1.119-1(b). Whether this exists depends on all of the facts and circumstances of the situation. The classic example is the employee who must be "on call" for the employer during meals.

        ii. Business premises: An employer's "business premises" is generally where the employee works. Reg. §119-1(c)(1). Standard business premises are easy to identify. Properties "nearby" the employer's premises probably do not qualify.

        iii. Condition of employment: This requirement is usually satisfied by showing that the employee is on call for the business of the employer. Reg. §1.119-1(b)(3).

3. Special rules and exceptions

    a. Qualified campus lodging: Employees of educational institutions are often provided nearby housing at below-market rent. The value of qualified campus lodging is excluded from the gross income of the employee. IRC §119(d)(1). However, the exclusion does not apply to the excess, if any, of the lesser of (1) 5% of the appraised value of the property; or (2) the average of rentals paid (by others than students and employees) for similar property, over the amount actually paid by the employee. IRC §119(d)(2).

    Example: Jenny is a professor at Kiawah University. The University provides Jenny and her family with a three-bedroom home near the University, at a rental of $540 per month, which is the University's standard rent to faculty for three-bedroom homes it owns. The

University rents similar homes for $1,000/month to non-employees. The appraised value of the home is $140,000.

Jenny has gross income to the extent of $12,000 (the value of the house provided to her) but she may be able to exclude a portion of this amount from gross income as qualified campus lodging. The lodging seems to qualify: the University appears to be a qualifying educational organization, and the home is located near the campus and is used as a residence.

But does the limitation pose a problem? The exclusion does not apply to the excess, if any, of the *lesser* of 5% of appraised value (5% × $140,000 = $7,000) or the average yearly rent for similar property (the amount paid by others, $12,000) over the amount Jenny actually pays ($6,480). Thus, Jenny must include in her gross income $520 ($7,000 − $6,480).

    b. Charges for meals: Some employers pay their employees a fixed amount for meals. This amount is excluded from the employee's gross income if the other requirements for meals are met, and the employee must make the payment whether or not he or she accepts the meals. IRC §119(b)(3)(A),(B).

4. Related material

    a. Deductions: For a discussion of deductions for business meals and entertainment, see Chapter 8(IV)(B).

    b. Business travel: For a discussion of deductions for lodging while away from home, see Chapter 8(IV)(D).

C. Statutory Fringe Benefits—§132

1. General rule: Section 132(a) excludes from the gross income of the recipient the value of any fringe benefit provided by the employer that qualifies as any of nine fringes: a no-additional-cost service, a qualified employee discount, a working condition fringe, a de minimis fringe, a qualified transportation fringe, a qualified retirement planning service, a qualified military base realignment or closure fringe, or an on-premises athletic facility. The value of a fringe benefit is its fair market value, minus the amount the employee is required to pay for it.

2. Definitional issues: The key to §132 is defining the nine fringes that qualify and determining whether a particular benefit fits within any of the exclusions.

    a. Employee: All of the exclusions require an employer-employee relationship. The employee's use of the benefit will qualify. For qualified employee discounts and no-additional-cost services, use by close family members and surviving spouses generally will also qualify for exclusion.

    b. No-additional-cost service: A no-additional-cost service is one regularly provided to the public by the employer, which the employer can provide to the employee without incurring significant additional cost (disregarding any amount paid by the employee). IRC §132(b).

    Example: Carlo is employed by Dolphin Airways as a counter clerk. All Dolphin employees and immediate family members are entitled to fly on Dolphin flights, on a standby (space available) status, for a flat fee of $5.00 per trip. Carlo and his wife take advantage of this by flying from Atlanta to Miami for $10.00 instead of the usual fare of $340.00. Although he has income (an economic benefit), the value of the benefit ($330) is excludable from gross income as a no-additional-cost service: Dolphin regularly provides this service to the public and incurs no additional cost by providing it to Carlo on a standby basis. In addition, Carlo's spouse's use of the benefit is deemed to be use by the employee.

c. **Qualified employee discount:** There are three requirements for a qualified employee discount.

    i. **An employee discount:** This is the amount of the discount to employees, determined by comparing the price paid by employees to the price paid by the general public. IRC §132(c)(3).

    ii. **Qualified property or services:** These are services and property (other than real estate and securities) that the employer sells in the ordinary course of business. IRC §132(c)(4).

    iii. **Limitation on discount:** The discount must not be in excess of a 20% discount for services. IRC §132(c)(1)(B). For property, the discount must not be in excess of the "gross profit percentage" at which the property is sold to the public. IRC §132(c)(1)(A).

    Example: Eliza is a professor for Giggleswick University, which offers her a 20% discount at the University Bookstore. For a representative period, the aggregate price to the public and cost of bookstore items was $100,000 and $65,000, respectively. Thus, the gross profit percentage is 35% (100,000 − (65,000/100,000)). Therefore, Eliza's discount is a qualified employee discount, as it does not exceed 35%.

d. **Working condition fringe:** This is a benefit to the employee that, if he or she had paid for it personally, would have generated a business deduction as a trade or business expense under §162 or as depreciation under §167. IRC §132(d).

    Example: Gerry is a tax lawyer in the employ of the firm of Smith & Jones. Smith & Jones provides Gerry with a looseleaf tax service and subscriptions to various tax magazines for his offices at both work and home. The cost to the firm is $2,600 per year. While Gerry has income (an economic benefit) as a result of this benefit, the $2,600 value is excluded from Gerry's gross income as a working condition fringe—if he had purchased these items personally, he would have been entitled to a deduction under §162 for the expenditure.

e. **De minimis fringe:** This is the provision of goods or services to the employee with a value so small that the accounting for the benefit would be unreasonable or administratively impractical. IRC §132(e)(1). A cash payment cannot be a de minimis fringe benefit.

    Example: Every year Ixnel Corporation gives its employees a holiday party, and each employee receives a turkey for the holiday season. The party and turkey are probably de minimis fringe benefits to the employees of Ixnel Corporation, as the benefit is small, and accounting for the benefit to each employee would be administratively impractical. Other examples include occasional use of employer photocopy machine, occasional taxi fare, supper money for overtime work, and occasional tickets for sporting or entertainment events. Items not considered de minimis would include season tickets for sporting or entertainment events or dues at a private club.

f. Qualified transportation fringe: This means employer-provided transit passes, transportation by van from home to office, or parking near the employer's premises, within specified dollar limits ($105 for a transit pass and $200 for parking, in 2005). IRC §132(f)(1).

g. Qualified moving expense reimbursement: This is the amount paid to an employee for expenses that would be deductible as moving expenses under §217. IRC §132(g).

Example: Ivan works for Ixnel Corporation, which transfers him from Pittsburgh to San Antonio. He incurs $5,000 in moving expenses for himself and his family. Ixnel Corporation reimburses him in the amount of $4,800, its ceiling on moving expenses. He may exclude the $4,800 as a qualified moving expense reimbursement, because this expense would qualify for deduction under §217. The additional $200 may be deductible under that provision as well.

h. Qualified retirement planning services: This includes any financial planning advice or consultation provided by an employer related to the retirement plan sponsored by the employer. IRC §132(m)(1)

i. On-premises athletic facility: The value of the facility to the employee may be excluded if it is on the business premises of the employer, is operated by the employer, and is used mostly by employees. IRC §132(j)(4).

3. Special rules and exceptions

a. Nondiscrimination: The exclusions for no-additional-cost services, qualified employee discounts, and qualified retirement planning services apply only if the benefit is available on substantially the same terms to all employees and the employer does not discriminate in favor of highly compensated employees. IRC §132(j)(1).

b. Other sections: Section 132 expressly does not apply to any fringe provided for in another Code section. IRC §132(l).

4. Related material

a. Moving expenses: For a discussion of the deduction for moving expenses, see Chapter 6(IV).

b. Business expense deductions: For a discussion of items deductible as business expenses or depreciation, see Chapter 7(II) and (III).

D. Insurance premiums and payments

Many employers pay the premiums on various types of insurance coverage for employees, and often their spouses and dependents. The employee will receive insurance payments directly from the insurer after submitting a valid claim.

1. Health insurance—§106

a. Employer-paid premiums: The employee excludes from gross income the premiums paid by the employer for coverage for the employee, spouse, and dependents under an accident or health plan. IRC §106.

i. Accident or health plan: This is a plan for payments to employees in the event of their personal injury or sickness. Reg. §1.105-5(a). It includes traditional insurance, HMO plans, and long-term care insurance.

ii. No dollar limitation: This applies regardless of the cost of the premiums.

iii. Definition of "dependent": The Working Families Tax Relief Act of 2004 (WFTRA), Pub. L. No. 108-311, 118 Stat. 1166, amended the definition of "dependent" to include new requirements for years after 2004. See Chapter 6 (XVII). In determining the exclusion for employer-paid health insurance premiums, the IRS does not intend to incorporate these new limitations, and thus the definition of dependent under pre-2005 law will apply. See Notice 2004-79, 2004-49 I.R.B. 898.

b. Benefits received by employee: When the employee receives benefits, the question is whether the employee must include them in gross income. Section 105(a) includes in the employee's gross income any amounts received for personal injuries or sickness that are attributable to employer-provided premiums or coverage (self-insurance). However, §105(b) excludes amounts otherwise included under §105(a) if they are to reimburse the employee for medical care for the employee or his or her dependents, and if the taxpayer has not deducted the amount under §213. Any amount paid for other benefits—such as wage replacement—are included in gross income.

Example: Karen works for the State Bar Association. The Association pays the premiums on her medical insurance, which are excluded from her gross income under §106. Karen incurs $4,000 of medical expenses resulting from an automobile accident. The insurance company reimburses her 80% ($3,200) of this amount. She may exclude this amount from her gross income, assuming she did not deduct it under §213. She may also seek to deduct the non-reimbursed $800 under §213.

i. Self-insurance plans: Some employers self-insure, i.e., they reimburse employees for medical expenses based on an established plan, rather than paying premiums to an insurance company. The employee excludes the benefits paid if they are for reimbursement of medical expenses. Such plans must not discriminate in favor of highly compensated individuals, or those individuals will not be able to claim the exclusion.

ii. Disability insurance: If the employer pays the premium (i.e., it is not included in the gross income of the employee), amounts received by a disabled employee will be included in his or her gross income. IRC §105(b). If the employee has included the premiums in gross income, or purchased the policy separately from employment, the amounts received pursuant to the policy will be excluded from gross income. IRC §104(a).

iii. Definition of "dependent": The Working Families Tax Relief Act of 2004 (WFTRA), Pub. L. No. 108-311, 118 Stat. 1166, amended the definition of "dependent" to include new requirements for years after 2004. See Chapter 6 (XVII). However, the Act specifically provided that in determining the exclusion for amounts received as a result of insurance, the definition of dependent under pre-2005 law will apply. WFTRA §207.

c. Health Savings Accounts: An employer may establish a health savings account for any employee who is covered under a high deductible health plan. This allows the employer to contribute to the plan amounts (up to a specified amount per year) that can be used to pay for the employee's health care expenses. The contribution is not included in the employee's gross income, and if distributions are used for qualified medical expenses, these distributions are not included in the employee's gross income. See IRC §223 and discussion at Chapter 6(IX).

2. Life insurance premiums: The employee excludes from gross income employer-paid premiums on group term life insurance in an amount not in excess of $50,000 of coverage. IRC §79(a). Group-term life insurance is life insurance (1) providing a general death benefit for each member of a group of employees, (2) which is paid for by the employer, and (3) the amount of which is based on a formula generally applicable to all members of the group based on age, years of service, compensation, or position. Reg. §1.79-1(a). Nondiscrimination rules limit this exclusion. IRC §79(d).

3. Group legal services: The employee may exclude up to $70 per year of either insurance to provide legal services or the value of legal services provided under a qualified group legal service plan. IRC §120(a).

E. Dependent care assistance—§129

1. General rule: An employee may exclude from gross income amounts paid by the employer for dependent care assistance pursuant to a qualified dependent care assistance program. IRC §129(a)(1).

2. Definitional issues

   a. Dependent care assistance: Dependent care assistance is the employer's payment of, or reimbursement of, an employee's payment of employment-related expenses for the care of a dependent unable to care for him- or herself. IRC §129(e)(1).

   b. Dollar limitation: A plan may provide any amount of assistance, but the employee may only exclude a maximum of $5,000 ($2,500 for married filing separately). IRC §129(a)(2)(A).

3. Special rules and exceptions

   a. Earned income limitation: The exclusion is limited to the earned income of the lesser earning spouse. IRC §129(b)(1)(B).

   b. Nondiscrimination: The plan must meet certain requirements, including that the plan not discriminate in favor of highly compensated individuals. IRC §129(d)(2).

   Example: Larry is a single father of one son, age 6. Last year he paid $2,000 in day care costs, for which his employer reimbursed him pursuant to a qualified dependent care assistance plan. Larry may exclude from his gross income the $2,000 in dependent care assistance he received from his employer as reimbursement.

4. Related material—dependent care credit: For a discussion of the tax credit for dependent care expenditures, see Chapter 13(V).

5. Summary: A taxpayer may exclude up to $5,000 of dependent care assistance provided by an employer. IRC §129.

F. Educational assistance

An employer's expenditures for educational assistance to employees will not be included in the employee's gross income. IRC §127(a)(1). Educational assistance is limited to $5,250 per employee. IRC §127(a)(2).

G. Adoption assistance

An employer can provide tax-free assistance up to $10,630 (in 2005) per child with respect to an employee's "qualified adoption expenses" pursuant to an employer's written adoption expenses program. This exclusion is phased out for employees with adjusted gross incomes between $159,450 and $199,450 (in 2005).

H. Frequent flyer miles

For some years, the Service took the position that frequent flyer miles accumulated by employees while on business travel—and subsequently used to purchase personal travel—constituted gross income to them. See also *Charley v. Commissioner,* 91 F.3d 72 (9th Cir. 1996). In 2002, the Service changed its position, holding that it will not assert that such awards are gross income to the employee. Announc. 2002-18, 2002-10 IRB 621.

I. Summary—Employment-related exclusions

See Figure 4A—Summary of Employment-Related Exclusions.

Figure 4A
Summary of Employment-Related Exclusions

Code Section of Exclusion	An employee may exclude from gross income certain benefits provided by the employer, including:
§119: Meals and lodging	Certain meals and lodging, subject to convenience of employer and business premises requirements
§132: Statutory fringe benefits	A number of specifically defined fringe benefits, such as de minimis fringes, working condition fringes, etc.
§106: Health insurance	Health insurance premiums paid by the employer
§79: Life insurance	Premiums on $50,000 of term life insurance paid by employer
§120: Group legal services	$70 per year of group legal services benefits
§129: Dependent care assistance	$5,000 of qualified dependent care assistance, subject to earned income limitation (see also IRC §21)
§127: Educational assistance	$5,250 of qualified educational assistance
§137: Adoption assistance	$10,630 (in 2005) of qualified adoption expenses

X. EDUCATIONAL INCENTIVES

A. Savings bonds—§135

Savings bonds are purchased from the U.S. Government in multiples of $50. They are "discount" bonds, i.e., their issue price is less than their redemption price at maturity. For example, a $50 savings bond costs $25 today, and is redeemable for $50 at maturity. The $25 difference between the issue price and redemption price is, of course, interest, which is includable in the gross income of the holder of the bond in the year of maturity. (The owner of a U.S. savings bond may elect to include the interest on a pro rata basis during the term of the bond, but most taxpayers do not elect this option.)

1. **General rule—Exclusion for educational expenses:** Section 135 excludes from the gross income of an individual any amount received upon redemption of any qualified U.S. savings bond. IRC §135(a). However, there are two significant limitations on this exclusion.

   a. **Limitation—Higher education expenses:** The exclusion of §135 is intended to reach taxpayers who use their bond proceeds for educational expenses. Therefore, if the redeeming taxpayer's qualified higher education expenses paid for the year are less than the total amount of proceeds from bonds redeemed during that year, the exclusion will be limited. To determine the amount excludable, multiply the interest income from the bonds redeemed during the year by a fraction, the numerator of which is the qualified higher education expenses of the taxpayer (or spouse and dependents) during the year, and the denominator of which is the aggregate proceeds of U.S. savings bonds redeemed during the year. IRC §135(b)(1).

   Example: Maureen purchased U.S. savings bonds for $25,000 (face value $50,000) in 1990. She later redeems them at face value and uses part of the proceeds for her son's college tuition. Her son qualifies as a dependent. In the year of redemption, her son's tuition is $10,000. Maureen is entitled to exclude from her gross income only a portion of the redemption proceeds otherwise includable in her income. The excludable amount will be limited to:

   $$\$25,000 \quad \times \quad \frac{\$10,000}{\$50,000} \quad = \quad \$5,000$$

   The remaining interest income ($20,000) will be included in Maureen's gross income.

   b. **Limitation—Modified adjusted gross income (MAGI):** The exclusion of §135 is intended to benefit only low- to middle-income taxpayers. Therefore, if the taxpayer's MAGI for the year exceeds $91,850 (joint return) or $61,200 (single return) the exclusion is reduced and is completely eliminated when MAGI reaches $121,850 (joint return) or $76,200 (single return)(in 2005). IRC §135(b)(2). This limitation cannot reduce the exclusion below zero. IRC §135(b)(2)(A). These limitations are indexed for inflation for future years.

   Example: To apply the income limitation, assume the same facts as in the previous example, except that the higher education expenses were $50,000 in the year of redemption and that Maureen's MAGI was $68,700. She files a return as a single individual. Because her MAGI is greater than the allowed amount, she will not be able to exclude the full $25,000 of interest. The reduction will be calculated as follows:

   $$\text{Amount of reduction} = \text{interest otherwise excludable} \times \frac{\text{``Excess'' MAGI}}{\substack{\text{specified amount} \\ \text{based on filing status}}}$$

   $$\text{Maureen's reduction} = \$25,000 \times \frac{\$68,700 - \$61,200}{\$15,000}$$

   The reduction amount is $12,500. Thus, Maureen will reduce the otherwise allowable exclusion by half, from $25,000 to $12,500. This will mean that, of the $25,000 in interest she earns upon redemption, only $12,500 of that amount will be includable in her gross income.

2. Definitional issues

a. **Qualified U.S. savings bond:** A qualified U.S. savings bond is a U.S. savings bond purchased after December 31, 1989 and issued to someone at least 24 years old. IRC §135(c)(1).

b. **Qualified higher education expenses:** Qualified higher education expenses are expenses of the taxpayer, spouse, or dependents in attending an eligible educational institution, which generally means an institution of higher education, whether college or vocational school. IRC §135(c)(2).

c. **Modified adjusted gross income:** MAGI is adjusted gross income, with the modifications listed in §135(c)(4).

3. Special rules and exceptions

a. **Effect of scholarships:** Qualified education expenses are reduced by the amount of scholarships excluded from gross income under §117 and exempt veterans' benefits. IRC §135(d)(1).

b. **Joint return:** Married individuals must file a joint return in order to claim the benefit. IRC §135(d)(2).

4. Related material

a. **Exclusion for scholarships:** For a discussion of qualified scholarships, see this Chapter, Section VII.

b. **Original issue discount (OID):** For a discussion of original issue discount, applicable to discounted bonds other than U.S. savings bonds, see Chapter 15(III).

5. **Summary:** A taxpayer may be able to exclude from gross income the interest on a qualified educational bond upon redemption, subject to the two limitations.

B. Section 529 Plans and Education Savings Accounts

1. **Section 529 plans:** The "§529 Plan" is a plan established under state law designed to create an incentive to save for education. Under this type of plan, the account owner designates a beneficiary who will receive the funds, for K-12 or post-secondary education. There is deduction for contributions, but the investment earnings accrue tax free, i.e., are not includable in the gross income of either the account owner or the beneficiary. IRC §529(c)(1). Section 529 allows distributions from certain qualified state tuition plans to be excluded from income if the distributions are used for qualified educational expenses. Section 529 plans discussed more fully in Chapters 15 and 16.

2. **Education savings accounts:** Formerly known as "education IRAs," these are accounts, usually held by banks or other custodians, to which taxpayers may contribute up to $2,000 per year (beginning in 2002). These accounts name a "beneficiary," who is the person whose education is being funded, for K-12 or post-secondary education. No deduction is available for these contributions, but income earned in these accounts is not subject to tax. IRC §530(a). Distributions from the account are tax-free to the extent the distributions are used for qualified education expenses. Education savings accounts are discussed more fully in Chapters 15 and 16.

XI. CHILD SUPPORT

Child support is excluded from the gross income of the recipient parent. IRC §71(c)(1). Child support is payment for the support of the payor's minor children. Id. Amounts not designated child support but which are tied to a contingency involving a minor child of the payor will be considered child support. IRC §71(c)(2).

Example: Todd and Susie are getting a divorce. Under the terms of the divorce decree, Todd will pay Susie $1,500 per month, and this payment appears to qualify as alimony under the federal definition. However, the decree also provides that the $1,500 payment will be reduced to $1,000 on July 18, 2002, which happens to be the date Todd and Susie's only child turns 18. The portion of the payment tied to the child turning 18 will be considered child support rather than alimony. Susie may exclude that portion from her gross income.

XII. GAIN FROM SALE OF STOCK

A taxpayer other than a corporation may exclude from gross income one-half of the gain on the sale of certain small business stock that the taxpayer has held for more than five years, up to the greater of $10 million, or ten times the taxpayer's adjusted basis in the stock. IRC §1202(a)(1). Qualified small business stock is stock in a C corporation engaged in a qualified active business, the aggregate assets of which do not exceed $50 million.

XIII. WHERE ARE WE GOING?

With this chapter's discussion of exclusions from gross income, we now have a sense of which items are included in (and excluded from) gross income. These are the items that are potentially subject to the federal income tax. We now turn to ***deductions***—the items that are subtracted from gross income in computing taxable income.

Quiz Yourself on
SPECIFIC EXCLUSIONS FROM GROSS INCOME

29. Upon settlement of her grandfather's estate, Rikki received a pair of antique carved mongooses worth $50,000. Her grandfather had won these in a poker game in India many years before. What are the tax consequences of this receipt to Rikki? _____

30. Tonika sued Dump-It-All, Inc. for illnesses she sustained as a result of a toxic waste dump near her home. She ultimately prevailed, receiving reimbursement for all her medical expenses and damages for pain and suffering. What are the tax consequences of these receipts to Tonika?

_____

31. DotComInc has debts of $1 million, property with a fair market value of about $50,000, and a net operating loss of $400,000. Negotiating with creditors, DotComInc obtains cancellation of $700,000 worth of debt. What are the tax consequences to the company of this cancellation?

_____

32. Assume the same facts as in the previous question. However, DotComInc files for bankruptcy, and the court discharges $800,000 of debt. What are the tax consequences to the company of the discharge? _____

33. Sheri is a flight attendant whose employer provides certain fringe benefits, including medical insurance for herself and her husband and the opportunity to fly free on a standby (seats available) basis for her and her family. What are the tax consequences of these fringe benefits to her? _____

34. Sheri is promoted to flight attendant supervisor. One of the perks of this position is an apartment near the airport where she is based which she is provided free of charge. The employer wishes to have Sheri available at a few moments' notice to deal with scheduling and other difficulties, but there aren't suitable facilities at the airport. What are the tax consequences of this benefit to Sheri? _____

35. Travis bought a home in Year One. He used it as his principal residence in Year One and Year Two. He then decided to change his life: He abandoned his career as a tax lawyer, got his private detective's license, and moved onto a houseboat in Florida. The house sat empty for a couple of years but he sold it in Year Five at a gain of $75,000. What are the tax consequences of this sale to Travis? _____

36. Ellen purchased U.S. savings bonds (Series EE) in 1992 for $50,000. In 2005, she redeemed them for $90,000. She paid $70,000 for books, tuition, and fees to commence studying a PhD program in archaeology in that year. She is a single taxpayer whose MAGI in the year of redemption was $64,200. _____

37. Lisa's employer provides her and her family with health insurance, and also provides disability insurance for Lisa. In Years 1 through 5, the employer spent $10,000 on these premiums for Lisa. In Year 4, Lisa became very ill. She incurred $25,000 of medical expenses, of which the insurance company reimbursed her for $20,000. Eventually, she was determined to be disabled, and now receives $2,000 per month under the disability policy. What are the tax consequences of these events to Lisa? _____

38. Tiffany's employer gives her a $100 gift certificate on her birthday. Is this included in Tiffany's gross income? _____

Answers

29. Section 102(a) excludes from gross income bequests and inheritances. Rikki can exclude from her gross income the value of the carvings. (Her basis in the carvings will be their fair market value as of the date of her grandfather's death. See Chapter 9.)

30. Tonika may exclude amounts received as reimbursement for medical expenses, unless she previously deducted them and obtained a tax benefit as a result. (See Chapter 11). Amounts received for physical injuries are also excludable from gross income (§104(a)) and thus all of these receipts are excludable from Tonika's gross income.

31. The adjustment in the amount of his indebtedness results in $700,000 of discharge of indebtedness income to DotComInc. However, because it is insolvent (liabilities exceed assets) it may exclude the discharged amount from gross income under §108(a), up to the amount of insolvency (which, in this case, is greater than the discharged amount). However, it must reduce its net operating loss to zero as a result of this discharge.

32. This discharge is excluded from DotComInc's gross income because IRC §108 excludes any discharge in bankruptcy from gross income.

33. Sheri may exclude from gross income the medical insurance premiums paid by her employer for her and her family (§106) and may exclude as a no-additional-cost fringe benefit (§132) the value of standby flights.

34. While Sheri might try to exclude the fair rental value of the apartment as lodging provided for the convenience of the employer under §119, because the lodging is not provided on the business premises of the employer, it does not meet the statutory requirements and must be included in Sheri's gross income.

35. Section 121 requires the taxpayer to use the home as a principal residence for at least two of the past five years in order to exclude the gain on sale from gross income. Travis' use of the home qualifies and therefore he may exclude the $75,000 of gain from his gross income. (This assumes that he has not used the exclusion during the past two years.)

36. On the redemption of the savings bonds (which are qualified because Ellen purchased them after 1990) she received $40,000 of interest income ($90,000 − $50,000). The amount she may exclude from gross income requires application of both limitations of IRC §135. First, the amount of interest income is multiplied by a fraction, the numerator of which is Ellen's qualified education expenses for the year ($75,000) and the denominator of which is the total amount of bond redemption proceeds ($90,000), or 83.33%. Thus, of the $40,000 of interest, she may potentially exclude only $33,332. Then, the MAGI limitation must be applied. Multiply the amount potentially excludable ($33,332) by a fraction, the numerator of which is the excess of Ellen's MAGI ($64,200) over the 2005 limitation amounts ($61,200 for a single taxpayer) or $3,000, and the denominator of which is the specified amount of $15,000 for a single taxpayer. Thus, the income limitation reduction is equal to $33,332 × 20% or $6,666. Of the $40,000 of interest she earned, only $26,666 is excluded from her gross income. The rest ($13,334) is included in her gross income as ordinary income.

37. Lisa may exclude the value of her employer's provision of insurance (both health and disability) from her gross income. IRC §106. She also may exclude the $25,000 of insurance reimbursements as they were for medical expenses. IRC §105(b). (The excess $5,000 not reimbursed by the insurance company may be deductible under IRC §213. (See Chapter 6(XV).) The disability payments she receives will be included in her gross income because her employer paid the premiums. IRC §105(b).

38. Yes. While birthday gifts are generally thought to be given out of generosity and affection, and would otherwise be an excludable gift under IRC §102(a), there is a specific provision (§102(c)) that provides that every transfer by an employer to an employee is compensation. It does not qualify as any of the fringe benefits under IRC §132. The closest possible fit is a de minimis fringe benefit. However, the IRS takes the position that gift certificates are not de minimis fringe benefits because they are like cash and accounting for them creates no more of an administrative burden than accounting for cash.

Exam Tips on
SPECIFIC EXCLUSIONS FROM GROSS INCOME

☛ Questions about exclusions focus on the taxpayer's receipt of something of value that would otherwise be included in the taxpayer's gross income.

   ☞ *Watch for:* Receipt of property, money, or some other benefit to the taxpayer that would be considered gross income under Section 61.

   ☞ *Analyze:* Is there a specific statutory exclusion that exempts it from gross income?

☛ Interpret exclusions narrowly.

   ☞ Make sure the purported exclusions precisely fit within the domain of the statute.

   ☞ If in doubt, don't exclude an item; include it in gross income.

☛ Many exclusions (and deductions) have complex limitations based on income. In a test situation, the limitation phase-out figures would usually be given to you and the goal would be to demonstrate your ability to understand how these limitations work and show that you comprehend the structure of the statute.

☛ Understand the difference between the exclusion for gifts for income tax purposes, and the so-called annual exclusion for gift tax purposes.

   ☞ A person can receive an unlimited amount of gifts, in terms of value, without including them in gross income.

   ☞ The gift tax exclusion is limited to a dollar amount ($11,000 in 2005); this is the amount any person may give to another person without counting against the donor's lifetime exclusion amount.

☛ **Remember:** Damages for nonphysical injuries are includable in gross income; damages for physical injuries are excludable; punitive and delay damages are included in the gross income.

☛ Section 108 provides a number of potential exclusions from gross income for discharge of indebtedness income.

   ☞ *Look for:* A discharge of debt situation that generates gross income to the taxpayer, but surrounding circumstances that make it seem somewhat "unfair" to tax the income.

   ☞ *Analyze:* Does some subsection of §108 apply? If so, are there corresponding reductions in tax benefits? Or, is there a gift that would protect otherwise includable discharge of indebtedness income from being taxed?

☛ Consider the employment situation carefully:

   ☞ *Look for:* Compensation income in the form of noncash items, such as medical insurance, fringe benefits, dependent care assistance or other benefits.

   ☞ *Analyze:* Is there a benefit to the taxpayer that would otherwise be included in his or her gross income? If so, is there a specific statutory exclusion that would prevent it from being included in the taxpayer's gross income?

CHAPTER 5

DEDUCTIONS—IN GENERAL

ChapterScope ───

Gross income is the starting point for computing a taxpayer's ultimate tax liability. But gross income is certainly not the tax base—the amount on which tax is levied. Certain deductions must be subtracted from gross income to reach taxable income, upon which the income tax is imposed. This chapter explores the concept of a deduction, and the next three chapters discuss various deductions in detail.

- **Definition of a deduction:** A deduction is a subtraction in the calculation of taxable income. Some deductions are subtracted from gross income in computing adjusted gross income (AGI), while others are subtracted from AGI in computing taxable income. In order to claim a deduction, a taxpayer must meet every requirement of the statute, and these statutes are narrowly construed.

- **Standard versus itemized deduction:** In computing taxable income, an individual taxpayer may claim either the standard or the itemized deduction. The standard deduction is an amount set by statute based on filing status, while the itemized deduction is the aggregate of a number of deductions that are available only if the taxpayer files a Schedule A on which he or she lists all of the available deductions.

- **Personal versus business deductions:** Section 262 denies a taxpayer any deduction for personal expenses except for deductions specifically allowed by statute. By contrast, taxpayers generally may claim deductions for the expenses of doing business. A commonly encountered theme is whether a particular expenditure is a personal (nondeductible) or business (deductible) expense.

- **Expense versus capital expenditure:** If an item is not currently deductible, it may constitute a capital expenditure, and the taxpayer may recover his or her investment in the item at some point during ownership of the asset.

I. WHERE ARE WE?

Having established what is—and is not—gross income, we now turn to deductions. These are subtractions from income that must be made to compute taxable income, on which the income tax is levied.

II. ROLE OF DEDUCTIONS

A. Deduction—Definition

A deduction is a subtraction from income in the calculation of taxable income.

1. Compare exclusion: If an item is excluded from gross income, it never appears in the calculation of taxable income. By contrast, if an item is deducted, it appears as a subtraction from income in the ultimate calculation of taxable income. An exclusion is appropriate for an income (inflow) item, while a deduction is appropriate for an expenditure (outflow) item.

2. **Effect:** The tax effects of an exclusion and a deduction are the same, although they reach the same result by different paths. An exclusion prevents an item from being included in gross income, thus protecting it from tax. A deduction "shelters" other income from tax—the subtraction from income potentially results in the same amount of income escaping tax.

3. **Compare credits:** Unlike a deduction, a tax credit is a dollar-for-dollar reduction in the amount of tax due. See generally Chapter 13.

   Example: Compare the effect of a $50 deduction and a $50 tax credit to a taxpayer in the 28% tax bracket. The $50 deduction will reduce the taxpayer's income by $50, reducing tax by $14 ($50 multiplied by the 28% tax rate). The $50 tax credit will reduce the taxpayer's tax by $50 because the tax credit is a dollar-for-dollar reduction in the amount of tax due. In this case, the tax credit is obviously more valuable to the taxpayer than the deduction.

4. **The upside-down subsidy:** Because a deduction reduces tax by the deduction multiplied by the tax rate (see example above), a deduction is more valuable to a high tax bracket taxpayer than a low tax bracket taxpayer. Thus, a deduction is sometimes referred to as an upside-down subsidy because in a graduated tax system, it offers a bigger benefit for the well-off taxpayer than for the poorer taxpayer. A tax credit, by contrast, confers the same dollar benefit on all taxpayers regardless of their tax rates.

B. Narrow construction

A deduction is available by statute only—as the courts often say, "by legislative grace." Courts interpret deduction requirements strictly, construing these statutes narrowly. *New Colonial Ice Co., Inc. v. Helvering*, 292 U.S. 435 (1934).

C. Role

Deductions occur in two steps of the computation of taxable income. See Figure 5A—Role of Deductions in the Computation of Taxable Income. Deductions that are subtracted in computing adjusted gross income (AGI) are known in the tax trade as "above-the-line" deductions. Deductions that are subtracted in computing taxable income are known as "below-the-line" deductions.

D. Adjusted gross income

1. **Computation:** A number of deductions constitute a subtraction from gross income to produce adjusted gross income. AGI is used as a measure for certain other deductions (such as medical expenses, casualty losses, and entitlement to certain tax benefits), and therefore its determination is important. Taxpayers generally seek to reduce AGI as much as possible because it is often used as a measure for limiting itemized deductions and other tax benefits.

2. **Principal deductions:** Section 62 defines adjusted gross income, allowing the following principal deductions from gross income.

   a. **Alimony:** A taxpayer may deduct the amount of alimony he or she pays. IRC §62(a)(10). See IRC §215 and discussion at Chapter 6(III).

   b. **Certain retirement savings:** A taxpayer may deduct certain contributions to an Individual Retirement Account (IRA) and other retirement plans. IRC §62(a)(6), (7). See IRC §219, and discussion at Chapter 6(V).

   c. **Certain health care expenses:** A taxpayer may deduct certain contributions to health care accounts. IRC §62(a)(16), (19) and discussion at Chapter 6(IX).

Figure 5A
Role of Deductions in the Computation of Taxable Income

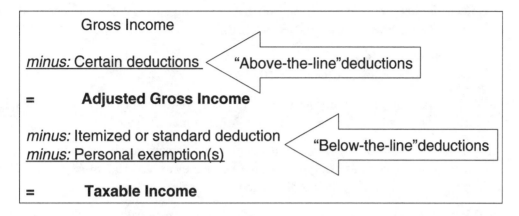

d. **Moving expenses:** A taxpayer may deduct qualifying moving expenses incurred in moving his or her household to take a new job. IRC §62(a)(15). See IRC §217 and discussion at Chapter 6(IV).

e. **Business losses:** If a taxpayer's expenses of doing business exceed the income from that business, the net loss will be deductible, subject to certain limitations. IRC §62(a)(1). See IRC §165(c)(1) and discussion at Chapter 7(II).

f. **Rent and royalty expenses:** A taxpayer earning rents or royalties that do not rise to the level of a trade or business may deduct certain expenses associated with that income. See IRC §62(a)(4) and discussion at Chapter 6(V).

g. **Certain employee expenses:** A taxpayer who is employed may deduct certain expenses from AGI. See IRC §62(a)(2) and discussion at Chapter 6(XVII).

h. **Capital losses:** A taxpayer's capital losses are deductible, subject to the limitations of §1211. IRC §62(a)(3). See generally Chapter 12.

i. **Interest on education loans:** The taxpayer's interest expense on education loans is deductible, subject to certain limitations. IRC §62(a)(17). See IRC §221(a) and discussion at Chapter 6(VII).

j. **Higher education expenses:** The taxpayer's expenditures for qualified tuition and related expenses are deductible, subject to certain limitations. IRC §62(a)(18). See IRC §222(a) and discussion at Chapter 6(VIII).

k. **Clean fuel vehicles:** A taxpayer who purchases a clean fuel automobile may deduct certain costs associated with it. IRC §62(a)(14).

E. **Taxable income**

1. **Computation:** A second group of deductions is subtracted from AGI to produce taxable income. The taxpayer may subtract either the standard deduction or the itemized deduction (but not both), and the sensible taxpayer will choose to deduct the larger of the two. Section 63 defines taxable income.

2. **Standard deduction:** The standard deduction is a statutorily fixed amount based on the tax-payer's filing status. See Chapter 6(XI).

3. **Itemized deduction:** The itemized deduction is the aggregate of a number of deductions, principally the following. See Chapter 6(XI).

    a. **Home mortgage interest:** A taxpayer may deduct qualified residence interest. See IRC §163, and discussion at Chapter 6(XII)(D).

    b. **Taxes:** A taxpayer may deduct state and local income and property taxes, and sales taxes (at least in 2004-05). See IRC §164 and discussion at Chapter 6(XIII).

    c. **Casualty losses:** A taxpayer may deduct the net personal casualty losses—the excess of casualty losses over casualty gains—to the extent they exceed 10% of AGI and $100 per loss event. See IRC §165(c)(3) and discussion at Chapter 6(XIV).

    d. **Medical expenses:** A taxpayer may deduct certain medical expenses to the extent they exceed 7.5% of AGI. See IRC §213 and discussion at Chapter 6(XV).

    e. **Charitable contributions:** A taxpayer may deduct contributions to certain qualifying organizations, subject to certain limitations. See IRC §170 and discussion at Chapter 6(XVI).

    f. **Miscellaneous expenses:** Certain expenditures (principally unreimbursed employee business expenses) are deductible only to the extent that they exceed 2% of a taxpayer's AGI. See IRC §67 and discussion at Chapter 6(XVII).

4. **Personal exemption:** Each taxpayer is entitled to claim a deduction for personal exemptions for him- or herself, a spouse (if a joint return is filed), and any qualifying dependents. This essentially exempts from tax an amount attributable to basic living expenses (although the personal exemption amount is not explicitly tied to a measure of those living expenses). See discussion at Chapter 6(XVIII).

III. COMMON THEMES OF DEDUCTION CONTROVERSIES

Just as inflows of value to a taxpayer generate a common question of whether that value must be included in gross income, outflows or expenditures generate their own common tax controversy themes.

A. An event

To qualify for a deduction, the taxpayer must have experienced an outlay, a loss, or some other event that results in a net outflow—and there must be little if any likelihood of recovery. Deductions are narrowly construed, and therefore the taxpayer's situation must fit within each requirement of a deduction statute to qualify for the deduction. A closely related question is *when* a taxpayer may claim the deduction—in what taxable year. See Chapter 11.

B. Personal versus business deductions

Throughout the deduction provisions of the Code, a common theme emerges—most personal expenses are not deductible, and business expenses generally are deductible.

1. **No deduction for personal expenditures:** Section 262 provides that no "personal living or family expenses" are deductible unless a specific statutory provision allows a deduction.

Although it can be difficult to identify a personal expense, in general, if an item has more than a minimal connection with a taxpayer's personal (as opposed to business) life, it is likely to be considered a personal expense. See generally Chapter 6.

2. **Deduction for business expenses:** Section 162 provides a deduction for most commonly encountered business expenses, and other provisions specify other types of business expenditures for which a deduction is allowed. See generally Chapter 7.

3. **Policy:** There are very different rationales for business and personal deductions.

   a. **Business deductions:** The income tax is generally a tax on net, rather than gross, income. Thus, the Code must provide a deduction for the expenses of creating business income in order to tax only the net increase in wealth of the taxpayer.

   b. **Personal deductions:** If deductions were allowed for all personal expenses, taxable income—the tax base—would be zero. It is sometimes difficult to articulate the rationale for the relatively few personal expenses that are deductible. The income tax often incorporates incentives for specific behavior (such as charitable contributions). It also seeks to tax income actually available to the taxpayer for discretionary expenditure, hence the deductions for alimony, casualty losses, and extraordinary medical expenses.

4. **Personal or business?** A commonly encountered theme in federal income tax is the question of whether an expenditure is a personal (nondeductible) or business (deductible) expense. Taxpayers generally try to characterize expenses as deductible business expenses, but the IRS may disagree, asserting that the expense has a closer connection with the taxpayer's personal life than his or her business activity and therefore is not deductible. See discussion at Chapter 7(II). Some types of expenditures have a close connection with both aspects of a taxpayer's life. These are particularly troublesome for tax purposes, and Congress has specifically addressed the tax treatment of some such items by statute. See generally Chapter 8.

C. Expense or capital expenditure?

Another commonly encountered theme is the question of whether an expenditure constitutes an expense or a capital expenditure. If an expenditure is an expense, it will generate a deduction, if the other requirements for deductibility are met. If, however, an expenditure is capital in nature (for the purchase or improvement of real property, for example), the cost or expenditure must be capitalized. This means that the cost is not currently deducted, but instead becomes part of the basis of the property. The taxpayer *may* be able to recover the cost through depreciation or similar deductions during ownership of the property. The line separating expenses from capital expenditures has never been crystal clear, and taxpayers' attempts to characterize an expenditure as a currently deductible expense rather than a capital expenditure (in order to claim the deduction as early as possible) generate a good deal of controversy. See discussion at Chapter 7(III).

IV. WHERE ARE WE GOING?

This chapter has introduced the concept and role of deductions and suggested some common themes in controversies between taxpayers and the IRS regarding deductions. The next three chapters examine various deductions in detail, beginning with the principal personal deductions.

Quiz Yourself on
DEDUCTIONS—IN GENERAL

39. Lee owns a small business, which he runs as a sole proprietorship. His view is: "What's the point of owning a business unless you can run all your expenses through it?" Therefore, he deducts all his living expenses (food, rent, vacations, etc.), in addition to his business expenses, on his Schedule C. What's wrong with that, if anything? _____

40. On his federal income tax return, Double Dip Dan deducted the standard deduction ($3,800) and his itemized deductions ($12,000). The IRS assessed additional tax. Why? _____

41. T.C. "Cat" Adorre is a Congressman. He is considering proposing a tax code change that would benefit taxpayers who incur expenses in adopting animals from shelters. You are his aide and official tax guru. He asks: "Would it be more beneficial for taxpayers to allow a tax deduction or a tax credit for these expenses? What's the difference, anyway? _____

42. Betty owns Hare Heaven, a salon where customers can get a haircut while their pets are also groomed. This year, she purchased dog-grooming equipment for a cost of $50,000. She deducted the entire cost on her tax return. Was this the right approach to these expenses? (Assume IRC §179 does not apply.) _____

43. What is the difference between adjusted gross income and taxable income? _____

44. Of the following, which are deductible from gross income in computing AGI and which are deductible from AGI in computing taxable income? Medical expenses, personal exemption, standard deduction, moving expenses, retirement savings, capital losses, net personal casualty losses, charitable contributions, alimony. _____

Answers

39. Section 262 disallows a deduction for all "personal, living, and family expenses" unless they are deductible under a specific statute. Most of Lee's living expenses (food, rent, etc.) will not be the subject of any statute allowing deduction. In any event, personal expenses (if deductible) would not be deductible on Lee's Schedule C as part of his business expenses, but elsewhere on his return (Schedule A). They also would be subject to all of the restrictions associated with these deductions. Incidentally, this is the kind of unreasonable return position that could result in penalties, even fraud charges, against Lee. See Chapter 1.

40. Dan is entitled to deduct *either* the standard deduction *or* the itemized deduction, but not both. In his case, because his itemized deduction of $12,000 is greater than the standard deduction, he should have deducted only the itemized deduction.

41. A deduction is a subtraction from income in computing taxable income, and its benefit to a taxpayer is equal to the taxpayer's tax rate multiplied by the amount of the deduction. A tax credit is a dollar-for-dollar reduction in a taxpayer's tax. Neither is absolutely "better" than the other, but a deduction does benefit higher income taxpayers (who are in a higher tax bracket) proportionately more than lower income taxpayers. By contrast, a tax credit generates the same dollar benefit for all taxpayers who are entitled to it.

42. Betty's purchase of equipment is a capital expenditure, not a deductible expense. Therefore, she cannot deduct it in the year of acquisition, but instead must recover the cost over time, through MACRS deductions. See Chapter 7.

43. Adjusted gross income is the amount computed by subtracting certain items from gross income. Tax is not imposed on AGI, but instead on taxable income, which is the amount computed by subtracting certain items from AGI.

44. *Deductible in computing AGI:* Moving expenses, retirement savings, capital losses, and alimony. *Deductible in computing taxable income*: personal exemption, standard deduction, personal casualty losses, charitable contributions, medical expenses, and net personal casualty losses.

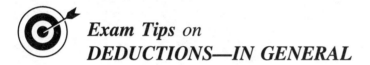

Exam Tips on *DEDUCTIONS—IN GENERAL*

Deduction questions involve an outflow of value from the taxpayer in question to another person.

☛ *Look for:* The taxpayer paying someone else for something, in cash or property, or experiencing some other outflow, as in a loss.

☛ *Analyze:* Is this item deductible? If so, how much is deductible?

If something is deductible, is it a deduction from gross income in computing adjusted gross income (an above-the-line deduction)? Or, is it deductible from AGI in computing taxable income (a below-the-line deduction)? Make sure you understand why the distinction is important.

☛ Deductions are construed narrowly. If in doubt, deny the deduction.

☛ The allowance of a deduction is not the whole story. *When* will it be deductible? (See Chapter 11.)

☛ Some outlays involve either deductions or credits—or both.

   ☞ Be ready to explain which is more valuable to the taxpayer. A credit is a dollar-for-dollar reduction in tax, so it is usually more valuable, while a deduction is potentially worth the marginal tax rate of the taxpayer multiplied by the amount of the deduction.

   ☞ *Remember:* A taxpayer cannot claim a credit and a deduction for the same dollar of outlay.

CHAPTER 6

PERSONAL DEDUCTIONS

ChapterScope ─────────────────────────────────

As discussed in the previous chapter, personal expenses are generally nondeductible. However, the Code allows deductions for a limited number of personal expenses. Some of these deductions constitute subtractions from gross income in computing adjusted gross income (AGI); others form part of the itemized deduction, which a taxpayer may claim in lieu of the standard deduction. This chapter discusses the specific requirements for deductibility of personal expenses.

- **Deductions in computing AGI:** A taxpayer may claim certain deductions from gross income in computing AGI. These include deductions for alimony paid, for qualifying moving expenses, for certain retirement savings, and for nonbusiness bad debts.

- **Standard deduction:** The standard deduction is a statutorily fixed amount that depends on the taxpayer's filing status.

- **Itemized deduction:** In lieu of the standard deduction, the taxpayer may claim the itemized deduction, which is the sum of a number of deductions. These include the deduction for qualified residence interest, for certain investment interest, for state and local income and property taxes, for extraordinary casualty losses, for certain medical expenses, and for qualifying charitable contributions. Certain miscellaneous expenses are also deductible if they exceed 2% of a taxpayer's AGI. A taxpayer's itemized deduction may be limited if his or her AGI exceeds a threshold amount.

- **Personal exemption:** A taxpayer is entitled to claim a personal exemption for him- or herself, a spouse (if filing jointly), and for any qualifying dependents.

I. WHERE ARE WE?

In calculating his or her taxable income, a taxpayer can claim a deduction for certain expenses. In the individual income tax course, personal deductions (as opposed to business deductions) are especially important. This chapter identifies these personal deductions in two categories: those that are deductible from gross income in computing AGI (above-the-line deductions) and those that are deductible from AGI in computing taxable income (below-the-line deductions).

II. ABOVE-THE-LINE AND BELOW-THE-LINE DEDUCTIONS

The first set of personal deductions discussed here are deductions subtracted from gross income in computing AGI, called in the trade "above-the-line" deductions. All other deductions are "below-the-line" deductions, meaning that they are deductible from AGI in computing taxable income. Taxpayers generally prefer above-the-line deductions because they reduce AGI, which in turn potentially increases certain itemized deductions (such as medical expenses) that use a percentage of AGI as a measure of deductibility.

III. ALIMONY

A. General rule

Section 215 allows a taxpayer a deduction for the amount of *alimony* or separate maintenance paid during the taxable year. This constitutes a deduction from gross income in computing AGI.

B. Definitional issue—Alimony

Alimony and "separate maintenance payments" are defined in §71. See discussion of alimony at Chapter 3(VI).

C. Special rule—Front-end loaded alimony

If alimony is front-end loaded, the payor must include the excess alimony payment in gross income in the third post-separation year. IRC §71(f)(1)(A). See discussion at Chapter 3(VI).

D. Related material

1. **Inclusion:** The recipient of alimony must include it in his or her gross income. IRC §71(a). See discussion at Chapter 3(VI).

2. **Child support:** Child support payments are neither deductible by the payor nor includable to the recipient. IRC §71(c). See discussion at Chapter 4(XI).

3. **Property settlements:** Transfers of property between spouses or ex-spouses pursuant to a divorce generally produce neither gain nor loss to the parties. IRC §1041(a). See discussion at Chapter 10(V).

E. Summary

The payor of alimony may claim a deduction for the amount paid during the taxable year. IRC §215.

Example: Calvin pays $1,000 per month to Melissa pursuant to their divorce decree. The $1,000 meets the requirements of the federal definition of alimony. Calvin may deduct $12,000 per year as alimony in computing his AGI.

IV. MOVING EXPENSES

A. General rule

Section 217 allows a deduction for certain moving expenses incurred by a taxpayer in connection with moving to a new place of employment. The taxpayer's new place of work must be at least 50 miles farther from his or her former residence than his or her former workplace was from that residence. This is a deduction from gross income in computing AGI. See IRC §217(a).

B. Definitional issues

1. **Moving expenses:** Expenses that may be deducted include the expenses of moving household goods and personal effects and of traveling to the new locale, but do not include meals. IRC §217(b)(1)(A), (B).

2. **Employment:** Employment includes self-employment for a sole proprietor or a partner in a partnership. IRC §217(f)(1), (2).

3. **Distance requirement:** The taxpayer's new place of work must be at least 50 miles farther from his or her former residence than his or her former work was from that residence. The taxpayer's commuting distance must have increased by at least 50 miles. Special rules apply for taxpayers with more than one place of work.

Example: Karen is employed in downtown Chicago. She commutes five miles to work in the city. She moves outside the city and takes a job with a new employer who is located 60 miles from her former employer. She will qualify for the moving expenses deduction because her commuting distance has increased by 55 miles, which is greater than the 50-mile distance minimum.

C. **Related material—Coordination with §132: Employer reimbursement**

If an employer reimburses an employee for all or a portion of the moving expenses, the employee will be able to exclude the reimbursement as a fringe benefit under §132. Any unreimbursed portion of otherwise qualifying expense would qualify for deduction under §217.

Example: Cliff, currently working in Boston, accepts a new job in Los Angeles. He incurs $7,000 in qualifying expenses of moving to California. His new employer reimburses him for $5,000 of these expenses. Cliff may exclude the $5,000 reimbursement from income (IRC §132) and may deduct the additional $2,000 from gross income in computing AGI (IRC §217).

D. **Summary**

A taxpayer may deduct certain qualifying moving expenses from gross income in computing AGI. IRC §217.

V. CONTRIBUTIONS TO REGULAR IRAs

An "Individual Retirement Account" (or IRA) is an account held in a bank, credit union, or brokerage firm for the benefit of a taxpayer to allow that taxpayer to save for retirement. Each year, the taxpayer may make a contribution to the IRA, which then earns interest or other earnings without tax as long as the funds are in the IRA. There are two kinds of IRAs: "regular IRAs" and "Roth IRAs." Section 219 allows a taxpayer to claim a deduction in computing AGI only for certain contributions to regular IRAs, not Roth IRAs. When the taxpayer withdraws amounts from a regular IRA, the amount that represents untaxed earnings is included in the taxpayer's gross income. When a taxpayer withdraws amounts from a Roth IRA, no amount is included in gross income.

A. **Contributions limited to earned income**

A taxpayer's maximum annual contribution to an IRA is the lesser of a specified dollar amount or the taxpayer's earned income (salary, wages, and consulting fees, for example). IRC §219(b)(1). A taxpayer may contribute the maximum amount, divided between a regular IRA and a Roth IRA as the taxpayer chooses, subject to certain income limitations applicable to Roth IRAs, but the taxpayer cannot exceed the annual maximum amount. The maximum dollar amount is scheduled to increase over time, as follows:

Year	Maximum Contribution (*Sunset 12/31/2010*)
2005–2007	$4,000
2008 and thereafter	$5,000 (indexed for inflation)

In addition, taxpayers who have attained age 50 in a particular year may contribute an additional $500 per year in 2005 and an additional $1,000 per year in the years 2006 and thereafter. (*Sunset 12/31/2010*)

B. Spousal IRA

A contribution may be made for a nonworking spouse if the spouses file a joint return, and the total earned income is at least equal to the contribution for both. IRC §219(c)(1), (2).

C. Participation in qualified plan

If the individual participates in an employer-sponsored qualified plan, the deductible amount will be reduced as AGI rises. When such a taxpayer's AGI reaches $60,000 (single) or $80,000 (joint return) (in 2005), the taxpayer cannot make a deductible contribution. IRC §219(g)(1), (2). The taxpayer may, however, make a nondeductible contribution to the regular IRA.

VI. LOSSES

Although §165(a) allows a taxpayer to claim a deduction for all "losses not compensated for by insurance or otherwise," §165(c) imposes significant limitations on the deductibility of losses for individuals.

A. Definition—Loss

A loss is an event that makes the taxpayer economically worse off than he or she was before the event. A loss must be realized, i.e., there must be a realization event that fixes the loss (see Chapter 9(III)(B)) and there must be no reasonable likelihood that the taxpayer will recoup or recover the loss.

B. Three types of deductible losses

Section 165(c) allows individuals to deduct only three types of losses.

1. **Trade or business losses:** Individuals may deduct losses incurred in a trade or business. IRC §165(c)(1). These losses result from a trade or business activity in which expenses exceed income but may be subject to certain restrictions under §§465 and 469. See generally Chapter 7 and Chapter 11(VII).

2. **Investment losses:** Individuals may deduct losses incurred in activities entered into for profit, even if the activity does not rise to the level of a trade or business. IRC §165(c)(2). This category includes losses from rental and royalty-generating activities, as well as losses on the sale or exchange of capital assets, such as real property, stocks, and other types of property. See generally Chapters 7, 9, 10, and 12.

3. **Personal casualty losses:** Individuals may deduct (generally as an itemized deduction) loss incurred in fire, storm, shipwreck, theft, or other casualty. See IRC §165(c)(3) and discussion at this Chapter, section VI(B)(3). Personal casualty losses are deductible from gross income to the extent of personal casualty gains. Any remaining losses (net casualty losses) are potentially deductible as part of the itemized deduction.

VII. INTEREST ON EDUCATION LOANS *(*Sunset 12/31/2010)*

A. General rule

Section 221 allows a taxpayer to deduct a certain amount of interest paid on any qualified education loan. This is a deduction from gross income in computing AGI. See IRC §221(a). The maximum amount of interest that can be deducted is $2,500 and is subject to a limitation based on modified adjusted gross income (MAGI).

B. Definitional issues

1. **Qualified education loan:** A qualified education loan is a debt incurred by a taxpayer that is incurred solely to pay qualified education expenses of the taxpayer or his or her spouse or dependents. The expenses must be paid within a reasonable time after the loan is incurred. The recipient must be receiving education as an eligible student.

2. **Eligible student:** The student must be an enrolled student at an acceptable college, university, or trade school.

3. **Qualified higher education expenses:** These include most of the costs of attending college, university, or trade school, including books, fees, tuition, room, board, equipment, and necessary expenses, including transportation.

4. **MAGI:** The deduction is subject to a limitation based on modified adjusted gross income. This is AGI, not considering the deduction for interest on education loans, with certain adjustments. These adjustments put back into AGI certain amounts that have been excluded or deducted under other Code provisions. To calculate MAGI for this purpose, start with AGI, and then:

■ **Add amounts excluded for:**

Social Security benefits (IRC §86)

Interest on U.S. savings bonds used for education (IRC §135)

Adoption expense assistance (IRC §137)

Certain foreign earned income (IRC §§911 and 931)

■ **Add deductions allowable for:**

Retirement savings (IRC §219)

Qualified higher education expenses (IRC §222)

C. Special rule—MAGI limitation

As modified adjusted gross income increases, this deduction is phased out. For single taxpayers, the phase-out begins at MAGI of $50,000 and when MAGI rises to $65,000 (in 2005) the entitlement to the deduction is completely eliminated. For joint filers, the corresponding amounts are $105,000 and $135,000 (in 2005). To determine the reduction amount, multiply the maximum allowable deduction (the lesser of $2,500 or the interest paid) by a fraction. The numerator of the fraction is MAGI minus $50,000 (for single taxpayers) or $105,000 (for joint filers). The denominator is $15,000 for single taxpayers and $30,000 for joint filers. The reduction amount is subtracted from the otherwise allowable amount to produce the deductible interest.

Example: Sabrina, a single taxpayer, pays $3,000 of interest on a qualified education loan for higher education expenses for her daughter Terri. Sabrina's AGI is $57,000, and she is entitled to claim a $3,000 deduction for an IRA contribution and $2,000 for an exclusion for employer-provided qualified adoption expenses. She will be entitled to a reduced deduction for interest on education loans of $500, calculated as follows:

- **Step One: Calculate MAGI.** Sabrina's AGI of $57,000 is increased by $5,000, i.e., $3,000 of retirement savings and $2,000 of adoption assistance. Therefore, her MAGI is $62,000.

- **Step Two: Apply the MAGI limitation.** Although Sabrina had $3,000 of education interest, she can only potentially deduct the maximum statutory amount ($2,500). Because Sabrina's MAGI is greater than the phase-out threshold, the amount of the deduction will be limited. To determine the amount of the reduction, multiply the maximum education interest ($2,500) by a fraction, the numerator of which is the amount by which her MAGI exceeds the threshold phase-out amount and the denominator of which is $15,000 (because she is a single taxpayer).

$$\$2,500 \times \frac{(62,000 - 50,000)}{15,000} = 2,500 \times 12/15 = \$2,000$$

Thus, the reduction amount is $2,000, so her maximum deduction will be $500 ($2,500 − $2,000).

D. Related material—Coordination with other education provisions

The amount expended for educational expenses must be reduced by any amount received as a scholarship, or which are excluded from gross income under IRC §127 (employer assistance), §135 (interest on U.S. savings bonds used for education), §529 (qualified tuition programs), or §530 (education savings account distributions). For a chart comparing the various educational incentive provisions, see Chapter 16(III)(D).

E. Summary

Taxpayers may take a deduction from gross income in computing AGI for up to $2,500 of interest on certain loans for education, subject to restrictions tied to income.

VIII. QUALIFIED EDUCATION EXPENSES *(*Sunset 12/31/2005)*

A. General rule

A taxpayer may claim a deduction for certain qualified education expenses paid during the year for education for the taxpayer or his or her spouse or dependents. IRC §222. The maximum amount that may be claimed is $4,000 in 2005. This provision is subject to a phase-out depending on modified AGI. Single taxpayers with AGI, as modified, of $65,000 or more are not entitled to the deduction; for joint filers, the phase-out amount is $130,000. This is a deduction subtracted from gross income in computing AGI.

B. Definitional issues

1. **Qualified education expenses:** Qualified tuition and related expenses are tuition and fees required to be paid to the enrolling institution for the enrollment or attendance of the taxpayer,

the taxpayer's spouse, or any dependent for whom the taxpayer is entitled to deduct a dependency exemption, at an eligible educational institution. Amounts paid for room and board, transportation, or similar personal expenses do not qualify. See IRC §25A.

2. **Adjusted gross income:** AGI is modified to add back the exclusion for certain foreign earned income (IRC §§911 and 931).

C. Related Material—Coordination with other educational incentives

If a deduction or exclusion is claimed for any expense under any other Code section, it cannot qualify for this deduction. IRC §222(c)(1). For a chart comparing various educational incentives, see Chapter 16(III)(D).

D. Summary

Taxpayers may claim a deduction in computing AGI for amounts expended for tuition and fees for higher education, subject to certain limitations based on income.

IX. CERTAIN CONTRIBUTIONS TO MEDICAL ACCOUNTS

Alarming increases in the costs of medical care and health insurance motivated Congress to establish two kinds of savings accounts for medical needs: the "Archer Medical Savings Account" (Archer MSA) and the "Health Savings Account" (HSA). Using either vehicle, a taxpayer may make deductible contributions, earnings grow tax-free, and qualifying distributions are excluded from the gross income of the taxpayer. Archer MSAs are less useful than HSAs because of the sunset provisions applicable to Archer MSAs. This discussion will focus on HSAs.

A. General rule

An eligible taxpayer may claim a deduction from gross income in computing AGI for the amount he or she contributes to an HSA, but the total contribution cannot exceed an amount based on the deductible of the taxpayer's health insurance or $2,650 (self-only coverage) or $5,250 (family coverage), whichever is less. IRC §223(a), (b)(1),(2).

B. Definitional issues

1. **Eligible individual:** To be eligible, the taxpayer must be covered under a "high deductible" health plan, which is a health plan with a deductible higher than $1,000 but less than $5,100 (self-only coverage in 2005) or for family coverage, between $2,000 and $10,200. IRC §223(c)(1). The taxpayer may not be eligible for Medicare. IRC §223(b)(7). While the taxpayer cannot have other health insurance, certain kinds of supplemental insurance—such as long-term care insurance—are disregarded. IRC §223(c)(3).

2. **Qualifying account:** The account must be established with a bank or other approved institution, and may only accept contributions in cash. The funds in the account can only be used for payment of qualified medical expenses of the taxpayer or his or her spouse and dependents. The account must be nonforfeitable, i.e., there must be no circumstances in which the taxpayer would have to give amounts in the account to someone else (other than a family member for medical expenses).

3. **Qualified medical expenses:** Distributions may only be used for these expenses, which are those described in IRC §213(d).

C. **Special rules and exceptions**

1. **Monthly determination:** Because health insurance is usually provided on a monthly basis, the amount a taxpayer may contribute also is determined on a monthly basis. A taxpayer may contribute and deduct one-twelfth of the annual deductible for any month he or she is eligible to make contributions. IRC §223(b)(2).

   Example: Matt has self-only coverage under a high deducible health plan with a deductible of $3,000 for the months of January through March of Year One. His coverage terminates in April. His maximum contribution to the plan is one-twelfth of the annual deductible ($250) for three months, or $750.

2. **Excise tax:** Amounts not used for medical expenses are included in gross income and a 10% excise tax is imposed on these distributions. IRC §223(f)(4).

D. **Related material**

1. **Distributions excluded from gross income:** Distributions from HSAs to pay for qualified medical expenses are excluded from gross income. IRC §223(f)(1). See Chapter 4(V)(B).

2. **Amounts grow tax-free within HSA account:** Earnings on investments in HSAs are not subject to tax. IRC §223(e)(1).

3. **Exclusion or deduction, not both:** If an employer establishes an HSA for employees, and makes contributions to it, these contributions are excluded from gross income of the employee, and cannot generate a deduction for the employee. The employee can only claim the deduction if he or she contributes to the account.

4. **Coordination with IRC §213:** Amounts paid from or distributed from an HSA may not generate an itemized deduction under IRC §213. The definitions under §213 govern what qualifies as a medical expense for which distributions can be used.

E. **Summary**

The potential benefit of an HSA is significant: it allows a taxpayer an above-the-line deduction for saving for health care expenses and the taxpayer can use these savings in any subsequent year without including distributions in gross income.

X. COSTS INCURRED IN CIVIL RIGHTS ACTIONS

Amounts received as damages for nonphysical injuries are includable in gross income. See Chapter 4(V). The costs of pursuing these claims—principally attorneys' fees—are deductible. Prior to the 2004 Act, these were deductible, if at all, as itemized deductions. The 2004 Act added an above-the-line deduction for attorneys' fees and court costs incurred by or on behalf of an individual in connection with any claim for unlawful discrimination and certain other federal claims. IRC §62(a)(19), (e).

XI. THE CHOICE: STANDARD OR ITEMIZED DEDUCTION

A taxpayer must choose either the standard or the itemized deduction. A sensible taxpayer will, of course, choose the larger of the two.

A. The standard deduction

1. **Basic amount:** The basic standard deduction is set forth in Figure 6A—Basic Standard Deduction. Standard deduction amounts are indexed for inflation.

Figure 6A
Basic Standard Deduction

Filing Status	2005 Amounts
Single taxpayers	$5,000
Married filing jointly	$10,000
Head of household	$7,300
Married filing separately	$5,000

2. **Additional amounts:** An elderly or blind taxpayer receives an additional amount of between $1,000 and $1,250 (in 2005) depending on his or her circumstances. IRC §63(c)(3).

B. The itemized deduction

When someone says that a taxpayer "itemizes," it means that he or she has decided to forego the standard deduction and claim the itemized deduction, which is the total of a group of deductions listed on Schedule A to the Form 1040, subject to various limitations. All of the deductions discussed in the following sections are itemized deductions.

C. Limitation on itemized deductions

If a taxpayer's AGI exceeds an "applicable amount," the overall itemized deduction will be reduced.

1. **Reduction:** The amount of the reduction is the lesser of (1) 3% of the excess of AGI over the applicable amount, or (2) 80% of the amount of the itemized deductions otherwise allowable. IRC §68(a).

2. **Applicable amount:** The applicable amount is $145,950 ($72,975 for married, filing separately) (in 2005) and is adjusted for inflation each year. IRC §68(b).

3. **Certain deductions not limited:** Certain itemized deductions will not be limited by this rule, including medical expenses (IRC §213, discussed at this chapter, §(XV)), investment interest (IRC §163(d), discussed at this chapter, (XII)(C)), and personal casualty or theft losses (IRC §165(c)(3), discussed at this chapter, (XIV)). IRC §68(c).

4. **Phase-out repeal scheduled** (*Sunset 12/31/2010*)**:** This limitation is scheduled for gradual repeal. In 2006–2007, a taxpayer will compute his or her limitation under the rules described above, and then will multiply this by two-thirds to obtain his or her actual limitation. In 2008–2009, the taxpayer will compute his or her limitation, then will multiply this by one-third to obtain his or her actual limitation. In 2009-2010, no limitation will apply. Unless Congress acts, the limitation will be put back into effect on 1/1/2011.

XII. INTEREST—§163

A. In general

Section 163(a) allows a deduction for interest paid or accrued during the taxable year. (For a discussion of the definition of interest, see Chapter 3(V)(C).) For interest other than trade or business interest, this is an itemized deduction. Section 163 also imposes significant restrictions on the deductibility of interest, for taxpayers other than corporations.

B. No deduction for personal interest

No deduction is allowed for "personal interest" paid by an individual. IRC §163(h)(1). Personal interest is interest other than trade or business interest, investment interest, qualified residence interest, and passive activity interests. Common examples of personal interest include:

- interest on credit card debt incurred for personal purposes,

- interest on car loans for cars not used for business purposes, and

- interest on loans (not secured by a personal residence) the proceeds of which are used for personal purposes.

C. Investment interest—§163(d)

1. **General rule:** For taxpayers other than corporations, the deduction for investment interest is limited to the ***net investment income*** of the taxpayer for the year. IRC §163(d)(1). If this limitation prevents the deduction of an amount of interest, the disallowed portion is carried forward and treated as incurred by the taxpayer in the next year. In that year, the same limitation and carryforward rules apply. IRC §163(d)(2). There is no time restriction on the carryforward.

2. **Definitional issues**

   a. **Investment interest:** Investment interest is interest on a debt the proceeds of which are used to acquire "property held for investment." IRC §163(d)(3)(A).

   b. **Property held for investment:** Property held for investment is property that produces dividends, interest, annuities, or royalties other than in the course of a trade or business. IRC §163(d)(5)(A).

   c. **Net investment income:** Net investment income is the excess (if any) of investment income over investment expenses. IRC §163(d)(4)(A).

i. **Investment income:** Investment income includes dividends, interest, royalties, etc. produced by property held for investment. IRC §163(d)(4)(B).

ii. **Investment expenses:** Investment expenses are all the deductions, except interest deductions, directly connected with holding property for investment, e.g., safe deposit box rental. IRC §163(d)(4)(C).

Example: Shikha takes out a $10,000 loan at 8% to purchase shares of stock in ABC Corporation, which is traded on the NASDAQ. In the first year of ownership, she receives $500 in dividend income and pays $800 in interest to her lender. She has no expenses associated with ownership of the shares. Because the interest is investment interest (it was used to purchase investment property, the shares), her interest deduction is limited to $500, the net investment income from the shares. The disallowed $300 in interest expense will be carried forward to the next year and may be deducted at that time, subject to the same limitation.

3. **Related material:** The recipient of the interest must include it in gross income, regardless of the limitation imposed on deduction by the payor. IRC §61(a)(4). See discussion at Chapter 3(V)(C). According to the legislative history of the 1986 Act, the investment interest rules are applied *after* the 2% floor on miscellaneous itemized deductions imposed by IRC §68(a). This means that investment expenses are first subject to the 2% floor rules, and only investment expenses that are allowable after application of that rule may be used in computing net investment income. However, in determining the disallowance imposed by IRC §68, expenses other than interest are to be disallowed first.

Example: Tony has AGI of $50,000 and itemizes. He has $3,000 of investment income, and the following expenses: $1,000 in investment interest; $900 in unreimbursed employee business expenses; and $700 in other allowable miscellaneous expenses subject to the 2% floor which are associated with his investment activities. Two percent of his AGI is $1,000, so his $1,600 of items subject to the 2% floor will result in a deduction of $600. The $900 in unreimbursed employee business expenses will be considered disallowed in full, and $100 of his other expenses will be disallowed. He will be entitled to use $600 of investment expenses to offset net investment income, as well as his entire $1,000 of investment interest.

4. **Summary:** The deduction for investment interest is limited to net investment income. IRC §165(d).

D. Home mortgage interest—§163(h)(3)

1. **General rule:** "Qualified residence interest" is deductible by taxpayers other than corporations. IRC §163(h)(3)(D).

2. **Definitional issues:** The key to understanding the general rule is understanding the definitions.

   a. **Qualified residence interest:** Qualified residence interest is any interest paid or incurred during the year on "acquisition indebtedness" or "home equity indebtedness" for any "qualified residence" of the taxpayer. IRC §163(h)(3)(A).

   b. **Acquisition indebtedness:** In order for a debt to qualify as acquisition indebtedness, it must meet three requirements.

   i. Use of funds: The indebtedness must be incurred to acquire, construct, or substantially improve any qualified residence. IRC §163(h)(3)(B)(i)(I).

   ii. Security: The qualified residence must secure the indebtedness. IRC §163(h)(3)(B)(i)(II).

   iii. Amount: A taxpayer's aggregate amount of acquisition indebtedness cannot exceed $1,000,000. IRC §163(h)(3)(B)(ii).

   Example: Carla purchases her principal residence for $250,000, paying cash of $50,000 and incurring a mortgage of $200,000. She may deduct the interest on the mortgage because it qualifies as acquisition indebtedness—debt incurred to acquire a principal residence.

c. Home equity indebtedness: In order for a debt to qualify as home equity indebtedness, it must not be acquisition indebtedness, and it must meet three requirements.

   i. Equity: The indebtedness must not exceed the fair market value of the residence minus the acquisition indebtedness on the residence. IRC §163(h)(3)(C)(i)(I), (II).

   ii. Security: A qualified residence must secure the indebtedness. IRC §163(h)(3)(C)(i)(I), (II).

   iii. Amount: A taxpayer's aggregate amount of home equity indebtedness cannot exceed $100,000. IRC §163(h)(3)(C)(ii).

   Example: Debra owns a home with a fair market value of $100,000, which is subject to a mortgage of $60,000. The local bank offers her an arrangement whereby she obtains a credit line of up to 90% of the equity in her home if she places her home as security for the credit. She takes advantage of this arrangement and draws on credit of $25,000. The interest on the credit of $25,000 is deductible as home equity indebtedness because it meets the three requirements: It does not exceed the equity in Debra's home; it is secured by the home; and it does not exceed $100,000.

d. Qualified residence: The qualified residence of a taxpayer is the principal residence of the taxpayer and one other residence designated by the taxpayer that the taxpayer uses for at least two weeks for personal purposes during the year. IRC §163(h)(4)(A)(i)(I), (II).

Example: Aubrey uses his home in Dallas as his principal residence. He also owns two vacation homes, one in Vail and one in Florida, and typically spends about three weeks at each vacation home during the year. All three homes have mortgages on them. Aubrey's principal residence is a qualified residence, and Aubrey will be allowed to designate one of his vacation homes as a qualified residence if he spends at least two weeks there during the year.

3. Special rules and exceptions

a. Construction loans: In a construction loan, the taxpayer typically receives temporary financing for the construction period and replaces that loan with a permanent mortgage (known as permanent financing) once the residence is completed. Because the taxpayer cannot occupy a residence under construction, the question arises whether construction financing will produce qualified residence interest. The regulations solve this problem by allowing a residence under construction to be treated as a qualified residence for the 24 months ending on the date on which the residence is ready for occupancy. Reg. §1.163-10T(p)(5)(i).

b. **Refinancing:** In a refinancing transaction, a taxpayer seeks a new loan to replace his or her old one. Although the new loan may be in the same amount as the old one, it is often the case that the new loan's face amount exceeds the balance of the old loan. The refinanced portion can qualify as acquisition indebtedness but only in the amount of the original loan balance at the time of refinancing. IRC §163(h)(3)(B)(i)(I), (II). Any amount in excess of the acquisition indebtedness may qualify as home equity indebtedness up to the $100,000 limit on the aggregate amount of home equity indebtedness. IRC §163(h)(3)(C)(i), (ii).

Example: Andy's principal residence has a fair market value of $250,000. He originally purchased it for $175,000, by paying cash of $50,000 and obtaining a mortgage of $125,000. Over the five years since purchase, he has reduced the mortgage to $100,000. With interest rates dropping, Andy wishes to refinance his mortgage and also hopes to access some of the increased equity in his home. To that end, he arranges for a new loan in the amount of $225,000. With this new loan, he repays the original mortgage of $100,000 and uses the additional $125,000 for personal purposes.

Of the new $225,000 loan, only $200,000 generates qualified residence interest. The refinancing of the original mortgage is acquisition indebtedness but only in the amount of $100,000, the debt existing at the time of refinancing. The additional $125,000 might qualify as home equity indebtedness because it is equal to the difference between the fair market value of the home ($250,000) and the amount of acquisition indebtedness on the home ($100,000). But the dollar limitation applies to limit home equity indebtedness to $100,000. The interest on the remaining $25,000 of the mortgage is not deductible.

c. **Points:** Points are essentially prepaid interest, paid to a lender in the year a loan is closed to obtain a lower interest rate. Taxpayers want to deduct points in the year of payment, and may do so, provided a number of requirements are met. The IRS has established a safe harbor, so that taxpayers may deduct points paid during a year if the following five requirements are met: (1) the points must be paid in cash in connection with the acquisition of the taxpayer's principal residence; (2) the closing statement must clearly designate the amount to be paid as "points," "loan origination fees," "loan discount," or "discount points"; (3) the points must be computed as a percentage of the stated principal amount of the loan; (4) the points charged must conform with general practice in the area; and (5) the points must be paid from cash provided at closing or in escrow, i.e., they must not be incorporated into the loaned sum. Rev. Proc. 94-27, 1994-1 C.B. 613. Points that do not fall within this safe harbor may still qualify, but the burden will be on the taxpayer to show that the amounts paid are truly prepaid interest rather than some other fee associated with the lending transaction.

4. **Related material:** For a discussion of gain or loss on the sale of a principal residence, see Chapters 4(VIII), for a discussion of trade or business interest, see Chapter 7(IV)(A).

5. **Summary:** See Statute Summary—§163(h): Qualified Residence Interest.

Parsing Step	§163(h)
General rule	Taxpayers may deduct qualified residence interest paid or incurred during the taxable year
Definitional issues	Qualified residence interest: (1) acquisition indebtedness (2) home equity indebtedness
Special rules and exceptions	Dollar limits: $1,000,000 & $100,000 Construction rules Refinancing
Related material	Gain or loss on sale of residence: §§1001, 165(c), 121
Summary	Taxpayers may deduct qualified residence interest.

XIII. TAXES—§164

Section 164 allows a deduction for certain taxes incurred by an individual. The potentially deductible taxes include state, local, and foreign real property taxes; state and local personal property taxes; state, local, and foreign income taxes; and (only in 2004–2005, unless Congress acts to extend this provision) certain state sales taxes. See IRC §164. A taxpayer may elect to deduct either his or her state income taxes or state sales taxes, but not both. A taxpayer electing to deduct sales taxes will deduct either the actual amount or an amount based on IRS tables to be published plus extra sales taxes paid for large-ticket items, such as cars or boats. See IRC §164 (b)(5). Federal income taxes, federal estate, and certain other taxes are not deductible. IRC §275. In certain situations, a taxpayer may choose to claim a tax credit for foreign taxes paid. See generally Chapter 13.

XIV. CASUALTY LOSSES—§165(c)(3)

A. General rule

A "casualty" occurs when a taxpayer's property is destroyed in a fire, storm, or similar event, or is stolen. A casualty can produce a gain or a loss. For example, consider property that the taxpayer bought for $1,000, but which appreciated in value to $10,000. It is stolen and the taxpayer receives insurance proceeds of $10,000. That taxpayer would have a casualty *gain* of $9,000—the difference between the insurance proceeds and the taxpayer's cost of the property. (See discussion of IRC §1033 in Chapter 10(IV). That casualty gain must be included in gross income. If that same property were not insured, however, the taxpayer would have a casualty *loss* of $1,000, because the measure of loss is the *lesser* of the decrease in fair market value or the taxpayer's adjusted basis in the property. Reg. §1.165-7(b)(1).

Section 165(c)(3) allows individuals to claim as a deduction losses of property arising from casualty events such as fires or storms—or tsunamis—or from theft, but of course there are limitations and special rules. In particular, the loss must exceed $100 per event, so that the amount of any loss must first be reduced by $100 before any other rules are applied. IRC §165(h)(1). Think of this as a "deductible," removing from the calculation the many small losses of everyday life. Then, the treatment of casualty losses depends on the total casualty gains and losses of the taxpayer during the year.

1. **More gains than losses:** If a taxpayer's personal casualty gains exceed personal casualty losses for the year, both the gains and losses are treated as capital gains and capital losses. This allows the taxpayer to offset the gains (included in gross income) with the losses (deductible from gross income in computing AGI).

   Example: Dave experienced two casualties during the year. First, his antique car was stolen. His basis in the car was $20,000, and it had a fair market value of (and was insured for) $30,000. Second, his cherished Native American marriage basket with a fair market value and basis of $5,000 (which was uninsured) was stolen. In this situation, Dave has more personal casualty gains ($30,000 − $20,000 = $10,000) than losses ($4,900). He includes the gain in gross income as capital gain and is allowed a deduction for the casualty loss of $4,900 as a capital loss, so that his net figure is a capital gain of $5,100.

2. **More losses than gains:** If personal casualty losses exceed gains, the amount of loss equal to the amount of gain is allowed as a deduction from gross income in computing AGI. The balance is potentially an itemized deduction, but only to the extent this loss exceeds 10% of the taxpayer's AGI. IRC §165(h)(2)(A)(i), (ii).

   Example—No casualty gains: Lindsay's personal collection of antiques, worth $150,000, is destroyed when her storage facility burns to the ground. She had a basis in them of $50,000. She did not have insurance. Lindsay's AGI is $75,000. Lindsay may claim a casualty loss as an itemized deduction in the amount of $42,400, calculated as follows:

   - *Step 1:* Determine the loss: $50,000 (the lower of basis or decrease in value).

   - *Step 2:* Subtract the $100 limitation: $50,000 − $100 = $49,900.

   - *Step 3:* Subtract the 10% AGI limitation. Ten percent of AGI is $7,500. Subtract this from $49,900 to obtain $42,400.

   Lindsay may claim an itemized casualty loss deduction of $42,400.

   Example—Casualty gains and losses: Kathy experiences two casualty events during the year. In the first event, her horse, Two Egg, is killed by lightning. Two Egg's basis was $10,000, and he was insured for his fair market value of $40,000. In the second event, a Ming vase with a basis and value of $50,100 was stolen. The vase was not insured. Kathy's AGI (disregarding these events) is $50,000.

   - *Step 1:* Include in Kathy's gross income the personal casualty gain of $30,000 ($40,000 insurance proceeds minus Two Egg's basis of $10,000).

   - *Step 2:* Subtract as a deduction from gross income in computing AGI the personal casualty loss equal to the amount included in gross income as a personal casualty gain. Kathy's personal casualty loss is the loss from the Ming vase ($50,100) minus the $100 deductible. Thus her casualty loss is $50,000. Of this amount, $30,000 is subtracted as a deduction from gross income in computing AGI.

   - *Step 3:* Compute the itemized casualty loss deduction by applying the 10% limitation to the balance of the personal casualty loss. This amount will be deductible to the extent it exceeds 10% of AGI. Ten percent of Kathy's AGI of $50,000 is $5,000. The remaining balance of the casualty loss ($20,000) is deductible to the extent it exceeds $5,000; thus the itemized casualty loss deduction is $15,000.

Summary: Kathy will be allowed a deduction of $45,000 of the total $50,100 loss; $30,000 as offsetting casualty gains and $15,000 as an itemized deduction.

B. Definitional issues: Casualty loss

A casualty loss requires a complete or partial destruction of property from a sudden, unexpected, and unusual event. IRC §165(c)(3), (h)(3)(B). There must be no reasonable possibility of recoupment. In order to claim a loss, the taxpayer must file an insurance claim if the property is insured. IRC §165(h)(4)(E).

1. **Cat owners, beware!** *Dyer v. Commissioner,* **20 T.C.M. 705 (1961):** When the taxpayer's Siamese cat destroyed a vase during a neurotic fit, a deduction for a casualty loss for the vase was denied, as the fit was not "of the same character" as a fire, storm, or shipwreck.

2. **Suddenness requirement:** Termite damage and similar gradual deteriorations do not occur with sufficient "suddenness" to constitute a casualty. See, e.g., Rev. Rul. 63-232, 1963-2 C.B. 97; *Meersman v. United States,* 370 F.2d 109 (6th Cir. 1966).

3. **Theft—***Mary Frances Allen,* **16 T.C. 163 (1951):** Theft must be proven, and the taxpayer bears the burden of proof. Merely losing an item of property does not generate a casualty loss. A theft occurs in the year of discovery.

4. **Corporate wrongdoing:** Some taxpayers have tried to claim a casualty loss when publicly traded stock they purchased for investment declined in value due to the wrongdoing of corporate officers. The courts and the IRS agree that no casualty loss exists in these circumstances. See, e.g., *Paine v. Commissioner,* 63 T.C. 736, *aff'd without published opinion* 523 F.2d 1053 (5th Cir. 1975).

C. Related material

1. **Casualty gain deferral:** For a discussion of the nonrecognition of gain on involuntary conversions, see Chapter 10(IV).

2. **Capital gains and losses:** For a discussion of the treatment of casualty gains and losses treated as capital gains and losses, see Chapter 12(III), (IV).

D. Summary

See Statute Summary—§165(h): Casualty Losses.

XV. MEDICAL EXPENSES—§213

A. General rule

Section 213 allows a deduction for medical expenses paid or incurred by the taxpayer for care of the taxpayer or his or spouse or dependents, to the extent these expenses exceed 7.5% of AGI. IRC §213(a). This is an itemized deduction.

Example: Lori's AGI is $45,000. This year she had medical bills of $25,000 associated with a complicated pregnancy. She is uninsured and paid this amount with her savings. To calculate

Statute Summary—§165(h)
Casualty Losses

Parsing Step	§165(h)
General rule	Taxpayers may claim an itemized deduction for net casualty losses incurred during the year.
Definitional issues	Casualty loss = fire, storm, shipwreck, etc.
Special rules and exceptions	Two limitations: $100 per event; losses 10% of adjusted gross income (AGI) Casualty losses deductible in computing AGI to extent of net casualty gain (treated as capital loss)
Related material	Net casualty gain includable in gross income: §61 Involuntary conversions: §1033
Summary	Taxpayers may claim a deduction for net casualty losses in excess of $100 per event and 10% of AGI.

Lori's deduction for medical expenses, subtract 7.5% of her AGI ($7.5\% \times 45,000 = \$3,375$) from her total medical expenses ($25,000). The result is her itemized medical expense deduction:

$$\$25,000 \text{ (medical expenses)} - \$3,375 \text{ (7.5\% of AGI)} = \$21,625$$

B. Definitional issues—Medical expenses

Medical expenses are expenditures for the diagnosis, cure, relief, or treatment of disease or bodily malfunction, for medical insurance, and for transportation and lodging while seeking care. IRC §213(d)(1)(A)-(C). See Figure 6B—Common Medical Expenses.

1. **Personal versus medical—*Ochs v. Commissioner*, 195 F.2d 692 (2d Cir. 1952):** Mrs. Ochs was very ill, and she and her husband enrolled their children in boarding school during her treatment and recovery. The Ochs family sought to deduct the boarding school tuition and fees as medical expenses.

   a. **Issue:** Were the tuition and fees for the children's boarding school medical expenses?

   b. **Result and rationale:** These expenses were personal expenses, not medical expenses. The expenses were made necessary not by the medical condition, but by the taxpayers' decision to have children.

2. **Cosmetic surgery:** Expenses of cosmetic surgery do not qualify as medical expenses unless the procedure is necessary to ameliorate a deformity arising from a congenital abnormality, a personal injury, or disfiguring disease. IRC §213(d)(9).

3. **Long-term care insurance:** Long-term care insurance is insurance to provide for the care of an individual who is chronically ill and needs assistance in daily activities. Medical expenses

includes a portion of the premiums paid for long-term care insurance. IRC §213(d)(10). In 2005, the amounts are as shown in the following table.

Attained Age Before the Close of the Taxable Year	Limitation on Premium Deduction
40 or less	$270
More than 40 but not more than 50	$510
More than 50 but not more than 60	$1,020
More than 60 but not more than 70	$2,720
More than 70	$3,400

4. Capital expenditures

a. In general: Expenditures for permanent improvements of a residence or for equipment may be medical expenses if specifically necessary for treatment of a medical condition. Reg. §1.213-1(e)(1)(iii).

Example: Patricia has a slipped disc in her back. After surgery her physician prescribed physical therapy and a special type of chair. Even though the expenditure for the chair constitutes a capital expenditure, it will probably still constitute a medical expense because it is medically necessary for the treatment of her condition.

b. Increases in value: If the improvement increases the value of the property, only the excess of the cost of the improvement over its effect on the increased value of the property will be considered a medical expense. *Hollander v. Commissioner,* 219 F.2d 934 (3d Cir. 1955).

Example—*Ramon Gerard,* 37 T.C. 826 (1962): Mr. Gerard's daughter had cystic fibrosis, and her doctor required her to restrict her daily activities to air-conditioned areas. The Gerards installed central air conditioning in their home and deducted the cost ($1,300) as a medical expense. The installation increased the value of the home by $800. Only the difference between the cost ($1,300) and the increased value ($800)—$500—is a medical expense qualifying for deduction.

C. Special rules and exceptions

1. Insurance: Amounts received as payments under insurance plans reduce a taxpayer's medical expenses. Reg. §1.213-1(a)(3)(ii). For example, a taxpayer who incurs $10,000 in medical expenses but receives an insurance reimbursement of $8,000 will consider only the unreimbursed $2,000 in applying the 7.5% limitation to compute his or her itemized medical expense deduction. Recall, however, that reimbursement from accident and health plans generally are not included in a taxpayer's gross income. See discussion at Chapter 4(IX)(D).

2. Child of divorced parents: Both divorced parents may treat their child as a dependent for purposes of claiming a deduction for the child's medical expenses. IRC §213(d)(5).

Figure 6B
Common Medical Expenses

Expenses	Deductible (subject to limit)	Nondeductible
Physicians, hospital, nursing fees	√	
Medical insurance premiums	√	
Nursing home fees	√	
Prescription medicines	√	
Nonprescription medicines		√
Chiropractor fees	√	
Physical therapy	√	
Dental fees: cleaning, filling, etc.	√	
Dental surgery	√	
Eyeglasses, contacts, exams	√	
Braces, splints, similar items	√	
Stop-smoking and similar classes	√	
Health club dues		√
Pregnancy-related health care	√	
Maternity clothing		√
Organ donor expenses	√	
Vasectomy expenses	√	
Abortion expenses	√	
Medical marijuana		√
Seeing eye and other service animals	√	
Doctor-prescribed weight loss programs	√	

D. Related material

1. **Health insurance premiums and proceeds:** A taxpayer may be able to exclude from gross income health insurance premiums paid by an employer and insurance reimbursements for expenses. See discussion at Chapter 4(IX)(D).

2. **Personal injury damages:** Compensation for certain personal injuries is excludable from gross income of the injured taxpayer. See discussion at Chapter 4(V).

3. **Health Savings Accounts:** Amounts distributed from HSAs to pay for medical expenses cannot generate a deduction under IRC §213. See IRC §223 and discussion, this chapter, Section IX.

XVI. CHARITABLE CONTRIBUTIONS—§170

A. General rule

Section 170 allows a taxpayer to claim as an itemized deduction charitable contributions made during the taxable year to qualifying charitable, educational, or religious organizations. IRC §170(a).

B. Definitional issues—Charitable contribution

1. **Charitable organization:** In order for a gift to be deductible, it must be made to a charitable organization.

    a. **Tax status:** Section 170(a) allows a deduction for contributions to certain entities, including the United States or a state or local instrumentality (if made for public purposes), and to religious, charitable, educational and similar organizations if no part of the net earnings of the organization inures to the benefit of any private shareholder or other individual. IRC §170(c).

    b. **Public policy—*Bob Jones University v. United States,* 461 U.S. 574 (1983):** Faced with the question whether a racially discriminatory private school could be a charitable organization, the Supreme Court concluded that a "charitable organization" is one that serves the public benefit and does not violate public policy. Racial discrimination was found to violate public policy, and therefore the organization was not charitable.

2. **Private benefit—*Ottawa Silica Co. v. United States,* 699 F.2d 1124 (Fed. Cir. 1983):** The taxpayer owned large parcels of real estate in a developing area. It donated a 70-acre site to the school district, knowing that the district would construct needed access roads that would make the taxpayer's remaining land more valuable. The taxpayer claimed a deduction for the fair market value of the land donated.

    a. **Issue:** Was the taxpayer entitled to a charitable deduction for the donated land?

    b. **Result and rationale:** No deduction was allowed because the taxpayer received a private benefit from donation of the land. A charitable donation assumes that the donor receives no benefit from the transfer. If the benefits received or expected to be received are substantial—i.e., greater than those inuring to the public from a charitable donation—the quid pro quo of the transfer removes it from the realm of deductibility.

3. **Development—*Hernandez v. Commissioner,* 490 U.S. 680 (1989) and Rev. Rul. 93-73, 1993-2 C.B. 75:** The Church of Scientology qualified as a charitable organization, so that donations to it were deductible by donors. Church of Scientology members pay fixed fees for "auditing," a religious process of becoming aware of one's spirituality through individual training with Church representatives. The IRS challenged the deductibility of such payments on the ground that they involved the receipt of a benefit.

   a. **Issue:** Are auditing fees paid to the Church of Scientology deductible?

   b. **Result and rationale:** The payments were not deductible because they constituted payment for services rendered rather than a donation.

      i. **Majority opinion:** The donors acknowledged that the payments were made for auditing but argued that the quid pro quo restriction should not apply to the receipt of a religious benefit. The Court found no such distinction in language of the statute or the development of the law in this area, and declined to advance it because of its implications for other types of purported donations.

      ii. **Dissent:** The dissent focused on the religious contribution exception, under which the IRS considers other types of payments for attendance at religious services (e.g., pew rents) as deductible contributions, rather than payments for services. According to the dissent, the majority's approach constituted discrimination against the Church of Scientology.

   c. **Rev. Rul. 93-73:** The IRS withdrew its prior ruling that payments for auditing by Church of Scientology members were nondeductible. It currently takes the position, contrary to *Hernandez,* that such payments are deductible.

C. Special rules and exceptions

1. **Amount:** The amount of the contribution is the amount of money or the fair market value of the property contributed. Reg. §1.170A-1(c)(1). The taxpayer must substantiate the value of contributed property and special rules apply to noncash donations such as vehicles or artwork.

   a. **Services:** There is no deduction for services performed for a charitable organization. Reg. §1.170A-1(g).

   b. **Expenses:** Unreimbursed expenses incurred on behalf of the charitable organization (including mileage, etc.) are deductible. Reg. §1.170A-1(g). The mileage rate, however, is 14¢ per mile (in 2005), rather than the higher business mileage rate.

   c. **Blood:** One cannot claim a deduction for the donation or sale of one's blood. *Lary v. United States,* 787 F.2d 1538 (11th Cir. 1986).

2. **Limitation for individuals:** The deduction for contributions by individuals is limited to a percentage of their contribution base.

   a. **Public charities—50%:** For organizations that qualify as public charities (generally schools, churches, governmental entities, and other publicly supported organizations), the limitation is 50% of the taxpayer's contribution base. IRC §170(b)(1)(A).

   b. **Private charities—30%:** For other organizations, the limitation is 30% of the taxpayer's contribution base. IRC §170(b)(1)(B).

    c. Definition—Contribution base: A taxpayer's contribution base is AGI computed disregarding the net operating loss deduction. IRC §170(b)(1)(F).

D. Related material

    1. Business expenses: For a discussion of the business expenses limitation for charitable contributions in excess of AGI limitation, see Chapter 7(II)(C).

    2. Tax-exempt organizations: While §170 allows a deduction for contributions to certain charitable organizations, §501 addresses the tax status of these entities themselves. Section 501 describes a number of organizations that are exempt from federal income tax, of which the most familiar are "§501(c)(3) organizations," which are religious, educational, or scientific entities.

E. Summary

A taxpayer is allowed an itemized deduction for the amount of cash and the fair market value of property donated to a qualifying charitable organization. For individuals the deduction is limited to 50% of AGI (less NOL carrybacks) for public charities and 30% for private charities. Corporations are limited to 10% of taxable income computed with certain adjustments.

XVII. MISCELLANEOUS EXPENSES—2% FLOOR

A number of expenses that comprise part of the itemized deduction are deductible only to the extent that, in the aggregate, they exceed 2% of the taxpayer's AGI. IRC §67(a). This is commonly referred to as "the 2% floor." Of these, the most important are employees' unreimbursed business expenses and expenses incurred in the production of income.

A. Employee business expenses

    1. Employees have a "trade or business": Employees are engaged in the trade or business of performing services for their employers. Thus, the ordinary and necessary expenses they incur (and are not reimbursed for) are deductible, but not on a Schedule C. Instead, these expenses are part of a taxpayer's itemized deduction, and are subject to the 2% floor.

    Example: Jill is a salesperson for Howdoyoudo, Inc., a dating introduction service. Her job involves a significant amount of travel and other expenses for which she is not reimbursed by her employer. In the year in question Jill's AGI was $150,000, and her expenses incurred as a salesperson were $75,000. Because Jill is engaged in the business of providing services to her employer, she may deduct her employment-related expenses, but only to the extent that these expenses exceed 2% of her AGI. Two percent of her AGI is $3,000, and thus she may deduct $72,000 of her expenses as an itemized deduction (assuming she has no other miscellaneous expenses).

    2. Allocation to the right activity: Because these expenses are itemized deductions subject to the 2% floor, taxpayers try to allocate them to a separate trade or business, in an attempt to fully deduct the expenses. The expense must be allocated to the event giving rise to the activity. For example, in *Test v. Commissioner,* unpublished opinion (9th Cir. 2002), a doctor who was an employee and also had a separate trade or business incurred legal fees and sought to allocate them to the trade or business in order to fully deduct them on her Schedule C. The court determined that the event giving rise to the need for legal advice related to the doctor's status as an employee rather than as the owner of the separate business. Thus, these expenses were an itemized deduction subject to the 2% floor.

3. **Common nonreimbursed employee business expenses:** Travel and entertainment; mileage; dues to professional associations; job search expenses in current occupation; home office deduction of an employee (see Chapter 8(V)), malpractice insurance premiums; equipment used in the business (see IRC §179 and discussion in Chapter 7(III)); clerical help; publications; and legal fees.

B. Investment expenses—§212

Section 212 allows a deduction for expenses associated with the production or collection of income, with the management or holding of property that produces income (but not in a trade or business), and with the collection or computation of tax. Commonly encountered expenses include:

- tax preparation or litigation fees; computer programs for tax preparation;

- safety deposit box fees;

- fees for investment advice;

- fees on brokerage accounts (but not commissions, which must be capitalized); tax advice; and

- attorneys' fees for nonbusiness lawsuits, unless covered under IRC §62(a)(19), discussed at this Chapter, Section (X).

XVIII. PERSONAL EXEMPTION—§151

A. Policy

The federal income tax is not intended to be levied on taxpayers who are at the subsistence level. Thus, the deduction for the personal exemption ensures that this amount goes untaxed.

B. How much?

1. **Basic amount:** The personal exemption is intended to approximate subsistence living expenses. For certain categories of taxpayers, it is increased to reflect their increased expenses. The personal exemption is set at $3,200 (in 2005) and increases with inflation.

2. **Phase-out:** The personal exemption is reduced as AGI rises above a certain level. If AGI exceeds a certain threshold amount, the exemption amount will be reduced by 2% for each $2,500 or a fraction thereof that AGI exceeds that threshold amount. IRC §151(d)(3)(A). For example, for 2005, the phase-out begins, and the exemption is completely phased out in the following fashion:

Filing Status	Phase-Out Begins	Phase-Out Ends
Married, filing jointly	$ 218,950	$341,450
Single	$145,950	$268,450

Example: Barbara and Wayne are married and file a joint return. Their AGI is $250,000. Without regard to the phase-out of personal exemptions, they would each be entitled to an exemption of $3,200 for 2005. However, because their AGI exceeds the threshold amount ($218,950), the exemption amount is reduced by 2% for each $2,500 or a fraction thereof that their income exceeds the threshold amount. As a result, their $6,400 combined personal exemption will be reduced to $4,736. This is because the excess of their AGI over the threshold amount is $31,050. This quantity divided by $2,500 results in 12.42, which is rounded to 13 and multiplied by 2% to obtain 26%. This is the reduction, i.e., a 26% reduction in the amount of personal exemptions to which Barbara and Wayne are entitled ($6,400 − (.26 × 6,400) = $4,763.

3. **Repeal of phase-out scheduled** *(*Sunset 12/31/2010)*: The phase-out of the personal exemptions is scheduled for repeal beginning in 2006. In 2006 and 2007, taxpayers will calculate their reduction, but reduce that reduction by one-third. In 2008 and 2009, taxpayers will reduce the reduction by two-thirds. In 2010 and thereafter, no reduction will occur. Unless Congress acts, however, the full reduction will come back into effect on 1/1/2011.

C. Dependents—Definition

The taxpayer receives an additional exemption for each "dependent." IRC §151(c)(1), (2). The Working Families Tax Relief Act of 2004 simplified the definition of dependent. A dependent is either a "qualifying child" or a "qualifying relative." IRC §152(a).

1. **Qualifying children:** These include the taxpayer's children and their descendants, stepchildren, or adopted children, but the child must be under age 19 (or if full-time students, age 24), who shares the taxpayer's principal abode for at least half the taxable year, and who does not provide more than half of their own support. IRC §152(c).

2. **Qualifying relatives:** These include most family members, including the taxpayer's spouse, children and their descendants (other than qualifying children), parents, siblings, aunts/uncles, and nieces/nephews, as well as others. A qualifying relative's gross income must be below the exemption amount, and the taxpayer must provide more than half the support of that individual. IRC §152(d).

3. **Ineligible individuals:** To be claimed as a dependent, the person cannot be married, filing a joint return and must not be a nonresident alien (unless domiciled in Mexico or Canada). If a person is claimed as a dependent on a taxpayer's return, that person is treated as having no dependents of his or her own. IRC §152(b).

4. **Divorced parents:** Generally, the custodial parent will claim the exemption, unless the parents otherwise agree that the noncustodial parent will claim the exemption, and certain conditions are met. IRC §152(e)(1).

XIX. WHERE ARE WE GOING?

This chapter has addressed personal deductions available to individuals. We now turn to the deductibility of business-related expenses, for both individuals and entities engaged in business activity.

Quiz Yourself on
PERSONAL DEDUCTIONS

45. Under the terms of their divorce decree, Tom will pay Nicole $10,000 per month as alimony and $1,200 per month as child support. Assume that the alimony meets the federal definition of alimony. May Tom deduct these payments? _____

46. Dorothy has AGI (without considering the following described events) of $200,000 for last year. During the year, her home in Kansas was destroyed by a tornado. The basis of the home was $250,000 and its fair market value was $500,000. Dorothy had no insurance on the home. What are the tax consequences of these events to Dorothy? _____

47. Assume the same facts as in the previous question, except that Dorothy also received $100,000 from an insurance company attributable to the theft of a very valuable pair of shoes. She had a basis of $20,000 in the shoes. What are the tax consequences to Dorothy, considering *both* events? _____

48. Avid whale watcher Molly decides to move to Seattle. She purchases a new principal residence on the ocean there for $1.5 million. She takes out a mortgage of $1.2 million from Friendly Bank, and pays for the balance in cash. She owns no other properties. May she deduct the interest on the debt? _____

49. Sam owns a parcel of property on which he has built a new home. During construction, he lived in a dilapidated home on the property. Under applicable land use regulations, only one home suitable for occupancy may exist on this parcel. Now that the new home is ready for its occupancy permit, Sam wants to donate the older home to the local fire department (a governmental unit) for a burning home exercise. By removing the old residence, the burning exercise will allow him to move into the new home. He intends to claim a deduction equal to the fair market value of the older home. May he do so? _____

50. Pete's hobby is auto racing. This year, he was in a car wreck and incurred $100,000 in medical expenses. His medical insurance company reimbursed $75,000 of these expenses this year, and he paid for the balance with a $10,000 distribution from a qualifying HSA and the rest with savings. His AGI is $250,000. May Pete deduct any of these medical expenses? _____

51. Tom locates, buys, and sells hard-to-find vinyl recordings for his employer, Oldies but Goodies, Inc. ("OBG"). Under the terms of his employment agreement, OBG will reimburse him for up to $2,500 of travel expenses associated with his sales activities. This year, Tom incurred $30,000 of such expenses, of which $2,500 were reimbursed by OBG. He also had $500 in other qualifying miscellaneous expenses. His AGI is $140,000. How should Tom treat these expenses? _____

52. Janet, a single taxpayer, has a complicated household. The following people live with her. Assume that none of these individuals plan to claim an exemption for themselves on their own tax return. For whom may she claim a personal exemption on her income tax return? _____

Her daughter, age 16;

Her son, age 23, a full-time college student who lives at college 9 months of the year;

Her stepdaughter from a prior marriage, age 18;

Her mother, age 86, who has Social Security benefits of $1,000 per month;

Her brother, who is currently unemployed;

A foster child, age 12;

Her single niece, age 30, who is visiting the United States for an extended period from her home in Mexico; and

An unrelated boarder, who pays Janet $1,200 month for room and board.

53. Mimi, a single taxpayer, is training to be an opera singer. In 2005, when her AGI was only $15,000, she paid $3,000 in tuition, books, and fees at an accredited university's singing program. She also paid an additional $2,000 for private singing lessons from an acclaimed teacher outside the university. Is any amount of these expenses deductible? _____

54. Catherine is employed by Hospital X, which has a qualified retirement plan in which she participates. Her AGI is $45,000. In 2005, Catherine would like to establish an IRA. May she do so, and if so, how much will be her contribution? _____

55. Donald tells Maurice: *"You're Fired!"* Maurice then incurs the following expenses: $10,000 in attorneys' fees in an unsuccessful attempt to sue his employer for breach of contract; $1,500 in job search expenses to obtain a similar position; $500 to a moving company to move his things out of his office at Donald's building; and $5,000 in psychological counseling to help him recover from this harrowing experience. Of these, which are deductible—and in what manner? What if Maurice says "I've had it with this business! I'm only going to take a job in a completely different profession . . ."? _____

Answers

45. IRC §215 allows Tom a deduction for alimony paid during the taxable year; this is a deduction from gross income in computing AGI. The child support is not deductible.

46. Dorothy's loss on her home is a personal casualty loss, in the amount of $250,000 (the lower of basis or value). However, personal casualty losses are subject to two limitations. First, in computing the deduction, each loss is reduced by $100. Second, personal casualty losses are deductible only to the extent they exceed 10% of AGI. Dorothy's AGI is $200,000, so the personal casualty loss of $249,900 is deductible to the extent it exceeds $20,000. Thus, her personal casualty loss is $229,900. This is a deduction on Dorothy's itemized return, i.e., available only to her if she itemizes, and therefore as a deduction from AGI in computing taxable income.

47. The theft of the shoes and receipt of the insurance proceeds is a constructive sale of that item, so Dorothy realizes $80,000 of gain on that transaction. This is a personal casualty gain. Personal casualty gains offset personal casualty losses, so that the net result is the net personal casualty gain (income) or net personal casualty loss (deduction). The net loss is $249,900 minus $80,000, or $169,900. To the extent this exceeds $20,000 (10% of Dorothy's AGI) it is deductible. Thus, $149,900 is deductible on Dorothy's itemized return, i.e., available only to her if she itemizes, and therefore as a deduction from AGI in computing taxable income.

48. Assuming that the property secures the debt, the interest on the acquisition indebtedness, up to $1,000,000 of debt, is deductible. Molly also may deduct the interest on an additional amount of debt ($100,000) as home equity indebtedness. The remaining interest will be nondeductible.

49. Sam is attempting to take a charitable deduction under §170 of the Code. Normally, a deduction for the fair market value of the property would be available to him (and it would be his burden to prove the value). However, in this case, Sam appears to be receiving something of value. Without the burn, he would be in violation of the land use laws, and would have to remove the older home in some way to make way for the new home. By donating the home, he avoids this cost and places his property in compliance with local law. Although this is a close case, Sam probably is not entitled to a deduction for this donation. However, if Sam could show that the costs of removal were nominal, he may be able to claim a deduction for the property donation.

50. The amount Pete received as reimbursement for medical expenses is not included in his gross income (see Chapter 3). The $10,000 distribution from the HSA is not includable in his gross income. The remaining $15,000 is deductible as an itemized deduction as medical expenses to the extent it exceeds 7.5% of his AGI. This 7.5% of AGI is $18,750, and because his remaining expenses are less than that amount, Pete may not deduct any amount as medical expenses as an itemized deduction.

51. The amounts Tom received as reimbursements of travel expenses are not included in his gross income. The excess amount ($27,500) is potentially deductible on his return. However, unreimbursed employee business expenses are deductible by the taxpayer only to the extent that they—along with all other expenses in this category of miscellaneous expenses—exceed 2% of the taxpayer's AGI. This amount is $2,800 ($140,000 × 2%). Thus, combining the $500 of miscellaneous expenses and $27,500 of unreimbursed expenses produces $28,000 of expenses. These are deductible only to the extent that they exceed $2,800. Therefore, $25,200 of these expenses are deductible. This is a deduction on Tom's itemized return, i.e., available only to him if he itemizes, and therefore as a deduction from AGI in computing taxable income. (These deductions might be limited in computing Tom's AMT; see Chapter 13.)

52. In order to claim a personal exemption for any of these people, they must qualify as Janet's "dependent," which requires that they either be a "qualifying child" or a "qualifying relative."

Janet may claim an exemption for her daughter as a "qualifying child," assuming that the daughter lives with Janet for at least half the year and doesn't provide over half of her own support. The stepdaughter may qualify, but perhaps not, since Janet no longer is married to the daughter's father (more inquiry is needed here). None of the others qualify as a "qualifying child" because of the residence test (the son) and the relationships test (everyone else).

The foster child and the boarder are not "qualifying relatives" because of the lack of formal family relationship to Janet. However, her son, brother, mother, and even her niece may qualify assuming that their gross incomes are less than the exemption amount ($3,200 each in 2005) and that Janet provides over half of their support. Although it would appear that Janet's mother's income is greater than the exemption amount, only a certain amount of her Social Security benefits will be included in gross income, and it is not clear how much that would be; further investigation is necessary. Even though Janet's niece may be a nonresident alien, she is domiciled in Mexico, and therefore she could be a qualifying relative.

53. Mimi may potentially deduct up to $4,000 of qualified education expenses under IRC §222. However, only $3,000 of Mimi's expenses qualify as higher education expenses, because the private singing lessons do not fall within the definition of such expenses of IRC §25A(f). She is probably not subject to any limitation based on modified AGI, as her AGI is only $15,000. Thus, she should be able to claim a deduction from gross income in computing AGI of $3,000. Mimi should investigate whether it is better for her to claim this deduction or one of the education credits of IRC §25A (see discussion at Chapter 16.)

54. Catherine may establish either a Roth IRA or a regular IRA and may contribute up to $4,000 to it, unless she is over age 50, in which her contribution could increase to $4,500. If Catherine establishes a regular IRA, she may deduct contributions to it, because although she participates in her employer's qualified retirement plan, her AGI is not more than $60,000. If she contributes to either kind of IRA, the contribution will grow tax-free until it is distributed to her after retirement. However, distributions from the regular IRA will be included in her gross income, while distributions from a Roth IRA will be excluded. She must decide whether it is better for her to take the deduction now and pay taxes later (in which case she would make a contribution to the regular IRA) or to forego the deduction now and receive tax-free distributions later (in which case she would make a contribution to the Roth IRA) or some combination of the two. Most taxpayers appear to prefer the Roth IRA approach.

55. Maurice may deduct (but only if he "itemizes"—i.e., claims the itemized deduction) the following: $10,000 of legal fees, $1,500 in job search expenses, and probably the $500 in moving costs to remove his items from Donald's office. All of these will be miscellaneous itemized deductions subject to the 2% floor. The $5,000 in counseling will be a medical expense, which will be deductible as an itemized deduction to the extent it exceeds 7.5% of Maurice's AGI. Maurice's job search expenses will only be deductible if he is looking for a position in his current occupation. Expenses for looking for a position "in a completely different profession" will be capital in nature and nondeductible.

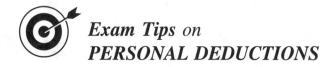

Exam Tips on
PERSONAL DEDUCTIONS

☞ Questions involving personal deductions deal with expenditures associated with a taxpayer's personal life. Address these separately from business deductions.

    ☞ *Look for:* Outlays by taxpayers for charity, health, etc.

    ☞ *Analyze:* Deduction-by-deduction—is this a deductible expense, and if so, how much is deductible?

☞ Know which deductions belong where: above-the-line or below-the-line.

☞ Most taxpayers described on law exams are "itemizers," i.e., they do not take the standard deduction, but instead take the deductions listed on Schedule A as itemized deductions.

☞ Many deductions have specific limitations tied to AGI.

    ☞ *Look for:* Charitable donations, medical expenses, casualty losses, educational loans, miscellaneous expenses, retirement savings.

☞ *Analyze:* Determine if the outlay is deductible at all; if it is, apply the limitations to determine the deductible percentage.

☛ *Don't* allow a taxpayer to claim *both* the standard and itemized deduction.

☛ Personal deductions are usually deductible in the year the outlay is made, if at all, not later. Timing issues are usually not a large feature of these questions. Nevertheless, as a precaution, think about *when* an amount is deductible.

☛ **Remember:** Construe deduction statutes narrowly. If in doubt, deny the deduction.

CHAPTER 7

BUSINESS AND INVESTMENT DEDUCTIONS

ChapterScope

Gross income includes net income from business, rentals, and royalties, and a net loss from these activities may be deductible. But to compute net income or loss, it is necessary to subtract from this income the various deductions associated with these activities. This chapter explores these deductions in detail.

- **Trade or business expenses:** Section 162 generally allows a taxpayer to deduct all of the ordinary and necessary expenses of carrying on a trade or business, but imposes restrictions on certain types of expenses.

- **Capital expenditures:** Section 263 prohibits any deduction for capital expenditures. Instead, the amount paid for a capital expenditure is "capitalized," i.e., it becomes part of the basis of the property. If the property is used for business or investment purposes, the taxpayer will recover that investment at some point during ownership of the property (through MACRS deduction, for example) or upon sale.

- **Capital recovery:** A taxpayer is entitled to recover his or her investment in property, i.e., to be taxed only (for federal income tax purposes) on the income from that property, not the invested capital in the property. The timing of capital recovery, however, is a matter for Congressional discretion and our tax system uses a number of different timing methods for capital recovery.

- **Modified accelerated cost recovery system (MACRS):** MACRS is the method by which tax-payers claim capital recovery on tangible business assets. The taxpayer claims an annual deduction computed by applying the "applicable recovery method" to the basis of the asset over the applicable recovery period, taking into account applicable conventions. A taxpayer claiming the deduction also reduces the basis of the asset by the amount of the deduction.

- **Amortization of intangibles:** Section 197 allows a taxpayer to amortize intangible assets such as goodwill, covenants not to compete, certain intellectual property, and similar assets on a pro rata basis over 15 years.

- **Certain other business deductions:** Specific Code sections allow deduction of certain other business expenses, such as interest, taxes, and bad debts.

- **Deductions attributable to nonbusiness, for-profit activities:** Some activities may not rise to the level of a trade or business, but nevertheless be entered into for profit. Certain deductions are allowable for these activities.

I. WHERE ARE WE?

For certain kinds of income, it is necessary to group all of the income and deductions attributable to that activity together to determine net income or net loss. This is what the Code requires for business, rental, and royalty activities. The income and deductions associated with each of these activities will be separately computed (on Schedule C for business and on Schedule E for rents and royalties) and the net result—whether net income or net loss—is reported on the Form 1040. See Figure 1A. To make this determination, understanding business and investment deductions is critical, and this chapter analyzes these kinds of deductions.

II. TRADE OR BUSINESS EXPENSES—§162

A. General rule

Section 162 allows a deduction for all the ordinary and necessary expenses paid or incurred in carrying on a trade or business or while away from home, and rental payments for property. There are five distinct requirements for deductibility under §162: "ordinary," "necessary," "expense," "of carrying on," and "a trade or business." These are discussed as definitional issues.

B. Definitional issues

1. **Ordinary:** The function of the ordinary requirement is to allow a deduction only for those amounts that are usual in business, thus distinguishing between expenses paid for business or other purposes.

   a. **Definition:** Ordinary means usual in the course of general and accepted business practice, arising from a transaction commonly or frequently encountered in the type of business involved. *Deputy v. DuPont,* 308 U.S. 488, 494–497 (1940).

   b. **Common situation—Reasonable compensation:** A closely held corporation may attempt to pay shareholder/employees unreasonably high salaries instead of reasonable salaries plus dividends. This is because the corporation can deduct the salary but not the dividend. The IRS may seek to recast a portion of the unreasonable salary as a dividend, based on the theory that the salary is not "ordinary."

      Example: Tomasina is the sole shareholder and CEO of Close Corp. Close pays her $1 million per year in salary, while comparable CEOs are paid $650,000. The IRS may seek to recharacterize this transaction as a salary payment of $650,000 to Tomasina and a dividend of $350,000. Only the salary component would be deductible as an ordinary and necessary business expense.

   c. **Debt repayment—*Welch v. Helvering,* 290 U.S. 111 (1933):** Mr. Welch had been an executive with a bankrupt company. When he became a commission agent in the same line of business as his former company, he voluntarily paid some of the company's unpaid debts in order to establish good relations with customers.

      i. **Issue:** May Mr. Welch deduct the debt payments as ordinary business expenses?

      ii. **Result and rationale:** These payments are not deductible because they are not ordinary expenses. An ordinary expense is one that is common and accepted within an industry, even if uncommon for a particular taxpayer. It is extremely rare in business for an individual to undertake the payment of an unenforceable debt, and therefore the payment was not ordinary and thus was not deductible.

   d. **Connection with business activity—*Gilliam v. Commissioner,* 51 T.C.M. 515 (1986):** Mr. Gilliam was a noted artist with a history of mental disturbance. Anticipating an anxiety attack prior to an airplane trip for professional purposes, Mr. Gilliam obtained a prescription for a new medication. During the airplane trip he became agitated and attacked another passenger—a side effect of the medication, probably. He was arrested and paid legal fees to defend both criminal and civil actions and also paid an amount in settlement of the civil suit.

    i. Issue: May Mr. Gilliam deduct the amounts he paid in connection with the criminal and civil suits?

    ii. Result and rationale: The amounts paid are not ordinary expenses of business and therefore are not deductible. Although Mr. Gilliam was traveling on business during which ordinary expenses might be incurred, these particular expenses did not arise from the business but from his personal medical condition.

2. Necessary: The function of the necessary requirement is to ensure the requisite connection between the expense and furtherance of the business. Necessary means "appropriate and helpful" to the business activity. *Commissioner v. Heininger,* 320 U.S. 467, 471 (1943). Courts are extremely reluctant to substitute their business judgment for that of business people and will disallow an expense as "unnecessary" only in extreme cases.

Example: Valerie owns a health food store. In order to improve the health of her employees and therefore their productivity, Valerie engages an aerobics instructor to come to the store three times a week to give a class at lunch time. Concerned about whether her employees' "past lives" are adversely impacting their current work habits, she also engages a psychic to attend the employees every Friday at 4:00. Valerie seeks to deduct the payment for both the instructor and the psychic. A court likely would allow the aerobics instructor expense as necessary, given the proven link between health and productivity. Regardless of a court's typical reluctance to second guess the decisions of a business person, a court likely would disallow the expense for a psychic, because of the absence of the necessary link between the business and the expense. It is more likely that Valerie is indulging her personal tastes than attending to business matters.

3. Expense: The "expense" requirement seeks to distinguish between expenses and capital expenditures. Only expenditures for expenses are deductible; amounts paid as capital expenditures are not. Instead, amounts that constitute capital expenditures are "capitalized," i.e., they become part of the basis of an item. See discussion at this chapter, at (III).

4. Carrying on: This requirement exists to prevent the deduction of expenses prior to the time the taxpayer commences a trade or business.

    a. Going concern: A taxpayer is carrying on a trade or business from the date that it is a "going concern." This requires regular activity in the pursuits for which the business was organized. *Richmond Television Corp. v. United States,* 345 F.2d 901 (4th Cir. 1965).

    Example: Carla is opening a coffee bar. She rents space, hires a contractor to remodel it, hires staff, and purchases inventory. Until she is ready to sell coffee to customers, however, Carla's coffee bar is not a going concern, and Carla may not deduct expenses incurred under §162.

    b. Pre-opening expenses—§195: Expenses that would be deductible but for the "carrying on" requirement may be deductible if the taxpayer properly elects to take advantage of IRC §195(a). A taxpayer may elect to deduct $5,000 in the year the business opens, but this amount must be reduced by the amount the total pre-opening expenses exceed $50,000. IRC §195(b). Any remaining amount must be amortized over 180 months (15 years), much like §197 intangibles (see this Chapter, Section III(G)).

Example: Sam is planning to open a restaurant. In the month prior to opening, he incurs $8,000 for salaries, utilities, and other expenses that would otherwise qualify as ordinary and necessary business expenses but cannot be deducted because the restaurant is not yet open for business. He may deduct $5,000 in the year of opening, and the remaining $3,000 can be deducted over 15 years ($200/year).

5. **Trade or business:** The principal function of the trade or business requirement is to distinguish the expenses of a taxpayer's business activities from other activities—principally personal activities. It also serves to match expenses of an activity with the income from that activity.

   a. **Judicial interpretation:** Neither the Code nor the regulations define a trade or business. To be engaged in a trade or business, a taxpayer must be involved in an activity with continuity and regularity and must have the primary purpose of creating income or profit rather than merely engaging in a hobby. See *Commissioner v. Groetzinger,* 480 U.S. 23 (1987).

   b. **Profit motive:** A trade or business requires a ***profit*** motive. The absence of profit motive indicates a personal activity. See IRC §183, and discussion at Chapter 8(III).

   Example: Sheila, a doctor, owns two champion Labrador retrievers. Last year she bred the female, sold three of the pups, and kept two for herself. She wishes to deduct the veterinary and other costs of breeding as a business expense to offset the income from the sale of the pups. This situation raises the question of whether she is carrying on a business of breeding dogs or is merely engaged in a personal hobby.

C. **Special rules and exceptions**

Section 162 is riddled with special rules and exceptions.

1. **Traveling expenses:** A taxpayer's reasonable expenses of traveling while away from home on business are deductible.

   a. **Home—IRS position:** The IRS interprets a taxpayer's home as (1) the taxpayer's regular or principal (if more than one regular) place of business; or (2) if the taxpayer has no regular or principal place of business, the taxpayer's regular place of abode in a real and substantial sense. If neither (1) nor (2) apply, the taxpayer's home is wherever he or she works. Rev. Rul. 73-529, 1973-2 C.B. 37.

   b. **One-year rule:** A taxpayer is not treated as being away from home on business if the period away exceeds one year. IRC §162(a)(3). The taxpayer's "realistic expectation" governs, so a taxpayer may deduct expenses (at least during the first year) for a job that is realistically expected to last less than a year, even if it continues longer. Rev. Rul. 83-82, 1983-1 C.B. 45; Rev. Rul. 75-432, 1975-2 C.B. 60; Rev. Rul. 60-189, 1960-1 C.B. 60.

   c. **Primary relation:** In order to generate deductible expenses, the travel must be primarily for business. Reg. §1.162-2(b)(1).

2. **Public policy:** Expenses that otherwise meet the requirements of §162, but the payment of which violate public policy, may not be deductible.

   a. **Bribes and kickbacks:** No deduction is allowed for illegal payments to any governmental employee (domestic or foreign) or illegal bribes or kickbacks to other persons. IRC §162(c).

b. **Fines:** There is no deduction for any fine or similar penalty paid to a government. IRC §162(f).

> **Example:** Careless Co. is indicted on charges relating to illegal dumping of chemicals. As part of settlement of the matter, Careless is required to pay a $20,000 fine. Careless will not be allowed to deduct the payment of the fine as an ordinary and necessary business expense.

c. **Treble damages:** There is no deduction for the two-thirds portion of antitrust damages attributable to punitive damages. IRC §162(g)(1),(2).

d. **CEO compensation:** There is no deduction for compensation of a CEO of a publicly traded company in excess of $1,000,000, unless the compensation is based on specified commissions or is tied to performance. IRC §162(m).

e. **Charitable contributions:** There is no deduction under §162 expense for an amount that would be a charitable contribution but is not deductible because of the percentage limitations of IRC §170. See discussion of charitable contributions at Chapter 6(XVI).

D. Related material

1. **Hobby losses:** If an activity is not engaged in for profit, significant limitations may be placed on the deduction of expenses associated with that activity. See IRC §183 and discussion at Chapter 8(III).

2. **Capital recovery:** If an amount is not deductible because it is not an "expense," its cost may be recoverable over the period of ownership of the property. See discussion this Chapter, Section III.

3. **Section 280E:** Section 280E disallows any deduction or credit for the expenses incurred in illegal drug trafficking.

E. Summary

Section 162 allows a deduction for ordinary and necessary business expenses, subject to certain limitations. See Statute Summary—§162.

III. CAPITAL RECOVERY FOR BUSINESS ASSETS

A. Capital recovery—In general

Section 263 disallows any deduction for capital expenditures, generally defined as "permanent improvements or betterments made to increase the value of any property or estate." Thus, if an expenditure constitutes a capital expenditure, the amount expended is capitalized and is added to (or constitutes) the basis of the asset. The taxpayer may *recover* this capital investment during the time he or she owns the asset if the Code specifically provides for such recovery, known as *depreciation* or *amortization*. The timing of this capital recovery is also governed by specific Code provisions. If capital recovery is not allowed during the years the taxpayer owns the property, or the taxpayer has not fully recovered his or her capital investment by the time he or she sells the property, the taxpayer may be able to recover his or her remaining economic investment in the property in the year of sale (through the computation of gain as amount realized minus the adjusted basis of the property sold). This concept is discussed in detail in Chapter 9.

Statute Summary—§162

Parsing Step	§162
General rule	Taxpayers may deduct the ordinary and necessary expenses of carrying on a trade or business.
Definitional issues	Ordinary Necessary Carrying on a trade or business Expense versus capital expenditure
Special rules and exceptions	Traveling expenses "away from home" No deduction for bribes, kickbacks, and fines CEO compensation >$1,000,000
Related material	Capital expenditures: §263 Capital recovery issues Personal expenditures: §262 Hobby losses: §183
Summary	In computing net income or loss from business, deduct all ordinary and necessary business expenses.

B. Matching principle

Appropriate capital recovery is said to "match" income and the expenses incurred to produce that income. See generally Chapter 11. For example, if a taxpayer purchases an apartment building to be rented to students, the taxpayer will earn rental income each year for a number of years. In theory, the property will be "used up" over those years, and so allocating a portion of the purchase price as a deduction each year will better reflect the taxpayer's true net income than either of the other capital recovery approaches: (1) allowing a deduction for the entire cost in the year of purchase; or (2) waiting until disposition of the asset for capital recovery to occur. However, the idea of a property being "used up" on some specific schedule is a fantasy: In fact, a property may rise in value over the period (some real estate, for example) or may fall in value much more quickly than its so-called recovery period (some computer equipment, for example).

C. Depreciable assets

Not all assets are subject to depreciation or amortization. Only those assets that are "used up" over time are subject to depreciation, or as the Code puts it, subject to "wear and tear." IRC §167(a). Fine art, for example, may not be depreciable. Raw land certainly isn't depreciable. Compare those examples with equipment, customer lists, or patents, all of which are "used up" over time.

D. Definition—Capital expenditure

Neither the Code nor the regulations offer a precise definition of a capital expenditure.

1. **Acquiring assets:** Costs incurred in acquiring or disposing of assets are capital expenditures. The price of an asset is obviously included in this category; also included are other expenses of acquiring the property.

Examples:

- The purchase price of a parcel of land is a capital expenditure.

- The commission paid on the purchase of corporate shares is a capital expenditure that is added to the price of the shares in determining their basis.

- Legal expenses in perfecting or defending title to real property are capital expenditures that are added to the basis of the property.

- Depreciation and other expenses associated with equipment used to build an asset are capital expenditures. *Commissioner v. Idaho Power Co.,* 418 U.S. 1 (1974).

a. **What is an asset?** The regulations offer examples of capital expenditures as including the costs of assets such as buildings, machinery and equipment, furniture and fixtures, and "similar property having a useful life substantially beyond the taxable year." Reg. §1.263-2(a). While it is easy to identify these assets, other assets are trickier. For example, when an existing business expands into new ventures, it is not entirely obvious what parts, if any, of the new business constitute capital expenditures.

   i. **Separate asset test:** In *Commissioner v. Lincoln Savings & Loan Assn.,* 403 U.S. 345 (1971), the Supreme Court held that when a separate and distinct asset is created, the amounts expended in doing so are capital expenditures.

   ii. **Exploring a new venture:** Expenses of researching, investigating, and considering acquiring a new venture are capital expenditures.

   Example: Deleen is the owner of Balloons 'R Us, a commercial ballooning outfit, which she operates as a sole proprietorship. Ballooning has whetted her appetite for adventure, and she is considering expanding into the long-distance travel arena. Over three months she expends considerable time and energy investigating the possibility of establishing an adventure travel endeavor as a division of Balloons 'R Us. She also incurs costs for telephone, subscriptions, client analyses, and similar items. Because the travel undertaking is a new venture, its costs are not deductible but are capital expenditures. Another way of viewing this is that Deleen may not deduct these costs because she is not yet "carrying on" a trade or business. The expenses may qualify as pre-opening expenses, and may be amortizable after opening under §195. For either argument (capital expenditure or pre-opening expense) the question is whether the move into adventure travel is a new undertaking (nondeductible) or merely an expansion of the existing business (deductible).

2. **Future benefits test—*Indopco, Inc. v. Commissioner,* 112 S. Ct. 1039 (1992):** Unilever sought to acquire National Starch (later renamed Indopco) in a friendly takeover. National Starch incurred a variety of expenses in connection with the transaction, including $2.2 million in investment banker's fees and about $500,000 in legal fees.

   a. **Issue:** Were the costs associated with the acquisition capital expenditures or deductible expenses?

   b. **Result and rationale:** These amounts were capital expenditures. The creation of a separate asset (see *Lincoln Savings*) is a sufficient, but not necessary, element to test whether expenditures are capital. If an expenditure creates a more than insignificant future benefit to the taxpayer, the expenditure is a capital asset, even if no separate asset is created. In this case, the benefits motivating the acquisition were to last for many years. Hence, the expenditures produced a significant future benefit and were capital expenditures.

3. **Education for new trade or business:** While education undertaken to improve skills in a current job are potentially deductible, education that qualifies a taxpayer for a new job or profession is a nondeductible capital expenditure. See Treas. Reg. §1.162-5.

E. Capital recovery

Unlike an ordinary business expense, a capital expenditure does not generate a deduction for the taxpayer in the year the expenditure is made. But a taxpayer will be allowed (at some point) to "recover" the capital invested in the asset. This means that the taxpayer will be able to offset income by the capital invested in the asset, either during ownership of the asset or upon disposition. Depreciation deductions, for example, allow a taxpayer to deduct a portion of the cost of an asset each year for a specified period; this deduction constitutes capital recovery. The timing of that recovery is critical. Taxpayers generally prefer capital recovery as early as possible because these deductions reduce the taxable income from the property during ownership. See generally Chapter 15.

1. **Constitutional issue?** The taxpayer has a constitutional right to capital recovery because the federal income tax is a tax on income—not capital. *Eisner v. Macomber,* 252 U.S. 189 (1920). The courts usually accept this principle without much discussion, proceeding on to the question of timing of capital recovery.

2. **Timing—Statutory issue:** *When* a taxpayer will be allowed to recover his or her invested capital is a matter for Congress' discretion. See, e.g., *Burnet v. Sanford & Brooks Co.,* 282 U.S. 359 (1931). There are three options, all of which are used in the Code for different types of assets.

   a. **Capital recovery first:** A taxpayer may be allowed to recover his or her capital investment before reporting any income from the asset. An example of this approach is contained in IRC §179, which allows a taxpayer purchasing tools and equipment for use in a business to deduct the cost of such equipment in an amount equal to the lesser of $105,000 (for 2005) or the taxable income from the business computed disregarding the §179 deduction. The maximum amount that can be deducted under §179 is $105,000. However, the limit for heavy SUVs is $25,000.

      Example: Wendall owns a furniture store. In 2005 he purchased a computer system at a cost of $35,000 to track accounting and inventory. In 2005 the furniture store produced $160,000 in taxable income without considering any deduction for the computer. Wendall's purchase of the computer is a capital expenditure, so he would not be entitled to claim a deduction under §162 for its cost. However, §179 allows him a deduction for the cost of the computer in the year of purchase. Thus, in 2005 he has fully recovered the cost of (capital investment in) the computer.

   b. **Capital recovery during ownership:** A taxpayer may be allowed to recover his or her capital investment on some schedule, apportioning the recovery over his or her ownership of the asset. This is the approach used to recover investment in tangible property (known generally as depreciation) or intangible property (known generally as amortization). For example, a purchaser of residential real property for investment will apportion the basis of the property over 27.5 years, deducting a proportionate amount year. By the end of that period, the taxpayer will have fully recovered his or her investment in the property.

Example: Spencer purchases a residential rental property for $100,000 on January 1, 1994. The property will be depreciated over 27.5 years. Thus, each year (disregarding, for now, any midmonth conventions) Spencer will be entitled to a depreciation deduction of $3,636 ($100,000 ÷ 27.5). By the end of the year 2021, if Spencer keeps the property, he will have recovered his full $100,000 investment in the property.

c. **Capital recovery last:** A taxpayer may be required to defer capital recovery until the end of his or her ownership of the asset. This is the system used for nondepreciable property such as raw land.

Example: Tyler purchases Blackacre, a parcel of raw land, for $250,000. He holds it for ten years and leases it to Fred for $10,000 per year. During that time Tyler is not entitled to any capital recovery because raw land is not depreciable. However, when Tyler sells it after ten years for $400,000, he will recover his capital upon sale because only his gain (profit) from the sale of the property is included in his gross income. Only the $150,000 difference between his sales price ($400,000) and his capital invested in Blackacre ($250,000) is included in his gross income.

F. **Modified accelerated cost recovery system (MACRS) deduction for tangible business assets**

MACRS is the method by which taxpayers claim capital recovery for tangible assets used in a trade or business or held for the production of income.

1. **Dual function of MACRS deduction:** The MACRS deduction has two functions:

   a. **Deduction:** The MACRS deduction is a deduction from gross income in computing AGI. IRC §167(a).

   b. **Basis reduction:** The amount of the MACRS deduction reduces the basis of the asset. IRC §1016(a)(2).

2. **Calculation of MACRS:** The MACRS deduction is computed by applying the applicable recovery method to the basis of the asset over the applicable recovery period, taking into account applicable conventions. While this sounds complicated, it is a relatively straightforward process if the definitions of these terms are kept firmly in mind.

   a. **Basis:** The basis of an asset is generally its cost, subject to some particular rules for property acquired other than by purchase. (See Chapter 9(III)(B).) Basis is adjusted downward for capital recovery deductions, producing "adjusted basis." IRC §1061(a)(2). Improvements are treated as separate assets generating their own MACRS deductions.

   Example: Debra purchases a rental home for $100,000. Over the next five years she properly claims $5,000 of depreciation (MACRS) deductions, reducing her basis to $95,000. She then adds a small apartment on the back of the rental house to increase the rental income from the property. She spends $25,000 on this addition. The original rental home will continue to be depreciated on its existing schedule. Debra will depreciate the addition on the 27.5-year schedule applicable to residential real property beginning on the date it is first rented. Thus, assuming Debra keeps the property, the original rental home will be fully depreciated (i.e., its basis will be zero) five years before the addition is fully depreciated. If Debra sells the rental home, she will use the collective basis of the home and addition at that time as her basis for determining gain or loss.

b. Recovery period: The recovery period of an asset is the period of years over which the taxpayer claims capital recovery for the item. Some recovery periods are set forth in the Code (e.g., for real property); for other types of property, the IRS publishes the recovery period. The recovery period might not have any relation whatsoever to the actual life of the asset, but is nevertheless mandatory in computing MACRS deductions. Recovery periods include:

   i. Residential real property—27.5 years recovery period: IRC §168(c)(1).

   ii. Nonresidential real property—39 years recovery period: IRC §168(c)(1).

   iii. **Qualified leasehold improvements—15 years:** IRC §168(e)(3)(E)(iv) (2005 only).

   iv. Qualified restaurant property—15 years: IRC§168(e)(3)(E)(v) (2005 only).

   iv. Other property: Other property can be 3-year, 5-year, 7-year, 10-year, 15-year, or 20-year property. See Rev. Proc. 87-56, 1987-2 C.B. 674, modified by Rev. Proc. 88-22, 1988-1 C.B. 785.

c. Conventions: The applicable convention expresses the beginning date for capital recovery. Recovery begins when the property is "placed in service," i.e., when it is dedicated to use in a trade or business. Reg. §1.168(d)-1(a). In addition, instead of creating the technical nightmare of computing daily portions of capital recovery for properties placed in service during the year on various days, the MACRS system adopts various conventions. These conventions deem a property to be placed in service at a specific time during the month, quarter, or year, regardless of when the property is actually placed in service.

   i. Midmonth convention: Taxpayers purchasing or selling real property are deemed to make the purchase or sale on the 15th day of the month in which the transaction occurs. IRC §168(d)(4)(B). Thus, if a taxpayer purchases real property on April 28, she is deemed to have purchased it on April 15 for MACRS purposes.

   ii. Half-year convention: For tangible property other than real property, the Code deems a purchase or sale to be made at the middle of the taxpayer's taxable year regardless of when during the year the transaction actually occurs. IRC §168(d)(4)(A). For example, if a taxpayer on a calendar year sells equipment on January 1, he is deemed to have sold it on July 1 for MACRS purposes.

   iii. **Midquarter convention:** If the aggregate bases of properties placed in service during the last quarter of the taxable year exceed 40% of the aggregate bases of all properties placed in service during the year, the half-year convention does not apply. Instead, a midquarter convention applies so that properties are deemed placed in service at the middle of the quarter in which they were actually placed in service. IRC §168(d)(4)(C).

d. Recovery methods: Three different recovery methods are available under MACRS for different types of property; the straight-line method and two accelerated methods.

   i. Straight line: Under a straight-line system, the MACRS deduction is taken on a pro rata basis over the recovery period for the property. The cost of the property is divided by the recovery period to determine the annual MACRS deduction. For example, if the cost of the property is $10,000, and the recovery period is 10 years, the MACRS deduction is $1,000 per year. The straight-line method *must* be used for buildings and their structural components, and for qualified leasehold and restaurant property. A taxpayer may elect to use the straight-line method for other assets as well.

ii. **Accelerated method—150% declining balance:** Under an accelerated system, a larger MACRS deduction is taken in the early years of the useful life of the property than in later years. Under the 150% system, the MACRS deduction is the adjusted basis of the property multiplied by 150% of the straight-line percentage. For example, if the straight-line percentage were 10% (i.e., each year the MACRS deduction under a straight-line system would allow 10% of the original cost of the property as the MACRS deduction) this accelerated method would allow 15% (150% of 10%). The straight-line percentage is recalculated each year by dividing into 1 the remaining useful life of the asset. In the year in which this method would produce a lower MACRS deduction than the straight-line rate, the taxpayer reverts to straight line. This method is applicable to 15- and 20-year property and property used in farming.

iii. **Accelerated method—Double-declining balance:** The MACRS deduction is the adjusted basis of the property at the beginning of each year multiplied by 200% of the straight-line percentage. For example, if the cost of the property is $10,000, and the recovery period is 10 years, the MACRS deduction under the double-declining balance method would be 200% of the straight-line deduction of 10% ($1,000), or $2,000. The straight-line percentage is recalculated each year, by dividing into 1 the remaining useful life of the asset. In the year in which this method would produce a lower MACRS deduction than the straight-line rate, the taxpayer reverts to straight line. This method is used for all properties other than real property and properties for which the 150% method is specified.

e. **Calculating the MACRS deduction**

i. **Straight-line system:** Under a straight-line system, the cost of the property is divided by the recovery period to obtain the annual MACRS deduction. If the property is held (or deemed held under the conventions) for less than a full year, the annual figure must be multiplied by the percentage of the year during which the taxpayer held (or is deemed to have held) the property.

Example: Dina purchases Whiteacre, an apartment building, on January 1, 2004 for $500,000. She holds it for two years, selling it on January 1, 2006. During her period of ownership, Dina may claim the following MACRS deductions:

2004: $17,455

This is calculated by taking the Whiteacre's cost ($500,000) and dividing it by the recovery period for residential real property (27.5 years) to produce an annual MACRS deduction of $18,182. However, because of the midmonth convention, Dina is deemed to have purchased Whiteacre on January 15, 2004, and thus she is entitled to only 11.5 months of depreciation during 2004. Multiplying the annual allowance ($18,182) by the percentage of the year she held Whiteacre (11.5/12 or 96%) produces her 2004 MACRS deduction of $17,455.

2005: $18,182

Since Dina held Whiteacre for the full year, she is entitled to the annual MACRS deduction for that year.

2006: $727

Dina sold Whiteacre on January 1, but the midmonth convention deems the sale to have occurred on January 15, 2006. She is therefore entitled to a half-month's MACRS deduction during 2006 equal to the annual MACRS deduction ($18,182) multiplied by the percentage of the year she held the property (0.5/12 or 4%) to produce her 2006 MACRS deduction of $727.

ii. Accelerated system: In the accelerated systems, the selected recovery method is applied to the basis of the property over the recovery period.

Example: On April 1 of Year 1, Chad purchases property with a 10-year recovery period at a cost of $50,000. Assume that the midquarter convention does not apply and that Chad is on a calendar year.

Chad first selects his recovery method—200% declining balance. Applying this to his basis in the property over its recovery period, Chad determines his annual MACRS deduction. For the first year, however, Chad is entitled to only half of the MACRS deduction because under the applicable convention he is deemed to have placed the property in service on July 1 of that year.

Straight-line method percentage: 10%

200% of straight-line percentage: 20%

Chad multiplies the percentage (20%) by the cost of the property ($50,000) to determine the full year's MACRS deduction for Year 1 of $10,000. But this must be halved, because of the half-year convention, to $5,000. The 20% percentage is applied to the adjusted basis of the property each year, until year 5, when the straight-line deduction would be greater than the double-declining balance deduction. The MACRS deductions for each year are contained in the table on the facing page.

f. Bonus depreciation: To create an incentive to invest in depreciable property (and thereby improve the economy) Congress sometimes enacts special bonus depreciation provisions that allow larger depreciation deductions in the year of purchase of equipment. For example, special 30% and 50% allowances were created for post-911 purchases made prior to January 1, 2005.

G. Amortization of §197 intangibles

Section 197 was enacted to end years of controversy between taxpayers and the IRS about the appropriate amortization of intangible assets acquired in the purchase and sale of businesses.

CHAD'S
MACRS DEDUCTIONS

Year	Basic (beginning of year)	MACRS	Comment
1	$50,000	$5,000	½ of full year's amount of $10,000
2	$45,000	$9,000	$45,000 × 20%
3	$36,000	$7,200	$36,000 × 20%
4	$28,800	$5,760	$28,800 × 20%
5	$23,040	$4,608	$23,040 × 20%
6	$18,432	$3,686	$18,432 × 20%
7	$14,746	$3,277	Switches to straight-line: $14,746 × (1 ÷ 4.5)
8	$11,469	$3,277	$11,469 × (1 ÷ 3.5)
9	$ 8,192	$3,277	$ 8,192 × (1 ÷ 2.5)
10	$ 4,915	$3,277	$ 4,915 × (1 ÷ 1.5)
11	$ 1,638	$1,638	$ 1,638 × 100%

1. **General rule:** A taxpayer may claim a deduction in computing AGI for any amortizable §197 intangible equal to the adjusted basis of the intangible divided by 15 years, and may begin claiming the deduction in the month of acquisition of the intangible. IRC §197(a). Like an MACRS deduction, a §197 amortization deduction reduces the basis of the asset in question. IRC §1016(a)(2).

2. **Definitional issues**

   a. **Section 197 intangible:** A §197 intangible includes goodwill, going-concern value, covenants not to compete, patents, copyrights, formulas or processes, and various other intangibles. IRC §197(d)(1).

   Example: Robyn purchases Kitty Kaverns, an established cat boarding business. In the purchase, Robyn acquires various tangible assets and also pays $15,000 for the goodwill of Kitty Kaverns. Assuming that the goodwill meets the requirements for an "amortizable §197 intangible," Robyn will be able to amortize this payment over 15 years, i.e., taking a $1,000 deduction each year. She will begin amortizing this intangible in the month of acquisition, so that her first year's amortization deduction will be limited to the number of months that she is open for business in that year.

b. Amortizable §197 intangible: An amortizable §197 intangible includes intangibles acquired after July 25, 1991 that are held in connection with the taxpayer's trade or business. IRC §197(c)(1). But the term does not include "self-created" intangibles and excludes interests in land, readily available computer software, and leases of tangible property. IRC §197(c)(2), (e)(2), (3), (5).

c. Covenant not to compete: In the sale of a business, the seller may promise the buyer not to engage in the same or similar business for a reasonable time after sale, in the same general geographic area as the sold business. This is called a "covenant not to compete."

Example: Trevor purchases a car detailing business from Drake. In connection with the sale of the business, Drake promises not to open any type of similar business within 60 miles of the purchased business for five years, and Trevor pays Drake $20,000 for this promise. This covenant not to compete is a §197 intangible, which Trevor amortizes over 15 years for an annual amortization deduction of $1,333. Notice that even though the covenant only runs for five years, Trevor must amortize it over the statutory 15-year period.

d. Goodwill: Goodwill is generally defined as the likelihood that customers will return to the old place of business, the tendency of an established business to continue. *Wilmot Fleming Eng. Co. v. Commissioner,* 65 T.C. 847, 860 (1976).

e. Going concern value: Going concern value is the value of an operational business, as compared with the cost of acquiring all of the components of the business and getting them going. *Los Angeles Gas & Elec. Corp. v. R.R. Comm. of Cal.,* 289 U.S. 287 (1933).

3. Special rules and exceptions: Section 197 has a number of special rules and exceptions, most of which are technical in nature and relate to the prohibition on the "churning" of assets to begin a new amortization schedule.

4. Related material: For a discussion of MACRS, see this chapter, (III)(G).

H. Section 179 election

Section 179 allows a taxpayer to treat the purchase of §179 assets (which would otherwise be treated as the purchase of a capital asset) as a current deduction. A §179 asset is any tangible property that is §1245 property and that is acquired by purchase for use in the active conduct of a trade or business. For example, computers, telephones, fax machines, tools, and similar items qualify for the §179 election. The taxpayer is limited to the lesser of a specified dollar amount or his or her taxable income from the business. In 2005, the allowable amount is the lesser of the taxable income of the taxpayer (computed without the §179 expense) or $105,000. However, this amount will be reduced by the amount by which the taxpayer's §179 property placed in service during the year exceeds $420,000 (2005 amount). A taxpayer must affirmatively elect the use of the provisions of §179. The basis of the property is reduced by the §179 deduction claimed for the property, resulting in a basis of zero for such property when the full price is subject to the election.

I. Capital recovery—Summary

The Code sections allowing capital recovery for business and investment assets are summarized in Figure 7A.

Figure 7A
Code Sections Allowing Capital Recovery for Business and Investment Assets

Code Section and Topic	Description
§179—Election to expense certain business assets	Taxpayers may elect to claim a deduction for up to $105,000 of tangible business assets (2005 amount), but $25,000 maximum for heavy SUVs.
§§167, 168—MACRS	Taxpayers claim depreciation (MACRS) deductions for depreciation of tangible business property not expensed under §179: straight-line (real property); accelerated methods (most personal property).
§197—Amortization of intangibles	Taxpayers claim 15-year straight-line amortization of §197 intangibles, including patents, goodwill, and covenants not to compete.
§195—Pre-opening expenses	Taxpayers claim a deduction for up to $5,000 of pre-opening expenses, but the amount is reduced by the amount over $50,000; remaining amounts amortized over 15 years.

IV. OTHER DEDUCTIONS

A number of specific Code sections allow a taxpayer to deduct particular expenses of carrying on a trade or business. Some of these expenses may also constitute a part of the itemized deductions for individuals when incurred as part of the taxpayer's personal life. However, when these expenses are "attributable to a trade or business carried on by the taxpayer," they are subtracted from gross income on the Schedule C because they are part of the computation of net business income or loss. See IRC §62(a)(1).

A. Interest

Section 163(a) allows a taxpayer to deduct "all interest paid or incurred within the taxable year on indebtedness." While §163(h)(1) disallows any deduction for personal interest, the definition of personal interest specifically excludes interest attributable to carrying on a trade or business. IRC §163(h)(2)(A). Thus, business interest remains fully deductible. For a discussion of nonbusiness interest as part of the itemized deduction, see Chapter 6(XII).

B. Taxes

Section 164(a) allows a taxpayer a deduction for certain taxes paid or accrued during the taxable year regardless of whether the taxpayer is carrying on a trade or business. For a discussion of nonbusiness taxes as part of the itemized deduction, see Chapter 6(XIII).

1. Deductible taxes: Deductible taxes include state, local, and foreign real property and income taxes, and state and local personal property taxes. State sales taxes are also deductible, at least in 2004-2005. IRC §164(a).

2. Foreign tax credit: Instead of deducting foreign taxes paid, a taxpayer may choose to claim a tax credit for certain eligible foreign taxes paid or accrued. IRC §901(a). See Chapter 13(VIII).

C. Losses

Section 165(a) allows the deduction of uncompensated losses sustained during the taxable year. Although §165(c) imposes significant limitations on losses incurred by individuals, §165(c)(1) allows a deduction for losses incurred in a trade or business. Thus, trade or business losses remain fully deductible for individuals. For a discussion of nonbusiness losses as part of the itemized deduction, see Chapter 6(VI).

D. Business bad debts

1. General rule: Section 166(a) allows a deduction for the portion of any debt that becomes worthless during the taxable year in the amount of the adjusted basis of the debt to the taxpayer. IRC §166(a), (b).

2. Definitional issues

    a. Debt: Section 166 governs debts that are not securities. These include ordinary promissory notes, open account loans, and other informal loans. IRC §166(e).

    b. Bad debt: A bad debt is one that is wholly or partially worthless, meaning that the reasonable investor would not view the debt as having any value at all.

    c. Business versus nonbusiness bad debts: A business bad debt generates a deduction for the taxpayer in computing net income or loss from business. A "nonbusiness bad debt" is treated as a loss from the sale or exchange of a capital asset, generating a capital loss. See generally Chapter 12.

        i. Business bad debt: To qualify as a business bad debt, a debt must be incurred in a trade or business and must become worthless in the course of that trade or business. Reg. §1.166-5(d).

        ii. Nonbusiness bad debt: A nonbusiness bad debt lacks the requisite connection to the taxpayer's trade or business. IRC §§166(d)(2)(A), (B). This arises in two principal contexts, shareholder loans and employee loans to companies. With respect to shareholder loans, it is clear that the ownership of stock is not a trade or business. *Higgins v. Commissioner*, 312 U.S. 212 (1941). Thus, loans made to corporations from stockholders are usually nonbusiness debts because they are not connected with a trade or business. *United States v. Generes*, 405 U.S. 93 (1972). With respect to employee loans, an employee is engaged in the trade or business of performing services for his employer. Therefore, if an employee makes a loan to the employer, and the dominant motivation for making the loan is to protect the employment relationship, the debt should be a business debt. The determination of the dominant motive will be based on all the facts of the situation. See, e.g., *Trent v. Commissioner*, 291 F.2d 669 (2d Cir. 1961).

        Example—Business bad debt: Dale is in the business of making short-term loans to students. In connection with this business, he lends Alicia $2,500. She fails to repay it on time and moves to India. Concluding that the loan is uncollectable, Dale claims a business bad debt deduction of $2,500, his basis in the loan.

Example—Nonbusiness bad debt: Dick is the owner of ABC Corporation, which is engaged in the business of making credit checks. He lends the corporation $10,000 to tide it over difficult financial times. When the corporation enters bankruptcy, Dick realizes that he will never collect this amount. He must deduct this loan as a nonbusiness bad debt because it lacks the requisite connection with a trade or business.

Example—Employee loan: Felicia is an employee and minority shareholder in Z Corporation. When the corporation falls on bad times, she makes a $15,000 loan to the company. When the company is unable to repay this debt, Felicia claims a business bad debt deduction. This will be the proper reporting position for the transaction if her dominant motive in making the loan was to protect her employment relationship. If the motive was to protect her stock value, the debt will be a nonbusiness bad debt.

E. Charitable contributions

A taxpayer engaged in a trade or business may claim a deduction for charitable contributions to qualifying organizations, subject to the limitations applicable to individuals and corporations. For a discussion of the charitable contribution deduction as part of the itemized deduction, see discussion at Chapter 6(XVI).

F. Standard mileage rate

In lieu of keeping track of all the exact expenses (gas, oil, etc.) of operating an automobile for business and claiming depreciation under the MACRS system, a taxpayer may opt to deduct an amount equal to the standard mileage rate multiplied by the number of business miles for which the automobile was used during the taxable year. For 2005 the standard mileage rate is 40.5¢ per mile.

V. RENTAL AND ROYALTY ACTIVITIES

Rental and royalty income is includible in gross income. See Chapter 3(V). The expenses associated with that income are deductible. But because these activities do not usually rise to the level of a trade or business, IRC §162 does not apply to allow these deductions. Instead, IRC §212(a) applies to allow deductions for the ordinary and necessary expenses paid or incurred during a taxable year for producing that income or for the management or maintenance of property. The terms "ordinary," "necessary," and "expenses" have the same meaning as they do in IRC §162 and the capital recovery provisions also apply to any depreciable or amortizable asset used in the rental or royalty activity. An individual taxpayer reports the income and expenses on a Schedule E, with the net result (income or loss) reported on the Form 1040. See Figure 1A.

VI. SPECIAL RULES FOR LOSSES

Net loss from business generates a net operating loss deduction that can be carried forward and back as a deduction to other years. See IRC §172 and discussion at Chapter 11(II)(D). In addition, there are significant restrictions on the deduction of losses arising from rentals, royalties, and businesses in which the taxpayer does not materially participate or with respect to which a taxpayer does not have money "at risk" See IRC §§465, 469, and discussion at Chapter 11(VII).

VII. WHERE ARE WE GOING?

Chapter 6 addressed purely personal deductions, and this chapter has explored purely business deductions. We now turn to expenses that have their "feet in both camps," that have both personal and business connections. The Code has a number of methods of dealing with such expenses, from bifurcating the expense into its component parts, to inquiring into the dominant connection, to disallowing all or a portion of the expense altogether. Chapter 8 illustrates these approaches for commonly encountered "mixed" expenses.

Quiz Yourself on BUSINESS DEDUCTIONS

56. Clean Machine is a sole proprietorship operating a mobile car detailing service. This year, the owner, Win, made a number of expenditures, as follows:

Wages to employees	$25,000
Waxes, soaps, etc.	$ 6,000
Licenses	$ 500
Parking fines	$ 600
Advertising	$10,000
Séance to get business advice from deceased father	$ 3,000
Legal fees to settle dispute with car owner	$ 5,000
Legal fees to quiet title to parking lot	$15,000
New van	$35,000

Which of these expenditures are deductible to Win? If not deductible, how should they be treated? _____

57. Jody purchased a rental house on July 1 of Year 1 for $55,000. She rented it for $3,000 in Year 1, and $6,000 in each of Years 2 and 3. She sold it on January 15, Year 4 for $80,000. Assuming no improvements to the home, what is her gain or loss on the sale? _____

58. Grant purchased a bagpipe store from Adam. He purchased all of the bagpipe inventory, a list of all the customers who loved bagpipe music, and obtained a promise from Adam not to engage in the retail bagpipe business for five years from the date of sale. He paid Adam $30,000 for the promise. How should Grant treat the $30,000 for tax purposes? _____

59. Baxter is a large animal veterinarian. In 2005, he returned to his hometown to open a practice. He spent $50,000 on equipment, and on June 1 hired an assistant, Penny, to whom he paid $2,500 per month. He spent $10,000 on fixing up his leased premises and another $5,000 on various miscellaneous expenses associated with opening his business. He was finally ready to open on August 1. His expenses after that date were $35,000. Which expenses are deductible, if any? How should nondeductible expenses be treated? _____

60. Lenore purchases the Wallflower Hotel on January 1, Year 1. She expects to be able to claim 12 months of depreciation for the hotel during Year 1. Is she able to do so? _____

61. Xavier makes a loan of $25,000 to Zena. Eventually, it becomes clear that Zena will never repay the loan. What is the proper tax treatment of the loan to Xavier if:

    ■ Xavier is Zena's father? _____

    ■ Xavier is Zena's employer? _____

    ■ Xavier is in the business of making loans to individuals? _____

62. Bennie is a law professor. This year, he traveled across the country to teach one semester at another law school. While there, he incurred expenses for rent, food, and utilities. He also incurred traveling expenses there and back. Are any of these expenses deductible to Bennie? _____

63. Wendy owns a wholesale pet rock business. She is considering opening a retail outlet, and expends $10,000 exploring this idea. She eventually does open the business. Is the $10,000 deductible? _____

64. Richard is a law librarian. He decides to go to law school. He wants to deduct the costs of his education. May he do so? _____

65. Peter is a Belgian lawyer. He came to the United States to earn an LLM, which took him two years. During the summer between school years, he worked as an associate at a large law firm. Peter wishes to deduct the cost of his LLM. May he do so? _____

66. Bonbon owns a rental house. She was paid rental income of $10,000. Her expenses were repairs ($1,500), property management ($3,000), and taxes ($2,500). She also spent $15,000 adding another bedroom to the home. How should Bonbon report these items? _____

67. What is the rationale for allowing depreciation deductions? _____

―――――――――――

Answers

56. IRC §162 allows a deduction for all of the ordinary and necessary expenses of carrying on a trade or business. Win's expenses for wages to employees, waxes, soaps, etc., and advertising would certainly fit within this category. The legal fees incurred in the dispute with a car owner would also qualify; even though they might be unique in Win's experience, legal fees are of the usual type of expenses incurred by businesspeople, and therefore considered "ordinary." Similarly, license fees are usually deductible, although there may be some question of when these are deductible (we don't know Win's method of accounting). Parking fines are not deductible, because IRC §162(f) prohibits a deduction for fines or illegal payments. The fees for the seance are almost certainly not deductible; although courts generally don't substitute their judgment for those of businesspeople, in this case, the expenditure would probably not be considered "ordinary" or "necessary." The legal fees to settle the dispute about title to the parking lot are properly capitalized; they are not deductible, but instead become part of the basis in the asset (fee title or lease). Similarly, the van is a capital asset which must be capitalized. However, a portion of the expense may be deducted under IRC §179, which allows up to $105,000 (in 2005) to be deducted instead of capitalized.

57. Jody's basis in the rental home must be adjusted downward to account for MACRS deductions allocable to it. Residential real property is deductible on the straight-line basis, over 27.5 years.

Therefore her annual depreciation deduction is $2,000 ($167 monthly). She is entitled to the following depreciation (MACRS) deductions:

Year 1	5½ months	$ 918
Year 2	12 months	$2,000
Year 3	12 months	$2,000
Year 4	½ month	$ 83
Total		**$5,001**

As a result, her basis is $49,999 and the gain on sale is $30,001.

58. The promise from Adam is a "covenant not to compete," one of the so-called §197 intangibles that must be amortized over 15 years—regardless of the actual term of the promise. Therefore, Grant will take a deduction of $2,000 per year for 15 years attributable to the covenant.

59. The amount that Baxter paid for equipment is a capital expenditure that, except for amounts properly deductible under §179, must be capitalized and depreciated under MACRS. The leasehold improvements are amortizable on a straight-line basis over 15 years. Of his $10,000 of pre-opening expenses ($5,000 to his assistant and $5,000 of miscellaneous expenses) only $5,000 is deductible in the year of opening. The rest is amortizable over 15 years. The expenses incurred after opening are deductible, assuming that they otherwise meet the requirements of being ordinary and necessary.

60. When a taxpayer acquires real property, he or she is deemed to have acquired it on the midpoint of the month it is acquired, regardless of the day on which it is actually acquired. The function of these conventions is to simplify MACRS calculations. Therefore, Lenore will be able to claim 11½ months of depreciation for Year 1, not a full 12 months.

61. Xavier would like to take a deduction for the bad debt. Ideally, he would like the debt to be a business bad debt, because that leads to an ordinary deduction, rather than a capital loss.

   ■ If Xavier is Zena's father, the first question is whether there is a debt at all, or if there were a debt, whether the "badness" of it is really the father making a gift to the daughter. If the debt is bona fide, and it is really a bad debt, it would definitely be a nonbusiness bad debt, as it is family oriented, not related to the business (absent other facts).

   ■ If Xavier is Zena's employer, there is a possibility that this could be considered a business bad debt if Xavier's primary motivation in making the loan was to further the business. If his primary motivation was to be a "nice guy," the debt is a nonbusiness bad debt.

   ■ If Xavier is in the business of making loans, the debt is a business bad debt.

62. Assuming Bennie's tax home is and remains at his home institution, his visit at the other school is a temporary job away from home. Therefore, Bennie traveled away from home on business, and is entitled to deduct his reasonable expenses while away from home, including rent, food (to a certain extent), and other expenses. These expenses are considered unreimbursed employee business expenses, deductible if he itemizes, but subject to the 2% limitation.

63. Wendy will probably be considered as creating a capital asset, because the retail outlet is a separate and distinct asset from the wholesale business. As such, these expenses must be capitalized, but some or all of them may qualify as pre-opening expenses, in which case up to $5,000 is deducted in the year of opening and the rest is amortizable over 180 months.

64. If Richard's job required him to earn a law degree, he would be able to deduct the costs of his law school education. However, if his employer did not require it, the cost would not be deductible because it would qualify him for a new profession. In the latter case, Richard's argument that his information would help him better carry out his current duties would probably fall on deaf Tax Court ears. See *Galligan v. Commissioner,* T.C. Memo. 2002-150.

65. A practicing lawyer who goes back to school to get an LLM can usually deduct these costs. But in *Weyts v. Commissioner,* TC Memo 2003-68, the court likened the summer internship as more akin to education and denied the deduction for education expenses.

66. Bonbon must report the rental income as part of her gross income but may deduct the expenditures for repairs, property management and taxes as ordinary and necessary expenses of the production of income under IRC §212. Thus, her net income, not considering MACRS deductions, will be $3,000. She will not be able to deduct the costs of the addition, as this is a capital expenditure. She will be able to claim MACRS deductions of some amount for the home and the addition, but these cannot be determined from the facts given.

67. Depreciation is allowed for capital assets, i.e., those that will last more than one year. To allow a deduction in the year of acquisition would result in a mismatch of income and the costs of producing the income over time—accelerating the deductions while the income would be reported over a number of years. Depreciation deductions match the "using up" of the asset to the income it produces over time. However, the schedule for depreciation (or amortization, for that matter) does not necessarily match up with the actual fall in value of the asset (if any); it is an approximation at best.

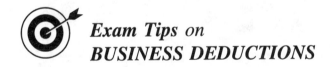

Exam Tips on BUSINESS DEDUCTIONS

Questions dealing with pure business deductions obviously involve a taxpayer's activities with respect to trade or business.

☞ *Look for:* Usually a sole proprietorship is illustrated in the basic income tax course, but a trade or business can be carried on by a corporation or partnership.

☞ *Analyze:* Identify the particular outlays. Analyze them expenditure-by-expenditure. Is an expenditure deductible, and if so, how much is deductible?

☛ Work through the four requirements to test deductibility: ordinary, necessary, incurred in carrying on (not pre-opening), and a trade or business. If an expense flunks any of these requirements, it is not currently deductible under IRC §162.

☛ Timing questions often arise in these questions.

☞ *Look for:* The taxpayer's method of accounting—cash or accrual (see Chapter 11).

☞ *Analyze:* If an expenditure is deductible, *when* is it deductible?

☛ Watch for expenses that have benefits for a longer period than the taxable year. Usually, these must be capitalized. If so, when will the taxpayer be allowed to recover the invested capital? Over time (as in MACRS) or upon disposition of the investment?

☛ MACRS questions involve some arithmetic skills. Intimidated or pressed for time? Explain how MACRS would be applied to the particular situation, and come back later to do the math if you have time.

☛ Some expenditures have both personal and business connections (see Chapter 8). In that case, usually some or all of the expenditure will be nondeductible.

CHAPTER 8

MIXED BUSINESS AND PERSONAL EXPENSES

ChapterScope

As discussed in the previous two chapters, the expenses of conducting business are generally deductible, while personal expenses are not (absent specific statutory authority). The previous two chapters have identified and discussed expenses that are clearly business or personal expenditures. Some expenses, however, do not fall neatly into these categories; they are connected with both the business and personal aspects of a taxpayer's life. The dual nature of these expenses raises the difficult tax question of whether they should be deductible in whole or in part. Congress and the courts have taken two different approaches to the problem. First, the expense may be assigned to one or the other category even though its ambiguous nature makes it less than a perfect fit in that category. Second, the Code may bifurcate the expense into its personal and business components, allowing deduction for the business portion and disallowing a deduction for the personal component. This chapter examines how these approaches are applied to a number of mixed business and personal expenses.

- **The origin test:** The origin of an expense determines whether it is most closely related to the business or personal aspect of a taxpayer's life.

- **Hobby losses:** Section 183 denies deductions in excess of income for activities not engaged in for profit. The regulations offer nine factors to be used in determining whether a taxpayer is engaged in an activity for profit or as a hobby.

- **Meals, entertainment, travel, and related expenses:** Section 274 imposes significant restrictions on the deductibility of certain items, such as meals and entertainment, travel, gifts, and related items, even if they have a significant connection with a taxpayer's trade or business.

- **Home offices and vacation homes:** A taxpayer using a personal residence as a rental or for business will incur expenses for personal as well as business use of the residence. Which will be deductible? Section 280A requires bifurcation of these expenses, and imposes significant restrictions on the deductibility of expenses to prevent a taxpayer from claiming a loss attributable to business use of a residence.

- **Luxury automobiles and listed property:** Automobiles and certain other types of property (computers, for example) are particularly likely to be used for business and personal purposes. Section 280F imposes restrictions on capital recovery deductions attributable to these properties.

I. WHERE ARE WE?

We are still working our way through deductions on the road to determining taxable income. These deductions, unlike the ones in the previous chapters, have a connection to both the taxpayer's personal life and the taxpayer's business or investment life. The question, then, is whether they are properly deductible, and if so, how—on Schedule C or E (business or rents/royalties) or elsewhere, perhaps as an itemized deduction?

II. ORIGIN TEST

The origin of an expense determines its nature as a business or personal expense.

A. *United States v. Gilmore*, 372 U.S. 39 (1963)

The taxpayer incurred legal expenses in a divorce action in which the primary issue of controversy was the protection of his ownership of a closely held corporation that also employed him. He argued that the legal expenses were deductible because they related to his business and employment relationships. The Supreme Court disagreed on the grounds that the "origin" of the expense was the divorce, a clearly personal or family matter. Because the origin of the expenses was personal, the expenses were not deductible, regardless of their connection with the taxpayer's business life.

B. Relation to "ordinary and necessary"

Section 162 requires that an expenditure be an ordinary and necessary business expense in order to be deductible. The definitions of "ordinary" and "necessary" function in part to distinguish personal expenses from business expenses, denying deduction for personal expenses even if they have some relation to the business activity. The origin test is more often used for extraordinary, nonrecurring expenses, while the ordinary and necessary definitions are used for ongoing expenditures. Their functions are similar, however, and both can be invoked to deny deduction for a personal expense incurred in business. For a discussion of §162, see Chapter 7(II).

Example: Carol, the sole proprietor of Candy-2-U, hires her son Adam to assist her in delivering candy baskets so that he may earn money for graduate school. She pays him five times the going rate for delivery persons, and seeks to deduct the expense on her Schedule C. In challenging this deduction, the IRS would likely rely on the argument that unreasonably high wages do not qualify as an ordinary expense. Instead, it is partly a payment for services (a deductible business expense) and partly a gift to Adam from Carol (a nondeductible personal expenditure). It would be equally correct to argue that the origin of the expense was partly business (the reasonable part of the wages) and partly personal (the relationship between mother and son). As a result, only the business portion of the payment would be deductible.

III. HOBBY LOSSES—§183

A. Policy

As discussed in Chapter 7(II)(B), a trade or business requires regular and continuous activity with the expectation of producing a profit. Most businesses are easy to identify; the taxpayer would not engage in them without some expectation of profit. However, some income-producing activities offer such significant recreational or personal benefits that they raise questions about the taxpayer's profit motive. If the activity is engaged in for profit, the expenses associated with the activity should be deductible. If the taxpayer does not have a profit motive, however, the activity is personal in nature, and expenses should not be allowed, at least not in excess of the income from the activity. Section 183 seeks to identify activities "not engaged in for profit" and restrict deductions associated with them.

B. Statutory analysis

1. **General rule:** A taxpayer engaged in an activity without a profit motive may only deduct certain expenses associated with that activity. These expenses are (1) those that are deductible (under other Code sections) without regard to a profit motive, and (2) expenses in an amount (if any) equal to the gross income from the activity, minus the expenses described in (1). IRC §183(a). Thus, the taxpayer is not allowed to generate a loss from activities not engaged in for profit, but is allowed to offset the income from the activity with expenses of producing the income.

   Example: John is a race car driver engaged in the activity as a hobby (not for profit). This year he earned $5,000 in race prizes, and had the following two categories of expenses. He had a casualty loss of $6,000 attributable to a crash, and expenses that would otherwise qualify as ordinary and necessary business expenses of $2,500. Assume that of the $6,000 casualty loss, $4,000 is deductible under §165(c) and (h). Since John is engaged in an activity without a profit motive, he may deduct only the deductible portion ($4,000) of the casualty loss (because it is allowable without regard to his profit motive) and $1,000 of the expenses that would be deductible if he had a profit motive. In computing the $1,000 deduction, John subtracts from his gross income from the activity ($5,000) the deductions allowable without regard to his profit motive ($4,000) to determine the allowable deduction ($1,000). The remaining $1,500 of expenses are nondeductible.

2. **Definitional issue—Activity engaged in for profit:** Whether a taxpayer is engaged in an activity for profit depends on all of the facts and circumstances of the situation. The courts emphasize that a taxpayer need have only a sincere and bona fide expectation of realizing a profit, regardless of the reasonableness of that expectation. *Golanty v. Commissioner,* 72 T.C. 411, at 425-426, (1979) *aff'd without opinion,* 647 F.2d 170 (9th Cir. 1981). The regulations specify nine factors to be examined in analyzing the taxpayer's profit motive. See Reg. §1.183-2(b).

   a. **Nine factors:** The regulations set forth nine factors, none of which are determinative, that are relevant in determining whether the taxpayer has (or does not have) a profit motive.

      i. **Manner of operation:** A taxpayer carrying on the activity in a businesslike manner, keeping books and records, running the business like other similar businesses, and changing methods of operation as necessary to increase profitability, indicates a profit motive. Reg. §1.183-2(b)(1).

      ii. **Expertise:** A taxpayer with expertise in the activity (or who develops or engages others with expertise) is more likely to be viewed as having a profit motive than one without such expertise. The taxpayer also should conduct business in accordance with the best practices of experts, unless he or she can show development of innovative methods for profitability. Reg. §1.183-2(b)(2).

      iii. **Time and effort:** A taxpayer devoting substantial time and effort to an activity is more likely to be considered as having a profit motive than one who dabbles in the activity, particularly if the activity is not particularly enjoyable. A taxpayer who engages others to conduct substantial activity may also be viewed as having a profit motive. Reg. §1.183-2(b)(3).

iv. **Assets that increase in value:** If assets used in an activity are reasonably likely to increase in value, this may indicate a profit motive. Reg. §1.183-2(b)(4).

v. **Similar success:** A taxpayer who has had success in similar ventures may be viewed as having a profit motive. Reg. §1.183-2(b)(5).

vi. **History of income or loss:** While losses during the start-up phase of a business may not indicate a lack of profit motive, losses that continue beyond this period suggest the absence of a profit motive. However, losses arising from unforeseen or unusual events (such as storm or fire) are not indicative of a lack of profit motive. Reg. §1.183-2(b)(6).

vii. **Amount of occasional profits, if any:** A taxpayer engaging in a venture in which profits, though occasional, would be large in comparison to losses and investment, would generally be viewed as having a profit motive. By contrast, a taxpayer engaging in a venture in which occasional profits would be small compared with losses and investment, would generally be viewed as lacking a profit motive. Reg. §1.183-2(b)(7).

ix. **Taxpayer's financial status:** A taxpayer who does not have substantial income or capital from other sources generally will be viewed as engaged in an activity for profit. By contrast, a taxpayer with substantial income from other sources may not be engaging in an activity for profit, particularly if the activity has personal or recreational elements. Reg. §1.183-2(b)(8).

x. **Personal pleasure or recreation:** A taxpayer who engages in an activity for personal purposes may be viewed as lacking a profit motive, especially when the activity involves recreation or other personal elements. However, enjoyment of one's work does not, alone, establish the absence of a profit motive. Reg. §1.183-2(b)(9).

b. **Application—*Nickerson v. Commissioner*, 700 F.2d 402 (7th Cir. 1983):** Nickerson purchased a farm in anticipation of retiring from the advertising business. The court examined the nine factors, ultimately concluding that Nickerson was engaged in the activity for profit as evidenced by his expectation that the farm would be profitable in future years, his engagement of a tenant farmer to clear and farm the land in his absence, his attempts to improve his expertise, and the absence of pleasurable activities on the fairly dilapidated farm.

3. **Special rules and exceptions—Presumption:** If the activity produces income for three out of the five consecutive years ending in the year in question, it is rebuttably presumed to be an activity engaged in for profit. IRC §183(d). Moreover, if the activity involves horse breeding, racing, showing, or training, the test is whether the activity showed a profit in two out of the seven consecutive years ending in the year in question. Id.

Example: Jan is engaged in the activity of breeding and training horses. She reports a loss from the activity in 2004, and the IRS challenges the deductions generating that loss, arguing that she did not have a profit motive in the activity. Jan had experienced losses in 1998, 1999, and 2002–2003. However, she had reported net income from the activity in 2000 and 2001. This income and loss history establishes a rebuttable presumption that her activity is engaged in for profit, for she reported net income in two out of the seven years ending in the year 2000. In order to successfully invoke §183's disallowance of deductions, the IRS must overcome the presumption and may attempt to do so using the nine factors of the regulations.

4. Related material

    a. Available deductions—No profit motive: In order to apply §183, it is necessary to understand what deductions are available even if the activity is not engaged in for profit. These can include certain interest, casualty losses, and other expenditures. See generally Chapter 6.

    b. Available deductions—Profit motive: If the taxpayer has a profit motive, all the deductions otherwise allowable are available, as discussed in Chapter 7.

5. Summary: A taxpayer engaged in an activity without a profit motive may not deduct a loss attributable to that activity. Instead, the taxpayer may only deduct certain expenses associated with that activity, up to the gross income from the activity. IRC §183.

Statute Summary—§183
Activities Not Engaged in for Profit

Parsing Step	§183
General rule	No deduction is allowed for expenses incurred in activities not engaged in for profit.
Definitional issues	"Not for profit" depends on all facts and circumstances; see nine factors in regulations.
Special rules and exceptions	Deductions allowed to extent of income from activity minus otherwise allowable deductions Presumptions 3/5 years; for horses 2/7 years
Related material	Business expenses: §162 Otherwise allowable deductions: §§163, 165
Summary	Deductions limited to income minus nonbusiness expenses, when activity is not for profit

IV. SECTION 274 RESTRICTIONS

A. General approach

Section 274 takes the general approach of denying deductions for certain expenses altogether, and denying deductions for other expenses unless the taxpayer shows that the expense was incurred in specified circumstances indicating that the expenditure was business-related.

B. Meals and entertainment expenses

Meals and entertainment expenses are subject to especially stringent rules in §274. "Meal" expenses are for food and beverages, including tips. "Entertainment" expenses are expenses for amusement, recreation, or entertainment, such as expenses of entertaining at nightclubs, theaters, sporting events, golf, and similar activities. Reg. §1.274-2(b)(1).

A taxpayer desiring to deduct any expense for meals or entertainment must run a gauntlet of tests for deductibility, and is likely to find that, in the end, only a portion of the expense is deductible.

1. General requirements

a. Ordinary and necessary expenses: In order to even begin the analysis of an expense under §274, the expense must meet the requirements of an "ordinary and necessary business expense" under §162(a). Section 274, then, focuses on the "business" aspect of the expenditure, subjecting it to more intensive scrutiny to determine if its connection with business is sufficient to justify a deduction. See Chapter 7(II)(B).

b. *Sorry*—Certain really fun expenses are nondeductible: Expenses associated with facilities for entertainment, amusement, or recreation, including dues for such facilities, are nondeductible. IRC §274(a)(1)(B). In addition, dues for clubs organized for "business, pleasure, recreation or other social purposes" are nondeductible. IRC §274(a)(3).

c. Special limitations: For meals, any amount that is "lavish" or "extravagant" or is incurred while the taxpayer (or a representative of the taxpayer) is not present is nondeductible. IRC §274(k)(1). For tickets, only the face value is deductible: Extra fees, whether imposed by legitimate ticket agents or scalpers, are not deductible. This is true for skyboxes, where only the face amount of the tickets, multiplied by the number of seats in the box, is deductible. IRC §274(l)(1). An exception is provided for charity sporting events, where the face amount of the ticket includes a donation.

2. Business connection tests

Section 274 accomplishes its purpose of determining whether there is a close connection between the taxpayer's business and the expenditure in question by imposing a business connection test on certain expenditures.

a. Exceptions: There are nine categories of expenses that are not subject to the business connection tests. These are assumed to have the requisite business connection. The nine exceptions are for expenses: (1) for food/beverages for employees in a cafeteria or other business setting; (2) that are treated as compensation; (3) that are reimbursed; (4) for recreation of employees, such as at the annual company picnic; (5) for employee, stockholder, or other business meetings; (6) for meetings of business leagues; (7) for food/entertainment generally available to the public, as in hot dogs and soda available at a sidewalk sale; (8) which constitute entertainment sold to customers; and (9) for prizes and awards for nonemployees. IRC §274(e)(1)-(9).

b. Stringent "directly related" standard: Under the first business connection test, in order to be deductible, the expenditure must be "directly related" to the active conduct of the taxpayer's trade or business. IRC §274(a)(1)(A). Expenditures made in a clear business setting, such as a "hospitality room" at a convention, will be considered directly related to the active conduct of the taxpayer's trade or business. Reg. §1.274-2(c)(4). Certain expenditures generally will not be considered directly related, such as expenditures for entertainment when the taxpayer was not present, and for entertainment offering substantial distractions (such as at sporting events, nightclubs, and cocktail parties). Reg. §1.274-2(c)(7). For expenditures outside a clear business setting, four requirements must be met that impose a standard quite difficult to meet.

i. Expectation of income: At the time of the expenditure, the taxpayer must have more than a general expectation of deriving some income or other specific benefit in making the expenditure, although the taxpayer need not prove that income or other benefits actually resulted from each expenditure. Reg. §1.274-2(c)(3)(i).

ii. **Active engagement:** The taxpayer must show that he or she actively engaged in a business meeting, negotiation, discussion, or other bona fide business transaction during the entertainment period for the purpose of obtaining income or other specific benefit. It is not necessary, however, that more time be spent on business than on entertainment. Reg. §1.274-2(c)(3)(ii).

iii. **Principal character:** The taxpayer must show that in light of all of the facts and circumstances of the situation, the principal character of the event was the active conduct of the taxpayer's trade or business. Reg. §1.274-2(c)(3)(iii).

iv. **Taxpayer and business associate:** The taxpayer must show that the expenditures were allocable to the taxpayer and a person(s) with whom the taxpayer is engaged in the active conduct of a trade or business. Reg. §1.274-2(c)(3)(iv).

Example: Jeff purchases two tickets to the local college basketball game and invites Cheryl, a sales representative of his major supplier, to join him at the game. It is Jeff's intent to try to negotiate a better price on certain supplies, and in fact the two discuss price during the less exciting moments of the game. While entertainment at sporting events is not generally considered to constitute "directly related" entertainment because of the substantial distractions, if Jeff can establish that in light of all the facts and circumstances of the situation, the principal character of the event was business-related, he will be able to deduct the cost of the tickets as a business entertainment expense. (This would require him to be able to prove that he and Cheryl principally discussed business during the event, perhaps because the game was so boring?) This will be a very difficult standard for Jeff to meet.

c. **Less stringent "associated with" standard:** Entertainment expenses that do not meet the directly related standard will be deductible only if they are "associated with" the active conduct of a trade or business and the entertainment directly preceded or followed a "substantial and bona fide business discussion." IRC §274(a)(1)(A).

i. **Associated with:** In order for an expense to be considered "associated with" the active conduct of the taxpayer's trade or business, the taxpayer must show that he or she had a clear business purpose in making the expenditure, such as to obtain new business or encourage the continuation of an existing business relationship. Reg. §1.274-2(d)(2). This encompasses expenditures for entertainment of persons close to those directly in a business relationship, such as spouses and other close family members. Id.

ii. **Substantial and bona fide business discussion:** Whether a discussion, negotiation, or meeting constitutes a substantial and bona fide business discussion depends on all of the facts and circumstances of the situation. The discussion must be substantial in relation to the entertainment, but it is not necessary that more time be spent on business than on entertainment. Reg. §1.274-2(d)(3)(i)(a).

iii. **What about conventions?** Committee meetings, lectures, panel discussions, and similar events at conventions generally constitute substantial and bona fide business discussions. Reg. §1.274-2(d)(3)(i)(b).

Example: Patricia is a tax lawyer who offers her consulting services to other lawyers and accountants on tax matters. She attends the ABA Tax Section meeting and participates in committee meetings and panel discussions. In the evening, she invites three other lawyers attending the meeting to see the touring production of "Cats." One of the lawyers regularly engages her for tax advice, and she would like the other two to do the same. This entertainment expense is probably deductible, as it is associated with the active conduct of Patricia's trade or business and occurs immediately after a substantial and bona fide business discussion at the convention.

    d. 50% deductibility rule: If an expense satisfies the requirements discussed above, it is potentially deductible. However, §274(n) provides that only *50%* of the amount potentially deductible as meal or entertainment expenses actually will produce a deduction. This is designed to allocate the expenditure between its necessarily business and personal elements (and, perhaps, to raise revenue).

        i. Exceptions: There are exceptions to the 50% rule. These generally follow the exceptions to the business connection tests, although there are some differences. Thus, the following expenses are excepted from the 50% limitation, as they are from the business connection test: (1) expenses treated as compensation; (2) reimbursed expenses; (3) expenses for recreation of employees; (4) expenses for food/entertainment generally available to the public; (5) expenses of entertainment sold to customers; and (6) expenses for prizes and awards for nonemployees. In addition, certain de minimis expenses, as determined under IRC §132, are not subject to the 50% rule, as are expenses of certain charitable events, and expenses of special kinds of employees. See IRC §274(n)(2).

        ii. So what? If one of the exceptions applies, the expense will be 100% deductible, not just 50% deductible.

C. Business gifts

No deduction is allowed for the cost of business gifts in excess of $25 per recipient per year. IRC §274(b)(1). For these purposes, a gift is a transfer that is excludible from gross income of the recipient under §102, and husbands and wives are treated as one person for purposes of the gift provisions. For a discussion of gifts, see Chapter 4(III).

D. Foreign travel

    1. General approach: If a business trip outside the United States is purely for business purposes, the expenses of travel will be fully deductible. However, if a portion of the trip is for personal purposes, an allocation must be made between the business and personal portions, and only the business portions will generate deductible expenses. If, however, the total travel time does not exceed one week, or the personal portion is less than 25% of the trip, no allocation will be required, and the expenses of travel will be fully deductible. Reg. §1.274-4(a).

    2. Conventions: Convention and seminar expenses are deductible only under §162 for a taxpayer's trade or business; no deduction is allowed for these activities for investment activities or other production of income. IRC §274(h)(7). In order to deduct expenses of attending conventions or meetings relating to his or her trade or business outside the North American area, the taxpayer must show that, considering all the facts and circumstances of the situation, it was as reasonable that the convention or meeting was held outside the North American area as inside it. IRC §274(h)(1).

        a. Four relevant factors: There are four factors to be considered in determining the reasonableness of having the convention or meeting outside the North American area: the purpose of the meeting and its activities, the purposes and activities of the sponsoring organization, the residences of the active members of the group and the places where other meeting have been held, and "such other relevant factors as the taxpayer may present." IRC §274(h)(1).

b. Cruising, anyone? A taxpayer may not take a deduction in excess of $2,000 for conventions or meetings on cruise ships in one calendar year, and special limitations apply to expenses incurred in "luxury" water transportation. See IRC §274(h)(2), (m)(1). In addition, in order to deduct expenses of conventions or seminars on cruise ships, the taxpayer must meet three requirements.

  i. Directly related test: The taxpayer must show that the meeting or convention was directly related to the active conduct of his or her trade or business. IRC §274(h)(2).

  ii. United States cruising *only***:** The taxpayer must show that the vessel was registered in the United States, and all ports of call were in the United States or possessions of the United States. IRC §274(h)(2)(A), (B).

  iii. Reporting requirements: The taxpayer must attach to his or her tax return information regarding the time spent on the trip, the itinerary, and the business engaged in on the trip. IRC §274(h)(5).

E. Substantiation requirements

Section 274(d) imposes significant substantiation requirements on taxpayers seeking to deduct expenses. The taxpayer must keep adequate books and records to support (1) the amount of any expense, (2) the circumstances under which it was incurred, (3) the business purpose of the expense, and (4) the business relationship to the taxpayer of the person(s) receiving the benefit of the expense. Congress granted authority to the Secretary of the Treasury to promulgate substantiation rules, and Treasury has done so. See Reg. §1.274-5T.

V. HOME OFFICES AND VACATION HOMES—§280A

A. General approach

Taxpayers may establish offices in their homes in order to deduct the expenses of a portion of the residence such as utilities, repairs—and especially depreciation. Or a taxpayer may rent out a vacation home for some period of the year, and seek similar deductions for that home. In both cases, the question is whether the taxpayer is really deducting personal expenses because the business use (in the home office case) is fictional or the percentage of expenses attributable to the rental of the vacation home is overstated. IRC §280A severely limits these kinds of deductions.

B. Statutory analysis—§280A

1. General rule: The complex general rule of §280A contains three parts: a disallowance of deductions, a restoration of certain deductions, and two potential limitations on allowable deductions.

  a. Disallowance of deductions: Section 280A(a) disallows any deduction for expenses of a "dwelling unit" that the taxpayer who is an individual or a corporation uses as a residence.

  b. Restoration of certain deductions: Section 280A(b) restores the deduction for expenses that are deductible regardless of whether the taxpayer is engaged in a trade or business, i.e., which are deductible under some other section of the Code (such as qualified residence interest). IRC §280A(c) restores the deduction for a specified portion of the expenses allocable to four different uses of the dwelling unit. The four qualifying uses are described below.

i.   **Certain business use:** Expenses allocable to a portion of the dwelling unit that is exclusively used on a regular basis as the place of business for any trade or business of the taxpayer are deductible. IRC §280A(c)(1)(A).

ii. **Storage use:** Expenses allocable to the use of the dwelling unit as storage for the taxpayer's inventory, if the business has no other fixed office or place of business, are deductible. IRC §280A(c)(2).

iii. **Rental use:** Expenses attributable to the rental of all or a portion of the property are deductible. IRC §280A(c)(3).

iv. **Day care facility:** Expenses attributable to the use of the property as a day care facility for children, the elderly, and those physically unable to care for themselves are deductible. IRC §280A(c)(4)(A). If the portion of the home used for day care is also used for personal purposes at other times, the statute requires an allocation of expenses based on time used in the day care business. IRC §280A(c)(4)(C). The section also imposes certain licensing requirements on these facilities in order for expenses to be deductible. IRC §280A(c)(4)(B).

c. **Two limitations:** Two separate limitations apply, depending on the use of the property.

i.   **Business, storage, day care, and certain rental use:** The first limitation applies to business, storage, and day care use of a dwelling unit, and to rental use where the taxpayer also uses the property as a residence. The deductions attributable to these uses cannot exceed the gross income from the use minus the sum of (1) the deductions allowable without regard to the allowed use and (2) the trade or business or investment expenses for the activity which are not allocable to the use of the property. IRC §280A(c)(5). These would include supplies, advertising, and other IRC §162 expenses that do not arise directly from the use of the home for business. In the case of rental activity, there usually wouldn't be any of these expenses, so the limitation would be gross rents minus the expenses allocable to the rental which are otherwise deductible without regard to rental. Amounts not deductible because of this limitation carry forward and may be deducted in the following year, subject to the same limitation. Id. The effect of these limitations is to prevent a deduction for business use of a home to create a loss for tax purposes.

Example: Kristan is an author with a home office that she uses exclusively for researching, writing, and editing magazine articles and talking with her editors on the telephone. Her income from writing for the year was $6,000. She had $2,000 of ordinary and necessary business expenses unrelated to her business use of her home. Her expenses that are attributable to her home office are as follows:

Home mortgage interest	$1,400
Property taxes	$1,250
Insurance	$ 375
Utilities	$ 150
MACRS (depreciation)	$1,600

Although §280A(a) disallows a deduction for any expenses associated with business use of a dwelling unit as a residence, certain of Kristan's expenses (her interest and property taxes) will be deductible under subsection (b), which allows a deduction for expenses that are allowable without regard to the taxpayer's trade or business. Moreover, at least a portion of the expenses associated with Kristan's use of her home office will most likely be deductible, as Kristan's use of the office exclusively as her principal place of business for writing qualifies as a use justifying deductions under §280A(c)(1)(A). These expenses, however, may be limited by §280A(c)(5).

Applying the limitation to Kristan's situation, the deductions attributable to the business use of her home will be limited to the gross income from the activity ($6,000), reduced by the sum of (1) the deductions attributable to use which are otherwise allowable regardless of her business use (the interest and taxes, $2,650) and (2) the trade or business expenses not attributable to the business use of the home ($2,000). This produces $1,350, which is the limit on deductions attributable to insurance, utilities and MACRS. The remaining $775 of these expenses will carry forward and be deductible in future years, subject to the same restriction.

ii. Personal use of rented property. The second limitation applies to rental property that is also used for personal purposes for even one day during the taxable year. The deductions attributable to the rental (other than expenses deductible without regard to rental) cannot exceed the expenses multiplied by a fraction, the numerator of which is the total number of days rented, and the denominator is the total number of days the property is used for either personal or rental purposes. IRC §280A(e).

iii. Ordering rule: If the overall limitation applies, expenses will be allowed in the following order: interest, taxes, trade or business expenses, and, finally, depreciation.

iv. Which limitation applies to rentals? If a dwelling is rented and is also used for the taxpayer's personal purposes, which limitation applies? If the taxpayer uses the dwelling as a residence, the IRC §280A(c)(5) limitation will apply, with the result that an overall limitation on the amount of deductions will be applied. If the taxpayer does not use the dwelling as a residence, but uses it for even one day for personal purposes, the limitation of IRC §280A(e)(1) will apply. This results in an allocation of expenses between personal and rental use, but no overall limitation.

2. Definitional issues

a. Dwelling unit: A dwelling unit includes any typical place of dwelling, including houses, apartments, and condominiums and also includes mobile homes, boats, and recreational vehicles. The term, however, does not include motels, hotels, and inns. IRC §280A(f)(1).

b. Use as a "residence": A taxpayer uses a dwelling unit as a residence if he or she uses it for personal purposes for a number of days during the taxable year that exceeds the greater of 14 days or 10% of the number of days the unit is rented at a fair rental. IRC §280A(d)(1).

Personal use is use by the taxpayer or his or her family, or rental to others at less than a fair rental value. IRC §280A(d)(2). But when a taxpayer spends substantially all day repairing the property, the day is not counted as a day of personal use. IRC §280A(d)(2).

c. **Place of business:** There are three ways a taxpayer may claim that a home office is a place of business, thus qualifying for the home office deduction. All three require that the portion of the residence used for business be used *exclusively* for business.

   i. **Principal place of business:** The portion of the residence may be regularly used as the principal place of business for a taxpayer's business. IRC §280A(c)(1)(A). This would be the case, for example, for writers or freelance editors who have no other place of business. A home office qualifies as a taxpayer's principal place of business if (1) the taxpayer uses the office to conduct administrative or management activities of the taxpayer's trade or business, and (2) there is no other fixed location of the trade or business where the taxpayer conducts substantial administrative or managerial functions of the business. These functions include keeping records, billing patients or other customers, setting up appointments, and forwarding written reports or orders. IRC §280A(c).

   Example: Steve is a self-employed golf teacher. He teaches students at several area golf courses and conducts golf seminars at various hotels around the area. From his home office, he sets up appointments, sends bills, and keeps records of each student's progress. Assuming Steve's home office is used exclusively for this purpose, he will be able to claim a deduction for his home office as the "principal place of business" of his golf teaching business.

   ii. **Meeting clients or customers:** The residence may be regularly used as the place where the taxpayer meets with clients or customers of the business. For example, a therapist might use a portion of her home as her office at which she meets patients. IRC §280A(c)(1)(B).

   iii. **Separate structures:** If the home office is located in a separate structure from the residence, it need only be "connected with" the trade or business in order to qualify, which imposes a lesser standard. IRC §280A(c)(1)(C).

d. **Allocable to such use—§280A(c)(5)(B)(i):** The limitation of §280A(c)(5) requires that gross income from a rental also used as a residence be reduced by the sum of the deductions "allocable to such use" otherwise allowable without regard to rental (such as home mortgage interest and property taxes) and the trade or business expenses not tied to the property itself (such as commissions). The example above assumed that the property was rented or used for personal purposes for each day during the year. If the property is vacant for any day during the year, there is a difference of opinion between the IRS and the courts on how to calculate the "otherwise allowable deductions," i.e., on the proper interpretation of the phrase "allocable to such use" in §280A(c)(5)(B)(i). This difference can have important implications for the amount of deductions allowable to a taxpayer.

   i. **IRS position:** The IRS position is that the allocation formula contained in §280A(e) should be applied to the §280A(c)(5) and §280A(e)(1) limitations so that the otherwise allowable expenses are multiplied by a fraction, the numerator of which is the number of days rented and the denominator of which is the number of days used. See Prop. Reg. §1.280A-3(c)(1).

   ii. **Courts' approach:** The courts allow mortgage interest and taxes to be multiplied by a fraction, the numerator of which is the number of days rented and the denominator of which is the number of days in the year (365). This reflects the fact that interest and taxes accrue on a daily basis, not just on days the property is used. While this results in a lower percentage for the allocable rental use, in fact it helps a taxpayer because the taxpayer may be able to take the rest of the interest and taxes as an itemized deduction, and this allows a greater amount of other expenses to be claimed under the overall limitation of IRC §280A(c)(5). See, e.g., *Bolton v. Commissioner,* 694 F.2d 556 (9th Cir. 1982).

Example: Josh owns a vacation home that he rents out for 180 days at $100 per day, and uses for personal purposes for 30 days. He has the following expenses:

Mortgage interest	$1,000
Taxes	$2,000
Repairs	$1,260
Depreciation	$5,000

Josh claims the itemized deduction. How much of these expenses may Josh deduct?

Because Josh used the vacation home as a residence (i.e., used it for the greater of 14 days or 10% of the rented days), the limitation of IRC §280A(c)(5) will apply. Thus, the total deductions allowable will be limited to the gross rents, minus the allocable share of expenses attributable to the rental activity. The "allocable" portion of interest and taxes depends on whether the IRS or courts' approach is taken. Compare the two below:

	IRS Approach	**Courts' Approach**
Percentage	180/210 = 86%	180/365 = 49% for interest and taxes 180/210 = 86% for other expenses
Gross rents	$18,000	$18,000
Interest and taxes	$2,580	$1,470
Overall limitation	$15,420	$16,530

Under both approaches, the amount of interest and taxes not claimed as part of this rental activity can (usually) be claimed as an itemized deduction on Schedule A. Josh itemizes, so he would claim the balance of such expenses as an itemized deduction.

Example: Assume the same facts as in the example above, except that Josh rents the property for 180 days but uses it for personal purposes for only 10 days. In that case, Josh has not used the property as a residence, so the limitation of IRC §280A(c)(5) will not apply, but the limitation of IRC §280A(e)(1) will apply. This limitation requires that the expenses be multiplied by a fraction representing the rental use of the property. The limitation does not apply to expenses deductible without regard to rental use (interest and taxes). Assuming the same approach to allocating expenses applies in the (e)(1) limitation as in the (c)(5) limitation, the percentage allocable to rental use is 95% (180/190). So, the following results would apply:

Expense	Deductible Percentage	Amount Deductible
Interest	100%	$1,000
Taxes	100%	2,000
Repairs	95%	17,000
Depreciation	95%	4,750
Total		$24,750

3. **Special rules and exceptions—15-day rental rule:** If the taxpayer rents a dwelling unit for fewer than 15 days during the taxable year, the income is excluded from the taxpayer's gross income, but no deductions associated with the rental are allowed. IRC §280A(g).

4. **Related material**

   a. **Hobby losses:** Sections 183 and 280A are similar in approach. Both prohibit a taxpayer from claiming a loss arising from certain activities. They are both potentially applicable to the same situation, in which a taxpayer is carrying on an activity not for profit, and claiming as part of the deduction expenses associated with business use of a home. Section 180A(f)(3)(A) provides that if a taxpayer uses all or part of a dwelling unit as a residence, §280A, not §183, will apply to potentially disallow deductions attributable to the property.

   b. **Otherwise allowable deductions:** In order to apply the restrictions of §280A, it is necessary to compute the deductions associated with personal use of a residence, which are allowable without regard to business use. See Chapter 6(VI), (XII), (XIII), and (XIV).

   c. **Profit-related expenses:** In order to apply the limitations of §280A, it is necessary to compute the potentially deductible expenses that require a business connection in order to be deductible. See, generally, Chapter 7.

   d. **Exclusion for gain on sale of principal residence:** IRC §121 allows a taxpayer to exclude from gross income all or a portion of the gain on the sale of a principal residence. However, the exclusion doesn't apply to gain attributable to previously deducted depreciation. See Chapter 4(VIII). So, taxpayers should think carefully about whether to claim a portion of their home as a home office or other business use, given that they will be giving up a portion of the exclusion on sale.

5. **Summary:** See Statute Summary—§280A.

Statute Summary—§280A

Parsing Step	§280A
General rule	Denial of deduction for expenses of dwelling unit used as residence, but: (1) Expenses deductible regardless of trade or business remain deductible, (2) Expenses attributable to 4 qualifying uses are deductible, (3) Two limitations on expenses associated with qualifying uses
Definitional issues	Dwelling unit/use as a residence Principal place of business "Allocable to such use"
Special rules and exceptions	15-day rental rule
Related material	Hobby losses: §183 Deductible personal expenses associated with residence: §§163(h), 165(h), 164 Deductible business expenses: §§162, 167, 168
Summary	If a taxpayer uses his residence for profit-generating activity, deductions associated with that use are likely to be limited.

VI. "LUXURY" AUTOMOBILES AND LISTED PROPERTY—§280F

A. Policy

While depreciation is only available for property used in a trade or business or held for investment, Congress felt the need to further restrict depreciation deductions for certain types of business or investment assets which are likely also to serve personal purposes. Thus, §280F imposes limitations on depreciation deductions for certain types of property, such as luxury automobiles and computers.

B. Statutory analysis—§280F

1. General rules: Before tackling §280F's general rule, recall that only property used predominantly in a trade or business or held for investment is depreciable under the MACRS system or potentially eligible for the §179 expense deduction. Thus, to the extent that property is used for both business/investment and personal purposes, only the portion of the property attributable to business use (expressed as a percentage of use, for example) is depreciable. In addition to this general principle, §280F imposes two additional limitations on depreciation of certain property.

    a. Limitation #1—Longer, slower capital recovery for "luxury" automobiles: The amount of MACRS deductions a taxpayer may claim for passenger automobiles is limited to a specified amount, adjusted for inflation (regardless of percentage of business use). IRC §280F(a). The result of this limitation is that the full cost of many automobiles is not recovered through depreciation deductions during the usual recovery period. Instead, §280F imposes a much longer, slower recovery period for most automobiles, although the restrictions are less onerous for certified clean-fuel vehicles. This reflects Congress's view that the "luxury" component of the cost of the automobile is a personal, nondeductible expenditure but that investment in clean-fuel vehicles should be encouraged. The term "luxury" automobile is used only in §280F's caption; it does not appear in the general rule. Instead, the MACRS limitations for automobiles are set at specified amounts, adjusted for inflation. From these limitations, one can derive the purchase price of the automobiles that Congress would consider to be luxury automobiles. In 2004, for example, any car that costs more than $14,800 would be considered a luxury automobile for purposes of the limitations of §280F.

For automobiles placed in service in 2004, the limitations are:

Maximum MACRS (or §179) Deduction for Automobiles Under IRC §280F (2004 Amounts)

Year	Regular Automobiles	Light Trucks, Vans, SUVs
Year placed in service	$2,960	$ 3,260
Second Year	4,800	5,300
Third Year	2,850	3,150
Every year thereafter	1,675	1,875

Example: Doug purchases a nonelectric automobile for use in his trade or business. It costs $25,000. Under the regular MACRS recovery period, using the 200% declining balance method and the mid-year convention, Doug would have been entitled to a MACRS deduction of $5,000 in the year he places the automobile in service. However, the §280F limitations apply to limit his first year MACRS deduction to $2,960. If the car had been an electric vehicle, however, the §280F limitations would not have applied to limit his deduction. Notice how Doug is placed on a longer, slower capital recovery schedule due to the §280F limitations for a nonelectric vehicle:

Year	Regular MACRS Deduction	Allowable under §280F (2004 Amounts)
1	$5,000	$2,960
2	8,000	4,800
3	4,800	2,850
4	2,880	1,675
5	2,880	1,675

[Continued]

Year	Regular MACRS Deduction	Allowable under §280F (2004 Amounts)
6	1,440	1,675
7	0	1,675
8	0	1,675
9	0	1,675
10	0	1,675
11	0	1,675
12	0	990

b. **Limitation #2—Listed property—Straight-line depreciation and recapture:** Listed property that is not used "predominately for qualified business use" must be depreciated using a straight-line method. IRC §280F(b)(1). If business use falls below 51% for listed property that was formerly used predominately in business, the taxpayer must recapture the excess depreciation and must use straight-line depreciation in the future. IRC §280F(b)(2). Recapture requires the taxpayer to include in his or her gross income the excess depreciation, i.e., the amount of depreciation claimed in excess of the amount that would have been allowable under the straight-line method. Id.

Example: Debi buys a computer for $2,500 to use partly in her trade or business of collecting and selling sports memorabilia and partly to stay in touch with friends and family through email. If her substantiated business use is not more than 50%, there are two results. First, the §179 expense deduction is not available. Second, the computer is "listed property." While MACRS would usually allow an accelerated method of depreciation for computers, the portion attributable to business use must be depreciated using the straight-line method. Therefore, if we assume that Debi will use the computer for business 40% of the time, her cost of $1,000 ($2,500 × 40%) will be depreciated over six years using straight-line depreciation, assuming a mid-year convention applies, as follows:

Year: $100
Year 2–5: $200 each year
Year 6: $100

2. **Definitional issues**

a. **For limitation #1—Longer recovery periods**

i. **Passenger automobile:** A passenger automobile is any four-wheeled vehicle that is manufactured primarily for use on public streets, roads, and highways, and is rated at 6,000 pounds or less unloaded vehicle weight (or for light trucks and vans, including

SUVs built on truck chasses, at 6,000 gross vehicle weight), but excludes certain working vehicles. IRC §280F(d)(5). The 6,000-lb figure effectively eliminates large SUVs and ¾+ ton pickups from the definition of a passenger automobile, and the limitations of §280F. Does this explain part of their popularity?

ii. Clean-fuel vehicle: The §280A limitations are tripled for passenger vehicles designed to run primarily on electricity. This is largely academic, as there are no candidates for this designation (in 2005).

b. For limitation #2—Listed property

i. Listed property: Listed property includes any passenger automobile, any other property used as a means of transportation (such as a boat, airplane, or motorcycle), any property of a type generally used for entertainment, recreation, or amusement (such as a DVD player), any computer or peripheral equipment, any cellular telephone, and any other property as specified by the Secretary of the Treasury. IRC §280F(d)(4).

ii. Excluded—Certain computers: Excluded from the definition of listed property is any computer or peripheral equipment used exclusively at a regular business establishment and owned or leased by the person operating the business. This includes home offices that qualify under §280A. IRC §280F(d)(4)(B). See discussion of home offices this chapter at Section V.

iii. Excluded—Transportation businesses: Also excluded from the definition of listed property is property used in a transportation business. IRC §280F(d)(4)(C).

iv. Predominantly used in business: A taxpayer must use property in a qualified business use for more than 50% of the use during the taxable year in order to qualify as predominantly used in a qualified business use. IRC §280F(b)(3). A qualified business use means any use in a trade or business, but does not include use for the production of income outside of a trade or business. IRC §280F(d)(6)(B).

Example: Erin purchases a personal computer. She uses it 45% for her writing business, 10% to manage her investments and rental property, and 45% for personal purposes. Her use of the property does not constitute "predominately for qualified business use" because her use in a trade or business of writing does not exceed 50%, and she may not add the 10% investment use in computing qualified business use. She will therefore be restricted to using the straight-line method for depreciation (but will be able to depreciate 55% of the property's cost because that percentage is attributable to use in a trade or business or for investment).

3. Special rules and exceptions

a. Leases: Lessees of listed property are subject to restrictions that place them on the same footing as owners of property. Thus, only a portion (known as the "allowable percentage") of the lease payments for listed property is deductible. IRC §280F(c).

b. Employee use: Use of listed property by employees is not considered business use unless the use is for the convenience of the employer and is required as a condition of employment. IRC §280F(d)(3). There must be a clear showing that the employee cannot properly perform the duties of employment without the property. Rev. Rul. 86-129, 1986-2 C.B. 48. This is a very difficult standard to meet.

Example: José is a law professor with an office at the law school with a computer supplied by his employer. José finds that he is much more productive in writing at home, and therefore he purchases a computer for use at home, under a special financing plan offered by his employer. José seeks to deduct the cost as a §179 expense. As an employee, however, he must show that the computer was for the convenience of his employer and was required as a condition of employment in order to deduct its cost. Even though his employer provides a special financing plan, this does not establish that the use was for the employer's convenience, and nothing in these facts suggests that José was required, as a condition of employment, to purchase a computer. Thus, it is unlikely that José will be able to deduct the cost of the computer as a §179 expense.

4. Related material

a. **Depreciation:** For discussion of depreciation in general, and MACRS in particular, see Chapter 7(III).

b. **Section 179:** Section 179 deductions are treated like depreciation deductions for purposes of §280F. IRC §280F(d)(1). If both §179 and §280F apply to the purchase of an asset, §280F trumps §179. For a discussion of §179, see Chapter 7(III)(E).

Example: Doug purchases an automobile (not an SUV or an electric vehicle) costing $35,000 for use in his trade or business of investment advising. Doug would normally be able to claim the entire amount as a §179 expense, unless the income limitations apply. However, §280F applies, so that his first year deduction is limited to $2,960 (2004 amounts).

c. **Too complex? Just use the auto mileage rate allowances:** As an alternative to claiming MACRS deductions and other operating expenses for automobiles, a taxpayer may claim the standard mileage rate allowance. A taxpayer who elects this method will not be subject to the restrictions of §280F on MACRS deductions for the year in which the election to use the mileage rate allowance is made.

5. Summary: See Statute Summary—§280F.

Statute Summary—§280F

Parsing Step	§280F
General rule	(1) Listed property not used predominantly for business must use straight-line depreciation (2) MACRS deductions for passenger autos limited to specified amounts
Definitional issues	Listed property: computers, transportation, recreational equipment, etc.
Special rules and exceptions	Rules for leases Employee use restricted
Related material	Capital recovery deductions: §§167, 168, 179 Auto mileage deductions
Summary	Capital recovery deductions for listed property and luxury autos are likely to be limited.

VII. GAMBLING LOSSES

A taxpayer may deduct gambling losses only to the extent of gambling income. IRC §165(d). Gambling losses in excess of gains are most properly viewed as expenditures for the personal enjoyment of gambling.

VIII. WHERE ARE WE GOING?

This chapter concludes our discussion of available deductions, having examined personal, business, and mixed-nature expenditures. We now turn to an in-depth discussion of a type of transaction that can generate gross income or deductible loss—transactions in property, including sales, exchanges, and transfers subject to debt.

Quiz Yourself on
Mixed Business and Personal Expenses

68. Shady Brokerage Company is being investigated by the SEC for allegedly recommending that clients buy stocks in various companies when in fact Shady's internal analysts recommended that they be sold. Selena is a broker at Shady, and also has fallen under investigation. Although Selena was ultimately cleared of all charges, she incurred $75,000 of legal fees defending herself. May Selena deduct these expenses? _____

69. Tom is engaged in the practice of law as a sole proprietor. During the year, he incurs a number of meal and entertainment expenses that he would like to deduct from his business income. These are:

Country club dues	$10,000
Golf greens fees (with clients):	$ 850
Restaurant meals (with clients):	$ 1,000
Sporting event tickets (clients attended as guests):	$ 3,500
Sporting event tickets (Tom did not attend; clients did):	$ 500
Annual employee picnic:	$ 1,600

May Tom deduct all or part of these expenses? _____

70. Billie, a cardiovascular surgeon, is considering buying a horse farm and several horses. She's allergic to hay, but her teenage daughters are avid riders, and she currently has to pay an expensive riding academy for her daughters to ride. Billie is a city gal, but longs for the country life. She understands that, at least in the first few years, farms are "losing propositions" but she thinks she can eventually turn a profit by having her daughters board and train other people's horses. In the meantime, she's looking forward to deducting the losses from the farm. You're her tax advisor. What do you tell her? _____

71. Rudy's principal residence is in New York City, but he has a second home in the Adirondacks. Each year, he spends four weeks there, and then rents out the home to vacationers for the rest of the year. In the past, Rudy has reported all of the rent received from the property in his gross income each year, and has deducted 100% of the expenses, including taxes, insurance, and repairs. He also has been depreciating the property on a straight-line basis over 27.5 years. Has Rudy's reporting position been correct? Why or why not? _____

72. Susan is a consulting psychologist in Boston. She occasionally sees patients as does a traditional psychologist, but most of her time is devoted to preparing for and testifying in trials as an expert witness. She owns a townhouse: The bottom floor is her office, and the top floor is her home. In her office, she sees patients, talks with lawyers in person and on the telephone, keeps records, bills insurance companies and lawyers, and does her research. She uses the office exclusively for work. May she deduct expenses associated with the home office? Why or why not? If she can deduct expenses, which ones are deductible? _____

73. Sharon is a professional golfer who enters many tournaments around the world. She properly deducts all of her travel expenses—airplane fare, rental cars, hotels, and other transportation. She spends so much time on the west coast (not her tax home) that she is considering buying a car to drive between west coast tournaments. She could also use it for occasional day trips between tournaments, but this would be a minor part of the car's use. The car she has in mind will cost $35,000. May she deduct the cost of the car? _____

74. Judy lives in Arizona. She rents out her home for one-half of each year while she is flitting around the world. She rents it to "snowbirds," who pay her a gross rent of $10,000 while Judy pays for all the utilities, repairs, pool cleaning, and other maintenance expenses. She doesn't claim any deduction for repairs, figuring that she would have to do those anyway, and none for depreciation. Judy reports the income and deducts all the out-of-pocket expenses that she actually pays for while the snowbirds are nesting in her house. Is this correct? _____

75. Debbie is an employee of ABC Company, which makes animated films for children. She is the "voice" for all ducks and other fowl-like creatures in these films. She recently had tonsillitis, and things didn't go so well. Her employer told her that her voice was no longer sufficiently fowl-like, and fired her, but she suspected—and ultimately proved—more sinister, discriminatory motives. Since then, Debbie's voice has enjoyed starring roles in other films, but she now works independently, not as an employee. Debbie sued her former employer and received $300,000 in damages for violation of a state anti-discrimination law, of which her attorney received $100,000 as her fee. May Debbie deduct these legal fees? _____

Answers

68. The origin of the expense rule determines whether an expense is personal or business-related. In this case, the origin of the expense is Selena's activity as a broker, i.e., her trade or business. While the consequences could have been intensely personal (jail time), it is the origin, not the consequences, of the expense that is relevant. Therefore, the legal expense should be potentially deductible. However, this expense is an unreimbursed employee business expense which is subject to the 2% floor of IRC §67. This expense will be deductible for regular tax purposes to the extent that it, combined with all of her other miscellaneous expenses, exceed 2% of Selena's AGI. It may be limited in computing the alternative minimum tax, however.

69. Tom's expenses can be analyzed in the following categories:

    a. Country club dues of $10,000: ***Nondeductible.***

Section 274(a) provides that dues to social clubs are nondeductible. Tom may not deduct this amount.

    b. Meals and entertainment $3,500: ***May be partially deductible.***

*Golf greens fees (with clients):	$ 850
*Restaurant meals (with clients):	$1,000
*Sporting event tickets (clients attended as guests):	$3,500

Meals and entertainment expenses must run a gauntlet of requirements in order to be deductible. First, they must be "ordinary and necessary business expenses" as determined under IRC §162. In this case, these are obviously ordinary expenses, as they are frequently incurred by business owners. They are of the type most business owners view as appropriate to their ability to obtain and retain business, and thus are "necessary." Tom is clearly carrying on a trade or business so there is no problem with pre-opening capitalization, and they do not create a specific benefit beyond the close of the taxable year, so they should not be capitalized under principles of *Indopco*.

Section 274, however, will impose additional requirements. First, with respect to meals, these must not be lavish or extravagant. The lavishness is of course, a question of fact. It appears that Tom was with the clients at the meals, so no restriction will apply because of his absence. Next, with respect to the tickets, only the face value of the tickets may be deducted. No facts exist to determine whether the amount is in excess of the face value. The requirement of §274 that may create problems is the business connection test. Tom may find it difficult to meet the "directly related" test because both sporting events and golfing provides the kind of significant distraction that would preclude meeting that test. However, if he can show that he had a specific expectation of generating income, that he engaged in an active business discussion during the event, and that in light of all the facts and circumstances, it was primarily a business meeting, he can meet the test. However, Tom may meet the less stringent "associated with" standard if he can show that he had a clear business purpose in engaging in the activity, and that a substantial and bona fide business discussion occurred in connection with the activity. It is more likely that he will meet this test.

If he can meet either business connection test, the amounts expended will still be subject to the 50% limit: Only 50% of the amount will be deductible.

    c. Sporting event tickets for events that Tom did not attend but clients did of $500: ***Nondeductible in full; possible business gift deduction.***

This expense might not even be considered an "ordinary and necessary business expense" under §162 because it appears to lack any connection to Tom's business. Assuming Tom could establish some connection sufficient to justify the expense under §162, the expense must nevertheless qualify under the more stringent provisions of §274. In the case of sporting event tickets where Tom did not attend, but clients did, it will be impossible for Tom to establish his right to deduct any part of the item as a meal and entertainment expense because the business connection test cannot be met—Tom cannot show a substantial and bona fide business discussion when he wasn't even there. However, Tom may be able to claim a business gift deduction for these tickets, subject to the limitations imposed on business gifts ($25 per person).

d. Annual employee picnic of $1,600: ***Fully deductible.***

This type of expense is clearly an "ordinary and necessary business expense" under IRC §162 (see discussion above). Moreover, it is not likely that this would be considered a "lavish" event given the amount expended. Expenditures for employee picnics and similar events are exempt from the business connection tests and from the 50% limitation. Therefore, 100% of the cost of this event would be deductible.

70. Billie Should be aware that the IRS may well challenge the deduction of losses from the horse farm as "hobby losses" under IRC §183 of the Code. This provision denies a deduction for expenses in excess of income for activities not undertaken "for profit." Whether an activity is engaged in for profit depends on the taxpayer's intention, as evidenced by the nine factors outlined in the regulations. No one factor is determinative. However, a number of factors may work against Billie, including:

  - *Time and energy spent on the activity:* As a surgeon, Billie probably has limited time to devote to the business. Relying on teenagers to handle the business is probably not a businesslike plan in the long run. She would need to engage a manager to handle the farm business.

  - *Similar success:* Billie apparently has no experience in these matters.

  - *Financial situation:* Billie has substantial income from other sources and doesn't need income from the farm to support her family. In fact, she could be expected to seek tax benefits from this activity.

  - *Personal enjoyment:* Billie "longs for the country life." She seems to want to support her daughters' wish to ride horses, which would suggest a personal, not profit, motive. On the other hand, she is allergic to hay, which would suggest little pleasure in a horse farm.

If Billie is to make the best possible case for deducting any loss, she should ensure that she takes a businesslike approach to this endeavor, researching best practices and getting the professional help she needs to run the operation. She should be able to show that the farm will increase in value, and that these operations can and do produce profits, even if her particular farm does not. It would be helpful not to have many years of losses in a row.

71. Rudy has been reporting the results of the summer home incorrectly. He is correct in including all of the income from the rental of the property. However, because the property is used partially for personal purposes, the expenses must be allocated between personal and business use. The deductible expenses attributable to the rental (other than expenses deductible without regard to the rental) cannot exceed the total expenses (other than expenses deductible without regard to the rental) multiplied by the percentage of the year the home is rented. While Rudy will be able to deduct all of the property taxes, because these taxes are deductible regardless of rental activity, the rest of the expense will be limited.

72. Susan would like to deduct the expenses of her home office, and it appears that she can do so. She uses the home office exclusively on a regular basis as the principal place of business for her practice. A home office qualifies as a taxpayer's principal place of business if (1) the taxpayer uses the office to conduct administrative or management activities of the taxpayer's trade or business, and (2) there is no other fixed location of the trade or business where the taxpayer conducts substantial administrative or managerial functions of the business. This would appear to be the case for Susan; although she travels to trials, her administrative work is done at the home office and there is no other *fixed* place of business for her practice. As to which expenses are deductible, Susan can already deduct (regardless of the home office) the interest on her mortgage and her property taxes on the property. But because it is a home office, she may also deduct repairs made to that portion of the property and, perhaps most important, she can depreciate that portion of the dwelling. Of course, when she sells the home, she will

not be entitled to the exclusion of IRC §121 on the gain from the sale of a principal residence for the portion used as a home office and depreciated.

73. Because Sharon will be using the car for business, its cost is potentially deductible—but the question is when and how those deductions could be claimed.

It appears that the car will be used for both business and personal purposes but that its predominate use will be in Sharon's business, Therefore, it is potentially subject to the §179 expense deduction, which would allow all of the cost to be deducted in the year of purchase (assuming that Sharon's income is sufficient). However, an allocation must be made between business and personal use, and only the amount allocable to business is subject to the §179 deduction. (We are assuming that the car is not an SUV for which the §179 deduction is limited to $25,000.) She would have to elect to treat the car as §179 property.

It may be that Sharon cannot claim the §179 deduction because of her income limitations. In that case, she would be required to depreciate the business portion of the car using the MACRS system, using a 5-year recovery period. She could select accelerated depreciation or straight-line, but she would probably prefer accelerated depreciation. For example, if the cost of the car is $35,000, the first year MACRS deduction would be $7,000, using 200% declining balance depreciation.

Whether Sharon is thinking of using §179 or the MACRS system, the limitations of IRC §280F may apply. That section limits the amount of depreciation deductions that may be claimed for so-called "luxury" automobiles, placing the taxpayer on a longer, slower schedule of depreciation, regardless of the amount of business use. Sharon's car would fall into that category. IRC §280F will apply, however, only if the car is a passenger vehicle (less than 6,000 lbs) or another of the listed vehicles.

74. Judy's approach is approximately correct, but not technically so. She also may be missing some important deductions to offset the rental income.

Because Judy's home is being used partially for personal purposes (when she is there) and partially for rental purposes, the expenses associated with the home must be bifurcated between personal and rental purposes. She should determine the total of these out-of-pocket expenses, including repairs, and allocate them between the two uses based on total amount of time in each use—half to rental and half to personal. She would then deduct the amount allocated to the rental use from the gross income from the rental, and if any amount is left over, she can claim a MACRS deduction associated with the rental use for the difference. While the MACRS deduction cannot create a loss, it can reduce her rental income to zero. Of course, this would reduce the basis in her home, and when she sells it, the exclusion of IRC §121 would not fully protect the gain from inclusion in her gross income. See Chapter 4(VIII).

75. Yes, probably—but how? These are not the kind of legal fees that Debbie could deduct as an above-the-line deduction, because the origin of the claim was state law, not federal anti-discrimination law. Debbie would like to deduct them on her Schedule C because they would be fully deductible. But they relate not to her trade or business that she is carrying on now, but instead to her relationship as an employee. Therefore, they are properly deductible on Schedule A, as a miscellaneous expense subject to the 2% floor. This may hurt Debbie when she calculates her AMT (see Chapter 13(III)).

Exam Tips on
MIXED BUSINESS AND PERSONAL EXPENSES

☛ Mixed business and personal expenses are often a major focus of deduction questions: they offer ample opportunities to test statutory skills.

   ☞ *Look for:* A taxpayer making an expenditure that benefits his or her business, yet is integrally tied to personal enjoyment or lifestyle (food, entertainment, vacations, home life, cars or trucks).

   ☞ *Analyze:* Find the applicable statute (e.g., §§183, 280A). Which approach does the statute take: nondeductible, partially deductible, deductible in full if requirements are met? Make sure the taxpayer's situation meets the applicable requirements in order to qualify for a deduction.

☛ **Remember:** It is not enough to have expended funds and met the statutory requirements for a deduction. The taxpayer has the duty of substantiating the deduction with adequate records.

☛ Most of the statutes contain objective tests. But IRC §183 is an "intent" test.

   ☞ *Look for:* Facts relevant to the nine factors evidencing profit motive.

   ☞ *Analyze:* Analyze each factor as to its particular impact on the taxpayer. Does the question ask you to be an advocate? Or an advisor?

☛ Use the origin of the expense test when there is no statute on point.

☛ IRC §280F offers ample opportunity for policy questions.

   ☞ Do the limitations make sense in an era of Humvees and big SUVs?

   ☞ Do you think this section is effective in achieving its goals? How do taxpayers likely change their behavior in response to the limitations on listed property, for example?

☛ **Remember:** Construe deductions narrowly. If in doubt, deny the deduction.

Chapter 9

TRANSACTIONS IN PROPERTY

ChapterScope _____

This chapter examines the rules governing the computation of gain or loss from transactions in property, such as sales, trades, and exchanges. This is important, of course, because gross income includes gains from dealings in property, and a loss on the sale or exchange of property may result in a deduction for the taxpayer.

- **An approach to property transactions:** Six straightforward questions address the issues that potentially arise upon the sale or exchange of property. First, has there been a transaction in "property"? Second, has a realization event occurred? Third, what is the taxpayer's realized gain or loss on the transaction? Fourth, what is the taxpayer's recognized gain or loss on the transaction? Fifth, what is the taxpayer's basis in any property (other than money) received? Finally, what is the character of recognized gain or loss on the transaction?

- **A realization event:** A realization event results in the taxpayer, as a result of an exchange of property, having a different legal entitlement than he or she had before the exchange.

- **Computation of realized gain or loss:** A taxpayer's realized gain is always equal to the difference between the amount realized on the transaction (what the taxpayer received) and his or her adjusted basis in the property transferred. Similarly, realized loss is equal to the difference between the taxpayer's adjusted basis in the property transferred and the amount realized on the transaction. Understanding the computation of adjusted basis and what is included in the amount realized is crucial to computation of realized gain or loss.

- **Transfers of encumbered property:** Transfers of encumbered properties raise special questions in the computation of both realized gain and loss and basis. Recognizing the common forms of transfers of such property is important in understanding the tax consequences to the seller, buyer, and creditor.

I. WHERE ARE WE?

We are now exploring in detail a certain kind of gross income or loss: income or loss from dispositions of property. Section 61(a)(3) includes these gains in gross income, so in a sense we are returning to the computation of gross income. Section 165(c) may allow an individual taxpayer to claim a loss on these transactions, so this is a deduction question as well. Special rules apply to the computation of gains and losses from property transactions, and these are explored in this chapter.

II. AN APPROACH TO PROPERTY TRANSACTIONS

The tax analysis of any property transaction can be addressed in six steps as illustrated in Figure 9A.

Figure 9A
An Approach to Property Transactions

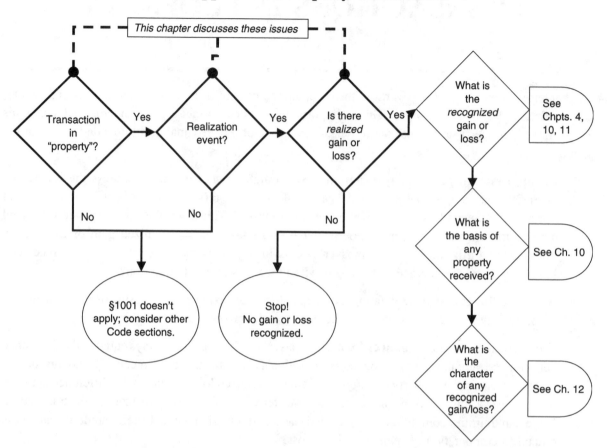

A. Step 1. Identify transactions in property

"Property" includes assets such as real estate, tangible personal property, and intangible property. This chapter does not address the disposition of inventory.

B. Step 2. Identify realization events

Gains and losses from dealings in property potentially occur when a taxpayer experiences a realization event. As discussed in detail below, a realization event occurs when a taxpayer transfers property and receives in exchange something giving the taxpayer different legal entitlements. Look for a taxpayer transferring an item of property (land, buildings, equipment, or personal property, to name just a few) in exchange for value of some kind, whether in money, other property, or services.

C. Step 3. Compute realized gain or loss

If a realization event in property has occurred, compute the taxpayer's realized gain or loss on the disposition. This is equal to the amount realized (the value of what the taxpayer received) minus the taxpayer's adjusted basis in the property transferred.

D. Step 4. Compute recognized gain or loss

If the taxpayer has a realized gain or loss, compute the taxpayer's recognized gain or loss, i.e., the amount of gain the taxpayer must include in gross income or the amount of loss the taxpayer may potentially deduct. As a general rule, all gains and losses are recognized. However, certain nonrecognition provisions of the Code defer recognition of gain or loss until the future. (See Chapter 10.) Moreover, the Code imposes significant limitations on the deduction of losses (see discussion at Chapters 6(VI) and 11(VII)). Determining whether any of these special rules apply is crucial in determining recognized gain or loss.

E. Step 5. Determine the basis of any property the taxpayer receives in the transaction

If the taxpayer receives only cash in the transaction, it will not be necessary to determine its basis. If, however, the taxpayer receives other property in the transaction, it is necessary to determine the basis of that property so that the taxpayer can later measure gain or loss on the disposition of that asset.

F. Step 6. Character

If gain or loss is recognized, another issue is the character of a gain or loss The character of gain or loss is discussed in detail in Chapter 12.

III. STATUTORY ANALYSIS—§1001

A. General rule

Section 1001(c) states that the entire amount of gain or loss on the sale or exchange of property must be recognized, unless some other Code section provides otherwise.

B. Definitional issues

1. **Property:** There is no definition of "property." As a starting place, state law defines real and personal property, but federal tax law is ultimately determinative of whether an item is "property." Certainly real property and tangible personal property qualify, as do many items of intangible property, such as copyrights or trademarks. Sometimes questions arise about contract rights qualifying as property. However, most items that one would normally consider property fall within the ambit of §1001(a). See §1222, discussed in Chapter 12.

2. **Sale or exchange:** Section 1001(c) requires a "sale or exchange" of property in order for gain or loss to be recognized. Section 1001(a) refers to a "sale or other disposition." Both require that the taxpayer have given up beneficial ownership of property in exchange for something else. Sales, exchanges (trades) of property, involuntary conversions, certain abandonments, and foreclosures qualify, but a gift of property does not because there is no sale or exchange. Mere increases or decreases in the value of property without disposition do not trigger §1001. See, e.g., *Lakewood Associates v. Commissioner*, 109 T.C. 456 (1997).

   a. **Realization events—*Eisner v. Macomber*, 252 U.S. 189 (1920):** The taxpayer received a stock dividend in which she received one additional share for every two that she owned. The Commissioner asserted that the stock dividend was income to her, even though the receipt of the stock dividend neither increased her proportionate interest nor resulted in her receiving any cash. The Court held that Mrs. Macomber had not "realized or received any income" as a result of the stock dividend, because all of the profits remained in the corporation. The Court relied on the 16th Amendment, an approach that is not favored today. Moreover, §305 now specifically provides for the tax treatment of stock dividends. However, the case is typically cited as the origin of the realization principle, i.e., that gains and losses must be realized before they will be recognized.

b. **Material difference—*Cottage Savings Association v. Commissioner*, 499 U.S. 554 (1991):** In the early 1980s, savings and loan institutions (S&Ls) held large numbers of low-interest loans whose value had plummeted during the interest rate rise of the late 1970s. While it would have made economic sense to sell these loans, doing so would have placed the S&Ls at risk of closure because they would have been required to report losses in excess of those allowed by their regulatory agency, the FHLBB. Eventually recognizing this problem, the FHLBB issued a regulation allowing S&Ls to exchange "substantially identical" mortgages without having to report losses on such exchanges for financial purposes. One such S&L, Cottage Savings, exchanged a 90% participation in 252 mortgages for a 90% participation in 305 mortgages in a transaction that qualified as "substantially identical " for regulatory purposes. Its basis in the loans transferred was $6.9 million, and it received loans with a value of $4.5 million in exchange. It therefore reported a $2.4 million loss for tax purposes. The IRS argued that Cottage Savings did not realize a loss, citing its long-standing administrative interpretation that the realization principle requires that the properties exchanged be materially different. In the IRS's view, the two mortgage groups did not meet this requirement. The Tax Court held for the taxpayer, and the Sixth Circuit reversed, on the grounds that the loss was not sustained during the taxable year.

i. **Issue:** Does the realization principle incorporate a "material difference" requirement?

ii. **Result and rationale:** The realization principle incorporates a material difference requirement, and all that is needed to satisfy this requirement is that the exchange confer different legal interests on the taxpayer than the taxpayer had before the transaction. Because the exchange resulted in Cottage Savings having different legal interests than it had before the exchange, the loss was realized. The Court gave deference to the Commissioner's interpretation of §1001(a) in Reg. §1.1001-1, which requires that properties exchanged be materially different in order for a realization event to occur. However, no deference was given to the IRS's interpretation of "materiality" because there was no prelitigation published interpretation of the issue. The IRS's approach of examining the facts and circumstances of the situation was inconsistent with prior case law, the goal of administrative convenience, and the structure of the Code. The minor argument that the loss was not "sustained" was rejected because the loss was bona fide.

iii. **Comment:** This case is an excellent example of how a court will properly give deference to the IRS's interpretation of the Code.

iv. **Subsequent developments—Reg. §1.1001-3:** Treasury subsequently issued a regulation that provides that any "significant modification " of a debt instrument results in a realization event in which the debt instrument is deemed to be exchanged for a new instrument with the new terms. Reg. §1.1001-3(b). This can result in gain, loss, and discharge of indebtedness income. A "modification" is any alteration of a legal right or obligation of the issuer or holder of a debt instrument. Reg. §1.1001-3(c)(1)(i). In order to be a "significant" modification, the changes must be economically significant in light of all of the facts and circumstances of the situation. Reg. §1.1001-3(e)(1). The removal of a co-obligor on a debt instrument, for example, is not significant. However, in Rev. Proc. 2001-21, 2001-9 I.R.B. 742, the IRS published procedures through which taxpayers can treat debt modifications which are not "significant" as realization events and take the tax consequences of these modifications into income over time.

c. **Realization event—Definition:** A realization event is a transaction—a sale, exchange, or other disposition for value—in which the taxpayer receives something materially different from that which he or she had before the exchange. To be materially different, the property received must confer different legal interests or entitlements on the taxpayer. This is an easy standard to meet, and most transactions will qualify as realization events.

Example: Ben owns Blackacre, a 20-acre parcel of raw land. Betty owns Whiteacre, a 20-acre parcel of raw land adjacent to Blackacre. Blackacre and Whiteacre are identical in all respects except location. If Ben and Betty exchange their properties, this will be a realization event because each will have different legal interests as a result of the exchange.

Example: Curtis owns a sports car, the purchase of which was financed by the credit union. When Curtis doesn't pay his debt, the credit union repossesses and sells the car. This is a realization event for Curtis.

3. **Computation of realized gain or loss:** Section 1001(a) defines gain or loss on the sale or other disposition of property. Realized gain is equal to the amount realized on the transaction minus the taxpayer's adjusted basis in the property transferred. Realized loss is equal to the taxpayer's adjusted basis in the property transferred minus the amount realized on the transaction. In calculating the realized gain or loss on a sale or other disposition, §1001 seeks to measure the taxpayer's economic profit or loss on the investment. Recall that a taxpayer need include only "income" in gross income (see discussion at Chapter 2(IV)) and thus will report only the income from the transaction in excess of his or her capital investment. Taxpayers who receive less in a sale or other disposition than their investment in the property sold may be entitled to claim a deduction for the loss on the transaction. Thus, the computation of realized gain or loss is designed to tally the taxpayer's gain or loss on the property at the time of the sale or other disposition.

a. **Amount realized:** In order to calculate the realized gain or loss, the amount realized must be determined. The amount realized is the total value that the taxpayer receives in the transaction in exchange for the property transferred. The taxpayer can receive cash, property, services, and the assumption of liabilities as part of the exchange. IRC §1001(b); Reg. §§1.1001-1, -2.

i. **Cash:** The most common transaction is a sale for cash. The taxpayer sells property to the other party in exchange for an amount of cash equal to the fair market value of the property. The amount of the cash is included in the amount realized.

Example: Erin owns Pinkacre, a parcel of raw land worth $100,000. She sells Pinkacre to Andrea for $100,000 in cash. Erin's amount realized on this transaction is $100,000.

ii. **Property received:** In many transactions, the taxpayer exchanges property for other property. In this situation, the amount realized includes the fair market value of the property received in the transaction.

Example: Tristan owns Blueacre, an apartment building. He exchanges Blueacre for Erin's Pinkacre, which is worth $100,000. (Because there is an exchange with no other property changing hands, we know that Blueacre and Pinkacre are worth the same amount, $100,000.) Tristan's amount realized is the fair market value of Pinkacre, $100,000.

iii. Services received: A taxpayer's amount realized includes the fair market value of any services the taxpayer receives as part of the transaction.

Example: Karin owns Blackacre, which is worth $15,000. She sells Blackacre to Pete in exchange for Pete paving her very long driveway. Karin's amount realized is the fair market value of Pete's services, which can be measured directly (what Pete would charge others for this service) or by the fair market value of Blackacre. Thus, Karin's amount realized is $15,000.

iv. Assumption of liabilities: In some transactions, the buyer will assume all or part of the seller's liabilities in connection with the exchange. In this situation, the amount realized includes the amount of the liability assumed. See section IV of this chapter for a detailed discussion of transfers of encumbered properties.

Example: Justin owns Yellowacre, an office building. It is worth $200,000, but is subject to a debt of $200,000. Justin transfers Yellowacre to Blake, and Blake agrees to assume the debt to which Yellowacre is subject. (Because the value of the property is the same as its mortgage, Blake will not pay any additional amount to Justin.) Justin's amount realized on this transaction is $200,000, the amount of the debt Blake assumed in connection with this transaction.

v. Amount realized equals total value received: Amount realized is the total of the cash received, the fair market value of the property or services received, and the liabilities assumed by the other party to the transaction. For arms-length transactions that include no gift component, the amount realized is always equal to the fair market value of the property transferred. Unless the facts suggest otherwise, you may assume that transactions occur between unrelated parties.

Example: Leah owns Blackacre, an apartment building. She sells it to William for $60,000 cash and a sports car worth $30,000. Leah's amount realized is $90,000, the total of the cash and the fair market value of the sports car received.

Example: Patrick owns Whiteacre, a parcel of raw land that is subject to a mortgage of $50,000. He sells it to Hillary for cash of $100,000 and Hillary's assumption of the $50,000 mortgage. (We can calculate the fair market value of Whiteacre at $150,000, the total value Hillary pays for it.) Patrick's amount realized on this transaction is $150,000, the total of the cash and assumption of the mortgage.

Example: Betsy owns an antique car worth $100,000. She sells it to Bill for $20,000 cash, a truck worth $30,000, and Bill's assumption of a liability for which Betsy is obligated of $50,000. Betsy's amount realized on this transaction is $100,000, the total of the cash ($20,000), the fair market value of the truck ($30,000), and the assumption of liabilities ($50,000).

b. Adjusted basis: In order to calculate realized gain or loss, the adjusted basis of the property transferred must be determined. The adjusted basis of property is its basis when acquired by the taxpayer and adjusted thereafter as required by §1016. Adjusted basis is the way the

Code keeps track of a taxpayer's unrecovered economic investment in property for purposes of calculating the taxpayer's gain or loss upon sale or exchange of the property.

i. **Cost:** For property acquired by purchase, the purchaser's initial basis is the cost of the property. IRC §1012. The cost of the property is equal to the amount of money paid for the property, the fair market value of the property or services given in exchange for the property, and the face amount of liabilities assumed in acquiring the property. For property received in exchange for services rendered, the cost is the amount of the income included in gross income as a result of the services transaction (known as tax cost basis). This discussion applies to property other than a taxpayer's inventory.

    Example—Cash: Bill purchases Blackacre for $100,000. His initial basis in the property is his purchase price, $100,000.

    Example—Cash and property: Allison purchases Whiteacre from Penny, giving Penny $50,000 cash and a parcel of raw land worth $60,000. Allison's initial basis in Whiteacre is its cost, or $110,000, equal to the cash plus the fair market value of the property given Penny to acquire Whiteacre.

    Example—Cash, property, liabilities: Frank purchases Blueacre by transferring to the owner $30,000 cash and a parcel of real property worth $50,000. Frank also assumes a $40,000 mortgage to which Blueacre is subject. Frank's initial basis in the property is equal to his cost, or $120,000 (the total of the cash, fair market value of the property, and the liability Frank assumes).

    Example—Tax cost basis: Mary Ann creates an estate plan for her client, who pays her with a sports car worth $20,000. Mary Ann includes the fair market value of the sports car received ($20,000) in her gross income, and her basis in the sports car is $20,000.

ii. **Property received from a decedent:** The basis of property received from a decedent is the fair market value of the property on the decedent's date of death or, if the alternate valuation date is elected, the value on that date (six months after the date of death). IRC §1014. Property can be received from a decedent by bequest or devise, by disclaimer, or through intestate succession. Property received in this fashion is often referred to as having a "*stepped-up basis,*" because generally property has a fair market value greater than its basis in the hands of a decedent just before death. However, the property could just as easily have a "stepped-down basis" if its fair market value were less than its basis just before death (although that is not a term in general usage). In that case, however, the decedent would have been well advised to sell the property before death, as the loss inherent in the property will be forever lost for income tax purposes if transferred by devise or inheritance. The date-of-death basis for property received from a decedent has been criticized because it completely exempts from income tax the economic benefit of the increase in value of the property during the decedent's lifetime. While a rationale often heard for this basis rule is that it prevents property from being subjected to both the income tax and the estate tax, this is hardly an adequate explanation. The estate tax, like the gift tax, is a tax on transfers that operates independently of the income tax. Note that in the gift area, the donee generally takes the donor's basis in the property, so that the donee will be taxed on the gain that occurred during both the donor's and the donee's ownership. Not so for property received by inheritance; neither the decedent nor the beneficiary will pay income tax on this gain. *Note:* The 2001 Act provides that when the estate tax is repealed, effective 12/31/09, the basis rules described here will be replaced with a carryover basis regime. Then, unless Congress acts, the rules described here will come back into effect on January 1, 2011. (What will actually happen, however, is anyone's guess.)

Example: Whitney receives 1,000 shares of XYZ stock pursuant to her grandfather's will. Her grandfather had purchased the stock in 1981 for $10,000, and at his death the stock was worth $150,000. Whitney's basis in the stock will be the value of the stock on the date of her grandfather's death, or $150,000.

iii. **Property received by gift:** As a general rule, if property is received by gift, the donee takes the property with the same basis that it had in the hands of the donor, increased by the portion of any gift tax paid by the donor. IRC §1015(a). If, at the time of the gift, the adjusted basis of the property in the hands of the donor is greater than the fair market value of the property, for purposes of determining loss on sale by the donee, the donee's basis in the property is the fair market value of the property at the time of the gift. Under this rule, if the donee sells at a gain, the general rule for determining the donee's basis applies. In order for the special rule to apply, the adjusted basis of the property in the donor's hands must exceed its fair market value on the date of the gift *and* the donee must sell at a loss. Property received by gift is generally referred to as having a *carryover basis,* at least if the special rule does not apply. Technically it has a *transferred basis,* which is a type of and is sometimes referred to as, *substituted basis.* See IRC §7701(a)(42),(43). These basis rules for gifts work in tandem with §102's exclusion from gross income for gifts. (See discussion at Chapter 4(III).) The donee does not really get a full exclusion of the value of the gift, because he or she takes the property with the donor's basis and may ultimately recognize gain or loss on the sale of the gift property. However, because the donee may be in a lower tax bracket than the donor, it may make sense in a family financial planning situation to cause the donee rather than the donor to realize the gain on sale. Moreover, a donor may not always be able to "give away" a loss by gifting loss property to the donee. If the donee sells at a loss, the donee will take as his or her basis the fair market value of the property as of the date of the gift rather than the donor's basis. Thus, in this situation, it may make more sense for the donor to sell the property, recognize the loss, and give the proceeds to the donee.

Example—General rule: Alan owns 1,000 shares of ABC stock in which he has a basis of $15,000. The stock is worth $100,000. Alan gives the stock to his daughter Caroline. Caroline will take her father's basis in the shares ($15,000) as her own basis.

Example—Loss property: Alex owns Blackacre, a parcel of raw land in which she has a basis of $50,000. The fair market value of Blackacre is $20,000 on the date Alex gives Blackacre to her sister Jessica. Jessica's basis in Blackacre under the general rule would be $50,000 (Alex's basis). This is the basis used for determining gain: If Jessica later sold Blackacre for $200,000, she would have a $150,000 gain. But, for purposes of determining Jessica's loss on any subsequent sale, the special rule applicable to loss applies because the property's fair market value was less than its adjusted basis in Alex's hands at the time of the gift. If Jessica sells Blackacre for $10,000, her basis would be $20,000, and she would have a $10,000 loss.

Example—No gain or loss: Assume the same facts as in the immediately preceding example. If Jessica sells Blackacre for any amount between $20,000 (its fair market value on the date of the gift) and $50,000 (Alex's basis), she will realize neither gain nor loss on the sale. This is because the basis for determining gain would produce a loss, while the basis for determining loss would produce a gain. For example, assume Jessica sells the property for $30,000. If she takes the basis for determining loss of $20,000, she has a $10,000 gain. If she takes the basis for determining gain of $50,000, she has a $20,000 loss. The regulations conclude that a taxpayer has neither gain nor loss in this situation. See Reg. §1.1015-1(a)(2), Example.

iv. Property received in divorce: The recipient of property pursuant to a divorce takes the property with the same basis the property had in the hands of the marital unit. IRC §1041(b)(2). These rules are discussed in detail at Chapter 10(V).

v. Exchanged basis property: In some transactions, a taxpayer gives up property in exchange for other property, and the basis of the property received is calculated in whole or in part by reference to the basis of the property transferred. This is known as "exchanged basis property." See IRC §7701(a)(44). For example, in a *like-kind exchange* under §1031, the property received takes a basis that is calculated by reference to the basis of the property transferred. Exchanged basis property is a type of, and is sometimes referred to as, substituted basis property. See IRC §7701(a)(42).

c. Adjustments to basis: A taxpayer must adjust his or her initial basis in property during ownership to reflect additional investment in the property and capital recovery with respect to the property. See IRC §1016.

i. Improvements: Improvements to property result in an increase in the basis of the property. IRC §1016(a); Reg. §1.1016-2.

Example: Tammy purchases Whiteacre, an office building, for $100,000. She then remodels the third floor of Whiteacre for leasing to a particular tenant, at a cost of $65,000. Her initial (cost) basis in Whiteacre was $100,000, and she adds to that basis her improvements of $65,000 for a total adjusted basis for the property and improvements of $165,000.

ii. Capitalized interest and taxes: A taxpayer may elect to capitalize, rather than deduct, otherwise deductible interest and taxes on property. IRC §266. If the taxpayer makes this election, the interest and taxes attributable to the property are added to the basis of the property. Id.

Example: Emilio purchases Blackacre, a parcel of raw land, for $50,000. He pays the seller $10,000 and promises to pay the balance in equal annual installments for five years with interest at 10%. Taxes on the land are $200 per year. Emilio may elect to capitalize the interest and taxes, so that his interest payments to the seller and the taxes paid are added to the basis of the property. Thus, in the first year after purchase, Emilio would add the $4,000 in interest and $200 in taxes to his basis, increasing his adjusted basis to $54,200.

iii. Cost recovery deductions: When a taxpayer claims a deduction for capital recovery (MACRS or amortization), the taxpayer must adjust the basis of the property downward by the amount of the capital recovery deduction claimed. See discussion of capital recovery at Chapter 7(III).

Example: Courtney owns Blueacre, a rental home that she purchased for $100,000. Over the first five years she owns the property, she claims $18,029 in MACRS deductions. This reduces her basis in the property so that her adjusted basis at the end of five years is $81,971.

Example: Tex owns Blueacre, a parcel of raw land that he purchased for $60,000 and with respect to which he capitalized $10,000 of interest and taxes. Tex sells Blueacre to Ashley for $40,000 cash plus stock worth $50,000. Ashley had a basis in the stock of $20,000. Tex's realized gain on the sale is the difference between the amount realized ($40,000 cash plus the fair market value of the stock, $50,000, or $90,000) and the adjusted basis in Blueacre (his initial basis of $60,000 plus capitalized interest and taxes of $10,000, or $70,000). Thus, Tex's realized gain is $20,000. His basis in the stock is the amount of value (in the form of Blueacre) that he paid for the stock, i.e., $50,000. Ashley has transferred stock in which her adjusted basis was $20,000 to purchase $50,000 of the property. She therefore has a realized gain of $30,000 on the stock transfer. Her basis in Blueacre is her cost, $90,000.

Example: Jan purchases Blackacre for $100,000. Over the years, she claims $30,000 of MACRS deductions with respect to Blackacre. She sells Blackacre to Adam for $150,000. Jan's realized gain on the sale is the difference between the amount realized on the sale ($150,000) and her adjusted basis in Blackacre ($100,000 − $30,000 = $70,000). Thus, her realized gain is $80,000. Adam's basis in the property he purchases is $150,000, his cost.

Example: Dustin sells his antique sports car to Beth. Dustin purchased the sports car for $20,000 and made $10,000 of improvements to it. Beth pays him $10,000 in cash and also agrees to assume a debt of $40,000 that Dustin owes. Dustin's realized gain is equal to the difference between the amount realized on the transaction ($10,000 cash plus the $40,000 debt assumption, or $50,000) and his adjusted basis in the car (his initial basis of $20,000, increased by the improvements to the property of $10,000, or $30,000). Thus, Dustin's realized gain is $20,000. Beth's initial basis in the car is her purchase price, $50,000.

4. **Recognition:** Recognition of gain or loss means that the taxpayer includes the gain in gross income, or that the taxpayer may claim the loss as a deduction. Section 1001(c) requires that all realized gains and losses are to be recognized, unless another Code section provides otherwise.

   a. **Nonrecognition provisions:** The Code contains numerous nonrecognition provisions that defer the recognition of realized gain or loss. These are discussed in Chapter 10.

   b. **Gain exclusion:** There are a few Code sections that exempt gain from recognition in whole or in part. For example, under certain conditions a taxpayer may exclude from gross income gain on the sale of his or her principal residence. IRC §121. See discussion at Chapter 4(VIII).

   c. **Loss restrictions:** The Code contains numerous provisions that restrict the deductibility of losses.

    i. Capital loss restrictions: Individuals may deduct capital losses only to the extent of their capital gain, plus $3,000 of ordinary income. IRC §1223. See discussion at Chapter 12(II).

    ii. Section 165(c): Individuals may deduct only certain types of losses. For example, losses on the sale of assets held for investment may be deductible, but a loss on the sale of one's home is not deductible. IRC §165(c). See discussion at Chapter 6(VI).

C. Special rules and exceptions—Part gift/part sale transaction

If a transaction is partially a gift and partially a sale, the transferor will be treated as having realized a gain in the amount by which his or her amount realized exceeds the adjusted basis of the property transferred. However, the transferor may not recognize a loss on the transaction, even if the amount realized is less than the adjusted basis of the property transferred. Reg. §1.1001-1(e).

Example: Dick has a $40,000 basis in Blackacre, which is worth $100,000. He transfers Blackacre to Jane, his daughter. Jane pays him $70,000 for Blackacre. This transaction is partially a gift because Jane paid Dick less than the fair market value of the property, and the other circumstances of the situation (intrafamilial transfer) suggest a gift. Thus, Dick has a realized gain of $30,000, equal to his amount realized ($70,000) minus his adjusted basis in Blackacre ($40,000).

D. Related material

    1. Nonrecognition provisions: A number of Code provisions override the general rule that all realized gains and losses will be recognized. See discussion in Chapter 10.

    2. Timing issues: The taxpayer's *taxable year* and *method of accounting* will determine when the taxpayer must include gain from dealings in property in gross income, and when he or she may deduct losses from dealings in property. When property is sold on the installment basis, the gain is taxed over the period during which the seller received payments. (See discussion at Chapter 11(V).)

    3. Character of gain or loss: The character of the gain from dealing in property will depend on the nature of the property sold or exchanged—as *capital* or *noncapital assets.* These issues are discussed generally in Chapter 12.

E. Summary

See Statute Summary—§1001.

IV. TRANSFERS OF ENCUMBERED PROPERTY

A. A few terms of art

    1. Liabilities incurred to purchase property: When a person wants to purchase property such as real estate and doesn't have enough money to do so, a bank or other person may lend the money to the purchaser to buy the property. The buyer usually puts some of his or her own money together with the loan proceeds to purchase the property from the seller. The debtor must usually give a security interest in the property to the lender in order to ensure repayment. If the debtor defaults, the lender will have the ability to sell the property and be repaid from the proceeds (commonly referred to as "foreclosure"). In many states, this is structured as a

Statute Summary—§1001

Parsing Step	§1001
General rule	All realized gains and losses are recognized, unless another Code section provides otherwise.
Definitional issues	Realization event Realized gain = Amount realized − Adjusted basis Realized loss = Adjusted basis − Amount realized
Special rules and exceptions	Part sale/part gift transactions
Related material	Nonrecognition provisions (see Chapter 10) Timing rules (see Chapter 11) Character issues (see Chapter 12)
Summary	Realized gain is included in gross income, and realized loss is deducted, unless the Code provides otherwise.

"mortgage" in which the debtor is the mortgagor and the creditor is the mortgagee. Deeds of trust, installment sales contracts, conditional sales contracts, and similar arrangements serve the same function as a mortgage in some jurisdictions but allow the creditor simpler mechanisms for selling the property if the debtor defaults. Here the term "mortgage" will be used to include mortgages and all similar arrangements. See Figure 9B—Typical Mortgage Transaction. As Figure 9B illustrates, there are really two different transactions occurring in this sale: the loan transaction (between the bank and the buyer) and the sale transaction (between the seller and the buyer). This would be true even if the seller were providing the financing; in that case, the seller would simply wear two hats: as seller and as the "bank."

2. **Recourse mortgage:** The most common type of mortgage debt is the "recourse" debt, which provides that if the debtor does not repay the loan, the lender may proceed against the debtor's assets for repayment without restriction except as provided under bankruptcy law or state anti-deficiency statutes. Thus, if the borrower does not repay the loan, the lender will seek satisfaction through foreclosure on the property and if that is not sufficient to satisfy the debt, the lender will seek additional payment from the borrower. The debtor's other assets are at risk for this type of debt.

Example: Jared purchases a home for $100,000, giving the seller $20,000 of his own funds and obtaining a recourse mortgage from Unfriendly Bank for $80,000. He repays $5,000 of the mortgage, but unfortunately an economic downturn causes the fair market value of the property to fall to $50,000. Jared defaults on the loan. Unfriendly Bank causes the property to be sold at foreclosure for its value of $50,000. Jared still owes $75,000 on the loan plus the expenses of the foreclosure sale of $3,000, for a total outstanding obligation of $78,000. The proceeds of sale are applied to Jared's outstanding obligation, reducing it to $28,000. If the state has an antideficiency statute, Unfriendly Bank cannot proceed against Jared for the $28,000. If no antideficiency statute exists, however, Unfriendly Bank will proceed to collect the $28,000

Figure 9B
Typical Mortgage Transaction

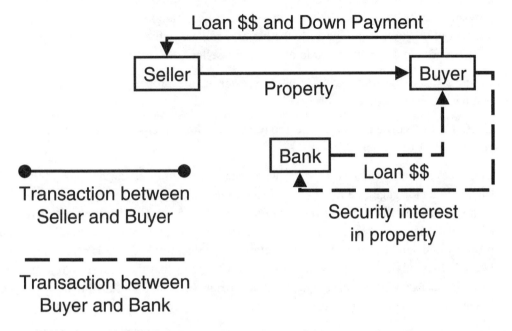

from Jared's other assets that are not otherwise protected. Jared might consider bankruptcy as an option for obtaining protection for some of his other assets.

3. **Nonrecourse mortgage:** A less common type of debt is the "nonrecourse debt," which means that the lender has agreed to seek satisfaction only from the property that secures the debt. Thus, if the value of the property is insufficient to repay the debt in full, the lender cannot proceed against the debtor's other assets for repayment of the balance. In a nonrecourse debt situation, the lender, rather than the borrower, bears the risk that the property will decline in value.

4. **Assumption of debt:** An assumption of debt occurs when another person explicitly agrees to be responsible for payment of a taxpayer's debt. For state law purposes, this may not relieve the taxpayer of his or her obligation under the debt, but for federal income tax purposes, it is considered a valuable benefit to the taxpayer and included in amount realized. Generally the lender must consent to another person's assumption of an outstanding debt.

5. **Transfer "subject to debt":** When an encumbered property is sold, most often the debt is repaid to the lender as part of the sale transaction. However, properties can be transferred "subject to the debt," which means that the seller will transfer the property to the buyer with the debt intact, and the buyer will become the obligor on the debt. This is an implicit assumption of debt, and has the same effect as an assumption of debt. Almost always, the lender must consent to a transfer of property subject to a debt.

B. The typical transaction—Sale of property and satisfaction of debt

In this very common transaction, the property's value is greater than the amount of the mortgage. The seller agrees to sell the property to the buyer for the property's fair market value. The seller repays the lender with some of the sales proceeds and keeps the rest. The seller transfers the property "free and clear" (i.e., without any debt associated with it) to the purchaser. The tax consequences to each party of this transaction are determined independently.

1. **Seller's tax consequences:** The seller will calculate realized gain or loss in accordance with the usual rules: amount realized (the purchase price) minus the seller's adjusted basis in the property. Recognized gain or loss will be equal to realized gain or loss, unless some Code provision limits recognition. Notice that the mortgage amount is irrelevant to the tax consequences of this transaction because the buyer is not assuming the mortgage. The repayment of the loan principal is not a taxable event to the seller.

2. **Buyer's tax consequences:** The buyer's basis in the property will be the buyer's cost of purchasing the property.

3. **Lender's tax consequences:** The repayment of the principal amount of the loan is not a taxable event to the lender:

Example: Sheila owns Blackacre, in which she has an adjusted basis of $60,000. Blackacre is subject to a mortgage of $50,000 from Friendly Bank and has a fair market value of $100,000. Brian purchases Blackacre from Sheila for $100,000 (cash). Sheila repays Friendly Bank with $50,000 of the sales proceeds, which releases its security interest so that Sheila can transfer the property to Brian "free and clear." She retains the remaining $50,000 as profit. See Figure 9C—Sheila's Sale of Blackacre. Again, this figure illustrates that there are two transactions occurring: the sale of property between Sheila and Brian, and Sheila's fulfillment of her promise to repay the loan to Friendly Bank.

Sheila's tax consequences: Sheila's realized gain on the transaction is $40,000, the difference between her amount realized ($100,000) and the adjusted basis of Blackacre ($60,000). Her recognized gain also will be $40,000, unless a Code provision limits recognition of that gain. The repayment of the principal amount of the loan is not a taxable event to Sheila.

Figure 9C
Sheila's Sale of Blackacre

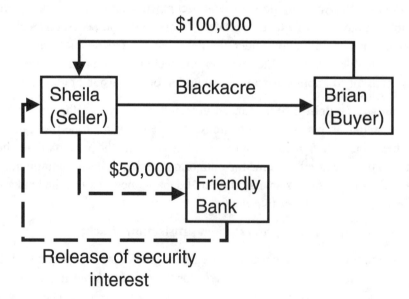

Brian's tax consequences: Brian takes Blackacre with a basis equal to his cost, or $100,000.

Friendly Bank: The repayment of the $50,000 principal amount of the loan is not income to the lender.

C. The assumption transaction—Buyer assumes the mortgage (or takes the property subject to the mortgage)

1. **The transaction:** In this transaction, the buyer, seller, and lender agree that the buyer will become responsible for the mortgage on the property as part of the purchase transaction. When the seller transfers the property to the buyer, the latter either expressly assumes the debt or takes the property subject to the debt. The buyer will pay the seller the "equity" in the property, i.e., the difference between the property's fair market value and the amount of the debt, if any. The property will secure the debt, and the seller may be released from this obligation. In some cases, the seller is not released, but in those situations the buyer indemnifies the seller from any loss related to repayment of the loan. For tax purposes, however, the seller is treated as having been released from the loan obligation. The buyer is treated as if the loan is now his or her own and that he or she has granted a security interest in the property to the lender. See Figure 9D—Assumption Transaction.

2. **Tax effects:** When the buyer assumes a mortgage for which the seller is liable, or takes property subject to debt, for tax purposes the assumption is treated as a transfer of value to the seller. See Figure 9E—Tax Effects of Assumption Transaction. This is why the seller is treated as having an amount realized that includes the assumption of the mortgage.

3. **Mortgage amount less than fair market value:** When the amount of the mortgage is less than the fair market value of the property, the seller's amount realized includes the debt assumed, regardless of the nature of the mortgage as recourse or nonrecourse. *Crane v. Commissioner,* 331 U.S. 1 (1947).

Figure 9D
Assumption Transaction

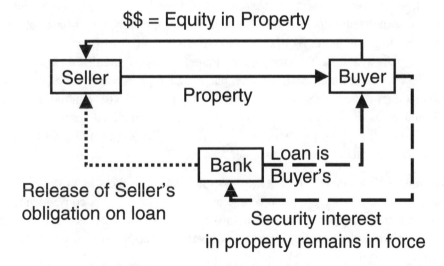

$$ = Equity in Property

Seller · Property → Buyer

Bank — Loan is Buyer's

Release of Seller's obligation on loan

Security interest in property remains in force

Transaction between Buyer and Bank

Transaction between Seller and Bank

Transaction between Seller and Buyer

Figure 9E
Tax Effects of Assumption Transaction

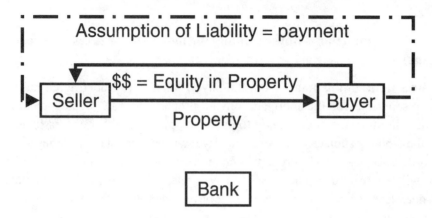

Tax transaction between
Seller and Buyer

Actual transaction between
Seller and Buyer

 a. Seller's tax consequences: The seller's amount realized will be the amount of money received, the fair market value of any property received, and the debt assumed by the buyer. The seller's realized and recognized gain or loss will be calculated under the usual rules.

 b. Buyer's tax consequences: The buyer will include in basis the amount of debt assumed plus the amount of money and the fair market value of property paid to seller.

 c. Lender's tax consequences: The lender will be unaffected by the transfer of property subject to the debt. From the lender's perspective, the loan remains outstanding.

 Example—Recourse mortgage: Sonny owns Parcel A of real property, which is subject to a recourse mortgage to Friendly Bank of $40,000. Sonny has a basis of $60,000 in the property, and it is worth $110,000. Sonny sells Parcel A to Becca for $70,000 cash, and Becca agrees to assume the mortgage on Parcel A. Sonny's realized gain on this transaction is $50,000. His amount realized is equal to the cash received of $70,000 plus Becca's assumption of the mortgage of $40,000, or $110,000. The amount realized minus his adjusted basis in Parcel A ($60,000) produces his realized gain of $50,000. Becca's basis in Parcel A is her purchase price: $110,000 ($70,000 cash plus $40,000 debt assumption). The transaction is not a taxable event for Friendly Bank.

 Example—Nonrecourse mortgage: Assume the same facts as in the previous example, except that the mortgage is nonrecourse in nature. The same tax consequences would result from this transaction because the nature of the mortgage as recourse or nonrecourse is irrelevant when the property's fair market value exceeds the amount of the debt.

 4. Nonrecourse mortgage exceeds fair market value of property: Because the lender bears the risk of a fall in value of property for a nonrecourse mortgage, a buyer might well purchase a property subject to a nonrecourse mortgage with a face amount greater than the fair market value of the property.

a. *Crane v. Commissioner,* **331 U.S. 1 (1947):** Mrs. Crane owned an apartment building that was subject to a nonrecourse mortgage. Over the years, she claimed depreciation deductions. She sold it to a buyer subject to the debt. Mrs. Crane claimed that her only gain was her equity in the building. She argued that her amount realized could not include the mortgage assumed because she did not benefit from the buyer's taking the property subject to the debt. The Supreme Court held that her amount realized included the amount of the nonrecourse mortgage. In that case the fair market value of the property exceeded the amount of the nonrecourse debt, and the Supreme Court observed that it did not rule on the result that would obtain if the property's fair market value were less than the debt encumbering the property.

b. *Commissioner v. Tufts,* **461 U.S. 300 (1983)**

  i. Facts: Because *Tufts* is a partnership case, it is helpful to simplify the facts by ignoring the partnership and assuming that Mr. Tufts owned the property individually. Mr. Tufts purchased an apartment building in 1970 by making a small cash outlay and obtaining a nonrecourse loan of $1,851,500. During his ownership of the property, Mr. Tufts claimed depreciation deductions in a total of $439,972. In 1972, the fair market value of the property was $1,400,000, and Mr. Tufts' adjusted basis in the property was $1,455,740. Because no principal payments had been made on the debt, its outstanding balance remained at $1,851,500. In 1972, Mr. Tufts transferred the property to Mr. Bayles, who assumed the nonrecourse mortgage. Mr. Tufts reported a $55,740 loss equal to the difference between his adjusted basis in the property and its fair market value.

  ii. Issue: How should the gain or loss on Mr. Tufts' sale be calculated? Specifically, must Mr. Tufts include in his amount realized the assumption of the nonrecourse debt by the purchaser of the property?

  iii. Result and rationale: Mr. Tufts must include in his amount realized the debt assumed, so that he realized a gain on the sale of the property equal to the difference between the face amount of the debt ($1,851,500) and the adjusted basis of the property ($1,455,740), or $395,760. The majority opinion gives deference to the Commissioner's decision to treat a nonrecourse mortgage as a "true loan." This treatment allows the mortgagor to include the amount in basis, and requires the mortgagor to include the debt in amount realized if assumed. Although the economic benefit analysis relied on in *Crane* might suggest a different result when the mortgaged property falls in value below the balance of the debt, the Court does not rely on the theory of economic benefit. Instead, the tax-payer's tax-free receipt of the loan proceeds and the inclusion of those proceeds in the basis of the mortgaged property requires consistent treatment upon sale of the property. Justice O'Connor concurred, but observed that the logical way to treat this transaction would be to bifurcate it into two different transactions: a sale of property and a discharge of debt. (See Figure 9F—Bifurcated Transaction—Justice O'Connor's Concurrence in *Commissioner v. Tufts.*) This results in a net gain of the same amount as in the majority's opinion ($395,760), but the character of the loss and gain are different. The sale transaction produces capital gain or loss, while the discharge of debt is ordinary income. In addition, the discharge of debt may be subject to exclusion under §108 (see discussion at Chapter 4(VI)). However, in deference to the IRS's interpretation, Justice O'Connor concurred in the result.

Figure 9F

Bifurcated Transaction—Justice O'Connor's Concurrence in *Commissioner v. Tufts*

Property Transaction		Discharge of Debt Transaction	
Amount realized	$1,400,000 (FMV)	Face amount of debt	$1,851,500
Adjusted basis	1,455,740	Debt satisfied	1,400,000 (FMV)
Loss on sale	**($ 55,740)**	**Discharge of debt**	**$ 451,500**

5. **Recourse mortgage exceeds fair market value of property:** As a practical matter, rational buyers will not assume a recourse mortgage greater than the fair market value of the property, because to do so would place the buyer's other assets at risk. However, several other transactions are common in this situation.

   a. **Discharge followed by sale:** The creditor (mortgagee) discharges the part of the debt in excess of the fair market value of the property, and then the debtor (mortgagor) transfers the property to the buyer subject to the remaining debt.

      i. **Tax consequences to seller/debtor:** The debtor has discharge of indebtedness income equal to the amount of the loan discharged, which is ordinary income and may be excluded under §108 if that section's requirements are met. Upon sale, the seller includes in the amount realized the portion of the debt assumed by the purchaser, and calculates gain or loss by subtracting his or her basis from the amount realized. This gain or loss will usually be capital.

      ii. **Tax consequences to buyer:** The purchaser of the property takes the property with a basis equal to the purchase price, including the debt assumed.

      iii. **Tax consequences to lender:** The lender has realized a loss in the amount of the debt forgiven (see discussion at Chapter 7(IV)(C)). Unless some Code provisions prohibit it, the lender may deduct this loss.

      Example: Sam owns Blueacre, which he holds for investment, with an adjusted basis of $400,000 and a fair market value of $500,000. It is subject to a recourse mortgage of $700,000 to Friendly Bank. Sam wishes to transfer Blueacre to Bonnie. After some discussion, Friendly Bank forgives the amount of the debt in excess of Blueacre's fair market value ($200,000) and Sam transfers Blueacre to Bonnie in exchange for Bonnie's assumption of the remaining $500,000 of debt. See Figure 9G—Sam's Sale of Blueacre. Notice that Bonnie does not transfer any cash to Sam, as he has no equity in Blueacre.

      Sam's tax consequences: Sam has discharge of indebtedness income of $200,000, which *may* be excluded from his gross income if §108 applies. His gain or loss on the sale to Bonnie is equal to his amount realized ($500,000) minus his adjusted basis in the property ($400,000), or $100,000.

      Bonnie's tax consequences: Bonnie takes Blueacre with a basis equal to her cost, $500,000 (the debt assumed). This is because she is treated as the debtor on the debt she assumed from Sam.

Figure 9G
Sam's Sale of Blueacre

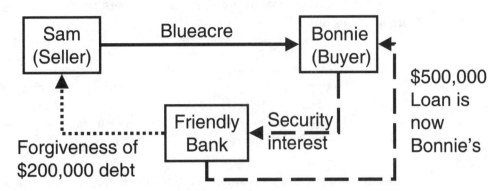

Transaction between Buyer and Bank

Transaction between Seller and Bank

Transaction between Seller and Buyer

Friendly Bank's tax consequences: The creditor may claim a loss in the amount of the debt discharged, or $200,000.

b. **Transfer to creditor in satisfaction of debt:** In this transaction, which is sometimes referred to as a nonjudicial foreclosure, the debtor transfers the property to the lender in full satisfaction of the debt. The lender then sells the property for its fair market value.

   i. **Tax consequences to seller/debtor:** According to Treas. Reg. §1.1001-2(a)(2), and (c), Example (8), and Rev. Rul. 90-16, 1990-1 C.B. 12, this transaction is bifurcated (as Justice O'Connor's concurrence in *Tufts* suggested). The sale transaction produces gain or loss equal to the fair market value of the property minus the debtor's adjusted basis in the property. The excess of the debt over the fair market value of the property is discharge of indebtedness income, which may be excluded if the requirements of §108 are met.

   ii. **Tax consequences to buyer:** The buyer will take the property with a basis equal to the buyer's cost in purchasing the property from the lender.

   iii. **Tax consequences to lender:** The lender takes a basis in the property equal to its fair market value. The lender may claim a loss on the amount of the debt discharged. On sale of the property, the creditor calculates gain or loss in the usual fashion. If the sale occurs immediately (no change in fair market value), the creditor will realize neither gain nor loss on the sale.

   Example: Sally owns Greenacre, which she holds for investment. Sally has an adjusted basis in Greenacre of $200,000, and its fair market value is $500,000. It is subject to a recourse debt of $900,000 held by Friendly Bank. Sally transfers Greenacre to Friendly Bank in full satisfaction of the debt. Friendly Bank then sells Greenacre to Ben for $500,000. See Figure 9H—Sally's Sale of Greenacre.

Sally's tax consequences: Sally must bifurcate this transaction into its sale and debt components. She realizes $300,000 of gain on the sale of the property, and also has $400,000 of discharge of indebtedness income that may be excluded if she meets the requirements of §108.

Sale of Property Transaction		*Discharge of Debt Transaction*	
Amount realized	$500,000 (FMV)	Face amount of debt	$900,000
− Adjusted basis	− 200,000	− Debt satisfied	− 500,000 (FMV)
= Gain on sale	$300,000	Discharge of debt	$400,000

Friendly Bank's tax consequences: Friendly Bank may claim a loss equal to the amount of debt forgiven ($400,000). The bank takes Greenacre with a basis of $500,000 and upon sale to Ben, realizes no gain or loss.

Ben's tax consequences: Ben takes Greenacre with a basis equal to his purchase price, or $500,000.

Figure 9H
Sally's Sale of Greenacre

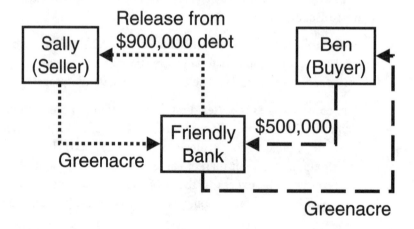

c. **Foreclosure sale:** In this transaction, the debtor defaults on the debt, and the lender forecloses on the property, causing the property to be sold and using the proceeds to satisfy part of the debt. Because the fair market value of the property is less than the outstanding debt, a portion of the debt will not be repaid. This transaction is treated as two transactions: the foreclosure sale and the disposition of the remaining debt. These two transactions often occur in different taxable years. See, e.g., *Aizawa v. Commissioner,* 99 T.C. 197 (1992), *aff'd unpublished opinion* 74 A.F.T.R. 2d ¶ 94,5493 (9th Cir. 1994). The amount realized is the fair market value of the property, which usually will be the foreclosure price (although not always—see *Frazier v. Commissioner,* 111 T.C. 243 (1998)). The lender facing a post-foreclosure deficiency has two options: to forgive the remaining debt or to proceed against the debtor's other assets for full payment (if allowed under state law).

i. **Tax consequences to seller:** The debtor realizes gain or loss on the sale of the property equal to the fair market value of the property sold minus the seller's adjusted basis in the property sold. The application of the proceeds to satisfaction of the loan is not a taxable event. If the lender forgives the debt, the debtor has discharge of indebtedness income equal to the amount of the forgiveness, which *may* be excluded from gross income by §108. If the lender proceeds against the debtor's other assets, the transfer of assets to the lender in satisfaction of the loan may generate gain or loss, if those assets' adjusted bases are different from their fair market values. Payment of the debt, however, is not a taxable event to the debtor.

ii. **Tax consequences to lender:** The full repayment of the loan is not a taxable event, but if the lender forgives any portion of the debt, the lender will be entitled to claim a loss on the transaction.

iii. **Tax consequences to buyer:** The buyer of the property will take it with a basis equal to its purchase price.

Example: Selena owns Pinkacre, with an adjusted basis of $20,000 and a fair market value of $100,000. Pinkacre is subject to a recourse mortgage of $150,000 for which Friendly Bank is the mortgagee. Unable to make payments on the debt, Selena defaults, and Friendly Bank forecloses. At the foreclosure sale, Bruce purchases Pinkacre from Selena for $100,000, and this amount is paid to Friendly Bank and is applied to reduce Selena's debt. Friendly Bank discharges the remaining $50,000 debt at a time when Selena's total debt exceeds her total assets by $100,000.

Selena's tax consequences: Upon sale of the property, Selena realizes and recognizes $80,000 of gain, equal to the difference between the sales price ($100,000) and her adjusted basis in the property ($20,000). The repayment of $100,000 of the loan is not a taxable event to Selena. When Friendly Bank discharges the remaining debt, Selena has discharge of indebtedness income in the amount of $50,000. Because she is insolvent by at least that amount, Selena may exclude this amount from her gross income but must reduce certain of her tax attributes.

Friendly Bank's tax consequences: The repayment of $100,000 of the loan is not a taxable event to the bank. It may claim a loss equal to the amount of debt forgiven, $50,000.

Bruce's tax consequences: Bruce takes Pinkacre with a basis equal to its purchase price, $100,000.

Example: Assume the same facts as above, except that Friendly Bank does not discharge the remaining $50,000 of the loan. Instead, pursuant to a judgment obtained by the bank in the next taxable year, Selena transfers another parcel of land, Whiteacre, to the bank in satisfaction of the remaining debt. Whiteacre has an adjusted basis of $70,000 and a fair market value of $50,000 in Selena's hand immediately prior to the transfer.

Selena's tax consequences: The tax consequences to Selena are the same as in the previous example, except that because Friendly Bank has not forgiven any part of the debt, she has no discharge of indebtedness income. In addition, however, in transferring Whiteacre to the bank, Selena realizes and recognizes (unless some loss recognition limitation applies) a loss of $20,000, equal to the difference between the debt satisfied ($50,000) and the adjusted basis of the property ($70,000).

Friendly Bank's tax consequences: As in the previous example, the repayment of the loan is not a taxable event to the bank. The bank takes Whiteacre with a basis equal to its purchase price (the amount of debt satisfied), or $50,000.

Bruce's tax consequences: As in the previous example, Bruce takes Pinkacre with a basis equal to his cost, or $100,000.

V. WHERE ARE WE GOING?

This chapter has examined the principles for computing realized gain or loss on the sale or other disposition of property. In general, realized or recognized gain or loss is recognized, so that a taxpayer must include in his or her gross income realized gain and is entitled to deduct (subject to certain limitations) realized loss. However, certain statutory provisions defer the recognition of realized gain or loss until a future date, and the next chapter discusses those statutes in detail.

Quiz Yourself on TRANSACTIONS IN PROPERTY

76. Al and Sal are avid sports memorabilia collectors. Al owns a baseball signed by Mickey Mantle. Sal owns a football signed by Joe Montana. Both purchased these items years ago and they have appreciated in value. They trade. What are the tax consequences to them of this trade? Disregard any nonrecognition provisions of the Code. _____

77. Taylor owns a collectible sports car, which she purchased many years ago for $10,000. It has appreciated significantly in value. Melique convinces Taylor to sell him the sports car, in exchange for Melique's promise to completely remodel Taylor's kitchen. Do either of these individuals have income or loss from this transaction? _____

78. What is the function of "basis"? Of "adjusted basis"? _____

79. Dick owns Bleak House, a bed-and-breakfast inn for literary types. He had an initial basis of $140,000 in this property, and has claimed $40,000 of depreciation deductions over the years. He agrees to sell the property to Tom for $300,000. What are the tax consequences of this sale to Dick? _____

80. Assume the same facts as in the preceeding question, except that Dick has a mortgage on Bleak House in the amount of $100,000. He agrees to sell Bleak House to Jerry. Jerry will pay Dick cash of $200,000 and Jerry's assumption of the debt on Bleak House. What are the tax consequences of this transaction to Dick? What is Jerry's basis in Bleak House? _____

81. Courtney purchased the Emerald Apartment Buliding for $1 million. She financed 100% of the purchase price through Very Friendly Bank, which loaned her the money on a nonrecourse basis.

Over the years, she properly claimed $250,000 of MACRS deductions with respect to the property. Unfortunately, the value of the property declined and became a stone around her neck. One day she simply marched into the bank, gave them the deed to the property and walked away. She had paid off only $50,000 of the debt so her mortgage balance was $950,000 at that time. The bank ultimately sold the property for $600,000. Courtney reported a $150,000 loss on this transaction on her tax return. Was she correct? _____

82. Linda purchased The Bates Motel for $500,000, the entire amount of which she financed with a recourse mortgage from a bank. Over the years she claimed $100,000 in depreciation deductions. Some spooky things happened at the motel, and it declined in value because few visitors wanted to stay there. Linda was unable to repay the debt. Last year, when Linda had a mortgage balance of $450,000, the bank foreclosed on the property. The property was sold for $200,000, all of which was applied to Linda's loan. The bank tried to collect the remaining $250,000, but ultimately decided it was uncollectible because Linda's debts were well in excess of her assets. The bank wrote off the debt. What are the tax consequences of this transaction to Linda? _____

83. Would the result in the previous question be any different if the bank and Linda had simply agreed that she would transfer the motel to the bank in full satisfaction of the debt? _____

Answers

76. As a result of this trade, Al and Sal both have realization events: What they received was different, qualitatively, than what they had before; they have different legal rights after the trade. Each has realized gain in the amount of the difference between the fair market value of what was received, and the basis of what was transferred. That gain should be recognized unless they can find a nonrecognition statute that applies. (See Chapter 10.)

77. This barter transaction results in income to both Taylor and Melique. Taylor has sold the sports car, and will recognize gain on that transaction equal to the difference between the fair market value of the sports car and its basis in Taylor's hands. (The value of the car is probably easier to determine than the value of the remodel.) Melique has received payment for services to be rendered, and must include the fair market value of the car in his gross income. Both Taylor and Melique would be wise to agree upon the fair market value of the sports car and report their two transactions consistently.

78. Basis represents the initial economic investment a taxpayer has in an item of property (or his or her deemed investment, as in the case of property received from a decedent). Adjusted basis reflects the initial basis, plus or minus, respectively, the capital recovery claimed or improvements made to the property after acquisition. In both cases, basis or adjusted basis is the starting point for measuring the capital recovery deductions a taxpayer may claim, and is the way of measuring gain or loss on ultimate disposition of the property.

79. Dick has a realized and recognized gain of $200,000, which is equal to his amount realized ($300,000) minus his adjusted basis in the property of $100,000 ($140,000 − $40,000).

80. Dick has a realized and recognized gain of $200,000, which is equal to his amount realized of $300,000 ($200,000 in cash plus assumption of the $100,000 mortgage) minus his adjusted basis in the property of $100,000 ($140,000 − $40,000). Jerry's basis is $300,000, which is equal to his purchase price: $200,000 in cash plus the assumption of the mortgage.

81. No. Courtney is thinking that her loss is equal to the difference between the fair market value of the property ($600,000) and her adjusted basis ($750,000). But this is incorrect. She should have reported a *gain* of $200,000. Under *Tufts,* Courtney is deemed to have sold the property and the amount realized is equal to the amount of the outstanding loan ($950,000). Her adjusted basis in the property is $750,000 ($1,000,000 – 250,000 of MACRS deductions). This produces a gain of $200,000.

82. Linda has two transactions in the year of foreclosure and writeoff. First, she has a sale of the property for $200,000. She had an adjusted basis of $400,000 in the property (her cost minus her depreciation deductions). This results in a $200,000 loss to her, which should be deductible under IRC §165(c). However, she also has $250,000 of discharge of indebtedness income. This may be excludable from Linda's gross income, however, if she meets any of the exceptions of §108(a), such as the insolvency exception.

83. The result would be the same, assuming that the value of the motel were $200,000 on the date of transfer.

Exam Tips *on*
TRANSACTIONS IN PROPERTY

Questions involving transactions in property involve sales, exchanges, trades, and other dispositions of property.

☞ *Look for:* A taxpayer giving up a property in exchange for something else—cash, other property, promises, services, assumption of liabilities.

☞ *Analyze:* Which taxpayer's tax consequences are you asked to analyze? Both, or just one of them? If both taxpayers are at issue, analyze them separately.

☛ *Careful: Don't jump right to the question of gain included in income, or loss deductible from income. Make sure there is a realization event, and that there is realized gain or loss, before asking what gain or loss is recognized.*

☛ If in doubt, consider a transaction a realization event. Most transactions are realization events.

☛ Compute realized gain by subtracting the adjusted basis of the property given up from the value of what the taxpayer receives. If the property received is difficult to value, refer to the value of the property given up.

☛ **Remember:** Rational, unrelated taxpayers will trade value-for-value and will adjust differences in value by paying or receiving additional property. If taxpayers are related, there may be a gift involved.

☛ Most realized gain is recognized (see Chapter 10). If in doubt, include it in income.

☛ Realized loss is recognizable only if there is a statute that allows it. See Chapters 6 and 7. Deductions are a matter of legislative grace, and are interpreted narrowly. If in doubt, deny the deduction of the loss.

CHAPTER **10**

NONRECOGNITION TRANSACTIONS

ChapterScope _____

The previous chapter addressed the computation of realized and recognized gain and loss from the sale or other disposition of property. As a general rule, gross income includes these gains, and a loss will generate a deduction if the other statutory requirements for a deduction are met. Congress has, however, determined that for some transactions, the time is not ripe for recognition of realized gain or loss. For these transactions, even though a realization event has occurred, recognition is deferred until a more appropriate time. Code sections that provide deferral of recognition of gain or loss for such transactions are called nonrecognition provisions and are the subject of this chapter.

- ■ **An approach to nonrecognition transactions:** The approach to sales or exchanges of property discussed above at Chapter 9(II) is equally applicable here, with special emphasis on steps 4 (gain and loss recognition) and 6 (calculation of basis).

- ■ **Section 1031—Like-kind exchanges:** Section 1031 mandates nonrecognition treatment for exchanges of like-kind properties, such as real property for real property, if certain requirements are met.

- ■ **Section 1033—Involuntary conversions:** Section 1033 allows nonrecognition of gain for conversions of property as a result of thefts, disasters, and condemnation actions, if certain requirements are met.

- ■ **Section 1041—Spousal and divorce transfers:** Section 1041 provides for nonrecognition of gain or loss on transfers between spouses and on transfers between former spouses if "incident to a divorce" and if certain other requirements are met.

- ■ **Other nonrecognition provisions:** A basic tax student should have a passing familiarity with a number of other nonrecognition provisions that generally receive only limited attention in the basic tax course. These include transfers to partnerships and corporations in exchange for interests in these entities, and certain other transfers.

I. WHERE ARE WE?

We are continuing our computation of gross income from the dealings in property, or losses from such transactions allowable as a deduction. A special group of statutes defer the recognition of all or part of the gain or loss for some kinds of transactions. If any of these statutes apply, all or part of the gain or loss will not be recognized by the taxpayer in the year of sale or exchange, but will potentially be preserved in the basis of the property received. So, this chapter is about gross income and deductions, as well as timing of the recognition of gains and losses.

II. AN APPROACH TO THE NONRECOGNITION PROVISIONS

A. An approach

The approach to sales and exchanges of property discussed in Chapter 9 is equally applicable to nonrecognition provisions. However, particular emphasis is placed on the calculation of gain recognition and the computation of basis.

B. Figure 10A—Six-step approach

1. **Step 1. Identify a transaction in property:** This is discussed fully in Chapter 9(III)(B).

2. **Step 2. Identify a realization event:** This process is discussed fully in Chapter 9(III)(B).

3. **Step 3. Calculate realized gain or loss:** This process is discussed fully in Chapter 9(III)(B).

4. **Step 4. Calculate recognized gain or loss:** This step is of crucial importance in discussion of nonrecognition rules. First, does any nonrecognition rule apply to defer gain or loss recognition? Consider carefully the requirements of the nonrecognition provisions, and construe them strictly. Second, what are the consequences to the taxpayer in terms of recognized gain or loss?

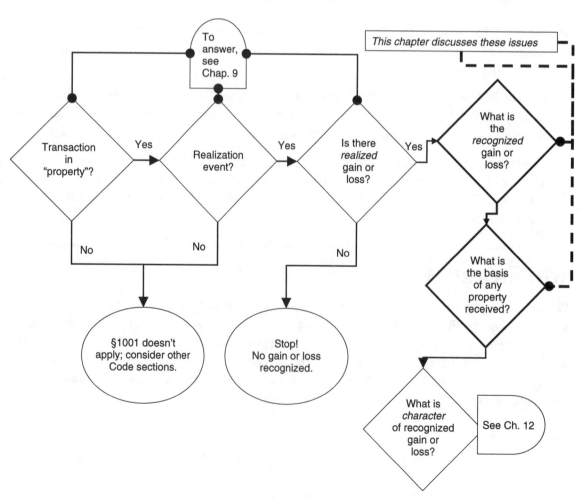

Figure 10A
An Approach to Property Transactions

5. **Step 5. Determine the basis of property received in the transaction:** In a nonrecognition transaction, property permitted to be received without recognition of gain or loss will take an **"exchanged basis"** specially calculated under the nonrecognition rule. Any **"boot"** (property other than property permitted to be received without recognition of gain) received will take a basis equal to its fair market value.

6. **Step 6. Determine the character of any gain or loss recognized:** See discussion at Chapter 12.

III. LIKE-KIND EXCHANGES—§1031

A. Recognizing this type of transaction

A like-kind exchange is exactly what it sounds like—a taxpayer exchanging one property for a property of like kind. Common examples include the exchange of real property for real property or the trade-in of equipment for other equipment. The taxpayer may also receive or transfer other types of property in the transaction and may assume or be relieved of liabilities in the exchange.

B. Policy

A variety of rationales are commonly offered for nonrecognition in like-kind exchanges.

1. **No change in investment:** The most commonly offered rationale is that because the taxpayer continues to hold the same kind of property, the time has not yet arrived to compute the economic gain or loss on the original investment.

2. **Liquidity:** Another rationale is that in a like-kind exchange, the taxpayer receives no cash, and thus paying the tax would be difficult. Notice that if **boot** is received, the taxpayer may have the cash (or other property that can be converted to cash) to pay tax. This rationale is criticized because taxpayers engaging in other types of trades do not have cash, but nevertheless must pay tax. See, e.g., barter transactions discussed at Chapter 2(II)(B).

3. **Fighting "lock-in":** The like-kind exchange rules may be a limited method of fighting the effect of "lock-in," i.e., taxpayers holding property simply to avoid paying tax. See discussion of lock-in at Chapter 12(II)(D).

C. Section 1031 statutory analysis—General rule

The general rule of §1031 is easy to state: A taxpayer engaging in a like-kind exchange recognizes neither gain nor loss on the transfer of property in the exchange, and takes the property received in the exchange with an exchanged basis. This general statement of the rule, however, captures neither the precise requirements for a like-kind exchange nor the full implications to the taxpayer of §1031 treatment. The sections below examine in detail the domain and effect of §1031's general rule before proceeding to other issues.

1. **Domain:** A like-kind exchange occurs if—and only if—the following five requirements are met.

   a. **Exchange:** A taxpayer must exchange property for property. IRC §1031(a)(1).

   b. **Not prohibited property:** The property exchanged must not be inventory, stocks, bonds, notes, securities or other evidences of indebtedness, partnership interests, interests in a trust, or choses in action. IRC §1031(a)(2).

c. Use of transferred property: The taxpayer must have held the property transferred for use in a trade or business or for investment. IRC §1031(a)(1).

d. Like-kind properties: The property received must be like kind to the property exchanged. IRC §1031(a)(1).

e. Use of property received: The taxpayer must intend to hold the property received for use in a trade or business or for investment. IRC §1031(a)(1).

2. Effect

a. Nonrecognition: In a qualifying like-kind exchange, the taxpayer does not recognize any of the realized gain or loss on the transfer of property unless he or she receives property not permitted to be received without recognition (known as boot). Section 1031's nonrecognition rule is mandatory; if a transaction qualifies as a like-kind exchange, the taxpayer recognizes neither gain nor loss.

i. Boot received—Gain recognition: If the taxpayer receives property not permitted to be received without recognition (boot), realized gain is recognized to the extent of the fair market value of the boot received. IRC §1031(b). In other words, realized gain is recognized in an amount equal to the lesser of the realized gain or the fair market value of the boot received. The receipt of boot triggers gain recognition because it represents a partial sale of the property. While the taxpayer has continued his or her original investment in a portion of the property (represented by the like-kind property received), the taxpayer also has discontinued this investment to the extent of cash or nonlike-kind property received. Thus, the taxpayer is treated as having sold a portion of the original property for purposes of gain recognition

ii. Loss not recognized: Loss is never recognized, even when boot is received. IRC §1031(c).

b. Basis: A taxpayer transferring property in a like-kind exchange may receive two types of property in the transaction: like-kind property and boot. See Figure 10B—Basis Calculation for Like-Kind Exchanges.

Figure 10B
Basis Calculation for Like-Kind Exchanges

To calculate basis of like kind property received:

Basis of Property Transferred

Plus   Gain recognized

Minus   Fair market value of boot received

Minus   Loss recognized

Plus   Additional investment in property (boot paid)

Basis of Property Received in the Exchange

Note: Boot received always takes a basis equal to its FMV

i. **Like-kind property:** The taxpayer's basis in the like-kind property received is equal to the basis of the property transferred, plus the gain recognized, minus the fair market value of the boot received, minus any loss recognized on the transaction, plus any additional amount invested in the property acquired. IRC §§1031(d), 1012. This is a form of exchanged basis, in which the basis of the property acquired is determined by reference to the basis of the property transferred. See IRC §7701(a)(44). The resulting basis will preserve, as of the date of the exchange, the realized but unrecognized gain or loss inherent in the property transferred in the exchange. Thus, if the property's fair market value remains unchanged until sale, the taxpayer will ultimately recognize upon sale of the property the gain or loss that went unrecognized in the like-kind exchange.

ii. **Boot:** The taxpayer's basis in any boot received is its fair market value. IRC §1031(d).

iii. **Loss taken into account in basis calculation:** Since losses are never recognized in like-kind exchanges, how can the basis calculation require a subtraction for losses recognized? This can occur if the taxpayer transfers property to the other party to the exchange that has an adjusted basis greater than its fair market value, and the taxpayer recognizes a loss on the transfer.

Example: Kay owns Property #1, which has a fair market value of $90,000 and an adjusted basis of $50,000. Kay wishes to trade Property #1 for Property #2, and the exchange would qualify as a like-kind exchange. However, Property #2 is worth $100,000, and therefore Kay must transfer $10,000 in boot to the other party. She does so by transferring a painting that she held for investment, which has a fair market value of $10,000 and an adjusted basis of $15,000. Assuming no other loss restrictions apply, she recognizes $5,000 of loss on this transfer. In computing her basis in Property #2, Kay will begin with her basis in Property #1 ($50,000) and the boot ($15,000), add the gain recognized (0), subtract the fair market value of boot received (0), subtract the loss recognized ($5,000) and add the boot paid (0, since she has already taken into account the painting in step 1). Thus, her basis in Property #2 will be $60,000. Another way to think about this problem is to imagine that Kay sold the painting to someone else for cash, recognized the loss independently of this transaction, and then exchanged properties, adding the cash from the painting sale to the mix. In that case, the basis of Property #2 would be the same ($60,000), calculated in a slightly different way: Start with the basis of Property #1 ($50,000), add the gain recognized (0), subtract the fair market value of boot received (0), subtract the loss recognized on this exchange (0), and add the boot paid ($10,000).

c. **Independent results for each taxpayer:** In order to qualify under §1031, a taxpayer must meet only the requirements discussed above. It is not necessary that any other party to the exchange meet these requirements. Thus, each taxpayer's tax consequences must be analyzed separately to determine whether he or she has made a qualifying §1031 exchange. The following examples illustrate the domain and effect of §1031.

Example: Alex owns Blackacre, a parcel of raw land she holds for investment. She has a basis of $30,000 in the property, and it is worth $100,000. Brenda owns Whiteacre, also a parcel of raw land, worth $100,000. Alex and Brenda exchange properties. Alex intends to hold Whiteacre for investment. What are the tax consequences of this transaction to Alex? Applying the five-step approach to this problem, consider the following questions:

Has there been a transaction in property? Yes. Real estate certainly qualifies as property.

Has there been a realization event? The exchange of properties certainly qualifies as a realization event, for both Alex and Brenda own materially different interests in property after the exchange than they did before the exchange.

What is Alex's realized gain or loss? Alex's realized gain or loss is equal to the amount realized on the transfer ($100,000, the fair market value of Whiteacre) minus her adjusted basis in the property transferred ($30,000) for a realized gain of $70,000.

What is Alex's recognized gain? This transaction falls within the domain of §1031 because (1) it is an exchange of properties; (2) Alex held Blackacre for investment; (3) the properties received are like kind (they are both raw land); (4) Alex intends to hold Whiteacre for investment; and (5) the properties exchanged are not prohibited property (they are real property). As a result, none of Alex's realized gain of $70,000 is recognized; she need not include any of this realized gain in gross income. Notice that Brenda's tax consequences are irrelevant to Alex's determination of whether she is entitled to like-kind exchange treatment.

What is the basis of Whiteacre in Alex's hands? Alex's basis in Whiteacre is equal to her basis in Blackacre ($30,000) plus the gain recognized if any (0), minus the fair market value of the boot received, if any (0), minus the loss recognized, if any (0). Thus, Alex's basis in Whiteacre is $30,000. Notice that this preserves the realized but unrecognized gain inherent in Blackacre at the time of the exchange. If, later, Alex sells Whiteacre for $100,000 in cash, she will recognize $70,000 of gain—precisely the amount that went unrecognized in the like-kind exchange. (If Whiteacre's value changes, of course, she will recognize a different amount of gain, but that amount will reflect her economic profit or loss on the investment of Blackacre *and* Whiteacre).

What is the character of Alex's gain? This is not relevant because Alex has no recognized gain. See discussion at Chapter 12(III).

Example: Assume the same facts as in the previous example, except that Whiteacre was worth only $90,000, so that in order to make the trade, Brenda would transfer Whiteacre plus $10,000 cash to Alex. What are Alex's tax consequences? In this situation, Alex's realized gain from the exchange is again $70,000. Her amount realized is the fair market value of Whiteacre ($90,000) plus the $10,000 cash, for a total amount realized of $100,000. Subtracting her adjusted basis in Blackacre ($30,000) produces the $70,000 realized gain. For the reasons discussed in the previous example, this transfer of Blackacre for Whiteacre qualifies as a like-kind exchange. The receipt of boot does not disqualify the like-kind exchange; it does, however, require the recognition of realized gain to the extent of the boot received ($10,000). As discussed in Chapter 12, that gain will be capital. Alex's basis in Whiteacre is equal to her basis in Blackacre ($30,000) plus the gain recognized ($10,000) minus the fair market value of the boot received ($10,000). Thus, her basis in Whiteacre is $30,000. Notice that this basis preserves the realized but unrecognized gain inherent in Blackacre ($60,000) at the time of the exchange. Thus, if Alex later sells Whiteacre for its current fair market value of $90,000, she will recognize the $60,000 of gain that was deferred in the like-kind exchange.

Assume the same facts as in the previous example, except that instead of giving Alex $10,000 cash to equalize the values of the two properties, Brenda transfers a sports car to her along with Whiteacre. The tax consequences to Alex will be the same as in the previous situation, except that she will be required to assign a basis to the sports car. That basis will be the sports car's fair market value, or $10,000.

Example: Christian owns DogAcre, a parcel of raw land. His basis in DogAcre is $40,000, but its fair market value is only $15,000. He trades DogAcre for David's parcel of raw land, CatAcre. CatAcre is worth $10,000, so David also transfers $5,000 cash to Christian. Christian held DogAcre for investment and intends to hold CatAcre for investment as well. What are the tax consequences of this transaction to Christian? This realization event causes Christian to realize a loss of $25,000, equal to the difference between his amount realized of $15,000 ($10,000 in the form of CatAcre plus $5,000 in cash) and his adjusted basis in DogAcre ($40,000). However, because this qualifies as a like-kind exchange, Christian will not recognize any of the realized loss. (Notice that this is the result even though Christian received boot.) Christian's basis in CatAcre will be equal to his basis in DogAcre ($40,000) plus the gain recognized, if any (0), minus the fair market value of the boot received ($5,000). Therefore, his basis in CatAcre will be $35,000. Thus, if Christian later sells CatAcre for $10,000, he will recognize the $25,000 loss that was deferred in the like-kind exchange. (Christian would probably have been better advised to sell DogAcre, recognize the loss, and purchase CatAcre for cash.)

D. Definitional issues

1. **Exchange:** The taxpayer must exchange his or her property for the other property; the transaction must not be—in form or in substance—a sale for cash followed by a purchase of like-kind property. The taxpayer cannot later change his or her mind and transform a sale of property into an exchange.

2. **Sale/Leaseback:** Because §1031 is mandatory, if a transaction is an exchange, no gain or loss will be recognized. This frequently arises in "sale/leaseback" transactions in which the taxpayer wants to recognize a loss on the sale. In a sale/leaseback transaction, a taxpayer owning property sells it to another person, who then leases it back to the original taxpayer on a long-term lease. When the dust settles, it can appear as if nothing much has changed. The question is whether a real sale occurred, or was the transaction an exchange of like-kind properties? See Figure 10C—Sale/Leaseback Transaction.

   a. *Jordan Marsh Co. v. Commissioner,* **269 F.2d 453 (2d Cir. 1959):** The taxpayer owned property with a basis of $4.8 million and a fair market value of $2.3 million. The taxpayer sold the property for cash, and then immediately leased the property from the buyer for a 30-year term, with an option to renew for 30 years. The taxpayer claimed a deduction of $2.5 million for the loss on the sale portion of the transaction. This transaction is called a "sale leaseback."

      i. **Issue:** Was this an "exchange" of like-kind properties (a fee interest for a leasehold that effectively constituted a fee because of its length), so that Jordan Marsh incorrectly reported a loss on the transaction? Or was it a "sale," giving rise to a properly deductible loss?

    ii. Result and rationale: Jordan Marsh sold the property and properly reported the loss. The transaction constituted a true sale for fair market value, and the subsequent lease was a true lease for fair rental value. These bona fide transactions must be respected for tax purposes. Thus, the sale/leaseback transaction could not be recharacterized as an exchange.

  b. *Leslie Co. v. Commissioner,* **539 F.2d 943 (3d Cir. 1976):** This case also involved a sale/leaseback transaction (see Figure 10C). The taxpayer constructed property with a cost of $3.187 million and sold it to Prudential for $2.4 million, deducting the difference of $787,000 as a loss. Prudential then leased the property back to the taxpayer for a 40-year term with two 10-year options to renew and options to purchase the property during the term of the lease.

    i. Issue: Was the sale/leaseback, in substance, an exchange of like-kind properties so that Leslie incorrectly reported a loss on the transaction, or was it a sale giving rise to a properly deductible loss?

    ii. Result and rationale: Leslie sold the property and properly reported the loss. The court examined the different approaches of the Second Circuit in *Jordan Marsh* and the Eighth Circuit in *Century Electric Co. v. Commissioner,* 192 F.2d 155 (8th Cir. 1951). In *Century Electric,* the court held that no valuation of the fee interest and leasehold interest was necessary, and that an exchange was to be found if the transaction constituted a reciprocal exchange of properties. In *Jordan Marsh,* the court valued the two property interests; if the payments made were based on fair market value, the transaction would be

Figure 10C
Sale/Leaseback Transaction

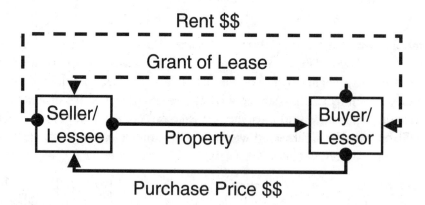

considered a sale rather than an exchange of properties. In *Leslie,* the court adopted the *Jordan Marsh* approach, and because the sales price and the rental price reflected fair market value, the transaction was a true sale and lease rather than an exchange.

3. Like kind: What constitutes "like-kind" property generates most of the controversy in §1031.

a. Statutory definitions: Section 1031 itself provides that certain properties are not like kind. Livestock of different sexes, and real property within and without the United States, are not like kind. IRC §1031(e), (h).

b. Regulations' definition: The regulations define like kind as having reference to the "nature or character" of the property rather than its "grade or quality." Reg. §1.1031(a)–1(b).

i. Depreciable personal property: The regulations offer a safe harbor for determining whether depreciable personal property held for use in a trade or business is of like kind. The regulations and other administrative guidance divide the world of depreciable personal property into "classes." An exchange of properties that are the same class is considered a like-kind exchange. Reg. §1.1031(a)–1(b). Exchanges of properties in different classes may still qualify as a like-kind exchange if the properties meet the general definition of like kind. Id.

Example: Fred owns an Apple computer system. He exchanges his system for an IBM system. Because computers are within the same class of business property, they are like-kind properties under §1031.

ii. Other personal property: Intangible and nondepreciable personal property, and personal property held for investment, must satisfy the more general like-kind test. The IRS's approach to personal property is apparently stricter than its approach to real property. See, e.g., Rev. Rul. 82–166, 1982–2 C.B. 190, in which an exchange of gold bullion held for investment for silver bullion held for investment was not a like-kind exchange, on the theory that silver and gold are intrinsically different metals and are used in different ways.

c. Real property: The regulations provide that a property's status as improved or unimproved is not material to the like-kind analysis, as it relates only to the quality of the real property, not its nature or character. Reg. §1.1031(a)–1(b). Thus, a taxpayer may exchange city real estate for a ranch or farm. Reg. §1.1031(a)–1(c). The regulations treat a lease of 30 years or more as equivalent to a fee interest, so exchanges of a fee interest for a long-term lease will be considered like-kind exchanges. Occasionally, the transfer of an interest in real property of a shorter duration for a fee interest raises questions, and a court faced with such a problem will compare the exchanged properties to determine whether they are substantially alike, examining the physical characteristics of the properties, "the nature of the title conveyed, the rights of the parties, the duration of the interest, and any other factor bearing on the nature or character of the properties. . . ." *Koch v. Commissioner,* 71 T.C. 54, 65 (1978). In a related context, the IRS has asserted that a building and land are not like kind. See Rev. Rul. 76–390, 1976–2 C.B. 243 (applying §1033(g), discussed at this chapter, section (IV)).

Example: Marsha owns an office building and the underlying lot. She trades this property for a marina located on a 99-year lease of shore property. This qualifies as a like-kind exchange, regardless of the different improvements and different uses of the two properties.

E. Special rules and exceptions

1. **Deferred and three-party (*Starker*) exchanges:** Deferred and three-party exchanges are based on *Starker v. United States,* 602 F.2d 1341 (9th Cir. 1979), in which the court allowed like-kind exchange treatment for a transaction in which the taxpayer's transfer and receipt of property were separated by a significant period of time. The essential problem addressed by these transactions is that the taxpayer holds property he or she wishes to exchange in a like-kind exchange, but the buyer who wishes to acquire the property has only cash, not like-kind property. A number of transactions have evolved to address this problem.

   a. **Solution 1—Buyer acquires like-kind property:** In this transaction, the buyer acquires like-kind property and then exchanges it with the taxpayer. This transaction is treated as a pure like-kind exchange, as there is no delay between the transfer and receipt of properties.

      Example: Alvin holds Blackacre for investment and wishes to exchange it for like-kind property to be held for investment. Becky wants Blackacre, but has only cash. Cecilia owns Whiteacre, which is like-kind property to Blackacre, and would be happy to sell Whiteacre for cash. Alvin would be happy to exchange Blackacre for Whiteacre. In the first step of the transaction, Becky buys Whiteacre from Cecilia for cash. Then, in the second step, Alvin transfers Blackacre to Becky in exchange for Whiteacre. From Alvin's perspective, this is simply a like-kind exchange. Notice that Becky could not claim like-kind exchange treatment for this transaction because she acquired Whiteacre for the purpose of transferring it to Alvin, which would not qualify as holding it for use in a trade or business or for investment. However, this will not matter to Becky, because her basis in Whiteacre is its cost. Moreover, Becky's tax treatment is irrelevant to Alvin's ability to claim like-kind exchange treatment for his transfer of Blackacre. See Figure 10D—Alvin's Exchange of Blackacre for Whiteacre.

   b. **Solution 2—Deferred exchange:** In a deferred exchange, the taxpayer first transfers his or her property to the buyer, in exchange for the buyer's promise to acquire like-kind property and transfer it to the taxpayer within a specified period of time.

      Example: Alvin owns and wishes to exchange Blackacre for like-kind property. Becky wants Blackacre, but has cash, not like-kind property. Alvin conveys Blackacre to Becky in exchange for Becky's promise to acquire and convey Whiteacre to Alvin within a stated period of time. Within that period of time, Becky finds Cecilia, who is willing to sell Whiteacre, which is like-kind property. She acquires Whiteacre from Cecilia and then conveys it to Alvin.

   c. **Solution 3—Deferred exchange with qualified intermediary:** If the taxpayer is understandably hesitant to transfer the property for a mere promise, he or she may transfer it to an intermediary. The intermediary will hold the property until the buyer acquires and transfers the like-kind property to the taxpayer or to the intermediary (who then transfers it to the taxpayer). Alternatively, the buyer may deposit funds with the intermediary, who will acquire suitable property. If the intermediary is related to the taxpayer, this could be viewed as a transfer for cash, so care must be taken that the transaction fits the requirements of statute and regulations for a "qualified intermediary," discussed below.

Figure 10D
Alvin's Exchange of Blackacre for Whiteacre

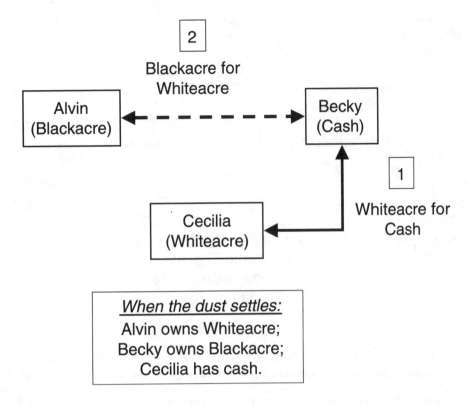

When the dust settles:
Alvin owns Whiteacre;
Becky owns Blackacre;
Cecilia has cash.

Example: Alvin owns and wishes to exchange Blackacre for like-kind property. Becky wants Blackacre, but has cash, not like-kind property. Becky would like Alvin to convey Blackacre to her in exchange for her promise to acquire like-kind property within a stated period of time. Alvin, however, is reluctant to convey Blackacre to Becky for her mere promise. In the first step of the transaction, Alvin conveys Blackacre to an intermediary, and Becky places funds equal to the fair market value of Blackacre with the intermediary. The instructions to the intermediary are to acquire acceptable like-kind property within a stated period of time. In the second step of the transaction, the intermediary acquires suitable like-kind property (Whiteacre) from Cecilia, paying Cecilia the cash previously deposited by Becky. In the third step of the transaction, the intermediary conveys Whiteacre to Alvin and Blackacre to Becky. In practice, Cecilia might directly transfer the property to Alvin, but in this illustration, the intermediary takes title and then transfers it to Alvin. See Figure 10E— Deferred Exchange with an Intermediary.

d. **Statutory and regulatory requirements:** In order for a deferred exchange to receive nonrecognition treatment, the property to be received by the taxpayer must be *identified* within 45 days after the taxpayer relinquishes his or her property, *and* must be *received* before the earlier of (1) the 180th day after the date the taxpayer relinquishes his or her property, or (2) the due date of the taxpayer's tax return for the year of the transfer of the relinquished property. IRC §1031(a)(3). The 45-day period gives the taxpayer time to find the right property, and the 180-day period gives the taxpayer the necessary time to inspect it, make an offer, and close the transaction.

FIGURE 10E
Deferred Exchange With Intermediary

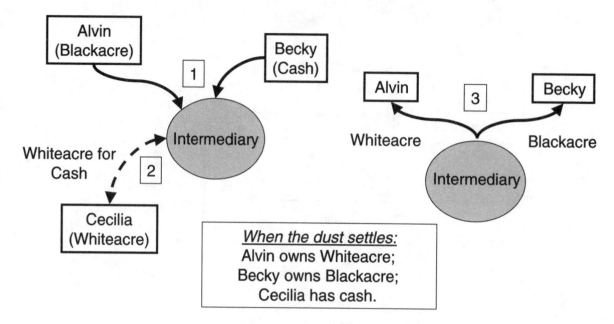

i. **Identification and receipt:** The regulations provide detailed rules regarding what constitutes adequate identification and receipt. Treas. Reg. §1.1031(k)-1.

ii. **Who may be an intermediary?** The danger of using a third party to hold the property and funds from the buyer is that the taxpayer may be viewed as being in ***constructive receipt*** of the funds so that the transaction would be viewed as a sale. See discussion of constructive receipt at Chapter 11(III)(B). The regulations identify what classes of persons may act as an intermediary so that the intermediary will not be treated as the agent of the taxpayer. Reg. §1.1031(k)-1(g). For example, a taxpayer's lawyer may not act as an intermediary. Reg. §1.1031(k)-1(k)(2).

e. **Another permutation—Reverse exchange:** At times the taxpayer may have identified the property to be acquired before the property to be transferred is identified. In this situation, the taxpayer may receive like-kind property before he or she transfers like-kind property; this is known as a "reverse exchange." The IRS has issued guidance creating a safe harbor for reverse exchanges in which a taxpayer may transfer property to a qualified intermediary while replacement property is being located, when the taxpayer has a genuine intent to engage in a like-kind exchange. Rev. Proc. 2000–37, 2000–40 I.R.B. 308, modified by Rev. Proc. 2004–51, 2004–33 I.R.B. 294.

2. **Effect of mortgages:** Property intended to be used in a like-kind exchange may be subject to a mortgage, and the first question in any exchange in which the encumbered properties are transferred is whether any party to the exchange is assuming those liabilities or whether property is being transferred subject to the liabilities. If so, special attention must be paid to the regulations setting forth the proper treatment of these liabilities.

a. **The rules:** The IRS provides guidance on the treatment of mortgages in regulations that are generally taxpayer-friendly, if somewhat complex.

i. Consequences to transferor of encumbered property: A transferor of encumbered property must include the liabilities assumed by the other party to the exchange as part of his or her amount realized in calculating the realized gain or loss on the exchange. See IRC §1001 and discussion at Chapter 9(IV). In addition, the liability assumed by the other party is considered boot to the party to the exchange transferring the encumbered property. This results in gain recognition (but see "**mortgage netting**," below) and must be treated as boot in the calculation of the basis of the like-kind property received.

ii. Consequences to acquirer of encumbered property: The party assuming a liability of the other party to the exchange is treated as transferring property in the amount of the liability. Thus, the amount of the liability is added to the basis of the property transferred in the exchange in determining the realized gain or loss on the exchange. This amount is considered an additional investment in the property for purposes of calculating the basis of the property received in the transaction.

iii. Mortgage netting: When both properties are subject to liabilities, only the taxpayer with net relief from liabilities is treated as having received boot, for purposes of gain recognition only. Reg. §1.1031(d)-2, Example (2). The full amount of the mortgages are considered (i.e., are not netted) in computing realized gain or loss and basis calculation, although the result will be similar to netting. Id.

iv. Mortgage netting and boot: The mortgage netting rule allows the party with net assumption of liability to avoid recognition of gain, but this applies only to the mortgage portion of the transaction. If that person receives other property (boot), the usual gain recognition rules will apply. Reg. §1.1031(d)-1, Example (2). In addition, the party with net relief from liability may reduce the amount of gain recognized by any boot paid in the transaction. Id.

b. Examples: Consider the rules described above, as applied in the following examples.

Example: Heather owns Blueacre, which has an adjusted basis of $60,000 and a fair market value of $100,000. It is subject to a liability of $20,000. Heather exchanges Blueacre for Mickey's Pinkacre (worth $80,000) in a qualifying §1031 exchange in which Mickey assumes Heather's liability. Heather's amount realized is the fair market value of Pinkacre ($80,000) plus Mickey's assumption of her liability ($20,000). Subtracting Heather's adjusted basis in Blueacre of $60,000 produces a realized gain of $40,000. Heather's recognized gain is $20,000, equal to the liabilities Mickey assumed in the transaction. Heather's adjusted basis in Pinkacre is equal to $60,000, calculated as follows:

Heather's basis in Blueacre	$60,000
+ Gain recognized	+20,000
– FMV boot (A/L*)	– 20,000
Basis of Pinkacre	$60,000

*A/L = assumption of liability.

Notice that Heather's $60,000 basis in Pinkacre preserves the unrecognized $20,000 gain on the original exchange. If Heather were to later sell Pinkacre for $80,000, she would realize and recognize the $20,000 gain.

Summary of Heather's Tax Consequences

Realized Gain	Recognized Gain	Basis of Pinkacre
$40,000	$20,000	$ 60,000 (basis of Blueacre) + 20,000 (gain) − 20,000 (boot) <u>$ 60,000 Basis of Pinkacre</u>

Example: Mildred owns Greenacre, with an adjusted basis of $40,000 and a fair market value of $80,000. Mildred exchanges Greenacre for Paul's Whiteacre in a qualifying §1031 exchange. Whiteacre has a fair market value of $110,000 and is subject to a mortgage of $30,000.

Mildred's realized gain is equal to $40,000, the difference between her amount realized ($110,000) and the sum of her adjusted basis in Greenacre ($40,000) and the amount of mortgage she assumes in the transaction ($30,000). Her recognized gain is zero because she received no boot in the transaction. Her basis in Whiteacre is $70,000, calculated as follows:

Mildred's basis in Greenacre	$40,000
+ Gain recognized	0
− FMV boot received	0
+ <u>Additional investment</u>	+<u>30,000</u>
Basis in Whiteacre	$70,000

Notice that Mildred's basis in Whiteacre preserves the realized but unrecognized gain ($40,000) on her transfer of Greenacre. If she later sells Whiteacre for $110,000, she will recognize $40,000 of gain on that sale.

Summary of Mildred's Tax Consequences

Realized Gain	Recognized Gain	Basis of Whiteacre
$40,000	0	$40,000 (basis in Greenacre) + 0 (gain) − 0 (boot) <u>+30,000 (liability assumed)</u> $70,000 Basis of Whiteacre

Example: Richard owns Blackacre, which has a basis of $100,000, a fair market value of $170,000, and is subject to a mortgage of $50,000. Richard exchanges Blackacre for Claudia's Yellowacre, which has a basis in Claudia's hands of $90,000, is worth $200,000, and is subject to a mortgage of $80,000. The exchange qualifies as a like-kind exchange under §1031 for both parties.

Richard Blackacre			Claudia Yellowacre		
FMV	=	$170,000	FMV	=	$200,000
AB	=	100,000	AB	=	90,000
Mortgage	=	50,000	Mortgage	=	80,000

Richard's Tax Consequences

- *Step 1:* **Calculate realized gain.** Amount realized minus adjusted basis of property transferred.

> $200,000 (FMV Yellowacre)
> + 50,000 (Liability Claudia assumes)
> $250,000 Amount realized
> *minus*:
>   100,000 (Basis of Blackacre)
> + 80,000 (Liability Richard assumes)
> $180,000 Basis of property transferred
>
> Realized gain = $70,000

- *Step 2:* **Calculate recognized gain.** Richard takes on an $80,000 mortgage and is relieved of a $50,000 mortgage. Therefore, because Richard has net assumption of liability, he recognizes no gain.

- *Step 3:* **Calculate Richard's basis in Yellowacre.**

Basis in Blackacre	$100,000
+ Gain recognized	+0
− Boot received (liability assumed by Claudia)	− 50,000
+ Boot paid (liability assumed by Richard)	+ 80,000
Richard's basis in Yellowacre	$130,000

- *Step 4:* Notice that this basis ($130,000) preserves the realized but unrecognized gain ($70,000) on the exchange of Blackacre.

Claudia's Tax Consequences

- *Step 1:* **Calculate realized gain.** Amount realized minus adjusted basis of property transferred.

$170,000 (FMV Blackacre)
+80,000 (Liability Richard assumes)
$250,000 Amount realized
minus:
   90,000 (Basis of Yellowacre)
+50,000 (Liability Claudia assumes)
$140,000 Basis of property transferred

Realized gain = $110,000

■ *Step 2:* **Calculate recognized gain.** Because Claudia experiences net relief from liability (she gives up $80,000 of liability and assumes only $50,000), she recognizes gain equal to the net relief, or $30,000.

■ *Step 3:* **Calculate Claudia's basis in Blackacre.**

Basis of Yellowacre	$90,000
+ Gain recognized	+30,000
− Boot received (Liability Richard assumes)	− 80,000
+ Boot paid (Liability Claudia assumes)	+50,000
Claudia's basis in Blackacre	$90,000

■ *Step 4:* Notice that this basis ($90,000) preserves the realized but unrecognized gain ($110,000 − 30,000 = $80,000) on the transfer of Yellowacre.

Summary of Richard and Claudia's Tax Consequences

	Realized Gain	Recognized Gain	Basis of New Property
Richard	$70,000	0	$130,000
Claudia	$110,000	$30,000	$90,000

Example: Assume the same facts as in the previous example, except that Claudia's property, Yellowacre, is worth only $190,000. Claudia transfers Yellowacre (subject to its mortgage) plus $10,000 cash to Richard in exchange for Blackacre (subject to its mortgage). Assume that the transaction qualifies as a §1031 exchange.

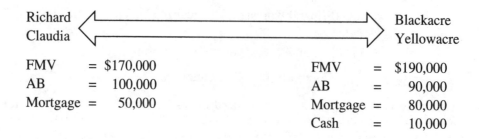

| Richard | | Blackacre |
| Claudia | | Yellowacre |

FMV   = $170,000   FMV   = $190,000
AB   = 100,000   AB   =   90,000
Mortgage =   50,000   Mortgage =   80,000
                          Cash =   10,000

Richard's Tax Consequences

- *Step 1:* **Calculate realized gain.** Amount realized minus adjusted basis of property transferred.

$190,000 (Yellowacre)
+10,000 (Cash received)
+50,000 (Liability Claudia assumes)
$250,000 Amount realized
minus:
$100,000 (Basis of Blackacre)
+80,000 (Liability Richard assumes)
$180,000 Adjusted basis of property transferred

Realized gain = $70,000

- *Step 2:* **Calculate recognized gain.** Richard recognizes $10,000 of the gain because he received that much boot in the form of cash, but the mortgage netting rule shields him from recognition of any gain on the mortgage.

- *Step 3:* **Calculate Richard's basis in Yellowacre.**

$100,000	(Basis of Blackacre)
+ 10,000	(Gain recognized)
− 10,000	(Boot received as cash)
− 50,000	(Boot received as A/L)
+ 80,000	(Boot paid as A/L)
$130,000	Basis in Yellowacre

- *Step 4:* Notice that this basis ($130,000) preserves the realized but unrecognized gain ($60,000) on the transfer of Blackacre.

Claudia's Tax Consequences

- *Step 1:* **Calculate realized gain.** Amount realized minus adjusted basis of property transferred.

$170,000 (Blackacre)
+80,000 (Liability Richard assumes)
$250,000 Amount realized
minus:
$90,000 (Basis in Yellowacre)
+50,000 (Liability Claudia assumes)
+10,000 (Boot paid)
$150,000 Adjusted basis of property transferred

Realized gain = $100,000

- *Step 2:* **Calculate recognized gain.** Claudia's net relief from liabilities of $30,000 would result in recognition of that amount of gain under the mortgage netting rule. However, Claudia may offset the $30,000 net relief from liabilities by the amount of boot she pays in the form of cash. Thus, she recognizes only $20,000 of gain.

■ *Step 3:* **Calculate Claudia's basis in Blackacre.**

$$\begin{array}{l} \$90,000 \text{ (Basis of Yellowacre)} \\ +20,000 \text{ (Gain recognized)} \\ -80,000 \text{ (Liability assumed by Richard)} \\ +50,000 \text{ (Liability assumed by Claudia)} \\ \underline{+10,000} \text{ (Boot paid—cash)} \\ \$90,000 \text{ Basis in Blackacre} \end{array}$$

■ *Step 4:* Notice that this basis ($90,000) preserves the realized but unrecognized gain ($80,000) on the transfer of Yellowacre.

Summary of Richard and Claudia's Tax Consequences

	Realized Gain	Recognized Gain	Basis of New Property
Richard	$ 70,000	$10,000	$130,000
Claudia	$100,000	$20,000	$ 90,000

F. Related material

1. **Personal use:** If any portion of the property is used for personal purposes, that portion cannot qualify for like-kind exchange treatment, and disposition of that portion would be subject to the usual rules applicable to sales and exchanges of property (or if used as a personal residence, perhaps to §121).

2. **Sale of principal residence:** If a taxpayer acquires property in a qualifying §1031 exchange, and subsequently converts its use to a principal residence, he or she must hold and use the property as the principal residence for at least five years in order to claim the exclusion under IRC §121. See Chapter 4(VIII).

3. **Character of gain:** The character of any gain recognized in a like-kind exchange is determined under the rules discussed at Chapter 12.

4. **Installment payment of boot:** If a transaction qualifies as a like-kind exchange, but boot will be received after the close of the taxable year in which the like-kind exchange occurs, special rules treat the taxable portion of the transaction as an installment sale.

G. Summary

See Statute Summary—§1031.

Statute Summary—§1031

Parsing Step	§1031
General rule	No gain or loss is recognized if taxpayer exchanges certain property held for use in trade or business or for investment for like kind property also to be held for use in a trade or business or for investment. (1) Boot: taxpayer recognizes gain (2) Exchanged basis rule
Definitional issues	Like-kind property
Special rules and exceptions	Deferred and three-party exchanges Effect of mortgages
Related material	Calculation of realized g/l: §1001 Character: §1221
Summary	No gain or loss recognized on like-kind exchange, unless boot received

IV. INVOLUNTARY CONVERSIONS—§1033

Section 1033 potentially allows a taxpayer to defer, in whole or in part, recognition of gain on the involuntary conversion of property if certain statutory requirements are met. (Notice that §1033 applies only to gain; losses from the involuntary conversion of property ("casualty losses") are the subject of §165(c)(3), discussed at Chapter 6(XIV).)

A. Recognizing this type of transaction

Look for a taxpayer's property being destroyed by a natural disaster such as flood, storm, earthquake, etc. If the taxpayer receives similar property, or receives insurance proceeds or other compensation and reinvests in similar property soon after the event, gain may be deferred. Proceeds received in a condemnation action, or under threat of condemnation, also qualify. Look for a taxpayer's property being taken under eminent domain or a taxpayer selling property in light of a realistic threat of eminent domain.

B. Policy

The following two rationales are often proffered for §1033.

1. **Same investment:** The taxpayer has not liquidated his or her original investment and the type of investment remains the same, even though the particular property is different. A similar rationale is offered for deferral in like-kind exchanges, but this rationale is perhaps more compelling in §1033 because of the involuntary nature of the transaction. Because the investment remains essentially unchanged, the calculation of gain or loss on the investment will be deferred until the taxpayer fundamentally changes the investment, e.g., sells the property.

2. "Yes, there *is* a penalty for piling on":   Another rationale is that a taxpayer experiencing an involuntary conversion has "suffered enough," and thus gain recognition should be deferred.

C. Section 1033 statutory analysis—General rule

1. Domain: There are three requirements for the application of §1033.

a. Property: The taxpayer's property converted in the transaction may be real or personal, fee or leasehold, and need not be held in a trade or business or held for investment. Cf. §1031, discussed above.

b. Involuntary conversion: Only certain types of events trigger gain deferral. These are discussed below as definitional issues.

c. Conversion and reinvestment: The taxpayer's property can either be converted into similar property or (more commonly) into money, usually insurance proceeds or damages for eminent domain. In the latter case, the taxpayer reinvests in similar property within the statutory two-year period to avoid recognition of gain. Conversion is the realization event for purposes of calculating realized gain or loss.

Example: Garland owns a vase with an adjusted basis of $20,000 and a fair market value of $100,000. It is insured for its fair market value. The vase is stolen, and Garland's insurance company pays him $100,000. This is the conversion of property into money, which is also the realization event for purposes of calculating his realized gain of $80,000.

2. Effect: If a transaction is within the domain of §1033, there are two principal effects: non-recognition of gain and an exchanged basis for the property acquired.

a. Conversion into similar property—Nonrecognition of gain: If the taxpayer's property is converted into property that is similar or related in service or use to the converted property, the taxpayer's realized gain on the involuntary conversion will not be recognized. IRC §1033(a).

b. Conversion into money—Election: A taxpayer whose property is converted into money may elect to recognize only that portion of the realized gain attributable to money not reinvested in property that is similar or related in service or use to the converted property. IRC §1033(a).

c. Basis: A taxpayer may receive property that is similar or related in service or use ("qualifying replacement property") in an involuntary conversion and may also acquire nonqualifying property.

i. Similar property: The basis of the "similar" property received in the involuntary conversion is an exchanged basis, calculated as follows:

> Basis of the converted property
> + Gain recognized
> − Amount of money not reinvested in
>   qualifying replacement property
> − Loss recognized
> _____
> Basis of qualifying replacement property

IRC §1033(b)

ii. Nonqualifying property: Nonqualifying property has a basis equal to its cost, or fair market value. IRC §1012.

d. Examples: The following examples illustrate the domain and effect of §1033.

Example: Pete's vacation home is destroyed by earthquake. His basis in the home is $60,000 and it was insured for its fair market value of $100,000. He receives insurance proceeds of $100,000 and immediately invests $100,000 in a similar vacation home. What are the tax consequences of this transaction to Pete? Pete realized a $40,000 gain, equal to the difference between his amount realized ($100,000) and the adjusted basis of the property ($60,000). However, because this transaction falls within the domain of §1033, he need not recognize any of that gain. His basis in the new vacation home is equal to the basis of the old vacation home ($60,000), plus the gain recognized (0), minus the un-reinvested insurance proceeds (0), minus the loss recognized on the transaction (0), plus any additional amount invested in the property (0). Thus, Pete's basis in his new vacation home is $60,000.

Example: Melinda owns a marina in southern Oregon. One dark and stormy night, while Melinda is visiting friends in town, a tsunami washes the entire marina away. Melinda's basis in the marina is $100,000, and it was insured for its fair market value of $500,000. In due course, Melinda receives the insurance proceeds and immediately purchases a marina in Florida (where there are no tsunamis) for $300,000.

Realized Gain	Recognized Gain	Basis of Florida Marina
$500,000 Proceeds −100,000 Adj. basis $400,000 Gain	$200,000 Un-reinvested proceeds	$100,000 old basis +200,000 unrecognized gain −200,000 proceeds not reinvested $100,000

Notice that the basis of the Florida marina preserves the realized but unrecognized gain ($200,000) on the conversion of the Oregon marina.

D. Definitional issues

1. **Involuntary conversion:** An involuntary conversion includes all of the usual natural disasters—fire, storm, flood, and earthquake. Theft and condemnation, or imminent threat of condemnation, also qualify as involuntary conversions, as does sale or destruction of livestock because of disease or drought. IRC §1033(d). The "suddenness" requirement of casualty losses under IRC §165(c) is not part of the test for an involuntary conversion. Rev. Rul. 59-102, 1950-1 C.B. 200.

2. **Similar or related in service or use:** The replacement property must be "similar or related in service or use." IRC §1033(a)(1), (2). However, for real property used in a trade or business or held for investment that is condemned or sold under threat of imminent condemnation, the replacement property may qualify as under the broader standard of §1031's "like-kind property" instead of the more restrictive standard of "related in service or use." IRC §1033(g).

   a. Similar or related in service or use: In order to qualify as "similar or related in service or use," the property must generally have the same physical characteristics, must be used in the same way as the previous property, and the taxpayer must have the same relationship to the property as he or she had to the previous property. This determination is made based on all of the facts and circumstances of the situation, including an inquiry into whether the taxpayer essentially has continued his or her investment. See, e.g., *Liant Record, Inc. v. Commissioner*, 303 F.2d 326 (2d Cir. 1962).

    i. Not similar—Rev. Rul. 76-319, 1976-2 C.B. 242: The taxpayer owned a bowling alley that was destroyed, and the taxpayer replaced the bowling alley with a billiard parlor. The IRS determined that a billiard parlor and a bowling alley were not "similar or related in service or use" because of their physical dissimilarities and dissimilar functions.

    ii. Similar—Rev. Rul. 71-41, 1971-1 C.B. 223: The taxpayer owned land and a warehouse leased to others. After it was destroyed, the taxpayer erected a gas station and leased it. The IRS determined that the gas station was similar or related in service or use because the lessor was in substantially the same passive relationship to both properties.

    iii. Owner/investor vs. owner/user: An owner/user must acquire similar property and use it for the same purposes. An owner/investor (who leased the property to others) appears to be under a different standard, whereby the properties must be similar, must present similar business risks, and must place similar demands on the owner—but the use need not be identical.

  b. Like-kind standard for certain properties: For real property used in a trade or business or held for investment that is condemned or sold under threat of imminent condemnation, the replacement property may qualify as like kind instead of "related in service or use." IRC §1033(g). The definition of like kind is the same under §1033(g) as it is in §1031. Reg. §1.1033(g)-1.

  c. Purchase of stock: The taxpayer may satisfy the similar property requirement by acquiring a controlling interest in a corporation that owns property "similar or related in use" to the converted property. IRC §1033(a)(2)(A). "Control" in this context means 80% or more of the combined voting power of all of the corporate stock entitled to vote. IRC §1033(a)(2)(E)(i).

3. Statutory replacement period: The taxpayer must replace the converted property during the period beginning on the date of disposition of the property (or the beginning of the threat of condemnation) and ending two years after the close of the taxable year in which the taxpayer realizes any portion of the gain or conversion. IRC §1033(a)(2)(B). A taxpayer may apply to the IRS for an extension of the statutory period. IRC §1033(a)(2)(B)(ii).

Example—Statutory replacement period: Richard owns a warehouse in Dallas, Texas. On July 1, 2000, a fire destroys the warehouse, and in August, Richard collects insurance proceeds. The conversion results in a realized gain to Richard. To avoid recognition of gain, he must reinvest in qualified replacement property before January 1, 2003, which is two years after the close of the 2000 year, in which he realizes the gain on the conversion. If the insurance proceeds had not been paid until January 2001, his replacement period would continue until December 31, 2004, because he would not have realized any gain until 2001.

E. Special rules and exceptions

  1. Definition—Presidentially declared disaster: A presidentially declared disaster is any disaster, in an area where a taxpayer's property is located, that resulted in a determination by the

President that the area warrants assistance under the Disaster Relief and Emergency Assistance Act. IRC §1033(h)(2).

2. **Presidentially declared disasters—Principal residence:** If a taxpayer's principal residence is involuntarily converted as a result of a presidentially declared disaster, the taxpayer has three benefits.

   a. **Extension of replacement period:** The taxpayer has four years, instead of two, to replace the property. IRC §1033(h)(1)(B).

   b. **Unscheduled property:** Gain on unscheduled property (personal property not separately listed on the insurance policy) is not recognized. IRC §1033(h)(1)(A)(i).

   c. **Common fund:** Insurance proceeds for property other than unscheduled property is treated as proceeds for a single item, and reinvestment in a variety of items of which at least one is similar or related in service or use is considered as a qualifying reinvestment. IRC §1033(h)(1)(A)(ii).

   Example: Alex's home is flooded and damaged, and many of her belongings destroyed. Her insurance company pays her $2,000 for a valuable painting listed on her policy and a lump sum of $43,000 for the rest of the damage. The President declares the flood a national disaster.

   Alex must recognize any gain she realizes on the painting, unless she reinvests in similar property. For the $43,000 lump sum, she need not allocate it between repairs and belongings or among the various belongings if she reinvests in home repair or replacement of assets over the statutory period, which is four years instead of the usual two.

3. **Presidentially declared disasters—Trade or business and investment property:** A taxpayer whose trade or business or investment property is destroyed in a presidentially declared disaster is allowed to reinvest in *any* tangible property of a type held for productive use in a trade or business without recognition of gain. IRC §1033(h)(2). The new property is treated as "similar" property to allow taxpayers whose businesses may have been closed for an extended period during such a disaster to invest in new businesses.

F. Related material

1. **Loss:** Section 1033 applies only to gains, not to losses. Losses from involuntary conversions may generate a deduction for a net casualty loss under §165(c)(3). The calculation of net casualty losses implicates §1033 because only *recognized* casualty gains are included in the definition of net casualty gains. See discussion at Chapter 6(XIV)(B).

2. **Section 121 exclusion:** An involuntary conversion of a principal residence of a taxpayer may generate gain that can be excluded (rather than deferred) under §121. See discussion at Chapter 4(VIII).

3. **Character:** For the character of recognized gain on the involuntary conversion of property, see generally Chapter 12.

G. Summary

See Statute Summary—§1033.

Statute Summary—§1033

Parsing Step	§1033
General rule	No gain is recognized if taxpayer's property is involuntarily converted into similar property; if converted into money, taxpayer may elect to recognize only portion of gain attributable to proceeds not reinvested in similar property within 2-year period.
Definitional issues	Involuntary conversion Similar or related in service or use 2-year replacement period
Special rules and exceptions	Presidentially declared disasters
Related material	Calculation of realized gain: §1001 Character: §1221 Losses: §165(c)(3), (h)
Summary	No gain recognized on involuntary conversion of property into similar property.

V. SPOUSAL AND DIVORCE TRANSFERS—§1041

A. Recognizing this type of transaction

Look for a transfer of property between spouses, or transfers made in connection with a divorce. Be careful to analyze cash payments separately if they qualify as alimony or child support.

B. Policy

Congress enacted §1041 in 1984 in response to three problems that arose when divorce transfers were treated as realization events. First, in a divorce, it is rarely clear exactly what a spouse "gives" in exchange for various items of property or other rights, thus the calculation of amount realized is unclear. Moreover, when what is exchanged is a nonmaterial right, basis calculation is impossible. Finally, taxpayers in community property and marital property states may be treated differently if such transfers are taxable events.

> **1. Prior law: Divorces as taxable events—*United States v. Davis,*** 370 U.S. 65 (1962): Mr. and Mrs. Davis were divorcing. Mr. Davis transferred 1,000 shares of DuPont stock to Mrs. Davis in satisfaction of all her marital rights under Delaware law.
>
> > **a. Issues:** Was this a taxable exchange, i.e., a sale? If so, what is the amount of gain recognized by Mr. Davis? What is Mrs. Davis' basis in the shares?
> >
> > **b. Result and rationale:** The transfer was a sale, resulting in a gain to Mr. Davis of the difference between the fair market value of the shares and his basis in them. Mrs. Davis took a cost (fair market value) basis in the shares. Mrs. Davis' rights in the stock under Delaware law were inchoate during marriage, not the rights of a co-owner. (This result might have been different in a community property state, where a spouse has a present interest in property.) Thus, she received the property by transfer from her husband. Since clearly this was not a gift, we must assume the parties acted at arms-length. She relinquished rights

equal in value to the fair market value of the shares. As a result, both parties must treat the transaction as a sale. (The Court did not need to reach the question of the wife's gain, if any; it would be difficult to assign a basis to the marital rights she relinquished.)

2. **1984 change:** The 1984 change made spousal and divorce-related transfers nontaxable events.

    a. **Simplification:** This removes the difficulties of assigning an amount realized to property transfers and determining the basis of nonmaterial assets.

    b. **Uniformity:** Taxpayers in community and marital property states are treated equally under this approach:

    c. **Private ordering:** In their division of property, taxpayers may determine who will pay the tax on various items.

C. Section 1041 statutory analysis—General rule

1. **Domain:** For §1041 to apply, a taxpayer must transfer property to a spouse, or to a former spouse, in a transfer that is "incident to a divorce." IRC §1041(a).

2. **Effect:** There are three consequences of a §1041 transfer.

    a. **Nonrecognition:** In a transfer meeting the requirements of §1041, the transferor recognizes no gain or loss. IRC §1041(a).

    b. **Basis:** The recipient of property takes it with the adjusted basis it had immediately before the transfer. IRC §1041(b)(2).

    c. **Gift:** The recipient of property is treated as if he or she received a gift, and so the recipient need not include the value of the property in his or her gross income. IRC §1041(b)(1). However, the basis rules for a gift are not used (§1041 has its own basis rules), and the transfer is not treated as a gift for gift tax purposes. IRC §2516.

    Example—Spousal transfer: Maria and Bob are married. Bob sells an office building with a basis of $50,000 to Maria. Maria pays him $100,000, the building's fair market value. Because this is a transfer between spouses, Bob does not recognize the $50,000 gain on the transfer, and has no income as a result of his receipt of $100,000. Moreover, Maria takes a basis of only $50,000 in the office building, even though she "paid" $100,000 for it.

    Example—Divorce transfer: Consider the facts of the *Davis* case, discussed above, under current law. Mr. Davis transfers stock with a basis of $100 and a fair market value of $1,000 to Mrs. Davis in full settlement of their divorce. Under current law, Mr. Davis would not recognize the $900 gain inherent in the stock. Mrs. Davis would not include the $1,000 value of the stock in her gross income, and would take the stock with a basis of $100, the basis it had prior to the transfer.

D. Definitional issues

1. **Spouses:** State law determines the legal status of individuals as married or unmarried, except when specifically that law is preempted by federal law. Individuals of the same gender cannot be married for tax purposes under the federal Defense of Marriage Act, Pub. L. 104-199, §3 (1996).

2. **Incident to a divorce:** A transfer of property is "incident to a divorce" if it satisfies either of two tests.

a. One-year rule: A transfer of property is incident to a divorce if it occurs within one year after the date the marriage is terminated. IRC §1041(c)(1).

b. Cessation of marriage: A transfer of property is incident to a divorce if it is "related to the cessation of marriage." IRC §1041(c)(2). A safe harbor is provided for transfers that are contemplated by the divorce decree and occur within six years of dissolution or thereafter if there is a good reason for delay. Reg. §1.1041-1T(b),Q-7. A property transfer made after one year after the marriage is terminated that is not mentioned in the divorce decree is rebuttably presumed not to be related to the cessation of marriage. The "divorce decree" will include subsequent judicial modifications of the decree or actions to carry out the transfers contemplated in the decree. See *Young v. Commissioner,* 113 T.C. 152 (1999), *aff'd* 240 F.3d 369 (4th Cir. 2001).

Example: Tim and Melissa are getting a divorce. Their divorce decree, issued July 1, 1995, provides that Melissa will be awarded Blackacre, and title should be recorded in her name as soon as possible. However, Blackacre is the subject of litigation as to title, and in fact the transfer to Melissa does not occur until September 2002. Regardless of the delay, this transfer would be related to the cessation of marriage and thus incident to the divorce because it was contemplated by the divorce decree, and there was good reason (litigation) for exceeding the six-year limit.

3. Indirect transfers: Indirect transfers of property may qualify for nonrecognition. A transfer to a third party on behalf of a spouse will qualify if it is specifically provided for in the divorce decree, or if it is requested or ratified by the recipient spouse. Reg. §1.1041-1T(c), Q-9. This transaction will be treated as the transfer by a spouse to the other spouse, and a transfer by the latter to the third party. Id.

E. Special rules and exceptions—Nonresident alien transferors

Section 1041 does not apply to transfers by spouses or former spouses who are nonresident aliens. IRC §1041(d).

F. Related material

1. Alimony: Property transfers are analyzed under §1041, while alimony payments are analyzed under §§71 and 215. These Code provisions often intersect. In divorces where one spouse receives cash, either at the date of the divorce or thereafter, and the other spouse receives property, the cash settlements are likely candidates for designation as "nondeductible and nonincludable" in the divorce decree. If so designated, they will not qualify as alimony; instead, their tax treatment is governed by §1041. While the transfer of cash does not, of course, generate gain or loss, §1041(b)(1) applies to exclude the cash from the gross income of the recipient. If, however, the payments are not designated as nondeductible and nonincludable, they are likely candidates for being "front-end loaded," and thus will generate spell-binding tax consequences in the third year after separation or divorce. See discussion of alimony in Chapter 3(VI)(B).

2. Child support: The tax treatment of child support payments is largely independent of the tax treatment of property transfers. However, if a child support obligation is satisfied by a transfer of property from one former spouse to another, §1041 may apply. If the transfer *is* incident to a divorce, nonrecognition rules apply. If the transfer is *not* incident to a divorce, the usual recognition rules apply. See discussion of child support in Chapter 3(VI) and Chapter 4(XI).

G. Summary

See Statute Summary—§1041.

Statute Summary—§1041

Parsing Step	§1041
General rule	No gain or loss recognized upon transfer of property between spouses or former spouses if incident to a divorce. Property takes same basis as it had before transfer; recipient has no income.
Definitional issues	Spouses Incident to a divorce: 1-year rule; "related to cessation of marriage"
Special rules and exceptions	Inapplicable to nonresident alien transferors
Related material	Alimony and child support: §§71, 215
Summary	Divorce is not a taxing event. No gain or loss recognized on transfer of property.

VI. OTHER NONRECOGNITION PROVISIONS

The Code contains a number of other nonrecognition provisions that are important in tax practice but generally receive only minimal attention in the basic federal income tax course. Students of basic tax should have a passing familiarity with the following nonrecognition provisions.

A. Transfers to partnerships and limited liability companies

In becoming a member of a partnership, a partner typically transfers money or other property to the partnership in exchange for an interest in the partnership. Similarly, a member of a limited liability company will transfer money or other property to the entity in exchange for a membership interest. These exchanges are realization events, of course, because the transferor has a materially different type of property before and after the transfer. Although a transfer of cash does not generate any gain or loss (it is the purchase of a partnership interest for cash), the transfer of property can generate realized gain or loss. However, §721(a) provides that neither the partnership nor the person who transfers property to a partnership in exchange for an interest in the partnership will recognize gain or loss on the transfer. This is equally applicable to limited liability companies treated as partnerships.

1. **Basis of partnership interest:** The transferor of the property receives a basis in the partnership interest equal to the basis of the property transferred. IRC §722.

2. **Partnership's basis in property:** The partnership takes the property with the transferor's basis. IRC §723.

3. **Related material:** Gross income includes a partner's pro rata share of income from a partnership, and a partner is entitled to deduct his or her pro rata share of loss, unless another Code provision restricts the loss. See discussion at Chapters 3(VIII)(B) and 11(VII).

Example: Melissa and Meganne form a partnership, M & M Associates. Melissa transfers Property A with a basis of $5,000 and a fair market value of $15,000. Meganne transfers Property B with a basis of $40,000 and a fair market value of $15,000. Each partner receives a 50% interest in the partnership. These transfers are realization events because both Melissa and Meganne have received a property interest different than they had before the transaction. As a result, Melissa has realized gain of $10,000, and Meganne has a realized loss of $25,000. Section 721, however, prevents recognition of any gain or loss. Each partner takes a basis in her partnership interest equal to the basis she had in the property transferred. M & M Associates recognizes no gain or loss on the issuance of the partnership interest in exchange for property, and receives the properties with the same basis that they had in the hands of the transferors. These results are summarized below.

Taxpayer	Realized G/L	Recognized G/L	Basis
Melissa	$10,000 gain	0	$5,000 in partnership interest
Meganne	$25,000 loss	0	$40,000 in partnership interest
M & M Associates (partnership)	0	0	$5,000 Property A $40,000 Property B

B. Transfers to corporations

As in partnerships, a person creating a corporation usually transfers money or other property to the corporation in exchange for shares in the corporation. This is a realization event, as a result of which the transferor may realize gain or loss. Section 351(a) provides that no gain or loss will be recognized on the transfer of property to a corporation if immediately after the transfer the group of persons that transferred property are in "control" of the corporation. In this context, "control" means the ownership of at least 80% of the corporation. IRC §368(c).

1. **Boot:** A taxpayer who receives money or property other than stock from the corporation as a part of the transfer will recognize gain, but not loss, on the transfer to the extent of the fair market value of the boot received. IRC §351(b).

2. **Services are not property:** The performance of services for a corporation in exchange for stock does not qualify for nonrecognition treatment. The service provider would be treated as having received compensation income equal to the fair market value of the stock received, and would take a basis in the stock equal to the amount included in gross income. IRC §351(d)(1). If the stock is restricted in some fashion (i.e., the service provider is not entitled to full enjoyment of it until some future date) §83 governs the tax treatment of the transferor. See discussion at Chapter 11(VI).

3. **Basis:** The transferor of property takes the shares with a basis equal to the basis of the property transferred, plus the gain recognized on the transaction. IRC §358(a)(1). Boot received takes a fair market value basis. IRC §358(a)(2).

4. **Corporate issuance of stock:** A corporation never recognizes gain or loss on the issuance of its own stock. IRC §1032(a).

5. **Corporate basis:** The corporation receives the property with the same basis as the transferor, increased by any gain recognized to the transferor. IRC §362(a).

   Example: Pauline and Sean form TinyCo. Pauline transfers property with an adjusted basis of $1,000 and a fair market value of $9,000, and Sean promises to perform services worth $1,000 for the corporation. The corporation issues 10,000 shares of stock worth $1.00 each, Pauline receives 9,000 shares, and Sean receives 1,000 shares. Pauline realizes $8,000 of gain on the transaction, equal to the difference between her amount realized (the fair market value of the stock received, $9,000) and her adjusted basis in the property transferred ($1,000). None of her realized gain is recognized, however, because the requirements of §351 are met: Pauline (the transferor of property) owns at least 80% of the stock in TinyCo immediately after the exchange. Pauline takes a basis of $1,000, equal to the basis in the property transferred plus her recognized gain of zero. Sean is not a transferor of property, because services do not qualify as property. He is treated as having been prepaid for services, so that he must include in his gross income the fair market value of the stock received ($1,000). His basis in the stock will be equal to the amount he includes in gross income ($1,000), under §1012(a). The corporation does not recognize gain or loss on the issuance of its own stock and takes Pauline's property with the same basis that she had ($1,000), increased by the amount of gain she recognizes (0).

C. Exchange of stock in same corporation

Section 1036(a) provides that a taxpayer will not recognize gain or loss on the exchange of common stock for common stock in the same corporation, or on the exchange of preferred stock for preferred stock in the same corporation.

Example: Chelle owns 1000 shares of Class A common stock in ABC Co. She has a basis of $1,000 in the Class A shares, and they are worth $10,000. Chelle receives an offer from ABC to exchange her 1,000 shares of Class A common stock for 1,000 shares of Class B common stock, which has essentially the same characteristics as her Class A and which have the same value. She exchanges her shares. Although Chelle has realized a $9,000 gain, she will recognize none of it because of §1036.

D. Exchange of life insurance policies

Section 1035 provides that a taxpayer will not recognize gain or loss on the exchange of life insurance contracts, within certain limitations usually beyond the scope of the basic federal income tax class.

E. Exchange of small business stock

Section 1045 provides that a taxpayer will not recognize gain on the sale of qualified small business stock held for more than six months if the proceeds are reinvested in other qualified small business stock within 60 days of the sale. Small business stock is stock in a C corporation engaged in an active business, but "small" is a relative term, requiring corporate assets of less than $50,000,000. IRC §1202(c).

VII. WHERE ARE WE GOING?

This chapter concludes the discussion of sales and other dispositions of property and the computation of realized and recognized gain or loss from such sales. The character of recognized gain or loss is discussed in Chapter 12, but first Chapter 11 addresses questions of the proper taxable year for a taxpayer to include items of income, or deduct expenses.

Quiz Yourself on NONRECOGNITION TRANSACTIONS

84. Al and Sal are avid sports memorabilia collectors. Al owns a baseball signed by Mickey Mantle. Sal owns a football signed by Joe Montana. Both purchased these items years ago and they have appreciated in value. They trade. What are the tax consequences to them of this trade? _____

85. Katherine owns Blackacre, in which she has a basis of $40,000. It has a fair market value of $100,000. Spencer owns Blueacre, in which he has an adjusted basis of $30,000. It has a fair market value of $90,000. Both Blueacre and Blackacre are parcels of land held for investment by their owners. Both parties intend to hold the property received for investment. Katherine and Spencer trade their properties, and as part of the trade Spencer transfers a sports car to Katherine. What are the tax consequences of this trade to Spencer and Katherine? _____

86. Assume the same facts as in the previous question, except that Spencer did not hold Blueacre for investment, although he intends to hold Blackacre for investment.

87. Assume the same facts again as in Question 85, except that Katherine and Spencer are married at the time of the transaction. What are the tax consequences to Katherine of this case? _____

88. Tony owns Rome Tower and Cleo owns Egypt Tower. Both are commercial office buildings. The properties have the following characteristics:

	Tony—Rome Tower	Cleo—Egypt Tower
Fair market value	$300,000	$180,000
Adjusted basis	$160,000	$200,000
Mortgage	$150,000	$0

Cleo transfers Egypt Tower to Tony. Tony transfers Rome Tower to Cleo, subject to its mortgage. Tony also transfers $30,000 to Cleo as part of this transaction. What are the tax consequences of this exchange to Tony and Cleo? _____

89. Let's take another look at Tony and Cleo from the previous question. Assume the following alternative facts:

	Tony—Rome Tower	Cleo—Egypt Tower
Fair market value	$300,000	$180,000
Adjusted basis	$160,000	$100,000
Mortgage	$180,000	$60,000

They exchange properties, each assuming the other's mortgage, with the lenders' approval. What are their tax consequences?

90. Harry and Sally are getting a divorce. Under the terms of their divorce decree, Sally will be deeded the marital home, which has a fair market value of $200,000 and an adjusted basis of $150,000. She will also receive stock in ABC Corporation with a fair market value of $100,000 and an adjusted basis of $175,000. Harry will receive the rest of the assets. What are the tax consequences to Harry and Sally of these transactions?_____

91. Donald and Ivanna are getting a divorce. In the divorce decree, the marital home is given to Ivanna in her sole name, with the proviso that it must be sold within eight years and the proceeds split 50/50. In the meantime, Donald must continue to pay the mortgage, taxes, insurance, and repairs. The home is sold eight years after the divorce and the proceeds are split between Donald and Ivanna. Donald insists that he has no gross income to report on the sale transaction. Is he correct?

92. Don owned a commercial fishing boat in Miami in which he had an adjusted basis of $200,000. It had a fair market value of $600,000. The fishing boat was destroyed by a hurricane in December of Year 1. In January of Year 2, Don received insurance proceeds of $600,000 from the insurance company. He spent the rest of Year 2 looking for a suitable replacement. In December of Year 2, he purchased a new fishing boat for $500,000. What are the tax consequences of these events to Don? What if he decided that the commercial fishing business was an industry of the past and the new boat was designed to take tourists on deep sea fishing trips?_____

Answers

84. Al and Sal have realized gain attributable to the trade. However, assuming that these properties are held by Al and Sal "for investment," §1031 will probably apply to defer recognition of the gain. The football and baseball are properties of a like-kind, and not the kind of property ineligible for like-kind exchange treatment (unless Al or Sal are in the business of collecting and trading memorabilia, in which case these items would be inventory to that person, and thus ineligible). If IRC §1031 applies, Al and Sal will not recognize the gain associated with the trade, and will take a basis in the new item equal to the basis in the old item.

85. Spencer and Katherine's tax consequences are analyzed separately.

■ *Katherine's tax consequences assuming qualification as like-kind exchange:*

Realized gain: $60,000 ($90,000 + $10,000 − $40,000)
Recognized gain: $10,000 (the value of the sports car)
Basis in Blueacre: $40,000

■ *Spencer's tax consequences assuming qualification as a like-kind exchange:*

Realized gain: $60,000 ($90,000 − $30,000)
Recognized gain: -0-
Basis in Blueacre: $40,000 ($30,000 + $10,000)

If Spencer's basis in the sports car were different from its fair market value, he would realize gain or loss on the transfer of the car. Realized gain would be recognized, but it is doubtful that loss would be recognized. Katherine's basis in sports car would be $10,000 (its fair market value).

86. If Spencer did not hold Blueacre for investment, all of his realized gain would be recognized because the transaction would not qualify as a like-kind exchange. This does not affect Katherine's ability to qualify for like-kind exchange treatment.

87. If Katherine and Spencer are married, §1041 prevents the recognition of *any* gain on the transaction for either party. Katherine will take any property she receives with the same basis as it had in the hands of Spencer.

88. This is a qualifying like-kind exchange. Therefore, the parties' tax consequences are as follows:

■ *Tony's tax consequences:*

Realized gain/loss: $140,000 ($330,000 − $190,000)
Recognized gain: $120,000 ($150,000 − $30,000)
Adjusted basis in Egypt Tower: $160,000

■ *Cleo's tax consequences:*

Realized gain/loss: ($20,000) ($330,000 − $350,000)
Recognized gain/loss: $ 0
Adjusted basis in Egypt Tower: $320,000

89. Notice in this case that because the "equity" in each property is the same ($120,000) there will be no transfer of the additional $30,000 from Tony to Cleo. The tax consequences to Tony and Cleo are summarized on the next page.

90. The transfers of property are almost certainly incident to a divorce, and therefore IRC §1041 applies to defer recognition of any gain or loss. Neither Harry nor Sally will have income as a result of these transactions, and each will take the property he or she receives with the basis it had immediately prior to the transfer. Therefore, Sally will receive the marital home with a basis of $150,000 and the ABC stock with a basis of $175,000.

91. He's probably right. Remember that IRC §1041 applies as between the parties to a divorce, not to sales to third parties. Who owns the property is a question of fact, and in this case, Donald has a strong case that Ivanna was the owner of the property so that its sale to a third party generated income to her, not to Donald. The division of the proceeds of the sale would probably be governed by IRC §1041, however, resulting in no income or a deduction to either party. Ivanna would probably be able to claim an exclusion under IRC §121, which Donald would not be able to do because he did not live in the home or own it for the time periods required. See *Suhr v. Commissioner*, T.C. Memo 2001-28.

Question No. 89: Tax Consequences to Tony and Cleo

	Tony	Cleo
Realized Gain/Loss	$140,000 Gain	$80,000 Gain
Recognized Gain/Loss	$120,000 (net relief from liability)	-0- (no net relief from liabilities)
Basis of New Property	$160,000 Old Basis +120,000 Gain recognized − 180,000 Cleo's A/L + 60,000 Tony's A/L $160,000	$100,000 Old Basis + 0 Gain recognized − 60,000 Tony's A/L +180,000 Cleo's A/L $220,000
Is this correct?	If sold for FMV (180,000), using this basis, Tony would recognize the realized gain that was not recognized : $20,000.	If sold for FMV ($300,000), using this basis, Cleo would recognize all of the gain that went unrecognized: $80,000.

92. The destruction of the fishing boat is a constructive sale of the fishing boat, in which Don realizes a gain of $200,000, which is the difference between the amount received from the insurance company ($600,000) and his adjusted basis in the boat ($200,000). However, he may defer recognition of this gain if he meets the requirements of IRC §1033. In order to qualify, he must reinvest the proceeds in similar property within two years. In this case, he probably qualifies, as he has purchased a commercial fishing boat within the requisite period. However, he did not fully invest the proceeds. Therefore, he will recognize $100,000 of gain, and his basis in the boat will be his old basis ($200,000) plus the gain recognized ($100,000), or $300,000. If he reinvests in a tourist fishing boat, he runs the risk that this will not be considered property similar in use, and therefore he may have to recognize all of the gain. This is a close case, and the IRS would be likely to assert that commercial fishing and tourist deep sea fishing tours are not "similar" uses.

Exam Tips on
NONRECOGNITION TRANSACTIONS

☛ Be able to articulate Congress's reasons for nonrecognition treatment for some—but not all—transactions.

☛ The nonrecognition statutes are relevant only if there is realized gain or loss on the disposition of property.

　☞ *Look for:* An exchange of one property for another, in which the taxpayer realizes gain or loss; usually in a situation in which the taxpayer hasn't fundamentally changed the nature of the investment.

☞ *Analyze:* Which taxpayer's tax consequences are relevant? One or both? Compute the realized gain or loss, and then ask if the requirements of a nonrecognition statute are met.

☛ Section 1031 is probably the most popular statute for testing, not only because it is important in tax law in general, but because it offers fertile ground for testing the student's knowledge of the requirements and consequences of the statute.

☞ *Look for:* Situations that raise questions about the taxpayer's use of the properties, or the like-kind nature of the properties.

☞ *Analyze: Each* requirement; make sure you analyze realized gain or loss, recognized gain or loss, adjusted basis in the property received in the exchange.

☛ **Remember:** Section 1031 is not optional. A taxpayer may not recognize loss on a transaction that qualifies as a §1031 exchange. A better way to recognize loss: Sell the old property and buy the new property with cash.

☛ Involuntary conversions can generate realized gain or loss.

☛ *Look for:* A disaster, or some event outside the control of the taxpayer that leads to the loss of property.

☛ *Analyze:* If realized gain (receipt of insurance proceeds, or exchange of properties), do the requirements of §1033 apply?

☛ If loss is realized, §1033 doesn't apply to that loss. Does §165 allow a deduction for a casualty loss? Are there both casualty losses and recognized casualty gains? Offset them.

☛ Divorces also offer fertile ground for testing.

☞ *Look for:* Divorce or separation and the transfer of money or property pursuant to the divorce.

☞ *Analyze:* Is this a transfer of property, or is it alimony or child support? If a transfer of property, the nonrecognition rules of §1041 will usually apply, but watch for special circumstances that would disqualify the transaction. Be sure to determine the basis of property received in the divorce. Is there alimony or child support? If so, who gets the deduction, and who must include payments in gross income?

CHAPTER 11

TIMING OF INCOME AND EXPENSES

ChapterScope

The previous chapters have addressed the issues of identifying and computing gross income and calculating available deductions. This chapter turns to the equally important question of *when* a taxpayer properly includes amounts in gross income or properly claims a deduction.

- **Importance:** Timing is important because of the understandable desire of taxpayers to defer for as long as possible the inclusion of items in gross income and to accelerate available deductions to the earliest possible year.

- **The annual accounting concept:** The federal income tax adopts an annual accounting system in which a taxpayer selects a taxable year and reports all income and deductions that occur in that year. The annual accounting concept can create results that seem unfair, particularly for transactions that do not fall neatly within a single taxable year. A number of doctrines and related Code sections have evolved to provide relief from the constraints of the annual accounting concept, including the claim of right doctrine, net operating loss carryovers, and the tax benefit rule.

- **Methods of accounting:** Every taxpayer has a method of accounting.

  - **Cash method:** Most taxpayers use the cash method of accounting, which provides simple rules based on receipt and payment for determining when to include items in gross income and when to deduct expenses.

  - **Accrual method:** A more accurate, but also more complex, method is the accrual method of accounting in which taxpayers include items in income or deduct expenses when the "all events test" is met. Special rules restrict the use of the cash method and impose limits on the deduction of expenses under both methods.

- **Accounting for inventories:** A taxpayer engaged in the business of selling goods will incur costs of acquiring or manufacturing the goods for sale. These costs, along with certain other costs of doing business, must be added to the cost of *inventory* in order to properly compute the taxpayer's income or loss from the sale of goods.

- **Installment method:** For certain sales of property in which payment is deferred, the taxpayer may elect to use the installment method of accounting, under which the gain is reported as payments are received under the contract for sale.

- **Section 83—Restricted property:** In certain situations, a taxpayer will receive property as compensation for services rendered, but the property will be restricted in some fashion to ensure the taxpayer's performance of the services. Section 83 provides specific rules for determining when the value of this property will be included in the taxpayer's gross income.

- **Restrictions on current deduction of losses:** Sections 465 and 469 impose significant restrictions on the deduction of certain losses. Section 465 limits losses to the amounts a taxpayer has *at risk* in an activity. Section 469 limits the deduction of ***passive losses*** to the amount of the taxpayer's passive income, allowing a taxpayer to deduct deferred losses only at the termination of the investment.

I. WHERE ARE WE?

Previous chapters have addressed issues surrounding identification of income and deduction and the computation of gain and loss. Underlying all of these issues has been a fundamental question that previous chapters have noted but deferred for later consideration: *In which taxable year does the taxpayer include an item in gross income or claim a deduction?* For many transactions, the proper timing of income and deduction will seem obvious. But for many transactions, particularly those that span more than one taxable year, the choice of the proper year for reporting income and deductions is problematic. As discussed in detail in Chapter 15, taxpayers seek to defer the inclusion of income items in gross income and to accelerate deductions; this produces tax savings that can be invested during the period of deferral. Even if, later, the taxpayer must include an item in gross income, or income is not sheltered by a deduction, the taxpayer will usually be better off economically by deferring income and accelerating deductions. Congress and the IRS, however, have the daunting task of ferreting out and preventing "inappropriate" income deferral and deduction acceleration strategies, i.e., those that result in an inaccurate reflection of a taxpayer's ability to pay. This chapter addresses the principles that have evolved to govern the timing of income and deductions, beginning with that most basic of concepts—the taxable year.

II. THE ANNUAL ACCOUNTING CONCEPT

The annual accounting concept is the principle that a taxpayer reports all of his or her income and deductions on an annual basis, reporting these items based on the facts as they exist as of the close of the taxable year in question.

A. Taxable years

Every taxpayer has a taxable year, either a ***calendar*** or ***fiscal year.*** IRC §441(b)(1).

1. **Calendar year:** Most individual taxpayers use the calendar year, which is a year that begins on January 1 and ends December 31. IRC §441(d).

2. **Fiscal year:** Some business entities use a fiscal year, which is a year other than a calendar year beginning on the first day of the month of any month but January (e.g., a year beginning July 1 and ending June 30). IRC §441(e). This is convenient for businesses (such as retailers) with a busy season at the end of the calendar year because they need not do year-end accounting during their busy season.

B. Why *annual* accounting?

The concept of annual accounting is merely an administrative convenience to allow the Commissioner to collect tax at regular, easily identifiable intervals. Reliance on annual accounting makes administrative sense, but this convenience often comes at the expense of a precise measurement of a taxpayer's ability to pay. Many of the issues raised by annual accounting exemplify the tension between the value of administrative convenience of an annual system of taxation and the value of fairness. For example, an annual accounting system has difficulty accurately measuring the true increase or decrease in a taxpayer's ability to pay from transactions that span more than one taxable year. While other systems might be imagined, they do not eliminate this tension. For example, a "lifetime tax return" (one income tax return reporting lifetime income and loss, filed at death) would accurately measure a taxpayer's ability to pay over a lifetime. But its preparation (and audit) would be a nightmare, and such a system would be unlikely to generate the revenues at regular intervals needed by government. As described in the sections that follow, the unfairness of the annual accounting system is often mitigated by special Code provisions that require the reporting of income and deductions over various years to more accurately reflect a taxpayer's ability to pay.

C. Difficulties with annual accounting

1. **The problems:** The concept of annual accounting can create numerous difficulties because transactions rarely fall neatly into a single year. Instead, many transactions continue over several years, and events in one year may implicate a reporting position taken in the previous year, or a taxpayer may be aware of events that may occur in later years that will undermine the current reporting position. Nevertheless, annual accounting requires tax returns to be filed as if a year stands independently of all other years.

2. **Transactional accounting—*Burnet v. Sanford & Brooks Co.*, 282 U.S. 359 (1931):** The taxpayer was engaged in the business of dredging the Delaware River. During 1913–1916, it received payments and expended funds in this endeavor. In these years, it reported the payments as income and deducted its expenses. In most years it showed a net loss; in one year it reported a profit. In 1915, it abandoned the work and sued for breach of warranty of the material to be dredged. In 1920, the taxpayer received damages of $176,271.88 that were measured by the total of the taxpayer's expenses over income from the project.

   a. **Issue:** Was the $176,271.88 includable in the taxpayer's gross income in 1920?

   b. **Result and rationale:** The $176,271.88 was includable in the taxpayer's gross income in 1920. Although the taxpayer argued that the amount could not be considered income because it experienced a loss on the entire contract from its inception in 1913, under the annual accounting system the events of other years are irrelevant in determining the tax consequences for the particular year. Thus, the court rejected transactional accounting in favor of annual accounting.

   c. **Comment—Court of Appeals approach:** The Court of Appeals was sympathetic to the taxpayer's argument, and allowed the taxpayer to exclude the $176,271.88 from gross income on the condition that it amend its prior years' returns to eliminate the deduction of expenses in those years. The Supreme Court's rejection of this approach reflects a general preference for not reopening prior years' tax returns.

D. Net operating loss (NOL) deduction

Section 172 provides a method of mitigating the impact of annual accounting. Under §172, the excess of expenses over income in a particular year may be claimed as a deduction (known as the net operating loss deduction, or NOL) in other years. In essence, the NOL rules allow a taxpayer "to set off its lean years against its lush years." *Lisbon Shops v. Koehler*, 353 U.S. 382 (1957). The specific rules of §172 are quite complex, but can be summarized as follows.

1. **Definition—Net operating loss:** A net operating loss (NOL) is the excess of allowable deductions over gross income, computed in accordance with special rules. IRC §172(c).

In computing the allowable deductions, the following modifications must be made to the usual deduction rules.

   a. **No NOL deduction:** In computing the excess of deductions over income, no deduction is allowed for an NOL carryover from another year. IRC §172(d)(1).

   b. **No personal deductions:** In computing the excess of deductions over income of an individual, no personal deductions are allowed, including personal exemptions and nonbusiness deductions such as medical expenses, casualty losses, and charitable contributions. IRC §172(d)(3), (4). For a discussion of personal deductions, see generally Chapter 6.

   c. **Capital losses:** In computing the excess of deductions over expenses, the deduction for capital losses is allowed only to the extent of capital gains. IRC §172(d)(2). For a discussion of capital loss deductions, see Chapter 12(II)(B).

2. **Carryover:** The NOL carries back to the two previous taxable years and forward to the succeeding 20 taxable years following the year of the loss. IRC §172(b)(1)(A). When carried to a particular year, it reduces taxable income in that year, potentially to zero. The loss must be applied to the earliest of the years first, and then in chronological order. IRC §172(b)(2). However, the taxpayer may elect to waive the entire carryback period and apply the loss to the carryforward years. IRC §172(b)(3). The Job Creation and Workers Assistance Act of 2002 provides that NOLs arising in 2001 and 2002 may be carried back five years, instead of the usual two. There are also longer carryback periods for certain kinds of liabilities that take a long time to accrue. See IRC §172(f).

   Example: Zelco, a corporation formed in Year 1, has the following results in Years 1-6:

Year	Income or (Loss)
1	10,000
2	20,000
3	(50,000)
4	10,000
5	(10,000)
6	30,000

An NOL may be carried back two years and forward 20 years. Zelco may carry the Y3 loss first to Y1. It may then apply it to Y2, Y4, and Y6, in order. The Y5 loss may only be applied to Y6, because all other years' income has been eliminated. The following chart shows application of the NOL if Zelco chooses to apply any of it to previous years.

Year	Income/(Loss) Before NOL	Application of NOL	Final Result Taxable Income
1	$10,000	($10,000)	0
2	$20,000	($20,000)	0
3	($50,000)	n/a	0
4	$10,000	($10,000)	0
5	($10,000)	n/a	0
6	$30,000	($10,000) Y3 ($10,000) Y5	$10,000

E. Claim of right doctrine

1. **Recognizing this type of transaction:** In claim of right situations, a taxpayer receives an amount that normally would be considered an item of gross income under the taxpayer's method of accounting, but there is some uncertainty about whether the taxpayer will later have to relinquish the income. In a later year, the taxpayer may have to repay the amount, in whole or in part.

2. **The problem:** The uncertainty about repayment raises the question whether the taxpayer should include the amount in gross income in the year of receipt or should wait and report the transaction when the uncertainty has been resolved. If the taxpayer must include the item in gross income, the question arises of how to treat the taxpayer if the funds must be relinquished later. While the taxpayer normally would be entitled to a deduction in the amount repaid, a deduction will not necessarily place the taxpayer in the same position as if he or she had never included the item in income, for two reasons. First, the taxpayer will have lost the use of the funds used to pay the tax from the first year. Second, if tax rates have fallen, the deduction will not generate a tax savings equal to the tax originally imposed on the same amount of income. (Of course, if tax rates have risen, the deduction will generate a greater tax savings, but this may or may not offset the loss attributable to the *time value of money.*)

3. **Claim of right doctrine—*North American Oil Consolidated v. Burnet,* 286 U.S. 417 (1932):** A taxpayer includes an item in gross income if he or she has a claim of right to it, regardless of uncertainties about subsequent relinquishment. A claim of right exists when the taxpayer has a colorable legal claim to the item of income and has it without restriction of disposition.

4. **Examples**

   a. *United States v. Lewis,* **340 U.S. 590 (1951):** In 1944, the taxpayer received a bonus of $22,000. In subsequent litigation, it was determined that he was not entitled to the full amount, and in 1946, he had to repay $11,000 to his employer. The taxpayer had use of the full $22,000 until repayment. The taxpayer was required to include the $22,000 in gross income in 1944. (As a corollary, when he had to repay the $11,000 in 1946, he was entitled to a deduction in that amount. The taxpayer received the income under a claim of right. The "mistake" as to his right does not relieve him of the obligation of reporting it in 1944, since he had a right to the income and received it without restriction. The subsequent event is addressed in the year it occurs.)

b. *Inductotherm Industries, Inc. v. United States,* **351 F.3d 120 (3d Cir. 2004), reporting an unpublished District Court decision:** The taxpayer argued that the U.S. government's blocking order with respect to income earned in Iraq resulted in a restriction on the taxpayer's right to that income, so that it should not be included in income. In fact, the taxpayer didn't deposit the funds in a blocked account, and the government did not enforce the blocking order. According to the court, a dormant or potential restriction on the use of funds does not rise to the level of a restriction that would prevent inclusion in gross income.

5. **Legislative response—§1341:** Congress enacted §1341 to provide relief to taxpayers like Mr. Lewis (see *United States v. Lewis* above). Section 1341 applies if a taxpayer has included an item in gross income in one year because it appeared that the taxpayer had an unrestricted right to that income, but in a later year the taxpayer had to repay some amount greater than $3,000. Recently, courts have disagreed on the basic requirement of whether there must be some dispute as to whether the taxpayer had a right to the income. See, e.g., *Cinergy Corp. v. United States*, 55 Fed. Cl. 489 (2002) (dispute must exist); *Dominion Resources, Inc. v. United States*, 219 F. 3d 359 (4th Cir. 2000). Section 1341 allows a taxpayer caught in a claim of right/ repayment situation to pay the *lower* of two differently computed taxes: (1) the tax that would have been paid if the taxpayer had never included the amount in gross income, or (2) the tax that would have been paid if the taxpayer had included the amount in the first year and deducted the repayment in the later year. The statute does this by computing the tax in the year of repayment by reference to these two options. The details of §1341 are formidable, and its computations are beyond the scope of most basic tax courses.

F. **Tax benefit rule**

1. **Recognizing this type of transaction:** In a *tax benefit rule* situation, the taxpayer deducts an item or claims a *credit,* based on the facts as they existed in the year of deduction or credit, and in a later year an event occurs which suggests that the prior deduction was incorrect. The classic example of this is the deduction of a *bad debt* by the taxpayer. In a subsequent year, the debtor repays the debt, and the question arises: Does the taxpayer have income as a result of the repayment?

2. **The problem:** The question raised by the tax benefit pattern is what impact the event in the later year should have on the taxpayer. One option would be to go back and amend the prior return. Not only would such an approach be administratively burdensome, it would also be theoretically incorrect if the taxpayer properly claimed the deduction or credit on the facts as they existed in that year. The proper result is to address the problem in the year of the subsequent event, so that the taxpayer may have income in that year. Thus, in the bad debt example, the repayment should logically be income, to offset the prior deduction. See Reg. §1.166-1(f).

3. **Judicial development of tax benefit rule—***Alice Phelan Sullivan Corp. v. United States,* **381 F.2d 399 (Ct. Cl. 1967):** In 1939 and 1949, the taxpayer made charitable contributions of property that was subject to a reversion if the charitable donee did not make charitable use of the

property. The taxpayer claimed deductions of $4,243.29 and $4,463.44 in those years, which created a total tax savings for the taxpayer of $1,877 in those years. In 1957, the property reverted to the taxpayer. The taxpayer originally did not include any amount in income as a result of the reversion, claiming that it was the nontaxable return of its own property, but ultimately asserted that the amount to be included in gross income in 1957 should be limited to the tax savings from the earlier years. This would essentially apply the earlier years' tax rate to the later recovery. The Commissioner argued that the sum of the prior deductions should be included in the taxpayer's gross income in 1957, thus requiring that the later year's tax rate be applied to the recovery.

    a. Issue: Should the amount included in gross income in 1957 be the tax savings from the prior year or the amount previously deducted?

    b. Result and rationale: The amount included in income in 1957 should be the sum of the deductions previously claimed. The court overruled *Perry v. United States,* 160 F. Supp. 270 (Ct. Cl. 1958), in which it determined that the recovery was income only to the extent of the prior tax savings. The ***annual accounting concept*** requires that income be determined without reference to events in other years and that the tax be computed without reference to earlier tax rates. While this may generate inequitable results, the court declined to legislate a different result.

4. Statutory analysis—§111: Section 111 is the codification of the tax benefit rule. As expressed, it is a rule of income exclusion and, conversely, a rule of income inclusion. It is discussed here in connection with timing rules because the annual accounting concept creates the need for such a rule.

    a. General rule—Domain: In order for the tax benefit rule to apply, there must be a ***recovery*** of an item in the current year that must relate to an item that was deducted or credited in a prior taxable year. IRC §111(a).

    b. General rule—Effect: The tax benefit rule of §111 may be expressed either as an exclusion from gross income or as an inclusion in gross income.

        i. Exclusion: Gross income does not include the recovery to the extent that the prior deduction or credit did not reduce tax in the prior year.

        ii. Inclusion: Gross income does include the recovery to the extent that the prior deduction reduced the tax in the year of deduction or credit.

        iii. "To the extent": The statute's use of "to the extent" is somewhat confusing, but the regulations clarify this. The amount of a recovery that is excluded from gross income is the "exclusionary amount." Reg. §1.111-1(a). The exclusionary amount is the amount of the prior deduction or credit that did not reduce tax in the prior year. Id. The rest of the amount of the recovery is included in gross income.

        Example: Two years ago, Rashon incurred $25,000 in damage to his home from a windstorm. He submitted a claim to his insurance company for payment. The insurance company informed him that this damage was not covered under the policy for a variety of reasons. Rashon claimed the expenses as a deduction on his income tax return for the year of the loss, but because of the limitations on casualty loss deductions imposed by §165(h), he deducted only $15,000 of the expenses. His taxable income after this deduction was $62,000. Believing he was wrongfully denied coverage, Rashon sued the insurance company. This year Rashon won, and received $25,000 in payments from the insurance company. Rashon must include the payment in his gross income to the extent that the previous deduction reduced his taxes two years ago. His delight at winning the lawsuit, therefore, will be tempered by the understanding that he must include $15,000 of the payment in his gross income.

c. **Definitional issues—Recovery:** A recovery is an event that is inconsistent with the assumptions underlying the prior deduction or credit. *Hillsboro National Bank v. Commissioner,* 460 U.S. 370 (1983). To be a "recovery," the event must be functionally related to the original deduction or credit. The repayment of a debt previously deducted as worthless is obviously inconsistent with the assumption that the debt is uncollectible, and thus repayment is recovery. See Reg. §1.166-1(f). Other, less obvious, events also may be recoveries.

Example: Paula is an artist. She rents a loft warehouse as a studio in which she paints and displays her paintings for sale. In October of year 1, Paula prepays nine months' rent, and properly deducts this amount as a business expense on her year 1 tax return, which she files in year 2. In March of year 2 Paula decides to move into the loft and begins using half of it as her personal residence. The conversion of a portion of the loft from business to personal use is a "recovery," as the use of the loft for personal purposes is fundamentally inconsistent with the assumptions underlying the deduction for rent, i.e., that the premises would be used exclusively for business purposes.

d. **Special rules and exceptions—Erroneous deduction rule:** A judicially created rule focuses on the impact of the propriety of the original deduction on the later recovery. The Tax Court has held that if the original deduction was erroneous, the later recovery is not included in gross income. See, e.g., *Streckfus Steamers, Inc. v. Commissioner,* 19 T.C. 1 (1952). However, the Second and Ninth Circuits have held that the propriety of the original deduction is not relevant in determining the inclusion of the later recovery for two reasons. First, there is no statutory authority for such an exception. Second, this places the IRS in the position of having to examine every return for errors in order to prevent recoveries from later being excluded from gross income. *Unvert v. Commissioner,* 656 F.2d 483 (9th Cir. 1981); *Askin & Marine Co. v. Commissioner,* 66 F.2d 776 (2d Cir. 1933).

e. **Related material**

   i. **Section 61 and related statutes:** In addition to being a timing rule, the tax benefit rule is a rule of inclusion in and exclusion from gross income. Thus, it is similar to §61 and related statutes addressing the inclusion of various items in gross income and should be studied in conjunction with them. See generally Chapters 3 and 4.

   ii. **Deductions and credits:** The application of the tax benefit rule requires that the taxpayer previously deducted or credited an item, and the propriety of that deduction or credit may also be implicated. Deductions and credits are discussed generally in Chapters 5 through 8 and 13, respectively.

   iii. **Claim of right:** The tax benefit situation is the inverse of the claim of right pattern. In the tax benefit situation, there is a deduction in one year and income in a subsequent year. In the claim of right situation, the taxpayer has income in one year, and a deduction in the later year. For a discussion of claim of right, see this chapter, section (II)(E).

III. METHODS OF ACCOUNTING

A. Functions of a method of accounting

The taxpayer's method of accounting determines in which taxable year items of income, gain, loss, deduction, or credit will properly be reported. There are two principal methods of accounting, the *cash method* and the *accrual method.* While the specific rules of the two methods are very different, they both set forth the rules governing the inclusion of income and the deduction of expenses. A taxpayer is required to report net income based on his, her, or its usual method of accounting, unless that method does not, in the view of the Commissioner, clearly reflect income. IRC §446(a). The Commissioner may impose some other method to ensure a clear reflection of income, and in litigation of such matters, the courts will not usually inquire as to whether there is some better method of computing net income, but instead will focus on whether the Commissioner has abused his or her discretion in requiring a taxpayer to use a particular method to clearly reflect income.

B. The cash receipts and disbursements method

The cash method focuses on when the taxpayer receives income or pays expenses, regardless of when income or expenses are due or owing. A taxpayer using the cash method of accounting reports income in his or her gross income when the income is received, actually or constructively. Reg. §1.451-1(a). A taxpayer claims deductions when he or she actually pays them by cash, check, or credit card. Reg. §1.461-1(a)(1). All individual taxpayers use the cash method in their personal lives, and many businesses (particularly service businesses) use the cash method as well.

1. **Income—Actual receipt:** Actual receipt means that the taxpayer receives cash or other property and is usually easy to identify. Look for an inflow to the taxpayer, in cash or property.

   Example: Carla, an attorney, uses the cash method of accounting and is a calendar-year taxpayer. She sends out her bills, which are due in 30 days, monthly. In October of year one Carla sends Client X a bill for $2,000, which is due in November. In fact, Carla receives payment from Client X in February of the next year. She properly reports the $2,000 in the year of receipt rather than the year the income was due.

   a. **Economic benefit doctrine:** In some situations, the taxpayer does not seem to actually receive any tangible or intangible property, but an event has occurred that makes the taxpayer better off financially than he or she was before. The question in these cases is whether the taxpayer has received an economic benefit sufficient to constitute income. This question is related to the timing question as well, because if a taxpayer has not received an economic benefit sufficient to trigger income, the next question is: At what time in the future will the taxpayer have income? A good example of this distinction is found in the case of *United States v. Drescher,* 179 F.2d 863 (2d Cir.), *cert. denied,* 340 U.S. 821 (1950). In that case, the taxpayer's employer purchased an annuity policy for the taxpayer's benefit. The issue in the case was whether the taxpayer had income in the year the policy was purchased. The court found that the taxpayer did have income in that year, but if it had found otherwise, the question would have been a slightly different one: When will the taxpayer have income—perhaps at the annuity starting date? See discussion of *Drescher* at Chapter 2(III).

   b. **Mere promise to pay not income:** A mere promise to pay, not represented by notes or secured in any way, does not constitute receipt of income for a cash method taxpayer. Rev. Rul. 60-31, 1960-1 C.B. 174.

2. **Income—Constructive receipt:** The cash method rule that income is reported when actually received might tempt taxpayers to direct that income not be made available to them until a later taxable year, thus deferring income. The constructive receipt doctrine provides that a taxpayer will be considered to be in constructive receipt of amounts over which he or she has a legal claim, and which are available to the taxpayer without ''substantial limitations or restrictions.'' See Reg. §1.451-2(a).

Example: Scott is a housepainter who uses the cash method and a calendar year. He agrees to paint Sue's house for a payment of $5,000, payable when the painting is complete. Scott completes the work in October, but when Sue starts to write the check, Scott says, "Sue, how about just holding off on that check until January, after the holiday rush, you know." Scott receives payment in January. Although the general rule of the cash method would require him to include the income in his gross income for the year of payment, he had a legal right to the income in the previous year, and in fact that income was made available to him in that year. As a result, he will probably be deemed in constructive receipt of the income for the earlier year.

a. *Amend v. Commissioner,* **13 T.C. 178 (1949), acq. 1950-1 C.B. 1:** In this case, the cash method taxpayer entered into a contract for the sale of wheat in which he would be paid in the year following the year of sale. The Commissioner argued that he should be charged with income in the year of sale, not the year of receipt, because the taxpayer *could have* contracted for payment in the year of sale. Given that the sale arrangement was legitimate, the taxpayer was not in constructive receipt of the payment because the taxpayer had no legal right to the funds in the year of sale under the arrangement as negotiated. The constructive receipt doctrine does not inquire into what arrangements *could have* been negotiated; it looks to the legal rights of the taxpayer under the deal as struck, assuming that the deal is legitimate and not a sham.

b. **Circumstances beyond the taxpayer's control—***Hornung v. Commissioner,* **47 T.C. 428 (1967):** The taxpayer was a professional football player using the cash method of accounting. For 1961, he was selected as an outstanding player by *Sport Magazine.* The prize was a Corvette valued at the astonishing price of $3,331.04. The Corvette was typically made available to prize recipients in New York on December 31 after the football game in which they were selected as the outstanding player. However, in 1961, the December 31 football game was played in Green Bay, Wisconsin, and the taxpayer did not receive the car until the following Wednesday. The taxpayer did not include the value of the Corvette in his gross income for 1962, presumably on the grounds that it was a gift, and the Commissioner sought to include this value in the taxpayer's gross income. However, the taxpayer abandoned the gift approach in this controversy, relying instead (in an interesting procedural twist) on the doctrine of constructive receipt. By arguing that the Corvette was includable in his 1961 (not 1962) gross income, the taxpayer was seeking to defeat the Commissioner's notice of deficiency for 1962. (Although not explicit in the case, 1961 was probably closed by the statute of limitations.) The court found that the doctrine of constructive receipt did not apply, because the taxpayer did not have "unfettered control . . . over the date of actual receipt." The circumstances that led to the taxpayer not having the car in 1961 were not in the taxpayer's sole control—December 31 was a Sunday; the dealership had not arranged for title to be transferred to *Sport Magazine;* the taxpayer had no indicia of ownership as of December 31. Thus, the taxpayer received the car in 1962, as the Commissioner argued.

    c. Deferred compensation—*Minor v. United States*, 772 F.2d 1472 (9th Cir. 1985): In this case, doctors entered into employment arrangements with a corporation to provide medical services in exchange for fees. The corporation and doctors agreed that a portion of each doctor's future fees would be paid into a trust. Each doctor's share of the trust amounts would be paid to him or her upon retirement, disability, or certain other events. Each doctor included only the fees he actually received in his gross income, and the IRS argued that the doctors should have also included the fees paid into the trust. Neither the IRS nor the court relied on the doctrine of constructive receipt because the arrangement was for fees that had not yet been earned, to which the taxpayer had no present legal entitlement. The contractual arrangement for these fees resulted in the doctors having no present right to the fees when they were actually earned, and under the doctrine of *Amend v. Commissioner*, the court will not inquire into the deal that might have been negotiated, but will instead rely on the deal that is actually struck. For additional discussion of *Minor*, see this chapter, section (VI)(C).

3. Deductions: A taxpayer using the cash method of accounting claims otherwise deductible expenses when they are paid, whether by cash, check, or credit card. Reg. §1.461-1(a)(1). Look for the year in which there is an actual outflow of resources from the taxpayer to another person to determine the proper year of deduction.

Example: This year, William is in an automobile accident and incurs $15,000 of medical expenses for which he is not insured. In December of this year he writes credit line checks to the doctors and hospital for these expenses. He repays the amount on his credit line in the next year. He will be able to deduct these expenses this year, if the other requirements for deductibility are met, because he has paid them during this year. In using his credit line, he is viewed as borrowing the funds and using the borrowed funds to make payment of the medical expenses.

4. Restrictions on the cash method: The cash method is unavailable to certain types of taxpayers and certain types of activities. These restrictions arose out of concern that *tax shelters* were using the cash method to defer income and accelerate deductions inappropriately. Thus, farming corporations and farming partnerships with corporate partners must ordinarily use the *accrual method* of accounting. IRC §447(a). Section 448 has a much broader scope, disallowing the use of the cash method for tax shelters, certain corporations, partnerships with corporate partners, and unrelated business activities of nonprofit entities. IRC §448(a). Section 464 prohibits farming syndicates from deducting certain prepaid expenses, requiring deductions for items such as feed, seed, and fertilizer to be claimed as these items are actually used. IRC §464(a). These sections are rife with technical definitions, exceptions, and special rules, making the selection of a method of accounting for a business entity a tricky process.

C. The accrual method

The accrual method focuses on the "all events test" for both income and deductions, although the test is a bit different for the two items. Under the accrual method, a taxpayer includes an amount in gross income when "all the events have occurred which fix the right to receive such income and the amount thereof can be determined with reasonable accuracy." Reg. §1.451-1(a). A taxpayer using the accrual method deducts a liability (i.e., an expense) when all the events have occurred that establish the fact of the liability, the amount of the liability can be determined with reasonable accuracy, and economic performance has occurred with respect to the liability. Reg. §1.461-1(a)(2). The accrual method is sometimes said to "match" deductions with the income they produce in a taxable year to clearly reflect the taxpayer's net income in a particular year. Although this matching principle is not always the rule for income and deductions under the accrual method, a significant acceleration of deductions or deferral of income from related transactions is likely to draw IRS attention.

1. **The deposit doctrine—*Commissioner v. Indianapolis Power & Light Co.*, 493 U.S. 203 (1990):** Indianapolis Power & Light Co. (IPL) required certain of its customers to make deposits as a condition of providing electricity. When a customer terminated its electric service, it could either pay the entire bill and receive a refund of its deposit, or apply the deposit to the final bill. The power company did not include the deposits in gross income when received, and the IRS argued that they were income in that year.

   a. **Issue:** Were the amounts called "deposits" includable in the taxpayer's gross income as advance payments for electricity, or excludable as deposits?

   b. **Result and rationale:** The amount deposited by the electric customers were deposits and therefore were excluded from gross income of IPL. These amounts were most like a loan from the customer to IPL which could be applied to the purchase of electricity at termination of service. IPL's ability to retain the deposit depended on two events outside its control, i.e., the decision of the utility customer to purchase electricity and to ultimately apply the deposit against the final bill.

   c. **Comment:** This case illustrates nicely the relationship between "whether" a taxpayer has income and "when" a taxpayer has income. If amounts called deposits are advance income, they are included in gross income in the year of receipt. If they are true deposits, the income is properly taken into account when and if IPL applies the deposit against the customer's bill.

2. **Income—Accrual method:** Under the accrual method, a taxpayer includes an amount in gross income when "all the events have occurred which fix the right to receive such income and the amount thereof can be determined with reasonable accuracy." Reg. §1.451-1(a). The actual date of payment may be relevant to this test but is not determinative. There are two requirements of the all events test, one focusing on the taxpayer's right to receive income and the second on the determination of the amount to be received.

   a. **Right to receive income:** In order for income to accrue, the taxpayer must have the right to the income under its contractual or other arrangements, regardless of actual receipt. *Spring City Foundry Co. v. Commissioner,* 292 U.S. 182 (1934). Therefore, if the right to the income depends on one or more future events (including the passage of time), the taxpayer does not include the amount in income until the contingency has been resolved. However, purely ministerial or formal contingencies (e.g., clerk approval or issuance of a check) do not prevent accrual.

   Example: Luis, a calendar-year, accrual-method taxpayer, sells a shipment of artificial carnations to Emily under a contract providing that she will pay for the shipment within 30 days of her receipt of payment from her principal retail florist customer, Frank. In Year 1, Luis ships the flowers to Emily and sends her a bill for $30,000. In Year 2, Frank pays Emily. In Year 3, Emily pays Luis. Luis must include Emily's payment in his income for Year 2. He need not include it in Y1, for he has no right to the income because the contingency (Frank's payment to Emily) has not occurred. He has the right to the income (which of course can be determined exactly) in Y2, and payment in Y3 is irrelevant.

b. Determinable with reasonable accuracy—*Georgia School-Book Depository v. Commissioner*, 1 T.C. 463 (1943): The exact amount due the taxpayer need not be ascertainable, but the amount must be determinable with reasonable accuracy. Doubts about collectibility can affect this determination. In *Georgia School-Book*, the accrual-method taxpayer was a broker who sold books to the state of Georgia's school system. The broker was entitled to an 8% commission payable when the state paid the publishers. The only source of payment was the state's Free Textbook Fund, funded from an excise tax on beer, which was insufficient to pay the schoolbook obligations. The taxpayer did not include any commissions in income until it received them, on the theory that the commissions were not earned until payment and there was no "reasonable expectancy" that they would be paid (until receipt) because of the insufficiency of the excise tax fund. The IRS argued that the taxpayer should have included the amounts in income in the year the books were sold.

   i. Issue: In the year of sale, could the amount to be received be determined with reasonable accuracy, given the difficulty the state of Georgia was having paying for the books?

   ii. Result and rationale: The court concluded that the taxpayer was required to include amounts in income in the year the books were sold. The court agreed with the IRS that in the year the books were sold, all events had occurred that fixed the right to the income (the taxpayer had performed all its duties under the contract), and the amount thereof could be ascertained with reasonable accuracy. Collectibility would not affect this determination, according to the court, unless the right were in litigation or the debtor were insolvent. Even though the state of Georgia was having administrative problems with its fund, there was no reasonable expectation that the amounts due would not be paid.

c. IRS's discretion to change methods—Advance payments: If the IRS believes that a taxpayer's method of accounting does not clearly reflect income, the IRS may assert that the taxpayer needs to change his or her method of accounting or the treatment of a particular item. The courts are likely to respect the IRS's determination in making such a change, and a good example of this is found in the treatment of advance payments.

   i. American Automobile Association v. United States, 367 U.S. 687 (1961): The AAA received prepayment of annual dues from members throughout each year. The payment of annual dues entitled the member to various services from AAA during the year, including towing, travel assistance, and other services. In accordance with its financial accounting methods, the AAA reported a portion of the prepayment as income in the year of receipt for tax purposes; amounts relating to the next year were reported in the following year. For example, if the annual dues were $60, and the AAA received the dues on October 1, 1952, the AAA would report $15 in 1952 and $45 in 1953. The IRS argued that the entire amount should be included in income in the year of receipt on the basis that the accrual of only a portion of the dues in the year of receipt did not clearly reflect income. The taxpayer's position was that only the portion of the dues allocable to services for a particular year should be included in gross income for that year, and that allocation of the dues between years matched income and deductions to clearly reflect income. The Court agreed with the IRS, on the basis that the uncertainty associated with the provision of services upon member demand and not at fixed intervals resulted in an artificial deferral of income. It also focused on Congress' apparent failure to enact a provision to change this result as indicative of Congress' approval of it.

ii. Compare—*Artnell Co. v. Commissioner,* **400 F.2d 981 (7th Cir. 1968):** In this case, the accrual method taxpayer sold season tickets for Chicago White Sox games. The taxpayer reported as income on season ticket sales in a particular taxable year only the portion of the sales price that was attributable to games during that year; amounts attributable to games in the next year were deferred to that later year. The IRS predictably objected, relying on the theory that was successful in *American Automobile Association.* The court agreed that the deferral of prepaid income *may* not clearly reflect income (the principle of *American Automobile Association*), but rejected the IRS argument that deferral of prepaid income to a future year would not clearly reflect income in this situation. The court distinguished the *AAA* case in two ways. First, the time and extent of services to be performed in the *AAA* case were uncertain; in baseball, by contrast, the dates for games were certain, except for rain dates. Second, the *AAA* Court suggested that Congress was aware of the problem for automobile associations but chose not to act to change the law as it existed. There was no similar recognition of the problem for baseball ticket sales, and the court could not infer a Congressional purpose to prevent deferral of prepaid income in that context.

3. **Deductions—Accrual method:** A taxpayer using the accrual method deducts a liability (i.e., an expense) when "all the events have occurred that establish the fact of the liability, the amount of the liability can be determined with reasonable accuracy, and economic performance has occurred with respect to the liability." Reg. §1.461-1(a)(2). The first two prongs of the test, fact of the liability and determination with reasonable accuracy, are often difficult to distinguish.

   a. **Fact of the liability—***United States v. General Dynamics Corp.,* **481 U.S. 289 (1987):** Under this test, all events must have occurred that fix the fact of the liability. The taxpayer must be under a legal obligation to make the payment, and that liability must not depend on future events, including the passage of time. As in the income situation, purely ministerial tasks will not prevent satisfaction of the all events test. For example, in *General Dynamics,* the accrual-method taxpayer maintained a self-insured medical reimbursement plan for its employees under which they submitted health-related expenses for reimbursement. The taxpayer was entitled to deduct amounts actually paid under the plan as compensation. For 1972, the taxpayer claimed that it was entitled to deduct an additional amount that it actuarially estimated would be paid for medical expenses incurred by employees during the year, but for which claims had not yet been submitted, reviewed, or paid as of the close of the year. The IRS argued that such a deduction was not allowable because all events had not occurred (submission of the claim, review, and payment) that would establish the fact of the company's liability to the employee. The Court agreed with the IRS, on the grounds that the mere prediction that events were likely to occur was not sufficient to satisfy the all events test.

   b. **Determination with reasonable accuracy—***Schuessler v. Commissioner,* **230 F.2d 722 (5th Cir. 1956):** The exact amount of the liability need not be determinable, but there must be some reasonable method for estimating the amount. For example, in *Schuessler,* the taxpayer sold furnaces with a guarantee that he would turn them on and off each season for five years. Purchasers paid a premium for this guarantee, and the taxpayer offered proof as to the cost of performing this guarantee each year. The taxpayer sought to deduct in the year of sale of each furnace the estimated costs of performing the guarantee, and the IRS objected on the grounds that this did not clearly reflect income. The court agreed with the taxpayer, allowing the deduction even though the amount was not determinable with "mathematical certainty." Id. at 724.

c. **Economic performance:** Section 461(h) provides that the all events test is not satisfied prior to the time "economic performance" occurs. What constitutes "economic performance" varies for the type of liability.

i. **Services and property provided to the taxpayer:** When a taxpayer incurs a liability for services or property to be provided by another person, economic performance occurs when the other person provides the services or property. IRC §461(h)(2)(A)(i), (ii). If the liability is for the taxpayer's use of property, economic performance occurs as the taxpayer uses the property. IRC §461(a)(2), (A)(iii).

Example: Adrian, an accrual-method taxpayer, leases a loft for use as an art gallery. Under the terms of her lease, Adrian must prepay two years' worth of maintenance fees in the amount of $5,000. While the all events test may be satisfied because the liability is fixed, and the amount can be determined with reasonable accuracy, economic performance occurs as the maintenance services are provided to Adrian over the two-year period. Therefore, she will not be able to deduct the $5,000 in the first year.

ii. **Services or property provided by the taxpayer:** If the liability represents the obligation of the taxpayer to provide services or property, economic performance occurs as the taxpayer provides the services or property. IRC §416(h)(2)(B).

Example: Consider the *Schuessler* case discussed above. Today that case would be decided differently because of the economic performance requirement. The taxpayer would be considered as satisfying the all events test as he performed the guarantees over the five-year period, rather than in the year of sale of the furnaces.

iii. **Tort and workers' compensation claims:** For tort and workers' compensation claims, economic performance occurs as payments are made to the plaintiff or claimant. IRC §461(h)(2)(C).

Example: Paul sues Gresham for a personal injury sustained in Gresham's business. They settle the claim on the terms that Gresham will pay Paul $15,000 per year for five years. While under prior law Gresham might have been able to deduct $75,000 (or at least the ***present value*** of the five $15,000 payments) at the time of settlement, the economic performance requirement results in Gresham satisfying the all events test as he makes the $15,000 payments over the five-year period.

iv. **Certain nonrecurring items:** The economic performance requirement will not bar deduction of certain nonmaterial items if economic performance occurs within a relatively short period of time after the close of the taxable year. IRC §461(h)(3).

IV. ACCOUNTING FOR INVENTORIES

A taxpayer engaged in the business of selling goods incurs costs in manufacturing or purchasing these goods. Taxpayers would prefer to deduct these costs as they are incurred, but this practice can result in costs being deducted before income is earned (thus mismatching income and deductions and inaccurately reflecting the taxpayer's income). A more accurate reflection would occur if the costs of producing each item were taken as a deduction when that item is sold; the costs of production would be subtracted from the income from the sale to produce the taxpayer's net income or loss from that particular sale. While such an approach is feasible for sales of big-ticket items such as automobiles or large-carat gemstones, it is unmanageable for the sale of less expensive or fungible goods. Thus, a taxpayer must have a system for accounting for *inventory.*

A. Requirement for inventory accounting

Section 471(a) authorizes the IRS to require a taxpayer to account for inventories in accordance with the best accounting practice in the trade or business and to most clearly reflect income. The IRS generally requires inventories to be kept for manufacturing, mining, and merchandising businesses, and service businesses also may be required to keep inventories in certain situations, but has recently expanded the taxpayers engaged in business who can use the cash method of accounting and thus deduct the costs of what might otherwise be inventory. See Rev. Proc. 2002-28, 2002-18 I.R.B. 815.

B. General approach—Cost of goods sold

A taxpayer who must keep inventories will subtract the *cost of goods sold* from gross sales for the year. The cost of goods sold is equal to the taxpayer's opening inventory, plus purchases during the taxable year, minus the closing inventory.

Example: Collin is a sole proprietor engaged in the sale of cellular telephones. In his first year of operations, he began with no inventory, purchased $10,000 of inventory, and closed his first year with $8,000 of inventory on hand. Assume no other expenses of doing business. Collin's gross sales were $9,000. Collin must keep inventory because he is in the merchandising business. His cost of goods sold is computed by beginning with his opening inventory (0), adding the purchases for the year ($10,000), and subtracting the closing inventory ($8,000). Thus, his cost of goods sold was $2,000. His income from the business is $7,000, computed by subtracting the cost of goods sold ($2,000) from the gross sales ($9,000).

C. What must be included in the cost of inventory?

In order to properly measure the cost of goods sold, a taxpayer must include the proper items in opening and closing inventory and in purchases made during the taxable year. Items properly included in inventory fall within two different categories.

1. **Finished and partly finished goods:** The taxpayer should include in inventory finished and partly finished goods and all raw materials on hand to manufacture goods, but only if the taxpayer has title to these goods. Reg. §1.471-1(a).

2. **Uniform capitalization rules:** Some taxpayers are required to allocate to inventory a portion of the direct and indirect costs of producing inventory. The rules governing allocation of these costs are contained in §263A and are known as the *uniform capitalization rules (UNICAP rules).*

   a. **Only certain taxpayers affected:** Although the UNICAP rules are comprehensive, certain taxpayers are excluded from their requirements.

      i. **Large taxpayers only:** The UNICAP rules apply to inventory for a taxable year unless the taxpayer has average annual gross receipts of $10 million or less during the three years prior to the taxable year. IRC §263A(b)(2)(B).

ii. **Certain professions excluded:** The expenses of farming are not required to be capitalized under the UNICAP rule. IRC §263A(d)(1). In addition, the "qualified creative expenses" of writers, photographers, and artists are not required to be capitalized. IRC §263A(h). These include research expenses for writers and artists' materials costs that would qualify as trade or business expenses.

b. **Inclusion in inventory of allocable costs:** A taxpayer subject to the UNICAP rules must include in the cost of inventory the direct and indirect costs allocable to that property. IRC §263A(a)(1)(A), (a)(2).

i. **Direct costs:** Direct costs include the costs of creating the product, including materials, wages, and payroll taxes for employees of manufacturing businesses. Reg. §1.263A-1(e)(2).

ii. **Indirect costs:** Indirect costs include processing costs, storage costs, and administrative and management costs. Reg. §1.263A-3. These costs must be allocated among inventory and added to its cost.

D. Identifying inventory—FIFO and LIFO

Once what is properly included in inventory is established, the taxpayer must determine which inventory is on hand at the end of the year. If inventory is particularly identified, this is not a problem. However, if inventory is accounted for on a collective basis, two methods are available for identification: **FIFO** and **LIFO.** These methods are not based on what the taxpayer *actually* sells; both methods deem the taxpayer to have sold certain property regardless of which property is actually sold.

1. **FIFO—First in, first out:** Under the FIFO method of inventory, the taxpayer is considered to have sold the oldest inventory first. A FIFO inventory system will increase taxable income if replacement costs are rising because it causes the taxpayer to have sold the oldest (and cheapest) inventory.

3. **LIFO-Last in, first out:** Under the LIFO method of inventory, the taxpayer is considered to have sold the most recently purchased or manufactured inventory first. In situations where replacement costs are rising, the LIFO method causes taxable income in a particular year to be lower than under the FIFO method. Ultimately, however, taxpayers using the two different methods will report the same amount of income, but will do so in different taxable years.

Example: Fifi, a taxpayer using the FIFO method of inventory, purchased three lots of widgets for resale: Lot 1 in year one at $100, Lot 2 in year two for $200, and Lot 3 in year three for $300. In year four, having made no previous sales, Fifi sells two lots of widgets for $1,000. Because she is using the FIFO method, Fifi would be considered to have sold lots 1 and 2 for a cost of goods sold of $300 and profit of $700.

Example: Lola is a taxpayer using the LIFO method of accounting. She makes the same purchases and sales as Fifi did in the previous example. Lola would be treated as having sold lots 3 and 2, for a cost of goods sold of $500.

Note: Lola will have income from business of $500 rather than the $700 computed under the FIFO method. However, both Fifi and Lola will ultimately report the same amount of income. Assume in the next year that both Fifi and Lola sell their remaining inventory for $700. Using the FIFO method, Fifi is treated as having sold Lot 3, producing income of $400. Lola, who uses the LIFO method, is treated as having sold Lot 1, producing income of $600. Thus, over the two years of sales, both Lola and Fifi have reported $1,100 of profit on these sales. However, if one considers the benefit of the time value of money, Lola is better off economically than Fifi, as Lola has deferred income until a later year. See generally Chapter 15.

E. Valuing inventory

Inventory is generally valued at cost, but a LIFO taxpayer may value inventory at the *lower* of cost or market value. Reg. §1.471-2(c). Thus, a LIFO taxpayer may reduce the value of inventory to its replacement cost, taking into account market fluctuations and decline in marketability of inventory.

F. Relationship to capital recovery

The notion of accounting for inventory is not only a timing rule, but also an example of capital recovery. (See discussion at Chapter 7(III).) A taxpayer is entitled to be taxed on his or her profit from business and to recover his or her economic investment in property. The cost of goods sold is the taxpayer's economic investment in inventory, and the process of accounting for inventory allows the taxpayer to recover that investment. It is presented here as a timing rule because accounting for inventories also determines the taxable year in which a taxpayer will report income from sales of inventory.

V. INSTALLMENT METHOD OF REPORTING INCOME

A. Recognizing this type of transaction

The ***installment method*** of reporting income is applicable to deferred payment sales, i.e., certain sales in which at least one payment occurs in a year after the year of the actual sale. IRC §453(b)(1). A deferred payment sale is really *two* interrelated transactions—a loan and a sale. When a seller agrees to deferred payments, the seller is actually making a loan to the buyer for the deferred portion of the purchase price. Therefore, the seller will expect to receive a market rate of interest on this loan, and will also expect full payment of the principal (the purchase price) under the terms of the contract. See Figure 11A—Deferred Payment Sale Transaction.

B. The installment method approach

In recognition of the two parts of any deferred payment sale, analyzing a deferred payment contract requires two steps.

1. **Interest:** If the deferred payment sale provides for adequate stated interest, that interest is includable in the gross income of the seller and *may* be deductible to the purchaser; the timing of inclusion of income, or the deduction of interest will be determined under the seller and buyer's methods of accounting. See IRC §61(a) and discussion at Chapter 3(V)(C), and IRC §163 and discussion at Chapters 6(XII) and 7(IV)(A). If the sales contract does not provide for adequate stated interest, the ***original issue discount*** and related rules may apply to impute interest to the transaction (see discussion at Chapter 15(IV) through (VI)).

2. **Principal:** The installment method is designed to allow the seller in a deferred payment sale to spread the recognition of gain from that sale ratably over the taxable years in which the seller receives payments under the sales contract. Thus, a portion of each payment received will represent a nontaxable return of the seller's basis, and the remaining amount will be income from the sale of the property. The details of this approach are discussed below.

Figure 11A
Deferred Payment Sale Transaction

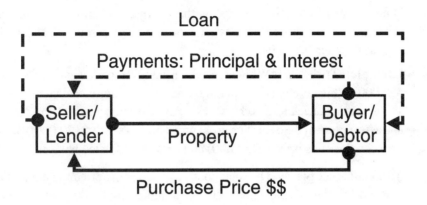

Sale transaction between
Seller and Buyer

Loan transaction between
Lender and Debtor

C. Statutory analysis—§453

1. **General rule:** Section 453(a) requires that income from an installment sale be reported using the installment method. Section 453 does *not* apply to losses on such sales; these losses may be recognized in the year of sale if the other requirements for loss recognition are met. See IRC §165, and discussion at Chapters 6(VI), 7(IV)(C), and generally at Chapters 9 and 10. Crucial to understanding this general rule is an understanding of the definitions of installment sale and installment method.

2. **Definitional issues**

   a. **Installment sale:** An installment sale is a sale of property in which at least one payment is due after the close of the taxable year in which the sale occurs. However, it does not include sales of inventory, sales by dealers of the property they hold for sale to customers, and sales of publicly traded stocks or securities. IRC §453(b)(2), (k)(2).

   Example: Maria owns Blackacre, a parcel of raw land that she holds for investment. She sells Blackacre to Chris for a sales price of $150,000. Under the terms of the contract of sale, Chris must pay Maria $50,000 upon sale, and the remaining $100,000 one year from the date of the sale with adequate interest. This is an installment sale because at least one payment is due after the close of the taxable year in which the sale occurs. If, however, Maria were a dealer in raw land, this transaction would not be an installment sale because dealer dispositions are not included within the definition of installment sales.

   b. **Installment method:** The income from an installment sale for any particular year is equal to the payments received during that taxable year, multiplied by a fraction known as the *gross profit ratio*. IRC §453(c). The numerator of the gross profit ratio is the "gross profit;" the denominator is the "total contract price." See Figure 11B—Installment Method Calculation.

i. **Gross profit:** The "gross profit" is the selling price minus the adjusted basis of the property. Reg. §15a.453-1(b)(2)(v). The selling price is the gross sales price, without reduction for any mortgages or any selling expenses. Reg. §15a.453-1(b)(2)(ii). Interest is not a part of the selling price, as the interest portion of the transaction is addressed separately. The adjusted basis is the adjusted basis computed under §1011. See discussion at Chapter 9(III)(B).

Example: Trisha owns Whiteacre, which has a fair market value of $150,000 and a basis of $30,000. Whiteacre is encumbered by a longstanding mortgage of $50,000. Trisha sells Whiteacre to Patrick for $100,000 cash, payable in ten years (with adequate stated interest) and assumption of the debt. The gross profit on this sale is $120,000, which is the difference between the sales price ($150,000) and Trisha's adjusted basis in Whiteacre ($30,000).

ii. **Total contract price:** The total contract price is the price to be paid under the contract, reduced by "qualifying indebtedness" assumed by the buyer, but not in excess of the seller's basis in the property. Reg. §15a.453-1(b)(2)(iii). For purposes of this computation only, the seller's expenses of sale, such as commissions and fees, are added to the basis of the property.

Example: In the previous example, Trisha sold Whiteacre for $100,000 in cash plus Patrick's assumption of $50,000 in debt. If the debt is qualifying indebtedness, the total contract price would be the price to be paid under the contract ($150,000) minus the portion of the debt up to Trisha's basis in the property ($30,000). Therefore, the total contract price would be $120,000.

iii. **Qualifying indebtedness:** Qualifying indebtedness is debt relating to the property that the buyer assumes as part of the transaction. Reg. §15a.453-1(b)(2)(iv). The property may be transferred subject to a debt, or the buyer may assume the debt in connection with the transaction. Qualifying indebtedness does not include the seller's expenses of sale or a debt functionally unrelated to the property; for example, it cannot be a consumer debt of the seller that the buyer agrees to assume as a part of the purchase price. Id. Finally, debt is not qualifying indebtedness to the extent it exceeds the taxpayer's basis in the property, or if the seller places an encumbrance on the property "in contemplation of disposition of the property."

Figure 11B
Installment Method Calculation

Amount included $=$ Payment $\times$ Gross profit ratio
in gross income

$$= \text{Payment} \times \frac{\text{Gross profit}}{\text{Total contract price}}$$

$$= \text{Payment} \times \frac{\text{Selling price} - \text{adjusted basis}}{\text{Selling price} - \text{qualifying debt}}$$

Amount excluded $=$ Payment $-$ amount included in gross income
from gross income

Example—Qualifying indebtedness: Frank owns Blackacre, which has a fair market value of $160,000 and an adjusted basis of $100,000. It is subject to a longstanding mortgage of $40,000. Frank sells Blackacre to Amy for a down payment of $50,000, Amy's assumption of the liability, and her promise to pay $70,000 in five years (with adequate stated interest). The total contract price in this scenario is $120,000—the sales price minus the qualifying indebtedness.

Example—Potentially nonqualifying indebtedness: Frank owns Blackacre, which has a fair market value of $160,000 and an adjusted basis of $100,000. Just before selling it to Amy, he uses Blackacre to secure a $40,000 loan from Friendly Bank. Pocketing the $40,000 in loan proceeds, he then sells Blackacre to Amy for a down payment of $10,000, her assumption of the $40,000 debt to Friendly Bank, and her promise to pay $110,000 over the next seven years (with adequate stated interest). The loan was placed on the property in anticipation of its sale, and is therefore suspect. As a result, the debt is probably not qualifying indebtedness and thus is not subtracted from the sales price in calculating the total contract price. In this scenario, the total contract price is the sales price.

Example—Partially qualifying indebtedness: Keelah owns Whiteacre, which has a fair market value of $100,000 and a basis of $30,000. Whiteacre is encumbered by a long-standing mortgage of $50,000. Keelah sells Whiteacre to Patrick for $100,000 cash, payable in ten years (with adequate stated interest), and assumption of the debt. The total contract price is the sales price ($150,000) minus the portion of the qualifying indebtedness ($50,000) in excess of the property's adjusted basis ($30,000). Thus, only $20,000 of the debt is taken into account in computing the total contract price.

c. **Payment:** Payment includes the receipt of cash and property, but not promissory notes or other "evidences of indebtedness" unless they are payable on demand, readily tradable on an established securities market, or secured by cash or a cash equivalent. IRC §453(f)(3), (4), (5). When the buyer assumes qualifying indebtedness on a property in excess of the seller's basis in the property, the difference is treated as payment in the year of the sale. Reg. §15a.453-1(b)(5) Example (3). The assumption of nonqualifying indebtedness is treated as payment in the year of sale. Reg. §15a.453-1(b)(3).

Example: Keelah owns Whiteacre, which has a fair market value of $150,000 and a basis of $30,000. Whiteacre is encumbered by a long-standing mortgage of $50,000. Keelah sells Whiteacre to Patrick for $100,000 cash payable in ten years and Patrick's assumption of the $50,000 debt. Although Patrick pays Keelah no cash in the year of sale, she is treated as having received payment equal to the excess of the qualifying indebtedness assumed ($50,000) over her adjusted basis in Whiteacre ($30,000), or $20,000.

3. **Special rules and exceptions**

a. **Election out:** A taxpayer may elect not to apply the installment method by so indicating on his or her tax return for the year in which the sale occurs. IRC §453(d)(1), (2). If a taxpayer elects out of the method, the recognized gain must be included in gross income in the year of sale. IRC §1001(c). This would be an appropriate strategy if the taxpayer had losses in the year of sale sufficient to offset the gain from the installment sale. The election out of the installment method is revocable only with the IRS's consent. IRC §453(d)(3).

b. **Contingent price sales:** In some situations, the sales price under a deferred payment sale is expressed as a measure other than a specific sum. At one time, the courts applied the "open transaction" approach to such situations, allowing the taxpayer first to fully recover his or her basis in the property sold, and once basis was fully recovered, to report any additional amounts received as income. This ensured that the taxpayer would recover his or her basis tax-free, but allowed significant income deferral—a much too generous approach, in Treasury's view. It also created difficult questions about when the open transaction approach should be allowed. The courts typically applied it when the amount to be received under the contract did not have an ascertainable fair market value, a standard that created more controversy than it solved. See, e.g., *Burnet v. Logan,* 283 U.S. 404 (1931). The regulations now provide specific rules for three types of contingent payment transactions, essentially making the "open transaction" doctrine obsolete. In all three situations, the regulations supply an assumption necessary to compute the gross profit ratio even though the sales price is uncertain. See Prop. Reg. §15a.453-1(c). As a result, courts are unwilling to apply the open transaction doctrine, even when the ultimate economic result of transaction is quite uncertain. See *Bernice Patton Testamentary Trust v. United States*, 2001-1 USTC ¶50,332 (Fed. Cl.), *aff'd per curiam unpublished decision*, 2002-1 USTC ¶50,277 (Fed. Cir.).

4. Related material

a. **Realized and recognized gain:** Inherent in the installment sale rules is the assumption that a realization event has occurred that has generated realized and ***recognized*** gain. See generally Chapter 9. A nonrecognition transaction (such as a like-kind exchange) in which a taxpayer receives boot after the close of the taxable year in which the exchange occurs can implicate both the nonrecognition rules and the installment sale rules, the correct combination of which takes tax complexity to new heights. See, e.g., IRC §1031(f). Fortunately this is beyond the scope of most basic tax classes.

b. **Section 453A—Interest charge:** A taxpayer with more than $5,000,000 in installment obligations due must, in certain circumstances, pay interest on the deferral of tax allowed by use of the installment method. IRC §453A(a).

c. **Disposition of installment obligations—§453B:** If a taxpayer sells or otherwise disposes of an installment obligation, he or she realizes gain equal to the difference between the basis of the installment obligation and the amount realized on sale. IRC §453B(a). The basis of an installment obligation is its face value minus the income not yet recognized by the holder of the obligation. IRC §453B(b). The amount realized is (a) the satisfaction amount, if satisfied other than by payment in full; (b) the sales price, if sold; or (c) the fair market value if transferred other than by sale or exchange. IRC §453A(a).

d. **Character of gain:** The character of the gain recognized under the installment method is determined under the usual rules as ordinary or capital. It will usually be capital, as sales of inventory or dealer property are excluded from the installment sale rules. For a discussion of the character of gain, see generally Chapter 12.

e. **Imputed interest:** If an installment sale does not provide for adequate interest, a market rate of interest may be imputed, giving rise to income for the creditor (seller) and a potential deduction to the debtor (buyer). See discussion at Chapter 15(IV) through (VI).

5. Summary and examples

a. Summary: See Statute Summary—§453.

Statute Summary—§453

Parsing Step	§453
General rule	Gain on installment sale is reported on installment method.
Definitional issues	Installment sale: at least one payment after year of sale. Installment method: payment × gross profit ratio = amount included in gross income; rest is return of basis.
Special rules and exceptions	Election out Not applicable to dealers Contingent payments sales
Related material	Calculation of gain: §1001 Interest charge: §453A Disposition of installment obligations: §453B
Summary	Report income from installment sales over period of payments, unless elected out.

b. Installment method calculations—Putting it all together: To compute the income of a taxpayer for an installment sale, first isolate and analyze the interest portion of the transaction. Then compute the realized gain, and determine the proper year for recognition by determining the gross profit ratio, which is the gross profit divided by the total contract price. Multiply the payments received during the year by the gross profit ratio. The resulting number will be the amount of the payment that is includable as gain from the sale for that year. The remaining amount of the payment will be a tax-free return of basis. By the last payment, the selling taxpayer will have recognized all of the realized gain on the sale and will have received a tax-free return of his or her basis as well.

Example: Jennifer sells Pinkacre to Sam for $150,000. Jennifer's basis in Pinkacre is $30,000. Under the terms of the contract of sale, Sam will pay Jennifer $50,000 in the year of sale and $50,000 on the first and second anniversaries of the sale with interest at 10% (which represents a market rate of interest).

Jennifer, a cash method taxpayer, will report her realized gain of $120,000 on this transaction, using the installment method. She will first deal with the interest side of the transaction. Since the contract calls for adequate stated interest, she will report the interest earned using her method of accounting, the cash method. Thus, she will include the interest in her gross income when she receives it, actually or constructively.

Jennifer will then compute her gross profit ratio, as follows:

$$\frac{\text{Gross Profit}}{\text{Total Contract Price}} = \frac{\$150{,}000 - \$30{,}000}{\$150{,}000} = 80\%$$

Jennifer multiplies the gross profit ratio by the payments she receives each year to determine the portion of the payment that is income and the portion that is a tax-free return of basis. Her total income should equal her realized gain on the transaction, and she should receive a tax-free return of her $30,000 basis. The chart below summarizes these results:

Year & Payment	× Gross Profit Ratio	= Income	Tax-Free Return of Basis
Year of Sale ($50,000)	× 80%	= $40,000	$10,000
1st anniversary year ($50,000)	× 80%	= $40,000	$10,000
2nd anniversary year ($50,000)	× 80%	= $40,000	$10,000
Total $150,000		**$120,000**	**$30,000**

Example: Denea owns a sailboat with a basis of $25,000 and a fair market value of $50,000. It is subject to a debt of $20,000, which Denea incurred to acquire the sailboat. Denea now wishes to sell the boat to Greg, who agrees to (1) pay her $5,000 at closing, (2) assume the debt, and (3) pay her $5,000 on January 1 of each of the following five years. The contract calls for adequate stated interest.

As a cash-method taxpayer, Denea will include the interest in gross income as she receives it, actually or constructively, and as the contract calls for adequate stated interest, it will not be necessary to recast any portion of the payments as interest. Denea's realized gain on the transaction is $25,000, the difference between her basis in the boat and its fair market value. She will report the income from the sale of the boat using the installment method. First, she calculates her gross profit ratio as follows:

$$\frac{\text{Gross Profit}}{\text{Total Contract Price}} \quad = \quad \frac{\$50,000 - \$25,000}{\$50,000 - \$20,000} \quad = \quad 83.3\%$$

She multiplies the payments received each year under the contract by the gross profit ratio. "Payment" in this scenario means the actual payments made, and none of the debt is considered payment in the first year because it is qualifying indebtedness. Notice that her total return of basis is $5,000, which is not her adjusted basis in the property. But if the acquisition debt ($20,000) that Greg assumes is added, this produces a basis of $25,000—her adjusted basis in the property. The installment method essentially allows the seller to recover this investment over time, as income is reported.

Year	Payment	Income	Return of Basis
Sale—Year 1	$ 5,000	$ 4,166	$ 834
Year 2	$ 5,000	$ 4,166	$ 834
Year 3	$ 5,000	$ 4,166	$ 834

[continued]

Year	Payment	Income	Return of Basis
Year 4	$ 5,000	$ 4,166	$ 834
Year 5	$ 5,000	$ 4,166	$ 834
Year 6	$ 5,000	$ 4,170*	$ 830
Total	**$30,000**	**$25,000**	**$5,000**

*Rounding adjustment.

Example: Trisha owns Whiteacre, which has a fair market value of $100,000 and a basis of $30,000. Whiteacre is encumbered by a long-standing mortgage of $50,000. Trisha sells Whiteacre to Patrick for his assumption of the debt plus $50,000 cash, payable in two installments of $25,000 on the fifth and tenth anniversary of the sale (with adequate stated interest).

Trisha will address the interest portion of the transaction independently of the gain on the sale, including the interest in her gross income when she receives it, actually or constructively. She will report her realized gain of $70,000 on the installment method. She calculates her gross profit ratio on the sale as follows:

$$\frac{\text{Gross Profit}}{\text{Total Contract Price}} = \frac{\text{Selling price} - \text{adjusted basis}}{\text{Selling price} - \text{qualifying debt}} = \frac{\$150,000 - 30,000}{\$150,000 - 30,000}$$

Thus, the gross profit ratio is "1," which means that all of the payments received will be treated as income until the taxpayer has recognized all of the income on the transaction. Thereafter, additional payments will be treated as a tax-free return of basis. In addition, the portion of the debt in excess of Trisha's basis ($20,000) will be treated as payment in the first year. The tax consequences of Trisha's sale are summarized in the chart below:

Year	Payment	Income	Return of Basis
Sale	$20,000	× 1 = $20,000	0
Fifth anniversary	$25,000	× 1 = $25,000	0
Tenth anniversary	$25,000	× 1 = $25,000	0
Total	**$70,000**	**$70,000**	**0**

By the end of the contract, Trisha has recognized her entire realized gain of $70,000, which is the proper result. The other totals may require an explanation. The total payment appears to be $70,000, but don't forget that the taxpayer has recovered the additional $30,000 of debt as well, for a total of $100,000—the fair market value of the property. Although she seems not to have recovered her basis, we must add to that figure the $30,000 qualifying debt assumed by Patrick, which produces her basis of $30,000.

VI. RESTRICTED PROPERTY—§83

A. Recognizing this type of transaction

As discussed in Chapter 2, gross income includes **compensation** received for services rendered whether the compensation is in the form of cash or property. The question of *when* the compensation is includable in the taxpayer's income is generally answered by the taxpayer's **method of accounting.** Sometimes, however, the taxpayer receives as compensation **restricted property,** i.e., property subject to significant restrictions on the taxpayer's ability to use or transfer it. Look for a compensation transaction in which the service provider receives not cash, but other property, and the property is subject to some restriction that makes it less valuable to the taxpayer. Transfers of stock or equity interests in other entities are frequently encountered in this context.

B. Whether, when, and how much

Transfers of restricted property raise significant questions not only of *when* the taxpayer must include the item as income but also *whether* the taxpayer has received income at all. The restrictions on the property may be so severe that in fact the taxpayer has not received any property interest at all. Moreover, *how much* income is also in question; the restrictions on use or alienability of the property will probably adversely affect its value. Section 83 resolves all of these difficulties by deferring taxation until it is clear that the taxpayer has received property. It then specifies the proper year for inclusion as well as how much income must be included.

C. Statutory analysis—§83

1. **General rule:** A taxpayer who receives property in connection with the performance of services must include an amount in his or her gross income. IRC §83(a). The amount included is the excess of the value of the property received over the amount the taxpayer paid for the property. Id. The taxpayer includes this amount in gross income in the first year in which he or she may transfer the property, or the rights are not subject to a **substantial risk of forfeiture.** Id.

   Example: Sonny is the CEO of Regency Park, Inc. As part of its incentive compensation plan, Regency Park transfers 1,000 shares of its stock to Sonny on the condition that he remain as CEO for four years. The stock is nontransferable for ten years. The stock received by Sonny is restricted property within the meaning of §83, and Sonny need not include its value in his gross income until the first year in which he is entitled to the stock without the performance of future services or may freely transfer the stock. This will occur at the end of four years, at which time Sonny will include the fair market value of the stock in his gross income (unless he makes a §83(b) election, discussed below).

2. **Definitional issues**

   a. **Transfers of property:** Property includes items other than money and unfunded and unsecured promises to pay money in the future. Reg. §1.83-3(e). A transfer of property occurs when a person acquires a beneficial interest in the property. Reg. §1.83-3(a)(1).

      i. **Economic benefit doctrine:** If an employer contributes assets unconditionally and irrevocably into a fund or trust to be used solely for the employee's benefit, the employee will be considered as receiving property. See, e.g., *Sproull v. Commissioner,* 16 T.C. 244 (1951), *aff'd per curiam,* 194 F.2d 541 (6th Cir. 1952).

ii. **Nonqualified deferred compensation plans—No economic benefit:** The regulations provide that funds set aside from the employer's creditors give the employee a beneficial interest in property. Reg. §1.83-3(e). Conversely, if the assets earmarked for an employee remain subject to the claims of the employer's creditors, they do not constitute a beneficial interest in property for the employee. Employers use this principle in creating ***nonqualified deferred compensation*** plans for employees. The employer and employee agree that the employee will provide services and will be paid for those services in the future (usually at retirement or at termination). Because the employee is generally not satisfied with the employer's mere promise to pay, the employer purchases an asset (such as an ***annuity*** policy) to secure the promise. The purchase of the asset, though earmarked for payment to the employee, is subject to the claims of creditors and thus does not constitute a transfer of property to the employee. Another very common structure for nonqualified deferred compensation is the employer's creation of a "grantor trust," to which the employer contributes funds that will ultimately satisfy the employer's obligation to the employee. The funds earn interest for the benefit of the employee. But because under the terms of the trust the assets of the trust remain subject to the claims of the employer's creditors, the employee need not include any amount in gross income until the amounts in the trust are paid to him or her. The employer is taxed on the interest earned by the trust, and the employer may not deduct any amount as compensation until payments are made to the employee. This arrangement is known as "nonqualified" deferred compensation because it is not subject to substantial regulations applicable to qualified plans that allow the employer to deduct contributions as made, allow amounts to earn interest tax free, and protect assets from the claims of creditors. (See discussion at Chapter 3(H)(1).) The trusts used in these arrangements are known as ***rabbi trusts*** because the first favorable ruling issued for such arrangements addressed a nonqualified deferred compensation plan for a rabbi. The American Jobs Creation Act of 2004 imposed additional requirements on nonqualified deferred compensation plans. See IRC §409A.

Example: Debra accepts a job as CEO of Happy Trax, Inc. (Happy). She and Happy agree that she will be paid $100,000 per year and that Happy will contribute an additional $20,000 per year to a grantor trust under which she is the beneficiary, but the assets of which remain subject to the claims of Happy's creditors. Assume the arrangement meets the requirements of IRC §409A. When she leaves Happy's employ, Debra will be paid all contributions made on her behalf plus earnings attributable to those contributions. Under this arrangement, Debra will not be required to include any amount in gross income until she receives distributions from the trust. However, Happy will be taxed on the earnings of the trust and will not be able to deduct amounts attributable to the trust until distribution to Debra.

iii. **Compare—Qualified plans:** The exception to this rule that an employer setting aside amounts for the exclusive and unconditional benefit of employees is income to them is in the qualified retirement plan arena. See Chapter 3(VIII)(A).

b. **Substantial risk of forfeiture:** A substantial risk of forfeiture exists when the person receiving the property must perform substantial future services in order to have full rights in the property. IRC §83(c)(1).

Example: Mark agrees to manage the apartment buildings of ABC Partnership in exchange for a 20% partnership interest. However, his rights in the partnership interest are conditioned upon his performing management services for five full years. The partnership interest is subject to a substantial risk of forfeiture. (Indeed, he may not even be a partner because of this requirement, but that discussion is for another course.)

c. **Transferability:** A person may freely transfer property only if the transferee's rights in the property would not be subject to a substantial risk of forfeiture. IRC §83(c)(2).

d. **"In connection with" the performance of services:** Property is transferred in connection with the performance of services if it is transferred to an employee or an independent contractor who is obligated to perform services or refrain from performing services. Reg. §1.83-3(f).

3. **Special rules and exceptions**

a. **Restrictions that never lapse:** Certain restrictions on property will never lapse, and therefore it will be impossible to value the property under the usual fair market value standards. In these circumstances, the agreement of transfer will usually provide a formula for valuing the property. If so, the formula price will be the fair market value for purposes of determining the amount to be included in income. Reg. §1.83-5(a).

b. **Employer's deduction:** The employer takes a deduction with respect to the transfer of property when the taxpayer includes the amount in gross income. IRC §83(h).

c. **Section 83(b) election:** A taxpayer receiving restricted property may elect to include the value of the property in gross income at the time received, rather than waiting for restrictions to lapse. If the taxpayer makes this election, he or she includes in gross income the excess of the fair market value of the property (computed without regard to restrictions) over the amount the taxpayer paid for the property. Id. This would be a rational choice for property whose value is relatively low in the year of transfer but which is expected to increase substantially prior to lapse of the restrictions on transfer. However, if the property declines in value, the taxpayer may not revoke the election. In any event, the taxpayer has only 30 days after transfer to make the election. IRC §83(b)(2).

Example: Joe is the accountant for a fledgling company, Zippy, Inc. Joe agrees to take restricted stock in Zippy in exchange for (1) a capital contribution of $10, and (2) providing accounting and financial services to Zippy over ten years. Because the value of Zippy stock is low in its early years, Joe might well be advised to make the §83(b) election. He would then include in his gross income the difference between the fair market value of the Zippy stock in the year he receives it (valued without regard to the restrictions on transfer to which the stock is subject) minus the amount he paid for it ($10). Joe's basis in the stock will be equal to the amount he paid for it plus the amount he included in gross income. Ten years later, when Zippy is fabulously successful and the restrictions lapse, the stock will be much more valuable, but Joe will not include any amount in gross income because of the lapse of the restrictions and because he had already included the value in income in the year of transfer.

4. **Related material**

a. **Basis:** The basis of property received as compensation for services is its cost. This includes the amount paid for the property plus the amount included in gross income as a result of §83. For a discussion of basis of property received as compensation for services, see Chapter 9(III)(B).

b. Constructive receipt: An alternative theory for challenging certain deferred compensation arrangements is the doctrine of constructive receipt. But see *Minor v. United States,* at Chapter 11(III)(B).

5. Summary: See Statute Summary—§83

Statute Summary—§83

Parsing Step	§83
General rule	A taxpayer who receives restricted property as compensation must include the excess of the value over the amount paid for the property in the first year in which the property is transferable, or the taxpayer's rights are not subject to a substantial risk of forfeiture.
Definitional issues	Transfer of property as compensation Substantial risk of forfeiture Transferability
Special rules and exceptions	Restrictions that never lapse Employer's deduction §83(b) election
Related material	Deferred compensation arrangements Basis of property: §1012 Constructive receipt
Summary	If a taxpayer receives restricted property as compensation, consider when, whether, and how much income the taxpayer has, applying rules of §83.

VII. SPECIAL RESTRICTIONS ON LOSS DEDUCTIONS

Two statutory schemes—the *passive loss* provisions of §469 and the *at risk* provisions of §465—potentially limit or disallow deductions for certain types of losses. These provisions are properly viewed as timing rules because they address a taxpayer's ability to claim a deduction for a loss in the year that it is incurred, and typically defer *loss deductions* to a later year. Although these provisions are technical in the extreme, a passing familiarity with them is important for the basic tax student.

A. Passive loss restrictions—§469

Section 469 prohibits individuals and certain other taxpayers from deducting a passive activity loss for any taxable year. IRC §469(a). The passive activity loss is the net loss (i.e., the excess of losses over income) from the taxpayer's "passive activities." IRC §469(d)(1).

1. Identifying passive activities: A passive activity is any activity of the taxpayer that is a *trade or business* but in which the taxpayer does not "materially participate." IRC §469(c). For example, a passive activity does not include income from investments, because the holding of investments does not rise to the level of a trade or business, but a taxpayer's participation as a silent partner in a horse breeding business would be a passive activity. In general, *any* rental activity is a passive activity generating passive income and loss, but there is an exception for rental real estate activities in which the taxpayer "actively participates," for up to $25,000 of otherwise passive loss. IRC §469(c)(7). Active participation is a slightly easier standard to meet, requiring that the taxpayer make management decisions, carry out services with respect to the property or arrange for others to perform such services in a significant and bona fide manner.

2. **Material participation:** The statute defines "material participation" as regular, continuous, and substantial participation, and provides a special rule that limited partners are not considered to materially participate except as provided in the regulations. IRC §469(h)(1), (2). The regulations' definition of material participation is extremely complex, offering a variety of different tests. The most familiar of these is the 500-hour test, under which the taxpayer is considered to materially participate in an activity only if he or she devotes 500 hours or more to the activity each year. Treas. Reg. §1.469-5T(a)(1).

3. **Deduction of passive losses:** A passive loss may be deducted only against *passive income,* i.e., income from a passive activity. IRC §469(d)(1).

   Example: Carol is a limited partner in a box car investment partnership and also is a member of a limited liability company that owns a coin laundry business. She does not materially participate in either venture. She has a $6,000 loss from the limited partnership investment, and she has $4,000 of income from the LLC owning the coin laundry business. Her passive loss of $6,000 may be deducted against the passive income from the LLC, but her $2,000 loss in excess of passive income is not deductible.

4. **Suspended passive losses:** Losses that cannot be deducted because of the passive loss rules carry forward indefinitely until a year in which the taxpayer has passive income. When the taxpayer disposes completely of his or her investment in the activity, suspended passive losses will not be treated as losses from a passive activity, and therefore will be deductible, subject to any other loss restrictions. IRC §469(g)(1). The amount of deductible loss is the excess of suspended passive losses over any net income or gain from all passive activities for the year. IRC §469(g)(1)(A).

   Example: Penny invests $100,000 in a cattle breeding enterprise from which she anticipates tax benefits but in which she does not have to actually ever see, touch, or communicate with any cows. She has no other investments in passive activities. In the first five years of the project, her share of the enterprise's income and deductions produce a net loss to her of $30,000 per year. These are passive losses, because although the underlying activity is a trade or business, she does not materially participate in the activity. Therefore, Penny may not deduct the losses, as she has no passive income. If in year six she sells her interest in the cattle breeding enterprise, she may deduct the excess of the suspended $150,000 loss over the income from disposition, and income from other passive activities will be treated as a loss from other than a passive activity.

B. At risk limitations—§465

Section 465 limits the amount of loss an individual and certain other taxpayers may deduct from certain activities to the amount the taxpayer has *at risk* in the venture. IRC §465(a)(1). Section 465 applies to businesses involving films or video, farming, leasing of personal property, certain oil and gas endeavors, and the holding of real property. IRC §465(b)(6), (c). The amount the taxpayer has "at risk" is equal to the amount of money and fair market value of property that the taxpayer has contributed to the business, and the amount for which the taxpayer could be held personally liable for contribution to the enterprise (or its creditors), reduced by any losses deducted in prior years for which the taxpayer was at risk. IRC §465(b). For real estate activities, the taxpayer may also be considered at risk for certain qualifying nonrecourse indebtedness, which greatly increases the amount at risk for certain taxpayers. See IRC §465(b)(6). Any losses disallowed by §465 carry forward and may be deducted if and when the taxpayer has additional amounts at risk. IRC §465(a)(2).

Example: Kerry invests in a filming enterprise by contributing $50,000 and promising to contribute another $40,000 if needed. He is not liable under contract or state law for any additional amounts in the venture. Kerry's share of losses from the venture is $60,000 in the first year. He may deduct these losses, as he is at risk by the amount of money he has contributed ($50,000) and the amount he has agreed to contribute ($40,000). If in the next year, Kerry's share of losses were again $60,000, he would be allowed to deduct only $30,000 of these losses, as his total amount at risk for that year would be reduced by the prior year's losses. The remaining $30,000 nondeductible loss would carry forward and would be deductible if Kerry were to contribute more money to the venture.

VIII. WHERE ARE WE GOING?

Previous chapters have addressed the computation of gain or loss from the sale or other disposition of property, and this chapter has discussed timing of that income or loss (as well as timing of other items of income and deduction). But a full analysis of gain or loss from the sale of property requires a determination of the *character* of income or loss as capital or ordinary. Chapter 12 turns to this very important question.

Quiz Yourself on *TIMING OF INCOME AND EXPENSES*

93. Why does the U.S. income tax system use an annual accounting system? _____

94. Jerry is a talk show host on a local radio station. He produces the show himself, and had income of $25,000 in each of Years 1, 2, and 3 from this activity. In Year 4, he experienced a loss of $30,000. In Year 5, the business had taxable income of $20,000. Can Jerry average these years' income to reflect his overall taxable income of $65,000? If so, how can this be done? _____

95. Sandy entered into a consulting contract for services with Rocky Corp. The contract said that Sandy was to be paid $100,000, but if its consulting services did not increase Rocky's sales of gravel and sand by 35% by the end of the next year, the consulting contract price would be reduced based on a formula. Sandy received $100,000 in Year 1, but had to repay $15,000 in Year 2. How should Sandy treat the receipt of income in Year 1? _____

96. Tom is a lawyer using the calendar year and the cash method of accounting. Tom performed work in December, and gave the client his bill, but the customer didn't pay until January. When will Tom properly include this payment in his gross income? _____

97. Consider Tom from the previous problem. What if Tom's client had showed up at his office on December 31 with a check but Tom refused to let him in? _____

98. Opie is a motivational speaker, using the calendar year and cash method of accounting. He paid otherwise deductible expenses of $5,000 this year, by paying $2,000 by check and $3,000 by credit card. He also owed the local office supply store $4,500 as of year-end. When will Opie properly deduct these amounts? _____

99. Oils R Us, an aromatherapy store, opened the year with $10,000 of inventory on hand. It purchased another $25,000 of products from suppliers, and its year-end count shows $12,000 of inventory on hand. It had gross sales of $50,000. What is its net income considering only inventory expense? _____

100. GoTown Recording Studios uses the calendar year and the accrual method of accounting. It engages Soundbites Corp. to provide mixing services in Year 2 for a stated amount. GoTown will pay Soundbites in two payments, one at the end of Year 1 and the second six months later in Year 2. When will GoTown properly deduct the payments to Soundbites? _____

101. Samantha owned Hideaway Hills, a ranch in California. Samantha is not a dealer in such property and the ranch is not her personal residence. She has a basis of $300,000 in the ranch. She sold Hideaway Hills to Darin for $1,000,000. Darin will pay her $200,000 per year, plus interest, for the next five years. When will Samantha report the gain on the sale of the ranch? Is there any other income to report? _____

102. Sara paid $5,000 of state income taxes and deducted this amount on her federal tax return for Year 1. This entire amount reduced her tax. In Year 2, she received a refund of $2,000 of those state income taxes. What are Sara's tax effects in Year 2? _____

103. Bev, a college basketball coach, inherited an apartment building from her mother. This year, it produced a net loss for tax purposes of $40,000. Bev wants to deduct this amount on her income tax return. May she do so? _____

Answers

93. The government needs some way to measure a taxpayer's income and collect the tax in predictable, objective, and fairly frequent intervals. The taxable year concept provides that technique.

94. Income averaging *per se* is not possible, but Jerry may carry back his net operating loss of $30,000 in Year 4 to Year 2 (applying $25,000, reducing taxable income to zero) and Year 3 (applying $5,000, reducing taxable income to $20,000). He does this by filing amended returns, and this carryback has the result similar to "averaging" his income.

95. In this case, Sandy had a colorable legal claim to $100,000 and must include that amount in income in the year of receipt. In the next year, it can invoke §1341 to pay the lower of the tax resulting from (a) computing the tax in Year 1 as if the $15,000 had never been included; or (b) including the income in Year 1 and deducting the repayment in Year 2.

96. Because Tom is a cash method taxpayer, he will include the payment in gross income in the year he receives it, Year 2. When he performed the services and sent his bill is irrelevant.

97. Tom would probably be in constructive receipt of payment, because he had access to the money and refused to take it.

98. Opie will deduct $5,000 for payments made, and it doesn't matter if they are made by check or credit card. He cannot deduct amounts owed at the end of the year because he has not yet paid them.

99. Oils R Us is required to account for inventories because it sells merchandise. It has $50,000 of gross income. Its cost of goods sold is computed by taking beginning inventory ($10,000), adding purchases ($25,000) and subtracting ending inventory ($12,000). Its cost of goods sold is $23,000. Therefore, its net income, considering only inventory costs, is $27,000 ($50,000 − $23,000).

100. As an accrual method taxpayer, GoTown generally deducts expenses when all events have occurred that determine the fact of the liability and the amount of the liability can be determined with reasonable accuracy. This test would normally lead to GoTown deducting the expense in Year 1. However, the economic performance rules are an overlay on the all events test. They provide that deduction cannot occur prior to economic performance. For the purchase of services, economic performance occurs when the services are provided. Therefore, GoTown may not deduct the payment until Year 2, when Soundbites provides the services.

101. Unless Samantha elects out of the installment method, she will report the gain realized on the transaction over the five-year period of payments. The portion of each payment that is income is determined by multiplying the payment ($200,000) by a fraction, the numerator of which is the gross profit ($1,000,000 − $300,000) and the denominator of which is the total contract price ($1,000,000). Thus, 70% of each payment, or $140,000, will be income. Moreover, Samantha must include the interest paid by Darin in gross income in the year it is received, assuming she is a cash method taxpayer.

102. Under IRC §111, the refund of the state income taxes is a recovery that may lead to inclusion of amounts in Sara's gross income. The exclusionary amount—the amount of the total $2,000 recovery that can be excluded from gross income—is the amount of the original deduction that did not reduce tax in the prior year. Since the entire amount was used to reduce tax, the entire amount of the recovery is included in gross income.

103. This is probably a passive activity loss, as it is produced from the activity of rental real estate. Therefore, Bev may deduct it against passive income, and depending on her AGI, Bev may be able to claim $25,000 of it as a deduction (§469(i)). If she cannot deduct the loss, it will be suspended and will carry over to the future until she can use it against passive income or she sells the apartment building.

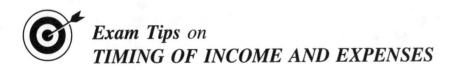

Exam Tips *on*
TIMING OF INCOME AND EXPENSES

☞ Questions of timing arise only *after* you have determined that there is an item of income or an expense that may be deducted. Don't get ahead of yourself by jumping straight to timing issues.

    ☞ *Look for:* Is there an item of income, and if so, how much? Is there an expense or loss that is deductible, and if so, how much?

☞ *Analyze:* Then, and only then, ask *when* is the income includable in the taxpayer's gross income, and when is the expense or loss deductible?

☛ Know what taxpayers are trying to do: Defer income and accelerate deductions. (See Chapter 15.) So, what's the Commissioner trying to do? (Accelerate income and defer deductions, when taxpayers try to play games!)

☞ *Look for:* Taxpayers playing games by accelerating deductions and postponing income. Look for situations in which taxpayers have access to income, but don't report it, or haven't yet made an economic outlay of some sort but still claim deductions.

☞ *Analyze:* Statutory and regulatory response to those games.

☛ When the facts describe a transaction occurring over two or more years, timing issues are likely to be important. If a result seems "unfair" to a taxpayer because of multiple-year transactions, timing issues are likely to be a big issue.

☞ *Look for:* Income in one year, and deductions in another; profit in one year, and losses in another; recovery of previous deductions; repayment of amounts received in previous years.

☞ *Analyze:* Chronologically—address the first year first, then later years, in order. Explain how the years affect each other, if they do. Think about claim of right, tax benefit, and NOL issues.

☛ Some kinds of property transactions raise important timing issues.

☞ *Look for:* Sales of property with deferred payment; stock or other property given to employees or others for services.

☞ *Analyze*: Over what period of time will income be recognized, or in what year will there be a sudden influx of income from property received in exchange for services?

☛ If a question describes the taxpayer's method of accounting, it may have important timing issues. Scan for the words cash method or accrual method.

☞ *Look for:* When is an amount paid, or received? When is the obligation due? Is there uncertainty about the amount?

☞ *If in doubt:* Include an amount in income and defer and expense, particularly for accrual method taxpayers.

☛ If a question describes the taxpayer's accounting year, it may have important timing issues. Scan for the words calendar year or fiscal year.

☞ *Look for:* Transactions occurring at the end of one year and the beginning of the next.

☞ *Analyze:* Chronologically—analyze first year first, then move to the next year. Explain how the two years affect each other, if they do.

CHAPTER 12

CHARACTER OF INCOME AND LOSS

ChapterScope ─────────────────────────────

Previous chapters have addressed issues surrounding the calculation of taxable income, including the identification of items of gross income and the availability of deductions. Several chapters have focused specifically on the computation of gain and loss on the sale or other disposition of property. This chapter turns to the important question of the *character* of income and loss as capital or ordinary for these transactions.

- **Importance of capital/noncapital distinction:** "Net capital gain" is taxed at a preferential tax rate, while ordinary income is subject to higher rates. Capital losses incurred in any taxable year may be deducted only against capital gains for that year plus $3,000 of ordinary income, for individuals.

- **An approach to characterization problems:** If gain or loss is recognized from the sale or exchange of property, the character of the gain or loss must be considered. Figure 12A offers an approach to characterization questions.

- **Capital gain and loss:** Gain or loss from the sale or exchange of a capital asset produces capital gain or loss.

- **Capital asset:** A capital asset is defined in §1221 as any asset, regardless of its business use, except for specifically enumerated items. Capital gain and loss is divided into categories, depending on the type of asset generating the gain or loss.

- **Section 1231 assets:** Real property and depreciable property used in a trade or business are "§1231 assets" and are subject to special rules for characterization. While these assets are generally not considered "capital assets" under the definition in §1221, §1231 supplies a taxpayer-friendly netting rule that, with some exceptions, can characterize net gains as capital and net losses as ordinary. Figure 12D offers an approach to determining §1231 gain or loss.

- **Special recharacterization rules:** Several special recharacterization rules apply to recharacterize capital loss as ordinary loss and capital gain as ordinary income.

- **Holding period:** The taxpayer's holding period for a capital asset determines whether gain or loss on sale will be long- or short-term capital gain or loss. Holding periods usually begin with the acquisition of an item, but in some transactions (such as gifts) the owner of the property will "tack" another holding period onto his or her own period of actual ownership of the property.

- **Calculation of net capital gain and net capital loss:** The calculation of net capital gain and net capital loss—and the tax rates applicable to net capital gain—requires a complex process from which the includable income or deductible loss is derived. Figure 12E provides a methodology for these computations.

I. WHERE ARE WE?

As we move to the computation of a taxpayer's actual tax, it is critical to identify the character of the individual's income or loss. This is because different kinds of income are subject to different tax rates, and some kinds of losses may be deducted only against certain kinds of income. The default category is ordinary income, but some income and loss may be capital in nature, raising these questions of tax rate and deductibility. This income and loss arises from the disposition of property, making the material in Chapter 9 critical as background to this discussion.

II. WHO CARES? THE CAPITAL/ORDINARY DISTINCTION

The distinction between capital and ordinary income and loss has implications for both gain and loss.

A. Income—Preferential tax rates

The 2005 tax rates imposed by §1 of the Code on individuals on ordinary income range from 10% to 35%. However, the rates imposed on "net capital gain" range from 5% to 28%, creating the *tax preference* for *capital gains.* IRC §1(h). Taxpayers usually seek to characterize income as capital gain in order to take advantage of this preferential rate.

Example: Last year, Margie's taxable income was $200,000, and she was taxed at the maximum rate of 35%. This year her tax situation is the same except that she sold some stock she held as an investment at a gain of $90,000. Because the stock is a capital asset in Margie's hands, its sale produces capital gain of $90,000. This will be taxed at a lower preferential rate rather than the 35% marginal rate applicable to Margie's other income.

B. Deductions—Limitations on deduction of capital loss

Section 1211 imposes significant restrictions on the deduction of capital losses.

1. **Corporations:** Corporations may deduct capital losses realized during a taxable year only to the extent of their capital gain income during that year. IRC §1211(a). Losses that cannot be deducted because of this limitation are called "net capital losses" and carry back to the previous three taxable years and forward to the five following taxable years, subject to the same limitation that such losses can only be deducted to the extent of capital gain income in those years. IRC §1212(a).

   Example: WellCo (a corporation) sells stock in its subsidiary, SickCo, incurring a capital loss of $250,000. WellCo has capital gain income from other transactions of $100,000. WellCo may deduct $100,000 of its capital loss. WellCo will be able to carry back the remaining $150,000 net capital loss to the previous three taxable years, and to the extent the loss is not used in the carryback, it will carry forward to the next five taxable years.

2. **Individuals:** Individuals may deduct capital losses recognized in a taxable year only to the extent of their capital gains for that year, plus the lower of $3,000 or the excess of capital losses over capital gains. IRC §1211(b). Losses that cannot be claimed because of this limitation are called "net capital losses" and carry forward indefinitely to the next succeeding taxable years. IRC §1212(b)(1). In each succeeding year, capital losses may be deducted to the extent of capital gain recognized in that year. In addition, in each succeeding year, the taxpayer is *deemed* to have a capital gain equal to the lesser of (1) $3,000 or the excess of losses over gains, whichever is lower; or (2) the taxpayer's adjusted taxable income. IRC §1212(b)(2)(A).

"Adjusted taxable income" means taxable income increased by the lower of $3,000 or the excess of capital loss over capital gain plus the personal exemption. IRC §1212(b)(2)(B). This deemed capital gain allows the taxpayer to deduct capital losses carried forward to future years, to the extent of capital gains in those years plus $3,000 of ordinary income in each year.

Example: This year, Bill had salary of $25,000. He also sold two blocks of stock. Sale of ABC stock produced a capital loss of $15,000. Sale of XYZ stock produced capital gain of $5,000. Bill would be able to claim $8,000 of his capital loss as a deduction in the year of sale, which is equal to the amount of capital gain in that year, plus $3,000 (the lower of $3,000 or the excess of capital loss over capital gain, $10,000). The remaining $7,000 of capital loss will carry forward to the next year, subject to these same limitations. If, for example, Bill's adjusted gross income (AGI) in that year were only $2,000, Bill would be allowed to take $2,000 of the loss in that year, and $5,000 of the loss would carry forward.

3. **Charitable deduction limitations:** Section 170(e) reduces the amount of a deduction for a charitable contribution of certain capital and noncapital assets. See discussion, Chapter 6(XVI)(C).

C. Taxpayer preference—Capital gain/ordinary loss

Given the favorable tax rates for capital gain and the restriction on the deductibility of capital losses, taxpayers typically prefer to characterize income as capital and loss as ordinary. The IRS typically responds that income is ordinary and losses are capital, and this conflict produces much of the judicial and administrative guidance in this area.

D. Policy

A number of rationales are offered for treating capital gain and loss differently than ordinary income and loss.

1. **Rationales for capital gains preference:** The following rationales are often offered for a capital gains preference. Each can be countered by questioning its empirical support, the related economic effects of the preference, and whether a more desirable route exists for addressing the particular problem.

   a. **General incentive:** This rationale suggests that reduction in the tax rate on investments will increase savings, investment, and economic prosperity.

   b. **Specific incentive:** This rationale suggests that a reduction in the tax rate for specific industries will increase investment in those industries.

   c. **Preventing "lock-in":** "Lock-in" occurs when a taxpayer holds rather than sells assets because of the tax that will be due on sale. Section 1014 increases the likelihood of lock-in, because holding an asset until death results in the heirs having a basis equal to the fair market value of the property on the date of death, thus avoiding income tax on the gain inherent in the asset. See Chapter 9(III). A capital gains preference is said to reduce lock-in by reducing the tax associated with sale.

   d. **Bunching:** Capital gains often accrue over many years, yet the gain is recognized in a single year. This "bunching" effect can result in the taxation of gain at the highest marginal rate in the year of recognition, even though the incremental gains might have been taxed at lower rates had they been recognized in the years they accrued. The capital gains preference is said to mitigate the impact of the bunching effect by allowing a reduced rate in the year of sale.

    e. Inflation: The recognized gain upon sale of a capital asset may not represent real gain, but instead may represent inflationary gains. The capital gains preference is said to mitigate the impact of inflation by lowering the tax in the year of sale. (Indexing the basis of assets for inflation is a common proposal to reduce the effect of inflation.)

2. **Rationale for limitation on capital loss:** Allowing a taxpayer to deduct capital losses without limitation would arguably give the taxpayer too much discretion to adjust his or her taxable income by selling only those capital assets that have declined in value.

E. Definitions

Characterizing income or loss as capital or ordinary requires reference to a number of definitions. Ordinary income or loss is the default category, i.e., unless an item of income or loss qualifies as capital gain or capital loss, it will be ordinary in nature. Characterization issues involve the interaction of a number of definitional issues, which are summarized here and discussed in more detail later in this chapter.

1. **Ordinary income:** Ordinary income is any gain from the sale or exchange of property that is neither a *capital asset* nor §1231 property. IRC §64.

2. **Ordinary loss:** Ordinary loss is loss from the sale or exchange of property that is not a capital asset. IRC §65.

3. **Capital asset:** A capital asset is any property held by the taxpayer (whether or not connected with the taxpayer's trade or business) except for eight categories of property, of which five are generally important in the basic tax course. See IRC §1221 and this chapter, section (III)(D).

4. **Capital gain net income:** Capital gain net income is the excess of gains from sales or exchanges of capital assets over losses from such assets. IRC §1222(9).

5. **Net capital gain:** Net capital gain is the excess of net long-term capital gain for the taxable year over net short-term capital loss for that year. IRC §1222(11).

6. **Net capital loss:** Net capital loss is the excess of losses from the sale or exchange of capital assets over the amount allowable as a deduction under IRC §1211. IRC §1222(10).

7. **Section 1231 gain or loss:** Section 1231 gain or loss is net gain or loss from certain kinds of property used in the taxpayer's trade or business. IRC §1231(a)(3).

III. AN APPROACH TO CHARACTERIZING GAIN OR LOSS AS CAPITAL OR ORDINARY

A. An approach to characterization problems

For any problem that potentially raises questions of the character of gain or loss, five straightforward questions can determine the nature of the gain or loss. These are illustrated in Figure 12A— An Approach to Characterization Problems. The first question is whether there has been a realization event from which income/gain or loss is recognized (see Box {1}). If the answer to that question is no, the problem is not one of characterizing gain or loss as capital or ordinary and one

Figure 12A
An Approach to Characterization Problems

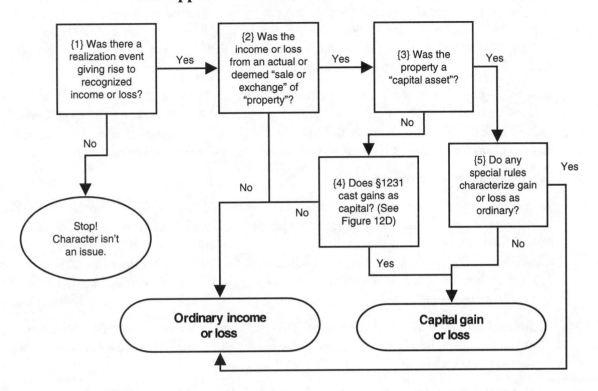

stops there. But if there is recognized income or loss, a closely related, yet distinct question arises—whether there has been a "sale or exchange" of "property" (see Box {2}). If there is no sale or exchange, recognized gain or loss will be ordinary in nature. But if a sale or exchange has occurred, the third question is whether the recognized gain or loss is from the sale or exchange of a capital asset (see Box {3}). The sale or exchange of noncapital assets usually generates ordinary income or loss, but whether §1231 applies must be considered to determine whether gains will be treated as capital under those special rules (see Box {4}). If the property is a capital asset, its sale or exchange generally will produce capital gain or loss. In the next step, however, one considers whether any special recharacterization rules recast capital gain or loss as ordinary (see Box {5}). If they do, the result will be ordinary income or loss. But if no recharacterization rules apply, the gain or loss is capital in nature.

B. Recognized gain and loss

In order for a taxpayer to have capital gain or loss, there must be a realization event (a sale or other disposition of property), and gains or losses from that sale must be recognized. This implicates §1001(a), which measures the realized gain or loss from the "sale or other disposition of property," and §1001(c), which requires recognition of gains or losses—unless otherwise provided in the Code. (See Chapter 9(III).) Moreover, the various provisions of the Code regulating the recognition of gain or loss, including the various nonrecognition provisions and §165(c), must be considered in determining whether realized gain is recognized. (See generally Chapter 10.)

Example—Gain: Janet owns Blackacre, a parcel of raw land, which she has held for investment for many years. She exchanges Blackacre for Whiteacre in a qualifying §1031 exchange in which she realizes $50,000 of gain but recognizes none of the gain. This realized gain is not capital in nature, because it does not result from a transaction in which gains are recognized. (Another way to express this is that the character of the gain is not relevant, since it is not recognized.) Later, when Janet sells Whiteacre in a transaction in which gain is recognized, her gain will likely be capital, and it will likely be long-term capital gain, because Janet will be able to add her holding period for Blackacre to her holding period for Whiteacre.

Example—Loss: Chen owns a principal residence with a basis of $100,000 and a fair market value of $90,000. He sells it for $90,000, realizing a $10,000 loss. However, §165(c) prohibits the deduction of this loss, and therefore this loss is not a capital loss. (Another way to express this is that the character of Chen's realized loss is not relevant because it is not recognized.)

C. Sale or exchange requirement

Section 1222 requires that there be a "sale or exchange of a capital asset" in order to generate capital gain or loss. The sale or exchange requirement is independent of the realization requirement implicit in §1001 (discussed above), and the two are frequently confused. The sale or exchange requirement is arguably a more stringent standard than the "sale or other disposition" language in §1001, and therefore a transaction might qualify as a "sale or other disposition" but fail to qualify as a "sale or exchange."

1. **Judicial definition of sale or exchange:** The courts typically construe a "sale or exchange" in its ordinary meaning, requiring "a giving, a receipt, and a causal connection between the two." *Yarbro v. Commissioner,* 737 F.2d 479 (5th Cir. 1984).

   a. **Involuntary sales or exchanges—*Helvering v. Hammel,* 311 U.S. 504 (1941):** Even an involuntary or forced sale, as in the case of foreclosure, can qualify as a sale or exchange for purposes of measuring capital gain or loss.

   b. **Transfer to legatee—*Kenan v. Commissioner,* 114 F.2d 217 (1940):** In *Kenan,* a legatee was entitled to $5,000,000 in value from a trust established by will. The trustees paid the legatee partly in cash and partly in appreciated securities. The court determined that the trustee's satisfaction of the legatee's claim with the securities constituted a sale or exchange of those securities resulting in capital gain to the trust. This transaction is best viewed for tax purposes as a deemed sale of the securities by the trustees for cash, followed by a deemed distribution of cash to the legatee.

   c. **Contract rights and judgments—*Galvin Hudson,* 20 T.C. 734 (1953), *aff'd sub nom. Ogilvie v. Commissioner,* 216 F.2d 748 (6th Cir. 1954):** The taxpayer purchased a judgment against a debtor. When the debtor settled the judgment by paying the taxpayer, the taxpayer claimed that he had capital gain to the extent that the amount received exceeded his basis (cost) in the claim. The court concluded that there was no sale or exchange when the taxpayer received payment, stating, "the judgment was extinguished without the transfer of any property or property right to the judgment debtor." Thus, the taxpayer had ordinary income in the amount of the receipt in excess of his investment in the judgment. The extinguishment doctrine continues to generate controversy. If a payment extinguishes a right altogether, there will be no sale or exchange. If a property right continues to exist, however, there may be a sale or exchange. *Gladden v. Commissioner,* 112 T.C. 209, 226 n.3 (1999) (water rights did not vanish where they reverted to the government; they survived, and "were reallocated to other users"), *rev'd on other grounds and remanded,* 262 F.3d 851 (9th Cir. 2001).

Figure 12B
Statutory Sales or Exchanges

Code Section	Topic	What Event Is the Deemed Sale?	Here's an Example:
165(g)	Worthless securities	When a security becomes worthless, it is deemed sold for $0.	Steve's 50 shares of ABC stock become worthless. He has a basis of $400 in them. He is deemed to have sold the stock for $0, realizing a loss of $400.
165(h)(2)(B)	Personal casualty losses and gains	If personal casualty gains exceed similar losses, the gains and losses are deemed to be from the sale of capital assets.	See Chapter 6(XIV)(C)(2). These gains and losses would be capital.
166(a)	Bad debts	Partial or entire worthlessness of a bad debt is treated as a sale of the debt for its value.	Jody lends Bob $10,000. The debt becomes worthless. Jody is deemed to have sold the debt for its value, $0, realizing a loss of $10,000.
1234A	Certain terminations	Cancellation, lapse, expiration, or termination of certain property that is a capital asset to the taxpayer is treated as sale or exchange.	Brenda has the right to acquire 1,000 German marks for a stated price. This option expires, and she is treated as selling the option for $0.
1235	Patents	Patent transfers are treated as a sale or exchange, even if payments depend on the productivity of underlying asset.	Tara transfers her patent for a better mousetrap to Steve in exchange for $1,000 plus 2% of sales in perpetuity. This is a sale of the patent.
1241	Lease cancellation	A lessee who receives money for cancellation of lease or by a distributor for cancellation of agreement is treated as selling the lease or agreement.	Lane is leasing office space from Gar. Gar pays Lane $10,000 to cancel his lease. Lane has sold the lease for $10,000.
1253	Franchises, trademarks, tradenames	A transfer of these items without retention of a significant interest is a sale.	Elyse transfers her tradename, Uncorked Wine Shop, to Emily for $1,000 with no continuing interest. Elyse has sold the tradename for $1,000.
1271	Debt instruments	Retirement of the debt instrument is a sale.	Prudence holds a note issued by ABC Co. ABC pays off the note. This will be treated as Prudence's sale of the note for the amount received.

2. **Deemed sales by statute:** Some transactions would not qualify as sales or exchanges under judicial interpretations of the term, but Congress has deemed them to be sales or exchanges by statute. See Figure 12B—Statutory Sales or Exchanges.

D. Capital asset requirement

In order for capital gain or loss to be generated, the sale or exchange must be of a capital asset. Section 1221 defines a capital asset as "property held by the taxpayer (whether or not in connection with his trade or business)" except for eight enumerated categories of property, of which only five are usually important in the basic tax course. Thus, an item of property is a capital asset *unless* it falls within any of these five categories.

1. **Property versus income:** In order to generate capital gain or loss, a transaction must involve a sale or exchange of "property." While property is not usually difficult to identify, some transactions, while crafted as sales or exchanges of property, are in substance merely prepayments of income from that property and therefore do not constitute sales or exchanges of the property itself. Courts look to factors such as whether there has been substantial appreciation in the value of the so-called asset over time and whether there is an investment risk of holding such an asset.

   a. **Lease cancellation—*Hort v. Commissioner*, 313 U.S. 28 (1941):** The taxpayer was the lessor of property. He and the lessee agreed to cancel the lease in exchange for a payment of $140,000 from the lessee to the lessor. The taxpayer claimed a loss on the transaction, asserting that the cancellation payment was less than the value of the lease canceled. The IRS disagreed and included the entire $140,000 payment in the taxpayer's gross income as ordinary income. The Court agreed with the Commissioner, on the theory that the payment was merely a prepayment of rent, which is includable in gross income under §61(a)(5), regardless of the fact that the lease itself constituted a property interest.

   b. **Sale of life estate—*McAllister v. Commissioner*, 157 F.2d 235 (2d Cir. 1946), *cert. denied*, 330 U.S. 826 (1947):** The taxpayer relinquished her life estate in a trust to the remainderman and agreed to the termination of the trust in exchange for a lump-sum cash payment. She reported a capital loss equal to the difference between the cash she received and the basis of her life estate, and the Commissioner disagreed, asserting that the entire payment was ordinary income to her under the principle of *Hort*. The court concluded that she had sold a property interest—her entire interest in the trust—citing *Blair v. Commissioner* for the principle that the gift of an income interest in the trust constitutes a valid transfer if it is not a "carved-out interest." See discussion of *Blair* at Chapter 14(III)(E). Thus, she realized a capital loss on the transfer.

   c. **Substitution of right to receive ordinary income periodically**

      i. ***Commissioner v. P.G. Lake, Inc.*, 356 U.S. 260 (1958):** A corporation owning a working interest in commercial oil and gas leases assigned to its president certain oil rights in exchange for the president's cancellation of a debt owed to him by the corporation. The debt was $600,000, and the right assigned was an oil payment right payable out of 25% of the oil from the corporation's working interest in two oil leases. The corporation reported the transaction as producing capital gain, and the Commissioner disagreed, asserting that the entire $600,000 should be included in the corporation's gross income as ordinary income. As in *Hort* (discussed above), the court viewed the transaction as the prepayment of income from the working interest, which should be taxable as ordinary income to the recipient.

ii. **Lottery proceeds:** Lottery winners—unhappy with the long-term payout of their winnings—often assign their rights to a third party in exchange for a lump sum. While taxpayers have repeatedly tried to characterize their gain as capital, the IRS and the courts have resisted these efforts, on the theory that the proceeds are simply a substitution for their right to receive what would otherwise be ordinary income—the lottery winnings. See, e.g., *United States v. Maginnis*, 356 F. 3d 1179 (9th Cir. 2004).

2. **Excluded categories of property:** Section 1221 excludes from the definition of capital asset properties in eight enumerated categories, of which five will be discussed here. A taxpayer generally will try to characterize property as *outside* these categories if its sale has generated a loss (in order to claim an ordinary loss), and property as *within* these categories if its sale has generated a gain (in order to claim capital gain). The challenge offered by §1221's specific categories is to determine whether a property fits within any one of them.

   a. **Inventory/stock in trade:** Section 1221(1) excludes from the definition of a capital asset stock in trade, inventory, and property held by the taxpayer for sale to customers in the ordinary course of business. These three types of property are referred to collectively as "inventory," although there may be some arcane differences among the three. The rationale for excluding these types of property from the definition of a capital asset is that sales of such assets should generate operating business income or loss.

      i. **Definition—*Malat v. Riddell*, 383 U.S. 569 (1966):** The taxpayer was a joint venturer in the purchase of a parcel of land, which was later subdivided and sold. The issue was whether the parcels sold were "property held . . . primarily for sale to customers 'in the ordinary course of his trade or business.' " Using the "plain meaning" rule of statutory construction, the Court defined "primarily" as "of first importance" or "principal," rather than using the IRS's proffered definition of "substantial." The Court remanded for reconsideration using this definition.

      ii. **Investors, traders, and dealers—*Van Suetendael v. Commissioner*, 3 T.C.M. 987 (1944), *aff'd*, 152 F.2d 654 (2d Cir. 1945):** The taxpayer's primary activity was the purchase and sale of stocks and other securities. The taxpayer reported the gains and losses as ordinary, on the theory that the assets were noncapital assets under §1221(1). When the Commissioner asserted that the assets were capital, the taxpayer argued that he was a dealer in securities, and thus the securities were noncapital assets.

         (a) **Issue:** Were the securities capital assets?

         (b) **Result and rationale:** The securities were capital assets. The court viewed the issue as the nature of the assets themselves, as capital or noncapital, rather than the status of the taxpayer as a dealer. The nature of the securities depended on whether the taxpayer held them primarily for sale to customers in the ordinary course of business. Several facts suggested that the taxpayer did not hold the securities in this manner:

         ■ He did not purchase them at wholesale;

         ■ He purchased small quantities;

- His portfolio was diversified; and

- He resold most of the securities to or through the same broker from whom he acquired them.

(c) **Section 1236—Safe harbor for dealers:** In order to generate capital gain or loss on sale of securities, dealers in securities must clearly identify securities as held for investment on the day the securities are acquired and must not hold them for sale in the ordinary course of business. IRC §1236(a), (b).

iii. **Real estate factual inquiry—*Biehenharn Realty Co., Inc. v. United States,* 526 F.2d 409 (5th Cir.), *cert. denied,* 429 U.S. 819 (1976):** The taxpayer purchased property in 1923 and over the years subdivided and sold parcels.

(a) **Issue:** Were the parcels capital or noncapital assets, i.e., were the lots property held by the taxpayer primarily for sale to customers in the ordinary course of its trade or business?

(b) **Result and rationale:** The lots were inventory (noncapital assets). The determination of this issue depended on the court's analysis of the seven factors enunciated in *United States v. Winthrop,* 417 F.2d 905 (5th Cir. 1969), as follows:

- *Number, extent, and continuity of sales:* The court considered this the most important factor, concluding that the sales were sufficient for noncapital treatment.

- *Extent of subdividing, developing, and advertising:* The taxpayer "vigorously improved" its subdivisions, suggesting noncapital treatment.

- *Taxpayer's efforts to sell:* While the taxpayer did not engage in traditional advertising, the court found this was not necessary to noncapital treatment when business was brisk, and the development activity itself attracted customers.

- *Character and degree of supervision and control over agents:* While use of independent agents may at times shield a taxpayer from the activities of those agents, the court suggests that this only applies when the agents have complete discretion over sales, which these agents did not have. In addition, the taxpayer itself made some sales without agents. Together, these factors suggested noncapital treatment.

- *Time and effort habitually devoted to sales:* The taxpayer argued that its business manager devoted only 10% of his time to real estate dealings, and most of that time was for management of rental properties. The court discounted this factor, on the theory that the time devoted to sales will not be determinative when business is brisk.

- *Use of business office:* The taxpayer shared a business office and employed the usual accouterments of business, suggesting noncapital treatment.

- *Nature and purpose of acquisition:* The Commissioner argued that the taxpayer's intent upon acquisition should be irrelevant, and the sole focus should be the activity at the time of sale. The court rejected this approach, preserving the possibility that prior investment intent will continue when external factors beyond the control of the taxpayer force sale of the property in circumstances that would otherwise suggest noncapital treatment. This did not save Biehenharn Realty Company, however, and the court concluded that the lots sold were noncapital assets generating ordinary income.

iv. **Section 1237—Safe harbor:** Section 1237 provides a safe harbor for taxpayers other than C corporations that improve and sell parcels of land. Under §1237, a tract of real property will not be treated as inventory if (1) the taxpayer has never held the tract as inventory and holds no other real property as inventory, (2) the taxpayer has made no "substantial improvement" to the property at the time of sale, and (3) the taxpayer held the tract for at least five years. IRC §1237(a). An improvement will not be considered to be a "substantial improvement" if the taxpayer held the tract for at least ten years; the improvements constitute the building or installation of water, sewer, and drainage facilities or roads that must be made in order for the tract to be marketable; and the taxpayer elects not to make any adjustment to the basis of the property as a result of the improvements. IRC §1237(b)(3). A special rule applies to characterize a portion of the gain on the sale of more than five lots as ordinary. IRC §1237(b)(1).

b. **Real and depreciable property:** Section 1221(2) excludes from the definition of a capital asset real property used in a trade or business, or property used in a trade or business that is subject to depreciation under §167. This is called "Section 1231 property." See this chapter, section (IV).

c. **Creative works:** Section 1221(3) excludes from the definition of a capital asset items such as copyrights, compositions, letters, or memoranda by a taxpayer who created them, hired others to create them, or received them in a transaction in which gain or loss was not recognized in whole or in part.

Example: Dave writes a book about federal court litigation. He holds the copyright. Big Publisher, Inc. wishes to acquire all rights to the book, and pays him $10,000 for the copyright. Because Dave created the work, the asset is not a capital asset in his hands and its sale generates ordinary income.

d. **Accounts/notes receivable:** Section 1221(4) excludes from the definition of a capital asset any accounts or notes receivable from the sale of inventory or stock in trade. In a sense, accounts or notes receivable of this kind are simply a transformation of inventory or stock in trade. Because sales of inventory or stock in trade generate ordinary income or loss, so too should dispositions of accounts or notes receivable from the sale of inventory.

Example: Connie's Crafts has accounts receivable of $40,000 for sales of silk flowers. As a cash-basis taxpayer, Connie's has a zero basis in the receivables. Connie's sells the accounts receivable to Friendly Bank for $35,000. This sale generates ordinary income rather than capital gain because the accounts receivable are not a capital asset.

e. **Supplies used in a business:** Section 1221(a)(8) excludes from the definition of a capital asset supplies customarily consumed by a taxpayer in his or her trade or business.

3. **"Related to" the trade or business—*Corn Products* and *Arkansas Best*:** Because sales of inventory and accounts receivable generate ordinary income and loss, the question arises

whether other types of income or loss that are closely connected with the taxpayer's trade or business should also generate ordinary income or loss. In *Corn Products* (1955), the U.S. Supreme Court arguably allowed property closely connected with a trade or business to be considered a noncapital asset. In *Arkansas Best* (1988), the Court held that the relationship between the taxpayer's business and the asset is irrelevant and interpreted *Corn Products* very narrowly to mean that inventory may include "inventory substitutes."

a. ***Corn Products Refining Co. v. Commissioner,* 350 U.S. 46 (1955), *rehearing denied,* 350 U.S. 943 (1956):** The taxpayer was in the business of manufacturing products from grain corn. To ensure a long-term supply of corn at a favorable price, Corn Products purchased "futures contracts" in corn. A futures contract is an agreement to buy or sell a specific amount of a commodity at a stated price on a specific date in the future. Thus, when it entered into a futures contract, it agreed to purchase corn at a specific price. If the corn prices in the general market were favorable, Corn Products sold these futures contracts and purchased grain as needed. In some years it realized a profit on the sale of the futures contracts; in others, it realized a loss. Because Corn Products Co. had net gains during the years from these contracts, it claimed that the gains and losses on the sales of the futures contracts were capital rather than ordinary, arguing that because the contracts were separate from its business of manufacturing corn products.

   i. **Issue:** Were the futures contracts capital assets, so that their sale generated capital gain or loss?

   ii. **Result and rationale:** The futures contracts were noncapital assets, which generated ordinary income or loss upon disposition. According to the Court, they were an integral part of the profits and losses generated by the business, which Congress intended to be taxed as ordinary income or loss. The Court construed the exceptions to capital asset status broadly to effectuate its view of Congressional purpose: to apply the preferential capital gains rate only to transactions that are not usual in the course of business.

b. ***Arkansas Best Corp. v. Commissioner,* 485 U.S. 212 (1988):** Relying on *Corn Products,* many taxpayers successfully classified items as "connected with" their trade or business (to produce ordinary loss) or "not connected with" their trade or business (to produce capital gain). Arkansas Best wanted to be one of these taxpayers. It purchased stock in a Dallas bank, which it ultimately sold at a loss. Some of the stock was purchased as an investment, but the taxpayer also purchased stock when the bank was having financial difficulties. The taxpayer asserted that the reason for these purchases was to protect its business reputation. The taxpayer argued that the latter block of stock was a noncapital asset, and thus the loss was ordinary because it was connected with its trade or business. The Commissioner asserted that all of the stock was a capital asset, generating a capital loss on sale.

   i. **Issue:** Was the stock purchased while the bank was in financial difficulty a capital asset?

   ii. **Result and rationale:** The stock was a capital asset. The Court rejected the interpretation of *Corn Products* as treating as noncapital any asset connected with a taxpayer's business, on the grounds that the specific language of §1221 ("whether or not connected with his trade or business") precludes any such inquiry. It thus rejected any inquiry into the taxpayer's motive in acquiring the stock. The Court viewed *Corn Products* as merely interpreting §1221(1)'s inventory exception to capital asset treatment: the futures contracts were substitutes for the raw material from which inventory was created and therefore were a type of inventory. Since in *Arkansas Best* the stock was not in any sense an "inventory substitute," it was a capital asset generating capital loss on sale.

E. Special recharacterization provisions—Recapture and small business stock

Recognized gain or loss on the sale or exchange of a capital asset will usually be capital. However, specific Code provisions may in certain cases recharacterize all or a portion of this gain or loss as ordinary. This section discusses two of these provisions: recapture and losses on the sale of small business stock.

1. Recapture—General approach: The recapture provisions potentially recharacterize gain on the sale of property as ordinary rather than capital as a means of "recapturing" (i.e., paying back) the benefit the taxpayer enjoyed when he or she claimed depreciation deductions with respect to the property, which reduces his or her ordinary income.

a. Section 1245—Personal property

i. General rule: Section 1245(a) provides that a taxpayer's gain on the disposition of "§1245 property" will be treated as ordinary income to the extent of the difference between the lower of (1) the taxpayer's "recomputed basis" or (2) the amount realized (for sales) or fair market value (for transactions other than sales), exceeds the taxpayer's adjusted basis in the property. Thus, the recapture amount (the ordinary income) will be the lesser of the realized gain or the depreciation claimed. For a three-step method for calculating the recapture, using the technical terms of the statute, see Figure 12C—Calculation of §1245 Ordinary Income.

Figure 12C
Calculation of §1245 Ordinary Income

Step 1:	Is the transaction a sale? If so, compute amount realized. If it is not a sale, determine the fair market value of the property transferred.
Step 2:	Determine the "recomputed basis," which is equal to the adjusted basis of the property transferred plus the cumulative depreciation claimed on the property.
Step 3:	Take the *lower* of the amount in Step 1 and Step 2, and subtract from it the adjusted basis in the property.

ii. Definitional issues: The key to understanding §1245 is grasping its definitions and applying them to the general rule.

(a) Section 1245 property: Section 1245 property is personal property that is used in a taxpayer's trade or business and certain other property (but not buildings or structural components of buildings). IRC §1245(a)(3).

(b) Recomputed basis: The *recomputed basis* of property is its adjusted basis plus all the depreciation attributable to the property taken by the taxpayer. IRC §1245(a)(2). For this purpose, depreciation includes all cost recovery deductions, including §179 deductions. IRC §1245(a)(2)(C).

> **Example:** Keith purchased a computer for $5,000 for business use. He claimed $2,000 of the cost of the computer as a §179 expense in the year he purchased it, and later claimed $600 of depreciation deductions with respect to the computer. His adjusted basis is $2,400 in the computer, and its recomputed basis is equal to the adjusted basis plus depreciation deductions claimed, or $5,000 (its original basis).

iii. **Special rules and exceptions:** Recapture does not apply in certain transactions that are otherwise tax-free, including transfers by gift and at death. IRC §1245(b)(1), (2). For certain transactions that are generally tax-free to the transferors, the recapture amount is limited to the amount of gain recognized on the transfer. IRC §1245(b)(3). A special rule that applies to like-kind exchanges and involuntary conversions requires recapture in the amount of the gain recognized plus the fair market value of any non-1245 property received that is not boot. See IRC §1245(b)(4).

iv. **Related material:** Section 1245 is intimately connected with the notion of capital recovery through depreciation deductions. Depreciation is discussed in Chapter 7(III).

b. **Section 1250—Real property:** Section 1250 requires that "additional depreciation" taken with respect to "§1250 property" be cast as ordinary income upon the sale of that property. IRC §1250(a)(1). Additional depreciation is the depreciation claimed with respect to an item of property in excess of the amount that would have been allowable had the taxpayer used the straight-line method of depreciation. IRC §1250(a)(2). Thus, §1250 recaptures only the accelerated portion of depreciation. Section 1250 was at one time of more importance than it is today. Because all buildings and their structural components placed in service after 1986 are required to be depreciated using the straight-line method, there is generally no additional depreciation to be recaptured on buildings placed in service after 1986. Disposition of a building placed in service prior to 1987 will generate §1250 recapture, but for the most part, §1250 is not of major importance today.

2. **Sale of depreciable property to related person—§1239:** If a taxpayer sells property that is depreciable to a controlled entity, such as a corporation in which he or she owns more than 50% of the stock, the recognized gain will be ordinary, not capital.

3. **Small business stock—§1244:** As a special incentive to investors in small businesses, §1244 allows a taxpayer to treat losses on the sale or worthlessness of stock in certain small business corporations as ordinary rather than capital losses.

a. **Only individuals and partnerships:** Only individuals and partnerships may take advantage of this provision, and only if they are the original holders of the stock. IRC §1244(a).

b. **Dollar limitations:** The maximum amount of the loss that can be treated as ordinary is $50,000 for a single taxpayer or $100,000 for a married couple filing a joint return. IRC §1244(b).

c. **Qualifying business stock:** The corporation issuing the stock must be a "small business corporation." It must issue the stock in exchange for money or other property (not services) and must have derived more than 50% of its income from active business sources within the five year period ending on the date of the loss. IRC §1244(c)(1). A small business corporation is one whose capital does not exceed $1,000,000. IRC §1244(c)(3).

d. Other technical requirements: Section 1244 also contains certain other technical requirements that are beyond the scope of most introductory tax courses.

Example: Alicia and Mike form AlMike Corp., each contributing $100,000 to the corporation in exchange for stock. AlMike is engaged in the business of selling prepaid telephone cards. After several years of profitability, a new telephone excise tax forces AlMike out of business, and Alicia and Mike's stock becomes worthless. Under §165(g), worthlessness would generate a capital loss of $100,000 for each shareholder. If, however, the stock qualifies as §1244 stock, Alicia and Mike will be able to treat at least a portion of this loss as ordinary rather than capital. Alicia is a single taxpayer, and therefore if §1244 applies, she may treat $50,000 of the loss as ordinary; the remaining $50,000 is a capital loss to her, subject to the usual restrictions. Mike is married, and therefore if §1244 applies, he and his wife may claim the full $100,000 as an ordinary loss on their joint return in the year of worthlessness.

IV. SECTION 1231—REAL AND DEPRECIABLE PROPERTY USED IN A TRADE OR BUSINESS

As mentioned in the last section, §1221(2) excludes from the definition of a capital asset real and depreciable property used in a taxpayer's trade or business. Alone, this would suggest that the disposition of such assets generates ordinary income or loss. However, §1231 specifically addresses the character of gain or loss from the sale of this type of property, offering the taxpayer-friendly rule that net gains are generally capital, and net losses are generally ordinary.

A. Policy

The taxpayer-friendly approach of §1231 was enacted to encourage taxpayers to sell or exchange their business properties during World War II.

B. General approach—§1231 Gains and losses

Figure 12D—Section 1231 Gains and Losses—illustrates the general approach of §1231. The first question is whether the property in question is "§1231 property" (see Box {1}). If not, §1231 does not apply, and the character of the gain or loss is determined under IRC §1221 and related sections. If, however, the property sold or exchanged is §1231 property, the next question is whether the recapture rules (see this chapter, section III(E)) applies, because any amount treated as ordinary income under IRC §§1245 or 1250 is not eligible for §1231 treatment (see Box {2}). Then, the taxpayer determines if the recognized losses from casualties involving §1231 assets exceed recognized gains from such casualties (see Box {3}). IRC §1231(a)(4)(C). If so, both losses and gains of this type are not included in the next step of the netting process, and their character will be ordinary. Reg. §1.1231-1(e)(3). If the casualty losses do not exceed gains, these gains and losses are incorporated into the next step. In this step, the taxpayer nets his or her §1231 gains and §1231 losses (see Box {4}). If a net loss is the result of the netting process, then all §1231 gains and losses for the year are treated as ordinary. IRC §1231(a)(2). If the result of netting is a net gain, then all §1231 gains and losses for the year are treated as capital unless a special recapture rule applies (see Box {5}). IRC §1231(a)(1), (c).

Figure 12D
Section 1231 Gains and Losses

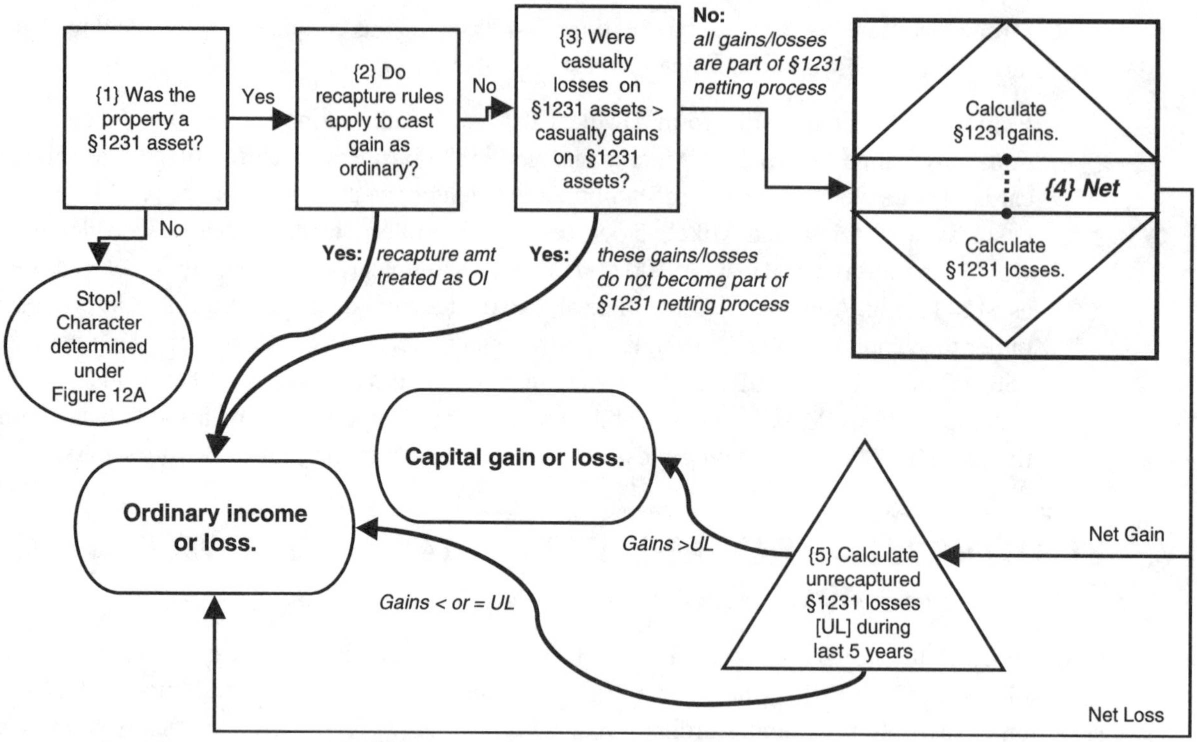

C. **Statutory analysis—§1231**

1. **General rule:** The general rule of §1231 is deceptively simple to state: If §1231 gains exceed §1231 losses for the year, all §1231 gains and losses are treated as capital. If §1231 losses exceed §1231 gains for the year, all §1231 gains and losses are treated as ordinary.

2. **Definitional issues:** The key to applying §1231 is understanding the definition of §1231 gains and losses and applying this understanding to the process described in Figure 12D.

   a. **The disposition of §1231 property generates §1231 gains and losses:** There are two types of §1231 gains and losses.

      i. **Sales of business property:** The most common is recognized gain and loss that arises from the sale or exchange of real or depreciable property used in the taxpayer's trade or business. IRC §1231(a)(3).

      ii. **Conversions:** Section 1231 gain or loss also includes gain or loss recognized on the involuntary conversion (including condemnation) of property which was used in the taxpayer's trade or business or of any capital asset held for more than one year and held in connection with the taxpayer's trade or business. IRC §1231(a)(3).

   b. **Property used in the trade or business:** Property used in the trade or business of the taxpayer means property that the taxpayer actually uses in the business, which is held for more than one year and which is either real property or property subject to depreciation, such as equipment. IRC §1231(b)(1). It does not include inventory.

c. **Two-step netting process:** *Netting* means subtracting losses from gains, and ending up with the net result, which is either a gain or a loss.

i. **Netting of involuntary conversion gains and losses:** If a taxpayer's recognized loss from the involuntary conversion of §1231 property by fire, storm, theft, or other casualty exceeds recognized gains from such events, the gain and the loss are excluded from the general process of netting §1231 gains and losses. IRC §1231(a)(4)(C); see Box {3} in Figure 12D. Instead, the character of these gains is determined under §1222 and related statutes, which will result in the taxpayer having an ordinary loss. Reg. §1.1231-1(e)(3). If losses do not exceed gains, both gains and losses are included in the general netting process. IRC §1231(a)(4)(C).

ii. **Netting of §1231 gains and losses:** All §1231 gains and losses are added up, and losses are subtracted from gains. The net result is either a net §1231 gain or a net §1231 loss.

Example: Warren experiences the following events with respect to properties A, B, C, and D, all of which are depreciable properties used in his trade or business. Property A is destroyed by fire, and Warren recognizes a $100,000 loss on this property. Property B is stolen, and Warren recognizes a $30,000 gain when he collects the insurance proceeds. He sells properties C and D, recognizing a $150,000 gain and $60,000 loss, respectively. In determining the character of these gains and losses, Warren will exclude from the §1231 netting process the loss and gain on the involuntary conversions of properties A and B because his recognized losses from such dispositions exceed gains. The character of the loss and gain on properties A and B will be determined under §1222. Since §1222 excludes from the definition of a capital asset depreciable property used in a trade or business, these assets are noncapital and produce ordinary gain of $30,000 and ordinary loss of $100,000. Warren will be able to deduct the loss attributable to property A under IRC §165(g) and this will offset the ordinary income from property B. Then, the netting process applicable to properties C and D will produce a net §1231 gain of $90,000, which will be treated as capital, assuming Warren has no unrecaptured losses (see below).

3. **Special rules and exceptions**

a. **Recapture:** If in any year, §1231 gains exceed §1231 losses, the general rule will characterize all §1231 gains and losses for that year as capital. However, the special loss recapture rule may limit this favorable characterization. If the taxpayer has had, within the previous five years, a §1231 loss that was characterized as ordinary, the current year's gain must be characterized as ordinary to the extent of that previous loss. IRC §1231(c)(1). This is known as a "recaptured loss," which only needs to be recaptured once. Id.

Example: In Year 1, Sandy opened her sandwich shop business. In that year, Sandy had §1231 losses in excess of §1231 gains of $5,000, and she reported a $5,000 ordinary loss. In Year 2, she had §1231 gains in excess of §1231 losses in the amount of $7,000. This gain would be capital under the general rule of §1231, except that Sandy is required to recapture the previous loss, so that she must treat $5,000 of her Year 2 gain as ordinary, and the remaining $2,000 is capital under the general rule of §1231. If in Year 3 Sandy has a net §1231 gain of $3,000, all of this will be capital because she has already recaptured the previous year's loss.

b. **Effect of §1211:** As discussed in section (II)(B) of this chapter, section 1211 limits the deductibility of capital losses to the amount of capital gain for the year and, for individuals,

$3,000 of ordinary income. However, in determining whether §1231 gains exceed §1231 losses, the §1211 limitation is ignored.

4. **Related material:** Section 1231 is intimately related to §1221. The category of property removed from the definition of capital asset by §1221(2) is the category specifically addressed by §1231. Thus, if one concludes that an item is not a capital asset because of §1221(2), one must consider how §1231 characterizes the gain or loss upon the sale of the asset. Also, the treatment of §1231 gains and losses of individuals must be considered in connection with the different categories of capital gain income.

5. **Summary**

   a. *Are we lost yet?:* When the process described above and in Figure 12D is complete, the taxpayer should have a net §1231 gain or a net §1231 loss. (Along the way, recapture amounts, casualty losses, and gains may have been separately segregated and gains may have been recaptured; those are separate from the basic net §1231 gain or loss.) If there is a net §1231 gain, it is included in the computation of net capital gain or net capital loss described in section V of this chapter. If the result is a net §1231 loss, it is an ordinary loss, which will be deductible as an ordinary loss on the taxpayer's tax return, unless some special rule denies or defers deductibility.

   b. **See Statute Summary—§1231**

Statute Summary—§1231

Parsing Step	§1231
General rule	If §1231 gains > §1231 losses, then all are capital If §1231 losses > §1231 gains, then all are ordinary
Definitional issues	§1231 gains and losses: business property
Special rules and exceptions	Involuntary conversion losses > gains Loss recapture rule; §1211
Related material	Capital asset definition: §1221 Casualty losses in a trade or business: §165

V. CALCULATING NET CAPITAL GAIN AND NET CAPITAL LOSS

There are two final steps in dealing with character issues. First, the taxpayer's net capital gain or loss must be determined. Then, the tax rate on net capital gain must be computed, along with the deductible net capital loss, if any.

A. An approach—Overview

The ultimate tax on capital gains and the availability of a deduction for capital losses depends on a number of factors: how long the taxpayer has owned the property before selling it (the "holding period"), the type of asset, the taxpayer's tax bracket for ordinary income, and when the property

Figure 12E
Process of Computing Net Capital Gain or Net Capital Loss

	Short-Term Capital Gain and Loss	Long-Term 28% Capital Gain and Loss	Long-Term 25% Capital Gain (Not loss)	Long-Term 15/5% Capital Gain and Loss & Net §1231 Gain	STEP – AS OUTLINED IN TEXT
A. Add capital gains in each category					*Step One—* See pages 288-291
B. Add capital losses in each category			(shaded)		*Step One—* See pages 288-291
C. *Net* the capital gains and losses in each category (A-B)			____, but not more than net §1231 gain.		*Step Two–* See page 291
D. Apply 28% loss (if any) to other categories	Does not offset	(shaded)	(1) From 28%:____ Net 25% LTCG remaining:__	(2) From 28%:____ Net 15/5% LTCG remaining:__	*Step Three—* See pages 291-292
E. Apply 15/5% loss (if any) to other categories	Does not offset	(1) From 15/5%:____ Net 28% LTCG remaining:__	(2) From 15/5%:____ Net 25% LTCG remaining:___	(shaded)	*Step Three—* See pages 291-292
F. Apply ST loss (if any) to other gain categories	(shaded)	(1) From ST:____	(2) From ST:____	(3) From ST:____	*Step Three—* See pages 291-292
G. Net capital gain *or* net capital loss remaining					*Step Three—* See pages 291-292
H. Max. tax rate or deduction?					*Step Four—* See pages 292 and Chapter 13

was purchased and sold. If this sounds complicated—*it is*. The best way to approach the problem is to divide it into a number of smaller steps. Figure 12E provides a chart that will organize these steps for any problem.

■ *Step 1:* First, identify and categorize the taxpayer's items of capital gain and capital loss into four different categories: short-term capital gain and loss, 28% capital gain and loss, 25% capital gain, and 15/5% capital gain or loss. (What's in these categories is described below.) These are Rows A and B in Figure 12E.

■ *Step 2:* Next, net each category of gain and loss. *Netting* means subtracting losses from gains, and ending up with the net result. For example, short-term capital gain is netted against short-term capital loss, and the result is either net short-term capital gain or short-term capital loss. Because there are no losses in the 25% category, there is no netting in this category; it will always result in either zero or a gain. In addition, the 25% gain cannot exceed a taxpayer's total net §1231 gain. This is Row C in Figure 12E.

■ *Step 3:* Losses in each category are used to reduce any net gains in other categories. There is a precise order in which losses must be applied against income, and this approach is discussed below. This is represented in Rows D, E, and F in Figure 12E. The result is a net capital gain or a net capital loss in each category. This is Row G in Figure 12E.

■ *Step 4:* Finally: "*so what*?" Net gains in each category are included in gross income, but they are taxed at special rates depending on the category. If the result is a net capital loss, individuals may offset $3,000 of ordinary income per year with these net losses, and the losses carry back and forward to past or future years to offset other gains, retaining their character in those years. Corporate taxpayers may only deduct capital losses against capital gains. This is Row H in Figure 12E.

B. Step 1: Categorize capital gains and losses

1. **Overview:** In this step, the taxpayer's capital gains and losses must be classified into two different kinds of gains or losses: short-term or long-term capital gains or losses. Then, all long-term gains and losses must be allocated among three different kinds of gain or loss: 28% capital gain or loss, 25% capital gain, or 15/5% capital gain or loss. See Rows A and B in Figure 12E.

2. **Holding period:** The calculation of net capital gain and net capital loss depends partly on the proper determination of the ***holding period*** (short- or long-term) for assets sold or exchanged during the taxable year. The period of time during which a taxpayer owns an asset (or is deemed to hold an asset) is the taxpayer's holding period. Holding an asset for one year or less qualifies as short-term, while holding it for longer than a year qualifies as long-term. IRC §1222. A holding period usually begins with the taxpayer's acquisition of an asset by purchase. For transactions other than purchases, however, a taxpayer may in certain cases be allowed to "tack" onto his or her actual ownership of an asset other periods of time during which he or she held other property, or another taxpayer held the property.

   a. **Exchanged basis property:** If a taxpayer receives property in an exchange that is totally or partially tax-deferred (such as IRC §1031 and §1033), the holding period of the property received in the exchange will include not only the taxpayer's actual ownership period of the property received but also the period during which the taxpayer owned the property given in the exchange. IRC §1223(1). This only applies if the property exchanged was a capital asset or §1231 property. Id.

Example: In a qualifying §1031 exchange, Edward exchanged Greenacre for Paul's Whiteacre, with Paul paying Edward an additional $10,000 to account for Greenacre's greater value. Edward recognized only $10,000 of his realized gain on the transaction, and Edward's basis in Whiteacre was determined by reference to his basis in Greenacre. Thus, Edward's holding period in Whiteacre included his period of actual ownership of Whiteacre plus the period of time during which he owned Greenacre.

b. **Transferred basis property:** If a taxpayer receives property in a transaction in which the taxpayer's basis is determined by reference to another person's basis in that same property, the taxpayer's holding period includes not only the period during which the taxpayer actually owns the property, but also the period of time during which the other person held the property. IRC §1223(2). This rule applies, for example, to gifts and property received in a divorce.

Example: Bruce and Demi are getting a divorce. The divorce decree provides that Demi will take the house and Bruce will take the stock in their family corporation in full satisfaction of all claims. In later determining the holding period of these assets, both Bruce and Demi will include in their holding periods the period of time that they held the stock and house as a married couple. This is because §1041 calculates the basis of the property in each former spouse's hands by reference to the basis of the property in the hands of the marital unit.

c. **Property received from a decedent:** A special rule allows a taxpayer to treat property as having been held for more than one year (regardless of a lesser period of actual ownership) if the basis of the property is determined under §1014 (property received from a decedent), and the taxpayer sells the property within one year of the decedent's death. IRC §1223(11). This allows heirs promptly to dispose of property they receive by inheritance without short-term capital gain treatment.

Example: Vicki inherited 1,000 shares of ZAZEL, Inc. from her grandfather. She sold them six months after receiving them, when they had risen in value. Vicki's actual holding period is six months, but she will be considered to have held the stock for more than one year under the special rule relating to property received from a decedent.

d. **Identification:** A taxpayer selling some but not all of a group of assets may designate which items he or she sells.

Example: Peter purchased 100 shares of ABC stock in each month of Year 1. In February of Year 2 he sells 50 shares at a gain. He may designate these 50 shares as from the lot purchased in January of Year 1 in order to ensure that the gain is long-term capital gain.

3. **Types of long-term gain or loss**

a. **Overview:** All long-term (not short-term) capital gain and loss must be placed into one of three categories. Both gains and losses for a particular kind of asset goes into that category, for later netting (see Step 2 above and Rows A and B in Figure 12E).

b. **28% capital gain and loss:** This category of gain and loss is made up mostly of gain and loss on the sale of "collectibles," such as coins, stamps, art, antiques, guns, gems, etc. This group also includes an amount equal to the gain excluded under IRC §1202(a), which applies to certain sales of small business stock. See Chapter 4(XII).

Example: Kate inherited a wine collection from her father. Her basis in the collection is $50,000 (the fair market value of this collection at the time of her father's death). She holds it for longer than one year and sells it for $80,000. The gain is 28% capital gain. If she had sold the wine collection for $40,000, she would have a $10,000 loss in this category.

c. **25% capital gain:** This category of gain is attributable to what is called "unrecaptured Section 1250 gain." This is long-term capital gain, which is not otherwise recaptured as ordinary income, attributable to the taxpayer's previous depreciation of real property. Note that this category does not include any losses. Section 1250 recapture is discussed at this chapter, section (E)(1). The unrecaptured §1250 gain cannot exceed a taxpayer's overall net §1231 gain, which is the excess of §1231 gains over §1231 losses.

Example: Peyton has owned an apartment building for many years. His basis in the building is $400,000. This year, he sells it for $900,000, realizing and recognizing $500,000 of gain. He had claimed $300,000 of depreciation on the property. Because he owned the building at a time when accelerated depreciation was available for real property, some of the gain on the sale is §1250 gain, which is recharacterized as ordinary income on sale. Let us assume this amount is $50,000 of the total $300,000 of depreciation claimed. As a result, the "unrecaptured 1250 gain" is the total depreciation taken ($300,000) minus the recaptured amount ($50,000), or $250,000. In this example, Peyton's "25% capital gain" is $250,000 and $100,000 is 15/5% gain (see below).

d. **15/5% capital gain and loss:** This category includes all capital gain and loss not included in the other two categories. In other words, it is the residual category; if gain or loss doesn't belong in either of the other two categories, it is placed in the 15/5% category. The 5% rate applies to taxpayers whose regular tax rate is 10% or 15%, thereby giving them the tax preference for capital gains (if taxpayers whose normal tax rate is 10% were subject to a 15% capital gains rate, the capital gain rate would impose an additional tax burden on them, instead of giving them a benefit; similarly, a taxpayer in a 15% bracket enjoys no benefit from a 15% capital gains tax).

Example: Mike sells ABC stock for $100,000. He has a basis of $50,000 in the stock. It does not qualify for the IRC §1202 exclusion. Because ABC stock is not a collectible, and it clearly isn't real estate subject to recapture, the gain on sale is included in the 15/5% capital gain category. If he had sold the stock for $30,000, he would have had a $20,000 loss in this category.

e. **Section 1231 gains and recapture**

   i. **Section 1231 gains:** As discussed in section IV of this chapter, net §1231 gains are treated as long-term capital gains. The IRS has stated that these should be characterized as 28%, 25%, or 15/5% gains and placed in the appropriate category, see Notice 97-59, 1997-45 I.R.B. 1, which would raise the entire operation to new heights of complexity. This is not what actually happens, however, so you are safe simply assigning a net §1231 gain to the 15/5% category—where it would probably be anyway.

   ii. **Loss recapture:** The loss recapture rule provides that if, in the previous five years, the taxpayer has had net §1231 losses, net gains are recharacterized as ordinary income until all those previous losses have been offset. As part of categorizing capital gains, the recapture rule must be applied to reduce gains in the various categories, in the order required by statute: 28%, 25%, and 15/5%. IRC §1(h)(8). Only after this recapture rule is applied can the next step commence.

C. Step 2: Netting within each category

In each category, capital gains and losses must be "netted." This means that gains are compared to losses, and the net result (positive, negative, or zero) is the "net" amount for that group. If losses exceed gains, the result will be a net loss. If gains exceed losses, the result will be a net gain. If the losses exactly equal the gains (not likely, but possible), the result will be zero. There are no losses in the 25% category, so that category will always have a positive or zero balance. See Row C in Figure 12E.

Example 1: Cindy has short-term capital gain of $10,000 and a short-term capital loss of $3,000. She has a net short-term capital gain of $7,000.

Example 2: Darla has a 28% capital gain of $50,000 and a 28% capital loss of $60,000. She has a net 28% capital loss of $10,000.

Example 3: Edward has a 25% capital gain of $30,000, a 15/5% capital loss of $20,000, and a 15/5% capital gain of $5,000. He has a 25% capital gain of $30,000 (there are no losses in this category), and a net 15/5% capital loss of $15,000. (Since there can only be gain in the 25% category, there is no netting in that category.)

D. Step 3: Apply net losses against net gains in other categories

1. **Overview:** After Step 2, a taxpayer will have either a net gain or a net loss in each category. Net losses in each category are then applied to reduce gains in the other categories to zero (but not below zero) in a particular order. Losses must be applied to reduce 28% gain first, then 25% gain, and finally to 15/5% gain, *in that order*. See Rows D, E, and F in Figure 12E for the order of applying losses.

2. **Apply (long-term) net 28% capital loss to other categories:** If a taxpayer has a net 28% capital loss, that amount will be applied to reduce net 25% capital gain, and then to reduce net 15/5% capital gain. It does not offset short-term capital gain. See Row D in Figure 12E.

   Example: Gerry has the following:

Net short-term capital gain:	$40,000
Net 28% capital loss:	($30,000)
Net 25% capital gain:	$20,000
Net 15/5% capital gain:	$ 4,000

   Gerry will apply the 28% net capital loss to reduce the 25% gain to zero, and will apply $4,000 of it to eliminate the 15/5% gain entirely. He ends up with a net 28% capital loss of $6,000. The 28% loss does not offset the STCG category.

3. **Apply (long-term) net 15/5% capital loss to other categories:** If a taxpayer has a net 15/5% capital loss, that amount will be applied to reduce net 28% capital gain, and then to reduce net 25% capital gain. It does not offset short-term capital gain. See Row E in Figure 12E.

Example: Hilda has the following:

Net short-term capital gain:	$40,000
Net 28% capital loss:	$30,000
Net 25% capital gain:	$20,000
Net 15/5% capital gain:	($40,000)

Hilda will apply the net 15/5% loss of $40,000 first to reduce the net 28% gain to zero, and will apply the balance to reduce the net 25% capital gain to $10,000. It will not affect the net short-term capital gain.

4. **Apply short-term capital loss to other categories:** If the taxpayer has a net short-term capital loss, and gains in any other category, the net short-term capital loss will be applied to reduce those gains. The short-term capital loss is first applied to reduce 28% gains, if any. Then, if any loss is left over, it is applied to 25% gain, if any. Finally, if there is still short-term capital loss left over, it is applied to 15/5% gain. This is Row F in Figure 12E.

   Example: Fritz has net short-term capital loss of $30,000. He has a $15,000 net 28% gain from the sale of collectibles, no 25% gain, and $50,000 of net 15/5% gain. Fritz will apply the short-term capital loss to reduce the 28% gain of $15,000 to zero, and will then apply the rest of the short-term capital loss to reduce the 15/5% gain by $15,000. As a result, he will have $35,000 of net 15/5% gain, no short-term capital loss and no net 28% loss.

5. **Wait! What about net 25% gain?** Because this category does not include losses, it will never generate a net loss that will be applied to the other categories. Gains in this category can, of course, be reduced by net losses from other categories, as illustrated in the above examples.

E. **Step 4: Apply the right tax rate (or claim the right deduction)**

1. **Overview:** After all the steps described above and in Figure 12E are completed, the result will be a net capital gain or a net capital loss in each category. The final question is the maximum tax rate on each of these kinds of gain or whether the taxpayer will be entitled to a deduction for a net loss. This is Row H in Figure 12E.

2. **Tax rates for net gain—in general:** The categories of capital gain and loss (28%, 25%, and 15/5%) also define their generally applicable maximum tax rate. Thus, net 28% capital gain (after application of losses from other categories) is taxed at a 28% rate, net 25% capital gain is taxed at the 25% rate. Net 15/5% capital gain is generally taxed at a 15% rate, unless the taxpayer's regular rate is 15% or 10%, in which case he or she can take advantage of the 5% rate. However, in each category, this rate is the maximum rate at which the gain will be taxed; if a taxpayer's rate applicable to his or her other income is lower, the gain will be taxed at that lower rate (after all, the tax preference for capital gains is intended to be a benefit to the taxpayer—not a punishment.) Net short-term capital gain is taxed at the rates applicable to ordinary income. See Chapter 13 (II)(B).

3. **Deduction for capital losses:** If the end result of the netting and loss application process is a net capital loss, the restrictions of §1211 apply. This process has already applied losses against capital gains, and so the taxpayer will be entitled to offset up to $3,000 of ordinary income with the loss, and the rest will carry to other years. The loss retains its categorization in future years. For example, an unused net 28% capital loss will retain its character as such, and will be applied in the same manner in a future year as if it has arisen in that year.

F. A comprehensive example

Eleanor, a taxpayer in the 35% bracket for ordinary income, experiences the following transactions in Year 1:

1. Sale of land held for more than one year: $50,000 loss
2. Sale of XYZ Stock held for less than one year: $30,000 loss
3. Sale of DEF Stock held for less than one year: $10,000 gain
4. Sale of sports memorabilia collection held for more than one year: $10,000 loss
5. Sale of wine collection held for more than one year: $15,000 gain.
6. Sale of Property #1, real estate, that she had purchased for $100,000. She had held it as a rental property, and had claimed $30,000 of MACRS deductions with respect to that property. She sold it for $140,000. This is §1231 property.
7. Net §1231 gain on the sale of equipment used in her trade or business: $10,000.

The chart on the following page, based on Figure 12E, summarizes the tax consequences of these transactions to Eleanor.

VI. WHERE ARE WE GOING?

This chapter concludes the discussion of the computation of a taxpayer's taxable income. By now, you probably are becoming a big fan of tax simplification. The discussion of tax rates on capital gains in this section will be revisited in the next chapter, as part of the larger discussion of tax rates on ordinary income and special alternative minimum tax rates.

Quiz Yourself on
CHARACTER OF INCOME AND LOSS

104. Your best friend is applying to be an IRS auditor. She's been studying for weeks and is very nervous about the upcoming test. She calls you and asks: "Why is it, exactly, that taxpayers seek to characterize income as ordinary and loss as capital?" Please answer her. _____

105. Wally is a sole proprietor engaged in the business of selling hand-carved duck decoys. Which of the following is *not* a capital asset in his hands: (1) his residence, (2) his supply of wood, (3) his stamp collection, (4) his antique tractor? _____

106. Wally (from the previous question) also owns a van in which he travels to country fairs to display his ducks. He has an adjusted basis of $35,000 in the van. He sells it for $25,000. What is the character of his loss on the sale, and how will he be taxed on it? Alternatively, what if in the same year he sold his display cabinets at a gain of $35,000? _____

107. John is a singer and songwriter. He has a collection of guitars and other musical instruments that he acquired from a famous singer many years ago. He purchased them for $50,000, and has taken $30,000 of depreciation on them. The instruments have appreciated in value and when his wife insists he get a "real job," he sells all of them for $100,000. What are the tax consequences to him of this sale? _____

108. Why are there two rates for the 15/5% category of net capital gain? _____

	Short-Term Capital Gain and Loss	Long-Term 28% Capital Gain and Loss	Long-Term 25% Capital Gain (Not loss)	Long-Term 15/5% Capital Gain and Loss
A. Capital gains	DEF Stock $10,000	Wine Collection $15,000	Property #1 $30,000	Property #1 $40,000 §1231 gain: $10,000
B. Capital losses	XYZ Stock ($30,000)	Memorabilia ($10,000)	NONE	Land ($50,000)
C. Net result (A-B)	Net STCL ($20,000)	Net LTCG $5,000	Net 25% LTCG $30,000	Net 15/5% LTCL ($10,000)
D. Apply 28% loss (if any) to other categories	NOT APPLICABLE: There is no 28% loss.		NOT APPLICABLE: There is no 28% loss.	NOT APPLICABLE: There is no 28% loss.
E. Apply 15/5% loss (if any) to other categories	Does not offset	From 15/5%: ($5,000) Net 28% LTCG remaining: -0-	(2) From 15/5%: ($5,000) Net 25% LTCG remaining: $25,000	
F. Apply S-T loss (if any) to other gain categories		NOT APPLICABLE: No 28% gain remaining	(2) From ST: ($20,000) Net LT 25% gain remaining: $5,000	NOT APPLICABLE: There is no gain to offset.
G. Net capital gain *or* net capital loss	**No net loss remaining in this category: fully applied to other categories.**	**No net gain remaining in this category: fully offset by losses from other categories.**	**Net 25% LTCG $5,000**	**No loss remaining in this category: fully applied to other categories**
H. Tax rate or deduction?	N/A	N/A	**25%**	N/A

109. Corrie purchased a house for $120,000. She used it as a rental, and properly claimed $30,000 of MACRS deductions with respect to it. In due course, she sold it for $150,000. How is she taxed on the gain or loss recognized from this transaction, and why? What if she had sold it for $80,000? _____

110. Andrea had the following transactions during the year: _____

    a.   Sale of land held for more than one year: $5,000 loss

    b.   Sale of ABC Stock held for more than one year: $15,000 gain

    c.   Sale of NOP Stock held for less than one year: $25,000 loss

    d.   Sale of stamp collection held for more than one year: $20,000 gain

    What are the tax consequences of this transaction to Andrea? _____

111. Bev is in the business of manufacturing basketballs. This year, the following events occurred with respect to equipment used in the trade or business: _____

    ■   Property A was destroyed by fire. Loss = $30,000

    ■   Property B was sold. She recognized a gain of $45,000 of which $10,000 was §1245 recapture income

    ■   Property C was sold. She recognized a $15,000 loss on that sale

    What are the tax consequences of these transactions to Bev?

112. In the previous question, what if Bev had experienced a net $5,000 §1231 loss in the previous year? _____

113. What are the principal arguments *for* having a tax preference for capital gain income? Against? Why are there substantial restrictions on the deduction of capital losses? _____

Answers

104. Tell her (gently) that she's got it backwards: Taxpayers seek to characterize income as capital and loss as ordinary. Capital gain income is eligible for preferential tax rates, which save the taxpayer significant amounts of money, as compared to the rates on ordinary income. On the deduction side, there are restrictions on the ability of taxpayers to take deductions for capital losses, while ordinary losses offset ordinary income. Therefore, taxpayers try to characterize income as capital and losses as ordinary.

105. The wood is part of his inventory or supplies and is therefore not a capital asset.

106. The loss on the sale of the van is an IRC §1231 loss because it is attributable to the sale of a depreciable asset used in Wally's trade or business. If §1231 losses exceed gains, the net loss is deductible as an ordinary loss. If §1231 gains exceed losses, they are taxable as capital gain. In this case, if there is only a loss on the sale of the van, it will be an ordinary loss for him. If gains on the sale of the displays exceed the loss on the sale of the van, the gain will be considered capital gain (probably 15/5% gain).

107. John has an $80,000 gain on the sale of the instruments. This would be considered §1231 gain, which would normally be taxed as a capital gain, since there is no reported §1231 loss. However, §1245 will require recapture of the depreciation of $30,000 as ordinary income. The rest would be capital gain, and probably would be considered 28% gain because these are collectible items.

108. The capital gains tax rate is supposed to be less than the rate for ordinary income. For taxpayers in the 15 or 10% bracket, a 15% capital gains rate would not be lower. Therefore, the 5% rate is available for taxpayers in brackets up to 15%.

109. The rental home is a capital asset in Corrie's hands. Her adjusted basis in the property is $90,000 ($120,000 – 30,000). Her gain on the sale is $70,000. None of this is §1250 recapture, so the amount treated as 25% long-term capital gain is equal to the depreciation deductions previously claimed, or $30,000. The remaining $40,000 is 15/5% long-term capital gain. Assuming no other transactions, she will be taxed at 25% on $30,000 of the gain ($7,500) and at either 15% or 5% on the remaining $40,000 gain. If Corrie's sales price had been $80,000, she would have recognized a $10,000 loss on this property, which would have been a 15/5% capital loss. No amount is treated as 25% gain or loss, as that category is triggered only when the taxpayer recognizes certain kinds of gain.

110. Andrea's tax consequences are summarized in the following chart:

	Short-Term Capital Gain and Loss	Long-Term 28% Capital Gain and Loss	Long-Term 25% Capital Gain (Not loss)	Long-Term 15/5% Capital Gain and Loss
A. Capital gains	-0-	$20,000	-0-	$15,000
B. Capital losses	($25,000)	-0-	-0-	($5,000)
C. Net result (A-B)	($25,000)	$20,000	-0-	$10,000
D. Apply 28% loss	NOT APPLICABLE: No loss		NOT APPLICABLE: No loss	NOT APPLICABLE: No loss
E. Apply 15/5% loss	NOT APPLICABLE: No loss	NOT APPLICABLE: No loss		NOT APPLICABLE: No loss
F. Apply S-T Loss (if any) to other gain categories		(2) From ST: ($20,000) Net 28% LTCG remaining: -0-	None	(4) From ST: ($5,000) Net 15/5% LTCG remaining: $5,000
G. Net capital gain *or* net capital loss	-0-	-0-	-0-	$5,000
H. Tax rate or deduction?	N/A	N/A	N/A	15/5%

111. All of these assets appear to be §1231 assets: They are depreciable property (equipment) used in a taxpayer's trade or business. Bev's casualty losses exceed casualty gains, so the loss is excluded from the computation of §1231 gains and losses. The gain on Property A is netted against the loss on Property B, but only $35,000 of the gain on Property A is included in the computation, because the recapture income is ordinary income and cannot be §1231 gain. The netting process produces a net gain of $20,000, which is considered capital in nature.

112. If Bev had experienced a $5,000 loss in the previous year that was characterized as an ordinary loss under §1231, a portion of her gain in the current year—up to that amount of loss—would be considered ordinary. Thus, $5,000 of her gain would be ordinary and the remaining $15,000 would be capital.

113. The principal arguments for having a capital gains preference (a lower tax rate on capital gain income) are: (1) a reduction in the tax rate on investments will increase savings, investment, and economic prosperity; (2) a capital gains preference is said to reduce lock-in (the tendency to hold on to assets rather than putting them to their best economic use) by reducing the tax associated with sale; (3) because capital gains often accrue over many years, requiring the gain to be recognized in a single year (the "bunching" effect) can result in the taxation of gain at the highest marginal rate in the year of recognition, even though the incremental gains might have been taxed at lower rates had they been recognized in the years they accrued, so a capital gains preference reduces the bunching effect; and (4) because the recognized gain upon sale of a capital asset may not represent real gain, but instead may represent inflationary gains, the capital gains preference mitigates the impact of inflation by lowering the tax in the year of sale.

The principal arguments against a capital gains preference is that it introduces new heights of complexity into the tax code, and of course, that it may not have the effects described above.

The rationale for a limitation on capital losses is that allowing a taxpayer to deduct capital losses without limitation would arguably give the taxpayer too much discretion to adjust his or her taxable income by selling only those capital assets that have declined in value.

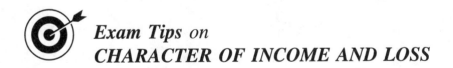

Exam Tips on *CHARACTER OF INCOME AND LOSS*

☞ Warning: Different professors have varying degrees of interest in the technical aspects of calculating net capital gain or loss. Some are happy if you know the different categories of capital gain and are content to leave the rest to a computer program. Others insist that you know the exact process—and can explain it as well as apply it. *Ask your professor about his or her approach.*

☞ Questions of character arise only after there is a determination that gain or loss has been recognized. If there is no recognized income or loss, there is no question of character.

☞ Be able to recognize when a taxpayer is trying to characterize income as capital or a loss as ordinary—and know why. Make sure the requirements for capital gain or loss are met (see Figure 12A).

☛ If there is a sale or exchange of an asset, determine what kind of asset it is: capital, noncapital, or §1231 asset.

☞ *Look for:* Is the taxpayer engaged in a trade or business?

☞ *Analyze:* Business assets are likely to be inventory (noncapital) and §1231 assets. Nonbusiness assets are likely to be capital assets. But the connection with the business isn't the determinative factor. (See *Arkansas Best*.) Study §1221 carefully for the definition of capital assets.

☛ Is there a "deemed" sale or exchange? Even if there is no direct sale, there still may be a sale or exchange leading to capital gain/loss. See Figure 12B.

☛ Know the different kinds of capital gain: 28%, 25%, and 15/5%.

☛ To get ready for any capital gain/loss calculation problem, have your friends pose various scenarios to you (and you to them). Don't stop until the process of Figure 12E is easy for you.

CHAPTER 13

TAX RATES AND CREDITS

ChapterScope

Previous chapters have discussed the computation of taxable income, including the identification of items of gross income and the allowances for deductions. This chapter turns to the crucial last steps in the calculation of the actual tax due—*tax rates* and *tax credits*.

Key concepts in this chapter include:

- **Tax rates applicable to individuals and entities:** Taxable income is multiplied by the appropriate tax rate to determine the tentative tax due (before credits). Tax rates depend on the amount of taxable income and, for individuals, the taxpayer's status as single, married, or head of household. Net capital gain and certain dividend income are subject to special tax rates.

- **Alternative minimum tax:** Taxpayers with certain tax characteristics are subject to an alternate method of computation of taxable income known as the alternative minimum tax or "AMT."

- **Tax credits:** A taxpayer subtracts available tax credits on a dollar-for-dollar basis to determine the actual tax due or refund owed the taxpayer. This chapter discusses the *dependent care credit*, *the earned income credit,* and certain *education credits* in detail, and highlights other available credits.

I. WHERE ARE WE?

In this chapter, we come to the end of the long process of calculating a taxpayer's tax liability: multiplying a taxpayer's taxable income by the appropriate tax rates (depending on type of income, amount of income, and the status of the taxpayer) and subtracting available tax credits. In many tax classes, the actual computation of tax is not emphasized, but embedded in that computation are important questions of the appropriate tax rates, the different taxing methods (regular versus AMT) and policy issues surrounding the appropriate tax rates.

II. TAX RATES

A. Policy

A variety of rate structures are theoretically possible, and selection of the appropriate rate structure generates a great deal of theoretical and political controversy.

1. **Progressive tax rates:** In a progressive rate system, the tax rate increases as taxable income increases, so that higher-income taxpayers pay proportionately more of their income as tax than lower-income taxpayers. The U.S. federal income tax system has historically been a progressive rate system. The major rationales for a progressive tax system include:

   a. **Ability to pay:** Taxpayers with more taxable income have a proportionately higher ability to pay.

b. Decreasing marginal utility: Drawing from the insights of economics, a taxpayer is thought to derive less enjoyment from every additional dollar of income. Thus, the theory goes, it hurts a high-income taxpayer less to pay a higher proportion of his or her income as tax.

2. Flat tax rates: In a flat tax rate system, the same rate is applied to taxable income, regardless of level. Thus, all taxpayers pay the same proportion of their incomes as tax.

3. Regressive tax rates: In a regressive tax rate system, tax rates decrease as income rises. Thus, lower income taxpayers pay proportionately more of their income as tax than higher income taxpayers. Sales taxes are generally thought of as regressive,

B. Current tax rates on ordinary income—regular tax (not AMT)

The 2005 tax rate structure is progressive within a limited range from 10% to 35%. The actual rate of tax depends on the taxpayer's taxable income and filing status.

1. Marginal rates: The tax rates are expressed as marginal rates, i.e., the rate of tax on the last dollar of taxable income. A taxpayer is taxed on the first portion of taxable income (e.g., $6,000 for a single taxpayer) at the lowest marginal rate, the next portion at the second lowest rate, and so on. As a result, the effective rate will be a blended rate of all applicable rates. When a taxpayer complains that additional income will "push me into a higher tax bracket" he or she is saying that the additional income is taxed at a marginal rate higher than the rate he or she previously experienced.

2. Effective rate higher—Phase-outs: The effective rate for high-income taxpayers may be greater than 35% because of the phase-out of the personal exemption (IRC §151(d)(3), see discussion at Chapter 6(XVII) and the overall limitation on itemized deductions (IRC §68, see discussion at Chapter 6(XI)).

3. Inflation adjustments: The taxable income amounts designated in §1 are adjusted each year for inflation, and the IRS publishes the new amounts to reflect these inflation adjustments. IRC §1(f). See, e.g., Rev. Proc. 2004-71, 2004-50 I.R.B. 1.

4. Single taxpayers—2005 rates: Unmarried taxpayers are taxed at the following rates:

Taxable Income	*Marginal Tax Rate*
Not over $7,300	10% of the taxable income
Over $7,300 but not over $29,700	$730 plus 15% of the excess over $7,300
Over $29,700 but not over $71,950	$4,090 plus 25% of the excess over $29,700
Over $71,950 but not over $150,150	$14,652.50 plus 28% of the excess over $71,950
Over $150,150 but not over $326,450	$36,548.50 plus 33% of the excess over $150,150
Over $326,450	$94,727.50 plus 35% of the excess over $326,450

Example: Ian is a single taxpayer. His taxable income is $69,700. His tax is $14,090 ($4,090 plus 25% of the amount by which $69,700 exceeds $29,700 (or 25% × $40,000 = $10,000)). Ian is said to be "in the 25% bracket," i.e., each dollar of additional taxable income will be taxed at a rate of 25%.

5. **Married couples filing jointly—2005 rates:** Married couples filing joint returns are taxed at the following rates:

Taxable Income	Marginal Tax Rate
Not over $14,600	10% of the taxable income
Over $14,600 but not over $59,400	$1,460 plus 15% of the excess over $14,600
Over $59,400 but not over $119,950	$8,180 plus 25% of the excess over $59,400
Over $119,950 but not over $182,800	$23,317.50 plus 28% of the excess over $119,950
Over $182,800 but not over $326,450	$40,915.50 plus 33% of the excess over $182,800
Over $326,450	$88,320 plus 35% of the excess over $326,450

Example: Carlton and Sally are married. Their joint taxable income is $252,800. Their tax is $64,015.50. This is $40,915.50 plus $23,100, which is 33% of the amount by which their taxable income ($252,800) exceeds $182,800 (or $70,000). This couple is in the 33% bracket, which means that each additional dollar of income is taxed at the 33% rate.

6. **Married filing separately:** A separate tax schedule is provided for married couples who file separate returns. These tax rates are usually unappealing, and you may have noticed that married couples filing separate returns also do not enjoy fully other tax benefits. Therefore, most couples file jointly. The primary reason couples file separately is to protect one spouse's assets from the other's tax liability (joint returns generate joint and several liability for the tax due, while separate returns do not).

7. **Surviving spouses:** Surviving spouses may use the more favorable tax rates for married taxpayers filing jointly. A surviving spouse is an unmarried taxpayer whose spouse died within the prior two years and who maintains a household for a dependent child. IRC §2(a).

8. **Heads of households:** Favorable rates are provided for "heads of households," i.e., unmarried persons maintaining a household in which a dependent lives during the taxable year. IRC §2(b).

9. **Children:** Children file their own tax returns reporting their incomes. In some circumstances their parents may report the child's investment income on their returns, or children's investment income may be taxed at the parents' tax rate. See discussion of the "kiddie tax" at Chapter 14(IV)(A).

10. **Entities**

   a. **Corporations:** Corporations are subject to tax on their ordinary income at rates ranging from 15% to 35%. IRC §11. Certain penalty taxes potentially apply, including the personal holding company tax and the accumulated earnings tax, which are beyond the scope of basic federal income tax classes.

   b. **S Corporations:** A corporation with a valid Subchapter S election (election to be taxed as a small business corporation) will not pay the §11 tax or any penalty taxes. IRC §1363(a). Instead, its shareholders will report the S corporation's income and loss on their own tax returns, much as if they earned the income or incurred the loss themselves. IRC §1366(a)(1). Certain special taxes apply to S corporations that are beyond the scope of the basic federal income tax class.

c. Partnerships (and limited liability companies taxed as partnerships): Partnerships are not subject to tax; instead, their partners report the income and loss from the partnership on their own tax returns, much as if they had earned the income or loss themselves. IRC §701.

d. Trusts: Estates and trusts are subject to tax on their taxable income at rates ranging from 15% to 35%. IRC §1(e). The 35% rate begins at taxable income of $9,750 (in 2005), so it is usually not a good idea to trap income in a trust; the goal instead is to have it taxed to the trust's grantor or beneficiary.

C. Tax rates on capital gains

1. **Maximum tax rates:** Preferential tax rates are available for net capital gain income. Chapter 12 describes the tax rates on capital gains and how the taxes on such gains are computed. Net capital gain can be of any of three types: (1) collectibles gain, taxed at a maximum of 28%; (2) unrecaptured §1250 gain, taxed at a maximum rate of 25%; and (3) all other net capital gain, taxed at a 15% rate, except for taxpayers whose regular tax rates are 15% or less, and in that case, the rate is 5%. These are *maximum* rates; if the taxpayer's regular tax rate is lower, that rate applies.

2. **Coordination with ordinary income rates:** The taxpayer's tax will be the *lower* of (a) the tax computed using the taxpayer's regular tax rate on all taxable income (including net capital gain) or (b) the tax computed using a bifurcated system: the regular rate on ordinary income and the various preferential rates on net capital gain.

   Example: Ken and Lynn are married taxpayers. This year, they have net capital gain income of $20,000 (collectible gain) and $10,000 (sale of stock in the 15/5% category). They have no ordinary income. Assume for illustration purposes that their standard deduction and personal exemptions total $10,000. The maximum tax on their capital gains will be $6,100 (28% of the $20,000 collectibles gain ($5,600) plus 5% of the gain on the sale of stock ($500)). But their tax computed using regular rates of tax is only $2,270 ($1,460 plus 15% of the amount by which their taxable income ($20,000) exceeds $14,600 ($810)). Thus, their tax is the lower of the two, i.e., $2,270.

   Example: Assume Ken and Lynn have the same capital gains and standard deduction as above, but their combined salary income is $202,800. In that case, the special rates on capital gains will produce a lower tax. The maximum rate on capital gains remains at $6,100. A tax computed at the regular rate on all income would produce a tax of $54,115.50. A tax computed using regular rates on ordinary income and the maximum capital gains tax produces a tax of $50,348.50. In this scenario, the preferential rates for capital gains help the couple reduce their tax, because their marginal rate for ordinary income is 33%, which is higher than the maximum rate for capital gains (28%).

D. Qualified dividend income

Although dividends qualify as ordinary income, certain dividend income is taxed at a special, preferential rate. Qualified dividends are taxed at 15% (or 5% for taxpayers whose effective rate is 15% or less). IRC §1(h)(11). A qualified dividend is a dividend (other than certain extraordinary dividends, or dividends from stock held for short periods of time) received from a domestic or certain foreign corporations. This provision eliminates the disparity between the gain on sale of stock and the dividends from such stock.

III. THE ALTERNATIVE MINIMUM TAX

A. Overview

The alternative minimum tax (AMT) was enacted to increase the fairness of the tax system by ensuring that all taxpayers, even those with the kind of income or deductions that receive favorable treatment under the Code, pay some minimum amount of income tax. Calculating the AMT requires a separate determination of "alternative minimum taxable income," which is the taxpayer's regular taxable income with some adjustments. The special AMT tax rates are applied to AMT income less an exclusion amount, and certain credits are subtracted. Then, a taxpayer's AMT is equal to the excess of the tentative minimum tax over the taxpayer's regular tax. A taxpayer subject to the AMT will pay two separate taxes: the regular tax and the AMT. The AMT is best thought of as a parallel tax system to the regular tax, which may impose a surtax on taxpayers—sometimes unexpectedly.

B. Alternative minimum taxable income (AMTI)

To calculate AMTI, begin with taxable income computed in the regular manner, and make a series of adjustments that put back into taxable income some items that were excluded (see Chapter 4) or deducted (see Chapters 6-8). The following are the most important adjustments, although there are others that are not usually so important in the basic tax class.

1. **Add some items that were excluded from gross income:** To calculate AMTI, add back into taxable income certain amounts that were excluded from gross income in computing the regular tax:

   a. **Section 1202 stock:** Seven percent of the gain on the sale of §1202 stock that was excluded from gross income for regular tax purposes is added back into taxable income. IRC §57(a)(7). After 2007, the amount is scheduled to be 42% of such exclusion.

   b. **Certain tax-exempt interest:** The tax-exempt interest on private activity bonds is added back into taxable income. IRC §57(a)(5). These include bonds used to finance mass transit, sewage facilities, and similar specialized activities.

   c. **Incentive stock options:** An incentive stock option gives an employee the right to acquire stock by exercising an option and paying less than the fair market value of the stock. The difference between the stock's market value and the exercise price is not included in regular gross income at the time of exercise, but it is included for AMT purposes, so it must be added back into taxable income. IRC §57(b)(3).

2. **Add some items that were deducted in computing taxable income:** For regular tax purposes, taxable income is the result of deducting certain items from gross income. These deductions are reversed in computing AMTI by adding back into taxable income deductions taken for the following:

   a. **Personal deductions:** Miscellaneous itemized deductions (see Chapter 6(XVII); standard deduction (see Chapter 6(XI); personal exemption (see Chapter 6(XVIII); and state and local income, sales, and other taxes (see Chapter 6(XIII). Medical expenses are deductible for AMT purposes only to the extent they exceed 10% (not 7.5%) of AGI, as computed for regular tax purposes. See Chapter 6(XV). Interest on a home mortgage is deductible for AMT purposes, but special rules apply so that only "real homes" (houses, condos, etc.) will qualify as personal residences, not boats, RVs, and the like. See Chapter 6(XI)(D).

Example: Judy has AGI of $100,000. She claimed $1,000 of medical expenses in excess of the 7.5% floor as an itemized deduction under IRC §213. In computing AMTI, she must apply at 10% floor rather than the 7.5% floor. Judy's total medical expenses must have been $8,500 ($7,500 attributable to the 7.5% floor plus the $1,000 amount properly deductible in excess of 7.5% of AGI). In computing AMTI, she will not be able to claim any medical expense because her medical expenses must be in excess of 10% of regular AGI (not AMT) to be deductible, and her total expenses are less than that floor. If Judy's deductible medical expenses for regular tax purposes had been $6,000, she would have been entitled to a deduction for AMT purposes of $3,500 (the excess of total expenses ($13,500) over 10% of regular tax AGI). In that case, in calculating the AMT, her AMTI would exceed her regular taxable income by the difference between the allowable deduction for regular tax purposes ($6,000) and the amount allowable for AMT purposes ($3,500) or $2,500.

   i. Depreciation: For AMT purposes, a taxpayer is generally required to use a longer, slower capital recovery method than for regular tax purposes. For 3-, 5-, 7-, and 10-year property, for example, a taxpayer would be required to use the 150% declining balance method rather than the 200% declining balance method. A taxpayer would then add the difference between the two in early years of ownership to taxable income in calculating AMTI.

     (1) Because real property is subject to straight-line MACRS deductions, no AMT adjustment is required for real property.

     (2) Bonus depreciation (see Chapter 7(III)) does not generate an AMTI adjustment.

     (3) Property subject to the §179 expense (see Chapter 7(III)) does not generate an AMTI adjustment.

  b. Losses: Certain restrictions apply to losses, including net operating losses (see Chapter 11(II)(D)) and passive activity losses. See Chapter 11(VII).

C. AMT tax rates

The first $175,000 of AMTI in excess of the applicable exemption amount is taxed at 26%. IRC §55(b)(1)(A)(i)(I). Any AMTI in excess of this amount is taxed at 28%. IRC §55(b)(1)(A)(i)(II). In addition, for a taxpayer subject to the preferential capital gains rates (see generally Chapter 12), a special AMT capital gains rate applies, ranging from 5% to 25%. IRC §55(b)(3).

D. Exemption amount

  1. Relatively low amounts: The exemption amount was originally designed to exempt mid- and low-income taxpayers from the AMT. However, because the exemption amounts are not tied to inflation, over the years the usefulness of the exemption amount has fallen, and many middle-income taxpayers find themselves caught within the AMT web. To make matters worse, Congress has flirted with the idea of *lowering* the exemption to pay for tax cuts in other areas. The current exemption amounts are as follows.

Status	Year 2004-2005
Single	$40,250
Married	$58,000

Example: Frodo, a single taxpayer, has AMTI of $150,000 in 2005. What is his tentative AMT? Frodo reduces his AMTI by the appropriate exemption amount ($40,250) and multiplies the result by 26%. His tentative AMT is $28,535.

2. **Phase-outs:** The exemption amounts begin to be phased out once AMTI reaches a certain amount. Once AMTI reaches $112,500 (for single taxpayers) or $150,000 (married taxpayers filing jointly) the exemption is reduced by 25% of the amount by which AMTI exceeds this amount. The exemption is fully phased out at the following levels:

Status	Year 2004-2005
Single	$273,500
Married	$382,000

Example: Joanne, a single taxpayer, has AMTI of $250,000. While her exemption amount would normally be $40,250, her AMTI is above the threshold phase-out amount ($112,500), so that her exemption amount is reduced by 25% of the amount by which her AMTI ($250,000) exceeds the phase-out amount ($112,500). Therefore, her exemption amount is reduced by $34,375 (15% × ($250,000 − $112,500)) so that her exemption amount is only $5,875.

E. Minimum tax credit

Some of the adjustments to regular taxable income in computing AMTI are timing adjustments: Some disallow deductions in early years, pushing them to later years; others accelerate income into an earlier year than is required for regular tax purposes. In later years, the taxpayer's tax liability as a whole will be overstated as these timing adjustments reverse themselves. For example, consider a taxpayer who incurred AMT because he or she was required to take a longer, slower MACRS deduction period for AMT purposes. In later years, the regular tax liability would be higher (less depreciation would be allowed) and for AMT purposes, the AMT tax would be lower (more depreciation would be allowed). To alleviate this problem, §53 allows a taxpayer a minimum tax credit against regular tax liability. The computation of the minimum tax credit—fortunately—is usually beyond the scope of the basic tax course.

F. Comprehensive example

In 2005, Tim and Val had a combined salary income of $90,000. Tim exercised a qualified stock option by paying $80,000 for stock worth $200,000. Their itemized deductions were $25,000 of which $6,000 was a miscellaneous itemized deduction (after taking into account the 2% floor) and $4,000 was a deduction of state income taxes. Thus, Tim and Val's taxable income for regular tax purposes was $58,600. Their regular tax liability was $8,060.

Calculating AMTI requires increasing taxable income as computed for regular tax purposes by adding: (1) the differential between what was paid for the stock option ($80,000) and the value of the stock itself ($200,000) or $120,000; (2) adding the miscellaneous itemized deduction of $6,000; (3) the deduction for state income taxes of $4,000; and (4) the personal exemptions of $3,200 each or $6,400.

This produces AMTI of $195,000.

Because AMTI exceeds $150,000 (the initial threshold amount for phase-out of the exemption), the exemption amount (usually $58,000) will be reduced by 25% of the amount by which AMTI exceeds this threshold amount, or $11,250. This leaves an exemption amount of $46,750.

Tim and Val's tentative AMT is 26% of their AMTI ($195,000) less their exemption amount of $46,750, or 26% × $148,250. This produces tentative AMT of $38,545. This exceeds their regular tax liability by $30,485, so their total tax liability is $8,060 of regular tax plus $30,485 of AMT.

When Tim sells the stock that he purchased through the stock option, the differential between option price and fair market value will be taken into account for regular tax purposes. At that time, he will probably be able to claim a minimum tax credit against regular tax to account for the timing differential in inclusion of income in the two taxes.

IV. TAX CREDITS—IN GENERAL

A tax credit is a dollar-for-dollar reduction in the amount of tax owed by a taxpayer.

A. Compare—Deductions

A deduction is a subtraction from gross income or adjusted gross income (AGI) in computing taxable income.

B. Why a credit? The upside-down subsidy problem

As a benefit to a taxpayer, a deduction is worth the amount of the deduction multiplied by the taxpayer's marginal tax rate. Therefore, in a progressive rate system, deductions are worth more to high-income taxpayers than to low-income taxpayers. Thus, deductions are occasionally referred to as "upside-down subsidies." By contrast, a tax credit is worth the same dollar amount to every taxpayer because it reduces tax on a dollar-for-dollar basis. Because a tax credit does not extend a larger tax benefit to higher-income taxpayers than to lower-income taxpayers, Congress may choose the credit vehicle in certain situations (e.g., the dependent care tax credit discussed below).

C. Refundable/Nonrefundable

A refundable credit can reduce the tax due below zero, generating a tax refund for the taxpayer. A *nonrefundable credit* can only reduce the tax to zero and thus will not generate a refund.

Example: Bo's income tax is $100, but he is entitled to a tax credit of $120. If the tax credit is refundable, he will receive a $20 refund. If the tax credit is nonrefundable, it will simply reduce his tax to zero.

D. Credit for tax withheld

Perhaps the most familiar credit is the credit for taxes withheld on wages. After computing the tax based on taxable income, the taxpayer subtracts from the tax due the amount of federal income tax withheld from wages, salaries, and bonuses. IRC §31(a)(1). This credit is a refundable credit, i.e., it can generate a tax refund.

V. DEPENDENT CARE CREDIT

The dependent care credit is designed to grant some tax relief to a taxpayer who incurs expenses to care for a dependent while the taxpayer works. (Remember that these expenses are not deductible because they are personal expenses. IRC §262.)

A. General rule

A taxpayer who maintains a household with at least one qualifying individual is allowed a tax credit in an amount equal to the "applicable percentage" multiplied by "employment-related expenses." IRC §21(a)(1). This is a nonrefundable credit.

B. Definitional issues

1. **Qualifying individual:** A qualifying individual is a dependent under the age of 13 for whom the taxpayer is entitled to a deduction as a dependent, or any other dependent or a spouse of the taxpayer who is physically or mentally unable to care for him- or herself. IRC §21(b)(1). The individual must live with the taxpayer more than half the year.

2. **Applicable percentage:** The applicable percentage depends on the taxpayer's AGI. For taxpayers with AGI of $15,000 or less, the applicable percentage is 35%. The applicable percentage drops by one percentage point for every increase of $2,000 (or fraction thereof) over $15,000 in AGI, but never falls below 20%.

3. **Employment-related expenses:** Employment-related expenses are expenses incurred for the care of a qualifying individual to allow the taxpayer to be gainfully employed. IRC §21(b)(2)(A).

   a. **Dollar limit:** Employment-related expenses are limited to $3,000 per year for one qualifying individual and $6,000 per year for two or more qualifying individuals. IRC §21(c). The maximum credit available is:

Adjusted Gross Income	Applicable Percentage	One Qualifying Individual	Two or More Qualifying Individuals
Up to $15,000	35%	$1,050	$2,100
$15,001 – $17,000	34%	$1,020	$2,040
$17,001 – $19,000	33%	$ 990	$1,980
$19,001 – $21,000	32%	$960	$1,920
$21,001 – $23,000	31%	$930	$1,860
$23,001 – $25,000	30%	$900	$1,800
$25,001 – $27,000	29%	$870	$1,740
$27,001 – $29,000	28%	$840	$1,680
$29,001 – $31,000	27%	$810	$1,620
$31,001 – $33,000	26%	$780	$1,560
$33,001 – $35,000	25%	$750	$1,500
$35,001 – $37,000	24%	$720	$1,440
$37,001 – $39,000	23%	$690	$1,380
$39,001 – $41,000	22%	$660	$1,320
$41,001 – $43,000	21%	$630	$1,260
$43,001 and over	20%	$600	$1,200

b. Earned income limitation: Employment-related expenses are limited to the lesser of the earned income of the taxpayer or the earned income of the taxpayer's spouse. IRC §21(d)(1). Students and disabled taxpayers are deemed to have $250 per month in earned income for one qualifying individual or $50 per month for more than one qualifying individual. IRC §21(d)(2).

Example: Timmy Sue has two children. She and her husband both work. Their adjusted gross income is $50,000. They incur $5,000 of expenses for the care of their children while they work. They may claim a tax credit of $1,000, equal to the applicable percentage (20%) multiplied by the employment-related expenses ($5,000).

C. Special rules and exceptions

1. **Mandatory joint return:** A married couple must file a joint return in order to claim the credit. IRC §21(e)(2).

   a. **Legal separation:** Legally separated spouses are not considered married for this purpose. IRC §21(e)(3).

   b. **De facto separation:** If a married individual files a separate return, bears over half the cost of maintaining a qualifying individual in the home, and the other spouse is not a member of the household for the last six months of the year, the individual will not be considered married and may claim the credit if otherwise qualified. IRC §21(e)(4).

2. **Caregiver information:** The taxpayer must provide identifying information (name, social security number, etc.) of the caregiver. IRC §21(e)(9).

D. Related material—Dependent care assistance

Section 129 allows a taxpayer to exclude from gross income up to $5,000 of dependent care assistance provided by an employer under a qualifying dependent care assistance plan. (See discussion at Chapter 4(IX)(E).) Sections 129 and 21 share a common goal of providing a tax benefit for taxpayers who incur expenses for the care of dependents so that the taxpayer can work. They also share some common definitions (dependent care assistance) and limitations (earned income limitation). But §129 offers an exclusion from gross income, while §21 provides a tax credit. Moreover, a taxpayer cannot claim the benefits of both provisions for the same dollar of expense. No credit is allowed for any amount that is excluded under §129. IRC §129(e)(7).

Example: Paul is a single parent maintaining a household for his two children, ages 6 and 8. His adjusted gross income is $40,000, and he incurs $6,000 of expenses for the care of his children while he works. Paul's employer maintains a qualifying §129 dependent care assistance plan that reimburses Paul for up to $2,000 of his child care expenses. Paul may claim an exclusion of $2,000 under his employer's plan. He cannot claim a credit for the amount he excluded from gross income under §129. Thus, his employment-related expenses are $4,000. Multiplying these expenses by his applicable percentage (22%) gives him a credit of $880. Alternatively, Paul may choose to claim the $6,000 of expenses as wholly applicable to the tax credit, forgoing the dependent care plan benefit entirely.

E. Summary

Section 21 allows a taxpayer a nonrefundable tax credit equal to the taxpayer's employment-related expenses (subject to limitations) multiplied by the applicable percentage. See §21 summary below.

Statute Summary—Section 21
Dependent Care Credit

Parsing Step	§21
General rule	Taxpayers with at least one qualifying individual may claim a credit equal to the applicable percentage multiplied by the employment-related expenses.
Definitional issues	Qualifying individual: dependent under age 13 or other dependent if unable to care for him- or herself Applicable percentage: 20%–35% depending on AGI Employment-related expense: expenses for care of qualifying dependent while taxpayer works or goes to school full time
Special rules and exceptions	Employment-related expenses limited to earned income and $3,000 for one qualifying individual or $6,000 for two or more qualifying individuals Cannot claim credit and exclusion for same expenses
Related material	Exclusion for dependent care assistance: §129 Earned income: §911
Summary	Credit available for expenses incurred in caring for certain dependents while the taxpayer works, limited in amount

VI. EARNED INCOME TAX CREDIT

The *earned income tax credit* is designed to grant a tax benefit to low-income working taxpayers.

A. General rule

A taxpayer must be an "eligible individual" to claim the credit. Calculating the earned income credit can be complicated, and it often leads to mistakes on returns. To compute the amount of the credit, first multiply the "credit percentage" by the taxpayer's earned income, up to a certain amount known as the "earned income amount." Then, subtract from that figure the taxpayer's "phase-out percentage" multiplied by the taxpayer's AGI, reduced (but not below zero) by the phase-out amount. These percentages and amounts vary depending on the income and family status of the taxpayer. Confused? Just use this formula:

Credit Percentage × Earned Income Amount

$\underline{- \text{ Phase-out Percentage} \times (\text{AGI} \times \text{Phase-out Amount})}$

Earned Income Credit

Example: Melinda, an eligible individual with no children, has earned income and an AGI of $7,000. She may claim an earned income tax credit of $192, computed as follows:

$$
\begin{array}{lr}
7.65\% \times \$5,220 & \$399.33 \\
\underline{- \quad 7.65\% \times (\$7,000 - \$6,530)} & \underline{-35.85} \\
\text{Earned Income Credit} & \mathbf{\$363.38}
\end{array}
$$

Example: Trudy, a married eligible taxpayer with one qualifying child, has earned income of $10,000 and AGI of $9,000. She may claim an earned income credit of $484, computed as follows:

$$
\begin{array}{lr}
7.65\% \times \$7,830 & \$598.99 \\
-\;\; 7.65\% \times (\$9,000 - \$16,370) & -0 \\
\hline
\text{Earned Income Credit} & \mathbf{\$598.99}
\end{array}
$$

B. Definitional issues

1. **Eligible individual:** An eligible individual is an individual with a qualifying child, or any other individual who meets the following three requirements.

   a. **U.S. residence:** The individual's principal place of abode must be within the U.S. for more than half the year. IRC §32(c)(1)(A)(ii)(I).

   b. **Age 25–65:** The individual must be at least 25, but not yet 65 during the taxable year. IRC §32(c)(1)(A)(ii)(II).

   c. **Not a dependent:** The individual cannot be claimed as a dependent on someone else's tax return. IRC §32(c)(1)(A)(ii)(III).

2. **Qualifying child:** The definition of a qualifying child is the same as the definition of a qualifying child for purposes of the personal exemption. See Chapter 6(XVIIII).

3. **Credit percentage:** The credit percentages are set forth in Figure 13A—2005 Earned Income Tax Credit Percentages and Amounts.

4. **Earned income amount:** Earned income includes income from wages, salary, and self-employment, but does not include investment income, alimony, or pension benefits. IRC §32(c)(2). The earned income amounts are set forth in Figure 13A. These amounts are adjusted each year for inflation.

5. **Percentages and amounts:** See Figure 13A.

Figure 13A
Earned Income Tax Credit Percentages and Amounts

Qualifying Children	Credit Percentage	Phase-out Percentage	Earned Income Amount	Threshold Phase-out/ Completed Phase-out— Single Filers	Threshold Phase-out/ Completed Phase-out— Married Filing Jointly
None	7.65%	7.65%	$5,220	$6,530 / $11,750	$8,530 / $13,750
1	34%	15.98%	$7,830	$14,370 / $31,030	$16,370 / $33,030
2 or more	40%	21.06%	$11,000	$14,370 / $35,263	$16,370 / $37,263

C. Special rules and exceptions

1. **Disqualified income limitation:** A taxpayer may not claim the earned income credit if he or she has disqualified income in excess of $2,700. IRC §32(i)(1). Disqualified income includes tax-exempt interest income, dividends, net rental and royalty income, capital gain net income, and net passive income. IRC §32(i)(2).

2. **Mandatory joint return:** For either spouse to claim the earned income tax credit, both must file a joint return. IRC §32(d).

3. **Anti-abuse provisions:** In response to perceived abuses of the EIC, the IRS has imposed a variety of measures to ensure that a taxpayer who claims the credit is eligible for it.

D. Related material

The earned income tax credit is part of an overall system designed to reallocate resources among taxpayers with different incomes. Thus, §32 is related to the system of progressive taxation and to welfare benefit systems outside the taxing arena.

E. Summary

Section 32 allows certain low income taxpayers with earned income a tax credit equal to the applicable credit percentage multiplied by their earned income, but the credit is phased out as income rises.

VII. EDUCATION CREDITS

A. In general

A number of Code sections provide special benefits for educational expenses. Two of these are in the form of nonrefundable tax credits: the HOPE credit and the Lifetime Learning credit of IRC §25A.

B. HOPE Scholarship credit

1. **Overview:** This is a credit of up to $1,500 for qualified expenses paid during the taxable year. IRC §25A(b)(1). The credit is available only for expenses for the first two years of post-secondary education at a qualified institution. IRC §25A(b)(2)(A). The expenses may be for the taxpayer, his or her spouse, or a dependent and is calculated on a per-student basis, so that a taxpayer might claim multiple credits if multiple students are involved.

2. **Application:** The credit is for expenses for tuition and fees, but not books, room and board, or nonacademic fees. IRC §25A(f)(1).

3. **Eligibility:** The student must be enrolled as a student in a qualified institution, and must be at least half-time. A student convicted of a drug-related felony will not be entitled to the credit. IRC §25A(b)(2).

C. Lifetime learning credit

1. **In general:** The lifetime learning credit is equal to 20% of the qualified tuition and related expenses of up to $10,000. IRC §25A(c)(1). This is a maximum amount per return, not per student, so that only one credit can be claimed on a return.

2. **Duration:** The taxpayer may claim the credit for any number of years, not just the two years available under the HOPE credit.

3. **Application:** The credit is for expenses for tuition and fees, but not books, room and board, or nonacademic fees. IRC §25A(f)(1). It is also available for expenses relating to any course of instruction at an eligible institution to acquire or improve job skills (but not as recreation). IRC §25A(c)(2)(B). The student need not be enrolled as a half-time student, but can take as little as one course.

D. Phase-outs applicable to both credits

1. **In general:** Both credits are phased out as modified AGI increases. This means that credit is only partially available to taxpayers with a certain modified AGI, and unavailable when modified AGI rises to a certain level.

2. **Modified AGI:** Adjusted gross income is modified by adding to it amounts excluded as foreign earned income under IRC §911. IRC §25A(d)(3).

3. **Phase-out amounts:** For 2005, the phase-out begins at AGI of $43,000 for single taxpayers. For married taxpayers filing joint returns, the phase-out begins at AGI of $87,000. These amounts are adjusted for inflation.

4. **Reduced credit:** In order to determine the available credit, multiply the otherwise available credit by a fraction, the numerator of which is the taxpayer's modified AGI minus the starting phase-out amount, and the denominator of which is $10,000 (for single taxpayers) or $20,000 (for joint returns). This amount is subtracted from the otherwise available credit to obtain the credit available to the taxpayer. IRC §25A(d)(1), (2). Confused? The following formulas may be helpful.

- *Step 1:* Determine the otherwise available credit, which is equal to 20% × allowable expenses, up to a specified amount.

- *Step 2:* Calculate the reduction amount, which is equal to:

$$\text{Otherwise available credit} \times \frac{(\text{Modified AGI} - \text{Initial phase-out amount})}{\$10,000 \text{ (single) or } \$20,000 \text{ (joint)}}$$

- *Step 3:* Determine the available credit:

$$\begin{array}{l} \text{Otherwise available credit} \\ - \text{ Reduction amount} \\ \hline = \textbf{Available credit, considering phase–out} \end{array}$$

E. Coordination of the credits

1. **No double credits for the same student:** While the taxpayer may claim both credits on the return for different students, the taxpayer cannot claim both credits for the same student. Prop. Reg. §1.25A-5(b)(1).

2. **Allocation to HOPE credit:** Amounts of qualified educational expenses that qualify under both credits are first allocated to the HOPE credit, then to the lifetime learning credit. IRC §25A(c)(2)(A).

Example: Ben and Ruth file a joint return reporting modified AGI of $25,000. Their son Adam is starting college this fall. They pay tuition of $3,000 and academic fees of $400. Assuming Adam is a dependent of Ben and Ruth, these expenses qualify as both HOPE credit expenses and lifetime learning credit expenses, so they are allocated to the HOPE credit. Ben and Ruth may claim a credit of 20% of these expenses, or $680.

Example: Beth is a single taxpayer with a modified AGI of $25,000. This year, she is enrolled in a qualified night law school on a half-time basis. She pays tuition of $12,000. These expenses do not qualify for the HOPE credit because they are not for the first two years of post-secondary education. They do qualify for the lifetime learning credit. She will be entitled to claim 20% of $10,000, or a $2,000 credit.

Example: Assume the same facts as in the above example, except that Beth's modified AGI is $45,000. Assume the phase-out amounts are the same as in 2005. In this case, Beth's credit must be reduced by an amount equal to the credit to which she would otherwise be entitled, multiplied by a fraction, the numerator of which is Beth's modified AGI minus the threshold phase-out amount and the denominator of which is $10,000. Thus, $2,000 is multiplied by 20% (($45,000 − $43,000) / $10,000) to produce the reduction amount of $400. Her otherwise available credit ($2,000) is reduced by $400, to $1,600.

VIII. OTHER CREDITS

The Code provides for various other credits for certain types of taxpayers or activities. While these are beyond the scope of many basic tax classes, the tax student may be required to have at least a passing familiarity with them.

A. Child tax credit

Section 24 allows a $1,000 credit for each qualifying child, with phase-outs tied to modified AGI in excess of $110,000 (married filing jointly) and $75,000 (single taxpayers).

B. Blind/elderly/disabled tax credit

Section 22 allows a taxpayer to claim a tax credit if he or she is at least 65 years old, blind, or is permanently and totally disabled. IRC §22(a). The credit is computed by multiplying 15% by the "§22 amount," which is set forth in the statute as ranging from $3,750 to $7,500 depending on filing status. IRC §22(a), (c)(2). The §22 amount is reduced by amounts (such as certain social security benefits) which are excluded from gross income, and is reduced as income rises. IRC §22(c)(3), (d). This credit is nonrefundable.

C. Foreign tax credit

Section 27 allows the taxpayer a credit for foreign taxes paid, to the extent the credit is allowed by §901. IRC §27(a).

D. Certain energy and research-related credits

A number of credits are available for certain energy and research-related activities. See IRC §§29, 30, 34, 40, and 41. These are generally nonrefundable credits.

E. Low-income housing credit

Section 42 allows taxpayers a tax credit for investing in certain buildings used for low-income housing. This provision, while technical in the extreme, basically allows a taxpayer a credit for a percentage of the basis of the property when it is placed in service. This is a nonrefundable credit.

F. Adoption expense credit

A taxpayer is entitled to a credit for qualified adoption expenses up to $10,630 per child. IRC §23(a)(1).

1. **Qualified adoption expenses:** Qualified adoption expenses include necessary adoption fees, court costs, attorney fees, and other expenses incurred for the principal purpose of the legal adoption of a child. IRC §23(d)(1)(H).

2. **When claimed:** The taxpayer claims the credit for adoption expenses incurred before the year of adoption in the year following the year they are paid, and for expenses incurred during or after the adoption year, in that year. For the credit for the adoption of special-needs children, the credit is available in the year of adoption. IRC §23(a)(2).

3. **Phase-out:** The credit is phased out for taxpayers with AGI greater than $15,945(2005 amount). IRC §23(b)(2)(A).

IX. WHERE ARE WE GOING?

This chapter concludes the analysis of the computation of a taxpayer's tax. This process began with the identification of gross income, continued through the subtraction of deductions, and concluded with the application of tax rates and subtraction of available credits. This discussion has made a very important assumption: that the "proper taxpayer" has been identified. The next chapter turns to that issue, examining the types of taxpayers subject to tax and various strategies taxpayers employ to direct income to related persons.

Quiz Yourself on
TAX RATES AND CREDITS

114. In 2005, Ray, a single taxpayer, sold some stock in which he had invested many years ago. He realized and recognized a $10,000 long-term capital gain. Ray wants to know how he will be taxed on this gain. Consider the following two alternatives: (a) Ray's taxable income (not considering this gain) is $260,000 or (b) Ray's taxable income (not considering this gain) is $12,000. _____

115. What is the rationale for the AMT? Give two examples of AMT adjustments that support this rationale. _____

116. Catherine, a single taxpayer, had the following items of income and deduction in 2005:

Salary income:	$97,200
Taxable interest income:	$3,000
Interest on tax-exempt bonds:	$2,000
Home mortgage interest on condo:	$5,000
State income tax:	$9,000
Medical expenses in excess of 7.5% of adjusted gross income	$1,000
Charitable deductions:	$2,000
Miscellaneous itemized deductions in excess of 2% floor:	$3,000

Will Catherine pay AMT? Why or why not? _____

117. A reckless newspaper reporter wrote a story about Becky that she was negligent in her duties as an employee of a child care facility. Becky sued the reporter and the newspaper for libel, and was awarded $300,000 in damages. Under Becky's agreement with her attorney, the attorney was entitled to 1/3 of this amount, or $100,000. What are the tax consequences of this transaction to Becky? _____

118. Candace is a single mother of two children, ages 6 and 8. Her AGI is $38,000. She spends $3,000 per year on child care while she works, and another $500 for their care while she travels as a volunteer for the American Cancer Society. What are the tax consequences to Candace of these expenditures? _____

119. Jordan has earned income and modified adjusted gross income (MAGI) of $10,000 and is a single father of one child, age 10. To what earned income credit, if any, is he entitled? _____

120. Kara and Jim are married, filing jointly. They have three children. Their MAGI is $25,000. Are they entitled to an earned income credit and if so, what is the amount of the credit? _____

121. George and Laura are married and file a joint return. Their modified AGI is $90,000. Assume the 2005 phase-out amounts are in effect. Laura is a full-time student in a graduate program in education at the local college. She paid $14,000 in tuition. Their daughter, Susan, is starting college, and they paid $20,000 in tuition and academic fees for her. She is a dependent of George and Laura. What tax credits are George and Laura entitled to claim on their income tax return? _____

122. Which is better for a taxpayer: a credit under IRC §25A, an exclusion from gross income under IRC §117, or a deduction for educational expenses under IRC §222? _____

Answers

114. Ray's long-term capital gain is properly categorized as 15/5% gain. If his taxable income not considering this gain is $260,000, he is in the 33% marginal bracket and this gain will be taxed at 15%. If his taxable income not considering the gain is only $12,000, he is in the 15% bracket and the gain will be taxed at 5%.

115. The rationale for the AMT is that every taxpayer—even those with activities that generate significant tax benefits in the form of deferred or excluded income or significant deductions—should pay some tax. For example, certain kinds of tax-exempt interest (from private activity bonds) are included in gross income for AMT purposes, while exempt for regular tax purposes. Also, depreciation on equipment is required to occur on a longer, slower schedule for AMT purposes than for regular tax purposes. Thus, taxpayers whose activities generate significant amounts of MACRS deductions, which reduce their taxable income and tax for regular tax purposes, will have larger AMTI in the early years of capital recovery.

116. To determine whether Catherine is subject to the AMT, first compute taxable income and tax for regular tax purposes, as follows:

Salary income:	$97,200
Taxable interest income:	$3,000
Gross income:	$100,200
(This is also adjusted gross income.)	
Minus: Itemized deduction	
Home mortgage interest:	$5,000
State income tax:	$9,000
Medical expenses in excess of	
7.5% of adjusted gross income	$1,000
Charitable deductions:	$2,000
Miscellaneous itemized	
deductions in excess of 2% floor:	$3,000
Total itemized deductions:	($20,000)
Minus: Personal exemption	($3,200)
Taxable income for *regular* tax purposes:	**$77,000**
Tax on regular taxable income:	**$16,066.50**

To determine whether Catherine will have to pay AMT, her taxable income is adjusted as follows to produce alternative minimum taxable income:

Taxable income for *regular* tax purposes:		**$77,000**
Plus:		
Tax-exempt interest on private activity bonds:	$1,000	
State income taxes:	$9,000	
Miscellaneous itemized deductions:	$3,000	
Medical expenses:	$1,000	
Personal exemption:	$3,200	
Total adjustments:	+ $17,200	
AMTI		**$94,200**
Minus: Exemption amount		($40,250)
Tax base for AMT		$53,950
× Tax rate for AMT (26%)		.26
AMT		**$14,027**

Because Catherine's regular tax liability ($16,066.50) is more than her alternative minimum tax liability ($14,027), she will not pay AMT. (However, this does not excuse her from calculating the AMT liability to determine if she is subject to this surtax.)

117. All of the award must be included in Becky's gross income, and her $100,000 of attorneys' fees is deductible on Schedule A as a miscellaneous itemized deduction for regular tax purposes, to the extent that these fees, plus any other miscellaneous itemized deductions, exceed 2% of her AGI. She cannot claim these as an above-the-line deduction because the award was not pursuant to the relatively limited category of claims that generate attorneys' fees eligible for such a deduction. See Chapter 6(X). For purposes of calculating her AMTI, however, none of the attorneys' fees are deductible because they are a miscellaneous itemized expense. This can generate significant AMT liability.

118. Candace can't deduct these personal expenses. IRC §262. However, she may be entitled to a non-refundable tax credit for dependent care expenses. She appears to qualify: She maintains a household with children; they are under the age of 13; she incurs expenses to care for them while she works. The amount expended for child care while she works as a volunteer ($500) would not be eligible for the credit. The amount of the credit will be a percentage of the lesser of her earned income, child care expenses, or the specified dollar amount of the statute based on the number of children ($6,000 for two children). The percentage is based on AGI. In Candace's case, she will be entitled to claim 23% of her actual expenses of $3,000, or $690 as the child care credit.

119. Jordan is entitled to claim the earned income credit because his income is within the earned income limitation. He has one qualifying child, and thus will be entitled to a credit of $2,813, computed as follows:

$$34\% \times \$10,000 \qquad \qquad \$3,440$$
$$-15.98\% \times (10,000 - 6,530) \qquad -15.98\% \times 3,470 = 554.50$$
$$\textbf{Earned Income Credit} \qquad \qquad \mathbf{\$2,885.50}$$

120. Kara and Jim may claim an earned income credit of $8,183. This is computed as follows:

$$40\% \times \$25,000 \qquad \qquad \times \$10,000$$
$$-21.06\% \times (25,000 - 16,370) \qquad -1,817$$
$$\textbf{Earned Income Credit} \qquad \qquad \mathbf{\$8,183}$$

121. All of these payments for tuition and fees are potentially available for the HOPE and lifetime learning credits. Laura's tuition is not available for the HOPE credit, because it is not applicable to the first two years of post-secondary education. However, she can take the lifetime learning credit for these expenses. Her credit would be equal to 20% multiplied by the maximum amount of expenses available in 2005 ($10,000), but may be limited by the family's AGI. In this case, the family's AGI exceeds the amount at which phase-out begins ($87,000). Thus, the credit would be reduced, and calculated as follows:

$$\$10,000 \text{ expenses} \times 20\% = \$2,000 \text{ (otherwise available credit)}$$

Reduction amount =
$$\$2,000 \times \frac{(90,000 - 87,000)}{\$20,000} = \$2,000 \times \frac{\$3,000}{20,000} = \$2,000 \times 15\% = \$300$$

Available credit:

Otherwise available credit	$2,000
− reduction amount	− 300
Available credit	$1,700

George and Laura may also take a credit for Susan's tuition. This is allocated to the HOPE credit, so that only $1,500 of a credit is available. The family cannot take both a HOPE credit and a lifetime learning credit for Susan, even though the expenses qualify for both credits.

122. This is one of those "trick" questions one sometimes encounters on tax exams. There is no one "best" education tax incentive, and the situation of each taxpayer should be considered before concluding that one or the other of these incentives is best. This question also raises the issue of "letting the tax tail wag the dog," or using one's common sense: A scholarship is always a good thing for the recipient, so the exclusion of IRC §117 is equally desirable as it excludes an amount from gross income, allowing it to escape tax altogether. As between a credit or a deduction, a credit reduces tax on a dollar-for-dollar basis, while the maximum value of a deduction is a taxpayer's marginal rate multiplied by the amount of the deduction. Therefore, a credit is usually preferable to a deduction. But if a taxpayer has ample other credits to reduce tax, a deduction may make more sense for that particular taxpayer. *Note*: the deduction of IRC §222 is scheduled to sunset at the end of 2005, so a part of this question may become moot, unless Congress acts to extend this education incentive.

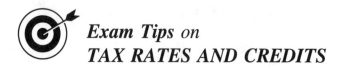

Exam Tips *on*
TAX RATES AND CREDITS

☛ The computation of tax is the *last* step in analyzing a taxpayer's tax consequences. It is not usually the case that law students are asked to actually compute the tax, but instead are asked to understand the concepts involved in tax computation.

☛ Know the differential in tax rates on ordinary income and capital gain (see Chapter 12) and qualified dividend income.

   ☞ *Look for:* A taxpayer with gain from dealings in property (not inventory) and other kinds of income, such as salary income.

   ☞ *Analyze:* Differentiate between the types of income and note the different tax rates that apply.

   ☞ *Note:* Most taxpayers one meets on exams have relatively high ordinary income levels, so that the preferential rates for capital gains will make a difference. However, when a taxpayer has low levels of ordinary income, and significant amounts of net capital gain in the 28% or 25% categories, the regular rates of tax will usually produce a lower rate than the capital gains rates. The capital gains rates are maximum rates; if the tax produced by the regular tax rates is lower, those rates will apply.

☛ Be able to compute AMTI using taxable income as the starting place.

  ☞ Know the adjustments to taxable income. Look for taxpayers who have relatively high itemized deductions or tax-exempt income, or can take advantage of significant income deferrals

  ☞ Be ready to explain the rationale for the AMT and comment on its effectiveness.

☛ Understand the difference between a credit, a deduction, and an exclusion, and the impact of each on a taxpayer.

☛ Be familiar with the numerous credits available to taxpayers.

  ☞ *Look for:* Adoptions, day care, low-income taxpayers.

  ☞ *Analyze:* Have the taxpayers met the specific requirements for claiming the credit? If so, is it limited by the taxpayers' income level?

☛ The bundle of education incentives available to taxpayers creates opportunities for testing.

  ☞ *Look for:* A taxpayer paying for higher education expenses, for the taxpayer or a spouse or child.

  ☞ *Analyze:* What incentives are available: exclusions, deductions, credits, deferral devices (see Chapter 14)? Are the specific requirements of the statutes met? What limitations apply, particularly with respect to income levels? Don't let the taxpayer "double dip," i.e., claim two benefits for the same dollars.

CHAPTER 14

IDENTIFYING THE TAXPAYER

ChapterScope

Previous chapters have focused on the computation of a taxpayer's taxable income and ultimate tax liability, from identification of income and deductions to the selection of the correct tax rate and subtraction of available credits. Thus far, the discussion has assumed that the taxpayer to report items of income and deductions has properly been identified. This is not usually a problem among unrelated taxpayers, whose individual self-interest will ensure that they do not overpay their taxes. However, related taxpayers may seek to transfer items of income and deduction among themselves in order to reduce the tax on the group as a whole. Both Congress and the courts have developed methods of combating this practice, which is the subject of this chapter.

■ **Persons subject to tax:** Individuals and legal entities are potentially subject to tax and must properly compute their income, deductions, and credits.

■ **Assignment of income principles:** Taxpayers in high tax brackets may attempt to shift (assign) income to a related person in a lower tax bracket. The assignment of income principle precludes many such attempts, taxing the assignor on the income.

■ **Statutory approaches:** Congress has enacted several statutory schemes to ensure that the "proper" taxpayer reports items of income and deduction. This chapter discusses §1(g) (known as the *kiddie tax*) and §482.

I. WHERE ARE WE?

This chapter returns to a question that underlies all of the income/deduction/credit/tax rate issues discussed previously in this book: Who is the proper taxpayer to report income or claim a deduction or credit, or to pay tax at a certain rate? This issue is discussed near the end of this book because you need to understand what "income" is before we can identify transactions involving the games that taxpayers try to play to reduce their overall tax by "assigning" income to others. But, conceptually, it is one of the first questions in analyzing any tax question. This issue is embedded in all of the tax statutes studied so far, but doesn't normally become explicit except in a few Code sections such as the "kiddie tax" or IRC §482. Therefore, it is up to the student of tax to ask the right question—Who is the proper taxpayer?—before tackling any tax problem.

II. "PERSONS" SUBJECT TO TAX

Both natural persons and legal entities are potentially subject to tax.

A. Adult individuals

Individuals are subject to tax at the rates described in §1 of the Code, generally ranging from 10% to 35%. (See generally Chapter 13.)

1. **Single individuals:** Single persons file a tax return, reporting their own taxable income. IRC §1(b), (c).

2. **Married couples:** Married couples can file a joint return, reporting their income and deductions together. IRC §1(a). They have the option of filing separate returns, but this is generally a less desirable option. IRC §1(d). State law generally determines who is "married" for purposes of the federal income tax, unless federal law preempts this definition. See, e.g., 1 U.S.C.A. §7 (defining marriage as between a man and a woman). The parties must be married on the last day of the taxable year in order to be considered married, except for surviving spouses, who may file a joint return for the year of the death of their spouse. IRC §7703(a).

B. Children

If children have sufficient taxable income to generate a tax, they must file their own tax returns separately from their parents.

1. **Child's services income:** Section 73 provides that a child's income from the performance of services is to be taxed to the child, not to the parent. IRC §73(a). This is true regardless of the parent's rights to the child's income under state law. Similarly, expenditures made to earn this income are considered those of the child regardless of whether the parent or child makes the expenditure. IRC §73(b).

2. **Kiddie tax:** Special tax rates may apply to a child's investment income, and in limited situations a child may report his or her investment income on his or her parents' return. See discussion this chapter at (III)(A).

C. Entities

A legal entity—such as a corporation, partnership, estate, or trust—may be subject to tax and thus may be required to report items of income and may properly claim items of deduction or credit.

III. ASSIGNMENT OF INCOME

The IRS may challenge taxpayers' attempts to assign income to another. The question in these situations is "Who must include an amount in gross income?"

A. Definition

Assignment of income is the attempt by a taxpayer to shift income to another person. This usually only occurs when taxpayers are related because the "assignor" of income is perfectly happy to have a relative enjoy the benefits of the income. That same assignor would be unlikely to arrange for an unrelated party to receive what is essentially a gift. Assignment of income issues do occasionally arise between unrelated parties. See, e.g., this chapter, section III(H).

B. Why assign income?

Progressive tax rates and the system of separate returns for related persons, taken together, create an incentive for a taxpayer in a high tax bracket to assign income to related taxpayers in lower brackets. The greater the progressive rates, the more incentive for assignment of income. Moreover, because related persons such as parents, grandparents, and children potentially file separate returns, it is possible to lower the overall tax of the group by reporting income on the separate tax return of a low-bracket member of the group.

Example: Alvin is a freelance artist. He is a taxpayer in the 33% marginal tax bracket, i.e., every additional dollar of income is taxed at 33%. His 21-year-old daughter, Beatrice, is in college and is in a 15% tax bracket. Alvin was planning to give Beatrice a $2,000 gift. Instead, he arranges for one of his clients to pay Beatrice (rather than Alvin) the purchase price of $2,000 for his latest project. By doing so, Alvin attempts to have the $2,000 taxed at Beatrice's lower rate than at his own higher rate. This will not work—Alvin must include the $2,000 in his gross income, and will be deemed to have made a gift of $2,000 to Beatrice. (However, if Alvin hired Beatrice to perform services, he could deduct reasonable amounts paid to her as compensation, and she would include those amounts in her gross income. This would achieve Alvin's desired result.)

C. Policy—Protection of integrity of progressive rates

The Code seeks to impose tax "fairly" on taxpayers, taxing similarly situated persons similarly *(horizontal equity)*. The tax rates are an integral part of identifying who is similarly situated to whom: Persons with similar taxable incomes are similarly situated and should be taxed similarly (at the same rates). If taxpayers could choose, without limitation, the person to whom income is taxed, the integrity of the progressive rate system would be undermined. As a result, the fairness of the system would be endangered.

D. Assignment of income from services

A taxpayer entitled to compensation income may attempt to shift that income to another person by private contract with the payor or assignee. Another route to the same result is the argument that state law gives another person significant rights to the income, and thus taxation should follow those state law rights by taxing that income to the other person.

1. **Diversion by agreement:** In this situation, a taxpayer enters into an agreement under which salaries or fees otherwise due the taxpayer will be paid to another person.

    a. **Rule:** Income is taxed to the person who earns it, regardless of arrangements made to channel it to another person.

    b. **Husbands and wives—*Lucas v. Earl*, 281 U.S. 111 (1930):** Mr. Lucas, an attorney, entered into a contract in 1901 with his wife that all property and salaries acquired by either of them would be "received, held, taken, and owned . . . as joint tenants, and not otherwise, with the right of survivorship." Mr. Lucas earned salary as an attorney in 1920 and 1921 and reported only half of it on his own return (at that time, husbands and wives filed separate returns).

        i. **Issue:** Should Mr. Lucas have reported the entire salary on his own return, or does the contract entered into with his wife vest half the income in her for federal income tax purposes?

        ii. **Result and rationale:** Mr. Lucas should have reported all of the income on his own return. Income is taxed to the person who earns it, regardless of "contracts however skillfully devised."

    c. **Parents, employers, and children—*Armantrout v. Commissioner*, 67 T.C. 996 (1977), *aff'd per curiam*, 570 F.2d 210 (7th Cir. 1978):** An employer established and funded a trust that paid the college tuition of children of employees. The parents (employees) had no rights in the trust, and if their children did not use the funds by age 21, they were no longer entitled to them.

i. **Issue:** Should the parents have included in their gross income the trust distributions used to pay for their children's college tuition?

ii. **Result and rationale:** The parents were required to include in their gross incomes the amount paid by the trust for the children's tuition. The trust arrangement constituted a device by which the parents attempted to divert compensation income they earned to their children. The parents earned the income, and they must be taxed on it.

iii. **Related issues:** This case raises interesting economic benefit and timing issues. The parents received an economic benefit (satisfaction of their obligation to pay their children's college) and therefore had an increase in their incomes. But *when* should the parents have included the amount in income? Three choices are: (1) when the plan was established, (2) when the rights vested, and (3) when the benefits were paid. The court did not address this issue.

2. **A contrast—Diversion by operation of law:** In some cases, governing law (state, federal, or foreign) sets forth rights of persons in items of property or income. The taxpayer may rely on these independently defined rights to assert that another person should report income.

a. **Rule:** State, federal, or foreign law determines the legal rights and duties from which federal tax consequences flow. If state law limits the rights of an individual to income in favor of another, that limitation will also limit his or her individual taxation.

b. **Community property—*Poe v. Seaborn,* 282 U.S. 101 (1930):** Husband and wife were residents of Washington, a community property state. Under Washington law, each spouse had an equal interest in community property, although the husband managed the property. They owned real and personal community property and had income from salary, interest, dividends, and the sale of real estate. Husband and wife each reported one-half of the income on their separate returns. (At that time, husbands and wives filed separate returns.)

i. **Issue:** Was the husband and wife's reporting position correct, or should the husband have reported *all* the income?

ii. **Result and rationale:** Each spouse was entitled to claim half of the income on his or her separate return. Under Washington law, each spouse had a right to half the income; the husband's rights to management were those of an agent. The right to the income under state law was dispositive of the incidence of taxation. *Poe v. Seaborn* arguably ignored the holding of *Lucas v. Earl* with respect to Mr. Seaborn's salary. However, the opinions might be reconciled by suggesting that state law determines who "earns" income; in the Seaborn situation, the "community" earned the income, not Mr. Seaborn.

iii. **Related issues:** *Poe v. Seaborn* led many states to adopt community property systems, and ultimately to Congress enacting the joint filing system for married persons.

E. Income from property

In these situations, an owner of income-producing property (e.g., stocks, bonds, real estate) gives the income or property to another person. The issue is which person—the donor or the donee—should include the income attributable to the transferred interest in gross income.

1. **Rule:** Attempts to transfer income of property independently of the property itself generally will be respected only if the income interest is transferred for its entire duration. Otherwise, the

donor will be taxed on the income, and will be deemed to have made a (nontaxable) gift to the donee.

2. *Blair v. Commissioner,* **300 U.S. 5 (1937):** William created a trust giving his son, Edward, a life estate in income of the trust. Edward assigned to his daughter, Lucy, an interest of about $9,000 per year in the trust. Edward later made similar assignments to his other children. The trustees distributed income directly to Lucy and the other children. The children reported the income they received from the trust in their gross incomes, but the IRS asserted that Edward should have included the income in his gross income.

   a. **Issue:** Should Edward have been required to include the income in his own gross income, or were the children correct in their reporting positions?

   b. **Result and rationale:** The children were correct in reporting the trust income in their gross incomes; Edward was not required to include it in his income. Edward transferred to his children the property interest he owned (an income interest in the trust), not the income from that property.

   c. **Comment:** This case illustrates the difficulty in distinguishing between property and income. Since the fair market value of property is simply the present value of its future income stream, the two are inextricably connected, thus creating this confusion.

3. *Helvering v. Horst,* **311 U.S. 112 (1940):** Dad owned negotiable bonds with interest coupons attached. Just before some of the coupons matured, Dad detached them and gave them to son. The son negotiated them, received the interest payments, and reported the income. The IRS asserted that Dad, not son, was the proper taxpayer to include the interest income in gross income.

   a. **Issue:** Who—Dad or son—should include the interest income in gross income?

   b. **Result and rationale:** Dad should have reported the interest income. The court relied on the realization concept, that Dad's gift of the coupons constituted enjoyment of the income, and thus income should be taxed to the person who obtains enjoyment of it. This rationale is not favored today.

      i. **Ripe fruit hanging on trees:** Dad essentially earned the income, because the coupons were so close to maturity when they were transferred. This case is the origin of the fruit-and-tree metaphor, which is vivid but generally unhelpful in analyzing assignment of income issues.

      ii. **Carved-out interest:** A better rationale is that Dad gave away only the income from the property, not the property itself, for less than the entire duration of the income stream. Thus, this was an inappropriate assignment of income.

   c. **Related issues**

      i. **Income/property distinction:** The court focused on the different interests in the bond: a capital interest (the right to be repaid the amount loaned) and the interest income (annual payments of interest to compensate the lender for the loan). While certainly both economics and tax law make a distinction between capital (principal) and income (interest), in fact the principal is merely the present value of the future income stream. Distinctions that rely on some essential difference between capital and income are probably destined to failure.

ii. **Timing:** In *Horst,* the interest payments were made in the same year as the transfer. If the interest payments had been made in the next year, the question would arise whether the transfer would have accelerated the income to Dad, i.e., required him to report the income in the year of transfer, even though the interest had not yet been paid. Subsequent cases have reached varying results on this issue.

iii. **Gifts—IRC §§102 and 1015:** Recall that a donee excludes from gross income the value of property received by gift and generally takes the donor's basis in the gift property. IRC §§102 and 1015, discussed at Chapters 4(III) and 9(III)(B), respectively. The combination of these rules allows a donor to transfer to the donee the unrealized appreciation in property, if the gift is of the full property. Special rules for the donee's basis in loss property, however, restrict the transfer of losses. See Chapter 9(III)(B).

4. **Qualified dividend income:** With tax rates on qualified dividend income at a low 15%, the incentive to transfer stock from high-bracket to low-bracket taxpayers is diminished.

5. **What's good for the goose—*Est. of Stranahan v. Commissioner,* 472 F.2d 867 (6th Cir. 1973):** The taxpayer was entitled to a large interest deduction in 1964, but he didn't have enough income in that year to use the deduction. The taxpayer agreed with his son to transfer to the son the father's right to dividends on certain stock owned by him, in exchange for a payment equal to the present value of the future dividend income. The taxpayer, relying on assignment of income principles to work for his benefit, included the payment in income and deducted the interest payment. Naturally, the IRS objected. The Tax Court found the transaction lacking in business motive, and essentially a loan, not a sale. It found that the taxpayer did not realize income as a result of the transaction with his son.

a. **Issue:** Did the taxpayer realize income on the sale, pursuant to assignment of income principles?

b. **Result and rationale:** Yes. Even though the tax benefit was the sole motive for the transaction, it was a bona fide sale with all of a sale's attendant risk and reward. The non-gratuitous nature of the transaction distinguishes it from *Helvering v. Horst* and related cases, and it must be respected for tax purposes. The taxpayer did assign the dividends, and receive payment in exchange, and the payment is includible in the taxpayer's gross income.

F. **Transformation of services into property**

In this situation, a taxpayer's services result in some item of income-producing property (often intellectual property) that he or she then gives to a related person. The issue is which person—the donor or the donee—should be taxed on the income from the property.

1. **Rule:** The assignment of the right to income alone arising from property created by services is an invalid assignment of income: The donor will be taxed on the income. By contrast, the transfer of the income-producing property itself is valid, resulting in the donee being taxed on the income. In order to qualify as "property," the transfer must include some bundle of legally enforceable rights (other than the right to collect income) given to the donee by the donor.

2. **Commissions—*Helvering v. Eubank,* 311 U.S. 122 (1940):** A retired insurance agent assigned renewal commissions to others, who subsequently collected the commissions. The court relied on *Horst,* holding that the insurance agent was taxable on the commissions when paid to the assignees.

3. **Patents—***Heim v. Fitzpatrick,* **262 F.2d 887 (2d Cir. 1959):** Mr. Heim invented a fancy bearing and applied for a patent. He then transferred the invention and patent application to a corporation owned by family members. Under an agreement with the corporation, Mr. Heim was entitled to certain royalties, retained some control over use of the invention, and retained a reversionary interest in the patent. He then transferred a portion of his interest in the agreement to his wife, son, and daughter (donees). The corporation paid royalties to Mr. Heim and the donees.

   a. **Issue:** Who should be taxed on the royalties due under the agreement—Mr. Heim or the donees?

   b. **Result and rationale:** The donees should be taxed on the income from the invention. Mr. Heim transferred income-producing property rather than merely assigning income from services rendered. The donees received not only the right to the royalties but certain legally enforceable rights relating to the invention and patents, including the power to bargain for royalties on new uses of the patent and the reversionary interest in the invention and patents.

G. What about transfers of property?

1. **Does the doctrine apply?** So far, the assignment of income doctrine has been applied to the transfer of services income, and the transfer of property that is essentially the culmination of a taxpayer's services. Will it apply to transactions purely in what is thought of as traditional "property"? Maybe. This also raises questions about what property really is.

2. *Salvatore v. Commissioner,* **29 T.C.M. 89 (1970)**

   a. **Facts:** Mrs. Salvatore inherited real property operated as a service station from her husband. She and her children ran it, dividing the income among themselves; she received what she needed for her support, and the children divided the rest. Texaco offered to buy the property, and Salvatore agreed. The sales price was to be divided, by family agreement, between Salvatore, up to the amount they estimated she needed for her lifetime support, and the rest to her children equally. To accomplish this, just before the sale, Salvatore made a gift of one-half of the property to the children, and she reported the gain only on her remaining one-half of the property.

   b. **Issue:** How much gain on the sale of the property is Mrs. Salvatore taxable on—all of it, or just one-half? In other words, who has income on the sale of the property: Mrs. Salvatore only, or Mrs. Salvatore and her children?

   c. **Result and rationale:** Mrs. Salvatore is taxable on all of the gain. She impermissibly assigned one-half of the income from the sale to her children. The children were treated as "mere conduits" for the income.

      i. **The gift:** The gift of the property was valid under state law; the deeds were recorded and all formalities respected. Mrs. Salvatore even paid gift tax on the gift. But the amount of the gift was conditional upon Mrs. Salvatore's need for income: If she had needed more, the gift would have been less.

      ii. **Fundamental principles:** If you continue in the study of tax, you'll see versions of this transaction again, in corporate tax (*Court Holding Company v. Commissioner,* 342 U.S. 331 (1945)) and throughout estate and gift tax. The fundamental principles: The substance of a transaction, not its form, governs its federal income tax consequences, and familial transfers are subject to special scrutiny.

3. **Choses in action:** A taxpayer may transfer to another the right to prosecute a claim and receive a recovery. If the transfer occurs when recovery is contingent and uncertain, the transferor will not be considered to have assigned the income. If the transfer occurs when payment is relatively certain, the transferring taxpayer must include the amount in gross income, and then is deemed to have transferred that amount to the transferee. *When* the right to payment becomes certain is a question of fact. See, e.g., *Doyle v. Commissioner,* 147 F.2d 769 (4th Cir. 1945).

H. Contingent fee awards—*Banks v. Commissioner,* ___ U.S. ___ (2005)

When a taxpayer hires an attorney on a contingent fee basis, such as in a personal injury lawsuit, the recovery is usually paid to the attorney, who deducts his or her fee and gives the balance to the client. In a personal physical injury case, of course, none of this amount is includible in gross income. But for nonphysical injury cases, all of the recovery must be included in gross income. Prior to *Banks,* many taxpayers argued that the amount paid to the attorney as fees was not included in gross income, and some courts agreed. In *Banks,* the Supreme Court held that all of the award—including the amount paid to the attorney—is included in the client/plaintiff's gross income for a nonphysical injury.

1. **What's the problem?** The taxpayer may claim a deduction for the attorneys' fees, but these are miscellaneous itemized deductions. This creates two problems. First, miscellaneous itemized deductions are subject to the 2% floor, rendering some of them nondeductible. See Chapter 6(XVII). Second, none of the miscellaneous itemized deductions are deductible in computing the AMT. See Chapter 13(III). As a result, many taxpayers receiving apparently large awards end up paying tax on all of the award, even though they didn't receive the portion attributable to attorneys' fees.

2. **Statutory response:** For certain kinds of nonphysical injuries, Congress has allowed an above-the-line deduction for attorneys' fees. See Chapter 6(X).

IV. STATUTORY RESPONSES TO ASSIGNMENT OF INCOME AND RELATED PROBLEMS

The previous sections have set forth the judicially developed assignment of income principles. Congress has also responded in a limited fashion to assignment of income problems.

A. Section 1(g)—"The Kiddie Tax"

Children are usually in a lower tax bracket than their parents and grandparents, and this creates an incentive for parents and grandparents to transfer income-producing property to them so that the income from the property is taxed at the child's lower rate. This type of planning is not precluded under assignment of income principles because the property itself is transferred to the child.

1. **Tax at parents' rate:** The kiddie tax reduces this incentive by taxing the child's "unearned income" at the parents' tax rate. IRC §1(g)(1).

2. **Only certain income:** The kiddie tax applies only if the following conditions are met.

   a. **Less than 14:** It is applicable only to children under the age of 14 with at least one parent living. IRC §1(g)(2).

b. **Unearned income:** The kiddie tax only applies to investment income, not earned income such as income from a paper route or film salaries. IRC §1(g)(4).

c. **Dollar amount:** The kiddie tax applies to investment income in excess of $1,600, so that the first $1,600 of the child's investment income is taxed at his or her lower rate. IRC §1(g)(4).

d. **Include in parental return:** The kiddie tax has a special option for parents to include their children's investment income on their own tax returns, in which case the child's income is taxed to the parents. IRC §1(g)(7).

B. **Reallocation of income and deductions—§482**

Section 482 is a broad statute, allowing the IRS to reallocate among members of commonly controlled businesses items of income, deduction, and credit if necessary to prevent evasion of tax or clearly to reflect income of the businesses. Although a detailed analysis is beyond the scope of most basic federal income tax courses, §482 should be noted as an effective tool for the IRS in ensuring that the appropriate taxpayer pays tax on various items of income.

V. WHERE ARE WE GOING?

This chapter has concluded the discussion of the computation of a taxpayer's tax liability (by identifying the proper taxpayer) and has introduced a common technique of tax planning (assignment of income). The next chapter turns to a fundamental financial concept—the time value of money—that motivates much of tax planning and generates congressional response to that planning.

Quiz Yourself on
IDENTIFYING THE TAXPAYER

123. Anakin is a consultant to international security firms. His son, Luke, is 25 years old and a full-time student at the University of the Republic. This year, Anakin hired Luke to assist him. Luke's duties were to call his dad periodically to consult with him about current events. Anakin instructed Empire, Inc., a firm that hired him, to pay to Luke the $100,000 fee earned for consulting this year, instead of paying it to Anakin. Will this plan be respected for tax purposes? _____

124. Danielle writes romantic novels. Her daughter Tiffany is 12 years old. Danielle requests that her publisher pay all the royalties on the book to be published this year to Tiffany, so that Tiffany can begin saving money for college. Her publisher does so, and reports Tiffany as the taxpayer on the required Form 1099. Is this correct? _____

125. Sam is Peter's grandfather. Peter's parents are living. Sam owns a number of bonds and regularly receives interest payments on these bonds. Sam directs the company that issued the bonds to pay Peter, rather than Sam, the interest on the bonds. The company does so. Who is taxed on this interest, and why? _____

126. Assume the same facts as in the previous question, except that the bonds are tax-exempt private activity bonds. Why would it matter who is taxed on these interest payments if they are tax-exempt? _____

127. Barbara is George's mother. Barbara owns a ranch in Texas. In Year One, she transferred an undivided 50% interest in the ranch to George, as a gift. In Year Ten, a buyer purchases the ranch for $2,000,000. Barbara and George each report one-half of the gain on the sale. Is this correct? _____

128. Brian files a lawsuit against Debbie alleging defamation of character. Prior to trial, Brian's health starts to fail. He assigns his rights in the action to Steve for a payment of $500,000. The trial and subsequent appeals result in an award of $5 million. Who, if anyone, must include this amount in gross income? _____

129. Kayla sues her employer for race discrimination. She hires an attorney on a contingent fee basis to represent her. Ultimately, the court enters a judgment of $500,000 against the employer. The lawyer's share of that is $165,000 for fees and $35,000 for costs, and Kayla receives $300,000. How should she treat this transaction for tax purposes? _____

130. Assume the same facts as in the previous question, except that the action was for slander rather than discrimination. What changes, if anything? _____

131. Spencer is age 12. He has a paper route, from which he makes $3,600 per year. He also has investment income of $3,000 per year from stocks and bonds given to him by relatives over the years. Spencer's parents are living. How will Spencer be taxed on his income?

Answers

123. Compensation income is taxed to the person who provides services, and it is not permissible to "assign" the income to someone else as Anakin has sought to do. Anakin and Luke may argue that Luke performed services for his father, and if so this raises two questions. First, who must report the payment from Empire? Because the contract was between Anakin and Empire, the appropriate reporting position is for Anakin to report the income from Empire, Inc. and then take a deduction for salary or wages paid to Luke. Second, what amount (if any) may be deducted for payments to Luke? Certainly not the entire $100,000. If the two taxpayers can prove that Luke actually provided valuable services, the fair market value of those services is deductible to Anakin. But this is a situation in which the transaction would be carefully scrutinized, because it appears that Luke did not provide any services.

124. Danielle has probably engaged in an inappropriate assignment of income. She transferred income from services (transformed into "property"—the intellectual property that gives rise to the income) to her daughter, who did not perform the services. However, she would argue that there is not an impermissible assignment because she transferred 100% of the income stream. However, without also transferring the intellectual property that gives rise to the income, she retains power over that income stream that would defeat her argument. If she can transfer the intellectual property itself (for example, if the rights to income arise from a copyright as opposed to a simple contract for services) she should be able to direct the income to Tiffany.

125. Sam is taxed on the interest. He cannot give away just the interest element. If he wants Peter to be taxed on the interest, then Sam must give Peter the bonds.

126. If the income is tax-exempt interest, it won't matter who is deemed to own it for regular tax purposes. But this kind of interest income may be included in alternative minimum taxable income, and therefore the assignment of income doctrine will apply.

127. It is probably correct. Although the *Salvatore* case might raise questions, in this case (1) the length of time between gift and ultimate sale; and (2) the absence of facts suggesting that Barbara's share was uncertain supports the taxpayers' position that the transfer was bona fide, and that the substance of the transaction is a sale by both Barbara and George of the property.

128. Brian's assignment of his claim will probably not result in an assignment of income because the claim is contingent and doubtful at the time of transfer. Thus, the transferee will properly include the amount in gross income. Because Steve has a basis in this action of $500,000, he will include only $4,500,000 in gross income; the rest will be a return of capital. Steve will argue that this is capital gain, but is unlikely to prevail. See Chapter 12 (III).

129. Under *Banks*, Kayla must include the entire amount of the award ($500,000) in her gross income when she receives it. (IRC §104(a) doesn't apply to exclude this award because this is a nonphysical injury.) However, Kayla will be allowed an above-the-line deduction (a deduction from gross income in computing AGI) for her attorneys' fees and costs.

130. In this case, Kayla must still include the $500,000 in her gross income, but is not allowed an above-the-line deduction in computing AGI for her attorneys' fees and costs. Instead, she can claim these as a miscellaneous itemized deduction, subject to the 2% floor of IRC §z 67. Assuming she had no other income or deductions that year, and that Kayla is a single taxpayer, here are her tax consequences:

Regular Tax Liability		AMT Liability	
Gross Income	$500,000	Taxable Income	$306,800
Minus:		Plus:	
Itemized Deductions	(190,000)	Itemized Deduction:	190,000
Personal exemption	(3,200)	Personal Exemption	3,200
Taxable income	$306,800	AMTI	$500,000
Regular Tax	**$88,243***	**AMT**	**$136,500****

Total Tax Liability:

$88,243	Regular Tax
$48,257	AMT
$136,500	**Total Tax**

*From tax tables
**26% of $175,000+28% of $325,000

131. Spencer will probably file his own tax return, but he does have the option of filing with his parents. His regular tax rate (10%) will apply to his earned income and up to $1600 of his investment income. But the remaining amount of investment income will be taxed at his parents' marginal rate.

Exam Tips on
ASSIGNMENT OF INCOME

☛ Even though the discussion of the assignment of income doctrine comes close to the end of this book, it is conceptually one of the first questions you should ask yourself in analyzing tax questions.

   ☞ *Look for:* Intrafamily transfers, usually from a senior generation to a younger generation, with the opportunity to lower taxes on the overall economic unit.

   ☞ *Analyze:* Has there been an impermissible assignment of income from one person to another? What is the result of this assignment? Is there a judicial doctrine or statutory "fix" that prevents this assignment?

☛ Use the smell test: Does it seem that the taxpayer is "getting away with something" by transferring income or property to another person? If so, the question probably involves an assignment of income problem.

☛ The assignment of income doctrine applies most often to services income.

   ☞ *Look for:* One person who performs services, but another receives the compensation, in money or other property. That other person just happens to be in a lower tax bracket.

   ☞ *Analyze:* Compensation income is taxed to the person who performs services. Then, that person is considered to have made a gift to the person who ended up with the income. However, if state, federal, or foreign law divides the income between two people—that will usually be respected.

☛ The assignment of income doctrine also applies to income arising from property.

   ☞ *Look for:* Assignments of dividends, interest, rent, royalties, etc.

   ☞ *Analyze:* Did the assignor transfer the underlying property or just the income stream? If only the income stream, it is likely to be an impermissible assignment of income.

☛ The *Banks* case is good fodder for testing, not only because it is a recent Supreme Court tax case, but also because it combines issues of gross income, deductions, and the AMT. Make sure you understand *Banks* and the stakes of the controversy.

☛ Remember two fundamental principles:

   ☞ Familial transfers are subject to particular scrutiny.

   ☞ The substance of a transaction governs its federal income tax consequences—not its form. If it seems too good to be true, it probably is.

CHAPTER 15

TIME VALUE OF MONEY: PRINCIPLES AND APPLICATIONS

ChapterScope _____

The previous chapters have focused on the issues surrounding the calculation of a taxpayer's tax liability; from identifying items of income, deduction, and credit, to identifying the appropriate taxpayer and tax rate. This chapter turns to a more general principle, the time value of money. The time value of money, simply expressed, is the notion that a sum of money will earn interest when invested. Thus, a dollar invested for one year at 8% interest will be worth $1.08 one year in the future (ignoring inflation). Time value of money principles are important in tax law for two reasons. First, some Code sections specifically incorporate time value of money principles in prescribing the proper tax treatment of certain transactions, principally those dealing with loans and similar undertakings. More generally, the time value of money often motivates taxpayers to engage in certain tax planning strategies, and understanding how the time value of money operates helps one understand these common strategies. This chapter explores both the specific and general applications of the time value of money in tax law.

Key concepts in this chapter include:

- **Time value of money:** This chapter introduces the basic concept of the time value of money and the calculation of present and future values.

- **Specific applications:** The Code specifically invokes time value of money concepts in prescribing the tax treatment of loans, debt instruments, and similar arrangements.

- **Deferral of income and acceleration of deductions:** Recognizing time value of money concepts, taxpayers typically seek to defer income as far into the future as possible and accelerate deductions to the earliest possible year. These form the basis of many common tax-planning strategies.

I. WHERE ARE WE?

This focus of this chapter isn't the Code, or administrative or judicial interpretations of questions of income or deduction or credit. Instead, we now turn to a principle underlying much of tax planning and legislative responses to that planning: the time value of money. As with the assignment of income principles discussed in the previous chapter, time value of money concepts appear explicitly only in a few places in the Code, mainly dealing with loan transactions. However, understanding how time value of money principles inspire taxpayers to take certain tax planning steps, and why the IRS and Congress are motivated to block these steps, is critical to understanding tax law in general.

II. TIME VALUE OF MONEY PRINCIPLES—THE BASICS

A. In general

The essence of the time value of money is expressed in the old adage, "A penny saved is a penny earned." But this only works if the saver doesn't stash the penny in a mattress. The alert saver will lend his or her penny to someone else, and that borrower will pay the lender for the privilege of using the penny during the period of the loan. Thus, the penny will earn more pennies for the saver, and given sufficient time, the saver will have dozens of pennies. The saver will have dozens, not just a few, because of the "miracle of compound interest." Compounding means that the lender earns interest not only on his or her principal sum but also on the interest earned. As a result of compounding, the investor will end up with many more pennies than the average person expects. The longer the investment period, and the higher the interest rate, of course, the more pennies will be earned. Add a few zeros, and this process becomes very interesting indeed.

Example: Leslie, age 50, invests $2,000 in an IRA. It earns interest at 12% compounded annually, tax-free. By the time she retires at age 60, her single $2,000 investment will have grown to $6,211. Had Leslie made her investment at 40, allowing twenty years for her investment to grow, she would have had $19,321 in her next egg. Had she invested $2,000 at age 20, allowing 40 years of growth, she would have had $186,916 at retirement.

B. Interest

Interest is the cost of using money. A lender charges a borrower interest for the privilege of using the lender's funds during the period of the loan, and thus the lender is said to "earn interest" on the loan. Interest is expressed as a percentage of the principal amount of the loan for a stated period, usually a year.

1. **Simple interest:** Simple interest is calculated as a percentage of the principal sum.

2. **Compound interest:** Compound interest is computed by applying the interest rate to both the principal sum and the accrued, but unpaid, interest. Compounding can occur at various intervals—typically daily, monthly, half-yearly, or annually.

   Example: Steve lends Andy $1,000 at 10% interest. If the loan provides for simple interest, the loan will generate $100 in interest each year that it is outstanding. If the loan provides for interest compounded annually, in the first year the loan will generate interest of $100. In the second year, the loan will generate interest of $110, which is calculated by adding the interest on the principal amount ($1,000 × 10% = $100) and the interest on the accrued but unpaid interest ($100 × 10% = $10).

3. **Market rate of interest:** A typical loan carries a "market" rate of interest, i.e., the interest rate at which loans of the same type are made in the general lending market. The interest rate depends on a variety of factors, including the repayment risk (a higher-risk loan comes with a higher interest rate) and the general availability of funds.

C. Future value of a stated sum

We can calculate what amount will eventually be created for any amount today, if we know the rate of return (interest rate) and period of time of investment. This is the "future value" of the principal sum (or any investment), calculated using the following formula:

$$FV = PV(1 + i)^n$$

FV = Future value
PV = Present value of invested (or loaned) amount
  i = interest rate
  n = number of years invested (or loaned)

Example—Loan: Larry lends Bob $10,000 at 10% interest compounded annually for five years. At the end of five years, Bob will pay Larry $16,129, calculated as follows:

$$FV = \$\,10{,}000 \times (1 + .10)^5$$
$$FV = \$\,10{,}000 \times (1.1)^5$$
$$FV = \$\,10{,}000 \times 1.6129$$
$$FV = \$\,16{,}129$$

D. Present value

Present value is the mirror image of future value, based on the same principles and derived from the same formula. Present value is the current value, given an assumed interest rate, of a right to a stated amount in the future. Differently expressed, it is also the amount that must be invested today, at a given interest rate and for a given period, to produce a stated amount. Present value can be computed using the following formula, which is simply the future value formula algebraically rearranged to solve for present value.

$$PV = \frac{FV}{(1 + i)^n}$$

$$PV = \text{Present Value}$$
$$FV = \text{Future Value}$$
$$i = \text{interest rate}$$
$$n = \text{number of years}$$

Example: Brenda is planning for her daughter's college education. She predicts she will need $100,000 in ten years and can earn 6% on her investment. She calculates how much she will need to invest ($55,800) as follows:

$$PV = \frac{\$100{,}000}{(1 + .06)^{10}}$$
$$PV = \frac{\$100{,}000}{1.7921}$$
$$PV = \$55{,}800$$

Example: Kate's employer offers her a bonus of either $75,000 today or $150,000 due in five years. Current interest rates are 8%. Disregarding taxes (and constructive receipt!) which offer is more valuable? To answer this question, the present value of the $150,000 five years hence must be calculated. Kate does so as follows:

$$PV = \frac{\$150{,}000}{(1 + .08)^5}$$
$$PV = \frac{\$150{,}000}{1.4684}$$
$$PV = \$102{,}150$$

The calculation shows that the five-year offer is the more valuable of the two, suggesting that Kate should accept the five-year offer.

E. Using present value tables

Instead of using the formulas above, the present and future values may be derived from commonly available tables. See Figure 15A.

1. **Future value:** The future value of a sum invested today is calculated using the tables by locating the entry found in the table at the intersection of the column representing the given interest rate and the row representing the given number of years to maturity. The sum to be invested is divided by that figure to determine the future value of the beginning sum.

   Example: Peter has $10,000 to invest at 10% for twenty years. To determine the future value of this sum, i.e., the amount he will have at the end of the 20-year period, divide $10,000 by 0.149. Thus, Peter will have $67,114 at the end of this period.

2. **Present value:** The present value of a sum available in the future also can be determined using the tables, given an interest rate and the number of years to maturity. To do so, multiply the sum available in the future by the entry found in the table at the intersection of the column representing the given interest rate and the row representing the given number of years to maturity.

   Example: Katherine is planning to retire in twenty years and estimates that she will need $1 million at that time. She can earn 8% on a one-time investment made today. How much must she invest today to have $1 million in twenty years, i.e., what is the present value of $1 million twenty years hence at 8%? To determine this, multiply $1 million by 0.215 to produce $215,000. Katherine must invest $215,000 today in order to have $1 million at retirement.

F. Other formulas

Many investors wish to know the future value of not just a single sum, but of a series of investments over a period of time. Others anticipate receiving an annual payment at some time in the future (an annuity) and wish to know the present value of those future payments. For these investors, other formulas and tables are available to determine present and future value. These are generally beyond the scope of the basic tax course, but are readily available in financial texts.

G. Code's use of time value of money principles

Although the Code does not import time value of money principles on a global scale, it does recognize these principles in a number of specific transactions principally relating to loans and similar undertakings.

1. **Federal rates:** Every month, the IRS publishes interest rates (known as the "applicable federal rate" or "AFR") which are used for computations under various Code provisions. There are many different rates, used for different purposes, but the major categories are the federal "short-term rate," (for obligations designed to be outstanding for fewer than five years), the "mid-term rate" (five through nine years), and the "long-term rate" (ten years or more).

2. **Tax over- and underpayments:** If a taxpayer overpays tax, the government will pay interest on the overpayment at a rate of the federal short-term rate plus 3%. IRC §6621(a)(1). If a taxpayer underpays tax, the taxpayer must pay interest at a rate of the federal short-term rate plus 3%. IRC §6621(a)(2).

Figure 15A
Present Value Table

Year	2%	3%	4%	5%	6%	7%	8%	9%	10%	12%	15%
1	.980	.971	.962	.952	.943	.935	.926	.917	.909	.893	.870
2	.961	.943	.925	.907	.890	.873	.857	.842	.826	.797	.756
3	.942	.915	.889	.864	.840	.816	.794	.772	.751	.712	.658
4	.924	.888	.855	.823	.792	.763	.735	.708	.683	.636	.572
5	.906	.863	.822	.784	.747	.713	.681	.650	.621	.567	.497
6	.888	.837	.790	.746	.705	.666	.630	.596	.564	.507	.432
7	.871	.813	.760	.712	.665	.623	.583	.547	.513	.452	.376
8	.853	.789	.731	.677	.627	.582	.540	.502	.467	.404	.327
9	.837	.766	.703	.645	.592	.544	.500	.460	.424	.361	.284
10	.820	.744	.676	.614	.558	.508	.463	.422	.386	.322	.247
15	.743	.642	.555	.481	.417	.362	.315	.275	.239	.182	.123
20	.673	.554	.456	.377	.311	.258	.215	.178	.149	.104	.061
25	.610	.478	.375	.295	.233	.184	.146	.116	.092	.059	.030
30	.552	.412	.308	.231	.174	.131	.099	.075	.057	.033	.015
35	.500	.355	.253	.181	.130	.094	.067	.049	.036	.019	.008
40	.453	.307	.208	.142	.097	.067	.046	.032	.022	.012	.004

To determine the present value of a future sum, multiply the sum by the figure at the intersection of the row indicating the year in the future and the column representing the interest (discount) rate.

To determine the future value of a present sum, divide the sum by the figure at the intersection of the row indicating the year in the future and the column representing the discount rate.

3. **Loan transactions:** Much of the time value of money material in the Code addresses loan transactions. When one unrelated party lends money to another, the lender charges interest on the loan at market rates. However, related parties may want to make interest-free loans to transfer value to the borrower, and sellers and buyers of property may want to characterize income as capital gain rather than ordinary income. Various provisions of the Code prevent this by imputing interest (which is ordinary income, of course) to loan transactions.

III. ORIGINAL ISSUE DISCOUNT (OID)

The OID rules are extremely complex and the following discussion focuses only on their highlights.

A. Policy

Sometimes a debt instrument will not provide for market interest payable annually during the period of the debt, but instead will build the interest payment into the final payment (repayment) of the debt. This strategy would offer two tax benefits for investors (creditors), the second of which specifically invokes the time value of money principle. First, the repayment in excess of the original amount loaned might be considered capital gain on the repayment of the debt. Second, the creditor might defer the inclusion of any amount in gross income until the end of the investment. The OID and related rules seek to preclude both of these "misstatements" of the economic realities of the loan.

Example: At a time when market interest is 10%, two corporations issue bonds. Alpha Corporation issues $1,000 20-year bonds bearing 10% annual interest. Investors purchasing these bonds pay Alpha Corporation $1,000 and receive (and pay tax on) their interest payments annually; in 20 years they will receive their initial $1,000 investment. Beta Corporation issues "deep discount" $1,000 bonds, in which the investors pay Beta Corporation $149, and in twenty years they will receive $1,000. No interest payments are due during the term of the Beta bonds. These two types of bonds are economically identical: each has a 10% rate of return, although the Alpha bonds pay currently, and the Beta bonds' payment is deferred until maturity.

The Alpha investors clearly must include the annual interest payments in gross income. When they receive their original $1,000 investment back in 20 years, they will have no gain or loss on the transaction.

Without the OID provisions, the Beta investors would not include any amount in gross income until maturity of the Beta bonds. They might also seek to characterize the $851 additional amount received as capital gain on the disposition of the bonds.

The OID provisions seek to tax the Beta investors in the same way as the Alpha investors, so that the Beta investors include a portion of the interest element of the bond ($851) in gross income each year until maturity. With each inclusion of interest, the Beta investors increase their bases in the bonds, so that upon retirement of the bond, they will have no gain or loss.

B. Original issue discount—Statutory analysis

1. **General rule:** The holder of certain debt instruments must include in gross income an amount equal to the daily portions of the original issue discount for each day on which the instrument is held. IRC §1272(a)(1). The amount of OID is the excess (if any) of the stated redemption price at maturity over the issue price. IRC §1273(a)(1). The OID provisions apply to debt instruments having original issue discount issued after July 1, 1982. IRC §1272.

   a. **Constant interest or economic accrual method of inclusion:** The effect of the OID rules is to treat the borrower as having paid the lender the interest accruing on the outstanding principal amount of the loan semiannually, and the lender is treated as having lent the interest back to the borrower, who then must pay interest on the original principal and also the re-lent interest. This concept of accruing interest on unpaid interest is commonly referred to as the "economic accrual of interest" or "constant interest."

b. **Effect to lender and borrower:** Under the transaction as described just above, the borrower may deduct the interest deemed paid (assuming the other requirements for deductibility are met), and the lender must include it in gross income.

c. **Allocating the OID:** The total OID must be allocated to the holder of the debt instrument on a daily basis by multiplying the "yield to maturity" by the "adjusted issue price," subtracting any "qualified stated interest." Reg. §1.1272-1(j). This amount is allocated on a daily basis within the accrual period. Reg. §1.1272-1(b)(1)(iv).

   i. **Yield to maturity:** A debt instrument's yield to maturity is the discount rate that, when used in computing the present value of all principal and interest payments to be made under the debt instrument, produces an amount equal to the issue price of the debt instrument. Reg. §1.1272-1(b)(1)(i). In computing the yield to maturity, the taxpayer must select an accrual period of one year of less, during which interest is compounded. Reg. §1.1272-1(b)(1)(ii).

   ii. **Adjusted issue price:** The adjusted issue price is the original issue price adjusted upward for the accrued, but unpaid, OID. IRC §1272(a)(4).

   iii. **Qualified stated interest:** Qualified stated interest is fixed-rate interest unqualifiedly due and payable at stated intervals of one year or less during the term of the indebtedness. Reg. §1.1273-1(c)(1).

2. **Definitions:** The following definitions offer only the general rules, which are subject to numerous technical exceptions.

   a. **Debt instrument:** A debt instrument includes a bond, debenture, note, or certificate or other evidence of indebtedness. IRC §1275(a)(1).

   b. **Stated redemption price at maturity:** The stated redemption price at maturity is the fixed amount that the debtor will pay the creditor to retire the debt. IRC §1273(a).

   c. **Issue price:** For bonds and similar instruments, the issue price is generally the offering price to the public for issuance of the debt instrument. IRC §1273(b).

   i. **Property:** For sales of property, the issue price is the stated principal amount if there is "adequate stated interest," i.e., the obligation bears interest at the statutorily prescribed **applicable federal rate,** discussed below. IRC §1274(a)(1).

   ii. **Other sales:** Otherwise, the issue price is the imputed principal amount. IRC §1274(a). The imputed principal amount is the present value of all payments to be made under the contract, using the applicable federal rate as the discount rate. IRC §1274(b)(1).

   d. **Applicable federal rate:** The applicable federal rate is the federal short-term, midterm or long-term rate, depending on the length of the obligation in question. The IRS publishes these rates periodically. IRC §1274(d)(1). The federal rates reflect the market rate of interest, rising and falling as do other rates of interest, such as the prime rate.

   Example—Bonds and similar instruments issued for cash: For bonds and similar instruments issued for cash, the OID rules compare the issue price (what the investor pays) with what the debtor will pay to retire the debt (repayment amount). The difference is OID, a proportionate share of which is included in the gross income of the creditor during the time he or she holds the debt. The creditor adds the OID to the basis of the debt instrument each year, so that by the end of the loan period, the basis is equal to the redemption price. Repayment, then, is a nontaxable event. Consider, for example, Carlotta, who purchases a 10-year bond from Delta Corporation for $508, under the terms of which Delta will pay her $1,000 in ten years with no interest payments due in the interim. Applying the OID rules, the issue price is $508 and the stated price at redemption is $1,000. The difference is $492, which is OID that Carlotta must include in her gross income on a constant interest basis during the time she holds the bond.

Example—Deferred sales of property: Applying the OID rules to deferred sales of property is problematic because it can be difficult to identify the issue price, i.e., the fair market value (true sales price) of the property. The first step in this analysis is determining whether the parties have provided in the transaction for market interest, measured by rates published quarterly by the IRS. If the stated interest is adequate, the OID rules won't apply. If there is not adequate interest, the Code imputes interest to the transaction at the applicable federal rate, thus isolating the interest element of the transaction. Any remaining payments constitute principal. Consider, for example, Zoe, who purchased Blackacre for $50,000 several years ago. Now it is worth $500,000. Zoe agrees to sell Blackacre to Alan. Because Alan does not have sufficient cash to purchase Blackacre, Zoe agrees to finance the purchase for two years. At a time when the applicable federal rate is 9%, Zoe and Alan agree that (1) the purchase price will be $594,050, (2) this sum will be due in two years, and (3) no interest will be payable under the contract.

In this contract there is obviously no adequate stated interest. Therefore, the OID provisions will recharacterize the transaction as first having adequate stated interest, using a standard market rate. Assuming a 9% rate, this would be $94,050. Zoe must include this interest in income over the term of the contract. The remaining amount would be principal, so Zoe's gain on the sale of Blackacre would be $450,000 ($500,000 − $50,000). To put this example in the language of the Code, the "issue price" of the instrument is the imputed principal amount of $500,000 (the present value of the $594,050 to be received two years hence, discounted at 10%). The "stated redemption price" is $594,050, so the OID is the $94,050 that is included in Zoe's gross income over the two-year term of the loan under the constant interest method.

3. **Special rules and exceptions:** The OID rules do not apply to certain types of transactions generally not considered abusive.

   a. **Farms/small businesses:** Sales of farms by individuals or small businesses where the purchase price is $1,000,000 or less are not subject to the OID rules. IRC §1274(c)(3)(A).

   b. **Principal residences:** Sales of principal residences are not subject to OID rules. IRC §1274(c)(3)(B).

   c. **$250,000 or less:** Sales involving total payments of $250,000 or less are not subject to OID rules. IRC §1274(c)(3)(C).

   d. **Cap on applicable federal rate:** The applicable federal rate is capped at 9% for debt instruments not in excess of $2,800,000 received in consideration for certain types of property. IRC §1274A(a).

4. **Related material**

   a. **Section 483—Imputed interest:** For deferred sales of property not subject to the OID rules, §483 will usually apply. See this chapter at section (V).

b. Below-market loans: Another potentially applicable section is §7872, dealing with below-market loans. See discussion of §7872, this chapter at section (VI).

c. Deductibility of interest: If the creditor must include an amount in income, there may be a corresponding deduction for the debtor. See discussion of interest deductions at Chapter 7(D)(1).

d. Basis: In sales of property, the imputed principal amount determines the buyer's basis in the property for purposes of depreciation and determination of gain or loss on subsequent sale. See Chapter 9(C).

5. **Summary:** See Statute Summary—OID.

Statute Summary—Original Issue Discount

Parsing Step	OID Rules
General rule	Holder of debt instrument must include daily portion of original issue discount in gross income
Definitional issues	OID = stated redemption price at maturity issue price Debt instrument
Special rules and exceptions	Certain (usually small) transactions excluded
Related material	§483, §7872 and interest inclusion in gross income
Summary	For most debt instruments, holder must include OID in gross income

IV. IMPUTED INTEREST—§483

Section 483 imputes to the creditor interest on certain loans made in connection with sales or exchanges of property that are not subject to the OID provisions.

A. Policy

A taxpayer who sells property to another for payments to be received in the future is essentially engaging in two different transactions—the sale of property and the lending of funds to the buyer. Because of the time value of money, a lender would be expected to charge interest on the loan. However, in the context of the sale of property, the tax preference for capital gains creates an incentive to "hide" interest in the purchase price of the property. This is because interest received by a creditor is included in gross income and taxed at the usual rates, but net capital gain from the sale of property will be taxed at a maximum 28%. As a result, sellers of capital assets might well attempt to characterize all or a large part of what is received as the sales price for property rather than interest. Section 483 prevents this by imputing to the transaction a market rate of interest.

Example: Jeff owns Blackacre with a basis of zero and a fair market value of $100,000. Blackacre is raw land that Jeff holds for investment. Wendy wishes to buy Blackacre, but cannot pay the entire $100,000 today. At a time when interest rates are 10%, Wendy agrees to pay Jeff $110,000 for Blackacre one year from now, but the contract provides for no interest to be paid. Because Jeff is in the 35% bracket, he would like to characterize the entire $110,000 as net capital gain subject to the maximum 15% tax rate. However, economically this transaction is a sale of Blackacre for $100,000 and the payment of interest of $10,000. Thus, Jeff will have $100,000 of capital gain and $10,000 of ordinary income after §483 is applied to the transaction.

B. Statutory analysis—§483

1. **General rule:** Section 483 applies when there is a contract for the sale or exchange of property under which at least one payment is due more than one year after the date of the contract and there is "total unstated interest." IRC §483(c). If §483 applies, the total unstated interest will be included in the creditor's gross income. IRC §483(a). The creditor will determine the timing of that inclusion based on his or her regular method of accounting. Reg. §1.483-1(a)(2)(ii).

2. **Definitional issue—Total unstated interest:** "Total unstated interest" is the excess of the total payments due under the contract over the sum of the present values of those payments and the present value of any interest payment provided for in the contract, using a discount rate equal to the applicable federal rate under §1274(d). IRC §483(b).

   Example: Betty, a cash-method taxpayer, owns Whiteacre with an adjusted basis of $100,000. At a time when market interest rates are 7%, she agrees to sell Whiteacre to Carl for $250,000 on the following terms: No cash down, the entire $250,000 due in three years, and no interest on the loan.

   Section 483 applies to this transaction because:

   - The contract is for the sale or exchange of property,
   - There is at least one payment due more than one year after the date of the contract, and
   - The OID rules do not apply because the price is not more than $250,000.

   Section 483 requires that Betty include in her gross income the total unstated interest ratably over the period of the time she holds the contract. The total unstated interest is equal to the excess of the payments to be received under the contract ($250,000) over the present value of those payments ($204,000, assuming a 7% interest rate). Thus, Betty must include in her gross income the $46,000 of interest on the contract when she receives it. The remaining amount ($204,000) will be payment for Whiteacre.

   Correlative effects of recharacterizing the transaction:

   - Carl may be able to deduct the interest deemed paid on the contract.
   - Carl's basis in the rental property is $204,000 (the imputed principal amount).
   - Betty's gain on the sale is Carl's purchase price of $204,000 minus her basis of $100,000, or $104,000.

3. **Special rules and exceptions**

   a. **Price limitation:** Section 483 does not apply to sales with purchase prices not exceeding $3,000. IRC §483(d)(2).

   b. **Maximum interest rate:** For a qualified sale (sale or exchange of land to a related party) with purchase price not exceeding $500,000, the maximum imputed interest is 6%, compounded semi-annually. IRC §483(e)(1).

4. Related material

    a. Coordination of §483 with OID rules: Section 483 does not apply to any debt instrument for which an issue price is determined under the OID rules of §§1273(b) or 1274. IRC §438(d)(1).

    b. Below-market loans: Certain transactions not subject to §483 may be subject to the below-market rules of §7872. See this chapter, section (VI).

    c. Deduction for imputed interest: A debtor who is deemed to pay interest under §483 may be entitled to deduct that interest, if the other requirements for interest deductibility are met.

    d. Calculation of basis to buyer and realized gain to seller: Section 483's recharacterization of the transaction necessarily affects the calculation of the amount realized and basis of the property.

5. Summary: See Statute Summary—§483.

Statute Summary—§ 483

Parsing Step	§483
General rule	Interest will be imputed to sales/exchanges of property with total unstated interest.
Definitional issues	Total unstated interest = total payments due − PV of payments plus stated interest
Special rules and exceptions	Inapplicable to sales price of $3,000 or less Qualified sale (price < $500,000) maximum 6% rate
Related material	OID, §7872, interest deduction, and basis rules
Summary	Watch for sales/exchanges with no interest or below-market interest: possible recharacterization to impute interest

V. BELOW-MARKET LOANS—§7872

Section 7872 provides that when a person makes a loan to another that provides for interest at a rate below the market rate of interest, the transaction may be recharacterized in order to ensure that the creditor includes the market rate of interest in gross income.

A. Policy

Low- or no-interest loans are often an important feature of a number of other relationships. Employers can compensate employees by providing them with interest-free or low-interest loans; shareholders of closely held corporations also often arrange for low- or no-interest loans to or from the corporation; relatives make a gift by providing a low- or no-interest loan. Section 7872 seeks to make the tax consequences of these arrangements match their economic substance, by imputing a market rate of interest to the loan and requiring certain correlative tax consequences as well (such as payment of compensation or the making of a gift).

B. Statutory analysis—§7872

1. **General rule:** Below-market demand, term, and gift loans are recharacterized so that the creditor includes the appropriate amount of interest in gross income. IRC §7872(a)(1).

   a. **Recharacterization of gift loans and demand loans:** Section 7872 treats the forgone interest as transferred from the lender to the borrower, and retransferred from the borrower to the lender on the last day of the taxable year. IRC §7872(a)(1)(A), (B). Each leg of the transaction must be characterized in accordance with its substance, i.e., gift, interest payment, compensation, etc.

   b. **Recharacterization of other types of below-market loans:** Section 7872 identifies the excess of the amount loaned over the present value of all payments to be received under the loan. It treats the lender as transferring this amount to the borrower on the date the loan is made. The below-market loan is then treated as having OID in the same amount. IRC §7872(b). The deemed transfer from the lender to the borrower must be characterized in accordance with its substance (as, for example, a gift or compensation). The characterization of the loan as having OID means that the creditor must include a ratable portion of the OID in gross income over the term of the loan.

2. **Definitional issues**

   a. **Demand loan:** A demand loan is a loan payable on demand of the creditor. IRC §7872(f).

   b. **Term loan:** A term loan is a loan payable on a certain date fixed or determinable by the loan instrument. IRC §7872(f).

   c. **Gift loan:** A gift loan is a loan in the context of which the creditor's forbearance of interest is properly viewed as a gift. IRC §7872(f).

   d. **Below-market loans:** A demand loan is below market if its stated interest is less than the applicable federal rate at the time of the making of the loan. IRC §7872(e)(1)(A). A term loan is a below-market loan if the amount loaned is greater than the present value of the payments due under the loan, using the applicable federal rate as the discount rate. IRC §7872(e)(1)(B).

      Example—Gift loan: Donna loans her son Edward $50,000 for two years, and the note provides for no interest at a time when the applicable federal rate is 10%. Since it is likely that Donna's forbearance of interest is intended as a gift, this is a gift loan. Section 7872 will characterize this transaction as a gift each year of $5,000 by Donna to Edward, and an identical payment of interest by Edward to Donna. As a result, Donna will include the $5,000 of interest income each year in her gross income. See Figure 15B.

      Example—Term loan: Dopey, Inc., loans Ellen, its chief executive officer, $100,000 interest-free for two years, at a time when the applicable federal rate is 10%. Section 7872 requires that this loan be characterized as the transfer of $20,000 by Dopey, Inc., to Ellen as compensation income on the date the loan is made, and Ellen must, of course, include this amount in her gross income. Thereafter, Dopey, Inc., must include the OID ($20,000) in its gross income, in accordance with its accounting methods. Ellen may have a deduction corresponding to this interest payment. See Figure 15C.

Figure 15B
Gift Loan—
Donna's Loan to Edward

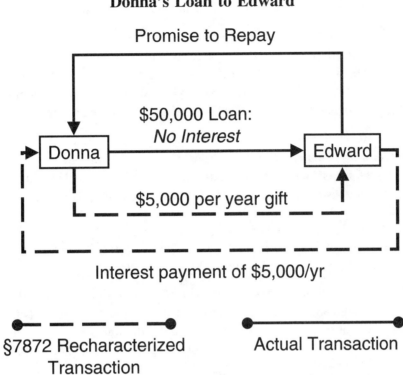

Figure 15C
Term Loan—Dopey, Inc.'s Loan to Ellen

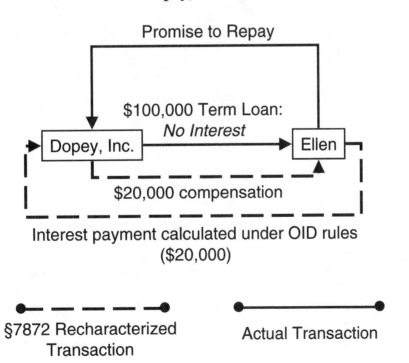

3. Special rules and exceptions

    a. Small gift loans: Section 7872 doesn't apply to gift loans between individuals if the total outstanding principal amount for all loans between them does not exceed $10,000. IRC §7872(c)(2).

    b. Income limitation: If the total amount of gift loans between two related parties does not exceed $100,000, the amount recast as interest income to the lender is limited to the investment income of the borrower. IRC §7872(d)(1). Investment income includes interest, dividends, royalties, and gains from the disposition of investment property. See Chapter 3(V).

    c. Small employee loans: Section 7872 doesn't apply to compensation-related and corporation-shareholder loans if the total outstanding principal amount of all loans made to the employee/shareholder does not exceed $10,000. IRC §7872(c)(3).

4. Related material

    a. Coordination of §7872 with §§483 and 1274: Section 7872 does not apply to any loan to which either §1274 or §483 applies. IRC §7872(f)(8).

    b. Gifts, compensation, dividends, and related transactions: Section 7872 recharacterizes a below-market loan in accordance with its economic substance. The tax consequences of this recharacterization must be analyzed in terms of the transfers deemed made, as gifts, compensation, dividends, or other transactions. See generally Chapters 2 through 4.

5. Summary: See Statute Summary—§7872.

Statute Summary—§ 7872

Parsing Step	§7872
General rule	Recharacterization of below-market demand, gift, and term loans to account for interest element and related transfers
Definitional issues	Below-market loan Demand loan Gift loan Term loan
Special rules and exceptions	Small loans excepted
Related material	OID; §483 Interest deduction and compensation, dividend inclusion rules Gifts—§102
Summary	Watch for low- or no-interest loan for possible recharacterization in accordance with economic substance.

VI. THE BASIC TAX STRATEGIES—DEFERRAL OF INCOME AND ACCELERATION OF DEDUCTIONS

A. In general

Time value of money principles inspire the most basic of tax planning strategies—the deferral of income and acceleration of deductions. A taxpayer who includes an amount in gross income without offsetting deductions must pay tax at his or her applicable rate. The amount of the tax is therefore unavailable for investment. If, however, the taxpayer can avoid the tax by deferring the income or accelerating deductions to reduce taxable income to zero, the amount that otherwise would be paid in tax will be available for investment, earning interest over the period of time before tax is due (if ever). Even if the taxpayer must ultimately pay the deferred tax, he or she will usually come out ahead by the end of the investment period, unless tax rates rise dramatically over the period of investment.

Example: Compare the tax and economic situations of two taxpayers, Alvin and Betty. Alvin has $100,000 in income, with no offsetting deductions and is taxed (for illustrative purposes) at a flat 30%. He pays $30,000 in tax, leaving $60,000 for investment. Assuming he invests this amount for five years at 6% (after tax), he will have $80,292 at the end of the five-year period.

Betty has the same $100,000, but is able to invest the full amount for five years, paying the $30,000 tax only at the end of the five-year period. At the end of five years, having invested the $100,000 at 6% (after tax), Betty will have $133,820. When reduced by the $30,000 tax, this will give her $103,820. The tax deferral has given Betty a benefit of $23,528 over Alvin. Even if tax rates were to rise over the five-year period, Betty would still come out ahead, unless rates were to rise to over 54%.

B. Achieving tax savings

In order to take advantage of the time value of money, the taxpayer seeks to generate tax savings through deferral of income and acceleration of deductions. Income deferral requires that the taxpayer have a sufficient ownership interest in funds so that they will be invested for his or her benefit, but that taxation of these funds not occur until a later year. Acceleration of deductions allows a taxpayer to offset current income, thus sheltering that income from tax and generating tax savings to be invested. Each of these is simply a timing strategy, moving to the future a tax that might be paid today. The time value of money suggests that this is a rational move, for the present value of a tax to be paid in the future is less than the same tax to be paid today. By contrast, the relentless taxpayer search for exclusions from gross income and for tax credits seeks to forever exempt a sum from taxation and thus increase either investment or consumption without the necessity to plan for payment of a future tax.

C. Income deferral strategies

Taxpayers employ a wide variety of income deferral strategies. Congressional, administrative, and judicial responses to these strategies are embodied in various Code provisions and their interpretations. The following sections point out some common income deferral strategies.

1. **Method of accounting:** A taxpayer's method of accounting determines the proper taxable year for the inclusion of income in gross income. The cash method will allow deferral of income until amounts are actually or constructively received, and a taxpayer in a business where customers are slow to pay might well prefer the cash method as a deferral device.

a. **Limitations on cash method:** Congress has placed a number of restrictions on the use of the cash method in situations where abuses of this method may arise. See Chapter 11(III)(B).

b. **Constructive receipt:** A cash method taxpayer may seek to defer the inclusion of income by arranging a transaction so that he or she does not actually receive the income. This strategy is limited by the doctrine of constructive receipt. See Chapter 11(III)(B).

2. **Realization principle:** The realization principle, which requires a realization event to occur before gains in property are recognized, defers gains to future years. While the realization principle itself is not a taxpayer strategy, it perhaps encourages taxpayers to make investments in properties (such as growth stocks or real estate) that tend to appreciate in value over time. That appreciation will not be included in gross income until a realization event occurs. (Of course, the realization requirement also works to prevent recognition of losses on such investments prior to a realization event, but taxpayers can usually overcome this by simply selling loss property in the year they wish to take the loss.) For a discussion of realization, see Chapter 9(III)(A).

3. **Nonrecognition provisions:** Various nonrecognition provisions specifically allow a taxpayer to defer the inclusion of income in gross income if certain specific requirements are met.

   a. **Like-kind exchanges:** Section 1031 of the Code allows a taxpayer to defer the recognition of gain on the exchange of certain property for like-kind property. See Chapter 10(III).

   b. **Involuntary conversions:** Section 1033 allows a taxpayer to defer income from the involuntary conversion of property into similar property. See Chapter 10(IV).

   c. **Divorce transactions:** Section 1041 allows a taxpayer to defer income from the division of property in divorce. See discussion at Chapter 10(V).

4. **Retirement planning:** Most of retirement planning is based on the notion of income deferral. For example, in a qualified plan, the employer's contribution to the plan is not included in the employee's gross income at the time of the contribution. The contribution earns interest, without tax, and the total amount is taxed to the employee as he or she withdraws it at retirement. Similarly, a taxpayer establishing an individual retirement account (IRA) will deduct (if qualified to do so) the contribution to the account. The contribution will earn interest without tax during the taxpayer's working years, and the entire amount will be included in the gross income of the taxpayer when he or she withdraws it at retirement. See Chapter 3(VIII).

5. **Saving for college:** The Code offers a wide variety of incentives for education savings. Some of these involve deferral of income techniques, in which saving can occur in ways that the income from the investment of funds is not subject to tax currently—or perhaps ever.

   a. **Education savings accounts:** Formerly known as "Education IRAs," these are accounts, usually held by banks or other custodians, to which taxpayers may contribute up to $2,000 per year (beginning in 2002). These accounts name a "beneficiary," who is the person whose education is being funded. The account owner can direct investments, i.e., purchase individual stocks or mutual funds. No deduction is available for these contributions, but income earned in these accounts is not subject to tax. IRC §530(a).

      i. **Cash/Age 18:** Contributions must be in cash and made before the beneficiary turns 18 (unless the beneficiary has special needs). IRC §530(b)(1).

      ii. **Treatment of distributions:** Any distribution is allocated between invested capital (tax-free) and income (potentially taxable) based on the rules of IRC §72, discussed at Chapter 3(V)(F). IRC §530(d)(1). The income is tax-free (i.e., excluded from gross income) to the extent that it is used to fund qualified education expenses. IRC §530(d)(2). If qualified education expenses are less than the amount distributed, the expenses are deemed to come proportionately from invested capital and income. IRC §530(d)(2)(B).

iii. Qualified education expenses: These are expenses for tuition, fees, books and supplies, not only for higher education but also for K-12 in a private, public or religious school. IRC §530(b)(4).

iv. 10% penalty tax: Amounts of income not used for qualified education expenses are subject to an additional 10% penalty tax, with certain exceptions. IRC §530(d)(4).

Example: Brittany receives a distribution from an Education Savings Account of $2,000. Under the rules of IRC §72, this is considered to consist of $500 of principal and $1,500 of income. Her qualified education expenses for the year are $1,000. Three-fourths of the qualified education expenses are considered to come from income $(1,500/2,000 \times 1,000 = \$750)$ and one-fourth from principal $(500/2000 \times \$1,000 = \$500)$. Therefore, of the $1,500 of income, she used only $750 for qualified education expenses, and must include the rest in gross income and must pay the 10% penalty tax as well on this amount.

v. Income limitations: Contributions to education savings accounts are subject to income limitations. For 2005, for married couples filing joint returns, the phase-out begins at $190,000 and is complete at $220,000. For single taxpayers, the phase-out amounts are $95,000 and $110,000. The reduction is computed by taking the contribution that would otherwise be allowed, and subtracting from it the "reduction amount." The reduction amount is the otherwise allowable contribution, multiplied by a fraction, the numerator of which is the excess of the taxpayer's modified AGI over the initial phase-out amount, and the denominator of which is $15,000 (for single filers) or $30,000 (joint filers). Modified AGI is AGI minus any foreign earned income excluded under IRC §911. Confused? Follow these steps:

Step 1: **Determine otherwise allowable contribution (lesser of $2,000 or actual contribution).**

Step 2: **Determine reduction amount.**

$$\text{Otherwise allowable contribution} \times \frac{(\text{modified AGI} - \text{initial phase-out amount})}{\$15,000 \text{ (single) or } \$30,000 \text{ (joint)}}$$

Step 3: **Determine actual contribution.**

Otherwise allowable contribution
- Reduction amount
Actual contribution

Example: Richard and Pat have one daughter, Cynthia, who is 12. Their modified AGI is $195,000. They want to contribute $2,000 to an education savings account for her. May they do so? The income limitations will apply, because their income is greater than the initial phase-out amount of $190,000. The contribution will be limited as follows:

1. Otherwise available contribution $2,000

2. Reduction amount

$$2,000 \times \frac{(195,000 - 190,000)}{\$30,000} = \$333$$

3. Available contribution = 2,000 − 333 = $1,667.

b. Section 529 Plans: A second type of savings vehicle is the "§529 Plan," which is a plan established under state law allowing college savings. Under this type of plan, the account owner designates a beneficiary, and cannot direct the investment, although usually choices are given based on investment preferences. There is no deduction for contributions, but the investment earnings accrue tax-free, i.e., are not includible in the gross income of either the account owner or the beneficiary. IRC §529(c)(1). Many states offer tax deductions for investments in their §529 Plans.

i. Cash: Contributions must be made in cash. IRC §529(b)(2).

ii. No contribution limits: Each plan establishes its own limits on contributions, which are usually well over $25,000 per year. There is no federal limit on contributions.

iii. Treatment of distributions: Any distribution is allocated between invested capital (tax-free) and income (potentially taxable) based on the rules of IRC §72, discussed at Chapter 3(V)(F). IRC §529(c)(3). The income is tax-free (i.e., excluded from gross income) to the extent that it is used to fund qualified education expenses. If qualified education expenses are less than the amount distributed, the expenses are deemed to come proportionately from invested capital and income (as in education savings accounts).

iv. Qualified education expenses: These are expenses for tuition, fees, books, and supplies, not only for higher education but also for K-12 in a private, public, or religious school. IRC §530(b)(4). It also includes the cost of room and board, within certain limits, for students who are enrolled at least half time. IRC §529(d)(3)(B).

v. 10% penalty tax: Amounts of income not used for qualified education expenses are subject to an additional 10% penalty tax, with certain exceptions. IRC §530(d)(4).

vi. No income limitations: Unlike most other education savings tax incentives, there are no income limits on the §529 Plan, so taxpayers of any AGI amount can take advantage of this kind of plan.

D. Acceleration of deduction strategies

From a taxpayer's perspective, claiming deductions should follow the voting-in-Chicago rule: *early and often.* A taxpayer expending funds for a deductible item wants to claim the deduction for that item in the earliest year possible and to the greatest extent possible. And if deductions can be claimed before (or without) an actual cash outlay, the taxpayer will be even better off. The following sections describe some common deduction acceleration strategies.

1. Method of accounting: A taxpayer's method of accounting determines the proper taxable year for claiming a deduction.

a. Cash-method strategies—Prepayments: A cash-method taxpayer cannot claim a deduction until an actual cash outlay is made, precluding a taxpayer from claiming a deduction prior to the year an actual cash outlay is made. But cash method taxpayers may try to accelerate deductions by making large prepayments (for rent or supplies, for example) applicable to several taxable years. The Code places certain restrictions on this strategy. See Chapter 11(III)(B).

b. Accrual method—Economic performance: Accrual-method taxpayers may seek to deduct amounts they owe before they actually pay them. While this is an acceptable practice under accrual method accounting, the Code prohibits certain deductions for accrual method taxpayers until "economic performance" occurs. See Chapter 11(III)(C).

2. Capital recovery: The taxpayer's preference for accelerated deductions is clear in the area of capital recovery. Under the theory of depreciation, a wasting asset actually becomes less valuable over its useful life, and the wise owner will be contributing to a fund each year the amount necessary to replace the property at the end of its useful life. (In reality, however, few owners actually establish such a fund, in part because the asset may actually be increasing in value or because the owner's planning horizon is not sufficiently lengthy to make this fund worthwhile.) The capital recovery period allowed for tax purposes on the property, however, may be shorter than its actual useful life, thus accelerating deductions for the taxpayer.

a. Section 179 expenditures: Section 179 allows a taxpayer a deduction for the cost of certain otherwise capitalizable assets in the year of purchase. See Chapter 7(III)(H).

b. MACRS: The recovery periods for assets covered by MACRS is set forth in the Code and administrative rulings. If the recovery period for an asset is shorter than the actual useful life of the asset, the taxpayer will enjoy an acceleration of deductions. See Chapter 7(III)(E).

c. Other capital recovery provisions: Sections 195 (addressing pre-opening expenses) and 197 (addressing the amortization of intangibles) provide capital recovery for expenditures that may benefit taxpayers. See Chapter 7(II)(B), (III)(G).

d. But consider recapture: The benefits of accelerated depreciation will be recaptured if the taxpayer ultimately disposes of the property for more than its adjusted basis. See discussion at Chapter 12(II)(E). Notice, however, that recapture only requires the recasting of capital gain as ordinary income. It does not take into account time value of money principles for the government's benefit by recognizing MACRS as a tax-free loan to the taxpayer.

3. Loss limitations: Various loss limitations restrict the ability of taxpayers to accelerate deductions by recognizing losses.

a. Capital loss restrictions: An individual may deduct capital losses only to the extent of capital gains plus $3,000 of ordinary income. See Chapter 12(II).

b. Passive loss restrictions: Passive losses may be deducted only to the extent of passive income; any additional amounts carry forward and may be deducted against future passive income or against any income at the termination of the investment. See discussion at Chapter 11. See also the discussion of tax shelters, this chapter, at section (VI)(E).

c. Nonrecognition provisions: If the requirements of the various nonrecognition provisions are met, taxpayers may not recognize loss on the transaction. See generally Chapter 10.

E. A note on tax shelters

The *tax shelter* industry of the 1970s and 1980s (prior to the enactment of §469 in the Tax Reform Act of 1986) sought to take advantage of many of these tax-planning strategies to allow taxpayers to reduce their tax by investing in limited partnerships and similar vehicles engaged in various tax-favored businesses. The case of *Commissioner v. Tufts,* discussed in Chapter 9(IV)(C), is a good example of a tax shelter. In this type of shelter, taxpayers would invest modest sums to purchase a limited partnership interest in a partnership that purchased real property. The partnership financed a large part of the purchase price with nonrecourse debt. The partnership would claim accelerated depreciation deductions based on its basis in the building (which included the amount of the debt). This, plus deductible interest payments, generally outstripped income from the building and generated large tax losses. The building was not declining in value as quickly as it was being depreciated. Thus, upon sale, a large gain would be generated, but most of the cash on sale would be dedicated to debt repayment. This typical tax shelter took advantage of the realization principle and accelerated capital recovery to generate significant tax savings for investors.

Although investors were perhaps aware that they ultimately would have to pay tax on the gain on sale of the property, the present value of this future tax was insignificant compared with the current gains generated by tax savings. (Most investors did not dedicate a portion of their tax savings to a fund to pay the ultimate tax liability.) Although the IRS pursued a number of strategies in combating tax shelters, §469 simply put them out of business in enacting the passive loss provisions discussed in Chapter 11(VII). The passive loss provisions are essentially a timing rule that suspend passive losses (i.e., make them nondeductible) until the taxpayer disposes of the investment entirely. At that time, losses may be offset against gains. But this timing rule removes the incentive for investing in these deals, as the loss is deferred until the gain is recognized.

VII. WHERE ARE WE GOING?

This chapter has begun the process of "pulling it all together" by showing how the time value of money principle inspires some of the most basic tax-planning strategies. The next chapter finishes that process by introducing a way to look at tax problems from a transactional viewpoint, to ensure that one asks the right questions in formulating tax advice.

Quiz Yourself on
TIME VALUE OF MONEY

132. Why should (and do) taxpayers care about the time value of money? _____

133. What is the present value of a promise to pay you $10,000 in five years, if the appropriate interest rate is 5%? What if the interest rate were 9%? _____

134. How much would you have to invest today to have $10,000 in eight years, if interest rates held steady at 6%? At 12%? _____

135. If you had $3,000 to invest today, and interest rates held steady at 4%, how much would you have at the end of 10 years? 15 years? 30 years? _____

136. Charles gives his son Harry a choice of receiving a gift of $50,000 today or a gift of $70,000 five years from now. Interest rates are holding steady at 8%. Which should Harry choose if he is a rational taxpayer? _____

137. Beverly is a doctor with a large income taxed at the highest federal and state tax rates. She tells you about an interesting offer that she has heard about from her broker. She has an opportunity to invest in a venture to locate and communicate with alien life forms. This has dazzling commercial potential. Start up costs would be large, and she would have to invest $75,000, but this would result in over $300,000 of losses, that would serve as deductions to her over the next five years. She could use them to offset her salary income. Beverly consults you about this idea. What do you say? _____

138. Marilyn and Joe report modified AGI of $200,000 on their joint return. They want to contribute $2,000 to an education savings account for their son, Steve, who is 12 years old. They also want to contribute $10,000 to a §529 plan. May they do so? _____

139. Ronald owned the Flying Z Ranch. Due to failing health, he sold the ranch to his good friend James for $1.5 million. The contract called for payment in a single lump sum in five years, with no provision for interest. Ronald's basis in the ranch was $900,000, so he simply reported $600,000 of capital gain in the fifth year when he received payment. At the time the contract was entered into, the applicable federal rate was 9%. Was Ronald's reporting position correct? What is James' basis in the ranch? _____

140. Joe's mother wants to lend Joe $10,000, interest-free. What will be the tax consequences of this loan? What if the loan were $100,000? $1 million? _____

141. Elmo purchases a bond from Cookies, Inc. in the face amount of $15,000. In five years it will pay him a lump sum of $21,037. How should Elmo report the tax consequences of holding the bond to maturity? What is the interest rate that Elmo is earning on this bond? _____

Answers

132. Taxpayers should (and do) care about time value of money principles because they affect the amount of tax they owe—specifically, by affecting the timing of taxes. Taxpayers seek to defer income as far into the future as possible (while still having access to it) in order to defer the tax on this income. Taxpayers want to contribute money to tax-deferred savings vehicles such as IRAs for this reason. A tax deferred vehicle may be a tax never paid (consider the impact of IRC §1014) and the present value of that future tax is less than its face amount. Taxpayers also want to accelerate deductions as much as possible, because these deductions reduce the taxes owed now.

133. The present value of a promise to pay you $10,000 in five years if the appropriate interest rate is 5% is **$7,840.** If the appropriate rate is 9%, the present value is **$6,500.** The appropriate interest rate should take into account the riskiness of the promise. A promise by the United States federal government (as in a savings bond) is essentially risk-free and would have a low interest rate. By contrast, a promise by a deadbeat (high risk) would carry a higher interest rate.

134. This is just another way to ask for the present value of a future sum. If you know you have a debt to pay in eight years of $10,000, you might set aside the present value of that debt (assuming an interest rate) and let that sum grow during the term so that you would have just the right amount to pay off the obligation. This is often how people save for college educations for children or for their own retirement, although they generally do that through periodic savings rather than putting aside a lump sum. At 6%, the amount you would have to put aside is **$6,270.** At 12%, you would only have to put aside **$4,040.**

135. If interest rates held steady at 4%, you would have:

10 years:	$4,437
15 years:	$5,405
30 years:	$9,740

136. For Harry to answer this question, he must compare the present values of the two gifts: the present value of $70,000 five years in the future or $50,000. Because gifts are not taxable, the taxes do not figure into the equation. He should take the gift today because the present value of the future gift is $46,670, less than the current gift. The present value is calculated as follows:

$$PV = \frac{FV}{(1+i)^n}$$

$$PV = \frac{\$70,000}{(1+.08)^5}$$

$$PV = \$47,670$$

This can also be calculated by using the table: multiply the future gift by the number at the intersection of 8% and five years, or 0.681. This produces the same number.

137. Beverly should run—not walk—away from this so-called "opportunity." Leaving aside the wisdom of such a venture, she will not be able to use the losses from the venture to offset her income from private practice. This would constitute a passive activity because it is certain that Beverly, a doctor, will not be actively involved in the business of contacting alien life forms (plus, the structure of the investment will probably ensure that it is a passive activity for her). The passive loss rules prevent a taxpayer from using "passive losses" to offset nonpassive income, so that the deductions from the venture would be useless to her until she disposes of the activity.

138. Marilyn and Joe may contribute any amount to a §529 plan. But their contribution to the education savings account will be limited because their modified AGI is greater than the initial phase-out amount for joint filers ($190,000). They may make a contribution of $1,333 to this account, as follows:

$$\$2,000 \times \frac{(\$200,000 - \$190,000)}{\$30,000} = \text{Reduction amount} = \$667$$

Contribution amount = $2,000 − 667 = $1,333

139. No. The Code will impute interest to this transaction. There are three potentially applicable Code provisions (IRC §483, §7872, and §1272 and its related statutes). Of these, §1272 applies because the purchase price exceeds $1 million. Section 1272 provides that the lender (Ronald) will be treated as receiving interest each year even though the contract does not call for interest. Thus, a portion of the capital gain will be recharacterized as interest, and Ronald will have to include the interest in his gross income as ordinary income in years one through five. His capital gain will be reduced accordingly.

Specifically, §1272(a) provides that the holder of the debt instrument will be treated as having original issue discount equal to the daily portions of the OID for each day during the year that the instrument is held. OID is the difference between the stated price at maturity and the issue price. IRC §1273(a). Section 1274 provides that the issue price for sales of property is the "imputed principal amount," which is the present value of future payments due under the contract. In making this determination, an appropriate discount rate is used. The applicable federal rate was 9%. Thus, the present value of the payment of $1.5 million five years hence was $974,912. Subtracting this issue price ($974,912) from the stated price ($1,500,000) produces the OID amount of $525,088. Ronald must include this amount in gross income over the five year period on the economic accrual of interest basis. His sales price for the ranch is only $974,912. As a result, Ronald's gain on the sale of the ranch is $74,912.

James' basis in the ranch is $974,912, the same as Ronald's selling price.

140. Joe's mother may lend him a total of $10,000 without interest because of the de minimis exception for gift loans. IRC §7872(c)(2)(A). If the loan is $100,000 or less, the transaction will be cast as a gift of the foregone interest (calculated at the applicable federal rate for long-term obligations) but the amount treated as included in the mother's income will be limited to Joe's investment income (i.e., his total of dividends, interest, etc.). If the loan is $1 million, neither of these exceptions apply. In that case, each year Joe's mother will be deemed to have made a gift of the foregone interest to Joe, who in turn transfers it to his mother as interest, which she must include in her gross income.

141. Elmo must include in his gross income a proportionate amount of the interest on the bond each year, and this will be ordinary income to him. The interest rate is 7% on this bond.

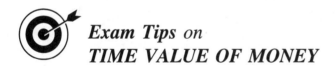

Exam Tips on
TIME VALUE OF MONEY

Most law exams do not ask pure time value of money questions like Questions 133 through 136 in "Quiz Yourself" of this chapter. Time value of money principles are embedded in other kinds of questions.

- ☞ *Look for:* A taxpayer's choice between two alternative receipts, or an opportunity to defer income or accelerate deductions.

- ☞ *Analyze:* Discuss time value of money principles to explain why a taxpayer would choose one alternative or plan over another.

- ☛ The statutory rules (OID, 483, 7872) are all based on making a loan transaction reflect economic reality: interest would be charged, and must be imputed if it is not stated.

☞ *Look for:* Loans, sales of property, etc. without an adequate stated interest rate.

☞ *Analyze:* Which section applies; what exactly does it impute; what are the results to the taxpayers? Analyze each side of the transaction separately.

The Education Savings Accounts and §529 Plans are just two of many education incentives, but are the two available to relatively higher income taxpayers. Consider these two benefits in connection with education deductions, the HOPE credit, and the Lifelong Learning Credit. See Chapters 13 and 16.

Math anxiety? Forget running the numbers. Discuss the theory of the time value of money, and what it causes taxpayers (and Congress) to do in a particular situation.

CHAPTER 16

RECOGNIZING RELATED TAX STATUTES: A TRANSACTIONAL APPROACH TO TAX

ChapterScope _____

Previous chapters have addressed the issues surrounding the calculation of a taxpayer's tax liability, from identification of income to the subtraction of tax credits. Chapter 15 broadened the perspective by focusing on the principle of the time value of money, showing how this concept informs not only specific tax statutes, but a number of common tax planning strategies. This chapter concludes the outline by offering a "transactional approach" to tax problems, to help the tax student approach unfamiliar tax problems systematically. First, this chapter suggests a methodology for approaching tax problems. It then applies this approach to five types of problems, showing how groups of Code sections and tax concepts work together in commonly encountered transactions.

Key concepts in this chapter include:

- **A problem-solving approach to the tax consequences of a transaction:** To analyze a tax question, consider using the STUDY TAX FIRST! approach. This approach offers a method of viewing facts and issues to fully analyze a tax transaction.

- **Commonly encountered transactions:** This chapter introduces five kinds of transaction that are commonly encountered in the real world and on tax examinations. These are compensation transactions, transactions in property, personal expenditure transactions, education savings, business transactions, and intrafamilial transfers. This chapter discusses the Code sections and tax concepts potentially applicable to each type of transaction and offers a chart of the STUDY TAX FIRST! approach to these types of problems.

I. WHERE ARE WE?

Unlike previous chapters, this chapter *isn't* about the determination of a taxpayer's tax liability. Instead, it is about tax problem-solving. Use it to systematize your approach to tax problems, and review it before doing practice problems. After you have completed some problems, review it again to see how you could improve your answers by making them more comprehensive or more focused.

II. A PROBLEM-SOLVING APPROACH TO TAX

Federal income tax is inherently a "transactional" subject. Tax issues do not arise from a taxpayer's private contemplation of the universe, but from two or more taxpayers engaging in a "transaction." In the broadest terms, a transaction is an event between two or more people in which some value changes hands. The goal of tax students and tax professionals alike is to determine the proper tax consequences to these transactions, either from a planning point of view in which the transaction has yet to occur or from a reactive point of view in which a transaction has occurred, but its tax consequences are unclear.

A. The STUDY TAX FIRST! approach

Determining the tax consequences of various transactions can be expressed in a process with three main steps. To remember these steps, simply recall this helpful hint:

STUDY TAX FIRST! See Figure 16A.

1. **What does it mean?** STUDY TAX FIRST! means to (1) STUDY the transaction; (2) identify the TAX problem; and (3) analyze the transaction using the FIRST! approach of analyzing the **F**acts, **I**ssues, **R**ules, asking "**S**o what?" and—when appropriate—offering **T**axpayer advice.

2. **Relationship to IRAC:** The alert student may recognize this as a variation of the issue, rule, apply to facts, conclude (IRAC) approach taught by law tutors. The STUDY TAX FIRST! approach, however, differs from IRAC in three important respects. First, STUDY TAX FIRST! incorporates learning theory, which suggests that comprehension of facts is insufficient for dealing effectively with complex problems. According to this theory, facts must be organized into patterns that suggest productive problem-solving approaches. The STUDY TAX FIRST! approach splits the factual analysis into two parts: comprehension of facts and organization of patterns to stimulate selection of Code sections likely to be applicable. Second, the STUDY TAX FIRST! approach is more detailed than IRAC. While IRAC simply states that a student must identify the issue, STUDY TAX FIRST! suggests six fundamental tax questions as an organizing principle for determining what issues are presented. Finally, STUDY TAX FIRST!

Figure 16A
STUDY TAX FIRST!

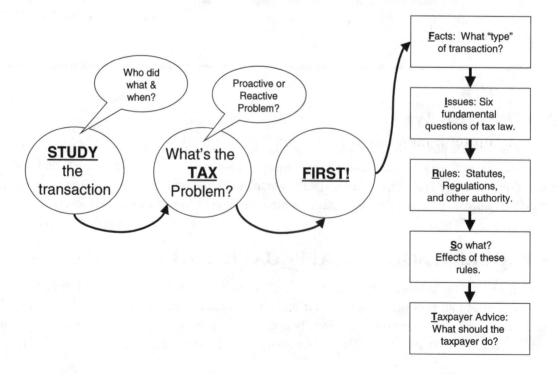

reminds the student of what the client requires—advice—making it helpful to the real world of tax lawyering.

3. **Taking tax exams:** This approach is intended for use in both exams and the real world. But use of this method for exam taking must be tempered by a student's understanding of his or her professor's emphasis on material in class. For example, the development of a reasonable return position is of crucial importance for a practicing tax lawyer in a planning situation but receives differing degrees of emphasis in the tax classroom. Some tax professors focus on this issue in discussing the ambiguity of tax law; some professors note the standard only in passing; others never mention it at all. The observant student will incorporate his or her tax professor's emphasis into studying for and writing exams.

B. Step 1. STUDY the transaction

The very first step in any tax problem is to understand the facts of a transaction. STUDY facts carefully, making sure you understand who did what, when, why, how, and with whom. In the kind of transactions that raise interesting tax questions, items or services may change hands in unexpected ways, and therefore it is often helpful to draw the transaction. See, for examples, Figures 9C and 9G in Chapter 9.

C. Step 2. What is the TAX problem?

In some situations, a professor (or client) may pose a very specific tax question. The question may be "Are these expenditures deductible?" Much more common in essay exams and in the real world, however, are calls for a general discussion of tax issues. These are posed as questions such as "Discuss the tax consequences of this (these) transaction(s)," or "Advise the taxpayer." These types of questions call for a broader range of advice in two different potential settings—the reactive problem and the proactive (planning) problem.

1. **Reactive problems:** In a "reactive problem," events have already occurred, and the problem is to determine the proper tax consequences of those events. When representing the taxpayer, the specific problem presented is typically either to create a return position for a transaction that has already occurred (i.e., determine how to report the transaction on a tax return), or to react to a challenge on audit. When representing the government, the typical problem is to determine if and how to challenge a taxpayer's return position or how to respond to a proposed transaction in a private letter ruling request. This type of problem is also occasionally raised as a government-client question in which the government seeks to draft legislation or regulations to combat a particular taxpayer strategy. This type of problem does not offer the option of changing the facts, but different interpretations of the existing facts are possible and indeed are the focus of such problems.

2. **Proactive (planning) problems:** In the proactive (planning) problem, a taxpayer typically is contemplating a transaction and seeks advice on how best to structure it. In this type of problem, there is flexibility to change some, but usually not all, of the facts. The specific problem will be to develop a plan that meets the taxpayer's goals and results in a reasonable return position. This type of problem is also sometimes presented as a government-client question in which the government seeks to draft new legislation or regulations to implement a new tax policy.

D. Step 3. FIRST! analysis—Facts, Issue, Rules, So what?, and Taxpayer advice

In this step, the student begins an in-depth analysis of the tax issues. FIRST! reminds the student of an approach to this analysis: **F**acts, **I**ssues, **R**ules, **S**o what?, and **T**axpayer advice.

1. **Facts—What is it?** In STUDYING the transaction, the student has grasped the essential facts of what happened in the transaction. This step adjusts the focus of the facts analysis, asking the student to identify the facts as a pattern—as an example of a particular "type" of transaction. The goal of this step is to see the patterns inherent in those facts, allowing the problem-solver to reduce the universe of potentially applicable Code sections and concepts to a manageable size for analysis. To illustrate, suppose that in STUDYING a particular transaction, the student grasps that Sue transferred property to Alvin in exchange for Alvin's performance of services. In analyzing these facts, the student recognizes this as a typical compensation transaction and a sale property transaction, allowing the student to consider a discrete number of Code sections and tax concepts for analysis. But remember these three tips in giving a name or type to a transaction.

   a. **Only a hypothesis!** Giving a name to the facts is simply a hypothesis that a transaction is of a certain type. As with any hypothesis, it can later be revised if further analysis suggests that the Code sections selected do not apply, or other facts are discovered to suggest that another type fits the transaction more precisely.

   b. **Complex transactions—More than one type:** A complex transaction may have two or more parts, of different types. Or a transaction may potentially fit within two different types, and its tax consequences must be considered under both. In such a situation, the tax student must decide which label is most appropriate for the transaction.

      Example: Mildred transfers a car to Sam to pay him for painting her house. He uses the car in business. He trades the car for a light truck, also to be used in the business. This is a compensation transaction, followed by a transaction in property (a possible like-kind exchange under §1031).

      Example: Mildred transfers a car to Sam, and we now discover Sam is Mildred's son. While the transfer of the car may be compensation income, it might instead be a gift. The alert tax student would analyze the transaction under both labels and would search for additional facts that would allow a definitive characterization.

   c. **Recharacterization:** Because the U.S. tax system is a self-assessment system, it is the taxpayer's responsibility initially to name or characterize his or her transactions. The taxpayer does so by taking a position on the tax return. Although the taxpayer is usually estopped from later changing this characterization of the transaction, the IRS may recharacterize all or a portion of the transaction in accordance with its economic substance. It is the substance, not the form, of a transaction that governs its federal income tax consequences. As a result, one must consider the possibility of the IRS asserting a different label if the economic substance of a transaction is different than its form.

      Example: Rick is an independent contractor who performs services for EDCO, a nonprofit organization. Rick and EDCO exchange parcels of raw land that they both hold for investment. Both intend to hold the parcels received for investment. The value of the property transferred by Rick is $100,000, and the value of the property he receives is $200,000, but Rick does not pay EDCO any additional amount. The parties would probably like to characterize this transaction as what it appears to be in form—an exchange of property that probably qualifies as a like-kind exchange under §1031. However, the differential in value suggests that there is another transaction occurring here. The prior relationship between Rick and EDCO would suggest that Rick may be receiving compensation income, and thus $100,000 of the transaction (representing the differential in value) should be analyzed as a compensation transaction.

2. **Issues:** The next step in the FIRST! analysis is to identify issues raised by the transaction. There are six fundamental questions to pose to determine the federal income tax issues in a transaction. See Figure 16B—Six Fundamental Tax Questions.

   a. **Who is the relevant taxpayer?** In most transactions, there are at least two taxpayers, and in some transactions, there are many more. As a general rule, the tax consequences to each taxpayer should be analyzed independently. Which taxpayer is your client? Or, in an exam-taking situation, in which taxpayer is the professor interested? Are the taxpayers involved in the transaction related to one another? Are there children participating in property or service transfers? Has any taxpayer attempted to "assign" income to another? These questions focus attention on which taxpayer's tax consequences must be considered. See generally Chapters 1, 13, and 14.

   b. **Does the taxpayer have income?** This issue raises questions of whether a taxpayer has income in a theoretical sense—has the taxpayer experienced an economic benefit? See generally Chapter 2. Once theoretical issues are resolved, §61 requires the inclusion of all income in gross income, but specific statutes may apply to exclude amounts from gross income. See generally Chapters 3 and 4.

   c. **What deductions may the taxpayer claim?** This issue raises the question of whether the taxpayer has made an outlay or incurred a loss that is potentially deductible. If so, the question is whether there is a specific statute to support the taxpayer claiming a deduction for the outlay or loss, and whether any limitations apply to the deductions. In general, deductions may be business-related or personal. Personal expenditures are not deductible without specific statutory authority. (See generally Chapter 6.) The usual expenses of doing business are generally deductible, but important constraints are also imposed on business deductions. See generally Chapters 7 and 8.

   d. **What is the character of income or loss?** If the taxpayer has income or loss, the gain or loss must be characterized as capital or ordinary. Ordinary income is subject to tax at rates up to 35%, but net capital gain is subject to a preferential tax rate as low as 5%. Moreover, capital losses are subject to significant restrictions and may be deducted only to the extent of capital gains plus, for individuals, $3,000 of ordinary income. See generally Chapter 12.

   e. **Timing issues. When must the taxpayer include an item in gross income, and when may the taxpayer claim a deduction?** Timing questions raises issues about when a taxpayer must include an item in gross income, and when the taxpayer may claim a deduction. Time value of money principles and taxpayers' planning strategies feature prominently in timing questions, raising technical questions regarding the taxpayer's taxable year, method of accounting, and various nonrecognition provisions. See generally Chapters 10, 11, and 15.

   f. **Rates and credits. What is the taxpayer's rate of tax, and is the taxpayer entitled to any credits?** These relatively straightforward questions raise issues about progressive tax rates, the kiddie tax, and whether the taxpayer may claim a tax credit. See generally Chapter 13.

Figure 16B
Six Fundamental Tax Questions

Fundamental Questions	Concepts and Important Code Provisions
Who is the taxpayer?	Definition of "taxpayer" Assignment of income principles Kiddie tax IRC §482
Does the taxpayer have income?	Theoretical notions of income IRC §§61, 71, 72, 79, 82, 83, 85, 86, 101–132, 1001
May the taxpayer claim a deduction?	Outlays and losses IRC §§162–197, 212–219, 262–263
What is the character of the taxpayer's gain or loss?	Definition of a capital asset Restrictions on capital losses IRC §§483, 1221, 1222, 1231, 1244, 1245, 1250
When must the taxpayer report items in gross income, and when may the taxpayer claim deductions?	Taxable year and annual accounting Methods of accounting IRC §§72, 446–448, 451, 453, 461, 464, 465, 469, 483, 1274, 7872
What is the rate of tax for the taxpayer, and may the taxpayer claim any credits?	Progressive rate system Preferential rates for net capital gain AMT Kiddie tax IRC §§1, 21, 25A, 27, 32, 56

3. **Rules—What tax concepts and Code provisions apply?** This step of the FIRST! process identifies the tax concepts and Code provisions potentially applicable to the transaction at hand. This requires identification of all potentially applicable provisions, i.e., knowing which Code sections generally apply for various types of transactions. Concepts and Code sections often work together in "families," and some of these are discussed later in this chapter (see this chapter, at section (III)). Identification, however, is necessary but not sufficient. The student must examine the specific domain of each potentially applicable concept and statute to determine whether a particular rule applies to the facts at hand.

4. **So what? Applying the rules:** This step of the FIRST! process applies the rules to the specific facts of the transaction. In this step, the relevant inquiry is "What are the tax consequences to the taxpayer?" or "What is the effect of the facts falling within a domain of a statute?" Applying the applicable tax concepts and Code provisions to the facts at hand produces the tax consequences to the taxpayer.

5. **Taxpayer advice:** In this final step of the FIRST! analysis, recall that the point of tax information in the real world is to advise a client—whether the taxpayer or the government—on tax issues. In this step, the student returns to the tax problem posed, offering advice to the client.

In developing this advice, the student considers the interests of the client and the constraints the client is under within the particular facts.

a. Return position: If a client is seeking advice on the proper reporting of a transaction on a tax return, the student offers advice on a reasonable return position. See Chapter 1(III).

b. Transaction structure: If a client is seeking advice on the proper structure of a transaction, the student offers that advice with a discussion of why a particular structure is the most appropriate. This can also implicate the taxpayer's return position, because only a transaction that results in a reasonable return position is acceptable.

c. Tax controversy: If a taxpayer is embroiled in a controversy, the student offers advice on possible responses to the controversy, including procedural issues (e.g., in which forum to litigate the matter; see Chapter 1(II)) and substantive issues (e.g., the proper interpretation of the facts and law).

d. Government advice: Although most tax exams involve advice to taxpayers (hence the term "taxpayer advice" in the FIRST! analysis), it is not unheard of to be asked to take the IRS's perspective or a legislator's perspective on a factual situation.

i. IRS advice: The IRS's job is to properly administer the tax system. It does so in two ways: pursuing tax controversies with taxpayers and promulgating administrative guidance with respect to the Code. In tax controversies, the IRS's role is to ensure that the taxpayer has properly included items of income and claimed the appropriate deductions and credits. Thus, advice to the IRS will center on the propriety of the taxpayer's return positions, and in controversies the IRS is likely to take positions that are mirror images of those taken by the taxpayer. In promulgating administrative guidance, the IRS's role is to issue "reasonable interpretations" of the Code, and in doing so, it will be considering the policy implications of the proposed guidance. See Chapter 1(II) and (V).

ii. Legislator's advice: A legislator will be examining the wisdom of a proposed change to the tax code. In doing so, he or she will consider the policy implications of a particular provision. See Chapter 1(V). In addition, a legislator may be reacting to a particular taxpayer strategy and IRS response, and must be cognizant of those strategies and interests. See generally Chapter 15.

III. APPLYING THE STUDY TAX FIRST! APPROACH TO COMMON TYPES OF TRANSACTIONS

This section analyzes five types of transactions that are common both in the real world and on tax exams. The discussion assumes that the student adequately STUDIES the transaction and identifies the TAX problem. The discussion focuses on the FIRST! step of the analysis to identify the common issues and "families" of tax statutes encountered in these transactions. Charts illustrate the Code sections and tax concepts for the six fundamental tax questions raised by each type of transaction.

A. Compensation transactions: See essay question 1 (p 383).

A very common transaction is the performance of services in exchange for something of value—cash, property, or some other benefit, including other services.

1. **Facts—Recognizing this type of transaction:** Look for a person performing services in exchange for value or a promise to transfer value. The most common transaction is payment in cash or check for services performed, but value also may be transferred in the form of property or other services. In some situations, payment may be deferred (which raises important timing issues). Be sure to distinguish compensation transactions from services performed as a gift in which the service provider receives no tangible value beyond the satisfaction of a good deed done (such as driving a friend's children to school).

2. **Issues—Summary:** The tax consequences of a compensation transaction must be considered from the perspectives of both the person who receives the benefit of the services (the payor) and the service provider. A compensation transaction essentially poses two tax questions. First, will the payor be entitled to a deduction for payment for services? Second, will the service provider include an amount in gross income, and if so, when? Once theoretical questions of whether the service provider has income and whether the payor has made an outlay are resolved, a variety of Code sections potentially apply to these transactions. See Figure 16C—Compensation Transactions.

3. **Tax consequences to payor:** The essential tax question for the payor is whether a deduction is available for the amount paid for services. The answer to this question depends in large part on whether the payment is related to the payor's trade or business. A deduction is generally not allowed for payments for services incurred for personal use. (See IRC §262, and discussion at

Figure 16C
Compensation Transactions

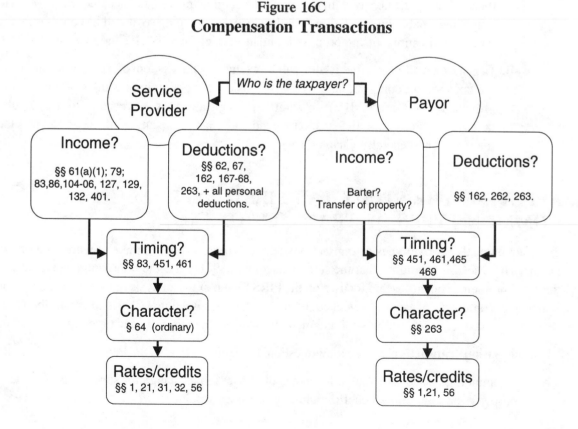

Chapter 6.) Payments for services relating to business, however, are generally deductible. If a deduction is allowed, important timing questions also arise.

a. **Income:** The payor generally does not have income questions arising from payment for services. In some situations, however, the nature of income that can be offset by the deduction is important. See IRC §469, and discussion at Chapter 11(VII)(A).

b. **Deduction:** The essential question for the payor in compensation transactions is whether the payor will be entitled to claim a deduction. A deduction will be available for the payment if it qualifies as an "ordinary and necessary business expense." (See IRC §162, and discussion at Chapter 7(II).) Important questions arise if the payment has some connection with the taxpayer's personal life; if so, its deductibility may be restricted. (See generally Chapter 8.) If the payment for services constitutes a capital expenditure, the amounts paid must be capitalized and included in the basis of the asset to which they relate (e.g., legal services to establish title to a parcel of real property). See IRC §263, and discussion at Chapter 7(III).

c. **Timing:** If a deduction is available for an expenditure, the subsidiary question is when the deduction is allowable. This will depend on the taxpayer's method of accounting and taxable year. A cash-method taxpayer will generally deduct an amount in the taxable year when it is paid. An accrual-method taxpayer will generally deduct an amount in the taxable year when all events have occurred that fix the fact of the liability, and its amount can be determined with reasonable accuracy, subject to the economic performance rules. See IRC §§451, 461, and discussion at Chapter 11(III). The payor's deduction for deferred compensation depends on the nature of the deferred compensation plan. See discussion at Chapter 11(VI). If deductions exceed income, the net operating loss may carry forward or back. See IRC §172 and discussion at Chapter 11(II)(D).

d. **Character:** A deduction for amounts paid for business-related service is a deduction from gross income from business, unless it is a capital expenditure. See IRC §263.

e. **Rates and credits:** Rates and credits for payors are not generally at issue. Note, however, the possibility of the dependent care credit for payors for dependent care services. See IRC §21, and discussion at Chapter 13(VI).

f. **Advice**

i. **Taxpayer advice:** The payor is usually seeking to increase and accelerate deductions associated with the payment of compensation. A typical issue in this area involves the different treatment of payors in qualified and nonqualified deferred compensation plans. In qualified plans, the payor may claim a deduction in the year a contribution is made to the plan, but in a nonqualified plan the payor cannot claim a deduction until the compensation is actually paid to the service provider. Notice here the differing interests of the payor and the service provider. See discussion at Chapter 11(VI)(C).

ii. **IRS advice:** The IRS will be determining whether the taxpayer is entitled to the deductions claimed in the year that they are claimed. In a controversy, the IRS will be likely to argue that the payor is not entitled to a deduction, or must defer the deduction to a future year.

iii. **Legislator advice:** A legislator must consider the propriety of changes in the tax law that would change payors' ability to deduct or claim a credit for amounts paid for services. For example, a common question for legislators is whether a deduction should be currently allowed for compensation to be paid in the future, under various sorts of retirement and related benefit plans.

4. **Tax consequences to service provider:** The essential tax questions for the service provider are: How much income, and when?

   a. **Income:** A service provider usually has income in the theoretical sense, as he or she receives something of value. If there is compensation income in the theoretical sense, it usually (but not always) is income in the sense of §61, which is the cornerstone of compensation transactions for service providers. (The major exception is imputed income from the provision of services for oneself or one's family, which may be income in a theoretical sense but which is not included in gross income. See Chapter 2(IV).) In addition, specific exclusionary statutes must be considered.

      i. **Section 61(a)(1):** Section 61(a)(1) provides that gross income includes "compensation for services including fees, commissions, fringe benefits, and similar items." Under this rule, the service provider must include in his or her gross income all types of compensation. See discussion at Chapter 3(II).

      ii. **Amount included:** Cash is included in gross income, of course, at its face value. When the value paid to the service provider is property or services, the service provider includes the fair market value of the services or property in gross income. See discussion at Chapter 3(II). The amount included becomes the basis in the property (known as "tax cost basis"). See IRC §1012 and discussion at Chapter 9(III).

      iii. **Exclusions and deferrals:** Specific Code sections address particular types of compensation income. Some offer an exclusion (such as payment for health insurance premiums or certain fringe benefits). Others offer deferral (as in deferred compensation arrangements).

   b. **Timing issues:** Individual service providers are typically cash-method taxpayers using a calendar year. Therefore, they report income in the calendar year in which they receive it. Payment by cash, check, or credit card is considered payment in cash, but a mere promise to pay is not income to these taxpayers until it ripens into something of value. See generally Chapter 11.

      i. **Restricted property:** If the property transferred to the service provider is subject to restrictions relating to the service provider's continued services, the service provider may either include it in income in the year of receipt at its value or include it in gross income in the year the restrictions lapse at its fair market value at that time. See IRC §83 and discussion at Chapter 11(VI).

      ii. **Retirement benefits:** The employee in a properly structured retirement plan does not include any amount in gross income until he or she receives payments under the plan. When distributions are made from the retirement plan, the employee includes the amount in income that has not been previously taxed. See discussion at Chapter 11(III).

   c. **Deductions:** A service provider in the marketplace is considered engaged in a trade or business and therefore may claim the usual expenses of doing business. Unreimbursed employee business expenses, however, are subject to the limitation that such expenses are deductible only to the extent that they (along with certain other miscellaneous expenses) exceed 2% of the taxpayer's AGI. See IRC §67 and discussion at Chapter 6.

d. Rates and credits: Service income is ordinary income subject to progressive tax rates for individuals. Two specific credits are potentially applicable to service providers. First, the earned income tax credit is available for low-income taxpayers. See IRC §32 and discussion at Chapter 13(VI). If the service provider in turn must hire dependent care services in order to work, the service provider may be eligible for the dependent care credit. See IRC §21 and discussion at Chapter 13(V).

e. Advice

   i. Taxpayer advice: Service providers seek to exclude items from gross income as their first choice in tax planning. But because exclusions are relatively rare for compensation income (beyond fringe benefit rules), service providers will seek to take advantage of the time value of money by deferring inclusion of compensation until future years. Consider the use of retirement plans and restricted property as methods of accomplishing this goal.

   ii. IRS advice: In examining a return, the IRS will be determining whether a taxpayer should have included an amount in gross income that he or she claimed was properly excluded or deferred. Thus, the IRS will be seeking to include items in gross income and to accelerate items of compensation income to the current year that the service provider claims are deferred to future years. The IRS may also challenge a taxpayer's deductions attributable to the business of providing services.

   iii. Legislator's advice: A legislator would be faced with a change that either includes certain service providers' income in gross income that is currently excluded, or excludes items that are currently included. For example, a legislator might be faced with the possible expansion of fringe benefits or other exclusions from gross income, or the amendment of timing rules regarding the inclusion of compensation income.

B. Transactions in property: See essay question 2 (p 383).

Transactions in property constitute a second major category of common transactions. These include sales, taxable exchanges, and various types of wholly or partially tax-free exchanges. The tax consequences of these transactions must be determined for the person who disposes of property (called here the seller) and for the person who acquires it (called here the buyer).

1. Facts—Recognizing this type of transaction: Look for a transaction in which there is an exchange, and the seller ends up owning an interest in property that is different than he or she had prior to the transaction.

2. Issues—Summary: The tax effects to both parties to the transaction—the seller and the buyer—must be considered in property transactions. The seller's realized and recognized gain or loss must be determined, and the buyer's basis in the property acquired must be computed. If the seller has also acquired property in the transaction, the seller's basis in that property must be determined. See Figure 16D—Transactions in Property.

Figure 16D
Transactions in Property

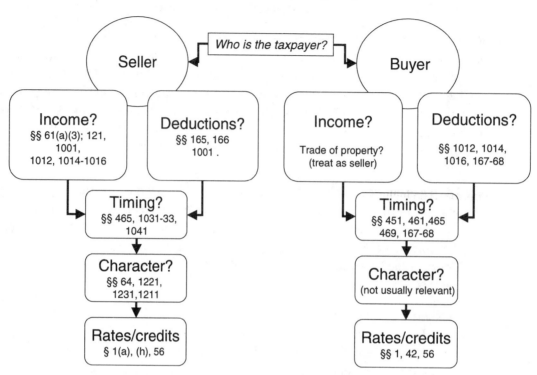

3. Tax consequences to seller: The essential tax question for the seller of property is determination of the amount and character of the gain (income) or loss on sale. (Notice that a purchaser of property can also be a seller if the purchaser transferred property rather than purchasing for cash.)

   a. Income: The starting point for the seller's income is §61(a)(3) that requires that the taxpayer include in gross income all gains from dealings in property. The seller's realized gain is equal to his or her amount realized minus the adjusted basis of the property transferred. Realized gain is generally recognized unless there is a statutory provision to the contrary. See IRC §1001(c) and discussion at Chapter 9(III).

   i. Amount realized: The seller's amount realized includes the money received, the fair market value of any property or services received, and the amount of any liabilities assumed by the taxpayer. Transfers of encumbered properties whose fair market value are less than their associated debt raise particularly challenging issues in determining amount realized. See IRC §1001(b) and Chapter 9(IV).

   ii. Adjusted basis: The seller must compute his or her initial basis and adjust it upward for improvements and downward for depreciation. See IRC §§1012, 1014, 1015, 1016, 1041 and generally Chapter 9.

   iii. Basis of property received: If the seller has accepted property other than cash in the sale, the seller must determine the basis of that property. The basis will usually be the cost of the property (fair market value of the property given in exchange) unless a nonrecognition rule requires a specially computed basis. See IRC §§1012, 1031, 1033, and 1041, Chapter 9(IV) and generally Chapter 10.

b. **Deductions:** Losses on the sale or exchange of property constitute a deduction, if allowed by statute. Potential restrictions on the deductibility of such losses include §§165 (general restrictions), 166 (losses on bad debts and worthless securities), 1211 (capital loss limitations), 465 (at risk limitations), and 469 (passive loss restrictions). See discussion at Chapters 6(VI), 7(IV)(C), 9(VII), 11(VII), and 12(II).

c. **Character:** The character of the gain or loss will be determined by the nature of the asset sold and its holding period. Capital assets will generate capital gain and loss, and noncapital assets will generate ordinary gain and loss. See IRC §§1221 and 1222. Section 1231 assets may generate long-term capital gain and ordinary loss if the requirements of that statute are met. See IRC §1231. Special limitations apply to the deduction of capital losses. See generally Chapter 12.

d. **Timing:** The inclusion of income or deduction of loss will depend on the taxpayer's method of accounting and taxable year. See discussion at Chapter 11(II) and (III). In addition, certain nonrecognition rules may apply to defer, in whole or in part, the inclusion of income or deduction of loss. See generally Chapter 10.

e. **Rates and credits:** The preferential rate for net capital gain may apply to recognized gain on the sale of property. See IRC §1(h) and discussion generally in Chapter 12. Credits are not usually at issue for the seller.

f. **Advice**

   i. **Taxpayer advice:** In advising a seller of property, tax advice generally focuses on the reduction and deferral of recognized gain and the acceleration of recognized loss. For example, a taxpayer contemplating sale of gain property held for investment might well be advised to engage in a like-kind exchange with respect to the property, in order to defer recognition of gain. Similarly, a taxpayer contemplating an exchange of loss property in similar circumstances would be better off selling the property and recognizing the loss rather than deferring it through a like-kind exchange. Alert tax advisors will also be on the lookout for strategies to exclude gain from gross income altogether, such as the exclusion of gain on the sale of a principal residence offered by §121. See discussion at Chapter 4(VIII).

   ii. **IRS advice:** The IRS will be determining whether a taxpayer properly calculated the realized and recognized gain or loss on a transaction, properly claimed a loss on sale of property, properly deferred items of income, and properly characterized the gain or loss as capital or ordinary. The IRS is likely to take positions that are mirror images of those taken by the taxpayer, claiming, for example, that gain is ordinary rather than capital.

   iii. **Legislator advice:** A legislator would be faced with the wisdom of changing the calculation of realized gain or loss, or the recognition provisions. For example, a legislator might well be faced with amendments to §1031 or §1033, expanding or limiting the domain of such statutes.

4. **Tax consequences to buyer:** The essential tax question for the buyer is generally his or her basis in the property acquired.

   a. **Income:** A purchaser who pays only cash or the assumption of liabilities never has any gain or loss on the purchase transaction. But a purchaser who transfers property will have realized gain or loss if the adjusted basis of the property transferred is different than its fair market value. In that situation, the purchaser is treated as having sold or exchanged the property, and the tax consequences are determined under the rules applicable to sellers. See generally Chapter 9.

b. Deductions: Deductions are not usually at issue in the sale or exchange of property situation, as expenses of sale paid by the purchaser are considered part of his or her purchase price. If the property is depreciable in the hands of the purchaser, the purchaser may begin to take depreciation or amortization deductions after placing the property in service. See IRC §§167, 168, and 197, and discussion at Chapter 7(III).

c. Character: Character of income or loss is not usually at issue for the purchaser of property. If he or she has transferred property and recognized gain or loss, the gain or loss will generally be capital. See generally Chapter 12.

d. Timing: The basis of the property acquired is equal to its purchase price unless a nonrecognition provision requires a special computation of basis. See IRC §§1012, 1031, 1033, 1041 and generally Chapters 9 and 10. The timing of the purchase is important for determining the beginning of the depreciation period for depreciable assets. Real property purchased for use in a trade or business or for investment is considered placed in service at the midpoint of the month in which it is actually purchased. Personal property purchased for use in a trade or business or for investment is considered placed in service at the midpoint of the taxpayer's year in which the property is actually purchased. See IRC §§168, 197 and discussion at Chapter 7(III).

e. Rates and credits: Tax rates are not usually an issue for the purchaser of property. If, however, the purchaser has recognized gain on the transfer of property to acquire the other property, that gain may be subject to the preferential rate for net capital gain. See IRC §1(h). Credits are not usually at issue for the purchaser of property except for certain low-income housing credits. See IRC §42 and discussion at Chapter 13(VIII)(D).

f. Taxpayer advice: Because a purchase for cash is not a taxable event, taxpayers generally require tax advice not on the computation of gain or loss created by the event but on the timing of purchases to maximize MACRS and other capital recovery deductions. Buyers also may seek advice on the proper structuring of property exchanges if they are not to pay the entire purchase price in cash.

C. Personal expenditure transactions: See essay question 3 (p 384).

A third major category of transactions involves situations in which the taxpayer makes expenditures or experiences losses not related to his or her trade or business or investments.

1. Facts—Recognizing this type of transaction: Look for expenditures by the taxpayer for personal and living expenses, and in particular, items such as medical expenses, charitable contributions, savings for various future needs, interest and taxes, child care, and adoption expenses. Look also for any other event that causes the taxpayer's personal (as opposed to business or investment) finances to be adversely affected, for these events may generate losses. Particularly relevant are losses from natural disasters such as storms, earthquakes, and fire. Consider as well the situation in which the taxpayer has received compensation, through insurance or otherwise, for expenditures or losses. In all of these situations, the professor is usually interested in the tax consequences to the person making the expenditures and receiving compensation, not others with whom the taxpayer interacts in making these expenditures. See Figure 16E—Personal Expenditure Transactions.

2. **Issues—Summary:** The central question in this type of factual situation is whether the taxpayer may deduct any part of his or her expenditures or losses. If the taxpayer has received compensation for any loss or expenditure, a related question is whether he or she must include that compensation in gross income. Relevant to both questions are timing questions: *When* may the taxpayer claim a deduction, and when must the taxpayer include an amount in gross income? Timing issues raise important time value of money issues, as taxpayers seek to defer income and accelerate deductions.

   a. **Income:** A taxpayer must include all income from whatever source derived in gross income. See IRC §61 and see generally Chapters 2 and 3. However, certain exclusions from gross income are particularly relevant in this context. These include compensation for personal physical injuries of §104 and for amounts received from accident or health plans. (See IRC §§104 and 105, and discussion at Chapter 4(V) and (IX)(D).) In addition, the tax benefit rule may apply to include in gross income (or exclude from gross income) recoveries of amounts that were deducted in previous years. See IRC §111 and discussion at Chapter 4(II)(F). Finally, certain savings vehicles (such as HSAs, IRAs, and education savings plans) offer the opportunity to defer, even exclude, amounts from gross income. See Chapter 6(V), (VIII), (IX).

   b. **Deductions:** A taxpayer may not deduct family and living expenses. See IRC §262, and discussion at Chapter 5(III)(B). However, the Code allows deduction of certain expenses,

Figure 16E
Personal Expenditure Transactions

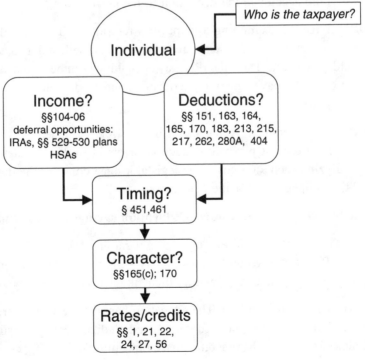

such as medical expenses (IRC §213), extraordinary casualty losses (IRC §165(h)), qualified residence interest (IRC §163(h)), certain taxes (IRC §164), and certain charitable contributions (IRC §170). In order to ensure a deduction, the taxpayer's facts must fit precisely within the domain of these statutes. See generally Chapter 6.

c. Character: The character of income and deductions associated with this type of transaction is not usually an issue. Income, if included, will usually be ordinary.

d. Timing: The taxpayer's method of accounting will generally determine when the taxpayer may claim a deduction or must include an amount in gross income. Since this type of transaction deals with a taxpayer in his or her personal life, normally the cash method of accounting will apply. The taxpayer will include amounts in gross income when received and will deduct amounts when paid, by cash, check, or credit card. See discussion at Chapter 11(III)(B).

e. Rates and credits: The preferential tax rate for capital gain is not usually applicable to this factual situation. However, the Code allows certain tax credits for amounts that are not deductible. These include the tax credit for dependent care expenses and the tax credit for adoption expenses. See IRC §§21, 24, 27 and discussion at Chapter 13(V) and (VIII)(B).

f. Advice

i. Taxpayer advice: Advice to taxpayers in these situations generally centers around determining whether they are entitled to a deduction and, if so, accelerating that deduction to the earliest possible year to allow a taxpayer to take advantage of the time value of money. For example, if a taxpayer incurs a liability to pay medical expenses in an amount that would generate a deduction for the taxpayer but does not have the cash to pay the bill currently, the taxpayer might be well advised to pay these expenses by credit card in December of one year rather than paying the bill in cash in the following year. This would accelerate the deduction to the current year.

ii. IRS advice: In examining a taxpayer's return, the IRS must determine whether the taxpayer is entitled to the personal deductions claimed, and if so, when those deductions should be allowed. Thus, the IRS may be making arguments that are the mirror image of those of the taxpayer, denying deductions and credits altogether or deferring them to future years.

iii. Legislator's advice: A legislator might well be faced with a proposal either to eliminate a current personal deduction or credit or enact a new deduction or credit. In analyzing such a proposal, the legislator must consider the tax policy, revenue, and political implications of the amendment.

D. A special kind of personal expenditure—Education savings and expenditures

1. In general: The recent spate of tax legislation regarding tax incentives for education savings and expenses offers fertile ground for testing, as well as real-world tax problems. This section summarizes those provisions and reviews their interaction.

2. Summary of education benefits: The education benefits are in the form of exclusions from gross income, deferrals of income, deductions, and credits. Every provision has its own special rules and almost every one has income phase-out limitations.

a. Exclusions/deferrals

   i. Education savings accounts and §529 plans: These offer opportunities to contribute to plans in which the investment income is tax-free. Withdrawals are excluded from gross income to the extent they are used for qualified education expenses.

   ii. Scholarships: Section 117 of the Code excludes from gross income amounts received for qualified scholarships.

   iii. Employer assistance: Section 127 of the Code allows an exclusion for up to $5,250 of employer-provided education expenses or reimbursement.

   iv. Interest on U.S. savings bonds: Section 135 of the Code allows an exclusion for the interest on U.S. savings bonds used for qualified education expenses.

b. Deductions

   i. Student loan interest: Taxpayers may be able to deduct up to $2,000 per year of the interest paid on student loans. IRC §221.

   ii. Deduction for higher education expenses: A taxpayer may be able to deduct up to $4,000 per year of higher education expenses, incurred prior to 2006. IRC §222.

c. Credits

   i. HOPE credit: A taxpayer may be able to claim a credit of up to $1,500 for tuition and fees for the first two years of post-secondary expenses. IRC §25A.

   ii. Lifetime learning credit: A taxpayer may be able to claim a credit of 20% of up to $10,000 of expenses for higher education. IRC §25A.

3. Income limitations—See Figure 16F: The 2005 income limitations for each kind of benefit are illustrated in the following chart. As income rises, fewer benefits are available, and the only benefits available for taxpayers with incomes in excess of $220,000 ($110,000 for single taxpayers) are the §529 plans, scholarships, and employer assistance.

Figure 16F
Income Limitations

Education tax incentive	Phase-out begins – 2005[*] (Benefit will be limited)	Phase-out ends – 2005 (Benefit no longer available)
HOPE credit IRC §25A	$ 43,000 Single $ 87,000 Joint	$ 63,000 Single $107,000 Joint
Lifetime learning credit IRC §25A	$ 43,000 Single $ 87,000 Joint	$ 63,000 Single $107,000 Joint
Student interest deduction IRC §221	$ 50,000 Single $105,000 Joint	$ 65,000 Single $135,000 Joint
Qualified education Expense deduction IRC §222	N/A	$ 65,000 Single $130,000 Joint

Figure 16F *[continued]*

Education tax incentive	Phase-out begins – 2005[*] (Benefit will be limited)	Phase-out ends – 2005 (Benefit no longer available)
Exclusion for interest from U.S. savings bonds IRC §135	$ 61,200 Single $ 91,850 Joint	$ 76,200 Single $121,850 Joint
Education savings accounts IRC §530	$ 95,000 Single $190,000 Joint	$110,000 Single $220,000 Joint
Section 529 plans IRC §529	No limit	No limit
Scholarships IRC §117	No limit	No limit
Employer assistance IRC §127	No limit	No limit

[*] For updated amounts for year after 2005, see www.speerhoyt.com

4. **Which sections apply? Sorting out the various incentives.** The relative newness of these provisions means that not all questions are answered with respect to how they are coordinated. But some basic principles apply.

   a. **Apply specific limitations first:** The AGI limitations are applied first to determine which incentives are available to the taxpayer. (See Figure 16F.) Each incentive has its special rules, so that the taxpayer may be eligible for some incentives, but not others. Analyze these first. Then, apply the following rules to determine the availability of the incentives, depending on the amount of qualifying educational expenses.

   b. **No double dipping:** The same expense cannot generate a benefit under two or more provisions.

   c. **Optional:** Taking a credit is optional, even if the taxpayer qualifies for it.

   d. **Ordering:** The ordering rule is best thought of as spreading the total qualified education expenses among the available incentives, in a particular order.

      i. **Exclusions:** Amounts attributable to scholarships and employer assistance excluded from gross income cannot be counted as qualified education expenses for other tax benefits.

         Example: Kristin receives a merit scholarship that covers $3,500 of her college expenses. She will not be able to claim this amount as qualified expenses suitable for a deduction under IRC §222, a credit under §25A, or as expenses with respect to 529 plans or education savings accounts. See IRC §§25A(g)(2) and 222(d)(1).

      ii. **Then—Section 529 and 530 plans:** If the taxpayer has taken a distribution from a §529 plan, or from an education savings account, any remaining expenses are allocated to those amounts, up to the amount the distributions.

iii. Then—Savings bond interest: If the taxpayer has redeemed U.S. savings bonds, any remaining expenses are allocated to that income up to the amount of the proceeds.

iv. Then—Choose: Do you want a credit or a deduction? The taxpayer can choose to take one of the credits of IRC §25A, not both, for a particular student. The taxpayer is not required to claim a credit if one is available. Any remaining expenses would be potentially available for deduction under §222.

Example: Rocky is a single taxpayer. He is going to law school at night and works during the day. In 2002, he had a total of $30,000 of qualified higher education expenses. His modified AGI was $25,000. Here's how he paid for his education:

- He received a merit scholarship for $5,000, which was applied toward tuition.

- He received a $15,000 distribution from a §529 plan, of which $5,000 was income and $10,000 was invested capital.

- He redeemed U.S. savings bonds in the amount of $5,000, of which $2,500 was income and $2,500 was invested capital.

- He paid $5,000 out of pocket.

Rocky is confused about the myriad tax incentives for education and wants some help. Which ones can he take? We first note that all the expenses are qualifying expenses under all the Code provisions, and that Rocky's AGI is such that none of the income limitations will apply.

- The scholarship is tax-free. Does not count as qualified education expenses for other purposes. This leaves $25,000 in expenses to allocate.

- He then should take $15,000 of expenses as offsetting the distribution from the §529 plan, so that 100% of that distribution is excluded from gross income. This leaves $10,000 of expenses to allocate.

- He could then take $5,000 of expenses associated with the redemption of the savings bond. This leaves $5,000 of expenses to allocate.

- He can't take the HOPE credit, because the expenses are not for the first two years of post-secondary education. But he could take the lifetime learning credit, which would allow him to take 20% of up to $5,000 of his remaining expenses, for a credit of $1,000 against his tax liability. Or, he could take a deduction under §222, allowing him a deduction of $3,000 of those expenses. Which is better for him? He is in the 15% bracket, which means that the credit saves him $1,000 in tax, while the $3,000 deduction generates a tax savings of 15% of $3,000—$450. He should take the credit.

Example: Assume the same facts as in the previous example, except that Rocky had only $15,000 of educational expenses, including the scholarship. He still received a $15,000 distribution from the §529 plan, and redeemed the $5,000 in savings bonds. (He used the rest of the money for noneducational purposes.) In this case, the scholarship is still tax-free, and uses up $5,000 of the expenses, leaving $10,000. This means that only a portion of the §529 plan distribution is tax-free. Of the distribution, $5,000 was income and the rest was invested capital. The $10,000 of expenses is allocated to the two categories, proportionately. This means that one-third is allocated to income ($3,333) and two-thirds to capital ($6,667), which in turn means that Rocky has $1,667 of income from the §529 plan distribution ($5,000 − $3,333). In addition, unless a special exception applies, the 10% penalty will apply to the nonqualifying portion of the distribution. All of the income from the redemption of the U.S. savings bond is income ($2,500) and there is no opportunity to claim a credit or deduction.

E. Business transactions: See essay question 4 (p 384).

A fourth type of commonly encountered transaction is the taxpayer engaging in sale of services or inventory for profit. See Figure 16G—Business Transactions.

1. **Facts—Recognizing this type of transaction:** Look for a taxpayer potentially engaged in business—the regular undertaking of business activity for profit. A taxpayer in this context may be an individual engaging in business as a sole proprietor, or may be an entity such as a partnership or corporation. When the taxpayer is an individual or S corporation, one must inquire as to whether the activity truly qualifies as a business, or whether it is merely a hobby. Look for sales income and for outlays for items used in the business.

2. **Issues—Summary:** The essential tax questions for business transactions are how much a taxpayer must include in gross income as income from business, when he or she must include it, what expenditures are deductible, and when they are deductible. Business transactions also can involve sales of property other than inventory, and these should be analyzed separately as sales or exchanges of property. In a business transaction, there will potentially be many other

Figure 16G
Business Transactions

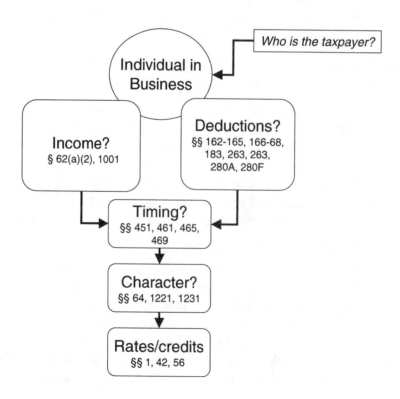

taxpayers involved (customers, suppliers, employees, and competitors) but business transactions questions typically focus on the net result of business activity to the taxpayer engaged in business.

a. Income: Section 61(a)(2) is the starting place for business taxpayers, who must include "gross income derived from business" in their gross incomes. See Chapter 7(III).

b. Deductions: A business taxpayer is entitled to a number of business-related deductions, including those allowed by §§162 (ordinary and necessary business expenses), 163 (interest), 164 (taxes), 165(c)(1) (losses incurred in a trade or business), 166 (bad debts), 170 (charitable contributions), and 172 (net operating losses). See generally Chapter 7. The taxpayer is not entitled to a deduction for capital outlays but will claim capital recovery with respect to these items during ownership of the asset. See IRC §§167, 168, and 197. See generally Chapter 7. Often embedded in business transactions questions are issues of whether an expenditure is truly a business expenditure or is personal and therefore nondeductible. Deductions may be limited if the activity is not engaged in for profit or if the deduction is attributable to listed property or other specially treated items (such as home offices or business entertainment). See generally Chapter 8.

c. Character: The character of business income is ordinary. It is important also to characterize the gains and losses on sales of property used in the business as §1231 property, which can lead to the taxpayer-friendly rule of gains as capital and losses as ordinary. See Chapter 12(IV).

d. Timing: In computing the net profit from sales of inventory, the taxpayer will deduct the cost of goods sold. See discussion at Chapter 11(IV). Amounts paid as capital expenditures will not generate a deduction but will generate capital recovery during ownership of the property. See discussion at Chapter 7(III). Finally, the taxpayer's method of accounting and taxable year will determine when he or she includes amounts in gross income or claims deductions. The cash-method taxpayer will include income when received and claim deductions when they are paid, subject to certain limitations. The accrual-method taxpayer will include amounts in income and claim deductions when the all events tests are met, again subject to certain limitations. See Chapter 11(III).

e. Rates and credits: Net business income, as ordinary income, is taxed at the usual rates, and the business owner may be entitled to claim certain business-related tax credits.

f. Advice

   i. Taxpayer advice: Most advice to business centers around identifying available deductions and helping accelerate those deductions to the earliest possible year to allow the taxpayer to take advantage of the time value of money. In giving this advice, the lawyer must provide guidance on the important questions surrounding the identification of capital expenditures and deductible expenses, the computation of MACRS and other capital recovery deductions, and the selection of an inventory identification method.

   ii. IRS advice: In examining a taxpayer's return, the IRS must determine whether the taxpayer has properly included all items of business income and claimed the proper deductions in the appropriate year. Thus, in a controversy, the IRS is likely to make arguments that are the mirror images of those made by the taxpayer: accelerating income, denying deductions and credits altogether, and deferring deductions and credits to future years.

iii. Legislator's advice: A legislator might well be faced with proposals that increase or decrease the number of business-related deductions. Deductions that have a personal flavor to them (such as meals and entertainment) are perennial congressional favorites for tinkering. In analyzing a proposal to change the deductibility of an item, the legislator must consider the tax policy, revenue, and political impact of the measure. In addition, Congress has shown interest in changing the timeframe for capital recovery, shortening the period to stimulate the economy. Some professors may test your ability to discuss the wisdom of these efforts.

F. Intrafamilial transfers: See essay question 5 (pp 384-385).

A fifth commonly encountered type of transaction is intrafamilial transfers, including gifts, bequests, life insurance, attempted assignments of income, and transactions occurring pursuant to a divorce.

1. **Facts—Recognizing this type of transaction:** This type of transaction is easy to recognize. Look for a transfer of value among family members (broadly defined) and in particular, transfers from the elder to younger generations. Look for a legal separation or divorce of a married couple, and transactions taking place because of or related to that separation or divorce.

2. **Issues—Summary:** This type of transfer must be considered from the points of view of the transferor *and* the transferee. The essential tax questions are whether the transfer is a taxable event to the transferor and whether the transferee must include any amount in gross income. These transfers also raise important questions regarding the federal estate and gift tax that are beyond the scope of the basic federal income tax class.

   a. **Gifts:** The transfer of property as a gift is not a realization event to the transferor, and therefore he or she does not recognize the gain or loss inherent in the property. The recipient of a gift need not include any amount in gross income, although the recipient must include any income from the gift in gross income. See IRC §102, and discussion at Chapter 4(III). The recipient of a gift generally takes the property with a basis equal to the basis the property had in the hands of the donor, increased by a portion of any gift tax paid by the donor. A special basis rule applies, however, to certain loss property. See IRC §1015(a), and discussion at Chapter 9(III)(B).

   b. **Bequests, devises, and inheritances:** The distribution of property pursuant to a specific bequest, devise, or inheritance is generally a taxable event to the estate, but if the estate transfers property to satisfy a monetary obligation, it may realize and recognize income. See IRC §1001(c) and discussion at Chapter 9(III). The recipient of property pursuant to a bequest, devise, or inheritance will exclude the value of that property from gross income. See IRC §102, and discussion at Chapter 4(III). The recipient will take the property with a basis equal to the fair market value on the date of the decedent's death or at the alternative valuation date six months later, if that date is elected. See IRC §1014, and discussion at Chapter 9(III).

   c. **Life insurance and annuities:** The payment of premiums on personal life insurance policies does not generate a deduction, as this is a personal expenditure. See IRC §262. The recipient of life insurance proceeds by reason of the death (or chronic or terminal illness) of the insured may exclude these amounts from gross income. See IRC §101, and discussion at Chapter 4(II). Annuity payments are taxed in accordance with the rules of IRC §72 that require a portion of each payment to be considered income and a portion as recovery of capital. See discussion at Chapter 3(V)(F).

   d. **Attempted assignments of income and the kiddie tax:** A taxpayer may attempt to assign income to a related individual in a lower tax bracket. Attempted assignments of services income will not be respected, and assignments of income from property will be respected only if they are not "carved-out interests" in property. See generally Chapter 14. The transfer of property to a child under the age of 14 may implicate the "kiddie tax," under which the child is taxed at his or her parents' tax rate on certain investment income. See IRC §1(g) and discussion at Chapter 14(IV)(A).

   e. **Divorce—Property settlements:** Neither spouse will recognize gain or loss on the transfer of property in a divorce-related transfer, if the requirements of §1041 are met. Neither spouse has income as a result of the receipt of property, and neither spouse claims a deduction for such transfers of property. The basis of the property after the transfer is the basis it had immediately before the transfer, not increased by any payments made in cash or property. See IRC §1041 and discussion at Chapter 10(V). Timing, rates, and credit issues generally do not arise until a former spouse disposes of property received in a divorce (which is treated as a property transaction, discussed above).

   f. **Divorce—Support payments:** There are two types of support payments with very different tax consequences to the former spouses.

   i. **Alimony:** A payment of alimony is deductible by the payor and includable in the gross income of the recipient. Front-end loaded alimony, however, generates an inclusion to the payor and a concomitant deduction to the recipient in the third post-separation year. Remember that a payment must meet the *federal* definition of alimony to be deductible; state law labels do not control the tax treatment of such items. See IRC §§71, 215 and discussion at Chapters 3(VI) and 6(III).

   ii. **Child support:** The payment of child support is not deductible by the payor and is not includable by the recipient (usually the custodial parent). See IRC §71 and discussion at Chapter 4(XI).

3. **Advice**

   a. **Taxpayer advice:** In advising families on intrafamilial transfers, attention should be focused on ensuring that the transfer itself is not a taxable event and that the recipient will not have unintended items of gross income. Care must be taken to properly compute the basis of the property transferred. In particular, advice in the divorce setting must take into consideration the inherent gain or loss in property transferred (which will ultimately be recognized upon sale of the property) and the impact of deductible alimony (and non-deductible child support) payments.

   b. **IRS advice:** In examining intrafamilial transfers, the IRS may assert assignment of income principles, along with determining whether the transfer fits within the domain of an exclusion or deferral statute.

   c. **Legislator's advice:** A legislator is likely to be faced with changes that make intrafamilial transfer more or less "taxing." The evolution of the kiddie tax is an example of the kind of question a legislator would be faced with, and in connection with which the legislator would be required to consider policy, revenue, and political implications.

Exam Tips on RECOGNIZING RELATED TAX STATUTES

☞ In solving a reactive problem, don't waste time on how the taxpayer "should" have structured the transaction, unless specifically asked to do so. Instead, fully consider the tax consequences of alternative interpretations of the facts and conclude as to which interpretation is most appropriate. Ethical issues (such as what would constitute a reasonable return position) can be embedded in this type of problem.

☞ When addressing a proactive problem for a taxpayer, consider first the taxpayer's tax and nontax goals and then consider alternative ways of accomplishing those goals, within the facts that are flexible. Propose alternative paths to solve the taxpayer's problem and analyze the tax consequences of each path. Choose the path that produces the best overall consequences for the taxpayer and explain why the other paths are less suitable. Ethical issues, including conflicts of interest and development of reasonable return positions, may well be embedded in proactive problems.

☞ Consider the call of the question carefully. In which taxpayer's tax consequences is the professor interested? If the professor is interested in fewer than all of the taxpayers in the transaction, focus on the others only to the extent that their tax consequences directly impact those in which the professor is interested.

☞ Look for an event that makes the taxpayer better off in an economic sense than he or she was before the event. Construe income broadly, and exclusions narrowly. In doubt as to whether an exclusion applies? Be sure to analyze the facts in the alternative.

☞ Look for the situation in which the taxpayer pays for an item or experiences an event that makes him or her worse off than the taxpayer was before. Then consider whether there is a specific statutory provision allowing a deduction for the item. Remember that deductions are a matter of legislative grace, and construe them narrowly. In doubt as to whether a deduction is available? Be sure to analyze the situation in the alternative.

☞ When a taxpayer has income or loss from dealings in property, be sure to address the character of that income or loss, and offer the implications of a particular classification.

☞ Timing questions are often hidden within the larger issues of income and deduction. Make a point of asking *"When?"* for any item of income or deduction a taxpayer claims. Moreover, remember that taxpayers prefer to defer income and accelerate deductions, and ask whether any of the principles governing the timing of income and deductions allow or prevent these strategies.

☞ Many tax professors are relatively uninterested in the calculation of the tax due and focus instead on an understanding of the progressive rate regime (in contrast to other potential tax regimes), the calculation of taxable income, and the domain of various tax credits.

☞ Any set of facts can raise a large number of potentially applicable tax statutes. Which ones do you discuss on an exam? If a tax statute is clearly inapplicable, do not squander valuable time discussing it. If the facts are clearly within a statute, discuss this succinctly. But at the heart of many tax questions lies a statutory "domain problem." A domain problem exists when the statute either contains some ambiguity in its terms that raises questions about whether the facts fit within its domain, or the facts themselves are ambiguous, which also raises questions about their inclusion in the statute's domain. These types of situations usually deserve an in-depth analysis in an exam situation, engaging in the process of statutory interpretation of ambiguous terms, or discussing alternative interpretations of the facts that cause them to fall within or without the domain of the statute.

☞ In addressing the tax consequence of applying a particular concept or statute, discuss each step in your analysis carefully. If performing some arithmetic feat, show how you reached your conclusion. If you have identified some ambiguity in the statute that causes you to be uncertain as to whether it applies, be sure to discuss the effects in the alternative of falling within and without the domain of the statute.

Essay Exam Questions

QUESTION 1: Samantha is currently employed full time as an engineer by Alpha Corporation in Boston. Beta Corporation of Salt Lake City has offered her similar employment, and Samantha is delighted because she is an avid skier and has always wanted to live and work near the ski slopes. Beta has offered the following salary and benefits (values are expressed as annual figures):

Salary	$100,000
Contribution by employer to qualified retirement plan	15,000
Moving expense reimbursement	2,500
Membership at country club	10,000
Annual consultation with financial planner	300
40% discount on computer equipment manufactured by Beta, up to $20,000 per year	20,000
Blackberry "Supreme"	1,000
Life insurance premium on $200,000 of group term insurance	800
Medical insurance premium for Samantha and her family (per month)	900

In addition, Samantha is given 1,000 shares of Beta Corporation stock; however, if she leaves within eight years, she has to give it back to her employer and cannot transfer it to any person other than the employer for ten years. She is eligible for adoption assistance of up to $10,000 per child (she is considering adopting a child from abroad) and she is told that the firm culture is such that she can expect a "significant gift" at the holiday season each year from her new boss, Amy. Finally, if Samantha travels for business, she can keep the frequent flyer miles.

Please discuss the tax consequences of Beta's offer to Samantha.

QUESTION 2: Mike is a former professional football player and manager of a local sporting goods store. His salary is $175,000 per year. He previously owned some land in Eastern Oregon which he inherited from his grandmother on March 2 of Year 1. At the time of her death, in Year 1, it was worth $368,000. Mike properly reported income and claimed expenses associated with rental of this land for livestock grazing. He kept the land until July 4 of Year 6, when he traded it with Bev for an office building plus $120,000. The office building was worth $568,000 at that time but was subject to a mortgage of $100,000 which Mike assumed. He intended—and did—hold the land and the office building for investment purposes, although he knew Bev was going to build a ranch for her personal use on the land. Over the years Mike paid off the mortgage. In December of Year 10 Mike sold the office building for $500,000. In that year he also sold some collectible sports memorabilia for $50,000 in which he had a basis of $10,000, and he sold some stock in ABC Corporation for $5,000. He had been given this stock by ABC Corporation years ago when he agreed to promote athletic shoes for that company. At that time, he had included $50,000 in gross income as the value of the stock. Finally, in year 10 he sold his personal playbooks to a collector for $50,000.

For Year 10, Mike reported a net long-term capital gain of $80,000 taxed at 15%. You are an IRS agent examining the return. Was he correct in his reporting of income?

QUESTION 3: Bill and Marion are married and have two daughters, ages 10 and 12. This morning they awoke to a startling realization: They had saved nothing for retirement, nothing for the college education of their children, and nothing for any unexpected health emergencies. Neither had thought much about this, because they are both covered by health insurance (but not a retirement account) at work, and retirement/college seemed just so far away. Having looked at their finances, they believe they could save a significant amount of money if they tried. Last year, their AGI (reporting on a joint return) was $150,000. Please advise them on the most tax-advantageous way to save for retirement, health, and their daughters' college educations.

QUESTION 4: Spencer is the owner of an Internet research business organized as a sole proprietorship. He uses the cash method of accounting. Last year, he recorded on his books $100,000 in sales of information to customers. As of December 31, he had received $75,000 in payments and $25,000 in oral promises to pay within 30 days from clients. He also incurred the following expenses:

Compensation to employees	$25,000
Advertising	5,000
Rent	12,000
Telephone & Internet	2,500
Taxes	2,000
Business entertainment	1,000
Insurance	3,500

He purchased a computer for $5,000 for exclusive use in the business and sold a used computer that had a basis of zero, for $1,500. He had originally purchased the computer for $10,000. Spencer also had a theft this year of some office equipment, with a fair market value of $1,500 and basis of $2,500. He received no insurance proceeds for this, as it was below his deductible amount. A flood destroyed some of his office art, which had a basis of $5,000 and a fair market value of $8,000. His insurance company paid him $8,000 for this loss.

Please advise Spencer on the tax consequences of these transactions. Do you have any suggestions for him to reduce next year's taxes?

QUESTION 5: This has been a difficult year for Sabrina. First, her mother died. Sabrina inherited the family home (worth $175,000). She also inherited some stock in XYZ Corporation (in which her mother had a basis of $50,000 and the fair market value of which is $125,000). Her mother named her as the beneficiary of an annuity. Sabrina is not sure she understands perfectly, but apparently her mother paid $80,000 for this annuity many years ago and received $5,000 per year for her lifetime (20 years). Sabrina will also receive that amount annually for a period of ten years. Sabrina sold the family home almost immediately for $190,000.

Also, Sabrina and her husband, Eli, separated amicably and are planning to get a divorce. During the separation, they have been sorting through their assets and they have transferred their home (worth $500,000, for which they paid $225,000) from their joint names to Eli's name, and their savings (primarily in the form of stocks held for many years) from Eli's name into Sabrina's name. (Sabrina expects that she would sell these soon.) The only remaining issue is alimony. They are considering the following alimony payments from Eli to Sabrina:

The year of the divorce	$50,000
The second year	$20,000
The third year	$10,000
The fourth year	$ 5,000
The fifth year	-0-

Sabrina wants to make sure that she is protected, so Eli will purchase a life insurance policy that will pay her these amounts if he dies. They agree that if Sabrina dies that Eli will pay these amounts into the college funds of their two children. They predict that Eli will be in the 35% bracket (federal) and Sabrina will be in the 28% bracket (federal) after the divorce.

Please advise Sabrina about the tax consequences of these events and if there is anything she should do to reduce her taxes before finalizing the divorce.

Essay Exam Answers

SAMPLE ANSWER TO QUESTION 1

This transaction involves the payment of compensation to Samantha in various forms, and the essential question for Samantha is whether she will be required to include each item of value in her gross income if she accepts Beta's offer and receives this compensation package.

As an initial matter, it appears that the job change would greatly benefit Samantha on a personal level because she has always wanted to work and live near the ski slopes. Although the job change would generate a benefit to her, this benefit is personal rather than economic and thus is not considered "income" in the sense of the federal income tax.

Similarly, while the benefit of keeping frequent flyer miles paid for by one's employer may technically be considered income to Samantha, the IRS position appears to be that the benefit of these miles is not includible in her gross income.

In this situation, Samantha will be receiving salary and other types of economic benefits. All of the items listed constitute an economic benefit to Samantha in exchange for her services and therefore are "income" in a theoretical sense. Section 61 requires that a taxpayer include in his or her gross income "all income from whatever source derived" and specifically includes compensation income in paragraph (a)(1). Thus, §61 requires the inclusion of all of the items listed in Samantha's gross income, unless a specific statute provides an exclusion for or deferral of these amounts. Samantha's salary income clearly must be included in her gross income. However, exclusions may be available for some components of her compensation package.

Retirement benefits: Contributions made by the employer to a qualified retirement plan are not includible in the gross income of the employee; instead, these amounts will (hopefully) grow tax-free, and Samantha will include amounts in her gross income when they are paid to her upon retirement. See IRC §401.

Moving expenses: The reimbursement for moving expenses is includable in Samantha's gross income. IRC §82. However, §217 allows a deduction for moving expenses of a taxpayer moving more than 50 miles from one job to another. Samantha meets the conditions of the deduction for moving expenses because her new job is more than 50 miles from her previous job, and she was a full time employee at Alpha and will be at Beta. IRC §217(c)(1), (2). Therefore, she may claim a deduction for qualified moving expenses, i.e., the costs of moving her household goods and personal effects and of traveling from Boston to Salt Lake City. IRC §217(a), (b). This constitutes a deduction from gross income in computing adjusted gross income (AGI).

Life insurance premium: An employer's payment of the premium on group term life insurance in excess of $50,000 is includible in the employee's gross income. IRC §79(a). Because the life insurance policy is in excess of that amount, the premium must be allocated between the excludible portion (attributable to $50,000 worth of coverage) and the includible portion (attributable to the remaining $150,000 worth of coverage). Samantha will include in her gross income the portion of the premium attributable to the $150,000 of coverage.

Medical insurance premium: Section 106 of the Code provides that gross income does not include the premiums paid by the employer for accident or health plans for employees. Thus, Samantha may exclude the premium for health insurance from her gross income.

Other benefits: The other benefits in Samantha's package must be examined under §132, which addresses fringe benefits provided by employers to employees. This section provides that certain specifically defined fringe benefits will be excluded from the gross income of the employee. But if an item is not described in §132 (and no other Code section excludes it), it will be included in the gross income of the employee under the general rule of §61(a)(1).

Computer discount: Section 132(a)(2) provides that gross income of an employee will not include any "qualified employee discount." Section 132(c)(1) defines a qualified employee discount as any "employee discount" that meets certain requirements. An employee discount is the amount by which the price of property sold in the ordinary course of business to the general public exceeds the price of that property to employees. IRC §132(c)(3). In order to be a qualified employee discount, the discount must not exceed the gross profit percentage for sales to customers. IRC §132(c)(1).

In Samantha's situation, Beta Corporation is offering a 40% discount on the equipment it sells to customers. This may constitute a qualified employee discount if the discount does not exceed the gross profit percentage. Additional information would be necessary to determine the gross profit percentage. If the discount does not exceed the gross profit percentage and if Samantha were to purchase computer equipment at a discount, the value of the discount would not be included in her gross income. If, however, Samantha were to purchase equipment at a discount and that discount exceeded the gross profit percentage, the amount of the excess would be included in her gross income.

Samantha might seek to deduct the cost of any computer she purchases for use in her employment. Section 280F imposes significant restrictions on the deductibility of such expenditures, requiring the employee's purchase to be a condition of employment and for the convenience of the employer. IRC §280F(d)(3). As Samantha will probably not be able to meet these tests (there is no evidence, for example, that her new employer is requiring her to purchase a computer) she will probably be precluded from deducting the cost of the computer as an unreimbursed employee business expense.

Blackberry "Supreme": The provision of this piece of equipment is not specifically addressed by §132. This benefit, however, potentially falls within two of the categories of excluded fringe benefits: de minimis fringes and working condition fringes. Section 132(a)(4) excludes from gross income "de minimis fringes," which are defined in §132(e) as any property or service of such small value that accounting for it would be unreasonable or administratively impractical. The value of the benefit in this case ($1,000) is not objectively small, and accounting for it would not be administratively impractical. Thus, the provision of the Blackberry probably would not fall within the exclusion for de minimis fringes.

More promising is the exclusion for working condition fringe of §132(a)(3). Working condition fringes are defined in §132(d) as property or services provided to an employee to the extent that, if the employee paid for such property or services, a deduction would be allowable under §162 or §167. Thus, the inquiry is whether, if Samantha purchased the Blackberry herself, she would be entitled to a deduction for these expenses as ordinary and necessary business expenses. This raises the question of what this equipment is for—business or personal use. If it is for personal use, it would not generate a deduction if she purchased it directly and thus would not constitute a working condition fringe. If, however, the Blackberry is to be predominantly for her business activities, the expenses attributable to the service agreement likely would generate a deduction under §§162 and 167 and would therefore qualify as a working condition fringe benefit.

Membership at country club: This benefit does not seem to fall within the purview of any of the six excluded fringe benefits. While the cost of such membership might seem to be a working condition fringe if Samantha intended to use the membership for business, §274(a) disallows any deduction for dues to such a facility and thus the expenditure would not qualify as a working-condition fringe. A special rule of

§132(j)(4) allows an employee to exclude the value of certain on-premises exercise and athletic facilities. Country club membership is clearly not within the purview of this statute, and thus the value of that membership would be included in Samantha's gross income.

Consultation with financial planner: This may constitute qualified retirement planning services, an excludable benefit under §132(m), if (1) the consultation is in connection with the retirement plan maintained by the company; and (2) Beta Corporation does not discriminate in favor of highly compensated employees in the provision of this benefit.

Adoption assistance: If Samantha does adopt a child, and takes advantage of this benefit, it will be excluded from her gross income under IRC §137.

Stock: When Samantha was given 1,000 shares of Beta Corporation stock, this was an economic benefit to her. However, she does not include it in her gross income until the first year in which she can either transfer it or it will not be forfeited if she leaves. Therefore, she will not have to include the value of the stock in her gross income until the ninth year, when her rights to it vest. She may, however, make a §83(b) election pursuant to which she includes the fair market value of the stock in gross income now, on the theory that it will be much more valuable later.

Gift? If the firm culture is such that she can *expect* a gift from her new boss at holiday time, is it really a "gift"? Moreover, IRC §102(c) provides that there is no possibility of a gift from an employer; such a so-called gift is compensation. In this case, however, the gift appears to be from *Amy*, not Beta Corporation, but the circumstances are such that it probably would be considered an indirect transfer from Beta to Amy to Samantha (and certainly if Amy is reimbursed for it).

Summary

Benefit	Amount	*Includible/Excludable/ Deferred?*
Frequent Flyer Miles	???	Excludable
"Gift" from boss	???	Probably Includable
Salary	$100,000	Includable
Qualified retirement plan	15,000	Deferred
Moving expenses	2,500	Excludable
Membership at country club	10,000	Includable
Annual consultation with financial planner	300	Potentially excludable
Discount (up to gross profit %)	20,000	Perhaps excludable
Blackberry "Supreme"	1,000	Partially excludable
Life insurance premium	800	Partially excludable
Medical insurance premium	900	Excludable
Adoption assistance	10,000	Excludable
Beta Corporation Stock	???	Deferred
Benefits of living in Utah	Priceless	Excludable

Advice

If Samantha wishes to improve her tax situation, she might explore other ways of deferring compensation income into the future, such as the use of other (perhaps nonqualified) retirement plans.

SAMPLE ANSWER TO QUESTION 2

Whether Mike correctly reported his situation requires a tracing of the tax consequences of his ownership of the land and the office building and combining that sale with other transactions in Year 10 that may (or may not) generate capital gain or loss.

When Mike inherited the land from his grandmother, he took it with a basis equal to its fair market value at the date of her death, which appears to be $368,000. He correctly did not depreciate this land, because land does not suffer "wear and tear." Apparently no improvements were made to the land.

The exchange with Bev was probably a like-kind exchange with respect to Mike (but not Bev—which does not matter to Mike, as the parties' tax consequences are determined independently). It was an exchange of property, of a type eligible for like-kind exchange treatment, and Mike held both the property he exchanged and the property he received for investment. Land and an office building are like-kind, as both are real property (assuming that the office building had at least some land with it).

If the transaction qualified as a like-kind exchange, in Year 6 Mike took the office building with a basis equal to his old basis in the land ($368,000) plus the gain recognized ($120,000), minus the fair market value of the boot received ($120,000) plus the assumption of liability ($100,000), which is treated as an additional investment in the property. Thus, his initial basis in the office building was $468,000. An office building is depreciable over 39 years ($12,000 per year or $1,000 per month), so he would have properly claimed MACRS deductions equal to the following:

Year 6: $5,500 (5.5 months because of the mid-month convention × $1,000)
Years 7-8-9: $12,000 per year
Year 10: $11,500 (11.5 months because of the mid-month convention × $1,000)

Total MACRS deductions = $53,000. The basis of the office building is $415,000 at the moment of sale. The sale for $500,000 therefore generates a recognized gain of $85,000.

To determine the tax effects of this sale, it is necessary to categorize this and the other dispositions of property as capital or noncapital assets.

Office building: Of the $85,000 of gain, the amount attributable to prior MACRS deduction is unrecaptured §1250 gain and is properly allocable to the 25% long-term category (because he has held it for more than one year). The remaining $32,000 of this gain properly belongs in the long term 15/5% category.

Sports memorabilia: Mike has a basis of $10,000 and a sales price of $50,000, generating a $40,000 gain. This is probably a 28% long-term capital gain attributable to collectibles.

Playbooks: This is not a capital asset (IRC §1221(3)) and generates ordinary income upon sale.

Stock: This is a long-term capital loss properly allocable to the 15/5% category. The amount of the loss is equal to the sales price ($5,000) minus Mike's basis of $50,000 (he had a tax cost basis in the stock equal to the amount of income he included in gross income upon receipt of the stock).

Applying the process of Figure 12E, the results are as follows:

	Short-Term Capital Gain and Loss	Long-Term 28% Capital Gain and Loss	Long-Term 25% Capital Gain (not loss)	Long-Term 15/5% Capital Gain and Loss & Net §1231 Gain	STEP— AS OUTLINED IN TEXT
A. Add Capital Gains in each category	-0-	$40,000	$53,000	$32,000	*Step One—* See pages 288-291
B. Add Capital Losses in each category	-0-	-0-		($45,000)	*Step One—* See pages 288-291
C. Net Result (A-B)	-0-	$40,000 gain	$53,000, but not more than net §1231 gain	($13,000) loss	*Step Two—* See page 291
D. Apply 28% Loss (if any) to other categories NOT APPLICABLE in this problem	Does not offset		NOT APPLICABLE to this problem	NOT APPLICABLE to this problem	*Step Three—* See page 291
E. Apply 15/5% loss (if any) to other categories	Does not offset	(1) From 15/5%: ($13,000) *Net 28% LTCG remaining: $27,000*	(2) From 15/5%: -0- *Net 25% LTCG remaining: $53,000*		*Step Three—* See pages 291-292
F. Apply S-T Loss (if any) to other gain categories NOT APPLICABLE to this problem		NOT APPLICABLE to this problem	NOT APPLICABLE to this problem	NOT APPLICABLE to this problem	*Step Three—* See pages 291-292
G. Net capital gain *or* net capital loss remaining	0	$27,000 gain	$53,000 gain	-0-	*Step Three—* See pages 291-292
H. Max. Tax Rate or Deduction?		28%	25%	-0-	*Step Four—* See page 292 and Chapter 13

From this analysis it is clear that while Mike was correct in his calculation of the amount of the gain ($80,000) but incorrect as to its proper rate. Because Mike's regular tax rate will be above 28%, he will be taxed on $27,000 at 28% and $53,000 at 25%, not at the 15% rate that he claimed.

SAMPLE ANSWER TO QUESTION 3

Dear Bill and Marion:

Welcome to the real world! Fortunately, there are a number of savings vehicles that will allow you to save for these purposes in a tax-advantageous way.

The umbrella strategy is to create savings that will grow tax-free and eventually be distributed with as little tax as possible. By deferring tax into the future, rather than paying it now, you can increase the dollars you end up with.

Let's begin with college savings: Because your children are not yet of college age, the two strategies you should consider are §529 and §530 plans. Section 529 plans are state-sponsored savings plans in which contributions are not deductible for federal income tax purposes (although some states do provide deductions). However, amounts contributed grow tax-free and distributions for higher education escape tax altogether. The state sponsoring such a plan hires an investment advisor to manage the assets, although you have flexibility in directing these investments. There is no limit on annual contributions for income tax purposes.

Section 530 (establishing the so-called Coverdell Education Savings Accounts) allows you to direct the investment, and the maximum annual contribution is $2,000 per year. There is no deduction for contributions, but again, amounts contributed grow tax-free and distributions for education are excludable from gross income. While there are income limits potentially restricting contributions, your AGI appears to be within the acceptable limits.

Retirement savings: First of all, you should look into whether your employers offer retirement plans at work. If so, join now, and contribute all you can. If not, you might consider establishing an IRA. Your income level is right on the cusp of being ineligible to make a contribution to a Roth IRA. A Roth contribution grows tax-free and distributions made after retirement are tax-free. This would be good for you, so it may make sense for you to find ways to reduce your income to below the Roth income limitations (which are $150,000 to $160,000 for joint filers). If you cannot qualify for a Roth IRA, you can still contribute to a regular IRA, although you cannot take a deduction for such contribution and earnings distributed later will be taxed to you.

Health savings: Let's take a look at your health plan at work. If it is a so-called "high deductible" health plan, you or your employer may be able to establish a health savings account to supplement your coverage. If you contribute, your contribution may be deductible; if your employer contributes, that amount is excludable from your gross income. The HSA itself is exempt from tax, and distributions for medical care are tax-free.

One more thing: Federal income taxes are as low as they have been in a long time, and the tax rate on qualified dividend income is only 15%. So, it makes sense to save *outside* of these vehicles. The tax rate isn't confiscatory and if tax rates rise (which many people believe they will) the tax will already have been paid on the income earned outside one of these accounts. This is particularly true for regular IRAs investing in stocks.

SAMPLE ANSWER TO QUESTION 4

This question raises issues regarding the deductibility of expenses incurred in a business and transactions in property relating to that business.

Sole proprietors report the income and deductions attributable to their businesses on Schedule C of their tax returns. Net income from business is includible in gross income (IRC §61(a)(2)), and net loss generates a deduction (IRC §165(c)(1)), subject to some limitations.

Spencer begins by including in his gross income his receipts from sales of information. (See timing discussion, below.) In order to qualify for any deduction, the expenditure must fall within the domain of a specific deduction statute. Potential deduction statutes are discussed below.

Ordinary and necessary business expenses: Section 162 allows a deduction for all "ordinary and necessary business expenses." This requires that the expenditure be usual in the trade ("ordinary"), have a reasonable likelihood of generating profit ("necessary"), be incurred for business and not personal reasons, and be incurred while the taxpayer is engaged in a trade or business ("trade or business"), and not be a capital expenditure ("expense"). Spencer's expenditures for compensation (if reasonable in amount), rent, advertising, and telephone/Internet would all seem to meet this requirement.

Business entertainment: While business entertainment may also seem to fall within the category of §162 expenses, special rules limit deductions for business entertainment. First, Spencer must establish that the entertainment item was "directly related to" the active conduct of his trade or business, or if the activity immediately preceded or followed a bona fide business discussion, was "associated with" the active conduct of his trade or business. IRC §274(a). Even if he meets this requirement, only 50% of the amount expended will be deductible. IRC §274(n). Spencer must substantiate his deductions for entertainment expenses, and additional information would be necessary to determine if he is eligible for any deduction.

Purchase of computer: The purchase of the computer is an outlay for a capital expenditure, because the computer is likely to generate benefits beyond the close of the taxable year. IRC §263. Thus, Spencer cannot take a deduction under §162 for this outlay. He may, however, deduct the cost of such items up to the lesser of $105,000 or the net income of the business disregarding this expense. IRC §179. If he elects to deduct the cost of the computer under §179, its basis will be reduced by the amount of the deduction (if he fully deducts the amount, the basis will be zero).

Taxes: Section 164 allows a deduction for income, real property, personal property taxes, and sales taxes, at least in some years. It is not clear what kind of tax Spencer paid, and further information is necessary to determine the deductibility of this expense.

Timing issues: Since Spencer uses the cash method of accounting for his business, he will include income in the year he receives it and claim deductions in the year they are paid. "Payment" includes payment by credit card, even if Spencer does not pay the balance to the credit card company. Thus, he should deduct those expenses that have been paid during the year and include income that he has received, but not the promises to pay from clients.

Sale of computer: Spencer's sale of the computer used in his business is the sale of a §1231 asset. However, we must first apply the recapture rule of IRC §1245 to recast as ordinary income any amount of accelerated depreciation claimed on the computer. It is not clear from the facts how much that would be, but let us assume for purposes of illustration that the recapture amount is $100. That amount is treated as ordinary income. The rest ($1,400) is §1231 gain.

As such, we must add up the §1231 gains and losses for the year, netting the two. Spencer had a theft loss of the equipment, with a basis of $2,500 and a fair market value of $1,500. If property used in a trade or business or for the production of income is totally destroyed, and if the fair market value of such property immediately before the casualty is less than its adjusted basis, the adjusted basis of such property is the amount of the loss. Reg. §1.165-7(b)(1)(ii). Therefore, Spencer's casualty loss is $2,500 on the theft. He also had a casualty gain of $3,000 due to the flood. Because Spencer's casualty losses are not greater than his casualty gains, all of the gains and losses are included in the computation of §1231 gains, as follows:

Sale of computer:	$1,400 gain
Theft loss:	$2,500 loss
Flood gain:	$3,000 gain
NET	**$1,900 gain**

This gain would be capital in nature. There is no indication that Spencer has unrecaptured losses in prior years that would treat any of this as ordinary income. This capital gain income would be taxed at 15% or 5% depending on Spencer's income (probably at the latter rate, although we do not know his exact tax rate).

Advice

Spencer might consider establishing some sort of retirement plan for his business to defer income to future years, or prepaying some expenses (within the limits imposed on prepayments) to accelerate deductions to earlier years.

SAMPLE ANSWER TO QUESTION 5

Inheritance: Sabrina will not have any income as a result of receiving the home and the stock and will take both of those assets with a basis equal to their fair market value on the date of death. When she sold the home she realized a capital gain of $15,000. Although she held the home for only a short period of time, she is treated as having a long-term capital gain because of IRC §1223(10), which offers a long-term holding period for inherited property so that heirs can more easily dispose of it. She cannot claim the IRC §121 exclusion because she did not live in the home or own it for the requisite period (which might have been a good planning strategy given that her own home is going to Eli).

The annuity is a different story. The income inherent in the annuity is "income in respect of a decedent" and there is no step-up in basis. At least a portion of each payment is taxable to Sabrina as she receives it. While in the usual case the rules of IRC §72 would apply so that a portion of each payment is income and a portion is a tax-free return of capital, in this case it is clear that Sabrina's mother had recovered her entire basis, so that all of the payments she was receiving were fully includible in gross income—and the same will be true for Sabrina.

Divorce: The transfers of property between spouses will not generate any tax liability, and each will take a basis in the property equal to the basis of the property immediately before the transfer. If Sabrina sells the stocks soon, she will realize and recognize long term capital gain or loss, while Eli may be able to exclude the gain on the sale of the residence because of IRC §121. Sabrina might ask herself if that is equitable, or should some adjustment be made because of the likelihood of an income tax due on her sale.

Payments that qualify as alimony for federal income tax purposes (regardless of whether they are called that for state law purposes) are deductible above-the-line by the payor and includible in the gross income of the recipient. The so-called alimony may not be alimony at all, at least for federal income tax purposes. Although it is paid in cash, and presumably will be incorporated into the divorce decree and they will not live together, there is one fly in the ointment: the liability survives—in some form—after Sabrina's death. This is potentially enough to ensure that it is not alimony, and if so, it would not be includible in Sabrina's income nor deductible by Eli. Sabrina might like this result but it is not the most tax-efficient result as Eli is in a higher tax bracket than Sabrina. If they are comfortable removing this provision, however, the amount payable should qualify as alimony.

The variance in the payments suggests a front-end loading problem. To determine the extent of the problem, we must calculate the "excess alimony payment," as follows:

Step 1   Calculate the excess alimony payment for the *second* post-separation year. $20,000 - ($10,000 + $15,000) = excess payment for second post-separation year = -0-

Step 2   Calculate the excess alimony payment for the *first* post-separation year.

$$\$50,000 - \left[\left\{\frac{\$(20,000-0)+\$10,000}{2}\right\} + \$15,000\}\right] = \text{excess payment for the } \textit{first} \text{ post} - \text{separation year}$$

$$= \$22,500$$

Step 3   Calculate the excess alimony payment, which is the sum of steps 1 and 2: $22,500

Step 4   So what? This would result in a deduction to Sabrina in Year 3 and an inclusion in Eli's income in that year.

Is this what the parties intend? Probably not. So, to avoid the front-loading problem, it is necessary that the payments not vary by more than $15,000 during the first three years. These payments could be restructured to be relatively equal over all years, or relatively equal in the first three years and a fourth year that is different. If Sabrina requires a large payment up front (for tuition, for example, if she is returning to school), a loan could be structured to fill the gap.

Table of Cases

Table of Statutes

Table of Internal Revenue Code Provisions

Table of Treasury Regulations

Index